Computers in Our World, Second Edition

Beverly E. Amer

THOMSON
COURSE TECHNOLOGY™
Australia • Canada • Mexico • Singapore • Spain • United Kingdom • United States

Computers in Our World, Second Edition

Beverly E. Amer

Senior Product Manager:
Kathy Finnegan

Product Manager:
Erik Herman

Associate Product Manager:
Brandi Henson

Print Buyer:
Fola Orekoya

Developmental Editor:
Fran Marino

Content Project Manager:
Aimee Poirier

Interior Design:
Kellee LaVars
Ken Russo

Illustrators:
Richard Herrera
Michelle French
Phillip Hajjar

Cover Design:
Marissa Falco

Photo Researcher:
Abigail Reip

Compositor:
GEX Publishing Services

Printed in the United States of America

1 2 3 4 5 6 7 8 9 10 QWD 11 10 09 08 07

For more information, contact
Course Technology
25 Thomson Place
Boston, Massachusetts, 02210

Or find us on the World Wide Web at:
www.course.com

ISBN-13: 978-1-4239-2515-6
ISBN-10: 1-4239-2515-7

Dedication

For every student and instructor with passionate curiosity. – Beverly

Cover photo (globe): Comstock Images/Jupiterimages; **Chapter 1:** Figure 1-1, Maximilian Stock Ltd. / Photo Researchers, Inc; Figure 1-2a, © Alistair Berg / Getty Images; Figure 1-2b, © Flip Chalfant / Getty Images; Figure 1-3, © Digital Vision / Getty Images; Figure 1-4, © David Young-Wolff / PhotoEdit; Figure 1-12, © Kyodo /Landov; **Chapter 2:** Figure 2-4, AP Photo/Rogelio Solis; Figure 2-8, Courtesy of Intuit; Figure 2-13, AP Photo/Nati Harnik; Figure 2-14, AP Photo/Jose Luis Magana; Figure 2-16, AP Photo; Figure 2- 17, AP Photo; Figure 2-18, AP Photo; **Chapter 3:** Figure 3-1a, ©Photolink/ Getty Images; Figure 3-1b, © Ingram Publishing / JupiterImages; Figure 3-1c, © Jupiter Images; Figure 3-1d, © Thinkstock /JupiterImages; Figure 3-2, AP Photo/Koji Ueda; Figure 3-4, Courtesy of Dolphin Medical, Inc.; Figure 3-5, Courtesy of Cygnus, Inc.; Figure 3-6, AP Photo/Toby Talbot; Figure 3-7, AP Photo/ Alex Dorgan Ross; Figure 3-8b, Courtesy of NOAA; Figure 3-10, Courtesy of Antarctic Meteorological Research Center Space Science and Engineering Center University of Wisconsin-Madison; Figure 3-13, Courtesy of NOAA/ Geophysical Fluid Dynamics Laboratory; Figure 3-14, Courtesy of American Wildlands; **Chapter 4:** Figure 4-4, © Michael Newman/ PhotoEdit; Figure 4-11, Dave Umberger/ Courtesy of Purdue News Service; Figure 4-12, Marc Levoy / Stanford University; Figure 4-13, Courtesy of Satellite Models; Figure 4-15a, Courtesy of Sony Electronics, Inc.; Figure 4-15b, Courtesy of Sony Electronics, Inc.; Figure 4-15c, Courtesy of Sony Electronics, Inc.; Figure 4-16, Courtesy of SanDisk Corporation; Table 4-2a, Courtesy of SanDisk Corporation; Table 4-2b, Courtesy of Kingston Technology Company; Table 4-2c, Courtesy of SanDisk Corporation; Table 4-2d, Courtesy of SanDisk Corporation; Table 4-2e, Courtesy of SanDisk Corporation; Table 4-2f, Courtesy of SanDisk Corporation; Figure 4-17, Courtesy of SanDisk Corporation; Figure 4-20, Courtesy of Digimarc Corporation; Figure 4-21, Courtesy of Digimarc Corporation; Figure 4 22a, Courtesy of Sony Electronics, Inc.; Figure 4- 22b, Courtesy of Sony Electronics, Inc.; Figure 4-22c, Courtesy of Sony Electronics, Inc.; Figure 4-24, AP Photo/The Journal Record, Mark Hancock; Figure 4-26, © Walt Disney/courtesy Everett Collection; Figure 4-27, AP Photo/Reed Saxon; Figure 4-28, Courtesy of ChampionChip/USA; **Chapter 5:** Figure 5-1, Courtesy of NASA; Figure 5-2, Courtesy of FHWA/NHTSA National Crash Analysis Center; Figure 5-3, Courtesy of FHWA/NHTSA National Crash Analysis Center; Figure 5-4, Courtesy of Sandia Corporation; Figure 5-7, Courtesy of Siemens AG 2003 Automotive; Figure 5-10, Courtesy of Eaton Corporation; Figure 5-11, © JupiterImages; Figure 5-12, Courtesy of The Tire Rack; Figure 5-13, Courtesy of Coby Electronics Corporation; Figure 5- 14, © Jason Reed/Reuters /Landov; Figure 5-19, © Roberta Casaliggi /istockphoto.com; Figure 5-23a, AP Photo/Daniel Hulshizer; Figure 5-24, © 2003 Corbis; Figure 5-25, AP Photo/Don Ryan; Figure 5-26, Courtesy of Irisbus North America; Figure 5-28, AP Photo/Michel Porro; Figure 5-31, Courtesy of IBM Corporation; Figure 5-32, Courtesy of Sgt. Michael Morford/U.S. Air Force; Figure 5-33, Courtesy of Clear®, www.flyclear.com; **Chapter 6:** Figure 6-1a, © 1999 National Academy of Sciences; Figure 6-1b, © 1999 National Academy of Sciences; Figure 6-1c, © Getty Images; Figure 6-2a, © Greg Pease/Getty Images; Figure 6-2b, Courtesy of Siemens AG; Figure 6-2c, Courtesy of Fujitsu; Figure 6-2d, Courtesy of Siemens AG; Figure 6-2e, Courtesy of Siemens AG; Figure 6-3, © Jupiter Images; Figure 6-13, Courtesy of LEGO, the LEGO logo and brick configuration are trademarks of the LEGO Group © 2003 The LEGO Group. The LEGO® trademarks and products are used with permission. The LEGO Group does not sponsor this publication; Figure 6-17, Courtesy of Apple; Courtesy of Microsoft Corporation; Figure 6-19, Courtesy of SMART Technologies, Inc; Figure 6-20, AP Photo/Fort Collins Coloradoan, V. Richard Haro; Figure 6-22, © Alan Levenson /Getty Images; Figure 6-25, © blue jean images/ Getty Images; Figure 6-27, © Nick White/Getty Images; **Chapter 7:** Figure 7-1, Robyn Beck/AFP/Getty Images; Figure 7-3, Courtesy of F-Secure Corporation; Figure 7-5, Courtesy of F-Secure Corporation; Figure 7-7, © 2003 John Pritchett; Figure 7-8, Courtesy of F-Secure Corporation; Figure 7-12, Courtesy of Norton by Symantec; Figure 7-19, Courtesy of F-Secure Corporation; Figure 7-20, AP Photo/ Magnus Johansson; **Chapter 8:** Figure 8-10, Courtesy of Sportvision, Inc; Figure 8-11, © Fred Prouser/ NewsCom/Reuters; Figure 8-14, Turnitin is a service of iParadigms, LLC; **Chapter 9:** Figure 9-8, Courtesy of American Power Conversion Corp.; Figure 9-9, Courtesy of American Power Conversion Corp.; Figure 9-12, © JupiterImages; Figure 9-20, © 1999 by Randy Glasbergen. www.glasbergen.com; Figure 9-23, Courtesy of Lavasoft;

Computers in Our World, Second Edition

Contents

PREFACE VI

CHAPTER 1 Computers in Business and Industry

MOVING INTO THE INFORMATION AGE 2
IN THE FACTORY 3
CAD, CAE, CAM 4
Manufacturing Resource Planning 4
Job Scheduling 5
Inventory Control, Shipping, and Warehouse Management 5
Industrial Robots 6
IN RETAIL SALES AND MARKETING 6
Point-of-Sale (POS) Systems 6
Payment Processing and Credit Authorization 7
Inventory Control Systems 7
Accounting and Finance Systems 8
Marketing and Sales 8
Database Marketing 8
Consumer Preferences 8
IN BANKING 10
Electronic Funds Transfer 10
Automated Teller Machines (ATMs) 11
Direct Deposit 12
Automated Clearing House (ACH) 12
Smart Credit Cards 13
Online Banking 14
Bill Payment Service 14
Bill Presentment 15
IN THE OFFICE 15
Going Paperless 15
Telecommuting 16
HUMAN FACTORS AND THE WORKPLACE 17
Ergonomics 17
Repetitive Stress Injuries 18
Computer Vision Syndrome (CVS) 19
QUALITY OF WORK LIFE 19
Employee Monitoring 19
Skilling and De-skilling 20
Worker Autonomy 21
Blurred Boundaries 21
LOOKING AHEAD 22
Employment and Unemployment 22
A New Economy? 23
Conclusion 24

CHAPTER 2 Computers in Government, Law Enforcement, and the Military

COMPUTERS AND THE GOVERNMENT 28
The Election Process 28
Conducting Polls 28
Communicating with Voters 29
Researching Candidates 30
Casting a Ballot: Computerized Voting Systems 30
United States Postal Service 33
Census Bureau 34
Internal Revenue Service 34
COMPUTERS IN LAW ENFORCEMENT 37
Tracking Evidence 37
Storing Criminal Records 38
Enforcing Traffic Laws 39
Tracking Stolen Vehicles 40
Finding Missing Children 40
Providing Wireless 911 41
COMPUTERS AND HOMELAND SECURITY 43
Tracking Citizens 43
Tracking Visitors 43
Surveillance Using Computer Vision Systems 44
Managing Crises Through Collaboration 44
COMPUTERS IN THE MILITARY 45
Deploying Unmanned Aerial Vehicles (UAVs) 45
Using Remote-Controlled Robots 45
Utilizing Precision-Guided Bombs 46
Tracking Troop Movement 46
Using Computer Simulations for Training 47
Conclusion 48

CHAPTER 3 Computers in Medicine and Science

COMPUTERS IN MEDICINE 52
Maintaining Patient History 52
Managing the Medical Practice 53
Improving Patient Diagnosis and Monitoring 54
Clinical Data Capture and Medical Imaging 54
Computer-Assisted Diagnosis 55
Accessing Pharmacy and Medical Information 56
Monitoring Patients 58
Technology in the Operating Room 58
Telemedicine and Telepresence Surgery 59
Medical Research and Training 60
Recognizing Patterns of Disease 60
Improving Medical Training 60
Credibility of Medical Information 61

COMPUTERS IN SCIENCE 62
Observation and Data Collection 63
Collecting Weather Data 63
Hunting Hurricanes 63
Remote Sensing 64
Data Classification and Analysis 64
Human Genome Project 65
SETI@Home 66
Data Modeling and Simulation 67
Forecasting the Weather 68
Environmental Impact Modeling 68
Geographic Information Systems 68
Conclusion 71

CHAPTER 4 Computers in Arts and Entertainment
COMPUTERS AND THE ARTS 76
Analog to Digital Conversion 76
Music 76
Composing Music 76
Playing and Recording Music 78
Editing Music 79
Performing Music 80
Distributing Music 80
Dance 82
Choreography and Notation 82
Motion Capture 83
Theater 84
Sculpture and 3-D Media 85
Graphic Arts 86
Photography 87
Behind the Scenes: Digital Photo Capture 88
Digital Photo Editing 90
Copyright Concerns 93
COMPUTERS IN ENTERTAINMENT 94
Television and Movies 95
Behind the Scenes: Digital Video Capture 95
Digital Video Editing 96
Colorization 99
Computer Generated Imagery and Animation 99
Sports 101
Conclusion 104

CHAPTER 5 Computers in the Transportation Industry
DESIGN AND MANUFACTURING 108
Design 108
Testing 108
Aerodynamics Testing 108
Crash Testing 109
Manufacturing 110
Inventory Control 110
AUTOMOBILES AND TRUCKING 111
Inside an Automobile 111
Fuel Injection and Other Functions 112
Antilock Braking System (ABS) 113
Collision Warning Systems 113
Night Vision 114
Smart Tires 115
Entertainment Systems 115
Smart Cars 116
ON THE ROAD 117
Computerized Mapping 118
Onboard Global Positioning Systems 118
Telematics 119
Route Optimization 120
Electronic Toll Collection 121
Intelligent Highways 122
TRAINS AND BUSES 124
AIRLINES 125
Air Traffic Control 125
Reservations and Ticketing 126
Self-Service Check In 127
Fuel Calculation 128
Training Using Flight Simulators 128
Conclusion 131

CHAPTER 6 Computers in Education
CHANGING TIMES, CHANGING SCHOOLS 136
The Factory Model 136
A New Model for a New Century 136
IMPORTANCE OF COMPUTER FLUENCY 137
COMPUTERS AS LEARNING TOOLS 139
Computer-Aided Instruction 140
Web-Based Training 141
Internet Resources 142
Programming Tools 143
Educational Games and Simulations 145
Software Tools 146
COMPUTERS AS TEACHING TOOLS 149
Presentation Tools 150
Communications Tools 151
E-mail 151
Mailing Lists 151
Newsgroups and Message Boards 151
Video Conferencing and Chat 152
Podcasting 152
Learning Management Systems 152
DISTANCE LEARNING 153
TECHNOLOGY IN THE CLASSROOM: BENEFITS AND OPPORTUNITIES 156
Benefits of Technology in the Classroom 156
Opportunities for Improvement 157
DEFINING AN INFORMATION AGE EDUCATION 159
Conclusion 160

CHAPTER 7 Computer Viruses and Computer Crime

COMPUTER VIRUSES, WORMS, and TROJAN HORSES 166
- Computer Viruses 166
- Types of Viruses 167
- How Viruses Work: Infection and Delivery 169
  - *Infection* 169
  - *Delivery* 169
- Trojan Horses and Worms 169
- Botnets and Zombies 171
- Hoaxes 171
- Protecting Your Computer 172
  - *Using Antivirus Software* 172
  - *Handling E-Mail* 174
  - *Disabling Macros* 175

COMPUTER CRIME 176
- Types of Computer Crime 176
  - *Unauthorized Access and Use* 176
  - *Hardware Theft* 177
  - *Information Theft* 177
  - *Intellectual Property and Software Theft* 180
- Methods of Committing Computer Crimes 182
  - *Obtaining Passwords* 182
  - *Salami Shaving* 184
  - *Data Diddling* 184
  - *Denial of Service Attacks* 185
- Identifying and Prosecuting Computer Criminals 186
  - *Who Is a Computer Criminal?* 186
  - *Prosecuting Computer Criminals* 187

Conclusion 190

CHAPTER 8 Computers, Law, and Ethics

LAW VERSUS ETHICS 194

COMPUTERS AND THE LAW 195
- E-Commerce Laws 195
  - *Digital Signatures* 195
  - *Online Advertising* 196
- Intellectual Property 198
  - *Copyright Infringement* 198
  - *Software Piracy* 201
- Objectionable Content 202
- Online Gambling 202
- Cyberlibel 203
- Cyberstalking 204

COMPUTERS AND ETHICS 205
- Ethical Decision Making: A Framework 206
- Ethics for Computer Professionals 206
  - *Codes of Ethics and Professional Conduct* 207
  - *Professionalism and Responsibility* 207
- Ethics in Business 207
  - *Advertising and Marketing* 209
  - *Digital Manipulation* 209
  - *Protecting Customer Data* 211
- Ethical Use of Intellectual Property 212
  - *Music, Movie, and Software Piracy* 212
  - *Plagiarism* 213

Conclusion 217

CHAPTER 9 Computers, Privacy, and Security

SECURITY CONCERNS 222
- System Failure 222
- Secure Internet Transactions and E-Mail 223

PRIVACY CONCERNS 223
- Collecting Customer Data 223
  - *Electronic Profiling* 223
  - *Opt Out and Opt In* 224
- Spam 224
- Online Activity Tracking 225
  - *Cookies* 225
  - *Spyware* 227
  - *Web Bugs* 227

PROTECTING SECURITY AND PRIVACY 230
- Privacy Laws 230
- Protecting Against System Failure 233
- Backing Up Data 234
- Defining a Disaster Recovery Plan 235
- Protecting Against Unauthorized Access and Use 236
  - *Firewalls* 237
  - *Intrusion Detection Software* 238
  - *Usernames and Passwords* 238
  - *Possessed Objects* 238
  - *Biometric Devices* 239
  - *Callback System* 239
  - *Audit Trails* 239
- Protecting against Hardware Theft 239
- Protecting Online Security and Privacy 240
  - *Using Data Encryption* 241
  - *Securing Internet Transactions* 242
  - *Securing E-Mail Messages* 244
  - *Reducing Spam* 244
  - *Limiting Personal Information Sharing* 244
  - *Managing Cookies, Spyware, and Web Bugs* 245

SECURITY AND PRIVACY IN THE WORKPLACE 247
- Employee Monitoring and Surveillance 247
- Legal Rights of Employers and Employees 248

COMPUTERS, SECURITY, AND PRIVACY: A BALANCING ACT 249

Conclusion 250

INDEX 253

Preface

Every day, a news headline touts the use of another new technology – a faster processor, an e-commerce technology, or a new storage media – thus adding one more topic to cover in an introductory computer concepts course. In an effort to cover the innumerable technologies related to computers, from bits and bytes to the latest Internet fad, the introductory computer concepts course all too often becomes an overwhelming exercise of memorizing the names, acronyms, and purposes of hundreds of devices and technologies. In the process, students can lose perspective on the practical applications of computers, as well as the important role computers play in their everyday lives.

Computers in Our World, Second Edition aims to help students regain that perspective by presenting a thorough and engaging look at how computers are used in our world today. Intended for use as a supplement to a computer concepts course or a lab applications course, this nine-chapter book assumes students have an understanding of basic computer concepts – and instead focuses on the use of computers in a wide range of industries and disciplines, including business, government, science and medicine, education, transportation, art, entertainment, and more. It also includes timely and relevant information on computer security, privacy, ethics, and the law as it relates to technology today.

Computers in Our World, Second Edition provides real-world examples that bring concepts to life, by illustrating the numerous places we interact with computers every day and the integral role they play in our lives. Social, ethical, security, and privacy issues raised by computers also are discussed, to encourage students to think critically about the impacts – both positive and negative – brought about by computers and technology.

Computers in Our World, Second Edition is divided into nine chapters. A summary of each chapter follows:

Chapter 1 Computers in Business and Industry An introduction to the impact of computers on all facets of business and industry, in a wide range of applications from the factory to the paperless office.

Chapter 2 Computers in Government, Law Enforcement, and the Military An overview of how computers have changed the face of government, law enforcement, homeland security, and the military.

Chapter 3 Computers in Medicine and Science A look at how computers are aiding new developments in medicine and science, from collecting data for scientific research to providing more efficient, higher-quality medical care to patients.

Chapter 4 Computers in Arts and Entertainment A review of computers as a tool in the visual and performing arts, including music, dance, theater, sculpture, the graphic arts and movies, and photography.

Chapter 5 Computers in the Transportation Industry An introduction to the use of computers in the transportation industry, from the manufacture of vehicles on the ground to the technologies keeping air traffic moving safely.

Chapter 6 Computers in Education An overview of the use of computers in education, as learning tools, teaching tools, and the basis of an entirely new type of classroom centered around student learning.

Chapter 7 Computer Crime and Viruses An introduction to the wide range of threats to computers, including viruses, Trojan horses, and worms, and the latest in security.

Chapter 8 Computers, Law, and Ethics An introduction to the laws and ethics related to computer usage – including cyberlibel, cyberstalking, and intellectual property issues.

Chapter 9 Computers, Privacy, and Security A discussion of technology's impact on privacy and security, including a review of potential issues and threats, and ways to safeguard systems, including backing up data, defining a disaster recovery plan, and practicing safe computing.

Computers in Business and Industry 1

Moving into the Information Age
In the Factory
- CAD, CAE, CAM
- Manufacturing Resource Planning
  - *Job Scheduling*
  - *Inventory Control, Shipping, and Warehouse Management*
- Industrial Robots

In Retail Sales and Marketing
- Point-of-Sale (POS) Systems
- Payment Processing and Credit Authorization
- Inventory Control Systems
- Accounting and Finance Systems
- Marketing and Sales
  - *Database Marketing*
  - *Consumer Preferences*

In Banking
- Electronic Funds Transfer
  - *Automated Teller Machines (ATMs)*
  - *Direct Deposit*
  - *Automated Clearing House (ACH)*
- Smart Credit Cards
- Online Banking
  - *Bill Payment Service*
  - *Bill Presentment*

In the Office
- Going Paperless
- Telecommuting

Human Factors and the Workplace
- Ergonomics
- Repetitive Stress Injuries
- Computer Vision Syndrome (CVS)

Quality of Work Life
- Employee Monitoring
- Skilling and De-skilling
- Worker Autonomy
- Blurred Boundaries

Looking Ahead
- Employment and Unemployment
- A New Economy?

Conclusion

While computers have had a major impact on a wide range of fields and disciplines, none has been more affected by the computer than business and industry. Almost every day you complete a business transaction that involves computer technology — whether it is the automatic teller machine at the bank, the bar code scanner at the supermarket, or the personalized text message you received this morning.

Today, businesses of all sizes use computers and technology in every aspect of commerce — from product design and manufacturing to sales, billing, and the final delivery of goods to customers. In this chapter, you will learn more about the use of computers in the factory, in retail sales and marketing, in banking, and in the office. The chapter also looks at how technology in the workplace affects your health, as well as the quality of your work life. Finally, the chapter looks ahead to review how technology will change the economy and employment in the future.

MOVING INTO THE INFORMATION AGE

The era in which we live – a world full of computers that define and shape our everyday leisure and business activities – often is referred to as the Information Age. The phrase, **Information Age**, along with the related idea of an **information economy** or the **new economy**, refers to the concept that instead of only producing tangible goods like shampoo, tires, and running shoes, businesses and industries are using information to help provide core services or are producing, processing, and distributing information as their main product.

The introduction of such new technologies as the transistor and the microprocessor powered the changes that define the Information Age. This shift, however, is not the first time new technologies have fundamentally transformed the world of work. Before the 20th century, humankind experienced two major paradigm shifts directly relating to the world of work: the Agricultural Revolution and the Industrial Revolution.

Thousands of years ago, humans fed themselves by hunting and gathering and were largely migratory. Over time, however, agriculture took hold as a practice. Farmers found they could produce the same amount of food from one acre that a hunter-gatherer could obtain from 100 acres. The invention of a new technology – a plow drawn by animals – made farming even more efficient, allowing communities to produce a surplus of food, introduce new crops, and free up people for other types of work. Over time, farms were organized into businesses, and farmers began using new fertilizers, artificial feed for animals, and new drainage systems. Technological improvements, such as the seed drill and threshing machine, continued to drive the agricultural economy (Table 1-1).

At the end of the eighteenth century, the Industrial Revolution unleashed the second radical change in the world of work. The shops of artisans and craftsmen were changed by new technologies that automated their work efforts. In the textile industry, the introduction of the flying shuttle and the spinning jenny accelerated the weaving process and began the mechanization of the textile industry. The introduction of the steam engine in 1763 changed the face of transportation, while other key innovations such as the telegraph, the sewing machine, the cotton gin, and electricity changed communications, manufacturing, and agriculture. With these technologies came an exponential increase in productivity, as each laborer could create many more products in the same time.

The newest revolution in the work world is the Information Age, whose origins started in the 1950s with the emergence of the transistor. Following in the footsteps of movies, radio, and television came such

TABLE 1-1 Major Societal Shifts

AGRICULTURAL REVOLUTION Inventions and Innovations	*INDUSTRIAL REVOLUTION* Inventions and Innovations	*INFORMATION REVOLUTION* Inventions and Innovations
■ Plow, seed drill, thresher	■ Steam engine	■ Movies
■ Selective breeding of livestock	■ Cotton gin	■ Radio
■ Removal of common property rights to land	■ Telegraph	■ Television
■ New systems of cropping, involving turnips and clover	■ Sewing machine	■ Transistor
	■ Transatlantic cable and telephone	■ Microprocessor
	■ Incandescent light bulb	■ Computers
	■ Induction electric motor	■ Satellites
	■ Diesel engine	■ Lasers
	■ First airplane	■ Fiber-optic technologies
	■ Model T Ford, assembly line	

Humankind has experienced three major shifts relating to the world of work. In each era, new technological inventions and innovations were at the heart of the social and economic changes. Today, many diagnostic tests and tools use computer technology to provide accurate and detailed clinical data.

inventions as the microprocessor, computers, satellites, lasers, fiber optics, networks, cellular phones, and more. Like the plow and the cotton gin, these technologies allow workers to work more efficiently and be more productive. By the 1990s, these technologies created a whole new way to work, allowing office workers to work from home while communicating via cellular phones, e-mail, and fax. In manufacturing, computer systems on the factory floor began providing up-to-the minute information to help firms make decisions on product design, inventory management, and shipping. Today, computer technologies are used in almost every business or industry. The following selections explore the use of computers in the factory, in retail sales and marketing, in banking, and the office.

@ISSUE: Resisting the Information Revolution

One of the key characteristics of the Information Age is constant change, with rapidly evolving technologies and new information being shared each day. With change, however, comes resistance to that change. The term **Luddite** sometimes is used to describe anyone who distrusts or fears the inescapable changes brought about by new technology. The term actually dates back to the early 1800s during the Industrial Revolution, when a group of English workers, gathered in protests led by a Ned Ludd, a weaver (who may or may not have been real). The Luddites rioted and destroyed stocking frames and other machines to protest the technological changes that they felt displaced craftsmen in favor of machines.

In the Information Age, Luddites continue to express concerns about the effects of computer technology, including the elimination of jobs, the isolation of workers, and the potential for invasion of privacy. In a world driven by and fascinated with computers, cell phones, the Web, and the latest new gadgets, the Luddites of today remind us to step back, review the effects of technology on our lives, and consider the potential downsides of computer technology. Some of the questions and concerns they raise include:

- The elimination of boundaries between work and home, as computers, cell phones, pagers, and PDAs make instant and round-the-clock contact possible
- Whether computers enhance or degrade the quality of working life for clerks and administrative staff
- The frustrations caused by increasingly complex computers and software
- The potential hazards of malfunctioning computers, such as losing your history paper when the computer crashes or the accident caused by an inaccurately timed signal on a commuter rail track
- Intellectual property theft of software, music, movies, images, and other works
- The reduction of face-to-face communication caused by e-mail
- Unauthorized access to personal information stored in large databases
- The digital divide, in which those who cannot afford computers will not be competitive in today's workforce
- The loss of jobs to automation, where computerized machines complete tasks once performed by individuals

These are just a few of the questions and concerns raised by the pervasive use of computers in our work and our lives. As with the stocking frames destroyed by the original Luddites, a technology itself might not be inherently harmful, but the application of the technology could have negative impacts. Today's Luddites are not maintaining that technology does not have positive effects, but they do suggest we should take a balanced view of how computing affects our lives, the lives of others, and the world around us.

IN THE FACTORY

Factories are where most of the products of everyday life are made, from the smallest microprocessor in your cellular phone to the jumbo passenger airplane. Computer technology has changed – and continues to change – the factory dramatically. While fewer individuals than ever work in factories, factories produce a wider range of products than ever before for a global customer base. Computer technology and automation are behind this, allowing factories to reduce design time, maximize the use of machines manufacturing the products, and track the shipping of products from order to final shipment.

CAD, CAE, CAM

Computer-aided design (CAD) is the use of a computer and special software to assist in product design (Figure 1-1). With CAD software, designers can use graphics and models to represent a product on screen, which allows them to produce more accurate drawings than those sketched on paper. CAD software also allows designers to modify a design, dynamically change product features, and perform calculations to optimize the design for production.

Using computer-aided design lets companies reduce the product design cycle, which can help companies get better products to market faster. For example, the product development team at Adidas-Salomon, the second-largest sporting goods provider in the world, must design up to 60 new shoe styles each year. For every new shoe, the time from idea to shipping product – referred to as the *cycle time* – is from 12 to 18 months. Most of that time is needed for manufacturing, which means the design team has only four to six weeks to design and create a prototype of a new shoe. Using CAD, designers can take a certain shape or a particular design requested by a customer and quickly determine if it can be manufactured. The CAD system also allows designers to rework designs quickly, creating three-dimensional models that are sent to show sales and marketing departments exactly how the shoe should look to appeal to customers.

Computer-aided engineering (CAE) uses computers to test product designs. Using CAE, engineers can test the design of a car or a bridge before it is built. These sophisticated programs simulate the effects of wind, temperatures, weight, and stress on product shapes and materials. CAE software gives designers and engineers the ability to analyze and verify their designs in the early stages of the product development process - when design alterations still are relatively easy and inexpensive. BMW realizes considerable time savings in the development and testing of a vehicle using CAE. Actual physical prototypes are built only after each individual component is checked and analyzed by BMW engineers with the help of CAE.

Computer-aided manufacturing (CAM) is the use of computers to direct the machines that produce and assemble a product. CAM production equipment includes software-controlled drills, welding, and tooling machines. Once a design is complete, computer-aided manufacturing helps speed the process of creating the actual product – even a product as simple as a chocolate kiss. Yorkshire Moulds, for example, uses computer-aided manufacturing to reduce the time required to manufacture highly detailed chocolate molds. The traditional time-consuming method of hand carving the models took almost two weeks. With the new digital process using CAD and CAM, the chocolate molds are created in just three days. Instead of sending physical models back and forth, Yorkshire Moulds now shares its digital models via e-mail, so that companies such as Hershey's and Cadbury can approve the size, shape, or specific placement of their logos on each mold. Once the designs are approved, Yorkshire Moulds uses computer-aided manufacturing tools and exports them directly to the machines that cut each molds – thus eliminating errors introduced by handcarving and reducing production time by 75 percent.

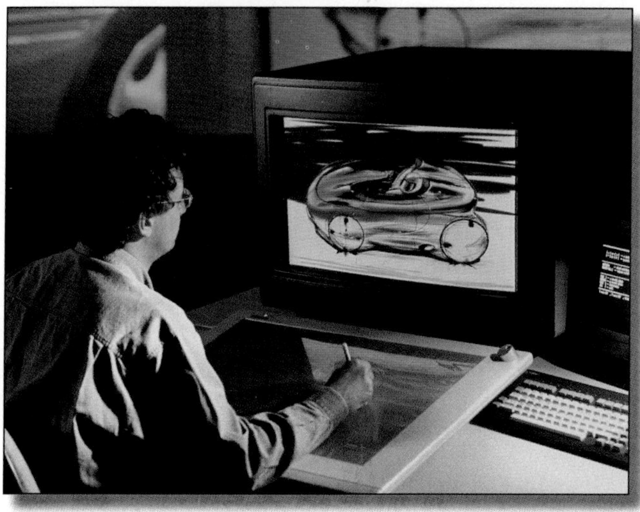

Figure 1-1 Using CAD software and digitizing tablet, designers from companies like BMW can use graphics and models to represent a product on screen, which allows them to produce accurate drawings and fine-tune them before actually producing models.

These software solutions – CAD, CAE, and CAM – can be combined into a **computer-integrated manufacturing (CIM)** system that incorporates the many different operations of the product design and manufacturing process.

Manufacturing Resource Planning

A wide range of software and computer technologies helps make factories more efficient in the scheduling, planning, and manufacturing process. Many of these tools come under the category of **manufacturing resource planning (MRP)** systems, which integrate various production and process control systems into a single computerized system. The components of an MRP system include: job scheduling, inventory control, shipping management, distribution, and warehouse management.

JOB SCHEDULING A **job-scheduling system** or **production-scheduling system** helps factory managers decide when to initiate production based on the supplies on hand and customer demand. During the winter holiday season, for example, a factory might receive a sudden increase in orders for the hottest new snowboard. The factory must respond rapidly in order to meet the demand, rescheduling production of other products for different times or other machines, while quickly moving the raw materials for the snowboard into place. Many production scheduling systems deliver real-time customer order information right to the factory floor, so that the snowboards – and other in-demand products – are immediately scheduled for production and hit the shelves before the snow melts. Another example is Dell Computer, a company that has a build-to-order process in which they customize and manufacture each computer according to the customer's order. Using this build-to-order process, Dell allows you to order a computer that exactly matches your required specifications via their Web site. Once Dell receives the order, the production scheduling system sends input to the inventory control system to pull the parts needed to build your new computer. The parts then are delivered to the assembly line, where the computer is manufactured and sent to the warehouse for shipping.

INVENTORY CONTROL, SHIPPING, AND WAREHOUSE MANAGMENT A key challenge for a factory and its warehouse is to manage inventory, so enough parts are available to continue production, without overstocking parts and having inventory that is obsolete or unused. Usually part of the organization's supply chain, an **inventory control system** tracks the current supplies of inventory and matches this against anticipated future orders to ensure that enough component parts, such as tires and brake pads, are available to manufacture the shipment of new trucks. Another approach to inventory management involves **just-in-time manufacturing**, which lets manufacturers purchase and receive components just before they are needed on the assembly line. For example, Dell's build-to-order process – which is an example of just-in-time manufacturing – helps prevent the company from being stuck with inventory that may become obsolete. Instead of having entire computers gather dust in a warehouse, Dell can place orders for or manufacture specific parts in direct response to an order, thus ensuring each part gets used and little inventory is wasted.

For those items in the warehouse, a **warehouse management system (WMS)** is used to track items received, generate pick lists to pack customer orders, label a package for shipping, and track its receipt by the customer. When you place an order for books over the Web, that order data is sent to a warehouse management system, which matches available stock to the order, enabling personnel to determine if your order can be filled immediately. Staff members with radio frequency-based handheld computers then pick each book for your order, scanning each bar code as they go, to confirm that the right title was selected (Figure 1-2). This information is transmitted back to the WMS, which deducts the inventory count for that item in real time. Based on the order size, the WMS references a database of boxes to determine which box size is appropriate for the order, and then automatically generates the shipping label. Once the box is shipped, the WMS might send a shipping confirmation back to the Web site, which e-mails this information to you to let you know the order is on its way. The end result is that you receive the order on time, with exactly the books you requested.

Figure 1-2 Order data from customers is sent to a warehouse management system, which matches available stock to the order, enabling the personnel to determine if an order can be filled immediately. Staff with radio frequency-based handheld computers then scan each item's bar code as they pick it for shipping.

Industrial Robots

Many factories also use industrial robots – computer-controlled machines designed to perform work that would be hazardous to people. To date, the greatest success in using robotics in the factory is in executing limited and repetitive actions, such as assembling simple industrial parts and performing jobs such as welding (Figure 1-3). Robotic arms, for example, are used to move heavy parts into and out of machines, while other robots are used to manipulate devices such as paint sprayers. Robots also are used in the warehouse to move heavy items from stacks of items and automatically pack boxes.

Figure 1-3 In today's factory, computer-controlled robots are used to move heavy parts into and out of machines and to control devices, such as welding tools and paint sprayers.

IN RETAIL SALES AND MARKETING

Computer technology has also changed the face of retail sales and marketing. The next time you head to the bookstore to browse for the latest bestseller and have a cup of coffee, notice all of the computers around you. Today, most retail sales locations – whether the department store, drugstore, toy store, or bookstore – are filled with computers and systems used to streamline the browsing and buying experience.

Point-of-Sale (POS) Systems

When you have finished shopping, you head to the checkout lane, where a cashier uses a point-of-sale system to complete your transaction and accept your method of payment. A **point-of-sale (POS) system** is a special kind of order-processing system that records purchases, processes credit or debit cards, and updates inventory.

In a grocery store, for example, the POS system is a combination of electronic cash register, bar code scanner, and printer. A **bar code scanner** is an input device that uses laser beams to read the **bar code** on a product (Figure 1-4). A bar code is an identification code that consists of vertical lines and spaces of different widths. The bar code represents data that identifies the manufacturer and the item. A bar code scanner reads data by scanning the width and spacing of the bars in the code. The bar code does not, however, contain price data. This is stored separately in the system. When the bar code is scanned, the data is matched to a file containing the price for that code, which then displays it on the POS terminal.

Figure 1-4 A bar code scanner reads a bar code by using a laser that detects the width and spacing of the bars. The bar code does not contain the item's price.

Different products use different types of bar codes. Retail and grocery stores use the **UPC (Universal Product Code)** bar code, while libraries use the Codabar bar code, and the United States Postal Service uses the POSTNET bar code. Books use the International Standard Book Numbering (IBSN) bar code, not only to identify book titles but also their various publication formats (hardcover, paperback, audiocassette, CD-ROM, and so on).

When the cashier scans the bar code on a product, a computer uses the manufacturer and item numbers to look up the price information and complete product name in the database. Then, the price of the item in the database shows in the display device, the name of the item prints on the receipt, and the item being sold is recorded so the inventory can be updated.

All sales are recorded in the central database as soon as they are finalized at the cash register, so that store managers can run reports to evaluate special promotions and spot fast-moving items. In larger store chains, the POS systems are connected over a network to allow managers to review the chainwide sales. The output from the POS serves as inputs to other systems, including payment-processing systems, inventory control systems, and accounting systems.

Payment Processing and Credit Authorization

If you use a credit or debit card to pay for your order, your payment request must be checked by a **credit-authorization system** before the transaction is completed (Figure 1-5). Today, many merchants allow you to swipe your card through a card reader, which reads your personal data from the magnetic stripe on the card. With a debit card, you also may enter a personal identification number (PIN) using a keypad. The POS terminal then uses a network connection to connect to a payment-processing service, which then sends the request on to your credit company or an **acquirer**, which is an organization that collects credit-authentication requests and provides retailers with a payment guarantee. When the acquirer gets the credit authentication request, it checks to see that the card number, expiration date, and PIN are valid; that the credit card is not over the limit; and that the card usage is not outside normal limits (a stolen card, for example, might have numerous transactions in a very short span of time). The PIN is compared against the database in the bank's computers. If everything is authenticated, the sale is approved and the acquirer sends back an approval code. If not, the sale is denied for that card and you must provide a new form of payment.

Inventory Control Systems

Information from the POS is fed directly into the inventory control system, so the warehouse is aware that replacement products need to be put on the shelves. The inventory control system provides a real-time look at the total count of products in the store and warehouse and provides alerts when designated reorder points set by the user are reached. When items are being stocked on shelves, hand scanners are used to scan the bar codes to update the inventory database and show that items are again available.

As stores get larger and the numbers of items stocked increases daily, more and more stores are allowing customers to access inventory databases over the Web to see what is in stock and where items can be located. Your local electronics store, for example, may provide a computer that allows you to search the inventory database for that store to see if a specific product is

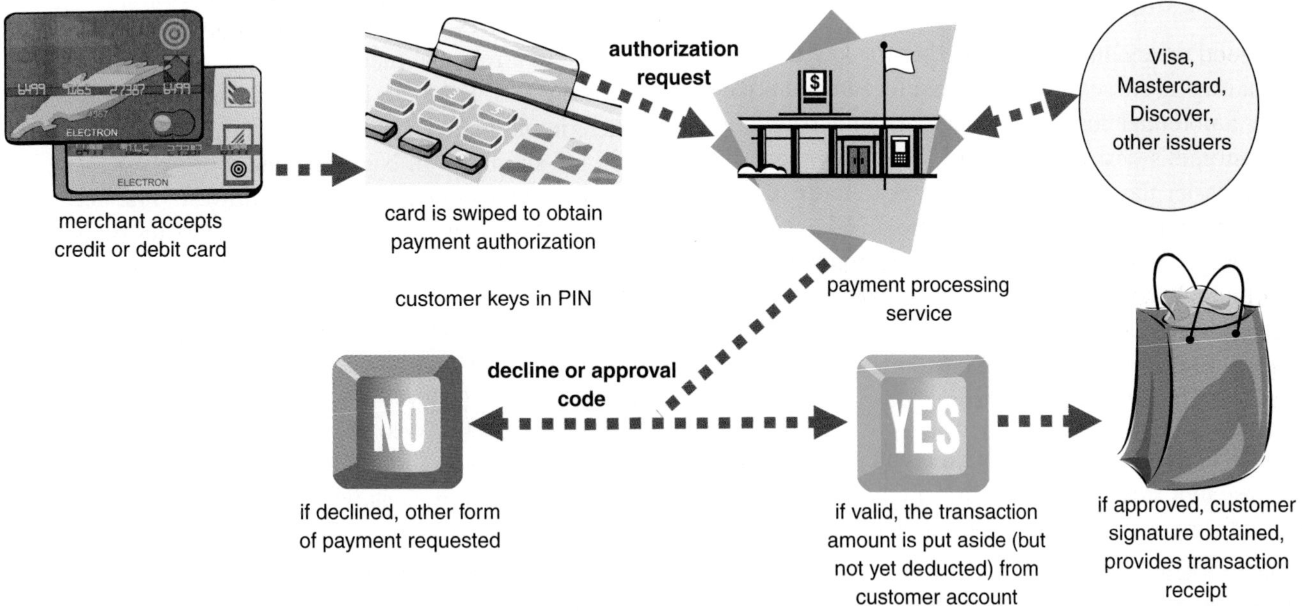

Figure 1-5 If you use a credit or debit card to pay for your order, your payment request must be checked by a credit-authorization system before the transaction is completed.

available and in stock. The retailer might even allow you to search for an item online and then reserve it for pickup at a local store (Figure 1-6). When you reserve the item, the inventory system decrements the count of available items by one, so the next customer has an accurate view of available inventory.

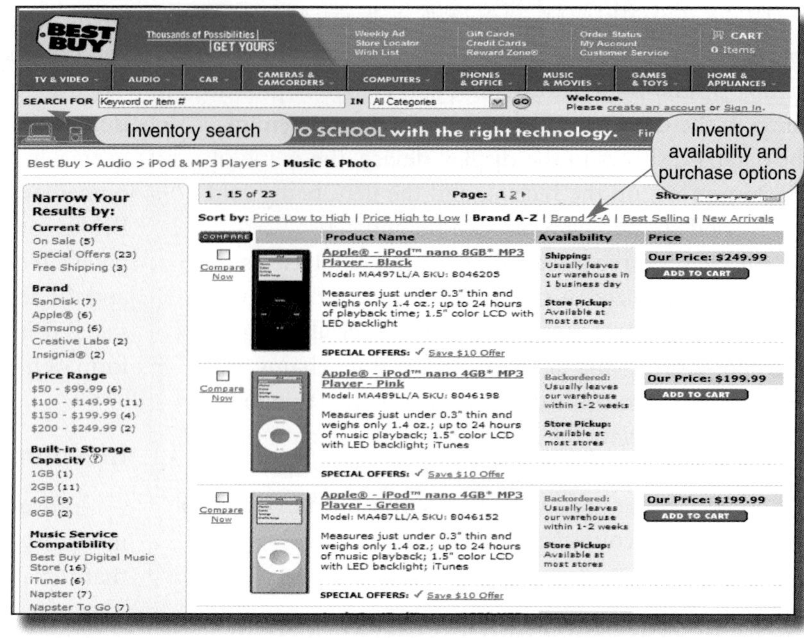

Figure 1-6 Retail stores, such as Best Buy, allow customers to search the inventory database to see if a specific product is available. Customers then can reserve the product for pickup at a local store.

Accounting and Finance Systems

Information from the POS is also fed in to a company's finance and accounting systems, so the company can track sales, returns, and other transactions. Computers and software help a company's accounting and finance groups, which are responsible for managing the company's money. Accounting departments track, analyze, and prepare reports covering every financial transaction that occurs within the company, while the finance department manages the company's money as efficiently as possible. Accounting software makes it easier to track and manage everyday transactions, such as sales and payments to suppliers. Financial software helps managers budget, forecast, and analyze the financial health of the business.

Marketing and Sales

A good salesman will tell you that the key to sales and marketing success is identifying, locating, and contacting a potential customer, along with understanding that customer's desires and needs. Computers have made it easier than ever for companies to more effectively market and sell products to a wider range of customers, while offering specific promotions tailored to individuals. The goal of creating a marketing database is to stay close to customers by recording and keeping an electronic record of customer contacts in an effort to improve all future contacts.

DATABASE MARKETING Each time you complete a purchase in a store or online using a credit or debit card, information about your purchase probably is stored in a large marketing database that later will be used to market additional products to you. This practice, called **database marketing,** allows companies to mine customer databases and create marketing lists to mail you catalogs or send you advertising e-mails. For businesses, having the ability to query databases and target their marketing efforts is a huge asset.

For example, rather than offering the same incentives to all customers, Ford Motors uses database marketing to determine which cars might benefit from a promotion and which will continue to be hot, even with a price increase. To do this, Ford collects daily sales data from dealerships and uses it as input for computer models that predict which incentives will be most tempting to customers. The output also shows what cars need a boost in a regional market – and what cars do not. Knowing this, Ford can focus their marketing dollars where it will matter, possibly offering a $3,000 rebate on a full-size truck in New England, but only a $500 rebate on that same truck in the Midwest. The net result is that Ford spends a lot less on rebates than their competitor, which helps lead to higher profits.

CONSUMER PREFERENCES Marketing databases not only help companies identify what you might like, they also give you a chance to tell a company your interests. Today, many retail Web sites have preference centers that allow customers to sign up for e-mail newsletters, promotions, or specific catalogs (Figure 1-7). Other sites give you the option to set up reminders for special occasions such as a friend's birthday. The Web site sends an e-mail to you a few days in advance of the occasion with possible gift ideas from their available products. Companies also can determine your preferences based on your past buying behavior. Amazon, for example, displays a

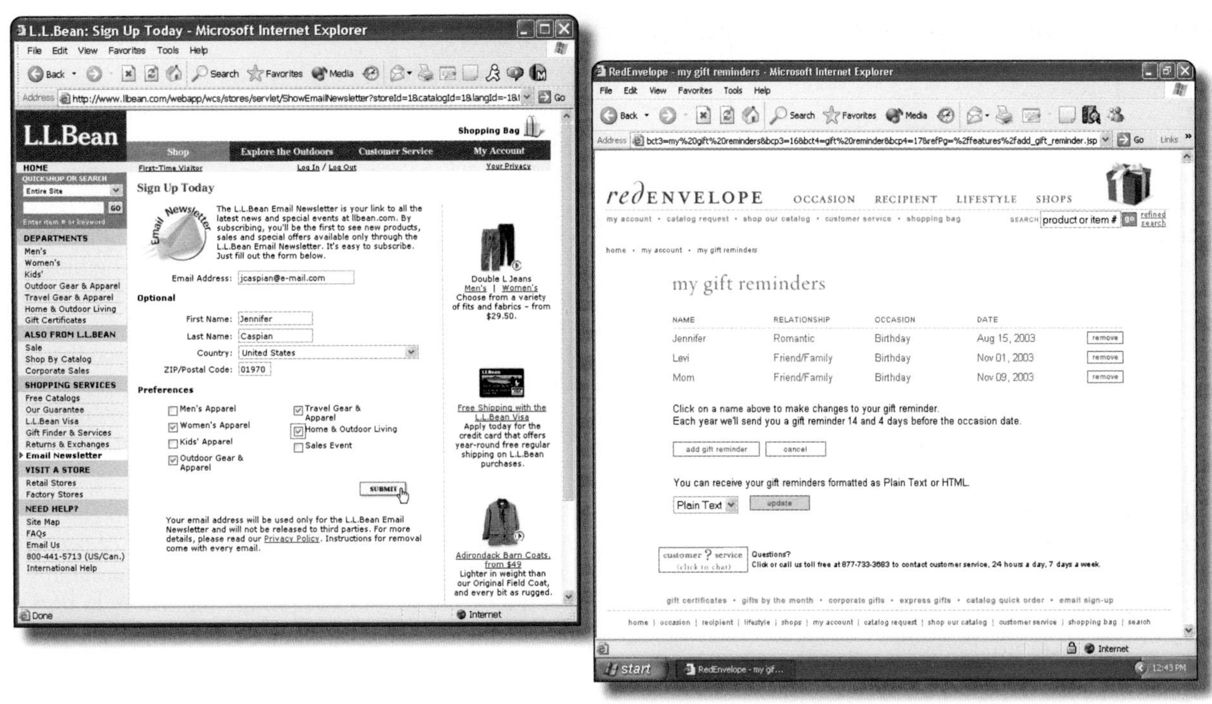

Figure 1-7 Today, many retail Web sites have preference centers that allow customers to sign up for e-mail newsletters or set up e-mail reminders for special occasions such as a friend's birthday.

recommendations page for you each time you visit the site, promoting specific products based on your past purchase (Figure 1-8).

Modern database marketing means you lose some control over information about yourself – information such as what books you read, what food you buy, and what types of music you like. It is important to read a firm's privacy policy to find out how they use the personal information you provide them. Companies, marketers, and government agencies simply may use your information to process your order or they may use it to market products, services, or promotions to you. They might, however, share your information with others, so that your e-mail is filled with **spam** – unsolicited, junk e-mail sent as part of an electronic mass mailing.

Some organizations offer you choices about how your personal information is used. For example, many marketers let you **opt in** to receiving marketing messages, which means you will not receive e-mails and other types of marketing messages unless you sign up and specifically request they be sent to you (many companies allow you to opt in via the Web site). You also can opt in to allow companies to share your personal information. Other firms allow you to **opt out** – that is, instruct them not to share your information with others or use it for promotional purposes. Marketing e-mails often include an opt-out link at the bottom that you can click to be removed from the mailing list; businesses also make opt-in and opt-out services available to customers online or over the phone.

Figure 1-8 Amazon uses your past purchases to identify other products you might be inclined to purchase.

Really Worth the Reward?

Pull your key chain or wallet out of your pocket and count the number of rewards or club cards you have, from grocery stores, drugstores, clothing stores, and gas stations. These cards provide many different benefits: discounts each time you shop, early notice of special sales, automatic entry into sweepstakes, coupons for items you purchase often, or recipes that include products you purchased. If you do not use your card for a while, the video store might even send you a special coupon to remind you to come back.

For retailers and marketers, club cards are a huge boon. Each time you use your card, the transaction information is stored in a database. By analyzing this data, retailers know who is shopping in the store and how they shop. They better understand your buying patterns (are you a one-time a week, full-cart grocery shopper or a three-times a week, express lane shopper?), as well as what items you buy. From there, the retailer can offer you relevant incentives to reward you and keep you coming back (free salsa with your tortilla chips?). Retailers also can focus on their best customers with discounts, special promotions, and gifts — and not waste marketing money on bargain hunters who only shop sporadically.

For some, however, there is a fine line between marketing and monitoring. For groups such as Consumers Against Supermarket Privacy Invasion and Numbering (CASPIAN), a club card is a registration and monitoring tool. When you fill out a form with your name, address, and phone number to receive a numbered card you have, in effect, been *registered*. The card number is kept in a database, along with your personal information. Each time you shop, the purchase history is stored with your information — a practice that is, according to CASPIAN, equivalent to *monitoring* or surveillance.

Each time you scan a club card at the POS system in a store, every item you purchase is recorded into a database linked with data from your card application. Eventually, based on many shopping trips over time, a picture of your shopping habits begins to emerge. This profile is linked to broader market segments based on age, income level, family size, and neighborhood. The real goal is to determine which customers bring in the most profit and then focus on the best customers.

Many shoppers are aware that this data is being tracked, and simply do not mind. For them, the benefits of discounts and promotions far outweigh whatever possible privacy invasions the card might represent. Privacy crusaders, however, warn that your shopping history ultimately could be used against you in ways you never imagined. For example, your employer might be able use your purchases of doughnuts as evidence that you do not fit their ideal profile for a health club employee. A tabloid reporter could reveal that a certain movie star was vain enough to rent his own movies or that a supermodel purchased a pregnancy test.

Someday, the data collected from your club card usage might even be used against you in a court of law. The precedent has been set: several club card programs have been required to turn over shopping history in response to a subpoena. In Los Angeles, a plaintiff was suing a supermarket, because he had fallen in the store and claimed he was unable to work as a result. He contended that the supermarket threatened to introduce shopping records showing alcohol purchases, to discredit him by implying that he had a drinking habit and was intoxicated at the time of the fall.

The concept of club cards to foster loyalty is not new. Coffee houses and sandwich shops have long had punch cards where you punch a hole for each purchase and ultimately get an item for free. For over 100 years, Green Stamps were given to customers at gas stations and supermarkets based on the total dollars spent; customers then could use the stamps to purchase items from local redemption centers.

The difference is the technology. These older programs stored no personal information about you or your shopping history. With the new cards, your shopping activity is tracked and can be linked to you. Once data about your shopping habits is stored in a database, it is accessible to anyone who legally has the right to use it (or anyone who gains unauthorized access). That may only mean it is used to offer you a 20 percent off discount on your next store visit — but it could mean something much more personal.

IN BANKING

For many, the face most customers associate with their bank is not the teller at a local branch; it is the keypad on an ATM or the home page of the bank's online banking Web site. Computers and technology have changed the banking industry in numerous ways – most noticeably, in a bank's use of computers to handle everyday transactions once managed by people.

Electronic Funds Transfer

At the core of the changes in the banking industry is a technology called electronic funds transfer. **Electronic funds transfer (EFT)** allows users connected to a network to transfer money from one bank account to another. Both businesses and consumers use EFT for a wide range of financial transactions. Businesses use EFT to purchase and pay for goods from vendors. Both businesses and consumers pay bills online by instructing their banks to use EFT to pay creditors. Other EFT transactions include withdrawing cash from an ATM, depositing a paycheck directly in an employee's account, or making a purchase in a store using a debit card.

AUTOMATED TELLER MACHINES (ATMS)

An **ATM**, or **automated teller machine**, is a self-service banking machine that connects to a host computer through a network, which ultimately connects to a bank's computer databases. For many people, the ATM is the only place they interact with their bank, and that interaction occurs outside bank branches, grocery stores, convenience stores, movie theaters, shopping malls, and gas stations – wherever banks place ATMs so customers can conveniently access their accounts.

While an ATM allows you to complete banking transactions – withdraw cash, deposit money, transfer funds, or inquire about an account balance, the ATM really is just a terminal with input and output devices (Figure 1-9). To access a bank account, you insert your plastic bankcard into the ATM's card reader, which reads personal data on the bankcard's magnetic strip. The host processor uses this information to route the transaction to the cardholder's bank. The ATM also asks you to enter a personal identification number (PIN), which verifies that you are the holder of the bankcard. Your PIN is **encrypted**, or encoded into an unreadable form, so that unauthorized individuals cannot read it. When your transaction is complete, the ATM prints a receipt for your records.

If you have requested a cash withdrawal, the host processor uses electronic funds transfer to move the correct amount from your bank account to the host processor's account. The host processor then sends a message to the ATM over the network, authorizing the machine to dispense the cash.

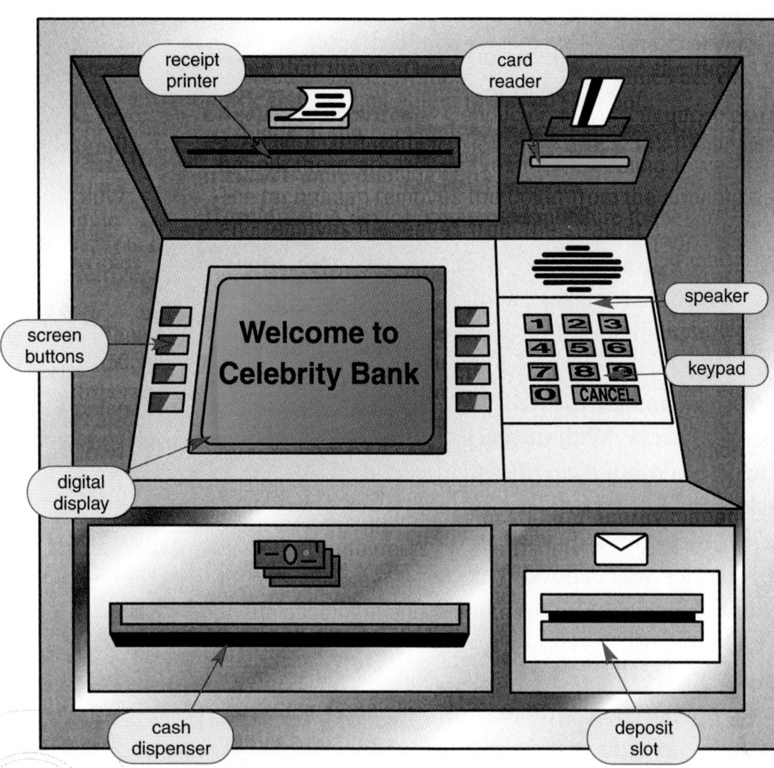

INPUT DEVICES	*OUTPUT DEVICES*
Card reader — Captures the account information stored on the magnetic stripe on the back of an ATM card for input to host processor	**Speaker** — Output sounds when key or area on touch screen is pressed
Keypad — Cardholder to input information to complete transaction and personal identification number (PIN)	**Display screen** — Displays messages to step the cardholder through the transaction process
Screen buttons — On some ATMs, display screen is also a touch screen with buttons that allow a cardholder to input transaction information and PIN	**Receipt printer** — Outputs a paper receipt as a record of the transaction
Deposit slot — Allows customer to input physical items for deposit	**Cash dispenser** — Dispenses cash in the amount of the transaction

Figure 1-9 An ATM has several input and output devices to allow you to complete a range of banking transactions.

DIRECT DEPOSIT When you first take a new job, the human resources person may ask if you would like to receive your paychecks via direct deposit. **Direct deposit** is a means by which an organization can transfer funds electronically to a specified bank, which then makes payments to accounts of individuals or companies. Many businesses use direct deposit to eliminate the need for paper paychecks. With direct deposit set up, you do not have to cash a check every week; instead, you receive a pay stub showing how much money was deposited in your account. The process of completing the direct deposit, as shown in Figure 1-10, is completely transparent to you; the paycheck simply shows up in your account at the end of each pay period. The government also uses direct deposit to distribute Social Security and Veterans benefits, and even tax refunds (Figure 1-11). Direct deposit has benefits for payer and payee: companies and government agencies save hundreds of millions of dollars in costs and productivity gains, and you save time and trips to the bank or ATM.

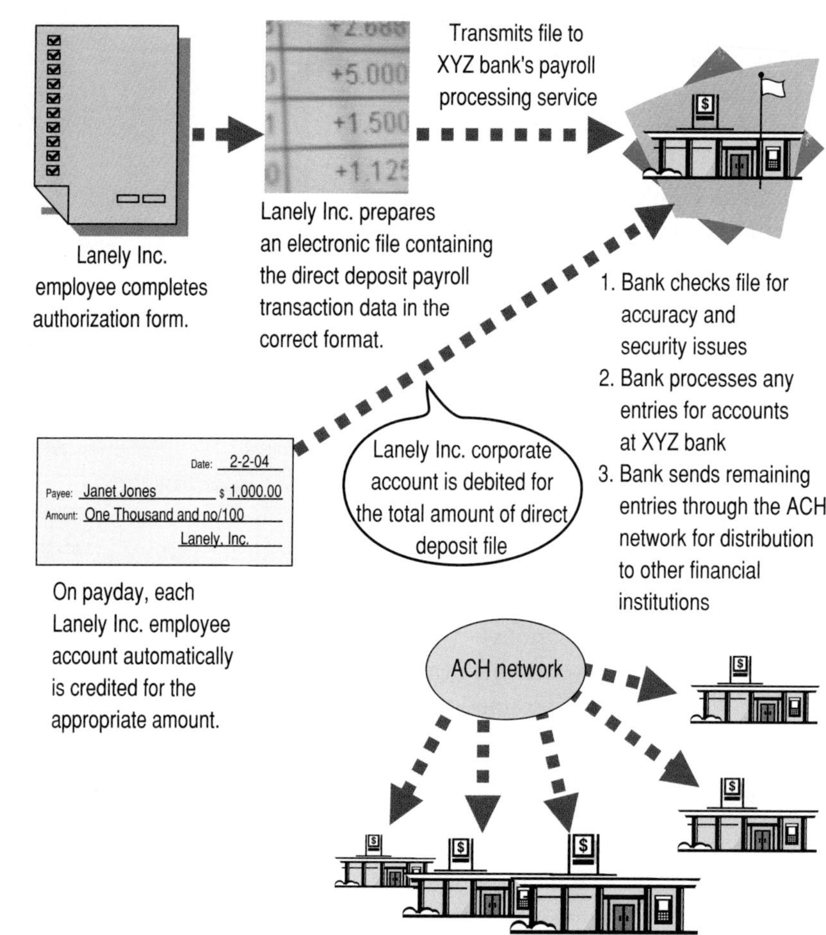

Figure 1-10 Many businesses use direct deposit to deposit employee paychecks in their personal accounts electronically.

59 Advance earned income credit payments from Form(s) W-2 . . . 59
60 Household employment taxes. Attach Schedule H . . . 60
61 Add lines 55 through 60. This is your **total tax** . . . 61

Payments
62 Federal income tax withheld from Forms W-2 and 1099 . . 62
63 2002 estimated tax payments and amount applied from 2001 return . 63
If you have a qualifying child, attach Schedule EIC.
64 **Earned income credit (EIC)** . . . 64
65 Excess social security and tier 1 RRTA tax withheld (see page 56) 65
66 Additional child tax credit. Attach Form 8812 . . . 66
67 Amount paid with request for extension to file (see page 56) 67
68 Other payments from: a ☐ Form 2439 b ☐ Form 4136 c ☐ Form 8885 . 68
69 Add lines 62 through 68. These are your **total payments** . . . 69

Refund
Direct deposit? See page 56 and fill in 71b, 71c, and 71d.
70 If line 69 is more than line 61, subtract line 61 from line 69. This is the amount you **overpaid** 70
71a Amount of line 70 you want **refunded to you** . . . 71a
b Routing number c Type: ☐ Checking ☐ Savings
d Account number
72 Amount of line 70 you want **applied to your 2003 estimated tax** 72

Amount You Owe
73 **Amount you owe.** Subtract line 69 from line 61. For details on how to pay, see page 57 73
74 Estimated tax penalty (see page 57) . . . 74

Third Party Designee Do you want to allow another person to discuss this return with the IRS (see page 58)? ☐ **Yes.** Complete the following. ☐ No
Designee's name Phone no. ( ) Personal identification number (PIN)

Sign Here
Joint return? See page 21.
Keep a copy for your records.
Under penalties of perjury, I declare that I have examined this return and accompanying schedules and statements, and to the be st of my knowledge and belief, they are true, correct, and complete. Declaration of preparer (other than taxpayer) is based on all information of whic h preparer has any knowledge.
Your signature | Date | Your occupation | Daytime phone number ( )
Spouse's signature. If a joint return, **both** must sign. | Date | Spouse's occupation

Paid Preparer's Use Only
Preparer's signature | Date | Check if self-employed ☐ | Preparer's SSN or PTIN
Firm's name (or yours if self-employed), address, and ZIP code | EIN | Phone no. ( )

Figure 1-11 If you provide your account information, the Internal Revenue Service (IRS) can deposit your tax refund directly into your checking or savings account.

AUTOMATED CLEARING HOUSE (ACH) Each time you use your ATM card to pay for a purchase, electronic funds transfer also is used to move the funds from your account back to your bank's account. That transaction takes place using an **automated clearing house (ACH)**, which is a company or group responsible for sorting automated payment instructions to allow the transfer of funds electronically. ACH is used any time a person or business authorizes another person or business to draw funds from your account. For example, your fitness center may use ACH to deduct your monthly membership fee from your account, or a retailer may use ACH when you make a purchase via their

Web site. The ACH network acts as the central clearing facility for all EFT transactions. You may have noticed that there is a slight delay between the time you make a purchase and the time the funds actually are removed from your account. During that time, the payments are held in computers on the ACH network, awaiting clearance to be sent to the appropriate bank.

Smart Credit Cards

A **smart card**, which is comparable in size to an ATM card or credit card, stores data on a thin microprocessor embedded in the card (Figure 1-12). Unlike the typical credit card, which has a magnetic stripe that stores data that cannot be changed, the data stored on a smart card can be updated instantaneously.

Smart cards initially gained favor due to growing concerns that magnetic stripe cards were easy to damage and did not provide protections against fraud. First introduced in Europe over a decade ago, smart cards originally were used as a stored value card for use with pay phones, to help reduce theft. As shown in Table 1-2, smart cards are used for a wide range of applications, some of which will be discussed later in this book. The use of smart cards as stored value cards, however, remains popular, as the cards are more convenient and safer than cash. In Tokyo, for example, more than 5.6 million people use smart cards to pay for their daily commute on the train.

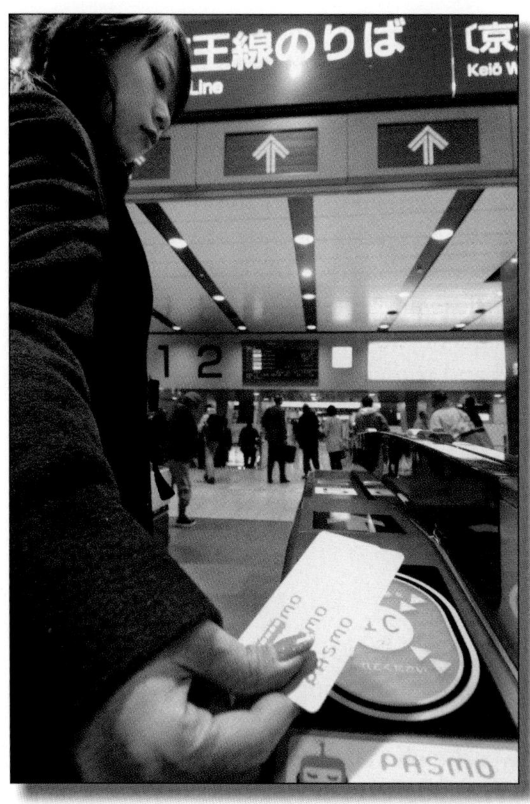

Figure 1-12 A smart card, which is comparable in size to an ATM or credit card, stores data on a thin microprocessor embedded in the card.

TABLE 1-2 Uses for Smart Cards

INDUSTRY/DISCPLINE	*APPLICATION*
Financial	■ Credit and debit cards, especially to allow secure payment over the Internet ■ Prepaid card for small purchases using vending machines, laundry, or photocopy machines
Health care	■ Card to carry medical information such as details of medical insurance coverage, drug sensitivities, medical records, and other information
Communications	■ Prepaid card for phone calls ■ Activation of programming on pay-per-view TV ■ Identifying caller on any GSM phone
Government programs	■ Carry Food Stamp and WIC food benefits instead of paper coupons and vouchers
Information security and physical access	■ Employee access card to protect access to computer systems ■ Employee access card to protect access to facilities
Transportation	■ Driver's license ■ Prepaid card for mass transit fare ■ Prepaid card for electronic toll collection systems
Retail and loyalty	■ Consumer rewards card to track customer purchase and redemption

Smart cards have a wide range of applications in many industries and disciplines.

Smart cards can be contact or contactless (Figure 1-13). A contact card must be swiped or inserted into a card reader. When a contact smart card is inserted into a card reader, the metallic pads of the card come into contact with the reader's metallic pins, thereby allowing the card and reader to communicate. The smart card and reader then are able to process the transaction. A contactless card, which only needs to come in close proximity to the card reader, uses a radio frequency to transfer information to and from the card and reader. The smart cards used for the commuter rail in Japan are contactless and work from up to four inches away from the reader. Most commuters do not even take the cards from their pockets or bags to pass through the turnstile.

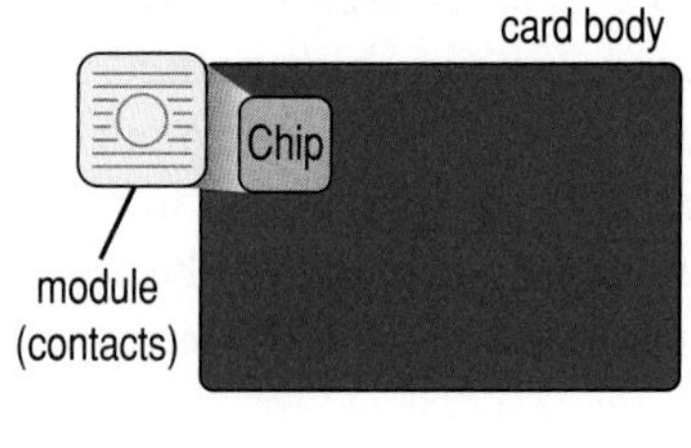

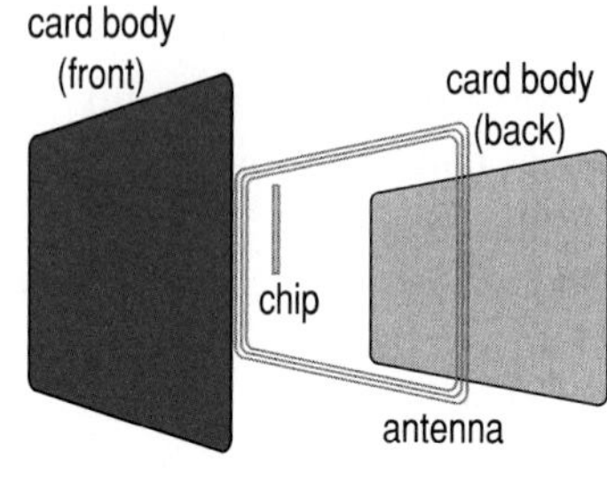

Figure 1-13 Smart cards can be contact or contactless.

Online Banking

In the past, a bank was largely a brick-and-mortar business, meaning that customers primarily conducted transactions in person at a physical location, over the phone, through paper-based communications, or, more recently, via an ATM. Today, many banks and credit unions are becoming brick-and-click businesses, that is, they offer online banking in addition to the services provided at the physical banking facilities. A brick-and-click business is any business that allows customers to conduct business or complete transactions at a physical location, as well as online. By contrast, a cyberbank, such as NetBank, is a virtual bank that has no physical facilities and offers products and services solely on the Internet.

Online banking is easy, convenient, and fast. Using online banking allows you to complete banking activities, such as those listed in Table 1-3.

For many, a common concern about online banking is related to the security of online banking transactions. While no online transactions are 100 percent secure and instances of fraud have occurred, the banking industry has been involved with securing electronic transactions for more than forty years, starting with electronic funds transfer (EFT) systems of the 1960s. Today, you can expect your online bank to use sophisticated security technologies to protect your personal information and to secure your online transactions. When shopping for an online bank, you should carefully review the bank's privacy policies and any security statements it provides.

TABLE 1-3

TRANSACTIONS AVAILABLE VIA ONLINE BANKING

- View real-time account balances and recent transactions.
- View a history of account activity.
- Search for individual transactions.
- Pay your bills.
- Transfer funds between accounts.
- Download transactions into personal financial management software such as Quicken and Microsoft Money.
- Issue a stop payment on a check.
- Order checks.
- Report a lost or stolen ATM card and request a replacement.
- Change personal information such as your address, phone number, and e-mail address.

Most online banking Web sites allow you to complete a wide range of transactions.

BILL PAYMENT SERVICE Many financial industry analysts think the most valuable use of online banking is online bill payment services. A **bill payment service** allows you to log on to a Web site and pay any number of bills from a range of vendors. In addition to online banks, e-businesses such as CheckFree, PayTrust, and Yahoo! Bill Pay offer bill payment services.

When you are ready to pay a bill online using an online bill payment service, you simply log onto your online bank or payment service's Web site, select a vendor from a list of vendors you created when you first established your account, and enter a payment amount and the payment date. On the scheduled payment date, your payment is debited from your bank account and transmitted to the vendor either by an electronic funds transfer or via a paper check. You also can set up recurring monthly bills, such as your cell phone bill or car payment, to be paid automatically on a specific day each month.

BILL PRESENTMENT More and more utilities, credit card companies, auto finance companies, and other businesses are using **bill presentment**, which is the process of sending bills electronically instead of mailing their customers paper bills or statements. Using bill presentment to send electronic bills, also called **e-bills**, can reduce substantially a company's billing costs. You can arrange to receive e-bills and then pay them electronically through your online bank account or bill payment service. Alternatively, you can pay your bill directly at the vendor's Web site.

IN THE OFFICE

Offices are at the center of the action in business and many other organizations. In today's office, technology is an integral part of the business. Almost every individual has a computer, a PDA (personal digital assistant), and a cell phone. Computers allow employees to store documents and spreadsheets on a network, so coworkers in different offices can review them at any time. Networked printers churn out high-quality presentations for the weekly board meeting. Fax machines and e-mail allow workers to communicate new advertising copy to a client, while receiving a signed copy of the latest contract.

Going Paperless

In the past, almost every activity in an office was recorded on paper. Memos were photocopied and distributed by hand, meeting agendas and handouts were distributed at the beginning of each meeting, and accounting information was kept by hand, in ledgers. For a creative department working on designs with a client, each iteration of the design had to be printed and shipped to the client for review – and then shipped back with comments.

Today, many offices have reduced paper in some areas of the business – and are working to be paperless. Archival information, such as tax returns and financial statements, are stored on disk or tape drives specifically designed for permanent storage. Paychecks are sent directly to individual's bank accounts using EFT and direct deposit. Many companies have corporate intranets (secure, online networks for employee use) that include online forms that employees can use to request vacations, send technical support requests, or update their address and contact information. Even the paper-laden process of completing a form for reimbursement of travel expenses is paper free: employees can fill out an online form from their computer, PDA, or cell phone, to itemize expenses and request reimbursement. The creative department can send new advertising layouts to a client using a PDF file, so the client can see exactly how the ad will look on the back cover of a magazine.

PDF, which is short for **Portable Document Format**, is an electronic file format that preserves formatting, fonts, and layouts so files can be viewed and printed on a variety of platforms or reader software, called Adobe Acrobat Reader. The PDF format also is greatly compressed, which means files are small enough to be sent quickly by e-mail or downloaded from the Web.

Many companies are creating annual reports in PDF for easy distribution to investors and shareholders. Others use PDF to make documentation for products, from cellular phones to washing machines, available to customers online (Figure 1-14). For creative, publishing, and advertising firms, PDF proofs can be e-mailed or posted to a Web site for download. Clients can make electronic comments directly in the file and e-mail them back in the space of hours, not days.

One of the first innovators in the move to a paperless office was Owens Corning, a fiberglass manufacturer. In 1997, the company designed its headquarters to be paper free. The office included no cabinets to file paper files; instead, they gave everyone computers with the same software so that everyone in the office could conduct internal business via an intranet or e-mail. Memos, news, and policy announcements are sent via e-mail and posted on the intranet; all forms are on the intranet as well. Owens Corning estimated that its corporate intranet would save $50 million a year, mostly by reducing the need for filing and faxing.

Despite the promise of a paperless office, however, most desks still are covered with documents and recycling bins are full of paper. Even Owens Corning still used paper for phone messages and, years later, found that the high cost of systems to support the paperless office offset some of the expected savings. Some studies show that, while technology could move offices closer to being paperless, the use of paper actually has increased.

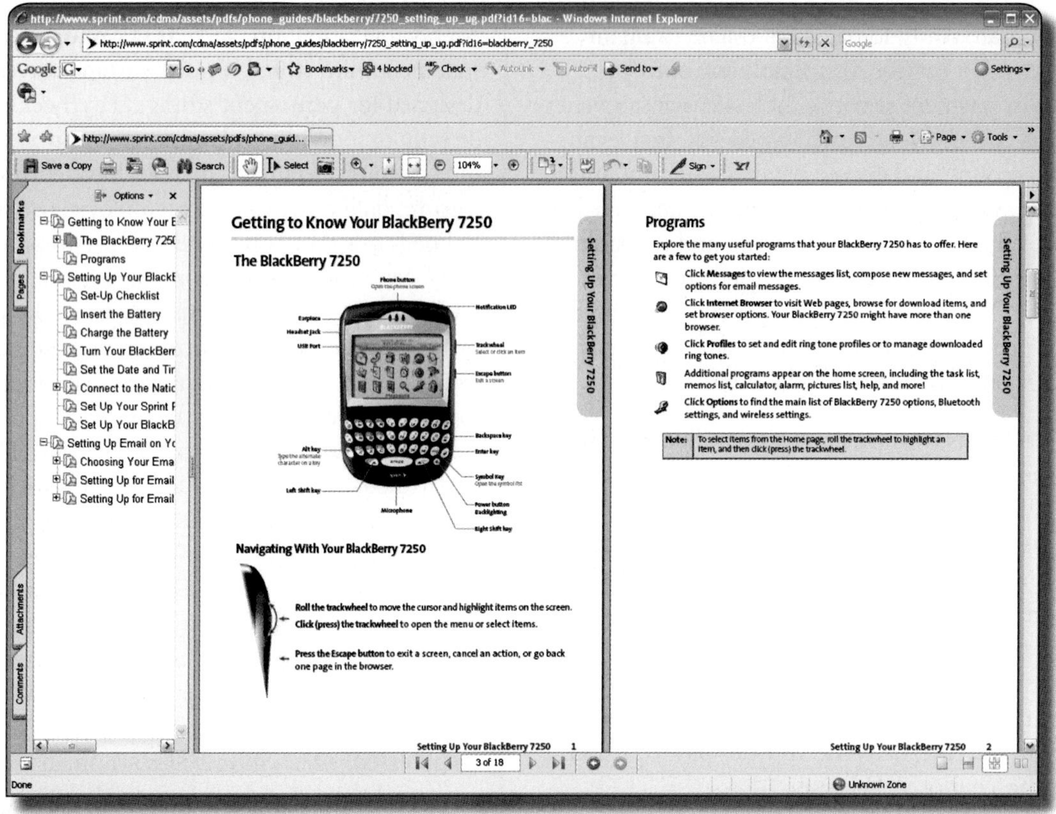

Figure 1-14 Many companies are using PDF files to make documentation for their products available online. Sprint PCS, for example, allows you to view a PDF version of the user guide for all of their cellular phones.

The use of the Web and e-mail, along with the ease of printing, has caused a rise in paper consumption of up to 40 percent in some offices. For many, e-mails and Web pages are easier to read when they are printed, which may be why employees, on average, print 33 Web pages each day.

Far from being obsolete, paper is the perfect medium for many work activities and provides a complement to digital documents. For now, the paperless office may remain more of an aspiration than a reality.

Telecommuting

One of the unique changes in the office brought about by computers is telecommuting. **Telecommuting** is a work arrangement in which employees work away from a company's office or other workplace, and communicate with the office using technology, including computers, video and telephone systems, fax machines, and high-speed network connections.

As shown in Table 1-4, telecommuting provides many advantages. For employees, telecommuting:

- Reduces commuting time, allowing employees to work during the time they normally would spend in a car
- Offers employees flexible schedules, which decreases absenteeism
- Allows employees to work for a company anywhere in the world

TABLE 1-4

ADVANTAGES	DISADVANTAGES
■ Reduces commuting time	■ Out of sight, out of mind to boss and coworkers
■ Provides flexible schedule and decreases absenteeism	■ Requires discipline and focus
■ Global employment opportunities	■ Puts onus on employee to initiate regular contact
■ Increased productivity	■ Perceived need to work hard to prove value
■ Creates higher morale	■ Reduces the socialinteraction of the office
■ Reduces stress	■ Initial cost to employer for set up
■ Reduces need for office space dedicated to individual employees	■ Often have to handle your own tech support

Telecommuting has several advantages and disadvantages.

- Increases productivity and improves quality, especially for jobs that demand a high degree of privacy and concentration; fewer interruptions can lead to better, faster results
- Creates higher morale and reduces stress by giving employees a sense of control over their work life

Telecommuting does have its disadvantages. Because their efforts are not directly visible to coworkers, a CEO might not appreciate the efforts of a telecommuter as much as the employee who arrives an hour early to the office each morning. Telecommuting also requires discipline. In the home, the distractions are numerous: housework, television, pets, and family. Employees who are successful working remotely must be self-motivated, able to focus, and comfortable defining their own work schedules to ensure projects are completed successfully. If telecommuters do not maintain regular contact with the office, managers also may feel they do not know what the worker is doing. To help combat this, telecommuters may believe that they need to work longer and harder than employees in the office, as a way of proving their value.

Telecommuters also miss the social interaction of an office and can experience feelings of isolation. Telecommuters also miss out on office gossip, which may mean being out of touch with important, but unofficial, matters that affect a company or a project. Telecommuters often also have to provide their own technical support. Even if the company has Help desk resources available, troubleshooting a computer or network problem must happen over the phone, rather than in person.

For many, a pure telecommuting job with no time in the office is not the ideal; instead, many workers want to work at home for only one or two days a week to focus on core projects or to handle personal responsibilities.

HUMAN FACTORS AND THE WORKPLACE

While computers and technology have had many positive impacts on the work world, using a computer also creates some new health issues and safety hazards. Problems such as repetitive stress injuries and computer vision syndrome are examples of some of the potential health problems caused by using computers for long stretches. Understanding these and other possible health risks – and how to prevent them – is a key step to healthy computing.

Ergonomics

The goal of **ergonomics** is to incorporate comfort, efficiency, and safety into the design of items in the workplace. Employees can be injured or develop disorders of the muscles, nerves, tendons, ligaments, and joints from working in an area that is not ergonomically designed.

Ergonomic studies have shown that using the correct type and configuration of chair, keyboard, display device, and work surface helps you work more comfortably and efficiently, while protecting your health. For the computer work area, experts recommend an area of at least two feet by four feet. Figure 1-15 illustrates additional guidelines for setting up your work area. Some

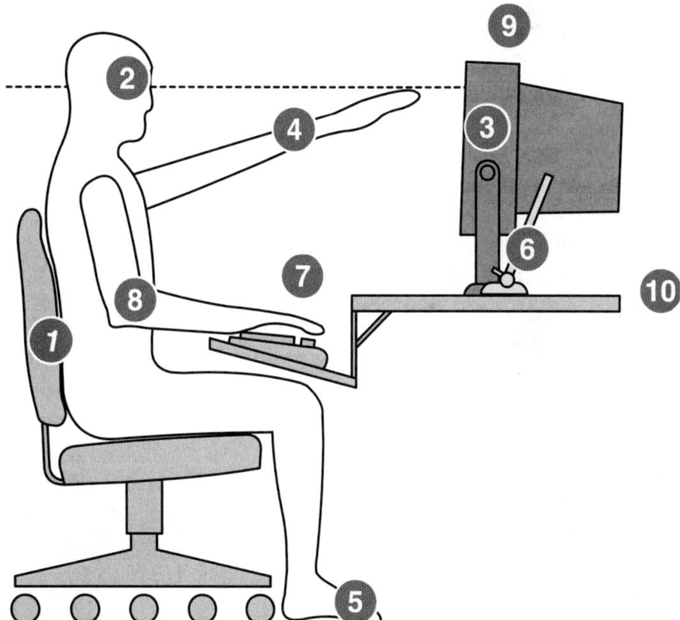

Figure 1-15 A well-designed work area should be flexible to allow adjustments to the height and build of individuals. Some other tips on setting up an ergonomically correct work area:

1. Use a good adjustable height chair with 4 to 5 legs for stability
2. Set the viewing distance to the monitor to 18 to 28 inches
3. Avoid glare on the screen (if needed, use an antiglare filter)
4. Sit at arms length from monitor
5. Place feet flat on floor or stable footrest
6. Use a document holder to place papers you are viewing as you work
7. Arms and wrists should be approximately parallel to the floor
8. Elbows should be relaxed, at about 90 degree angle to the floor
9. Center monitor and keyboard in front of you
10. Use a stable work surface and stable keyboard tray

also find that using desks where the desktop is thick glass and the monitor sits below the desk provides a comfortable work environment.

The way you organize the elements of your workplace to fit your individual needs is the most important consideration in working comfortably. For instance, organize your desk to reflect the way you use work materials and equipment, so that the things you use most regularly, such as a mouse or telephone, are within easy reach. Above all, vary your tasks and take periodic breaks to help reduce the possibility of discomfort or fatigue.

Repetitive Stress Injuries

Many computer input and output devices have features that address ergonomic issues. For example, some keyboards have built in wrist rests, while others have a design specifically intended to prevent repetitive stress injuries. A **repetitive stress injury (RSI)**, such as carpal tunnel syndrome, is caused when muscle groups complete the same repetitive actions, over and over again. In the past, RSIs were common among factory workers who performed the same task on an assembly line for hours a day. Today, RSIs are just as common among office workers. Computer keyboards are a major source of RSIs, resulting from constant typing at fast speeds. Mice and trackballs also cause injuries from the long periods spent using the input device. Other health problems caused by poorly designed work areas include back, neck, shoulder, and foot pain.

Symptoms of an RSI include stiffness or burning in the hands, loss of strength in the hands, and pain in the upper back, shoulders, or neck. Correct typing technique and posture, the right equipment setup, and good work habits are important for prevention of RSIs. These and other preventative tips are listed in Table 1-5.

TABLE 1-5 Tips for Healthy Computer Use

TIP	*DESCRIPTION*
Use correct posture.	You should not have to slouch or stretch to reach the keys or read the screen. Anything that creates awkward reaches or angles in the body will create problems. Relax and shift positions frequently.
Increase your font sizes and use easy-to-read colors.	Small fonts encourage you to hunch forward to read. Use color schemes easy on the eyes, particularly shades of gray for text documents.
Type gently.	Do not press hard on the keyboard; use a light touch. Also, use two hands to perform operations with two keys (such as CTRL+X).
Keep a light grip on the mouse.	Hold the mouse lightly; don't grip it hard or squeeze it. Place the pointing device where you don't have to reach up or over very far to use it; close to the keyboard is best
Take a break.	Take time to stretch and relax. This means both momentary breaks every few minutes and longer breaks every hour or so. Pace and plan your computer work.
Listen to your body.	If you are experiencing pain, it could be a first sign that your work area is not well-designed. Stop and evaluate the pain; take time to learn what is comfortable for you as you work.

These simple tips can help you avoid RSIs from working at a computer.

Computer Vision Syndrome (CVS)

Studies show that from 50 to 90 percent of computer users experience the symptoms of computer vision syndrome (CVS) at one time during their lives. CVS is caused by screen glare, improper lighting, monitor settings that are hard on the eyes, and even a need for glasses. Symptoms of computer vision syndrome include eyestrain or eye fatigue, dry or burning eyes, increased sensitivity to light, blurred vision, headache, and pain in the shoulders, neck, or back.

The symptoms and problems of CVS, however, usually can be alleviated by good eye care and changes in the work environment. Some tips for reducing CVS include using a high-resolution monitor, positioning the center of the monitor about 18 to 28 inches away, arranging the light to avoid glare, and stopping periodically to rest your eyes. Although blinking is a reflex, you blink less often when looking at a computer than when reading or performing other tasks. Remember to blink often when using your computer to avoid dry eyes or blurred vision. Regular visits to an eye doctor to check your vision also can help you avoid eyestrain while working at your computer.

QUALITY OF WORK LIFE

Many believe that technology has, in general, improved the overall quality of life and, in particular, increased the quality of work life. Technological change has decreased work time and reduced danger for workers, while creating better goods and services at lower prices for consumers. Employees can use technology to gain access to information from around the world; telecommunications makes working from anywhere at any time a reality.

Technology also has had a negative impact on the quality of work life. Employee monitoring, for example, reduces morale and causes employee stress, while new technologies force entire sets of workers to find their skills no longer are current. This section reviews a few aspects of work life altered by technology: employee monitoring, skilling and deskilling, worker autonomy, and the blurring of boundaries between work and home.

Employee Monitoring

Employee monitoring involves the use of computers to observe, record, and review an employee's use of a computer. Employee monitoring can track communications such as e-mail messages, the Web sites an employee visits, the amount of time an employee spends away from the computer, and, with keystroke monitoring, how many keystrokes per hour the employee is performing. Many software programs exist to help employers monitor their employees. Further, the law establishes that it is legal for employers to monitor your use of their computer equipment and your time at the workplace.

As more employees are granted Internet access, more companies also are using employee monitoring tools to help ensure network security and guarantee that employees are not using computers in a way that might damage the company's reputation. Other employers use monitoring to help manage productivity. For example, employers can place time limits or other restrictions on Internet access to ensure that employees do not waste time sending personal e-mail or browsing the Web.

E-mail is a hotly debated topic when it comes to workplace privacy. Laws relating to the privacy of your e-mail at work are not well defined, but several workplace privacy court cases have been decided in favor of the employer, stating that if an e-mail system is used at a company, the employer owns it and is allowed to review its contents. Messages sent within the company, as well as those sent outside of the company, can be subject to monitoring by your employer.

Because the topic of monitoring is a sensitive one, many companies publish policies explaining that they have the legal right to monitor employees' computer use and that, by accepting employment, employees acknowledge that right. Most companies do not abuse their right to monitor employees; they only want to protect themselves from any illegal or harmful use of their network and computer systems.

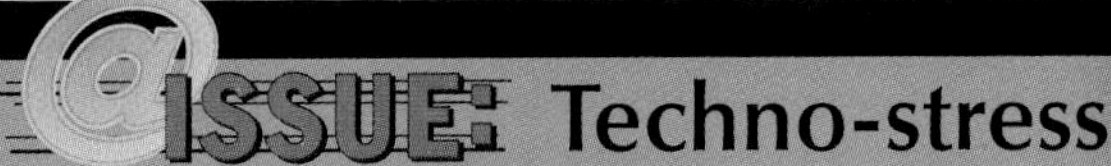

Techno-stress

Technology makes many things in your personal and business life more streamlined, productive, and less stressful. For example, instead of arriving at the airport for your business trip only to find your flight is delayed, you can check the flight departure times on the Web — and have an extra cup of coffee at home. After using a Web site to check traffic on the route to the airport, you use your PDA to e-mail the client about the delay and then call the limo service on your cellular phone to reschedule your pick up. Your presentation, which you deliver using PowerPoint slides and projector, is flawless. Instead of having you fly out for a follow-up meeting next week, you agree to set up a Web conference.

Recent research, however, suggests that technology also adds stress to our lives in some obvious and some subtle ways — a phenomenon called techno-stress. For example, the same technology that allows you to keep in touch with the office on your business trip also creates additional stress. Although you have spent a day with the client, you still have eight voice mail messages to hear and 32 e-mails to address at the end of your long day. Technology also allows you to take on many tasks simultaneously. At any point in the work day, you might be found talking on your cellular phone, sending e-mail, and printing the latest sales figures. The net result is that you cannot focus on any one thing, and you feel compelled to continue to do many things all at once, all of the time.

Your concentration and effectiveness are undermined further by the constant contacts from coworkers and clients. Recent studies have shown that you will be interrupted by electronic communications, such as e-mails, pages, or faxes at least three times an hour. Further adding to your stress is the computer itself, which crashes right as you complete an important memo, thus causing you to lose all of your hard work. You still do not fully understand the new accounting software installed a few weeks ago, so it takes you three times as long to complete the month-end numbers for the chief financial officer as it did with the previous software.

For employees who are being monitored, the stresses are less subtle — and can manifest themselves in health problems. Electronic monitoring puts pressure on employees to perform, which often makes them feel as if the employer does not trust them, and causes employees to worry about losing their jobs. In factories and offices where computer systems are used to monitor the number of items made per hour or the number of words typed per minute, the stress can take a physical toll. When workers feel compelled to meet set quotas, the repetitive motions that cause damage to joints and tendons increase and workers become prone to carpal tunnel syndrome and back pain.

Consider your recent experiences with technology. Did the technology make your life easier, or did it add to your stress? Techno-stress can creep up, when you least expect it. Maybe the next time you feel as if technology is causing you unnecessary stress, try to slow down and use technology for something that makes you smile: send a quick text message to a friend, view pictures from your last vacation, or plug in your MP3 player and listen to a favorite song.

Skilling and De-skilling

Computers and technology are at the core of a debate about whether the use of technology in the workplace helps increase the skill of workers by allowing them to learn and utilize constantly changing technology, or results in the deskilling of workers, due to automation that creates highly rigid jobs with narrow scopes. **De-skilling** is the process by which the tasks that workers do are fragmented to a point where a worker loses sight of the larger purpose of the job – he or she simply executes the task.

Many espouse the de-skilling side of the debate, arguing that managers exploit new technologies to help them control workers. This idea, first brought forth by the Marxist Harry Braverman in the early 1970s, remains popular today with those who believe managers computerize the workplace in order to tighten controls at every turn. They also suggest that computerization degrades work at the lowest levels of the office hierarchy, where jobs are the most routinized and the division of labor is the most rigid. Data entry clerks, such as telephone travel agents, insurance claims clerks, and word-processing specialists, for example, are forced into jobs that use one type of software for a single job task – jobs that are unsatisfying, uncreative, and monotonous.

Others emphasize the potential for computers to upgrade work and enhance employee skills. For them, an office rich in computer technology is one rich in opportunity. Instead of spending time on routine tasks, office workers can use computers and other technologies to speed through these tasks – and then focus on more interesting and creative work. For examples, office workers and professionals can use word processors to create mailings quickly and spreadsheets to track sales accurately. E-mail allows workers to communicate faster; the Internet and a company's databases place information at workers' fingertips. By helping to speed these routine tasks, office workers can focus on bigger-picture questions, such as how to analyze sales data to map regional sales trends or create a new advertising campaign for the latest product.

Worker Autonomy

Autonomy is self-directing freedom, and especially moral independence. In the workplace, worker **autonomy** is the freedom of workers to contribute to the overall goals of the organization, as well as to their own personal goals.

The extent to which computers help to foster or inhibit worker autonomy varies by industry, sector, and occupation. For manufacturing workers, better technology in the workplace has benefits and drawbacks. In some places, workers are more autonomous. State-of-the-art information technology at one Harley-Davidson plant, for example, allows workers on the factory floor to make production decisions that previously only would have been made by managers. The plant also gives network access on the shop floor to update workers on time and attendance, quality control issues, and the plant's production level. The end result is that workers are engaged in the process and feel a sense of personal responsibility for the results.

Others suggest that the use of technology in the factory strips employees of their autonomy. By using production-scheduling systems to define exactly what tasks are next in a particular process, employers can standardize activities and keep a tight rein on workers to drive maximum efficiency.

In service work, computers give employees more access to the information they need to complete their jobs. Customer service or Help desk employees now have large databases of information immediately available to help them quickly retrieve a customer's account information and determine the most appropriate way to handle the customer issue. Further enhancing autonomy in the service sector is the fact that many companies outsource their customer service to telecommuters, who connect to the company network remotely. These same workers, however, often find technology confines them to routine jobs with little opportunity for creativity.

Blurred Boundaries

As devices such as PDAs, cell phones, and computers become more powerful and more portable, you may find that you depend on them in unanticipated ways – quickly looking up a phone number while away from your desk, getting an e-mail that the shipment of new inventory has arrived, or checking your voice mail on the way home. These tools significantly change the way individuals work and live, extending the employees' focus on work and allowing them to work from anywhere, at any time. That, however, can be precisely the issue: today's technologies make it increasingly difficult for people to separate themselves from work, as the boundaries between work and home life become blurred.

Recent research found that 20 percent of workers keep in touch with the office while on vacation. Cell phones, laptops, and pagers are the most common devices used. 77 percent of workers aged 22 to 34 check personal e-mail while on vacation; 39 percent check work e-mail. 60 percent of people over 60 check e-mail on vacation. Other studies showed that employees who use the Internet regularly work longer hours in the office – and are more likely to work additional hours at home.

We are so used to being available at any time that we must be reminded to turn off our cell phones and pagers before church, movies, concerts, or school classes begin. More seriously, the time that individuals used to have for themselves is encroached on by work. Evenings once reserved for family and friends now often include at least one visit to the computer to check e-mail. Coworkers, managers, and clients can contact you on the weekend, on vacation, in the middle of dinner, and just about anywhere else, all as part of the ethic that dedicated employees always are accessible via their "electronic leash." On the surface, it looks as if individuals are being highly productive, but the reality is that employees risk burning out. What's interesting is that over half of U.S. workers do not take all their vacation time each year, yet 77 percent report feeling burned-out on the job. Workers wonder if the office will survive without them, if they'll be replaced while away, or whether co-workers who aren't vacationing will be resentful. At the other end of the spectrum, though, are those employees who don't want to be reached. Nine percent of workers have lied to their employers, claiming they couldn't be reached on vacation, to minimize the guilt associated with not checking in while gone.

Employers are starting to realize that employees and the self-employed need to have down time to recharge – and that the "always on" lifestyle causes more stress and strain than individuals realize. Employees also are recognizing that, because technology lets you accomplish your work more efficiently, many people end up taking on too much and thus always feeling rushed or behind. As is increasingly clear, the key is to reach a balance. As shown in Table 1-6, individuals can take steps to re-establish boundaries between work and home – first and foremost, simply by turning off the technology for a while.

LOOKING AHEAD

The work world of today looks far different from how it looked 50 years ago – and it is difficult to imagine what the workplace will look like another half century from now. In a perfect world, technology and the Internet will greatly improve the world of work, so that individuals never have to commute to work, robots handle any dangerous factory jobs, and a computer recording a conference call generates memos and status reports automatically. For many, the workplace of the future offers much opportunity for highly productive and satisfying work, aided by computers and technology. For others, the future and the new economy do not hold such hope.

Employment and Unemployment

Technology constantly changes both existing and emerging jobs. When computers originally were introduced into all facets of the factory, the office, and the retail store, many low-skilled production and service jobs requiring less education vanished – causing some to suggest that technology creates a condition of increasing unemployment.

No one can deny that technological change has displaced workers. As new technology makes the old obsolete, the new technology completely changes job descriptions and can eliminate occupations – but, in turn, it creates new opportunities. Over the last century, declines in the number of production jobs have been offset by increases in office and service jobs. Instead of machinery, these workers' tools are the telephone, the computer, e-mail, and the Internet.

The U.S. Department of Labor projects that 8 of the 10 fastest growing jobs between now and 2010 will be

TABLE 1-6

TIPS TO CREATE WORK-HOME LIFE BALANCE

- Turn off the technology. Define the times when you are working – and when you are not. Also allow for a middle area, where you are less accessible, but not completely out of contact (for example, during your commute). During the times when you are not working, turn off the cellular phone, computer, and PDA.
- Discuss your availability with your boss, coworkers, and clients. Create a proposal and, as needed, modify it to meet your needs and your coworkers' needs.
- If possible, do not bring work home. If you must, set aside a specific time frame during which to work on it.
- Work with your team members to set agreed upon boundaries. If everyone agrees to not check e-mail on vacation, it makes it easier to maintain that behavior.
- Create time for yourself at least once or twice a week. Take time to fully disconnect all of your technology gadgets and take a walk with the dog, read, or go see a show.
- Take your lunch break. A break during the day can be a terrific stress reliever.

Several simple actions can help you reestablish the boundaries between your work life and home life.

computer related. The demand for computer-related occupations will continue to increase as a result of rapid advances in computer technology and the ongoing demand for new computer applications, including those for the Internet and intranets.

Other jobs – even those considered to be nontechnical – will require an understanding of how to use technology. Administrative workers must understand word processing, accounting, and human resources software, along with how to set up teleconferences and book travel reservations online. Truck drivers use global positioning systems to determine the fastest route to their delivery destination. Food service workers use computer terminals to input customer orders and generate end-of-day sales numbers. By 2008, nearly half of all American employment will be in industries that either produce or use computer technology.

For the other 50 percent of Americans not working in technology-rich jobs, however, wages may continue to fall as the only work available to them may be low-paying service-sector jobs with few advancement opportunities. Even today, this trend is seen in many major U.S cities, and the problem continues.

Technology can significantly improve the lives of those who have the skill and education to adopt it – and further separate those who do not. This gap between those who have access to computers and those who do not is referred to as the **digital divide**. Some liken it to the days of the Industrial Revolution, when unskilled workers were forced into dangerous, tedious, low-paying jobs in factories. Today, however, underskilled workers are force to accept underpaid jobs in service industries instead of in factories. The social, ethical, and legal implications of the digital divide will be discussed later in the book.

A New Economy?

In the end, the solution to the problem is difficult. Technological change is a key part of progress for any society. Going as far back as the Agricultural Revolution and the Industrial Revolution, technology always has and always will continue to create change. Along with the change will be the inevitable shifts in available jobs and the skills required to hold those jobs. Can you imagine life today if we had stopped the invention of the stocking frame to save the job of Ned Ludd – or if we held back from light bulbs out of consideration for the candle makers? Paradoxically, the jobs that the Luddites so feared they would lose to the new machines did not vanish – by the end of the nineteenth century, textile mills were employing at least one hundred men for every one employed at the beginning of the century.

For workers then and now, the challenge is to keep skills as current as the available jobs.

Today the Information Age has brought its own revolution, resulting in an entirely new set of rules in the economy.

The old sources of competitive advantage – access to raw materials, transportation routes, or customer markets; low costs; and a large labor pool – are becoming less important. In an economy in which information is the raw material and the best selling product, these other factors are less key. Instead, the most important factors are having networked computer systems that provide efficient access to information to help foster innovation and creativity, and the educated workforce to use these systems.

Finally, the most valuable input for many firms is the skills and talent of their workforce. In the past, workers often held one job and followed a company from location to location. Today, you are likely to hold many jobs over your lifetime, each for a shorter period. Each time you change a job, you have the opportunity to move ahead and redefine your work. In today's technology-rich new economy, your ability to move up the corporate ladder is helped by a solid understanding of computers, technology, and their applications.

CONCLUSION

In this chapter, you learned about the transition from an agricultural to an industrial and, finally an information-based economy, and the changes that transition has brought. You learned about the use of computers in business and industry, including the use of computers in the factory, in retail sales and marketing, in banking, and in the office. After learning how ergonomics can help minimize health issues related to computing, you then were introduced to the various ways computers impact the quality of work life. Finally, you learned more about how computers may change work in the future, creating new jobs that require a solid understanding of computers, technology, and their applications.

KEY TERMS

acquirer
automated clearing house (ACH)
automated teller machine (ATM)
autonomy
bar code
bar code scanner
bill payment service
bill presentment
computer-aided design (CAD)
computer-aided engineering (CAE)
computer-aided manufacturing (CAM)
computer-integrated manufacturing (CIM)
credit-authorization system
database marketing
de-skilling
digital divide
direct deposit
e-bills
electronic funds transfer (EFT)
employee monitoring
encrypted
ergonomics
Information Age
information economy
inventory control system
job-scheduling system
just-in-time manufacturing
Luddite
manufacturing resource planning (MRP)
new economy
opt in
opt out
PDF (Portable Document Format)
point-of-sale (POS) system
production-scheduling system
repetitive stress injury (RSI)
smart card
spam
telecommuting
UPC (Universal Product Code)
warehouse management system (WMS)

CHAPTER REVIEW

Multiple Choice

Select the best answer.

1. _____ integrate various production and process control systems into a single computerized system.

a. Computer-aided design (CAD) systems
b. Point-of-sale (POS) systems
c. Computer-aided engineering (CAE) systems
d. Manufacturing resource planning (MRP) systems

2. A(n) _____ helps factory managers decide when to initiate production based on the supplies on hand and customer demand.

a. inventory control system
b. job-scheduling system
c. distribution system
d. warehouse management system

3. _____ use(s) the UPC (Universal Product Code) to identify different items.

a. Retail and grocery stores
b. Libraries
c. The United States Post Office
d. all of the above

4. Spam is _____.

a. an organization that collects credit-authentication requests
b. the use of bill presentment to send electronic bills
c. unsolicited, junk e-mail sent as part of an electronic mass mailing
d. a science that incorporates comfort and efficiency into workplace design

5. An ATM (automated teller machine) allows you to _____.

a. withdraw cash and deposit money
b. transfer funds
c. inquire about an account balance
d. all of the above

6. Unlike a typical credit card, a smart card _____.

a. has a magnetic stripe that stores data that cannot be changed
b. stores data that can be changed
c. is large and immoveable
d. cannot interact with computers or other automated systems

7. _____ is an electronic file format that preserves document integrity so files can be viewed and printed on a variety of platforms using reader software.

a. ACH
b. PDF
c. WMS
d. EFT

8. For the computer work area, ergonomics experts recommend having _____.

a. two feet by four feet
b. four feet by eight feet
c. eight feet by sixteen feet
d. sixteen feet by thirty-two feet

9. A _____, such as carpal tunnel syndrome, is caused when muscle groups complete the same actions over and over again.

a. posttraumatic stress injury (PSI)
b. computer vision syndrome (CVS)
c. repetitive stress injury (RSI)
d. workplace pathology syndrome (WPS)

10. Employee monitoring involves the _____.

a. use of computers to observe, record, and review a worker's use of a computer
b. electronic transfer of funds to a worker's bank account
c. use of computers to mine worker databases and create marketing lists
d. practice of working away from an office and communicating via technology

Chapter Review

Short Answer

Write a brief answer to each of the following questions.

1. How is the Information Age similar to the Agricultural Revolution and the Industrial Revolution?
2. How are CAD (computer-aided design), CAE (computer-aided engineering), and CAM (computer-aided manufacturing) different?
3. Why do businesses and consumers use electronic funds transfer (EFT)?
4. What are the advantages and the disadvantages of telecommuting for an employee?
5. How does the use of computers affect worker autonomy?

Web Research

Use a search engine such as Google (google.com) to research the following questions. Then, write a one-page, double-spaced report or create a presentation, unless otherwise directed.

1. Some people and companies cringe when they hear the word **ergonomics**, fearing the high costs required to make a workplace more user-friendly. Many experts point out, however, that creating a more comfortable workplace does not have to involve a great deal of money. Use the Web to discover some low-cost ways to construct a more ergonomically sound workplace.
2. Several companies, including Microsoft, have donated money to bridge the **digital divide**. Yet, some commentators insist that concern about the digital divide is overblown, and others even maintain that the digital divide is a myth. Use the Web to research the extent of the digital divide and what problems, if any, the digital divide poses.

Group Exercises

Working with a group of your classmates, complete the following team questions.

1. In 2003, a new virtual world appeared on the Internet called Second Life. This 3-D virtual environment for work and play, created solely by its residents, has started to see the presence of corporate entities populating its communities. For example, Manpower Inc. recently launched an island online to help Second Life residents with virtual employment issues. The Vancouver Police Department has its own virtual police force online to help with recruiting real-world cops. Inter-Continental Hotels' Crowne Plaza has a virtual conference center there. Some people argue the need for having a real "first life" before engaging in a computerized "second" one. Others see this as an extension of social networks such as MySpace and Facebook. As a team, research the Second Life community's history, membership options, costs, and competitors. What are the pros and cons of joining? If you know someone who has joined, interview them about their experience. Use the Web to find out what other companies are joining the Second Life community, and why. Prepare a PowerPoint presentation containing your findings.
2. A popular saying is, "You can't take it with you." In the modern workplace, however, sometimes you must use technology to take it — your job — with you wherever you go. Have each member of your team interview someone who uses technology (such as cell phones, notebook computers, and PDAs) as part of his or her job. Find out how the individual uses technology, and how technology makes the individual's job, and life, easier or more difficult. Then, meet with your team and prepare a PowerPoint presentation illustrating both the benefits, and problems, associated with using technology to blur the boundaries between an individual's personal and professional life.

Computers in Government, Law Enforcement, and the Military 2

Computers and the Government
- The Election Process
  - *Conducting Polls*
  - *Communicating with Voters*
  - *Researching Candidates*
  - *Casting a Ballot: Computerized Voting Systems*
- United States Postal Service
- Census Bureau
- Internal Revenue Service

Computers in Law Enforcement
- Tracking Evidence
- Storing Criminal Records
- Enforcing Traffic Laws
- Tracking Stolen Vehicles
- Finding Missing Children
- Providing Wireless 911

Computers and Homeland Security
- Tracking Citizens
- Tracking Visitors
- Surveillance Using Computer Vision Systems
- Managing Crises Through Collaboration

Computers in the Military
- Deploying Unmanned Aerial Vehicles (UAVs)
- Using Remote-Controlled Robots
- Utilizing Precision-Guided Bombs
- Tracking Troop Movement
- Using Computer Simulations for Training

Conclusion

Nowhere are computers more pervasive than in the government, law enforcement, homeland security, and the military. The federal government — which most consider to be a paper-laden bureaucracy — is using technology to launch a new paperless era, in which you can do anything from tracking your Social Security benefits to submitting your tax return with a few mouse clicks. Law enforcement, which long has relied on human intelligence to solve crimes, is applying computer technology to help local, state, and federal agencies more effectively prevent and solve criminal cases. For departments focused on providing homeland security and military protection, computers are indispensable tools, supplying key information quickly in a crisis, while offering tools to help protect citizens and soldiers during war.

In this chapter, you will learn more about how the government uses computers to streamline the electoral process, speed the delivery of mail, help gather and analyze census data, and handle millions of tax returns. After reviewing how law enforcement officials use computer technology to track evidence, enforce traffic laws, and locate stolen goods, you will see how other technologies help officers find missing children and route emergency help to any 911 caller. The chapter also looks at how computers help ensure homeland security, by tracking visitors to the country, offering collaborative tools for crisis management, and providing surveillance at the country's borders. Finally, you will learn about the use of cutting-edge computer technologies by the military — including devices that observe and explore dangerous areas and simulations used to train new recruits for combat.

COMPUTERS AND THE GOVERNMENT

The government – including local, state, and federal – is the largest user of computers in the world. Like other businesses, the government uses computers and software to streamline office functions, make information available to citizens via Web sites, manage budgets, handle employee payroll, and process vast numbers of applications and forms for government benefits, driver's licenses, passports, change of address, and more. In addition, the government collects, stores, and analyzes huge quantities of data, including labor statistics, laws and regulations, trademarks and patents, every book indexed in the Library of Congress, and the American Memory collection of primary source materials concerning the history of the United States (Figure 2-1).

The federal government (along with state and local governments) also uses computers for many specialized tasks, such as supporting elections, sorting and posting millions of packages at the U.S. Postal Service, collecting and storing Census Bureau data, and handling tax returns at the Internal Revenue Service.

The Election Process

In the past, federal, state, and local elections relied on hand-counted paper ballots or, more recently, mechanical lever-based machines. To get their message out to voters, candidates held public debates or purchased television time for advertising.

Today, computer technology is used to support and automate many aspects of the electoral process. For example, in any campaign headquarters, campaign staff members use text messaging and e-mail to communicate with each other and possible voters, while employing desktop publishing software to create flyers and mailings to send to potential supporters. Other staff members might use accounting software to monitor the amount of money spent on advertising, travel, and staff payroll, or to forecast the total donations needed to support future campaign expenses. More specialized programs, such as fundraising software, allow candidates to track donor's names, addresses, e-mail addresses, and gift amounts and create the mailing lists used to send appeals for more funds.

Outside headquarters, computers are used in almost every aspect of the electoral process, including conducting campaign polling, providing information to potential voters via Web sites, blogs, podcasts, text messaging, and e-mails, researching an opponent's record, registering voters, and predicting voting results. Computerized voting systems also are used to record votes, count ballots, and tally outcomes.

CONDUCTING POLLS The practice of conducting polls to gauge public opinion on an issue dates back to the 1960s, when President John F. Kennedy conducted polls to determine the best way to present his civil rights agenda. At that point, polling was so unusual that Kennedy took precautions to keep the polls and the results quiet. Since then, polling has become a mainstay of the political process before, during, and after elections.

In general, **political polling** is a process funded by candidates, in which a small group of qualified voters are asked questions specific to the topic about which

Figure 2-1 The government uses computers to help complete a wide range of tasks, from handling internal tasks to making information available to the public.

pollsters want to gather data: an issue, a candidate, or an upcoming election. The answers given by the voters then are used to predict how a larger group of voters will act.

The process of developing and responding to poll results relies heavily on computers. For example, to start the polling process for a congressional campaign a polling consultant uses software to design, create, and edit surveys for paper and the Internet. The consultant uses the software to input the types and content of the questions, the order of the questions, and how they should appear on paper or on screen (Figure 2-2a). The output is a completed survey to use in a poll.

In the past, the polling took place in person, by mail, or, most likely, by telephone. However, as more individuals screen or block unknown telephone calls, pollsters are turning to e-mail and the Internet to conduct polls. For example, during a campaign season you might receive an e-mail from Harris Interactive to invite you to participate in a poll. The e-mail includes a link to an online poll, where you answer questions presented on Web pages. Unlike telephone surveys, the online questionnaires can incorporate graphic, audio, or even video clips. Your responses are collected in a database and, as needed, merged with results gathered via telephone or mail.

With the data collected and entered into the database, the consultant uses decision-support system tools to analyze the data and determine how specific demographic groups (such as single women under 35, registered Republicans under 40, or Latino men living in Essex County) responded to questions about certain issues. The system generates views of the data and other reports (Figure 2-2b). Based on these results or output, the candidate can craft and deliver multiple campaign messages targeted to each group.

Many people, however, are critical of the validity of polls, especially Internet polls. The critics note that input gathered online comes from a group limited to those with computer access, and thus does not reflect the reactions of a true cross-section of voters. For instance, Americans aged 65 or over are most likely to vote – but only a small fraction of that group is online.

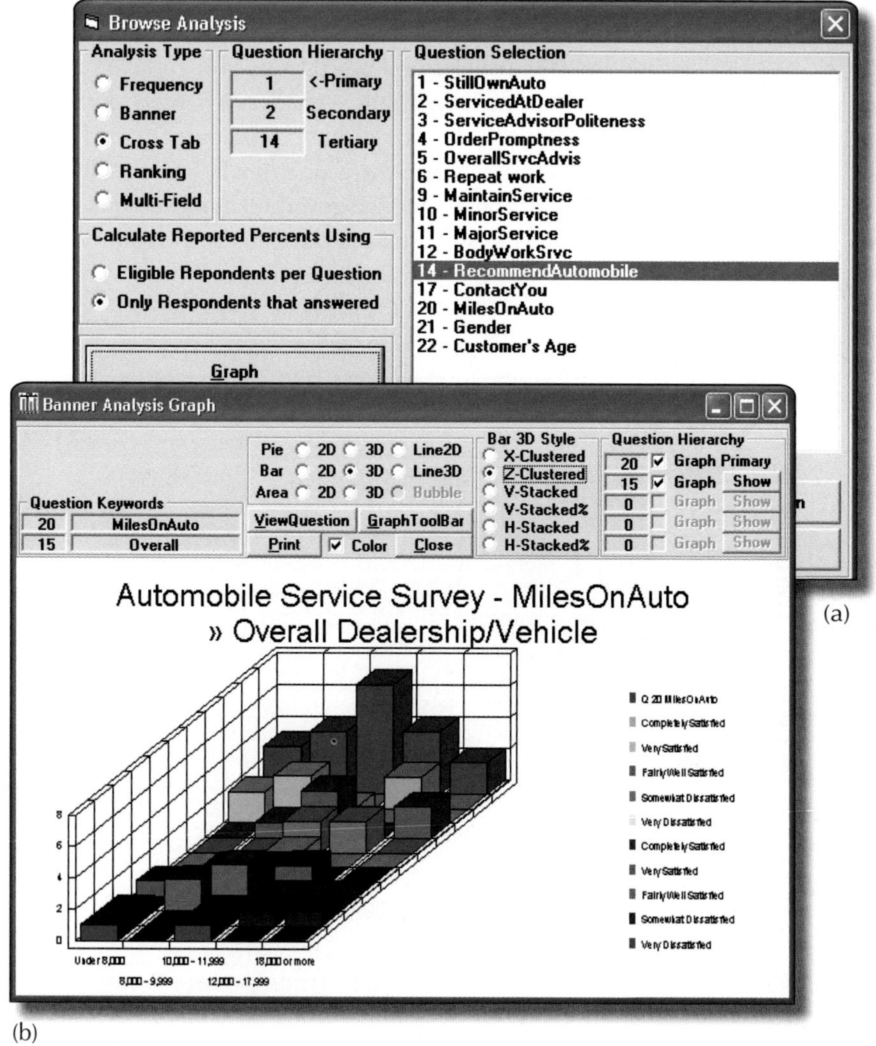

Figure 2-2 Survey software packages are used to (a) create the questionnaires used in polls, and then, (b) help analyze and chart the results.

COMMUNICATING WITH VOTERS

Computers and the Internet have changed the political process by making it easier than ever to communicate with voters. The use of Web sites to reach voters first gained popularity when Republican nominee Bob Dole ended his closing remarks at the initial presidential debate of 1996 by referring people to his Web site. For many, this was the first time they considered getting campaign information from a candidate via the Internet – and the response was huge. Traffic to the Dole Web site increased to 2 million hits the day after the debate and traffic remained high throughout the campaign.

In every political season since then, candidates have increasingly relied on Web sites, e-mail, and chat rooms to keep voters updated on their view and the latest news. In fact, for the 2008 presidential campaign, Hillary Clinton chose to enter the race, not with a press conference, but with the words, "I'm in" posted on her Web site on January 22, 2007. Her announcement also included a video message to Americans articulating her position. For the 2006 mid-term elections, more than 60 million Americans, or 25% of the total population, relied on the Internet for political news and information. For citizens under age 36, the percentage was 35%. With over 70% of total survey respondents citing convenience as a major reason for using the Internet for gathering political news, the expectation is that these numbers will only increase, especially during presidential election years. Today, almost every major candidate maintains a Web site, where they provide information on their career histories and political positions, and encourage their supporters to sign up for volunteer work, donate money online, and pass along e-mail endorsements to friends and newspapers. Chat rooms allow voters to pose questions directly to a candidate, so they can learn more concerning specific subjects about which they are concerned. The White House, for example, regularly holds chat sessions to allow you to pose questions directly to key members of the presidential staff.

Many political Web sites also provide interactive tools to help engage citizens. For example, to promote a tax cut plan a politician can create a Web site with an online calculator that allows visitors to see how much the tax cut would save them each year.

RESEARCHING CANDIDATES The Web simplifies the process of researching information on a candidate. For example, at C-Span's Web site you can check the voting records for any member of Congress, as well as search a campaign finance database to see who has donated money to federal candidates. The Web site also has bulletin boards that allow you to share your thoughts on a candidate or learn how other people reacted to a recent debate (Figure 2-3).

Voters are not the only ones using the Web to learn about candidates; candidates themselves can use the Web to learn more about their opponents. Web sites, such as www.thomas.loc.gov, list any bill introduced into Congress, along with the bill's supporters. Using this information, candidates can highlight the voting records of opponents and spotlight any contradictory statements or positions that an opponent has had in the past, or, based on poll results, might be currently communicating to voters. Members of a candidate's staff also can read numerous news sources in print and online to cull quotes that might be used to discredit an opponent. Having collected this information, staff members use word processing, collaboration, or database software to organize and store the information for use later in the campaign.

CASTING A BALLOT: COMPUTERIZED VOTING SYSTEMS In the country's early history of elections, voting systems largely were paper based or used mechanical devices, such as the machines with levers you pulled to indicate your vote. Since the mid-1960s, however, many polling places have used computerized punch card devices. With a **punch card system**, you mark your paper ballot by punching out bits of paper, called chads, using a stylus. With the chads removed, the punch card then is fed into a computerized counting machine that records the vote.

In 2000, the electoral process was brought to a halt by hundreds of hanging chads – chads not entirely punched from the card – that could cause a computer to read a vote incorrectly. When the winner finally was decided almost one month later, the government moved quickly to introduce more sophisticated computerized voting systems and avoid any more historical election snafus.

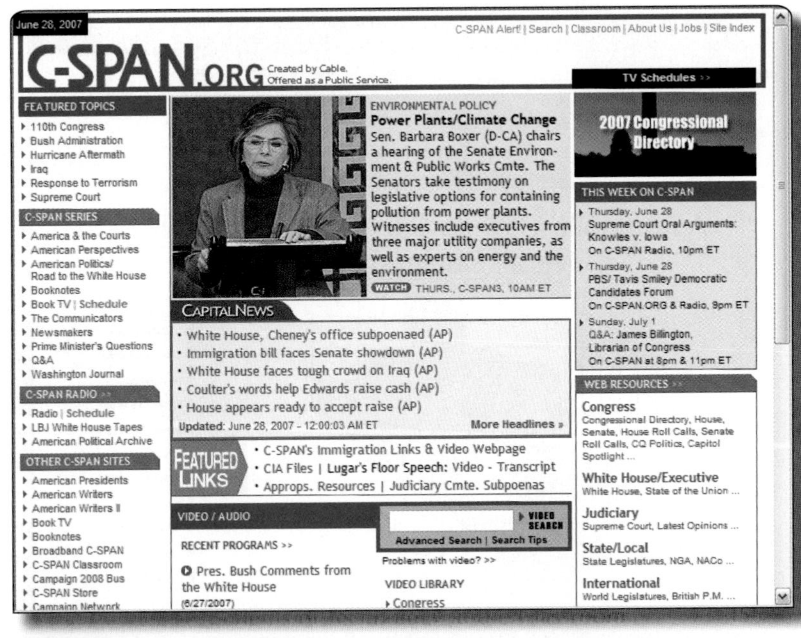

Figure 2-3 The C-SPAN Web site includes community bulletins boards that allow you to share your thoughts on election events.

Newer types of computerized voting systems include optical mark recognition, direct recording electronic (DRE) machines, and Internet-based voting systems (Table 2-1). With **optical mark recognition systems** (also called optical scanning systems or mark-sense systems), you fill in circles, squares, or other shapes printed on a paper ballot to indicate your vote. The optical mark recognition device scans the paper, detects the darkest mark for each question on the ballot, and records that as the vote. Similar systems are used widely for standardized college entrance exams.

Direct recording electronic (DRE) machines are computers that allow you to enter your vote by pressing buttons or touching images on a touch screen (Figure 2-4). The touch screen displays a list

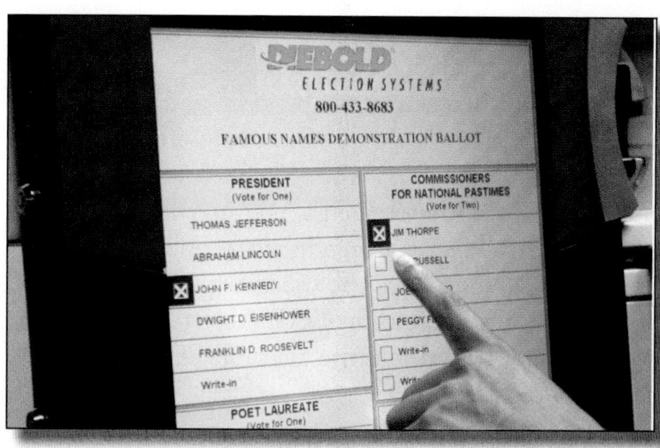

Figure 2-4 Direct recording electronic (DRE) machines allow you to enter your vote by pressing buttons or touching images on a touch screen.

TABLE 2-1

VOTING SYSTEM	*DESCRIPTION*	*PROS AND CONS*
Punch Card	Voters mark their ballots by punching holes in paper cards using a stylus. Punch cards then are fed into computerized counting machines.	*Pros:* Easy to use, most voters are accustomed to using such cards *Cons:* The bits of paper that are removed when a card is punched, called a chad, often do not become completely detached from their cards when prescored cards are used. These hanging chads can work their way back into place in the punch card, thus blocking holes and causing the computer to read the vote incorrectly
Optical Mark Recognition	Paper ballots printed with circles, squares, or other shapes that voters fill in to mark their votes. Optical scanning technology is used to detect the marks on each ballot.	*Pros:* Easy to use, most voters are accustomed to using such cards. Scanning machine can notify voters if their ballot is improperly marked, giving them an opportunity to remark their ballots. *Cons:* May require specific type of writing instrument, such as soft lead pencil (most also require red ink to not be used).
Direct Recording Electronic (DRE) Machines	Computer terminals that allow voters to enter their votes by pressing buttons or touching images on a computer screen. DRE machines can display images as well as text.	*Pros:* Easy to use, if well designed. More accessible to illiterate or disabled, because graphics can be used to support text. System does not allow voter to make unambiguous choices; thus no questions on intended vote can arise. *Cons:* More expensive than punch card and mark-sense systems. Also, because there are no physical ballots that can be recounted or examined manually, a DRE system must be thoroughly tested prior to an election to ensure proper operation. Votes also must be recorded on two or more backup devices, in the event the system is corrupted. Power outages can bring the system down; the system should be capable of running on batteries or emergency generators.
Internet-Based Voting	Allows users to cast a vote from any computer connected to the Internet (either at home or at a polling place). The ballot then is transferred via the Internet to a centralized tallying center.	*Pros:* Can eliminate the expenses associated with setting up and staffing remote voting locations, make voting more convenient for voters and eliminate the need for separate absentee ballot systems. *Cons:* Can raise security and privacy concerns, as well as concerns about people selling their right to vote to others. Finally, until everyone has Internet access and/or knows how to use a computer to vote, polling places will be required.

Several types of computerized voting systems are available today.

of candidates or ballot questions. To enter your vote, you press the correct location on the touch screen, which responds to your finger pressure and records your vote. Keyboards also are included with the DRE machines to allow you to type write-in votes. To eliminate potential fraud with DREs, you may be given an electronic card when you sign in at the polling place. Before casting your vote, you must swipe the card in a card reader connected to the DRE. Votes are counted by a computer, and results are available almost instantly at the end of Election Day.

Soon, you may provide your vote via the Internet. **Internet-based voting systems**, or **online voting systems**, allow users to cast their ballots via a Web site, using any Internet-connected PC. Although not widespread, Internet-based voting systems already are in use. For example, in March 2000, Arizona's Democratic Party held the first binding U.S. election in which voters could vote online instead of going to the polls or mailing in votes. To provide security for the online vote, all registered Democrats were mailed a PIN number. When a voter accessed the Web site, that PIN number, along with several personal questions, was used to confirm the voter's identity. Once confirmed, voters submitted their ballot by clicking the buttons on the Web page. Voter response to the Internet-based system was very positive – nearly half of the ballots cast in that election came via the Internet. Other countries, such as the United Kingdom and Estonia, are taking steps to make online voting available for the country's general elections. Recent research shows that turnout levels among young voters – the group least likely to head to the polls on Election Day – could improve significantly if they had the option to cast their ballot electronically.

As outlined in Table 2-2, computerized voting systems bring many benefits to the election process, including the ability to count ballots quickly, improve the accuracy of election results, and reduce election fraud. However, computerized voting systems also raise new apprehensions about security, reliability, the opportunity for fraud, and equal access. As you learned in Chapter 1, some Americans do not have access to the Internet – a concept called the digital divide – and this causes concern. For example, when the Democratic Party ran its presidential primary election in Arizona online, the U.S. Justice Department expressed anxiety about minority voters being locked out of the election process, simply because they did not have access to computers. To counter these concerns, polling places also remained open during the election, so that every registered voter could participate in the election process.

TABLE 2-2 The Benefits of Computerized Voting Systems

BENEFIT	*DESCRIPTION*
Simplify and streamline the voting process	Can reduce the time it takes to count ballots and obtain election results. Results can be calculated almost immediately after the polls close.
Improve accuracy of election result	Can provide more accurate results than can be provided by hand count. Inaccuracies introduced as a result of voters' unclear ballot marks can be eliminated.
Reduce election fraud	Unlike paper ballots, electronic ballots cannot be lost or destroyed before they reach the tallying location. Computerized voter registration logs also make it easier to identify people who should not be registered or who attempt to vote using someone else's registration.

Computerized voting systems can bring many benefits to the election process.

Computerized Voting: Vote Early, Click Often?

Elections — while a core part of a democracy — may always present security and fraud challenges. In one of the most well-known cases of suspected voting fraud, Chicago's Mayor Richard M. Daley is rumored to have encouraged the stuffing of Chicago ballot boxes with votes for John F. Kennedy (including votes cast by citizens long dead), helping Kennedy win by more than 450,000 votes. The widespread fraud perhaps is summed up best in a phrase coined by mobster Al Capone, who noted — on an earlier Election Day in Chicago — that voters were encouraged to "vote early, vote often."

While computerized voting systems do have benefits over older paper-based and punch card systems, the introduction of computers into the electoral process raises additional concerns. For example, errors or malicious code in the software may allow unauthorized users to gain access to the system or allow files to be modified inappropriately. Even after the software has been installed and tested, a programmer may make unauthorized modifications to the code — perhaps altering the touch screen on a DRE to record all votes for the same candidate regardless of which button is pressed. Further, election officials could abuse their privilege to access the software — accepting bribe money to access the system and alter total vote counts in favor of a candidate.

Computer failures also may result in lost or altered data, or the physical security of computerized voting equipment could be compromised. What happens, for example, if the database servers storing the results were damaged in an electrical fire? These and other scenarios point to the critical importance of regularly backing up the computers that accept, store, and tally votes — and storing the backup in a separate location.

Finally, if election information is transferred electronically, confidential transmissions may be intercepted, modified, or blocked. For instance, a hacker might be able to read the transmissions as votes are coming in and then call a candidate to offer an election fix in return for a fee or a job in the new administration. Further, like the stuffed ballot boxes that some think won the election for Kennedy, many wonder about the difficulties in ensuring that the person clicking the Submit button on a Web page ballot really is who he or she claims to be — and that they vote only once.

All of these issues have possible solutions. For example, systems that can be accessed by multiple officials should log any system access, so that potential fraud can be traced back to a specific user. Possible solutions for voter authentication include PIN numbers, smart cards, or **biometric devices**, such as fingerprint readers, that authenticate a person's identity by translating a personal characteristic, such as a fingerprint, into a code and comparing it with a digital code stored in a computer. Data transmissions should be encrypted, or encoded, into an unreadable form, so that unauthorized users cannot intercept it. Backups of all critical system data and components should be part of the overall system.

As Internet-based systems and other electronic voting systems gain widespread use, however, those who want to commit fraud probably will find some way to manipulate the systems. Even as sophisticated security controls are put in place to limit access and reduce fraud, just as quickly hackers find holes in the system that they can exploit. In the end, while computerized voting systems can provide controls not imaginable in a time of paper-based votes, it is quite possible that the next case of election fraud will cause some pundit to coin a new phrase — only this time it will be "vote early, click often."

United States Postal Service

The United States Postal Service (USPS) makes deliveries to about 146 million addresses every day. The Postal Service serves customers from almost 37,000 retail locations nationwide, and handles some 213 billion letters, advertisements, periodicals and packages a year. Given the enormous volume of mail it must handle, the USPS relies on computer technology to streamline its operations, speed mail sorting, and offer better products and services to its customers.

For example, mail sorting has changed dramatically since the days when all mail was sorted manually. Today, machines and computers perform tasks necessary to sort the huge daily volume of mail. After you drop a letter in the mailbox, a mail carrier picks up the letter and delivers it to the closest sorting facility. A machine then separates your letter from thicker mail that must be sorted manually and moves it down a conveyor belt to an **optical character recognition (OCR) system**, which is a technology that relies on artificial intelligence to recognize patterns and read handwritten, typed, or computer-printed characters from documents and translate the images into a form a computer can process. The OCR machines at the sorting facility can read the addresses you have written on the envelope, look up the address in a database, and then apply an 11-digit POSTNET bar code that indicates the delivery address (Figure 2-5). Next, the letter moves on to a bar code sorter, which reads the POSTNET bar code and routes the mail to a different location in the facility, based on delivery address.

Figure 2-5 The USPS uses 11-digit POSTNET bar codes that indicate the delivery address to help route mail to its correct location quickly.

Finally, the letter travels to a delivery point bar code sorter, which reads the 11-digit POSTNET bar code on your letter and places the mail into a carrier's mail bag in the order the carrier walks or drives the route.

By using sophisticated computerized equipment and bar codes, the USPS can process mail faster and more accurately, at less cost. Using these systems reduces the cost of processing 1000 pieces of mail from $40 to $2.50. To pass these savings back to customers, the USPS offers discounts to companies that include POSTNET bar codes on the mail before it arrives at the sorting facility.

In addition to using computers to help sort mail and ensure delivery, the United States Postal Service uses computers to provide better products and customer service. For example, at the USPS Web site, you can find ZIP codes, locate nearby post offices, calculate postage costs for a package, change your address, or make arrangements to have the post office hold or forward your mail. You also can buy stamps and have them shipped to your home or link to a licensed PC Postage vendor, such as Stamps.com, that allows you to buy and print stamps or shipping labels directly from your computer. If you'd rather customize your stamps with photos of your family, pets, wedding, or recent vacation, authorized vendor www.photo.stamps.com will do the job and ship your stamps directly to you via – what else? – the USPS (Figure 2-6).

Figure 2-6 Licensed digital postage vendors such as photos.stamps.com can create unique stamps using customers' own photos

Census Bureau

In 2000, you or your family probably received a census form in the mail from the U.S. government. After completing the form, which asked questions about who lives in your house and about your town, you mailed it back to the government. Every ten years since 1790, the U.S. government has taken a count of the U.S. population in a decennial census. Computers and technology have changed the process of taking the census entirely. During the first U.S. census in 1790, federal marshals traveled by horseback from town to town to count the population. In 1890, the government began using simple machines to tabulate census data. In 1990, the bureau captured census forms on microfilm, which was scanned into computers, although bureau workers had to type in any handwritten information.

For Census 2000, the Census Bureau was challenged with counting all 275 million Americans in six months and making the information available to citizens via the Bureau's official Web site (Figure 2-7). To do this, the Census Bureau used more than 10,000 computers, ranging from PCs to a supercomputer. To speed the process of inputting the data, the Census Bureau used optical mark recognition forms that could be scanned electronically. Census 2000 also introduced limited use of the Internet to gather census data. Once the data was entered, powerful computers tabulated the data collected by the census questionnaires. The bureau also used an image-capture system to store images of forms and help process poorly completed forms, allowing census workers to access forms electronically to deal with bad handwriting or poorly marked bubble choices (instead of having to find one original paper form among millions).

For the 2010 census, the Census Bureau is spending $600 million on 500,000 handheld computers and networked computer systems to help workers conduct the census. The handheld computers would have a database of streets, houses, and addresses to those people who have not filled out the census forms, and give census workers directions to find them. As they interview citizens, the census worker will be able to input the data, which later will be uploaded to the main Census Bureau database.

Internal Revenue Service

The Internal Revenue Service, like the US Postal Service, handles huge volumes of information, in the form of around 230 million tax returns each year. The IRS relies on computers for numerous activities, including processing returns, reviewing returns for possible audit, accepting payment, and providing refunds using direct deposit.

Computers have changed the way taxpayers work with the IRS. In the past, Americans had to complete their tax returns by hand, using paper forms. Today, **tax preparation software** guides individuals, families, and small businesses through the process of filing taxes (Figure 2-8). Tax preparation software programs, such as Intuit TurboTax and H&R Block's TaxCut, ask you a series of questions and then create your completed tax forms. The software also analyzes the forms to search for potential errors or places where you may have missed deductions. Once the forms are finished, you can print the necessary paper work and mail it to the IRS – or submit it electronically.

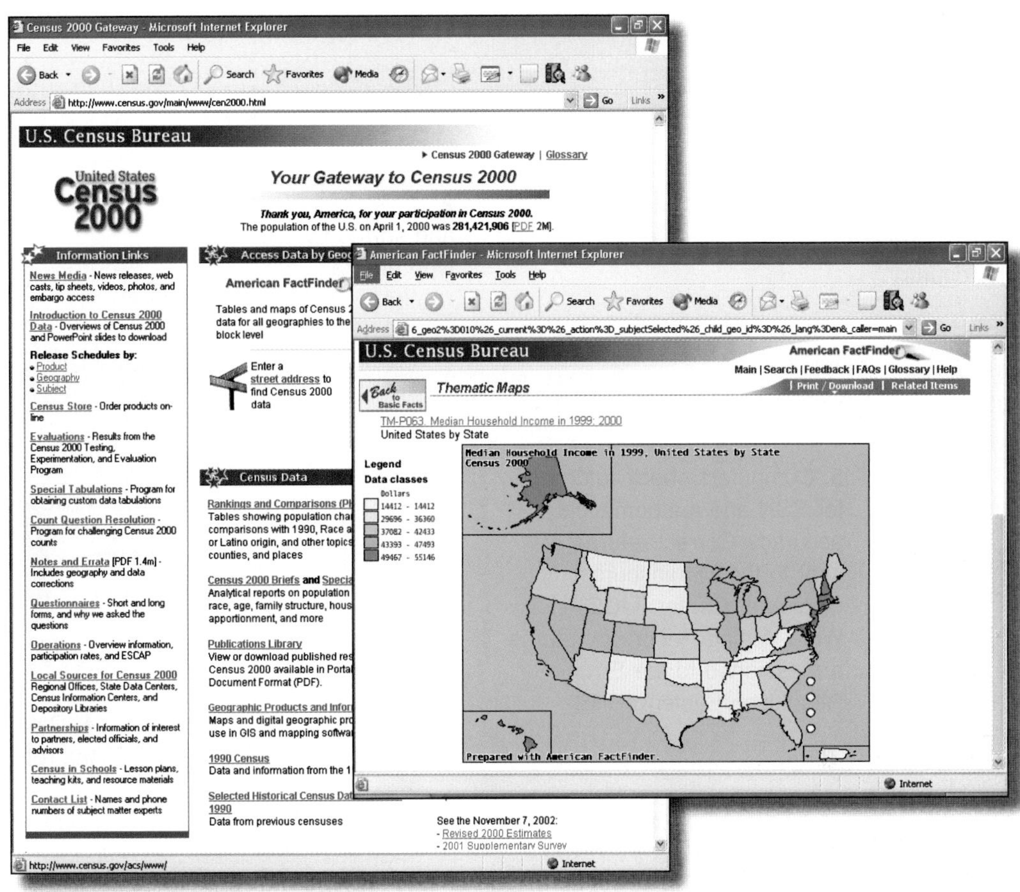

Figure 2-7 All of the Census 2000 results are stored in searchable databases accessible via the Census Bureau Web site, which also provides data organized geographically in maps.

If you mail in a paper copy of your tax return, an IRS employee enters every piece of information on your tax form into a computer system (Figure 2-9). The system checks returns for correct Social Security numbers and mathematical accuracy; if the returns are correct, this information then is stored in large magnetic tape machines. A second file that includes refund information is sent to disbursing centers, which handle the process of sending you your refund.

IRS **e-File** allows you to complete and submit your tax return over the Internet. With e-File, you can complete your tax return using tax preparation software and then submit the final forms electronically. Alternatively, you can complete your entire return online, via a tax preparation Web site, and then submit the completed return over the Internet to the IRS. Because the IRS does not have to reenter all

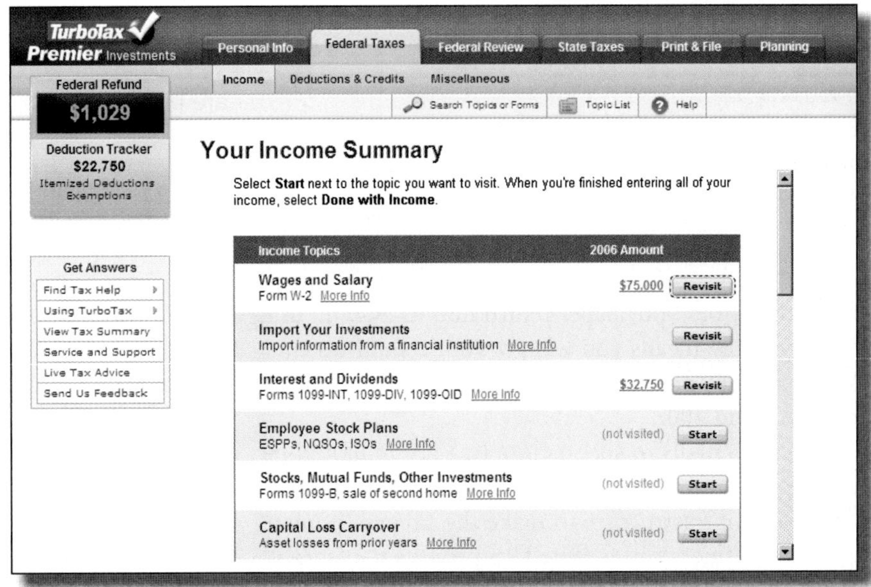

Figure 2-8 Today, tax preparation software, such as Intuit TurboTax and H&R Block's TaxCut, guides individuals, families, and small businesses through the process of filing taxes.

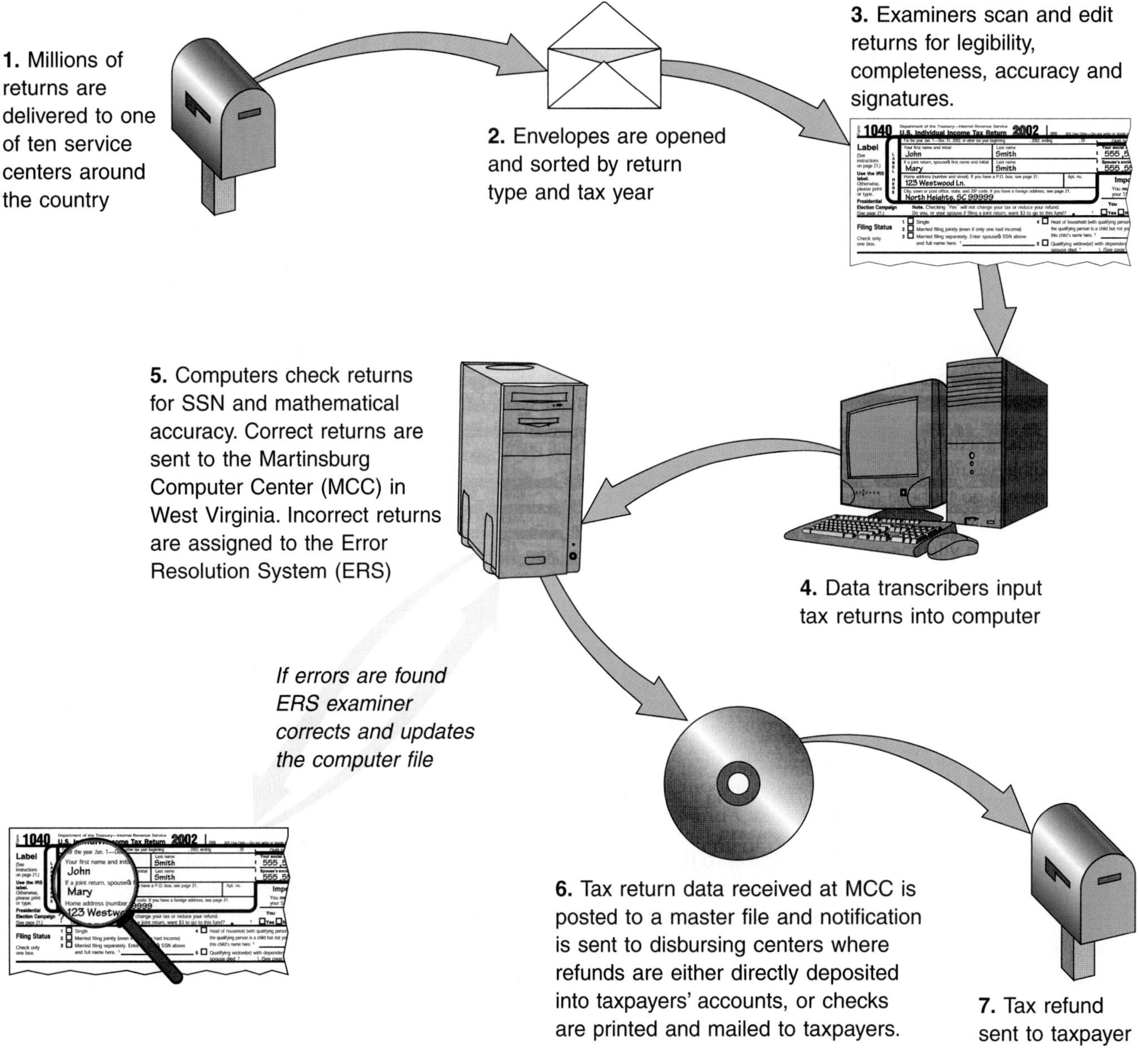

1. Millions of returns are delivered to one of ten service centers around the country
2. Envelopes are opened and sorted by return type and tax year
3. Examiners scan and edit returns for legibility, completeness, accuracy and signatures.
4. Data transcribers input tax returns into computer
5. Computers check returns for SSN and mathematical accuracy. Correct returns are sent to the Martinsburg Computer Center (MCC) in West Virginia. Incorrect returns are assigned to the Error Resolution System (ERS)
If errors are found ERS examiner corrects and updates the computer file
6. Tax return data received at MCC is posted to a master file and notification is sent to disbursing centers where refunds are either directly deposited into taxpayers' accounts, or checks are printed and mailed to taxpayers.
7. Tax refund sent to taxpayer

Figure 2-9 If you mail in a paper copy of your tax return, the IRS processes the form, reviews it for accuracy and then, as needed, sends you a refund using the above steps.

of the data from your paper return into its system, using e-File typically means you will get your refund faster. Approximately 35% of taxpayers used the electronic filing process in 2007.

The IRS plans to spend close to $410 million during the next few years to modernize its information technology infrastructure to make the process of managing its business easier. The IRS projects that this investment will lead to increases in annual revenue of $699 million – more than paying for the project's cost.

Using computer technology also helps the IRS process refunds more efficiently. For example, as you learned in Chapter 1, you can specify that you want to receive your refund via direct deposit, which means the IRS transfers the refund electronically straight to your bank account. The IRS.gov Web site also includes a feature that allows you to track the status of your refund, using your Social Security number and file status information.

The IRS relies on its Web site to provide helpful information and tools to taxpayers, such as federal tax codes and forms available in PDF format, information on where to find your local IRS office, tax calculators to help you determine what you owe, e-File information, and more. In recent years, during the height of the tax season right before April 15, the IRS.gov Web site receives almost 90 million hits.

The IRS also uses computers to determine if returns should be audited. A computer program numerically scores every individual tax return and some corporate tax returns to determine if they should be reviewed manually. If your return is selected and has an error, the computer automatically prints and addresses a discrepancy notice that is mailed to inform you of the error.

Although computers are widely used by the IRS, many of the agency systems are outdated and are in the process of being upgraded. By 2012, the IRS will implement a Customer Account Data Engine (CADE) system, which will allow IRS employees to post transactions and update taxpayer accounts from their desks. These updates will be available immediately to anyone who has authorized access to the data. An imaging system also will be used to scan and store electronic images of selected paper tax returns. Tax information for more than 200 million individual and business taxpayers will be kept in the CADE system. Today, correspondence often is not available to customer service representatives when they interact with customers. With the imaging system, employees will be able to see an electronic image of your return so they can answer your questions more effectively.

COMPUTERS IN LAW ENFORCEMENT

In today's police force, standard issue for new officers includes a PDA along with a badge. For some time, laptop computers have been standard in most squad cars (and even on some motorcycles), so that officers can receive information from headquarters while on the road. Other offices are using PDAs to reduce the time used writing tickets, filing accident reports, and completing other routine police work. These PDAs also include a magnetic scanner that reads the bar code on a driver's license and downloads information on warrants, restraining orders, driving records, and criminal histories.

Computers also are used by law enforcement officials to support a wide range of tasks, including tracking evidence and criminal records, enforcing traffic laws, quickly communicating information about missing children, and ensuring a rapid response to 911 emergency calls.

Tracking Evidence

A crime scene can have thousands of pieces of physical evidence: a bullet casing, a scrap of cloth, or a crumpled receipt. Any one of these pieces of evidence may be the key to constructing a criminal case, and the evidence needs to be kept safe, organized, and accessible.

Today, police departments are using computer databases and other technologies to manage evidence in evidence-tracking systems. As evidence is brought in, police enter complete documentation about the evidence into a handheld computer, which wirelessly transmits the information to the evidence database. The handheld computer then prints out a bar code sticker that the officer affixes to the evidence container. Once this label is in place, a quick scan of the bar code will access the evidence database and display information about what the item is, what case it belongs to, and where and by whom it was collected. Each time the item is scanned, the scan is logged in the database so officials can know exactly who handled the evidence at any point in time, in case questions about possible evidence tampering arise.

Databases also are used to monitor other types of evidence, including DNA. For example, the FBI's Combined DNA Index System (CODIS) is a database with three levels of DNA data: local, state, and national. When DNA evidence is gathered from a crime scene, the DNA profile is entered into the CODIS system. CODIS uses two key indexes: the forensic and offender indexes. The forensic index contains DNA collected as crime scene evidence, while the offender index includes DNA profiles of individuals convicted of violent crimes. CODIS allows federal, state, and local crime labs to compare DNA profiles electronically, so that they can better identify and convict previous offenders.

Another incredibly valuable database system used by law enforcement is the Integrated Automated Fingerprint Identification System, usually referred to as AFIS (pronounced *ay-fis*). The system allows law enforcement officials to search for and match fingerprints collected from previous arrests. Today, instead of using ink and fingerprint cards to take fingerprints, a scan system captures fingerprint images electronically. After capturing the image, an officer enters the data normally found at the top of a fingerprint card – name, date of birth, and arrest information – using the scan system keyboard. This data, along with the digital fingerprint images, is transmitted to a central AFIS system that can be accessed by officials around the country to identify the owner of fingerprints left at the crime scene.

Storing Criminal Records

Technology has made searchable databases of criminal records widely available to law enforcement agencies, including officers on the street. For example, the FBI's National Crime Information Center (NCIC) database is a computerized index of criminal justice information, such as criminal records and information on fugitives, stolen properties, and missing persons. After arresting a subject, law enforcement officials can access the database to see if other warrants for the subject's arrest are open or if the subject's name is connected with other crimes.

Another FBI system – the National Instant Criminal Background Check System (NICS) – was established to help gun dealers perform background checks on prospective firearms buyers to ensure that convicted felons, among others, cannot buy guns from a dealer. When a customer wants to buy a gun, the firearms dealer calls a toll-free number that connects the dealer with the state Bureau of Identification. An operator then runs a query for the purchaser's name. The query searches through several different databases, including a state criminal database, the federal NCIC, an outstanding warrant database, and a few other state databases. To ensure the full effectiveness of the system, records in the database must be updated and as accurate as possible – a delay in entering data could mean that a criminal leaves a store with a new gun. For this reason, many states have waiting periods before a customer can actually take a gun from a store, just to be sure that all of the latest data has been entered in the database. Historically, the denial rate is around 1.4% of total applicants.

Other databases are used to make relevant information about sexually violent offenders available to the public. The murder of seven-year old Megan Kanka led to the passage of Megan's Law, which requires people convicted of certain sexual offenses to register with local law enforcement agencies, for the rest of their lives. Information in the database includes the offender's name, aliases, photograph and physical description, ethnicity, date of birth, scars, marks and tattoos, registered sex offenses, and county and zip code based on last registered address. In order to make this information available to the public, many communities make the sex offender database available online (Figure 2-10).

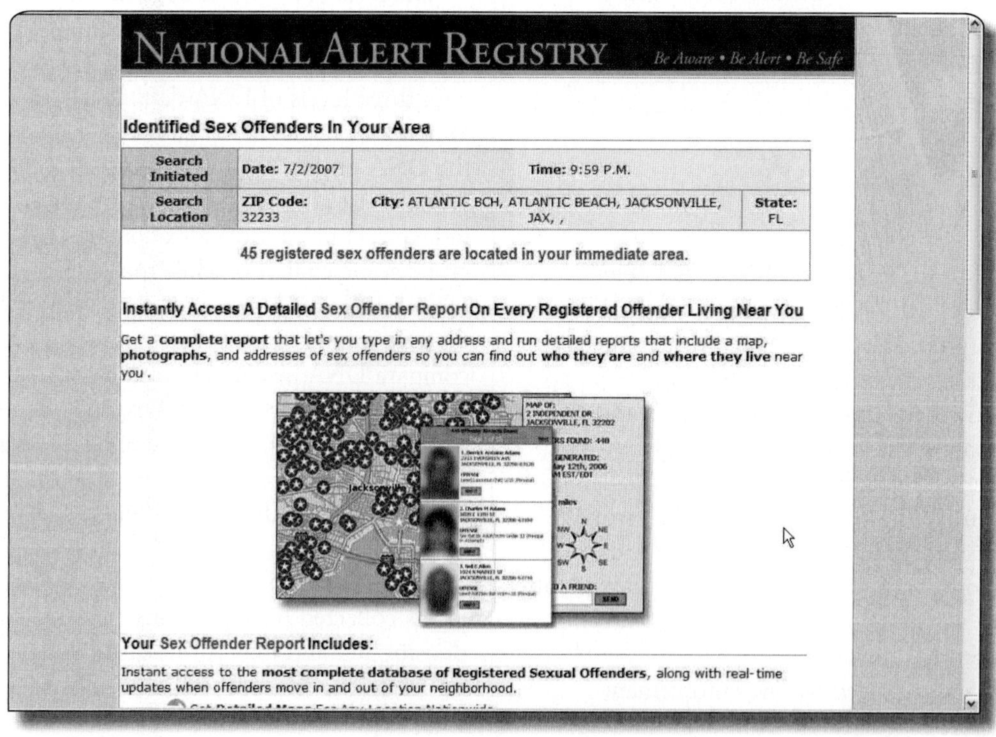

Figure 2-10 Many communities, such as the one shown here, are making sex offender databases available online as part of their response to Megan's Law.

Enforcing Traffic Laws

Even traffic lights are using computer technology to ensure that you (or other drivers) do not run a red light. Red-light systems include three key elements: one or more digital cameras, one or more triggers, and a computer. In a typical system, cameras are positioned at the corners of an intersection so they can photograph cars driving through the intersection (Figure 2-11). Each red light has a trigger, or a sensor loop, which is a length of electrical wire charged with an electrical current to generate a magnetic field. When a car passes over the sensor loop, it changes the magnetic field and sets off the trigger.

The computer is the core of the system: it is connected to the cameras, the triggers, and the traffic light and constantly monitors the traffic signal and the triggers. If your car moves over the sensors loops at a particular speed when the light is red, the computer instructs the cameras to take two pictures to document the violation – one as you enter the intersection and one when you are in the middle of the intersection.

To document the violation fully, the computer adds the date, time, intersection location, and other information to the digital photo. With this information and photos of the infraction, the police have everything they need to charge you for running the red light.

If you do get a citation for running a red light, speeding, or parking next to a fire hydrant, at least computers make paying your fine easier. You can access information regarding your citations and parking tickets

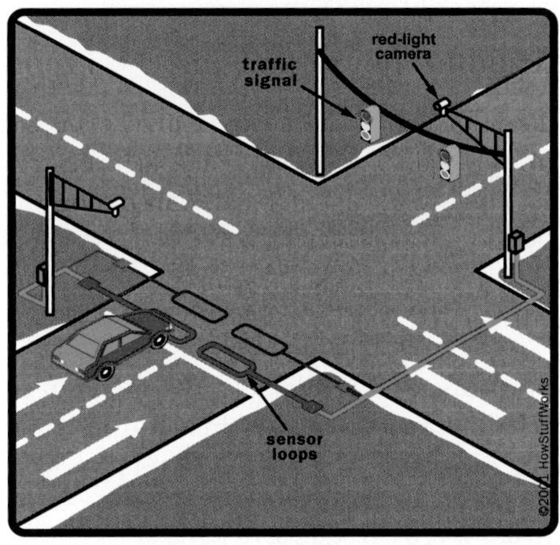

1. Each traffic light has a trigger, or a sensor loop, a length of electrical wire buried just under the asphalt with an electrical current to generate a magnetic field.

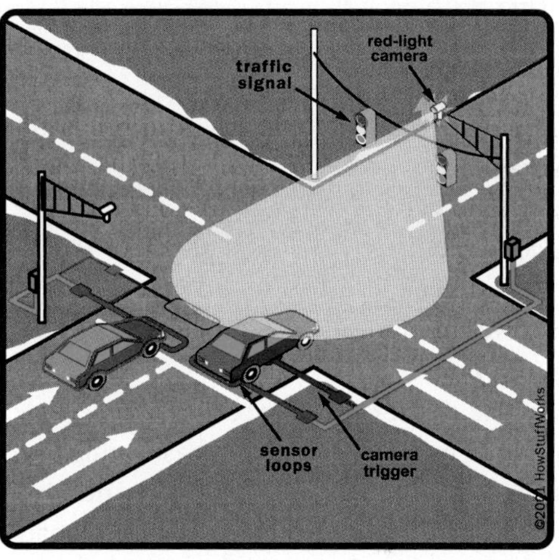

2. If your car moves over the sensor loops when the light is red, the computer automatically instructs the camera to take two pictures to document the violation – one as you enter the intersection –

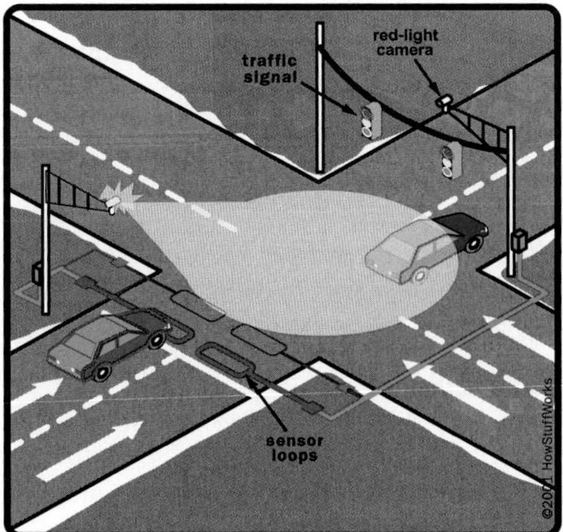

3. – and one as you are in the middle of the intersection to capture your car proceeding through the intersection (and your license plate number).

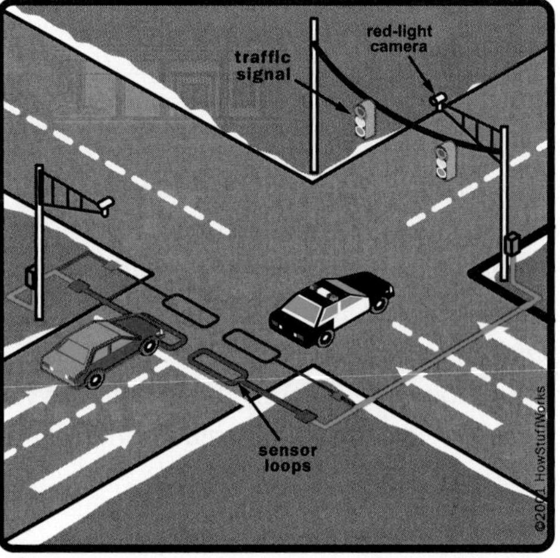

4. With the photos, along with information on date, time, and the intersection, the police have everything they need to charge the driver or the car owner.

Figure 2-11 Red-light systems rely on computer technology to catch drivers who run red lights.

online by going to a Web site and entering your citation number (Figure 2-12). If there is a balance due on the citation, you can enter your credit card information and submit payment online.

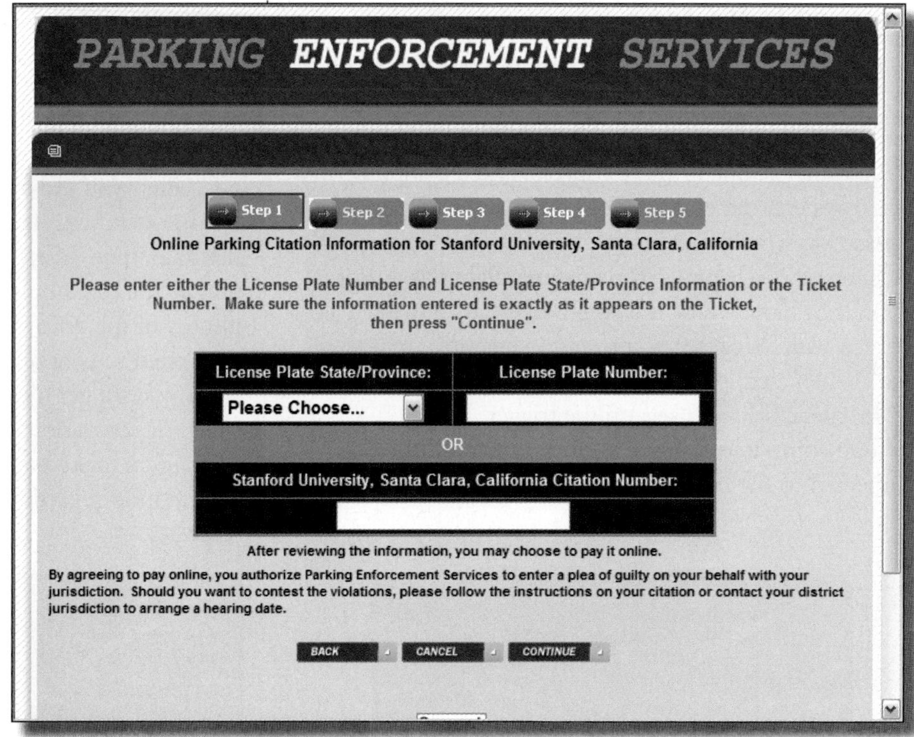

Figure 2-12 Computers even have made paying your citations simple, allowing you to access and pay your citations and parking tickets online.

Tracking Stolen Vehicles

Vehicle theft is the most expensive property crime in the United States: the 1.2 million cars stolen annually cost consumers more than $8.6 billion. You can protect your car from thieves using a stolen vehicle recovery system called LoJack. With the LoJack system, a wireless radio-frequency transceiver about the size of a chalkboard eraser is placed somewhere in your car (the installer does not tell you where the transceiver is located). When you report your stolen car to the police, the incident is entered into the National Crime Information Center database, which allows police to match the vehicle identification number of your car with your LoJack device and then automatically send a signal to the device on a special FM frequency. This signal activates the LoJack device hidden in your car, which in turn sends out a homing signal to a special tracking computer in police squad cars. The tracking computer displays a map with arrows to show police which way to steer their cruiser to locate the stolen vehicle. LoJack is the only stolen vehicle recovery system used by police.

You can further protect your car from theft by purchasing a system that uses a motion sensor and a uniquely coded key pass to detect unauthorized movement of the vehicle. When you are driving the car, the key pass identifies you as an authorized user. If the vehicle is moved without the key pass present, however, a notification is sent to you via phone, cell phone, e-mail, text messaging, or pager.

Finding Missing Children

Computers also are being used in the race to find missing children. The AMBER Alert system, for example, is a missing child alert system created to issue an immediate notification to the public so they can help recover missing or abducted children and teenagers before they can be harmed. All 50 states now have participation plans in place.

While the AMBER (which is short for America's Missing: Broadcast Emergency Response) Alert programs are relatively new, the technology that underlies the system is not. The technology is the Emergency Alert System (EAS), which is known to most television viewers as a loud beep followed by a weather warning or the "This is only a test" warning message.

When a law enforcement agency decides to issue an AMBER Alert, an officer first faxes key information – pictures of the missing child, the suspected abductor, a suspected vehicle and any other information available – to radio stations designated as primary stations under the Emergency Alert System. These stations immediately interrupt their programming to broadcast the alert on the air. The alert begins with a burst of data coded by a low-speed modem; the burst is followed by the familiar eight-second alert tone, spoken emergency information, and instructions. Another burst of data then terminates the message.

EAS boxes at hundreds of radio and television stations are tuned to the primary radio stations and receive the data burst. The data burst tells the EAS box to read the data header being sent, determine what kind of alert is being sounded, and then interrupt programming to broadcast the message on the air. The thousands of other stations tuned to these broadcaster do the same, until the message has filtered to almost every television and radio station in the area. Newer technologies are being applied to ensure that news outlets also get the alerts quickly. A new satellite communications system, for example, will link state emergency officials directly with television stations, so that police can send images of children straight to television stations for broadcasting.

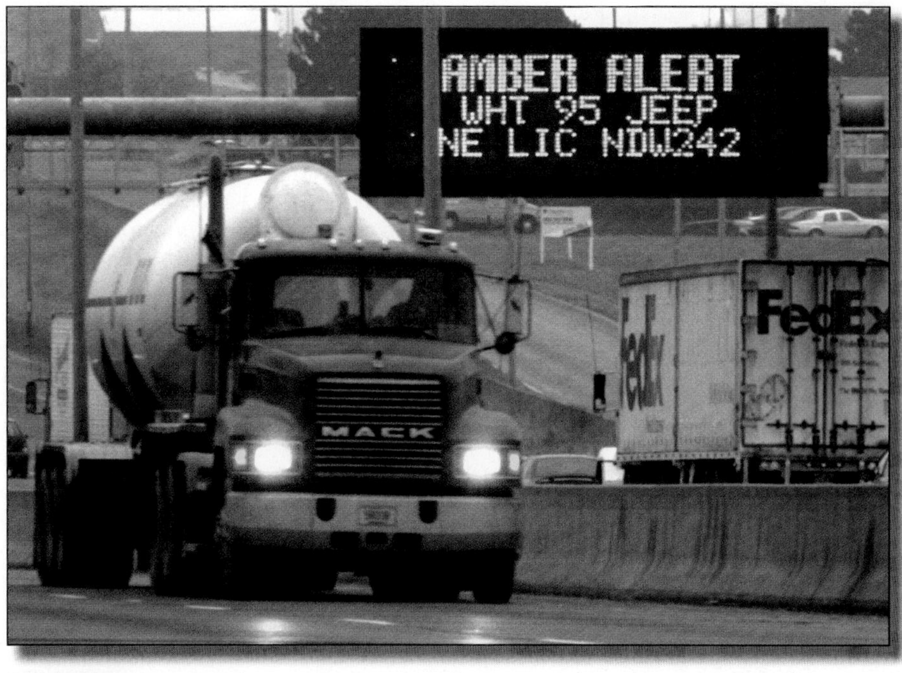

Figure 2-13 Amber Alert messages are displayed on dynamic message signs that enable transportation officials to type in a child kidnapping alert.

Other AMBER Alert messages are displayed on dynamic message signs that enable transportation officials to type in any information they want, including an alert on a child kidnapping (Figure 2-13). Law enforcement officials and staff from the National Center for Missing and Exploited Children (NCMEC) also provide alerts via e-mail, mobile phones, pagers, or AOL Instant Messenger. Alerts also are displayed as headers on Web sites, with the message content pushed from central servers to each Web server hosting a Web page with the AMBER Alert header. And you can even sign up for wireless AMBER alerts if you are interested in receiving them.

Providing Wireless 911

For years, individuals have dialed 911 to connect to emergency personnel. When you dial 911, the call automatically is forwarded to a public-safety answering point (PSAP), also called a 911 call center. The operator takes key information, such as the type of emergency and your location, and then dispatches the appropriate emergency personnel. Most areas have **Enhanced 911 (E-911)**, which automatically displays two key pieces of information – your telephone number and the address where your telephone is located – on the 911 operator's computer monitor as he or she answers the call. The Enhanced 911's automatic number identifier (ANI) and automatic location identifier (ALI) databases provide these two pieces of information.

The problem with wireless 911 calls is that mobile phones are not associated with one fixed address; callers can be located just about anywhere. In 2006, approximately 150 million calls were made to 911; 50 million of those calls were made on cell phones (and the number is expected to rise). The Federal Communications Commission (FCC) thus ruled that all cellular phone providers must equip their phones with global positioning system (GPS) receivers so that 911 operators can pinpoint your location when you call from a cell phone.

With the wireless 911 system, the GPS receiver in the phone receives signals from GPS satellites. When you make a 911 call from your cell phone, the operator's computer links to the automatic location identifier (ALI) database to get specific address information based on the latitude and longitude data from the GPS receiver, so that the operator can send emergency personnel right to your location. The FCC now requires all wireless carriers to ensure that 95% of their customers' phones be E911-capable.

ISSUE: Getting Chipped

For several years, pet owners around the globe have had a small microchip implanted in their beloved dogs and cats. Encoded on the microchip is a specific code number unique to the owner's pet, which is registered in a database along with the cat or dog's breed, age, sex, and, most importantly, the owner's name, address, and telephone number. To date, approximately 1.5 million pets have had a microchip implanted. With the microchip implanted, if your dog Spot gets lost and ends up at a veterinarian or animal shelter, any staff member can use a special hand scanner to read the chip, access your contact information, and call you so you can retrieve Spot.

Now, parents will have the opportunity to get similar chips for their children, and concerned adults can choose to get their very own chips. In about seven seconds, a physician can implant a microchip carrying a unique identification number in your arm. If you are in a car accident, emergency technicians can scan the microchip to access a medical records database to determine if you have any drug allergies or to get contact information for your family or friends.

Using technology to track, monitor, and store information about people is not entirely new. For several years, Applied Digital Solutions has sold a tracking and monitoring system called Digital Angel, which consists of a device similar to a wristwatch and a module worn on the belt. Digital Angel is used for a range of applications, such as allowing family members of Alzheimer's patients to locate a patient anywhere in the world. The Digital Angel can track if you fall, if the temperature around you changes dramatically, and even if you leave a specific area. A call service then sends an alert via e-mail to your key contact's cell phone, computer, pager, or PDA. The alert includes GPS information that pinpoints your location to within 75 feet. Already, more than 30 states use similar satellite surveillance systems to keep track of former prisoners. Parolees wear a wireless GPS-enabled ankle bracelet which allows law enforcement to trace them continuously. The system can provide alerts to parole officers if wearers go places they shouldn't, such as elementary schools for sex offenders, or bars for drunk drivers. Law enforcement officials report that the cost — about $5 a day compared to $50 a day in prison — is worth it.

The next generation of these devices comes in the form of an implantable microchip called the VeriChip, which is a $200 microchip about the size of a grain of rice. After a unique 16-digit identifier is encoded on the microchip, the VeriChip is implanted under the skin with a large needle device (Figure 2-14). A tiny transmitter on the chip sends out the data when it is scanned, so that medical personal can obtain key information about your medical past. Many people who suffer from illnesses or allergies are enthusiastic about the VeriChip, knowing that the information accessible via the microchip could help save their lives. For entirely different reasons, members of Mexico City's attorney general's office have had chips implanted to provide greater security to government offices housing key computer systems holding sensitive data used for fighting crime. Other uses of the chip have huge positive potential. Soldiers with a VeriChip could have their location tracked during war, as could journalists on assignment in dangerous locales. Jailbreaks could be eliminated, as wardens could use VeriChip technology to track prisoner locations on their office computer. However, use of the chip for social reasons may raise some eyebrows. In Barcelona, the Baja Beach Club nightclub offers to implant chips (during the daytime) in patrons who don't want to wait in line or carry cash in the future. These chips are scanned at the door for entry, and at the bar so customers can make purchases that will be added to their accounts.

Critics of the chip claim that the implants are frighteningly reminiscent of bad science fiction movies, and privacy advocates wonder out loud about how the technology might be abused. Overprotective or abusive parents could make their children virtual prisoners by tracking their every move. A suspicious wife might want to implant microchips in her husband to track his movements. A dictator might use the microchips to track and round up any citizens who oppose his regime.

In the end, many privacy and legal questions about the VeriChip have yet to be answered fully. Many wonder if the desire to protect our loved ones is worth curtailing their freedom. Others want to know who decides whether or not you get a chip — you, your parents, or a law enforcement agency? If your parents implant a chip in you, at what age do you have the right to remove the chip? Who has access to data transmitted from the chip?

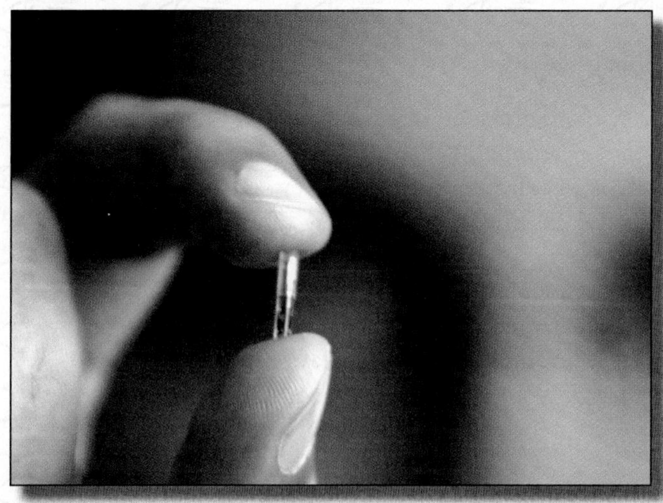

Figure 2-14 After your medical and personal information are encoded on the rice-sized microchip, the VeriChip is implanted under the skin with a large needle device.

@ISSUE: Getting Chipped *(continued)*

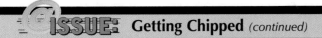

For now, these questions remain unanswered as VeriChip makers focus on the less controversial process of distributing VeriChip scanners to hospital emergency rooms and working with medical-device makers to bundle the chip with pacemakers and other appliances. In the meantime, Spot happily continues through his days, complete with the microchip that gives you a sense of security. The next time you give him a scratch behind the ears, ask yourself: would you want to have a VeriChip as part of your life? Just how secure does that make you feel?

COMPUTERS AND HOMELAND SECURITY

After the attacks in New York on September 11, 2001, homeland security became a renewed focus for the government and citizens alike. Computer technology is playing a key role in keeping the country safe, by helping to track citizens and visitors to the country, to provide good communication during national crises, and to protect the United States' borders.

Tracking Citizens

Beginning in 2005, the U.S. State Department began issuing passports to U.S. citizens bearing an RFID chip. The chip contains an identification number and a digital signature – numbers assigned to the chip when the passport is issued – in addition to a digital facial image and all the personal data currently found on the information page of a passport. All this data is stored in a central government database. Once the chip is printed and embedded in the passport, it cannot be altered. When citizens present their passports at U.S. ports of entry using the special readers needed to collect the data, the system makes note of the entry. Since passports are valid for up to ten years, it will take some time for all citizens' passports to be converted to the new format, giving the State Department time to fully implement the necessary RFID technology at all ports of entry. Critics contend that chips can be read by unauthorized scanning devices from as far away as 30 to 65 feet, without the passport holder's knowledge or consent. Government officials state that the chips are readable only when in close proximity to their chip readers. Damage to the chip, via tampering or exposure to water, can render it useless, requiring processing the "old fashioned" way.

Tracking Visitors

Tracking U.S. citizens is just one concern for homeland security officials. One of the biggest problems is one that has been aggravated by the use of computers: the easy availability of fake identification documents. Using expensive laser printers and desktop publishing software, counterfeiters can create credible passports, Social Security cards, birth certificates, and driver's licenses. Of the many millions of people who visit the United States each year, it can be difficult to know who is using real documents and who is using fake documents.

To thwart the use of fake documents, the United States has implemented a new system, called the U.S. VISIT (Visitor and Immigrant Status Indication Technology) system, which is designed to make it easier for legitimate tourists, students, and business travelers to enter the country, while making it more difficult to enter illegally.

The core of the U.S. VISIT system is a database of biometric identifiers. The system would require foreign students, tourists, and business travelers to supply two biometric identifiers – a digital fingerprint and a digital photograph – when entering and leaving the country. The biometric identifiers are stored in the U.S. VISIT database, along with information on the visitor's visa, nationality, and other personal data. Each time visitors use a passport or visa to exit or enter the country, their identifiers are matched against those in the database to verify their identity. The tracking system is intended to make it easier for immigration officials to spot visitors whose 90-day visas have expired and help tourists, students, and business travelers enter the United States more quickly by using biometric identifiers to verify their identities. There are currently 116 airports, 15 seaports, and 154 land ports of entry participating in the system.

Foreign students with visas attending schools in the United States also must provide personal information as input to the Internet-based SEVIS (Student and Exchange Visa Information Service) system. SEVIS is intended to help the government to ensure that foreign students and exchange visitors enroll and stay enrolled in courses at the school. Prior to SEVIS, colleges and universities had to submit paperwork for each student attending their schools. With the SEVIS system, administrative staff at a school can input student data and print bar-coded forms via the SEVIS Web site – or the school can upload student data in a batch, directly from the school's computer systems to the SEVIS systems. The data entered by a school resides on a central database maintained by the Bureau of Citizenship and Immigration Services (BCIS), which is accessible by schools via the Web. Schools can update student records via the SEVIS Web site. The data then is used to alert the BCIS if students who enter the country fail to enroll at the school they are supposed to attend or if students drop out of their programs. Many have expressed criticism of the new system, fearing invasion of privacy. Others note that the system has experienced technological problems including data transfer issues that result in lost information, delays in processing simple forms, and personal information being sent to the wrong individuals.

Surveillance Using Computer Vision Systems

The U.S. Bureau of Customs and Border Protection is stepping up security on the U.S. and Canadian border – the longest contiguous border in the world – by implementing a computer vision system at ports of entry along the border. The computer vision system, which is a new type of video surveillance system, uses hundreds of digital video cameras along the 3,987 mile border to see and analyze unusual activities or movements in real time. The surveillance system software uses artificial intelligence to analyze the data gathered by the video cameras. The software reviews the digital video feeds in real time for any unusual objects or activity – perhaps a large truck without license plates or people climbing over a fence. If the system identifies something suspicious, it immediately sends alerts to computers and wireless devices, such as PDAs, so that enforcement agencies can respond promptly. Other applications of computer vision systems like this include monitoring restricted areas, such as parking lots, for unauthorized vehicles, packages, or other objects, and controlling access to secure locations by checking movement around entrances and exits.

Managing Crises Through Collaboration

The Homeland Security Department also relies on computer technology – specifically a Web-based collaboration system – to help track and manage events during a crisis. Following the September 11 attacks, New York officials used a Web-based collaboration system to coordinate and manage the city's response. In 2003, NASA used the system to track over 10,000 pieces of debris from the Space Shuttle Columbia disaster. The system also is designed to help manage bioterrorism threats, natural disasters, and other crisis situations.

A Web-based collaboration system allows everyone involved to share critical information in real time (Figure 2-15). Authorized users can enter information about specific incidents, so that others can view information related to the event. Once the incident is logged into the system, it is placed on a map along with an incident report. The system also provides comprehensive situation reports for all agencies, status and damage reports for critical facilities, and even staffing assignments to handle recovery and response efforts.

All of this information is accessible from a wireless laptop or networked computer. The system also sends alerts to handheld computers, to notify individuals that new information is in the system, so that remote users know to log into the system using a laptop or PC.

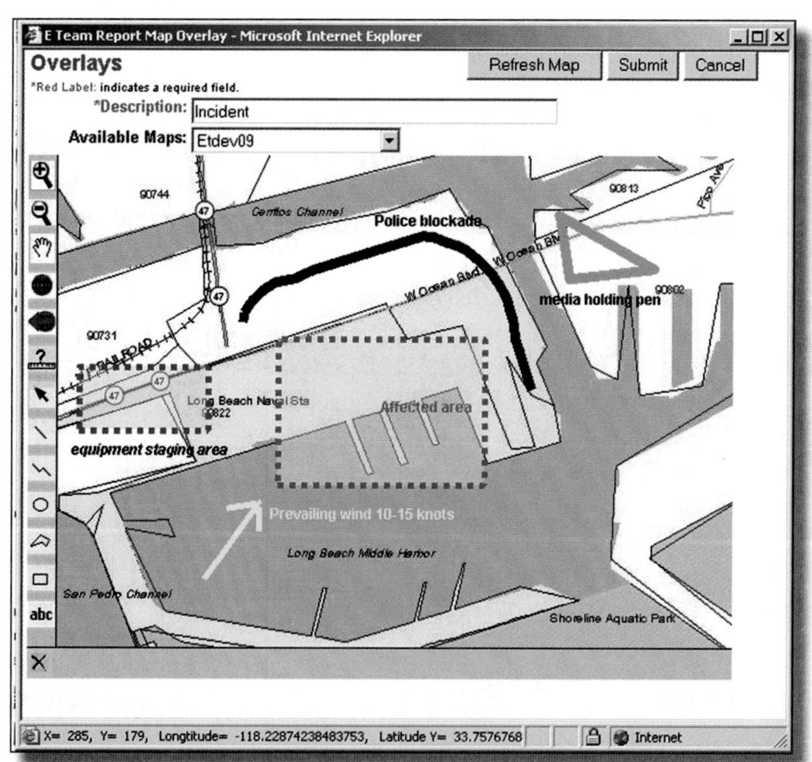

Figure 2-15 To help aid crisis management, the Homeland Security Department and other agencies use a Web-based collaboration system to share computerized incident maps in real-time.

COMPUTERS IN THE MILITARY

The United States military is continually working with technology firms and research organizations to improve the technologies behind military equipment and systems. Historically, wars and conflicts have brought many new products into commercial use by citizens. For example, duct tape first was used widely in World War II, when the U.S. military utilized hundreds of rolls to seal ammunition cases and hold together broken parts. After the war, everyone had a roll of duct tape to handle whatever job was needed. During the first Gulf War, troops used global positioning system (GPS) technology to navigate in sandstorms and at night. Today, boaters, sportsmen, and transportation services use GPS.

Today's military continues to set trends in the computer and technology field. U.S. troops in Iraq, for example, use rugged laptops equipped with the latest wireless technologies to communicate with each other and those back home. Other recent advances in military equipment include portable unmanned aerial vehicle (UAVs), remote-controlled robots, precision-guided bombs, the use of GPS to track trucks and troops over rough terrain, and using computer simulations for training.

Deploying Unmanned Aerial Vehicles (UAVs)

During Operation Iraqi Freedom, intelligence gathering was aided by **unmanned aerial vehicles (UAVs)** used to provide surveillance over cities by day and by night (Figure 2-16). These lightweight, remote-controlled drones each have a GPS for determining location, a chemical-agent detector, and a miniature camera (either color or night vision) that relays live video images to the pilot and mission navigator, to a video recorder, or even to other remote ground receivers. The UAVs are ideal for surveillance in crowded city areas. Because they are small, they are less noticeable than pilot-navigated surveillance planes or larger UAVs, which can be shot down. In the near future, these small UAVs may be used by the police for surveillance, by oil companies to check pipelines for leaks, or even by news organizations to get sweeping vistas of sports events.

Using Remote-Controlled Robots

Remote-controlled robots provide the military with eyes, ears, and feet in small or hazardous locations where it is impossible or unsafe for soldiers and emergency personnel to go. During the hunt for Osama bin Laden, newer remote-controlled robots, called PackBots, were used to explore caves in Afghanistan. These same robots were used in Operation Iraqi Freedom to crawl through buildings and look for signs of ambush (Figure 2-17). The newer versions of remote-controlled robots have numerous detectors – cameras, microphones, sonar, infrared sensors, and laser scanners – to allow the robot to react to its environment and turn away from walls, respond to sounds, and so on. Other specialized sensors – such as those used to search for chemical agents – also can be added to the 40-pound PackBots. Each $45,000 PackBot has a radio antenna and a network hub that allows it to receive remote-controlled signals and send video and other data back to the local command center. Today, police in several cities are testing the use of PackBots in hostage situations.

Scientists currently are working on a different type of robot, one that can steer a vehicle without human help. In wartime, these robots could drive trucks in convoys to deliver humanitarian aid or to return tired troops from the warfront to camp. Commercial applications might involve using the robots to harvest grain or mine coal. The robots would rely on neural networks, which are trained to pilot the vehicle, as well as GPS, magnetic sensors, and digital cameras to help the robot locate its position and transmit visual indication of its location.

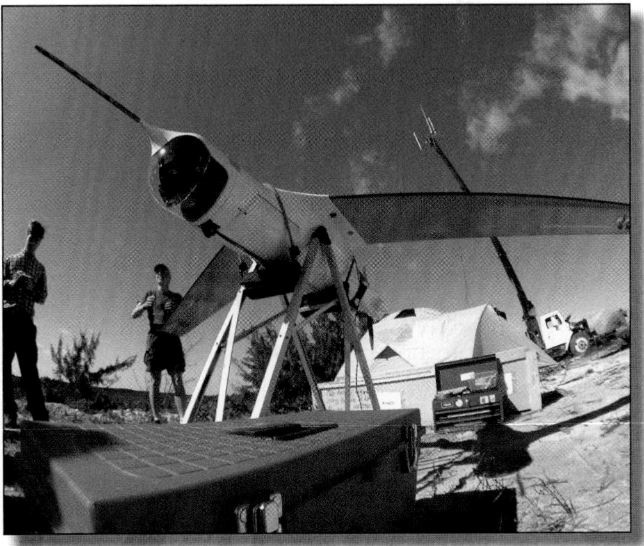

Figure 2-16 Unmanned aerial vehicles (UAVs) are used to provide surveillance. Each UAV is equipped a miniature camera that relays live video images to the pilot and mission navigator.

Figure 2-17 Remote-controlled robots, called PackBots, were used in Operation Iraqi Freedom to crawl through buildings and look for signs of ambush.

Utilizing Precision-Guided Bombs

Another technology pioneered by the military is **smart bombs** – bombs that can be guided to their targets using satellite-guidance capability (Figure 2-18). Smart bombs (more technically referred to as precision-guided bombs) are self-guiding weapons intended to maximize damage to the specific target, while minimizing civilian casualties and collateral damage. Modern smart bombs use signals from GPS satellites to determine their location and make necessary adjustments, which gives them the pinpoint accuracy needed to destroy a car directly beside a bridge, but leave the bridge undamaged.

Today's smart bombs can be directed to within three feet of a target from heights of over 20,000 feet. Because they rely on GPS (and not laser systems, like older bombs), bad weather, smoke, and debris do not limit the bombs' ability to hit the desired target. The precision of a smart bomb, however, depends on how well the specific target location has been mapped and whether the pilot has programmed the proper coordinates correctly into the weapon. This data requires human intelligence information, which may not always be accurate. Critics of the smart bomb question if we should turn over control of such deadly devices to technology. Proponents note, however, that the GPS technology provides more accurate targeting than dumb bombs that do not utilize technology.

In several years, the same precision-guidance technology used in the smart bombs may be used to allow pilots of commercial airliners to better guide their planes and to improve air-traffic control. The sensors used in smart bombs also could cause your car to brake when a dog runs out into the road – before you even see it or have a chance to react.

Tracking Troop Movement

The military continues to benefit from GPS – not only to track UAVs and guide bombs, but also to track trucks and troops. Troops often find themselves in locations with few landmarks, such as a desert with vast expanses of sand and terrain that remains unchanged for miles. GPS can be used to help the troops accurately determine their location and their enemy's position. Using GPS to locate units precisely also allows commanders to coordinate the actions of different units on the ground, in the air, or at sea. To ensure that the enemy does not benefit from the same systems, the United States also is developing jamming systems that reduce the effectiveness of enemy GPS guidance systems.

Rescue and emergency response is another area where GPS can prove invaluable to the military. By determining the location of a casualty during operations, emergency response teams can use GPS to reduce

Figure 2-18 Modern smart bombs use signals from GPS satellites to determine their location and adjust as needed, which gives them pinpoint accuracy.

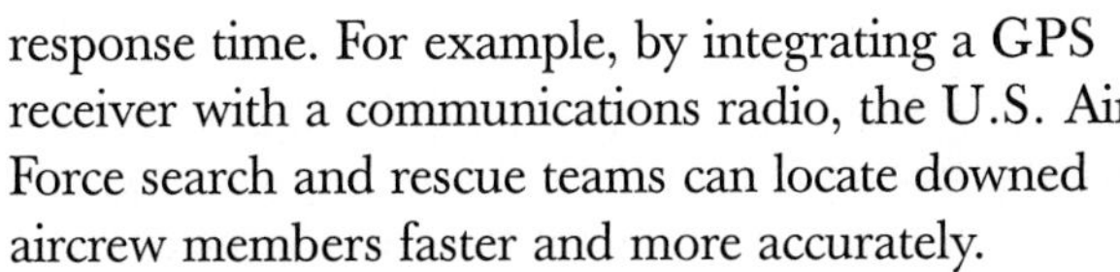

response time. For example, by integrating a GPS receiver with a communications radio, the U.S. Air Force search and rescue teams can locate downed aircrew members faster and more accurately.

Other military applications of GPS include GPS-guided cargo packages that can be dropped from the air by a transport aircraft to service troops on the ground. The cargo packages have parasails controlled by GPS receivers that can modify the trajectory of the package so it falls to a specific location. The supplies thus land at a precise remote location, while the transport aircraft and crew quickly travel back to a safer range.

Using Computer Simulations for Training

Effectively training soldiers for combat involves giving them an opportunity to experience the time spent in complicated and expensive military vehicles. However, live training inside battle tanks, aircraft, and ships can be dangerous and extremely expensive. Computer simulation, on the other hand, can provide many of the same benefits as live training without the associated risks and costs.

A **computer simulation** uses computers and software to create a realistic experience that helps show how events might occur under certain conditions. As you will learn in Chapter 3, scientists often use simulations to predict the weather or analyze other environmental developments. The primary goal of the computer simulations used by the military is to provide a realistic representation of battle conditions, so that soldiers trained by simulation can apply their experience to an actual battlefield.

Typically, a military training simulation involves modeling the experience of being inside a tank, helicopter, jet fighter, or naval vessel. A single computer simulates each military vehicle. By connecting two or more computer simulators, a soldier training in a tank simulator in California can fight against a soldier training in an Apache helicopter simulator in Connecticut. With thousands of soldiers participating from computer simulators, entire battles can be replicated.

Using computers for training simulations has several benefits. First, soldiers can practice a scenario repeatedly and learn from mistakes without additional cost or danger. Further, the computer simulator records every event in sequence, so that supervisors can review and replay portions of the exercise to offer feedback and analysis. Finally, with many simulators a supervisor can change variables in real time – for example, by adding a sandstorm to a simulated battlefield – to test soldier's reactions and response time. The realism of a simulation, however, depends on the accuracy of the assumptions provided by experts and the algorithms coded by programmers. If the assumptions and algorithms are incorrect, the simulation itself may create an unrealistic situation, which has little value as a training exercise.

CONCLUSION

In this chapter, you learned how computers have changed the electoral process. You discovered how key government branches and agencies, such as the United States Postal Service, Census Bureau, and Internal Revenue Service, use computers to streamline their processes and provide better service to citizens. You also learned how law enforcement uses computers and technology to maintain databases to track evidence and criminal records, enforce traffic laws, communicate information about missing children quickly, and incorporate GPS technology into cellular phones to ensure a quick response to a 911 emergency call. After reviewing how computers are used to help ensure homeland security by tracking visitors to the country, you also learned about the government's use of Web-based collaborative tools to share information in a crisis and how computer vision systems help to protect the country's borders. You learned how the military uses sophisticated computer technologies, including UAVs and remote-controlled robots to observe and explore dangerous areas, GPS to guide smart bombs to a specific target and to help guide soldiers, and computer simulations to train new recruits for combat.

Key Terms

biometric devices
computer simulations
direct recording electronic (DRE) machines
e-File
Enhanced 911 (e-911)
Internet-based voting systems
online voting systems
optical character recognition system (OCR)
optical mark recognition systems
political polling
punch card system
smart bombs
tax preparation software
unmanned aerial vehicles (UAVs)

Chapter Review

Multiple Choice

Select the best answer.

1. Critics of the validity of online polls note that the polls _____.
   (a) cannot incorporate graphic, audio, or video clips
   (b) collect only voter responses without any demographic information
   (c) gather input from a group limited to those with computer access
   (d) all of the above

2. When sorting mail, the USPS uses a(n) _____, which relies on artificial intelligence to recognize patterns and read handwritten, typed, or computer-printed characters from documents and translate the images into a form a computer can process.
   (a) optical mark recognition (OMR) systems
   (b) magnetic-ink character recognition (MICR) systems
   (c) optical character recognition (OCR) systems
   (d) bar code scanning (BCS) systems

3. The Internal Revenue Service (IRS) Web site provides taxpayers with all of the following assistance *except* _____.
   (a) federal tax codes and forms in PDF format
   (b) analysis of forms for errors or discrepancies
   (c) the address of a local IRS office
   (d) tax calculators to determine what is owed

4. The _____ was established to help gun dealers perform personal history checks on prospective buyers to ensure that convicted felons cannot buy guns.
   (a) Combined DNA Index System (CODIS)
   (b) National Instant Criminal Background Check System (NICS)
   (c) Automated Fingerprint Identification System (AFIS)
   (d) National Crime Information Center (NCIC) database

5. A key element of red-light systems is a trigger, which is a _____.
   (a) digital camera mounted on a light standard
   (b) computer database that stores information on traffic violators
   (c) stylus that adds pertinent information to the digital photo
   (d) length of electrical wire buried just under the asphalt

6. The _____ is a missing child alert system, created to issue an immediate alert to help recover missing or abducted children.
   (a) Amber Alert system
   (b) LoJack system
   (c) Emergency Broadcast System (EBS)
   (d) Automatic Number Identifier (ANI) system

7. The core of the U.S. VISIT system is a database of _____, such as digital fingerprints or iris or retinal scans.
   (a) bar codes
   (b) global positioning systems
   (c) artificial intelligence
   (d) biometric identifiers

8. New passports issued to U.S. citizens contain _____ which holds, among other things, personal data about the passport holder.
   (a) a bar code
   (b) infrared sensors
   (c) an RFID chip
   (d) digital fingerprints

9. A precision-guided bomb, also called a _____, is a bomb that can be guided to its target using satellite-guidance capability.
   (a) smart bomb
   (b) GPS bomb
   (c) intelligent bomb
   (d) rapid air defense bomb

10. The military continues to benefit from _____, not only to track UAVs and guide bombs, but also to track trucks and troops.
   (a) bar code scanners
   (b) global positioning systems (GPS)
   (c) biometric identifiers
   (d) artificial intelligence (AI)

Chapter Review

Short Answer

Write a brief answer to each of the following questions.

1. What are the pros and cons of using human-implantable microchips such as the VeriChip?
2. What is the POSTNET bar code and how is it used?
3. What are some ways that the IRS uses computers?
4. How do gun dealers use the National Instant Criminal Background Check System (NICS)?
5. What are the benefits of using computer simulations for military training?

Web Research

Use a search engine such as Google (google.com) to research the following questions. Then, write a one-page double-spaced report or create a presentation, unless otherwise directed.

1. The use of online voting systems has been the subject of much debate since the 2000 presidential election. Critics and proponents both are vocal about the viability of such systems. What is the current status of implementing such a system on a nationwide basis? Which states have experimented with this type of voting system, and which states have systems in development? What issues have they faced, and how would you recommend they be handled in the future? Use this information to prepare a position statement for or against online voting systems.
2. More than 50 cities use **red-light cameras** to catch traffic violations at intersections. The cameras can be a boon to city coffers — New York City's red-light cameras made $5.4 million in their first year. Some people feel, however, the cameras violate an individual's constitutional right to face his or her accuser. Use the Web to learn more about the advantages and disadvantages of using cameras to monitor intersections.

Group Exercises

Working with a group of your classmates, complete the following team questions.

1. Advocacy Web sites promote a political candidate, position, or issue. Although these Web sites can be sponsored by an individual, usually they are sponsored by a group, such as the Democratic National Committee or the Republican National Committee, or an association, such as the Society to Protect Human Rights or the Society for the Prevention of Cruelty to Animals. How effective are these Web sites? Have each member of your team visit a different advocacy Web site. Note the candidate or position being promoted and consider why the Web site is, or is not, effective. Then, meet with your team and prepare a PowerPoint presentation explaining what advocacy Web sites should, and should not, do to convince a reader of the soundness of a candidate or cause.
2. Law enforcement agencies can use computers to track evidence, store criminal records, enforce traffic laws, find missing children, and trace emergency calls. How does your local police department use computers? Contact your local police department (call the number in the telephone book, *do not* call 911) to arrange an interview for your team with an officer on how the department uses computers. Find out how the department uses computers now, and if any computer-related innovations are being contemplated for the future. Then, meet with your team and prepare a PowerPoint presentation showing how your local police department uses, and plans to use, computers in law enforcement.

Computers in Medicine and Science 3

Computers in Medicine
- **Maintaining Patient History**
- **Managing the Medical Practice**
- **Improving Patient Diagnosis and Monitoring**
  - *Clinical Data Capture and Medical Imaging*
  - *Computer-Assisted Diagnosis*
  - *Accessing Pharmacy and Medical Information*
  - *Monitoring Patients*
- **Technology in the Operating Room**
- **Telemedicine and Telepresence Surgery**
- **Medical Research and Training**
  - *Recognizing Patterns of Disease*
  - *Improving Medical Training*
- **Credibility of Medical Information**

Computers in Science
- **Observation and Data Collection**
  - *Collecting Weather Data*
  - *Hunting Hurricanes*
  - *Remote Sensing*
- **Data Classification and Analysis**
  - *Human Genome Project*
  - *SETI@Home*
- **Data Modeling and Simulation**
  - *Forecasting the Weather*
  - *Environmental Impact Modeling*
  - *Geographic Information Systems*

Conclusion

The disciplines of medicine and science involve similar steps, such as making an assessment of the cause of an occurrence — whether a new disease or a hole in the ozone layer — and then collecting and analyzing data to better understand why that occurrence happened. After confirming the reason for the occurrence, a course of action typically is recommended. In medicine, the recommendation might involve a physician telling a patient to exercise and take a prescription drug for a few weeks. In a scientific study, the recommendation might involve scientists suggesting regulations to limit the release of greenhouse gases into the atmosphere.

Over the last few decades, computer technology has transformed the disciplines of medicine and science — completely altering the way data is collected, analyzed, communicated, and stored. In this chapter, you will learn more about the use of computers in medicine to maintain patient histories and manage the medical practice, as well as to improve patient diagnosis and monitoring. After looking at technology in the operating room and seeing how telemedicine is making health care available at a distance, you will learn how computers are used in medical research and training. Finally, the question of how to assess the credibility of medical Web sites is reviewed. You also will learn about the use of computers in science to help with observation and data collection, data classification and analysis, and data modeling and simulation.

COMPUTERS IN MEDICINE

When you visit your physician for a routine examination, he or she is likely to greet you carrying a PDA, along with a stethoscope. As you review your medical history and the reason for the current visit, the physician may enter notes into a software application on the desktop computer. After your visit, the physician might print and hand you a sheet listing prescription information together with any special instructions, along with an e-mail address you can use to send any questions you might have.

In today's technology-rich field of medicine, the doctor's office and hospital are filled with computers, printers, PDAs, and other technology devices. This explosion of computer usage in the world of health care often is referred to as **medical informatics** – the application of computers, communications, and information technology to all fields of medicine, including medical care, medical education, and medical research. Using computers in medicine and health care helps doctors more effectively manage their practices. Both doctors and patients can use computers to collect and interpret data, and make subsequent actions as a result. For example, physicians can access online drug databases to learn more about possible side effects of a new prescription drug or view results from the latest clinical trials. Patients can access Web sites to learn more about health and wellness or find out how to cope with an illness. Furthermore, e-mail has completely changed communications among physicians and between physicians and their patients, making doctors accessible at any time, even from miles away.

Maintaining Patient History

One of the biggest challenges of any medical practice or hospital is keeping accurate and up-to-date patient records. For years, health care professionals relied on paper-based patient records to track patient visits, prescriptions, medical history, and recommended follow-up care. With paper-based patient records, your medical history evolved as a series of written notes from a physician, along with data, such as laboratory test results.

As medicine became increasingly advanced and specialized, however, the use of the paper-based record became progressively more inefficient. First, a patient record only can be at one place at one time. If a doctor takes the patient records to review with a specialist, a lab technician does not have access to the records that might alert her to possible adverse reactions to certain tests. Paper-based patient charts also have to be pulled and refiled every time a phone message, lab report, or accounting update needs to be documented. In many cases, the result of having charts handled by many different people may be misplaced medical records.

Computers can help change this slow, costly, and error-prone part of the medical process into a relatively streamlined procedure. A **computer-based patient record (CPR)** is a patient record maintained electronically. It allows all data on a patient to be stored in one place, in computerized form. Also referred to as an *electronic medical record (EMR)* or an *electronic patient record (EPR)*, a CPR includes a patient's medical history, prescriptions, and health insurance information. Because it is electronic, it also can include digital X rays, video of recent surgery, or recorded notes from the physician. The computer-based patient records are entered, stored, and maintained with the help of an **electronic medical record (EMR) system**, which is computer-based, patient records and documentation management software for the health care industry.

If you are the patient, the experience of visiting a physician using an EMR system is apparent as soon as you walk into the waiting room. Instead of photocopying an insurance card, the receptionist scans your insurance card, along with the new patient datasheet that forms the basis of your chart. Examination rooms include computers, conveniently positioned so that both you and the doctor can view and discuss your chart and medical history. The physician also can pull up any other pertinent documents, such as X rays or referral-letters that have already been scanned and stored in the practice's main database. If your visit involves lab work, the physician can connect to the computer system at the lab to pull up your results.

If the physician prescribes a new medication, the EMR system automatically generates a list of potential drug interactions. After a physician enters the prescription data, the EMR system can calculate drug dosage based on your weight, write the prescription, and print it, so you can pick it up as you leave the office. The EMR system also generates a sheet that you can take home regarding your diagnosis and any special instructions – a huge help in keeping you and other patients safe. Close to 25% of the nation's hospitals have fully implemented an EMR, and another 65% have plans to do so in the coming years, so the digital records collected by your doctor can be used to augment your hospital treatment records should you ever be admitted to the hospital.

Managing the Medical Practice

Running a medical practice involves much more than providing health care to patients; it also involves billing, handling insurance claims, scheduling, and more. An EMR system helps a physician address some of these needs. The physician can sit at the computer and enter all information into the chart during the examination. The EMR then links the information with the appropriate codes for the billing department. Using the EMR system cuts out the time-consuming process of dictation, transcription, and coding for billing and insurance claims. The claims manager can print the already coded records from the EMR system to file claims. Some insurance carriers even allow and encourage claims to be filed electronically.

In addition to EMR, billing, and insurance systems, physicians also use scheduling systems to schedule patient appointments and automatically print out reminder cards to mail to patients. Some physicians rely on PDA software that permits mobile input of new patient chart data, review of clinical records, and review

@ISSUE: Keeping Your PHI Private

Information privacy refers to the right of individuals and companies to deny or restrict the collection and use of information about them. In the past, information privacy was easier to maintain because information was kept in separate locations, not in large databases in various organizations. Your medical information — often referred to as your **personal health information (PHI)** — also was easier to keep private, as the paper documents that made up your patient record were accessible only to hospital staff.

Today, your medical information is stored in numerous databases, from the physician's EMR system to the hospital's lab testing database to the insurance provider's records system. Besides information about your health, these records may include information about family relationships, substance abuse, and even transcripts from counseling sessions.

While this information should only be accessible to authorized users, the use of technology to store and manage patient health information has caused many to raise questions about just how private health care data really is. For example, using databases to store large amounts of data means that, if the database is accessed illegally, countless patient records can be compromised. Further, electronic data is gathered, exchanged, and transmitted more easily than data on paper records. Sharing data with third parties is as simple as sending an e-mail. Concerns increasingly were expressed that information from your medical records might negatively impact your ability to get health insurance or keep you from obtaining loans, being admitted to schools, or even getting a job.

In response to the increased concern about the privacy of health care information, Congress enacted HIPAA. **HIPAA**, which stands for the **Health Information Portability and Accountability Act of 1996**, is a privacy law designed to protect personal information in consumer health records. HIPAA, which informally is called the Privacy Rule, protects consumers from having their personal health information exploited by insurance companies, employers, or anyone else who could try to misuse, disclose, or publish that information.

Patients now have the right to receive notice of privacy policies; request restrictions or receive a record of disclosures; and change or update their records at any time. However, even after the Privacy Rule was amended and finalized in 2003, the law still allows the use of health information for marketing without patient consent — which means you remain a target for coupons for the latest allergy medication, based on your prescription records from the past decade, as long as the marketing communication does not use personally identifiable and protected health information.

Most feel that HIPAA not only is good for patients, but also is a benefit for health care providers, who can avoid possible lawsuits and build patient loyalty by respecting patient privacy. The law puts patients back in control of most of their PHI, giving them the right to determine who can review it and when. Better security on electronic data also reduces the risk that their records might be stolen or examined by unauthorized people.

Others, however, suggest that the stringent rules required by HIPAA might become more of a hindrance than a help to most patients. For example, hospital patients must sign a notice before information about their condition or the location of their room is released to anyone, including family members. Even florists delivering to patients who have not signed a release are not allowed to deliver flowers to the patient's room. The law also may further complicate the already slow process of filing an insurance claim. Insurance companies may not have access to information needed to process a claim, thus forcing patients to deliver that information personally. And with the growth of Wi-Fi networks, some concern has been voiced over security and the potential for interception of confidential patient data as it streams invisibly across the radio waves surrounding clinics and hospitals.

In the end, everyone agrees that patients should have control over their medical records and PHI. With the computerization at the core of many changes in medicine, defining standards around privacy and security is a first and much-needed step to ensuring the information that has been protected by doctor-patient confidentiality for years remains just that: confidential.

and entry of schedules, patient demographics, procedure or diagnosis codes, billing, and more. The technology frees the medical practitioner from paper-based documentation and the need to spend time checking in with the office or running between locations to get vital information. Reporting is another key element in medical practice management software. Reports generated from the medical practice management software can help the physician monitor patient outcomes over time; other reports can help billing and insurance managers track completed or overdue payments.

Improving Patient Diagnosis and Monitoring

Computers have revolutionized patient diagnosis, making available new tools and machines to allow for the capture and analysis of patient data to help determine the source of a health problem. Computers also are at the heart of improved patient monitoring, where numerous new developments help ensure a patient's vital statistics can be monitored continuously, either in the hospital or at home.

CLINICAL DATA CAPTURE AND MEDICAL IMAGING Today, many diagnostic tools widely used in medicine rely on computer technology to provide accurate and detailed clinical data to allow physicians to make a sound diagnosis. Several of these tools are described in Table 3-1. For example, computers allow for the automatic capture of the electrical activity of the heart and the brain. **Electrocardiograms (ECGs or EKGs)** are used to record the electrical activity of the heart, show any abnormal rhythms, or detect heart muscle damage. The systems typically consist of a screen to monitor the heart functions (Figure 3-1a), along with a printer for obtaining hard copy results. EKG systems may also contain databases to archive patient results.

Other computer devices used in the diagnostic process include machines focused on obtaining medical images. Using ultrasound, for example, a computer analyzes sound waves reflected back from structures in the body (Figure 3-1b). Magnetic resonance imaging (MRI) provides a way to take images inside the body by using a powerful magnet and transmitting radio waves through the body (Figure 3-1c). The resulting images appear on a computer screen for viewing by the physician. Even the often-used X ray has benefited from advances in computer technology, which allow a digital X ray to be taken. Using a digital X ray means a health care professional does not have to wait for the film to be developed; instead, the physician or radiologist can look at an image as it is being taken and make an immediate diagnosis (Figure 3-1d).

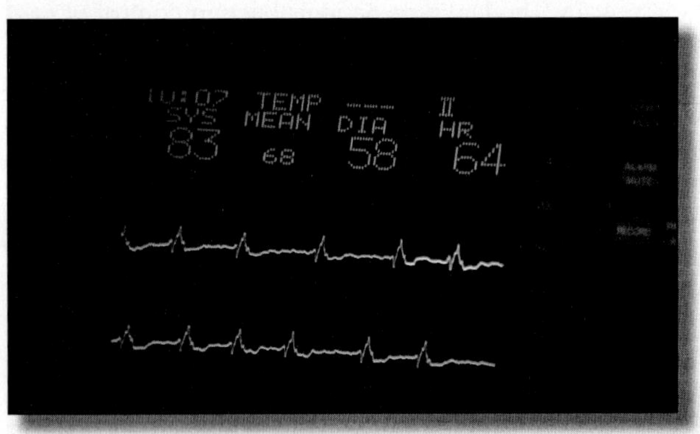

(a) EKG

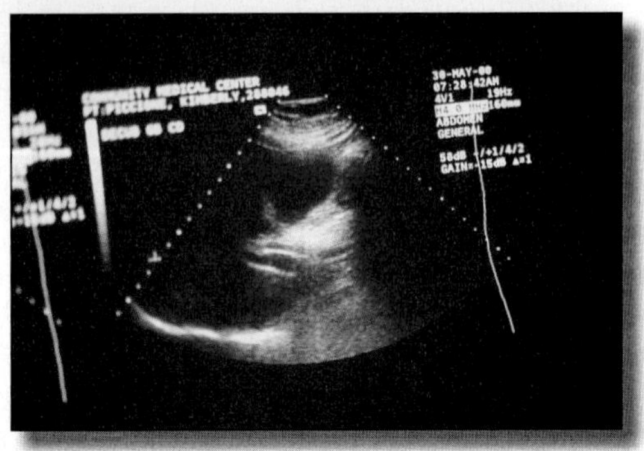
(b) Ultrasound

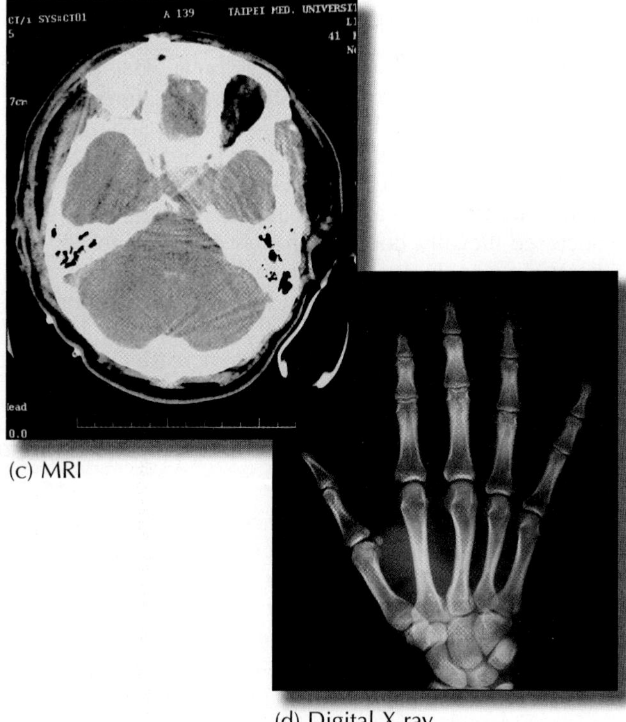
(c) MRI

(d) Digital X ray

Figure 3-1 In the diagnostic process, computers allow for the capture of clinical data, such as the electrical activity of the heart and the brain or views of bones, tissue, and other structures.

TABLE 3-1 Medical Tests that Use Computer Technology

DIAGNOSTIC TEST	*DESCRIPTION*
Electrocardiogram (ECG or EKG)	A test that records the electrical activity of the heart, shows abnormal rhythms, and detects heart muscle damage.
CAT scan	Also called a CT scan or computerized axial tomography (CAT) scan, an imaging test in which many X rays are taken of a part of the body from different angles. A computer combines these images to produce cross-sectional pictures of internal organs.
Magnetic resonance imaging (MRI)	A method of taking pictures of the inside of the body. Instead of using X rays, MRI uses a powerful magnet and transmits radio waves through the body; the images appear on a computer screen as well as on film. Like X rays, the procedure is physically painless, but some people find it psychologically uncomfortable to be inside the MRI machine.
Ultrasound	A method of gathering images using reflected sound waves to produce a picture of organs and other structures inside the body. During an ultrasound test, a small handheld instrument called a transducer (that emits and detects high-pitched sounds beyond the range of human hearing) is passed back and forth over the area of the body being examined. A computer analyzes and converts the reflected sound waves into a picture on a video monitor. The images produced by ultrasound are called a sonogram, echogram, or scan. Pictures or videos of the ultrasound images may be saved for a permanent record.
Electroencephalography (EEG)	A method to record the electrical activity of the brain. Sensors (electrodes) are attached to the head and connected by wires to a computer. The computer records the brain's electrical activity on paper as wavy lines. Certain brain abnormalities can be detected by observing changes in the normal pattern of the brain's electrical activity.
Digital X rays	A method of gathering images that uses a sensor placed next to the X-ray site. Within seconds, the X ray is displayed in sharp, vivid detail on a computer screen. Because of this short exposure time, the amount of X-ray radiation is reduced by as much as 90 percent. Once the X-ray image is on the computer, it can be enhanced for a more precise diagnosis, saved for later use, or sent to insurance companies or specialists, as needed.

Today, many diagnostic tests and tools use computer technology to provide accurate and detailed clinical data.

Electron beam tomography (EBT) and computerized axial tomography (CAT) scanning can be used for "whole body scanning," a technique for capturing a digital picture of the patient's entire body in one session. Considered somewhat controversial by the FDA (which does not certify or approve technologies associated with whole body scans) and some in the medical profession, this type of scan can provide a virtual diagnostic view inside the patient without using surgery or other invasive means to make a diagnosis. Most of the controversy does not surround the technology itself, but rather the benefits and its role in effective detection of disease. In some cases, abnormalities detected are not life-threatening yet create undue stress and concern for the patient.

As technology continues to advance, even more unique diagnostic tools are available to health care professionals. For example, a pill-sized camera that patients swallow allows doctors to travel virtually through a patient's small intestine to detect ulcers and tumors. More effective than CAT scans or X rays, and much less invasive than previously available diagnostic tests, the pill camera can allow doctors to find and repair problem areas before the patient experiences major problems.

COMPUTER-ASSISTED DIAGNOSIS **Computer-assisted diagnosis (CAD)** is the use of computer programs designed to aid health care professionals in diagnosing a medical problem. After a patient's symptoms, signs, and test results are entered, along with a possible diagnosis, the CAD system either confirms or excludes a diagnosis. The CAD system also may offer suggestions for subsequent medical tests to further narrow the diagnosis.

Systems used to support computer-assisted diagnosis often are decision support or expert systems. DXplain, for example, is a decision support system designed to provide a physician with a ranked list of diagnoses that might explain or be associated with the clinical data. In Japan, scientists at Osaka University have created a robotic "toddler" designed to move like a human child between the ages of one and three years old (Figure 3-2). Using 56 actuators in place of muscles, 197 sensors for touch, small cameras for eyes, and an audio sensor, researchers are hoping the robotic child will help them gain a better understanding of how toddlers learn language, recognize objects, and develop basic communication skills. The robot, called CB2, is 4 feet tall, weighs 73 pounds, uses an artificial vocal cord for speech, and can change facial expressions. Can you envision a robot like this eventually being used to assist in pediatric medical diagnoses?

Computer-assisted diagnosis systems also can help physicians analyze medical imagery. Medical images, such as MRIs or even photos, are difficult to analyze because they contain structures without well-defined edges or corners. To simplify the process, a CAD system can help physicians better detect irregularities – for example, to help detect changes in the eye that might lead to macular degeneration.

As a patient, you might worry that a computer is performing the work of the doctor, all the while knowing computer systems are susceptible to errors resulting from programming issues or outright failure. It is important to recognize that while CAD systems are designed to improve the process and outcome of clinical decision making, they cannot replace or overrule a physician's judgment or a physician's diagnosis.

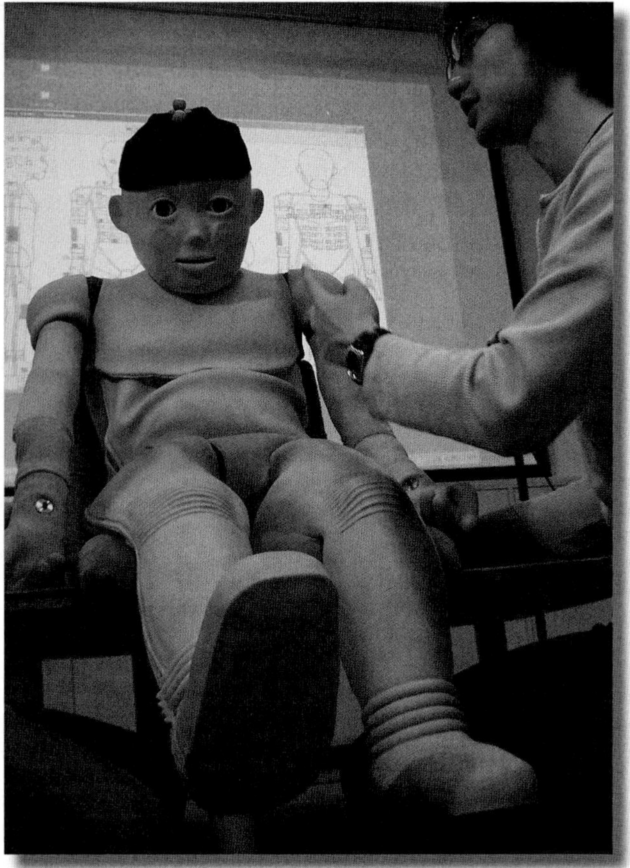

Figure 3-2 Scientists at Osaka University in Japan have created a robotic toddler, named CB2, to help better understand child development.

ACCESSING PHARMACY AND MEDICAL INFORMATION Every day, physicians must make informed decisions on a wide range of prescription drugs and other pharmaceuticals, based on disease treatment options, drug interactions, and drug cost. In the past, physicians relied on books, such as the *Physician's Desk Reference* (PDR), to research specific prescriptions. The printed materials, however, often were out of date as soon as they were printed.

Today, much of this content is available on the Web, which provides an up-to-date and more easily searchable form of the content in the book volumes. For example, all of the content in the *Physician's Desk Reference* now is available online at PDR.net. Doctors and nurses can use the Web site to decide what to prescribe based on illness, patient history, drug cost, and drug characteristics – including drug interactions and side effects. The Web site also includes a tool to search for possible drug interactions and the latest news on drugs recently approved by the Food and Drug Administration (FDA).

To ensure that physicians have the same information at their fingertips while doing rounds in the hospital, many physicians have wireless PDAs with software, such as the PDR or ePhysician's eDR (Figure 3-3). The databases can be updated via an Internet connection, so they remain as current as possible.

Just as technology has made pharmacy databases more available, it also has made medical research and medical databases from a number of reliable, reputable sources more accessible, as shown in Table 3-2. The MEDLINEplus Web site, for example, provides a database of references and abstracts from the world's largest medical library, the National Library of Medicine. Other Web sites are focused on specific areas of medical practice. OncoLink, for instance, is focused on cancer treatment.

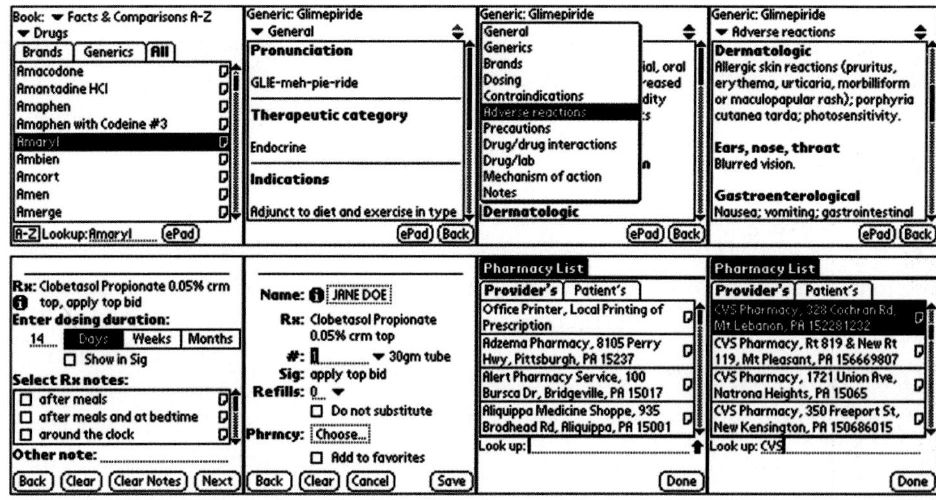

Figure 3-3 Physicians can use PDA software, such as ePhysician's eDR, to look up drug information, check for drug interactions, and then complete and transmit a prescription to the pharmacy and their office systems.

TABLE 3-2 Most Popular Web Sites for Medical Information

WEB SITE	*ADDRESS*	*DESCRIPTION*
PDR.Net	www.pdr.net	Provides an online, searchable database of drug information and potential drug interactions, along with news and information on recent approvals of new drugs
MEDLINEplus	www.medlineplus.gov	Provides a database of references and abstracts from the world's largest medical library, the National Library of Medicine. The Web site provides information on over 740 diseases and conditions, lists of hospitals and physicians, a medical encyclopedia and a medical dictionary, and links to thousands of clinical trials
TOXNET	toxnet.nlm.nih.gov	Provides several integrated toxicology and environmental health databases, information on hazardous substances, how to handle human exposure, waste disposal, and more
Centers for Disease Control and Prevention	www.cdc.gov	Provides a wide range of information on new and existing diseases; traveler's health information on specific destinations; health data; and news for physicians and patients
healthfinder	www.healthfinder.gov	Provides patient-friendly information from the Department of Health and Human Services, covering prevention and wellness, diseases and conditions, alternative medicine, and more
OncoLink	www.oncolink.com	Provides content focused on helping cancer patients, families, and health care professionals get accurate information on cancer causes, treatments, and coping resources
WebMD Health	www.webmd.com	Provides easy-to-understand information on a wide range of health, wellness, and nutrition information, along with tools for managing your health and supporting those with illnesses
Yahoo! Health	health.yahoo.com	Provides health centers for specific illnesses, a drug index, links to locate a doctor in your area, and more

Medical Web sites can be an excellent source of information for physicians and patients alike.

Patients also can use the Web to become better informed about their illnesses – whether to verify what doctors tell them regarding a course of treatment or prescription drugs, to educate themselves before they go to the doctor so they know what to ask, or to find others experiencing the same illnesses in chat rooms. Web sites, such as WebMD and MedlinePlus.gov, provide easy-to-understand information so that patients and their families can better understand and cope with an illness.

MONITORING PATIENTS Computers also provide new tools to help monitor patients after a diagnosis is made, during surgery, and throughout the course of treatment. For example, after a patient has a stroke, slight changes in basic vital signs can cause long-term damage. To ensure continuous, real-time monitoring, hospitals can replace the labor-intensive process of monitoring patients' vital signs with sophisticated mobile monitors. The monitors measure heart rate, blood pressure, temperature, respiration, and blood oxygen levels, displaying the results on a screen and sounding an alarm if any levels go outside the normal range. The data from the monitors also is stored in a computer database for later analysis.

In the emergency room, operating room, and recovery area, one of the most useful monitors is the pulse oximeter, which is used to monitor a patient's blood oxygen levels and pulse rate (Figure 3-4). The pulse oximeter consists of a probe attached to the patient's finger or earlobe, which is linked to a computer that displays blood oxygen saturation and heart rate. Some pilots even carry small finger pulse oximeters connected to their PDAs to detect the early onset of hypoxia, a deficiency of oxygen reaching the tissues of the body due to changes in altitude. Detecting hypoxia early protects them from such effects as dizziness or mental and muscle fatigue.

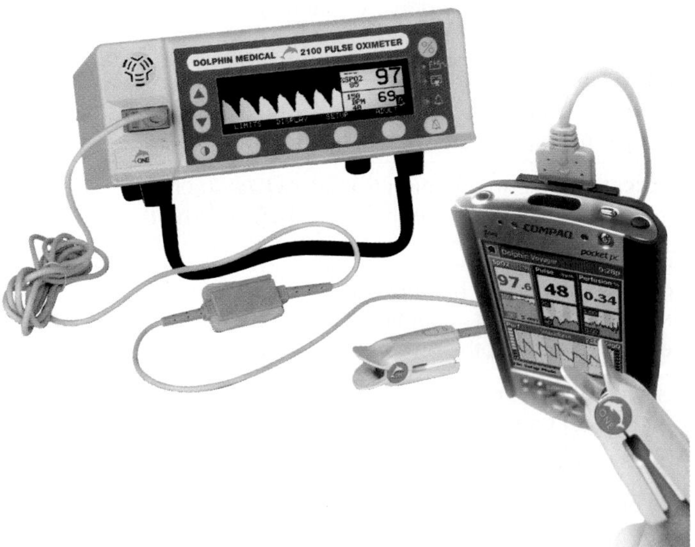

Figure 3-4 Pulse oximeters are used to continuously monitor a patient's blood oxygen levels and pulse rate. Handheld devices can be equipped with pulse oximeter software and a probe to provide a fully functional and highly portable pulse oximeter.

Once a patient leaves the hospital, the monitoring does not end. For example, after treatment, it may be necessary for cardiac (heart) patients to use a Holter monitor, a portable EKG that continuously monitors the heart's electrical activity. Diabetes patients have used finger prick tests for years to monitor and control their blood sugar levels. With computer technology, a patient can wear a device, such as a GlucoWatch G2 Biographer, which looks like a regular watch with an LCD display (Figure 3-5). The patient snaps a small single-use sensor into the back of the watch and wears it on the forearm. After calibrating the watch with a measurement taken from a finger prick test, the Biographer is set to sound an alarm when blood sugar levels are too high, too low, or are likely to be too low in about 20 minutes. The technology isn't foolproof, because perspiration can trigger a reaction in the sensor, which means heavy work and sports may cause the device to skip readings, instead of running the risk of displaying a false measurement.

Technology in the Operating Room

Along with the diagnostic and monitoring tools already described, the operating room of any hospital relies on numerous technological advances to ensure the highest quality patient care. **Computer-aided surgery (CAS)** involves the use of computers and other technologies to assist a surgeon at all points in the operative process, including planning, surgical navigation, and treatment.

For example, with **image-guided surgery** surgeons can use preoperative MRIs, CAT scans, and other images to understand the shape of tissues in a surgical area. In very delicate surgery, such as neurosurgery on the brain, such techniques allow for less invasive and shorter procedures and reduce the risk that regions of the brain might be compromised. Newer techniques in image-guided surgery even take into account possible changes in the shape of tissues during the operation and distort the images accordingly.

Endoscopy is a surgical technique that involves the use of an endoscope, which is a special viewing instrument that allows a surgeon to see images of

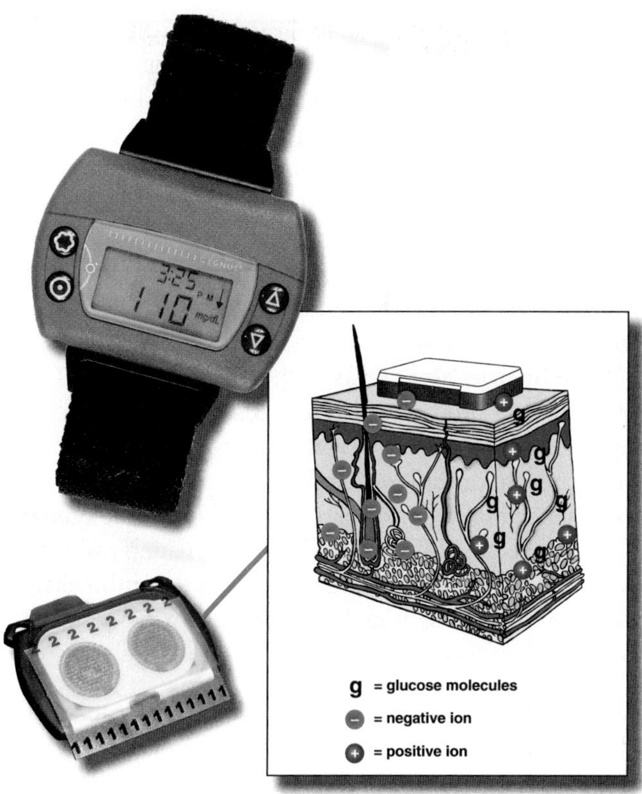

Figure 3-5 A G2 GlucoWatch consists of two main parts: a watchlike device that measures blood sugar (glucose) and a plastic part that snaps into the watch and sticks to your skin. The gel discs collect the glucose; the watch measures the glucose every ten minutes and sounds an alert if the reading is abnormal.

the body's internal structures. An endoscope consists of two basic parts: a tubular probe fitted with a tiny camera and bright light, which is inserted through a small incision; and a viewing screen, which magnifies the transmitted images of the body's internal structures. During surgery, the surgeon watches the screen while moving the tube of the endoscope through the surgical area.

Still other CAS systems involve the use of robots to help perform very delicate procedures. In an endoscopy, for example, a surgeon might use a console along with table-mounted robotic arms to perform surgical tasks. Using the console, the surgeon controls the right and left arms of the robot to move the surgical instruments. A third arm helps to position the endoscope, to provide the surgeon with a close-up view of the surgical area.

Telemedicine and Telepresence Surgery

Imagine if a surgeon could be transported instantly from a hospital to a rural area, a battlefield, or an accident site. This scenario is becoming a reality with telemedicine and telepresence surgery. **Telemedicine** is the use of advanced computer technology to help health care processionals consult with each other and work together on cases, regardless of where the patients, medical professionals, and relevant clinical data are located. Telemedicine allows medical experts around the world to share their experience and knowledge to improve patient care. With telemedicine, physicians can use live Internet and videoconferencing technologies to share digitized images such as X rays, CAT scans, and EKGs (Figure 3-6). Because these images can be electronically stored and transmitted worldwide by computer, mobile clinics can go to remote areas to give examinations and take digital X rays, which can be transmitted back to the main hospital for immediate diagnosis.

One of the most valuable uses of telemedicine is that it allows doctors in remote areas, such as rural locations or a battlefield, to consult with specialists at medical centers. For example, in a recent application of telemedicine, physicians in Virginia assisted with the anesthesia in a gall bladder surgery performed on a patient in Ecuador. The telemedicine was made possible by a satellite link from a clinic in Ecuador to an anesthesiologist in Virginia, who watched the patient's vital signs on

Figure 3-6 Physicians can use live Internet and videoconferencing technologies to share digitized images such as X rays, CAT scans, and EKGs.

her computer screen while communicating with the anesthesiologist who was in the operating room.

Still other telemedicine applications involve Internet-based remote monitoring systems for patients with chronic illnesses. These patients can use standard Internet connections and online forms to submit measurement results, such as blood pressure, body weight, or blood sugar levels, along with digital photos of problem areas, such as burns or other wounds. A patient can avoid numerous trips to the hospital, but the doctor or nurse still can track the patient's progress daily.

Telepresence surgery involves the use of robots to perform surgery, while the surgeon controls the robot from a remote location. Precision robotic arms are suspended over the area where the patient undergoes surgery. The arms are linked to a remote site, where the surgeon manipulates the surgical instruments connected to the robot. In the military, telepresence technology soon may help medical units deliver care to the front lines. Using a telepresence surgical unit mounted in an armored ambulance, surgeons – operating remotely from a safe location – will be able to provide lifesaving care to wounded soldiers in the combat zone.

Medical Research and Training

In addition to supporting patient care in diagnosis, surgery, and ongoing monitoring, computers also contribute to the learning process in the field of medicine – whether training students on new procedures or helping to recognize patterns of disease within a city around the world.

RECOGNIZING PATTERNS OF DISEASE In our incredibly mobile world, disease can travel quickly from one city or country to another. **Epidemiology** as a discipline is concerned with the distribution, cause, and control of disease across time and geography in human populations. Today, thanks to computer technology, data regarding a specific disease can be collected into a database and computers can process and analyze the vast quantity of data to look for patterns in the spread of the disease.

The National Cancer Institute, for example, tracks the epidemiology of thousands of cancer cases around the United States, using computer databases to store the data and software to analyze and map the data based on certain criteria. The software looks for possible patterns in the incidents of cancer, so that researchers can better understand differences in cancer rates and plan cancer control programs.

Larger cities and health centers are developing computer systems to recognize patterns of disease associated with outbreaks or epidemics. For example, during a scare about SARS (Sudden Acute Respiratory Syndrome), the New York Syndromic Surveillance System caught the increase in disease. Each day, the system analyzes more than 50,000 pieces of data, including calls, emergency room visits, and drugstore purchases, sifting them by symptom, time, and place for patterns that might escape human notice. The system routinely picks up patterns of disease that never would have been caught by human analysis alone.

The Internet also assists in the data collection process, as health care providers around the world can rapidly share information with each other – and can share prevention tips with individuals around the world. As discussed later, however, one should take the time to evaluate the credibility of medical information on the Internet and Web – especially as related to outbreaks, which tend to cause high levels of concern – before acting on the information.

IMPROVING MEDICAL TRAINING Computer technology fundamentally has changed the nature of medical training and education. Virtual reality (VR) simulators, for example, allow students and trainees to believe that they are interacting with a patient. The simulator has sensing instruments that detect the user's movements. The program then computes the changes and projects the correct response onto the screen. As the user works with the VR training system, the computer can collect data on the user's performance for later review.

While VR does provide excellent visual training, in many medical applications, a surgeon relies upon both visual and haptic feedback to complete an operation successfully. **Haptic feedback** is any feedback relating to or based on the sense of touch, such as the feel of a surgical scalpel on tissue. Newer training simulators use haptic feedback to recreate how injecting a needle into a patient actually feels – thus better preparing the student for the actual act.

In an even more realistic form of training with haptic feedback, Army medics training at Fort Sam Houston learn to deal with realistic wounds inflicted on a high-tech mannequin, known as SimMan (Figure 3-7). SimMan, an amazingly lifelike human patient simulator, is life-sized and has an artificial pulse, mechanized lungs, and plastic bones. Plastic veins in the dummy bleed fake blood from wounds, while plastic bones stick out from a broken leg. Each dummy is wired to a laptop computer that monitors and changes vital signs and then challenges trainees by dropping blood pressure or collapsing a lung. Each time the medic touches the body, the computer records what procedure was performed and what effect it had. For

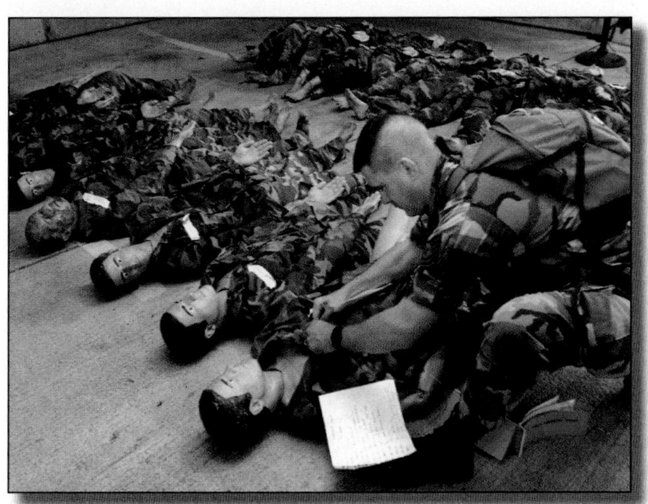

Figure 3-7 Army medics get to practice their skills on SimMan, a high-tech patient simulator that trains them to deal with battlefield injuries and humanitarian needs, such as delivering a baby.

example, administering drugs causes a realistic reaction to the drug. Spending time in the classroom with these dummies is good practice for saving real soldiers in combat.

All of these training tools, whether virtual reality or simulations involving dummies, allow surgeons to practice hundreds of procedures prior to patient contact, and the practice carries no risk to live patients. Since doctors with less experience are more likely to make errors, using computerized tools for training can lead to a more highly skilled and better prepared staff of medical professionals.

Credibility of Medical Information

As the use of the Internet has increased, the number of Web sites about health care information has grown quickly. Today, numerous Web sites provide information on how to find a good physician, eat a healthy diet, and get the proper exercise. Other Web sites allow you to review information about a specific illness or medical condition. Your primary source of health care information should be your doctor or other health care professional. However, if you are looking for health information online, you can choose from hundreds of Web sites.

In addition to researching specific medical, health, diet, and fitness topics, you can review Web sites to look into hospital services, to evaluate enrollment options and coverage of health insurance providers, and fill prescriptions at online drugstores. Web sites such as Yahoo! Health Find a Doctor or AMA Physician Select can help you find a local doctor. The Web sites of health care organizations such as the National Cancer Institute and American Stroke Association also provide information about how to find support groups for a particular illness or disability.

As you browse through all of these Web sites, however, be aware that not all online information is accurate or up to date. Many health-oriented Web sites have substantial gaps in the availability of key information, as well as conflicting information. Others fail to provide information about the authority and credentials of the individuals offering health advice, or do not clearly state possible commercial interests behind their claims.

With these concerns in mind, how should you evaluate health-oriented Web sites? The credibility of the content at these Web sites first should be evaluated using the basic steps outlined in Table 3-3, which involve identifying the sponsoring organization or author, establishing that the content is timely and objective, and comparing the content with that from other, similar sites.

Most people who go online to find health information rely on popular search tools to locate health-oriented Web sites; yet, some health care professionals suggest you should ask a trusted source, such as your doctor or nurse practitioner, to recommend health-oriented Web sites. Another alternative is to look for accredited Web sites, such as those accredited by the Health On the Net Foundation (HON) and the American Accreditation HealthCare Commission (URAC). The Web site standards required by these agencies include an editorial review process to ensure content accuracy; internal processes to guarantee privacy, security, and Web site quality; and the full disclosure of possible relationships with manufacturers or other commercial interests.

Another resource to help you evaluate medical Web sites is the CAPHIS (Consumer and Patient Health Information Section) Web site. CAPHIS evaluates health-oriented Web sites based on a number of criteria, including credibility, disclosure, sponsorship and authorship, and design, and then lists the highest-rated Web sites as part of the CAPHIS Top 100.

As you review information on the Web, watch out for false health care reports and health hoaxes. Unfortunately, it is all too easy to circulate false information via the Internet. You can find a list of current false health reports and health hoaxes at the Centers for Disease Control and Prevention (CDC) Web site. Finally, before acting on any information you gather from a Web site, consult a physician to ensure that the information you have gathered is accurate, effective, and will keep you on the road to good health.

TABLE 3-3 Tips for Evaluating Health-Related Web Sites

AUTHORITY	■ Examine site addresses and Web page headers and footers to determine the sponsoring organization or author of the site and then determine whether the sponsor or author has authority or expertise in the area. ■ Look at the date the site published the information. Out-of-date pages may not present the most recent developments or up-to-date information. ■ Look for primary sources. A primary source is any document, item, or other data that comes from a first-hand, authoritative resource. ■ Do not assume that government or education sites are always authoritative. For example, sites with the .edu top-level domain represent educational institutions, but a Web page may be the work of a student rather than a researcher or expert.
OBJECTIVITY	■ Determine whether the information is fair, whether any biases are stated clearly, or if the information is skewed toward commercial interests. ■ Look for links to other sites, and read background information about the author or organization. For example, when looking for information about a new prescription drug, you should weigh whether the site bases its recommendations on scientific evidence or whether the site profits by promoting the sale of the drug.
SCOPE	■ Evaluating the scope of a site — that is, the depth of coverage and the amount of detail provided — can help determine the value of its information. Although not a perfect approach, you can judge the accuracy of information on one site by comparing its scope with several other sites. ■ One technique for determining scope is to compare several sources on the same topic. If a Web site is missing information or conflicts with numerous other sites on a particular topic, it may be a less valuable source of information. ■ Look for detail and depth of coverage, as well as citations or references to other sources.
DESIGN AND FUNCTIONALITY	■ Pages that display mistakes in grammar or spelling, poor organization, or broken images and links may indicate a poor quality source.

Because the Internet offers anyone the opportunity to publish information, you must assess the credibility of the information presented on the page carefully — especially when it is health-related information.

COMPUTERS IN SCIENCE

Science involves the pursuit of knowledge about the world around us, from the smallest particle of physical matter to the vast expanse of planets that make up the universe. The process of science generally follows a series of steps known as the **scientific method**, a procedure by which scientists work to construct an accurate representation of the world. The scientific method involves:

1. Observing some occurrence or aspect of the world or identifying a problem
2. Developing a hypothesis to explain this occurrence
3. Determining how to test the hypothesis
4. Collecting data and then analyzing data to prove or disprove the hypothesis
5. Concluding whether or not the hypothesis was correct

Over the past few decades, computer technology has revolutionized science and the research process defined by the scientific method. Computer technology has given scientists powerful new tools to support the basic activities of the scientific method, including observing the world, collecting data, and then classifying or analyzing that data. Computers also allow scientists to create highly accurate models or simulations of the real world to test their ideas.

The speed and power provided by computers lets scientists tackle scientific questions that they previously never would have been able to investigate, such as mapping the entire set of genes that define humans or searching for signals from extraterrestrials. Today, computer technology plays such an integral role in science, it is unlikely you could find a scientist or a research project that did not use computer technology in some way to support or further the research process.

Observation and Data Collection

As noted earlier, a key part of the scientific method is observing and collecting data to better understand some aspect of the world. Computers and communications devices have transformed the data collection process, making it possible to gather data automatically and store or transmit it for immediate analysis. Computers even allow researchers to gather data around the clock from remote locations around the globe (and even under the ocean).

COLLECTING WEATHER DATA All weather forecasts begin with observations of what the weather is doing all over the world. The data collected from low-tech devices such as rain gauge buckets, along with computer-based devices such as weather balloons, radar, and satellites are used as the basis for weather forecasts updated continuously each day.

For example, each day, weather balloons are launched from over one thousand sites around the world. The weather balloons travel high into the atmosphere, carrying high-tech instrument packages, called **radiosondes**, that collect data about the upper atmosphere (Figure 3-8). The radiosondes measure temperature, humidity and air pressure at various altitudes, along with wind speed and direction. They then transmit this data via radio waves to a receiving station that receives and stores the data in a computer database. The National Weather Service launches close to 75,000 radiosondes annually, yet fewer than 20% are ever found and returned for reconditioning and reuse.

Weather radar also helps to collect weather data, by sending out a beam of energy and then measuring how much of that beam is reflected back. Rain, snow, sleet (and even bugs) reflect back more of the beam and are indicated by a bright color.

Satellites referred to as Geostationary Operational Environmental Satellites (GOES), which orbit the Earth about 22,000 miles above the equator, gather even more precise data. Each GOES has a sounder that measures temperature and humidity at various altitudes, along with a camera that takes and then sends back the photos that accompany the evening news weather forecast and the weather updates on Web sites like weather.com.

HUNTING HURRICANES Having computers to help collect data automatically is of enormous value to the meteorologists and scientists seeking to learn more about what happens during a hurricane. Any time a hurricane endangers a location in or near the United States, the National Oceanic and Atmospheric Administration (NOAA) sends out its hurricane hunters – airplanes that routinely fly into the types of weather most pilots avoid. The planes essentially are scientific laboratories with wings: the planes include a probe at the front to take in air for measurement; a cone at the rear that includes weather radar; and numerous instruments to collect basic weather data such as temperature, humidity, and wind speed and direction, as well as the amount of water and ice in clouds. The plane itself houses computer workstations for up to ten scientists, who can analyze the collected data in mid-flight (Figure 3-9). Using satellite links, the hurricane hunter planes transmit the collected data back to the hurricane center in Miami, Florida, along with radar photos that show details of the hurricane's structure. Meteorologists and scientists use this data to assess the hurricane's movement and determine any possible impact to cities and towns.

Figure 3-8 A weather balloon helps measure basic weather information. The weather balloon works by:
(1) Lifting a radiosonde about 20 miles into the atmosphere
(2) The radiosonde measures temperature, humidity, and air pressure.
(3) The balloon pops and the radiosonde is carried back to earth by parachute.

REMOTE SENSING The GOES satellites play an important role in data collection using remote sensing. **Remote sensing**, which is the use of remote devices to track and record data, is used to gather a wide range of data, including hazardous waste, beach erosion, wildlife populations, and atmospheric and weather changes and patterns.

Figure 3-9 A hurricane hunter resembles a cargo plane, except for the radar dome on the belly of the plane. Inside, the plane houses computer workstations for scientists, who can analyze the collected data in mid-flight.

For example, across Antarctica automatic weather station (AWS) units help support meteorological research and climate prediction. Each of the hundreds of AWS units measures air temperature, air pressure, wind speed, and wind direction (Figure 3-10). The AWS unit is controlled by a small computer, which updates the data approximately every ten minutes and then later transmits the data to a NOAA satellite, which receives the data and stores it in a data collection system. The data then is relayed to ground stations around the world for communication to scientists and meteorologists.

Remote sensing also is used to track the weather along coastlines of the United States. The National Data Buoy Center, for example, maintains and monitors over one hundred buoys and Coastal-Marine Automated Network (C-MAN) stations that serve as weather sentinels of the sea and coasts (Figure 3-11). The moored buoys and C-MAN stations measure wind speed, direction, and gust; barometric pressure; and air temperature as well as sea surface temperature and wave heights. Each hour, the buoy or C-MAN relays the data via satellite to a ground station, which sends the data on to the National Weather Service, which then sends the data over the Internet to world meteorological centers and interested scientists and individuals via the Web.

Another use of remote sensing is the DART system, which uses moored buoys with seismic sensors at the bottom of the Pacific and Atlantic Oceans to track the earthquakes that trigger tsunamis. These huge tidal waves are a major threat to coastal communities: once they reach shore, tsunami waves can be up to 100 feet high. For this reason, the Deep-ocean Assessment and Reporting of Tsunamis (DART) system was launched in 2003. Each moored buoy in the DART network has a device called a bottom pressure recorder (BPR) that measures the water surface levels (Figure 3-12). Every hour, the computer device attached to the BPR transmits the data to the surface buoy. The surface buoy retransmits the data to a satellite, which transmits the data to a ground station and on to the Tsunami Warning Centers. With the data from the DART system, the warning centers can identify tsunamis early enough to issue warnings or start evacuating coastal towns. Shortly after deployment, DART successfully recorded a 7.5 magnitude undersea earthquake near Alaska in November, 2003. The NOAA determined it would not impact U.S. coastline, however, and avoided a Hawaiian island evacuation, saving an estimated $68 million in lost productivity. Following the devastating 9.0 magnitude earthquake that triggered the December 26, 2004 Indonesian tsunami off the west coast of Sumatra, the NOAA was given nearly $47.8 million to expand its monitoring systems that help provide early warning for U.S. coastal areas.

Data Classification and Analysis

After data is collected, it must be organized, or classified, so that it can be analyzed. Computers have provided scientists and researchers with the power to classify and analyze vast quantities of data more quickly and accurately than ever before.

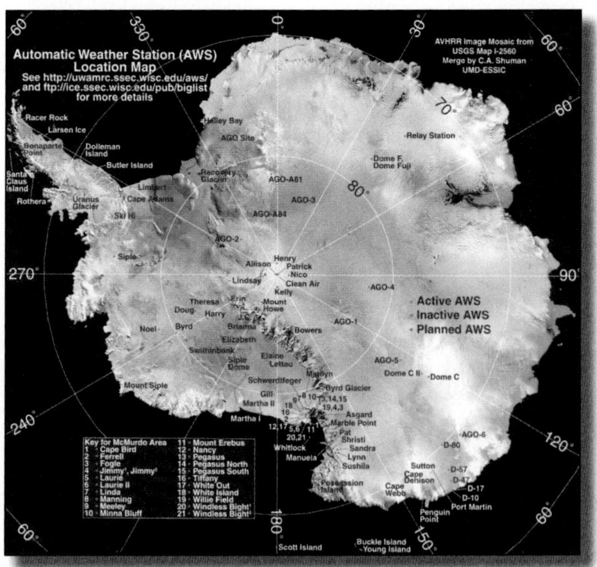

Figure 3-10 Hundreds of automatic weather stations located across Antarctica measure weather data and transmit it back to a data collection center.

HUMAN GENOME PROJECT The Human Genome Project is just one of many examples of how computers can speed the classification and analysis process. Officially begun in 1990, the Human Genome Project was a 13-year effort coordinated by the U.S. Department of Energy and the National Institutes of Health to identify all of the genes in human DNA. Advances in technology allowed the project to be completed in 2003, two years ahead of schedule. A **genome** is the blueprint for an organism, encompassing the organism's entire set of DNA, including its genes. A **gene** defines the characteristics of any organism, including how you look, how you behave, and even how you fight off a cold.

DNA is made up of similar chemicals, or **bases**, that are repeated billions of times throughout an organism's genome. The human genome, for example, has around three billion pairs of bases in each cell. The order of the bases defines the diversity of the biological universe – dictating whether an organism is a person, an ear of corn, or a golden retriever.

In the Human Genome Project, after collecting the raw data about the billions of bases in the human genome, researchers used powerful computers to sort through the billion bits of DNA contained in every human cell to identify the approximately 30,000 genes that define our physical traits and many of our behaviors. The first results of this classification process were published in 2000, but the analysis process continues. Scientists from 35 groups in 80 organizations worldwide use this vast collection of information to try to analyze the instructions contained within each of the genes and the role of formerly "junk DNA," which recently was found to have a more active biological function than previously thought by researchers.

This massive database promises to revolutionize medicine in the coming decades. After mapping the human genome, researchers learned that the genetic differences between any two people are relatively small. Yet, knowledge about the effects of DNA variations among individuals can lead to revolutionary new ways to diagnose, treat, and someday prevent thousands of illnesses, such as diabetes, cancer, multiple sclerosis, schizophrenia, and more. It also might allow physicians to screen patients to determine if they are at risk for certain diseases or whether they might react adversely to a particular drug.

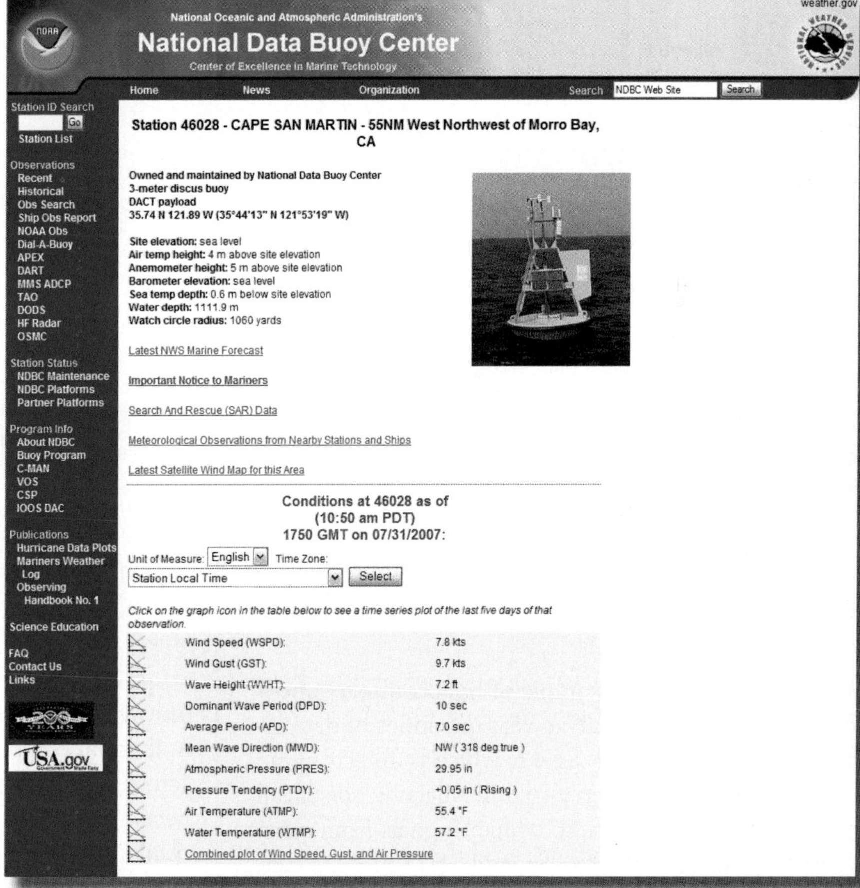

Figure 3-11 Real-time data from the buoys and C-MAN stations is posted on the National Data Buoy Center Web site for use by scientists, fishermen, boaters, surfers, and more.

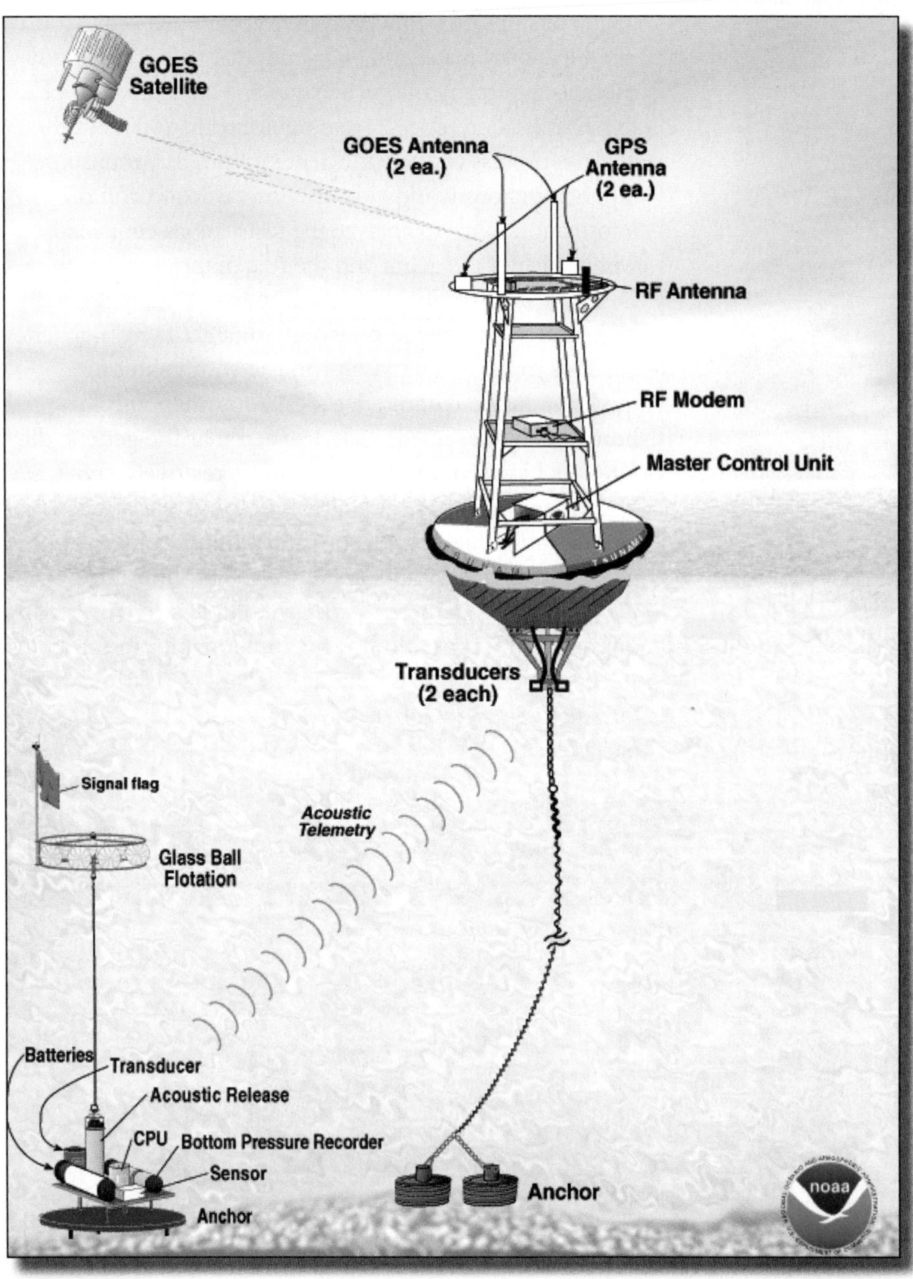

Figure 3-12 Each moored buoy in the DART network has a bottom pressure recorder that measures the water surface levels and then transmits that data across an acoustic link to the surface buoy hourly. The surface buoy retransmits that data to a satellite, which finally transmits the data to a ground station.

SETI@Home Another example of how computers help scientists classify and analyze vast quantifies of data is the SETI@home project. **SETI**, which is an acronym for the search for extraterrestrial intelligence, specifically involves the search for radio or light signals from other civilizations in the universe. Several SETI projects currently operate at different observatories around the world, including the well-known SETI@home.

SETI@home relies on the concept of **distributed computing**, in which the collective processing power of one or more computers is used to complete a large processing task, such as analyzing vast quantities of collected data. In the SETI@home project, the Arecibo radio telescope in Puerto Rico continuously collects radio signals from the atmosphere and has gathered massive amounts of data. The data, however, still must be analyzed to determine if any of the signals are, in fact, signals from extraterrestrials. This analysis would require tremendous amounts of time on the world's largest, fastest, and most expensive supercomputers. Instead of spending the money to have one huge computer complete the analysis of the radio signals, the SETI@home project turned to distributed computing.

With distributed computing, instead of running a single large computer for a long time, thousands of small computers are used for short periods of time. The SETI@home project accomplishes this by distributing a simple data processing program in the form of a screen saver, which individuals can run on their personal computers. The program allows the SETI@home server at the University of California, Berkeley, to connect and send a batch of data, called a work-unit, via the Internet to any one of the thousands of individual computers running the screensaver. The screensaver program analyzes the data and then connects back to the SETI@home server to transfer the results of the data analysis. The work-units for each computer are tracked in a large database in Berkeley.

So far, the project has not heard from any extraterrestrials, but the search goes on. In the meantime, other programs are using distributed computing models to analyze huge databases of information. One program is conducting cancer research, while another is testing new flu vaccines to find a cure.

Data Modeling and Simulation

Sometimes, one of the best ways (or perhaps the only way) to test a theory is to build a model and then test that model against real data or a realistic sample that you create. Computer and information technology can be used to create a **computer model** or representation used to help visualize just about any object, organism, or process. As you learned in Chapter 2, a computer simulation shows how the model operates under certain conditions. For instance, instead of crashing a car against a brick wall, it is more cost efficient and safer to build a computer model of the car and then develop a computer simulation of the crash.

Models and simulations also are useful when it is physically impossible to view the data firsthand. For instance, to try to forecast the weather, meteorologists must rely on computer models of how the weather will behave in the next week, because they cannot observe the future's weather. The same is true of models and

ISSUE: Is Your DNA A-OK?

The value of the Human Genome Project — creating treatments customized to your DNA to help cure or eliminate disease — is undeniably positive. The database, however, also opens up many ethical questions. Some worry that the knowledge eventually unlocked by the Human Genome Project could be used for less than desirable purposes, such as testing to ensure only "perfect" babies are born or discrimination based on your genetics. Imagine, for example, if colleges screened prospective students based on a particular gene that was linked to intelligence — or individuals with a gene predisposing them to cancer are denied health insurance before ever getting the disease?

Those scenarios are far-fetched, perhaps, but — thanks to the Human Genome Project and other genetic research — they are not impossible. In fact, it will not be long before each of us has our own genetic bar code to present when we go to the doctor or into the drugstore — and that is cause for concern for many health care professionals and privacy advocates.

Some of the questions raised by the Human Genome Project include:

- *Privacy and fair usage of genetic information* — Who should have access to personal genetic information, and how will it be used? Should insurers, employers, courts, schools, adoption agencies, or law enforcement agencies have access to an individual's genetic information?
- *Psychological impact or labeling based on genetic differences* — For example, if there is no cure for a disease, should people be tested to determine whether they might later develop that disease? Would you want to know?
- *Reproductive issues* — Should fetal testing include genetic testing to estimate the risk of developing diseases, such as cancer or Alzheimer's disease, as an adult? Or to screen for desirable or undesirable physical and mental traits?
- *Quality control and reliability of testing* — How will genetic tests be evaluated and regulated for accuracy, reliability, and utility? What are the implications of invalid or unclear tests?
- *Issues around genetically modified foods* — How do we know these foods are safe for humans and the environment? Will the world have to rely on just a few companies for food? Should humans tamper with nature and mix genes among species?
- *Commercialization and property rights* — Who owns genes and other pieces of DNA? How can you give a patent on a basic building block of life?

Politicians and medical policy makers will have to move quickly to keep up with the genetic researchers. In an effort to do so, the U.S. Department of Energy (DOE) and the National Institutes of Health (NIH) devote up to 5 percent of their annual Human Genome Project budgets toward better understanding the ethical, legal, and social issues (ELSI) surrounding availability of genetic information.

Still, even with all of the positive possibilities, gene-based treatments — like any new treatment — have risks. In January 2000, for example, the Food and Drug Administration shut down gene therapy trials for a liver disease treatment at the University of Pennsylvania because of the death of a research subject.

Like all new scientific advances, the discovery of a new aspect of the world raises numerous questions as it forces us to redefine how we always have thought about the world. When Copernicus first suggested that the sun, not the earth, was the center of the universe, most challenged the idea because it forced them to ask and answer tough questions they did not wish to address. The Human Genome Project is similar in this regard: along with the benefits of this amazing breakthrough come serious questions that must be answered.

simulations used to predict the impacts of pollution on the coastal areas or earthquakes along fault lines.

FORECASTING THE WEATHER Weather forecasts provide critical information about the weather to come. There are many different techniques involved in weather forecasting, from relatively simple observation of the sky to highly complex mathematical models run on computers.

As previously noted, all weather forecasts begin with observations of what the weather is doing all over the world. The data collected from low-tech devices and computer-based devices is then fed into supercomputers that use mathematical models of the atmosphere to make predictions. In the United States, the National Weather Service operates these computers.

Today, the National Weather Service manages and refines the computer models continuously, to make them as accurate as possible. Almost all weather forecasts use the forecasts resulting from these models – whether a newspaper, weather Web site, or meteorologist you see every morning on the local news.

Even with the most refined models and fastest computers, meteorologists cannot forecast day-to-day weather for more than about a week ahead of time. The atmosphere is just too complex – and, although the computer-generated models are a tremendous aid to forecasters, the models still require human analysis. Human forecasters study the output from models over a long time period and then compare the output from the models to the actual forecast in order to help fine-tune the models.

Many new models currently are being developed, including models to forecast and understand the behavior of hurricanes, thunderstorms, and other severe weather outbreaks. Supercomputers, for example, helped the NOAA successfully predict the path of Hurricane Katrina, which devastated New Orleans and the Gulf Coast of the U.S. in August, 2005. Once these models are developed, forecasters will be able to issue better and more timely warnings and advisories.

ENVIRONMENTAL IMPACT MODELING Computers also are used to model the impacts various occurrences, such as hurricanes or human actions, have on the environment. For example, the Geophysical Fluid Dynamics Laboratory (GFDL) has pioneered computer modeling research for two decades, with the goals of better understanding weather phenomena, such as El Niño, as well as to model the progress of ozone depletion and global warming.

Over the past few decades, scientists have noticed an increase in ocean heat, which is one of the key characteristics of global warming. Using computer models, the scientists at GFDL were able to pinpoint greenhouse gases introduced into the atmosphere by emissions from cars, factories, and so on as a significant factor in global warming.

GFDL then went on to create computer simulations of how the increase in ocean heat will affect the earth over the long term. In response to greenhouse gas warming, the water in the world's oceans will expand, thus causing sea level to rise. GFDL's computer simulations show that, as greenhouse gas levels double or quadruple, the sea level would gradually continue rising for centuries, rising about one to two meters (approximately three to six feet) after 500 years. Figure 3-13a illustrates the effect of a hypothetical sea level rise of one, two, four, or eight meters. The red areas in Figure 3-13a indicate regions of the southeastern United States that would be below sea level under such sea-level rise scenarios. (For reference, the volume of ice in the Greenland and Antarctica ice sheets is equivalent to a sea level rise of 7 and 73 meters – 23 feet and 240 feet – respectively). Another computer simulation showed that a persistent rise in greenhouse gases could lead to an excessively dry southeastern United States, which could significantly reduce the production of corn, wheat, cotton, tobacco, and other crops grown in these important farming regions (Figure 3-13b).

GEOGRAPHIC INFORMATION SYSTEMS A **geographic information system (GIS)** is a computer system capable of assembling, storing, manipulating, and displaying data that is geographically referenced – that is, data identified by its location. A GIS can be used for a huge range of applications, including resource management, scientific research, and development planning. For example, a GIS might allow a wildlife commission to map the impact of temperature on certain fish populations. A GIS also might allow emergency planners to calculate emergency response times in the event of a natural disaster by mapping out the best routes for emergency personnel to get in and the best evacuation routes for citizens to get out.

A geographic information system helps to connect where things are – the geographic information – with what things are – the descriptive information. Unlike a flat paper map, a GIS can present many layers of descriptive information laid out over a geographical location. Each layer of a map in a GIS can represent a different set of data (Figure 3-14). For example, a baseline layer might be a map of the Puget Sound area;

the next layer might show the fish population based on commercial catches; a third layer might show temperature levels; a fourth might show pollution levels; and so on. Using the GIS, you can add and remove layers to control the amount and type of information on the map at one time. This allows you to combine various data points to study possible relationships.

GIS software ranges from basic mapping software that allows businesses to map sales and branch locations to complex software capable of managing and studying large protected natural areas. The key components of a geographic information system are:

- Tools for entering geographic information, such as addresses
- Tools for inputting or using graphics files as baseline maps
- A database management system (DBMS)
- Tools that create maps you can examine, query for more information, or print

Using a GIS can help people make better decisions in many disciplines. Geographic data can be gathered and organized to support the business strategy of an organization or to help health care professionals link disease rates to specific locations. For example, geographic information systems have been used to analyze whether the use of pesticides or other toxic chemicals may have contributed to the number of breast cancer cases in the Cape Cod area of Massachusetts. Government agencies, such as the Arizona Department of Environmental Quality, use geographic information systems to analyze air and water quality, including possible groundwater contamination. Real estate agents in large metropolitan areas have used geographic information systems to help potential home buyers narrow their searches to appropriate communities based on housing costs, commute times, air quality, schools, and other factors. And restaurant chains regularly rely on GIS analysis of traffic patterns, community demographics, location of competition, and planned roadway construction to determine what street corner is best for their next outlet.

As you will learn in later chapters, geographic information systems also have valuable applications in business, government, the military, law enforcement, and more. In fact, almost anywhere you turn in your daily life, a GIS may have played a role. The paper used for the morning newspaper, for example, likely came from a wood product company that uses a GIS to ensure their

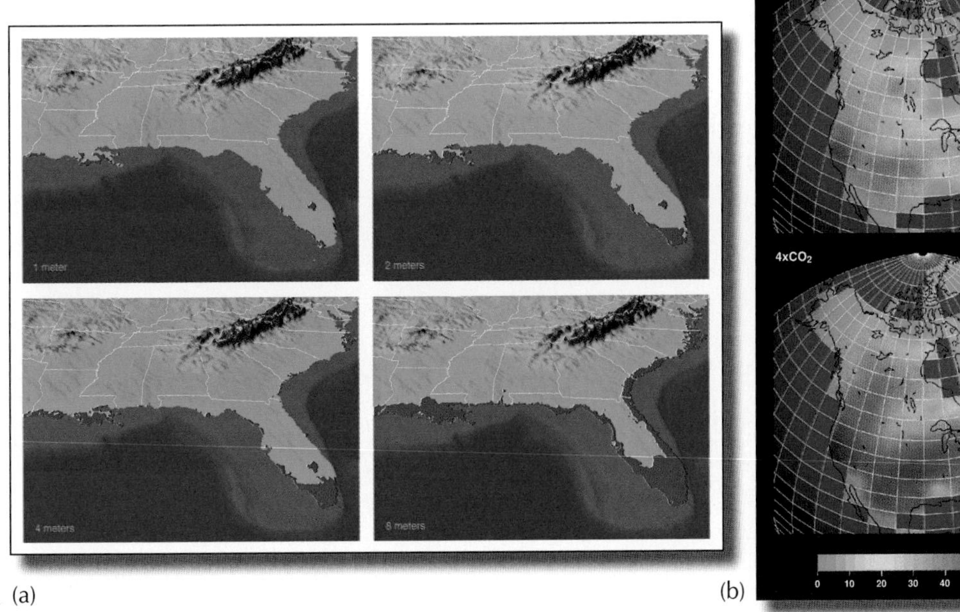

Figure 3-13 (a) Computer models are used to simulate the effects of sea level rise caused by global warming. The graphical model shows how a sea level rise of one, two, four, and eight meters would leave the areas in red under water.
(b) A second computer model shows how the increased global temperature would reduce soil moisture, resulting in an excessively dry southeastern United States.

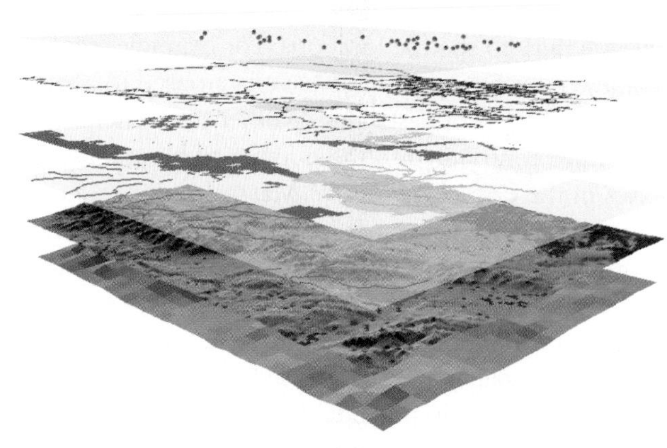

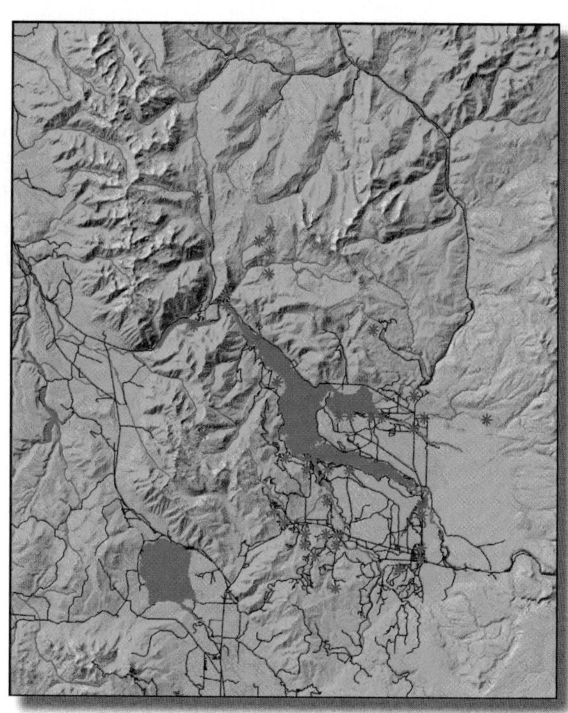

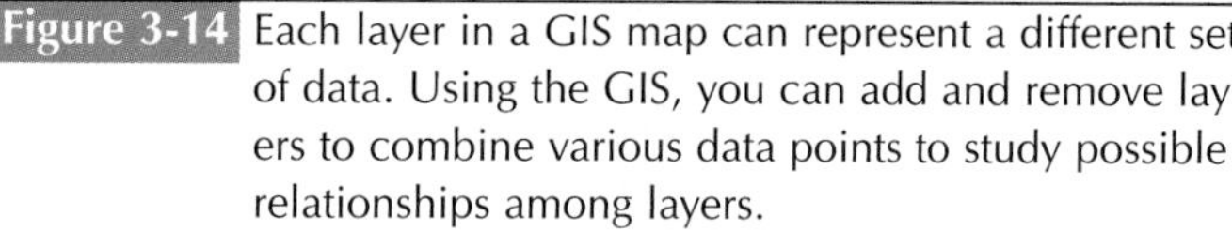

Figure 3-14 Each layer in a GIS map can represent a different set of data. Using the GIS, you can add and remove layers to combine various data points to study possible relationships among layers.

forestry work does not impact water, soil, or other sensitive environmental areas. To obtain the water you use to boil pasta for dinner, the water utility used a GIS to identify appropriate sources of clean water. Land and conservation organizations use geographical information systems to track and manage habitats, shoreline, and coastal erosion – so that you can have a long weekend visit to the shore, with clean water, plentiful fish, and wide beaches.

CONCLUSION

In this chapter, you learned about how the use of computers in medicine and science has fundamentally changed the process of data collection, analysis, and communication. You learned how computers are used in medicine to maintain patient history and manage the medical practice, as well as to improve patient diagnosis and monitoring. After learning more about how computer technology contributes in the operating room and how telemedicine is making health care available at a distance, you learned how computers are used in medical research and training. You also learned more about how to assess the credibility of health-oriented Web sites. You learned about the use of computers in science to help with observation and data collection, and the ethical, social, and legal issues such data collection can raise. Finally, you learned about how computers help scientists in the process of data classification and analysis, as well as in data modeling and simulation to help determine potential effects based on a set of data.

Key Terms

bases
computer-assisted diagnosis (CAD)
computer model
computer-aided surgery (CAS)
computer-based patient record (CPR)
distributed computing
electrocardiogram (ECG) or (EKG)
electronic medical record (EMR) system
endoscopy
epidemiology
gene
genome
geographic information system (GIS)
haptic feedback
Health Information Portability and Accountability Act (HIPAA)
Human Genome Project
image-guided surgery
information privacy
medical informatics
personal health information (PHI)
radiosondes
remote sensing
scientific method
SETI
telemedicine
telepresence surgery

Chapter Review

Multiple Choice

Select the best answer.

1. A computer-based patient record (CPR) is a patient record maintained electronically that includes _____.

(a) a patient's medical history
(b) prescriptions
(c) health insurance information
(d) all of the above

2. Using a(n) _____ system cuts out the time-consuming process of dictation, transcription, and coding for billing and insurance claims.

(a) CAD
(b) EMR
(c) CAS
(d) PHI

3. Computer-assisted diagnosis often is supported by _____ systems.

(a) decision support or expert
(b) scheduling or billing
(c) virtual reality or haptic feedback
(d) all of the above

4. Some pilots even carry small finger _____ connected to their PDAs to detect the early onset of hypoxia, a deficiency of oxygen reaching the tissues of the body due to changes in altitude.

(a) pulse oximeters
(b) remote sensor
(c) electrocardiograms
(d) GlucoWatches

5. Endoscopy is a surgical technique that involves the use of _____.

(a) preoperative images to understand the shape of tissues in a surgical area prior to the surgery
(b) a special viewing instrument that allows a surgeon to see images of the body's internal structures
(c) satellite links for communicating with anesthesiologists in the operating room
(d) simulators that allow medical trainees to believe that they are interacting with a patient

6. One of the most valuable uses of _____ is that it allows doctors in remote areas, such as rural locations or a battlefield, to consult with specialists at medical centers.

(a) epidemiology
(b) telemedicine
(c) haptic feedback
(d) computer simulation

7. Newer training simulators use _____ to recreate how injecting a needle into a patient actually feels — thus better preparing the student for the actual event.

(a) epidemiology
(b) telemedicine
(c) haptic feedback
(d) computer simulation

8. The first step in the scientific method involves _____.

(a) collecting data and then analyzing data to prove or disprove a hypothesis
(b) concluding whether or not a hypothesis is correct
(c) observing some occurrence or aspect of the world or identifying a problem
(d) developing a hypothesis to explain an occurrence

9. Weather balloons travel high into the atmosphere, carrying high-tech instrument packages, called _____, that collect data about the upper atmosphere.

(a) radiometers
(b) satellites
(c) radiosondes
(d) radiographies

10. Key components of a geographic information system are _____.

(a) tools for entering geographic information such as addresses
(b) a database management system (DBMS)
(c) tools for inputting or using graphics files to use as baseline maps
(d) all of the above

Chapter Review

Short Answer

Write a brief answer to each of the following questions.

1. How do physicians use electronic medical record (EMR) systems during a patient visit?
2. What is a geographic information system, and how is it used?
3. How can you evaluate the credibility of health-oriented Web sites?
4. What is remote sensing, and how is it used?
5. How is a computer model different from a computer simulation?

Web Research

Use a search engine such as Google (google.com) to research the following questions. Then, write a one-page double-spaced report or create a presentation, unless otherwise directed.

1. The Web is a valuable source of valid health information, but it also supplies a host of **health related hoaxes** — such as the belief that an ingredient in many shampoos causes cancer or the insistence that poisonous perfume samples had been sent through the mail. Use the Web to find out about at least one very believable, and one barely believable, health-related hoax.

2. Time, space, and economic constraints prevent us from seeing many things, but with **computer simulations** we can see things that we thought we could never experience. With computer simulations, we can fire a medieval catapult, fly a jet, or walk on one of Jupiter's moons. Use the Web to discover different ways that people use computer simulations.

Group Exercises

Working with a group of your classmates, complete the following team questions.

1. If you are diagnosed with a medical problem, friends may suggest that you "get a second opinion" and obtain additional information. This is good advice — as long as the opinion or information you get is reputable. The Web can be a fine source of medical information, but it is important to evaluate the credibility of that information. Choose a health concern in which your team is interested, then have each member of your team visit a Web site related to the concern. Use the standards presented in this chapter to evaluate the quality of the Web site. Then, meet with your team and prepare a PowerPoint presentation showing which Web sites provided the best and worst information, and explain why.

2. Local media outlets — television stations, radio stations, and newspapers — all supply weather forecasts. Sometimes, forecasts for the same day are different, because different media sources may rely upon different sources. Forecasts may come from an in-house weather department, or from a weather service to which the media outlet subscribes. Have each member of your team call a local media outlet and determine the source of its weather forecasts. Visit the source of the forecasts to learn about the technology used to analyze the weather, and the people who make the predictions. Then, meet with your team, compare your findings, and prepare a PowerPoint presentation illustrating how weather forecasts are made, what technology is used for the forecasting, and what obstacles and opportunities exist for improving weather forecasting in the future.

Computers in Arts and Entertainment 4

Computers and the Arts
- **Analog to Digital Conversion**
- **Music**
  - *Composing Music*
  - *Playing and Recording Music*
  - *Editing Music*
  - *Performing Music*
  - *Distributing Music*
- **Dance**
  - *Choreography and Notation*
  - *Motion Capture*
- **Theater**
- **Sculpture and 3-D Media**
- **Graphic Arts**
- **Photography**
  - *Behind the Scenes: Digital Photo Capture*
  - *Digital Photo Editing*
- **Copyright Concerns**

Computers in Entertainment
- **Television and Movies**
  - *Behind the Scenes: Digital Video Capture*
  - *Digital Video Editing*
  - *Colorization*
- **Computer-Generated Imagery and Animation**
- **Sports**

Conclusion

The idea of computers as a core part of the arts is new for some. Art, in the view of many, is a creative and often physical process that is free-form, and thus cannot benefit from the inherently logical processing of a computer. Today, however, computers and other technologies are an integral part of the arts and entertainment world, helping artists to translate a world full of information into unique creative works or polished music videos. The computer serves as a tool in the artistic process. A costume designer can use a computer to help in drawing patterns, while a sculptor might use it to create 3-D models of a new project. A composer can use software to create new music and then produce printed sheet music to share with the quartet that will play the new concerto. Photographers can capture photographs and edit them into entirely new scenes, while television and movie producers can create a vast range of special effects and script parts for completely computer-generated characters.

In this chapter, you will learn more about the use of computers in arts and entertainment. After reviewing the process of converting analog data to digital data, you will learn how computers affect music, from creating new music to recording and distributing the music around the world. You also will learn how dance, theater, and sculpture are changed by the use of computers to enhance and refine the craft. Computer graphics and digital photography also are reviewed, along with the ethical questions and copyright concerns computer technology bring to the fore. Next, you will learn how cutting-edge computer technologies are used in the television and movie industries, including software to edit footage, add new special effects, colorize older movies, and create animated characters. Finally you will learn how computers are used in sports to help athletes and officials improve their performances.

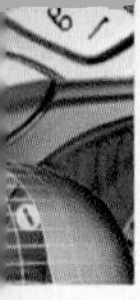

COMPUTERS AND THE ARTS

Artist is a broad term – it includes visual artists, theater artists, dance artists, musicians, sculptors, and more. As noted earlier, for these artists the computer is a tool to aid in producing drawings, to place notes on a music staff, to add special visual effects to a digital photo, or to insert a unique sound in a musical composition. Sculptors also use computers to help create models before the artist begins the process of making the 3-D physical form.

Analog to Digital Conversion

Before exploring the use of computers in the arts, you should understand the process of converting analog data to digital data. Data is processed in one of two ways: analog or digital. Generally, humans process analog data – that is, continuous wave patterns of light and sound that represent data to the eyes and ears. People hear sounds when their ears pick up pressure waves created by vibrating objects. They see objects and color when light waves interact and strike their eyes. For example, when you see a moving subway car, the sight and sound transmit to your eyes and ears in waves, or smooth up-and-down patterns. Originally, radio, television, and film used analog technology to transmit data, such as a song, an episode of a weekly program, or a moving picture.

A personal computer, by contrast, is digital. Computers process data as bits (0s and 1s) that represent a positive (on) and nonpositive (off) state. If sound and light waves are analog and a computer is digital, how does a computer record a photograph of a stunning landscape, play music through speakers, or show the car chase in your favorite action movie on a computer screen? The key lies in analog-to-digital conversion and digital-to-analog conversion. A computer converts all analog input into digital values before processing the data. To output the information, the computer converts the digital data back to analog form.

Many computer components, such as a modem, sound card, and a video card, perform these conversions. For example, a modem converts the computer's digital signals to analog signals (called modulation) to be sent over telephone lines. When the analog signal reaches its destination, another modem recreates the original digital signal (demodulation). This allows the receiving computer to process the data. The next time you dial up using a modem, pick up the telephone. The loud, screeching noise you hear is the sound of digital data after being converted to analog sound waves.

To experience analog-to-digital conversion via a sound card, try using the Windows Sound Recorder to record a digital audio clip of your analog voice. The sound card connects to the microphone, which is an analog input source. The diaphragm in the microphone collects the analog sound waves and converts them into an electrical signal. The signal flows to the sound card's analog-to-digital-converter. The **analog-to-digital-converter (ADC)** converts the signal into digital (binary) data of 1s and 0s. The digital data flows to the **digital signal processor (DSP)**, which compresses the data to save space. Finally, the DSP sends the compressed data to the processor, which stores the data in WAV, MP3, or other audio file format.

To play a recorded sound, such as a WAV, an MP3, or a CD track, the computer reverses the process. The processor retrieves and sends the digital data to the DSP to be decompressed. The DSP sends the decompressed, digital data to the sound card's digital-to-analog converter. The **digital-to-analog converter (DAC)** converts the digital data back to an analog voltage for output via a speaker or headset. This process happens very quickly, seeming almost instantaneous to a listener.

Throughout the chapter, you will see how the use of computers in the arts requires analog-to-digital conversion and the reverse, in order to capture the motion, sound, and sights of the real world into the art forms of music, dance, theater, sculpture, graphic arts, and photography.

Music

Computer technology is becoming an integral part of nearly every aspect of music. Musicians use computer technology to create, compose, and perform music. The digital recordings of a musical performance can be manipulated and processed down to the level of individual notes – allowing a producer to edit out slight imperfections in an artist's voice or remove background noises. For example, if you have listened to a CD with a live concert recording, the background crowd noise probably has been edited out digitally using audio editing software. The finished digital recording is recorded on optical media, such as CDs, or via the Web.

COMPOSING MUSIC The process of composing music is an iterative one, where artists may write a few notes on paper, play those notes on a guitar to listen to the melody, change the notes to a slightly different key, try humming those bars, and so on. While some artists complete the composition process entirely before performing a song, others actually might improvise a song first and then later transcribe that performance into a set of sheet music. With new computer hardware and software, artists have the flexibility to compose and create music in almost any fashion they choose.

Music notation software, such as Sibelius and Finale, allows you to create sheet music electronically. You can use notation software to produce new compositions, such as a new jazz tune. To compose the song using notation software, you first set up a **score**, which is a series of staves on which all the different instrumental or vocal parts of a musical work are written. Using the software, you can select any number of instruments or voices and a time signature (Figure 4-1). For the jazz tune, you might decide to choose several instruments, such as the trumpet, a string bass, a piano, drums, and a saxophone, and a time signature of four beats per measure. The software automatically sets up the score based on your input.

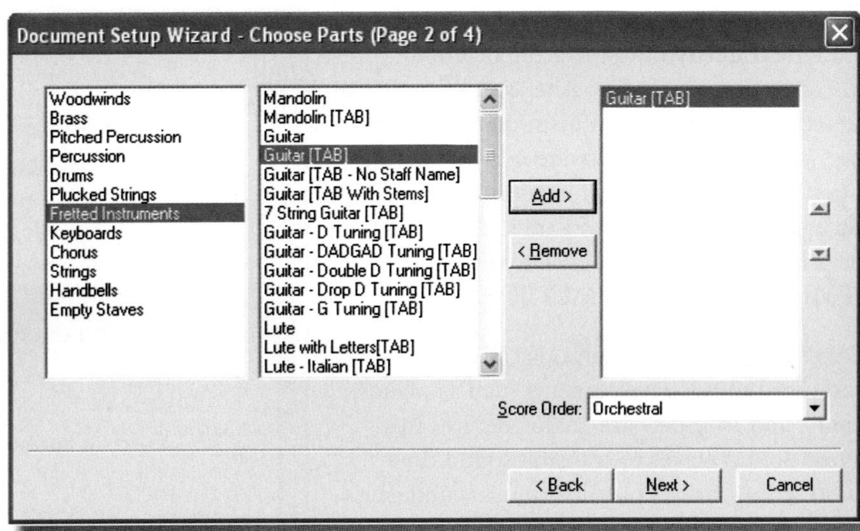

Figure 4-1 Using notation software, you can select any number of instruments or voices and a time signature for your new composition.

Figure 4-2 Some notation software allows you to scan printed sheet music, such as a Brahms song, which you then can edit, print, or post to the Web.

Next, you enter notes for the song. Typically, notation software allows you to input notes by:

- Clicking note buttons and then clicking them on to a staff in the score
- Typing notes on your computer keyboard or playing a tune on a MIDI keyboard connected to the computer's sound card
- Importing existing MIDI files
- Scanning printed sheet music, such as an existing classical tune (Figure 4-2)

As you enter notes for a melody of the lead saxophone, the software automatically will harmonize your melody and create your piano, string bass, and drum accompaniments, adding a nice jazz rhythm to your tune. Guitarists and other instruments with frets use a unique type of notation, called TAB or tablature, which uses notation for chords instead of standard music notes on a score. Many notation software packages also support creating TAB. Musicians enter notes as they would any other score – by entering via keyboard or mouse or connecting a MIDI guitar – so that that the notation software automatically can create the TAB.

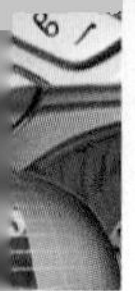

Most notation software also allows you to type lyrics directly onto the score or import full verses from a text file. After you have entered the notes for each instrument in the song, you can use the software to play the tune so you can hear your new creation, and then edit it, as needed. Once you are satisfied, you can print the score – and even save it as HTML to publish to the Web (Figure 4-3).

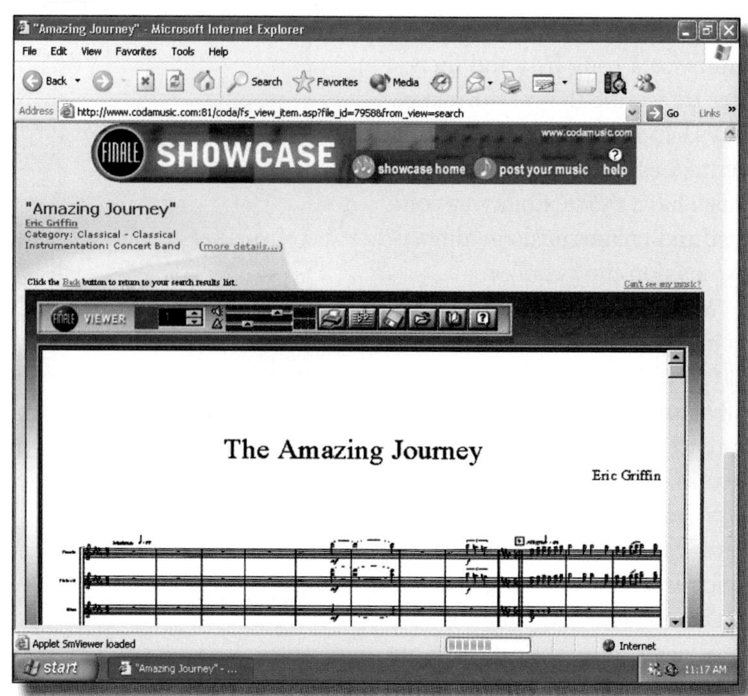

Figure 4-3 Files created using notation software can be posted to the Web as HTML files or to special Web sites, such as the Finale Showcase, where artists can post sheet music files for shared viewing, playing, transposing, and printing.

PLAYING AND RECORDING MUSIC

Traditional musical instruments such as pianos, guitars, and trumpets are analog devices that rely on sound waves to transmit sound. In a studio setting, artists play instruments and sing into microphones that transmit the sound to a computer. Inside every microphone is a diaphragm that collects the sound waves and creates movement in a plate, wire, or other component that converts the sound wave into an electrical voltage. This signal, in turn, is sent to an ADC converter, which converts the electrical voltages that correspond to analog sound waves into digital or numeric values that can be stored in the computer's memory and processed. This data is transmitted to a computer wirelessly or via a cable that attaches to a port on the sound card. Each performer or artist has his or her own microphone, and the sound of each voice or instrument is recorded as a track, or unique stream of digital sound.

Some of the sounds in today's music are not just recorded on computers – they are created using computers. For example, using a synthesizer, musicians can generate the complex tones of many instruments. A **synthesizer**, which can be a peripheral or a chip, creates sound from digital instructions input by the user, either via a standard computer keyboard or devices resembling an instrument.

The signals from a synthesizer are input into the computer via a MIDI port. A **MIDI port** is a special type of serial port that connects the computer to an electronic musical instrument or other input device, such as an electronic piano keyboard (Figure 4-4). **MIDI** (pronounced *MID-dee*) is short for **Musical Instrument Digital Interface** and is the music industry's standard for how to represent music in digital form, as well as for how devices, such as sound cards and synthesizers, represent sounds electronically. MIDI actually has three components: a MIDI port to connect an input device, the MIDI protocol or language, and the file format, called Standard MIDI.

Figure 4-4 An electronic piano keyboard is an external MIDI device that allows users to record music, which can be stored in the computer.

As noted, a computer with a MIDI port has the capability of recording sounds (data) that have been created by a synthesizer and then processing the data to create and output new sounds. The **MIDI protocol** is a series of instructions or messages that describes the action of a musical performance. The MIDI message encodes these actions, such as pitch and volume, as bytes of digital information. Each message instructs the synthesizer which sounds to use, which notes to play, and how loud to play each note. For example, to sound a note in MIDI language you send a Note On message; you can turn off the note by sending a Note Off message. Other MIDI messages include those to tell an instrument to change volume or change the sound (for example, from a guitar sound to an organ sound). The synthesizer then generates the actual sounds.

When the MIDI messages are saved so you can play them back later, they typically are saved in a format called the Standard MIDI format. The Standard MIDI files differ from the raw MIDI instructions in that they are time-stamped to ensure they play back in the correct sequence. Standard MIDI files typically are the primary source of music in many popular PC and CD-ROM games and your cellular phone's ring tone, because just about every personal computer now is equipped to play Standard MIDI files.

Figure 4-5 MIDI instruments allow a range of controls and features that are not available on conventional instruments. For example, you can set each drum pad to generate a different drum sound or special effect. Buttons on a MIDI wind instrument allow you to change the octave or even change the sound from a clarinet to a saxophone or flute.

A **sequencer** is a software program or dedicated device that records, processes, edits, and plays back MIDI data through a MIDI instrument or computer speaker. To record a MIDI file, you play a note on a MIDI keyboard, guitar, or other instrument connected to the computer (Figure 4-5). The sequencer records the data, including the length, volume, pitch, and other information about that note. Sequencing software allows you to record MIDI data in multiple tracks for a single recording, such as the bass, guitar, and keyboard.

Most film and TV scores, as well as popular recorded music, are written and performed using electronic keyboards and other MIDI-equipped musical instruments. Thanks to advances in digital sampling and synthesis technologies, the orchestra playing behind that big-screen blockbuster movie is more likely to be the product of MIDI than a real orchestra with dozens of instruments.

EDITING MUSIC Each day thousands of musicians, composers, engineers, and producers use audio-editing software to record and master CDs, score and post soundtracks for film and television, and create music for the Internet. **Audio-editing software** lets you modify audio clips, including music, and produce studio-quality soundtracks and songs (Figure 4-6). Audio-editing software works like a musical word processor, in that it has cut, paste, copy, and other editing functions that allow an artist to modify a track in any song. Most audio-editing software also includes features of a sequencer to allow you to edit, mix, and incorporate MIDI tracks with other audio tracks.

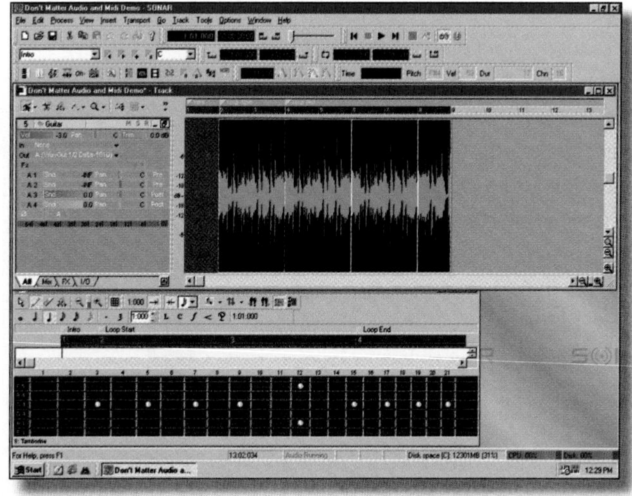

Figure 4-6 Audio-editing software lets you combine multiple tracks of songs and create special effects such as reverb, delay, or a looped sound of a chorus behind a melody.

With audio-editing software, you can combine multiple tracks of songs and create special effects such as reverb, delay, or a looped sound of a chorus behind a melody. The software also can generate rhythms that complement the melody of a song. You can adjust the song by changing the speed or tempo; adding or changing notes; or modifying pitch, tone, and timbre to create an entirely new sound. For example, you can play a song on a MIDI keyboard at 60 beats per minute, but then play in back at 120 beats per minute using audio-editing software. Because MIDI messages contain individual instructions for playing each individual note of each individual instrument, you actually can change just one note in a song or orchestrate an entire song with entirely different instruments. With live artists, you would have to bring the entire band back into the studio to rerecord any needed tracks. The end result of the recording and editing process is a final song, soundtrack for a video game, or television score, which then is printed as sheet music for performance or recorded to a CD or other medium for distribution.

PERFORMING MUSIC Computers are helping artists in the performances of their art as well. Computer-controlled amplifiers and speakers, for example, output sound from their instruments, while computers at the soundboard are used to balance the sound, ensure microphone volumes are correct, and create special lighting and sound effects.

Computers also help train musicians to perform better. In a unique application of technology to music, a facility at Arizona State University uses technology to help students learn the subtle movements required to be a world-class conductor. The system, known as the Digital Conducting Feedback System, gives you a chance to practice conducting without a live orchestra. During each training session, you stand in front of a mirror and a digital video camera records your conducting. You then put on a customized set of spandex sleeves that have pockets to hold four pairs of electrodes. These electrodes are placed in precise locations designed to capture key points of arm movement.

As you start to conduct a song, a computer algorithm monitors the movements of your arms. Based on your movements, the computer generates the sound of an orchestra. If your movements are technically correct, the digitally created orchestra sounds in perfect harmony and pitch. By experiencing the response of the digital orchestra in the lab, you learn to adjust your movements to generate the best sounding output from the orchestra. The electrodes also transmit your movement data to the computer, where your conducting performance is recorded for later analysis.

DISTRIBUTING MUSIC Computer technology has made distributing and accessing music easier than ever. Higher-quality digital music is recorded and distributed on optical media, such as CDs and DVDs, instead of tape cassettes. Users can purchase music online and download MP3 files directly to a hard disk, allowing them to listen to the music immediately from their computer or to transfer the music to an MP3 player. Some music publishers and musicians have Web sites that allow you to download sample tracks for free, to interest you in buying the entire CD. Other Web sites, such as the iTunes Music Store from Apple, allow you to purchase a single song or an entire CD and then download the tracks to your hard drive or MP3 player (Figure 4-7).

A few years ago, peer-to-peer (P2P) file sharing networks such as Napster, Grokster, Morpheus, and KaZaA, were popular sources for obtaining copyright-protected material. The music industry took notice, and has vigorously focused efforts on protecting its copyrights using both formal lawsuits and "pre-lawsuit" campaigns aimed at increasing awareness of copyright law and stemming the tide of outright violations. A **copyright** – which protects any tangible form of expression – gives authors and artists exclusive rights to duplicate, publish, and sell

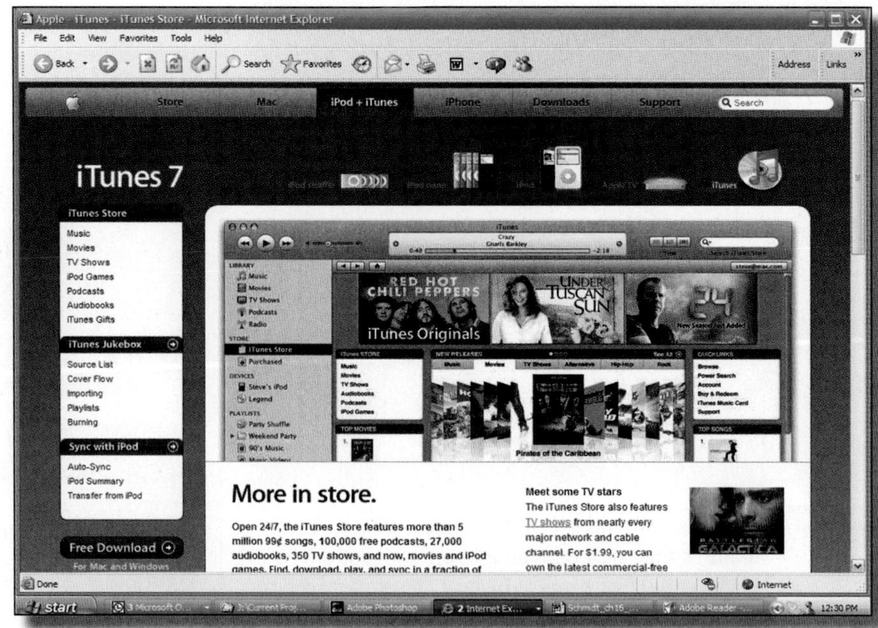

Figure 4-7 The iTunes Music Store has hundreds of thousands of songs that you can search by genre, new releases, exclusives, and more. You can preview any song for free and then buy a single song or the entire CD.

their materials. Shortly after the turn of the century, P2P file-sharing networks exploded in popularity as a means for people to share music, video, and other files stored on their personal computers. Unfortunately, many users of these P2P file-sharing networks are sharing material – music, movies, and software – that is protected by U.S. copyright law. In fact, the major trade organizations for the music and movie industries – the Recording Industry Association of America (RIAA) and the Motion Picture Association of American (MPAA) – continue to work aggressively to stop the piracy of copyrighted material by suing the P2P file-sharing networks. Napster, sued by the RIAA, effectively was shut down in July 2001 by court order. The Napster Web site now offers a subscription-based download service that complies with the law. Both Morpheus and KaZaA post statements regarding respect for copyright on their home pages. Grokster.com's file-sharing approach was ruled illegal by the Supreme Court and now posts a stern message on its home page to all viewers stating that there are "legal services for downloading music and movies" and that their service "is not one of them."

@ISSUE: Copyright Wars: The RIAA Wants You

It appears that the fight to stop copyright violation via file sharing is working, although not as much as the RIAA and MPAA might hope. One independent survey found that, in 2005, 28% of U.S. teens bought their music from legal sources; in 2006 the number had risen to 35%. Yet nearly two-thirds still report use of illegal sources. For years, the file-sharing networks and their defenders suggested that the software itself does not infringe on any copyright protection. Unlike Napster, whose exchange system did violate copyright laws by placing MP3s in one centrally indexed list, the software used to support P2P file-sharing systems only allows users to connect with each other for open exchange of files. As defenders of the P2P file-sharing networks have argued, the software itself is not in violation of copyright law: the users are.

When 28 entertainment companies filed suit against Grokster in 2003 (MGM Studios v. Grokster), the plaintiffs hoped the courts would agree that software distributors should be held liable for the use of their product. The Ninth Circuit court, however, agreed with Grokster and co-defendant StreamCast (developer of Morpheus) that users, not the software, were to blame. The case was appealed to the Supreme Court, and in 2005, the Supreme Court set aside the Ninth Circuit Court's ruling, stating that, indeed, the software developers were liable.

There are a couple of interesting elements in this case. First, in the original court case, the defendants successfully relied on an earlier landmark case ruling from 1984 - Sony v. Universal City Studios, Inc., better known as the "Betamax Ruling." In this case, the courts determined that distributors of devices, such as Sony Betamax VCRs, could not be held liable for users' infringement of copyright as long as the device was capable of sustaining "noninfringing" uses. Since the VCR could be used in such a manner to play home movie tapes or record non-copyrighted content, Sony was not liable.

Yet when MGM appealed the decision to the Supreme Court, the climate was different. Not only did the Court set aside the Ninth Circuit court ruling, they also created a new doctrine of copyright infringement liability called "inducement." To be found guilty of inducement, a defendant must intentionally distribute and promote its product for use in copyright infringement by third parties. Grokster was found liable under this new doctrine.

The ruling does not affect the use of P2P file-sharing networks for noninfringing uses such as sharing of research information (the original intent of some file-sharing networks), public domain films, historical recordings and digital educational materials, digital photos, shareware and freeware (Linux, for example), user-created audio and video files (podcasts), and a few other uses.

The RIAA didn't waste any time going after those who used P2P networks to obtain music files without paying for them. To get the message out, RIAA started an education initiative by sending thousands of instant messages to file swappers on Grokster and KaZaA, warning them that downloading copyrighted files is a criminal act and reminding them that they easily can be identified and prosecuted. RIAA also has hit college students with lawsuits, accusing them of running illegal file-sharing services on internal college networks — lawsuits that left several students working to pay off $12,000 to $15,000 worth of fines they each owe for swapping unauthorized music online. In recent months, the music trade group also sent letters to universities and large corporations alerting them to potential copyright abuses on their networks. As of 2007, the RIAA has continued its vigorous defense of its copyrights by issuing "pre-lawsuit" letters to numerous college and universities in the United States. These letters inform officials that the RIAA is planning to file a copyright infringement suit against one or more of its students or employees. The letters request that administrators pass the letter along to the appropriate network user.

In an effort to stop students and employees from using their networks to swap files illegally, universities and businesses have cracked down, monitoring network traffic or strengthening firewalls. To ensure that students understand their stance on copyright issues, many colleges and universities post acceptable use policies on their Web sites explaining that any activity that infringes on copyrights is not acceptable use of campus computing resources (Figure 4-8).

(continued)

@ISSUE: Copyright Wars: The RIAA Wants You *(continued)*

At the end of the day, despite legal wrangling on both sides of the copyright war, file sharing of copyrighted material is illegal. If you download a file that you do not have the license to own you are breaking the law. It remains to be seen, however, just how far the music industry will go to ensure you are identified and prosecuted to the fullest extent of the law. One thing increasingly is clear, however: in the copyright wars, you — and not the P2P file-sharing services — may be the enemy the industry is targeting.

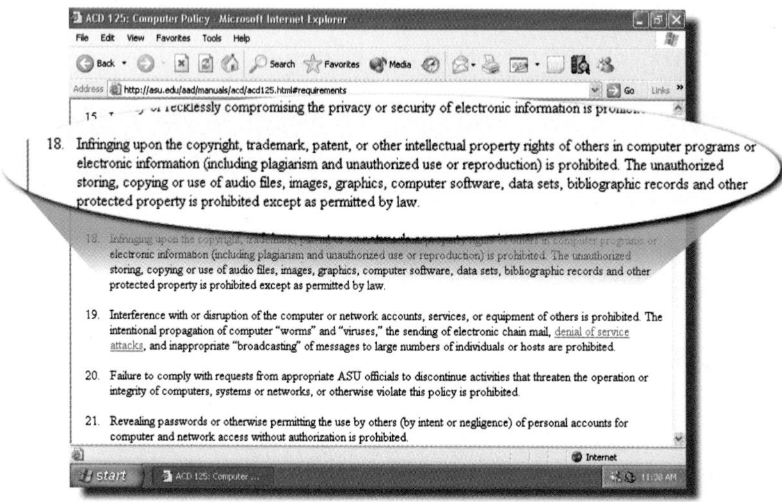

Figure 4-8 Many colleges and universities post acceptable use policies on their Web sites to communicate with students that any activity that infringes on copyrights is not acceptable use of campus computing resources.

Dance

In the world of dance, computers increasingly play an important role, allowing dancers to choreograph dances; reproduce their movements using computer notation and digital video, and use motion capture technology to create virtual dance partners and musical scores.

CHOREOGRAPHY AND NOTATION Just as music involves a series of notes, dance involves a series of steps. Dancers can use a computer program, called **dance notation software**, which captures movement as a series of symbols so that it can be shared with others. A dancer uses a dance score just as a musician uses a music score; the dance score allows each artist to learn the work without being influenced by someone else's artistic interpretation, and allows the dance to continue to be performed.

Several different types of dance notation are in use today – including Eshkol-Wachman Movement Notation, Benesh, and Labanotation. Software packages created around each of these dance notation methods allows dancers to use the computer keyboard and mouse to input notation for a particular dance. LabanWriter and CALABAN, for example, include tools to allow choreographers and dancers to notate their works using the Labanotation dance notation (Figure 4-9). The completed notation provides guidelines for future staging of the work.

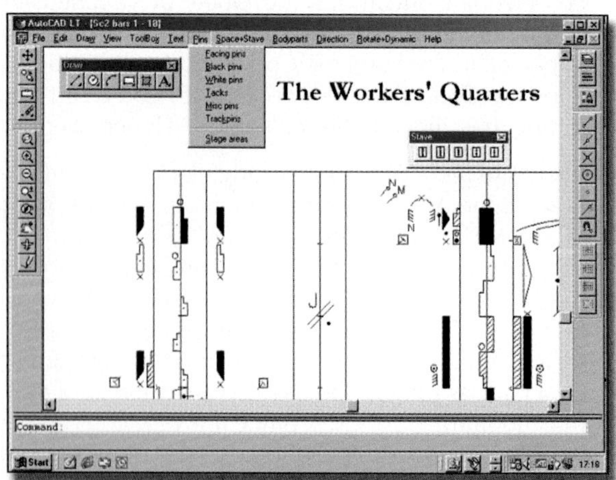

Figure 4-9 Software helps dancers notate dances for future reference. Using a special version of the AutoDesk AutoCAD software, called CALABAN, users can notate a dance called The Workers' Quarters using Labanotation symbols.

Choreographers use animation software packages to create choreographed animations of dances. For example, LifeForms Dance software includes templates of basic dance moves and tools to create mirror images of dancers, as well as 100 ballet positions and transitions that are used to script ballet choreography. Using LifeForms, the choreographer can plan the movements of individual dancers, view the interactions of all the dancers from different perspectives, and adjust each dance sequence in relative time (Figure 4-10).

In addition to capturing choreography using dance notation and animation, dancers can use other computer-based tools to document a dance fully. Computer technology allows any aspect of a dance – including electronic documents outlining the historical basis, the costumes, and production information such as costume, set, and light designs; digital audio of the musical score; and digital video of the performance – to be digitally recorded and stored on CDs or DVDs. The dance notation even can be synchronized to the digital video to show exactly the steps that created a particular move. This documentation process results in a complete electronic record of a dance, so that future performers have all the information needed to recreate a performance.

MOTION CAPTURE Dancers also rely on a technology called **motion capture** to record and analyze their dance movements, and even to create virtual dance partners and musical scores based on the movements. Several technologies are available for motion capture, including optical, inertial, and AC and DC magnetic. DC magnetic motion capture generally provides more accurate capture than the other technologies because the sensors do not need line of sight and are not affected greatly if other metals, such as steel or aluminum, are located near the sensors.

How does motion capture work? In a DC magnetic motion capture system, a transmitter is located at the center of a measured space that encloses an electromagnetic field. To start the process of motion

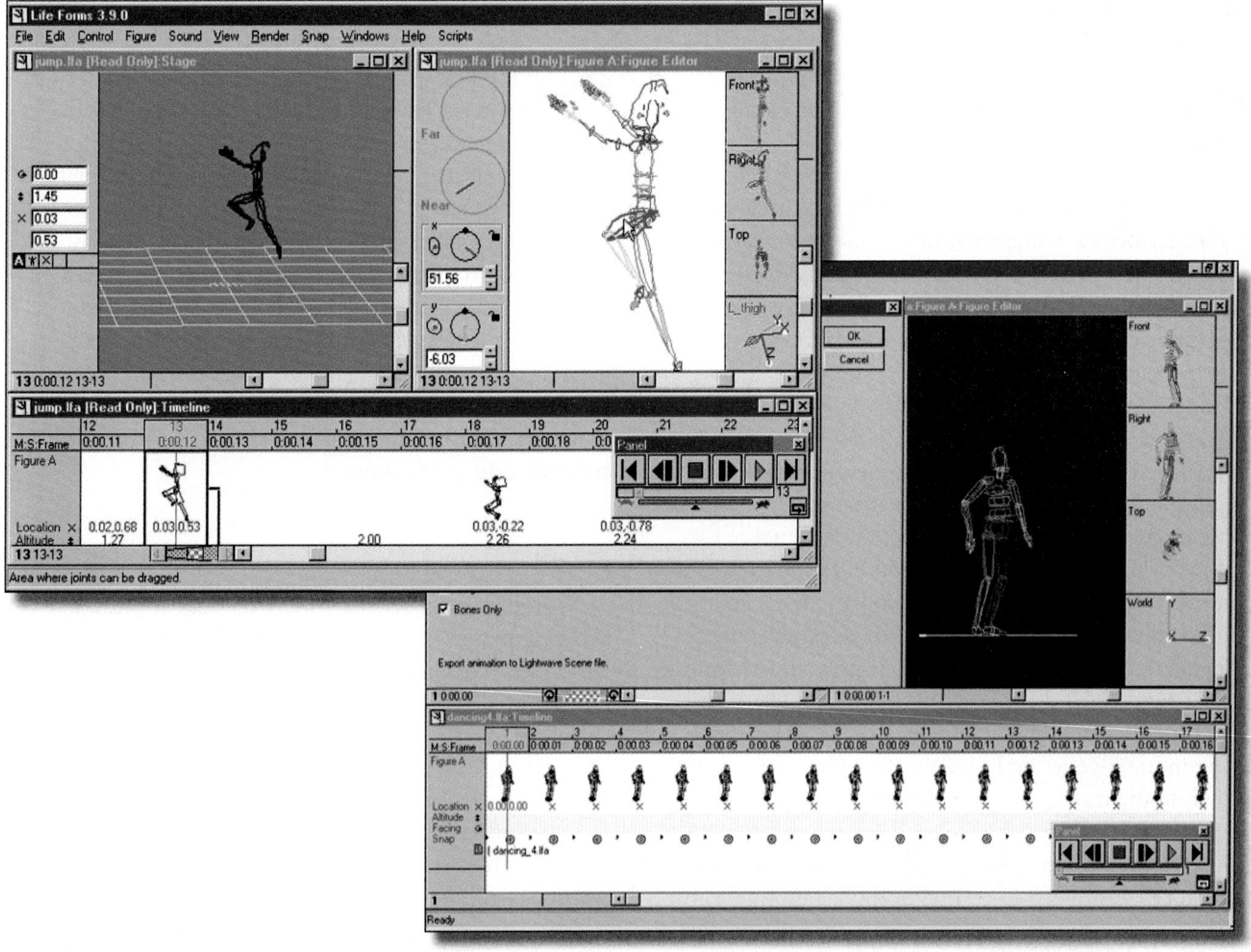

Figure 4-10 Using LifeForms software, a choreographer can plan the movements of dancers using computer-generated animations.

capture, a performer must secure magnetic sensors to various points on his or her body. A simple way to attach the sensors is to have performers wear a motion capture body suit with sensor holders where sensors are mounted (Figure 4-11). Performers also can wear peripherals, such as data gloves, which capture subtle movements such as hand gestures.

The sensors on the suit and peripherals use the electromagnetic field to measure their spatial relationship to the transmitter in the center of the measured space. In recording a dance, for example, you could attach up to 20 sensors to key points on several dancers. As the performers complete a motion, the motion capture system tracks the position and orientation of each magnetic sensor over 100 times per second to identify the location of the performers' bodies in space. This rapid tracking records every bodily motion and provides highly accurate capture of movements such as a leap, a pirouette, a rond de jambe, or a two-step.

Figure 4-11 Dancers and athletes rely on a technology called motion capture to record and analyze their movements. Computer animators can map these motion on to 3-D models to create lifelike amination.

Input from these sensors is transmitted to a recording device via cables (a tethered system) or via wireless connections (an untethered system). In an untethered or wireless system, input from the sensors travels over sensor cables to a battery-powered electronic unit mounted in a small, lightweight backpack worn by the performer. Channeled tubes and closures on the body suit and peripherals secure and guide the sensor cables into the electronic unit. A wireless system thus allows performers to complete complex motions without tangling cables.

The motion data captured by the sensors then is sent over a wireless connection to a base station for final processing. This data instantly can be mapped to the corresponding features of a computer-generated animated character to give them the exact movements of the live performers. Because many motion capture systems can track up to 90 sensors, a developer can create four or five animated characters and then track and map movements to multiple characters as several performers interact with each other.

Using this technology, one dancer can dance with 3-D computer-generated models of another dancer based on the movements acquired from a real dancer using motion capture. As the real, live dancer dances, the 3-D generated dancer can appear on a screen behind the dancer. Using a 3-D computer model allows a choreographer to use movements a human cannot complete, such as diving into the floor and vanishing from sight. Other applications of motion capture use sensors to transmit the position of a dancer's body to a computer. The computer software interprets the movements and then uses the information to control sound, lighting, and other effects. A particular leap by a dancer might cause lights to brighten, while a slower fluid movement of the arm could trigger a specific audio file to play as background music. A dancer defines the timing and action of those effects, based solely on his or her movements. While using such technology during a live performance, timing is critically important. If the timing of the dance if off slightly, the computers may not be able to adjust and thus the music and effects will be out of sync with the performers.

Theater

Computers are used in many aspects of theater, allowing key elements of a theatrical production – lights, sets, costumes, and sound – to be created, modeled, and tested in advance of the live performance. Computer-aided design (CAD) software, for example, is used to help with stage design. Using the software, the designers can create 3-D models of sets and then use these models as guides as they create the physical objects, either by hand or using computer numerical controlled (CNC) milling machines.

Stage lighting also relies on computer technology, including CAD software. For years, creating lighting effects was labor intensive and slow, requiring many technicians to adjust and move lights manually. Computers have automated much of the stage lighting process, allowing changes to unfold as slowly or quickly as possible to make effects, such as a sunrise or an explosion, more believable. A click of a button instructs computer-controlled lights to move into position for the next cue. Today, lighting technicians and designers also can use CAD software to design a lighting scheme and then play it back to watch the resulting effects, without even setting foot onstage.

Computers also help sound designers, who use a computer-controlled soundboard and software programs that manage multiple input tracks and effects, allowing operators to balance sound more effectively and create stunning effects. During scene changeovers, the sound designer can cover the noise by cueing digital music to play through speakers placed throughout a theater. The software also knows when singers, actors, and actresses are offstage and automatically turns off their microphones (the safest way to ensure any backstage gossip does not get piped out to the audience).

For the costume designer, cast measurements are stored in the computer so that, for the next production, the designer can plug the correct measurements into CAD software and then design and print a pattern for any part of the costume needed.

Theater box offices also use software to handle ticket sales. Either via telephone or over the Web, the software allows customers to specify the show they would like to see, select seats from a seating chart, and pay for the tickets. Box office staff can use the same software to report by day on sales or available seats for a particular show; to print labels to mail customers their tickets; or to calculate commissions earned by promoters.

Sculpture and 3-D Media

Sculpture is another art form that has benefited from the use of computers. In the past, a sculptor created a work using only a medium such as wood or marble, the appropriate tools needed to shape the medium, and a trained eye.

Today, as a sculptor, you may rely on computers to help with several aspects of the artistic process. Sculptors use CAD software, like that used in product design, and other types of 3-D modeling software to create a digital model of an object that they want to sculpt. That 3-D model then serves as a guide as the sculptor creates the art in a physical medium, such as marble.

As a sculptor, you also can use 3-D scanning to scan an existing object and then recreate the object. Once the object is scanned, you can use CAD or 3-D modeling software to manipulate the digital model to enlarge, reduce, or alter the object. If desired, you then can use the scan as a model to create art from a physical medium. A 3-D scanning system was used in the Digital Michelangelo project, whose goal was to digitize Michelangelo's sculptures for archive and future study. These 3-D scanners sweep a fine line of laser light across the sculpture's surface (Figure 4-12). The scanner captures the shape of the laser line as it curves across the unique features and chisel marks of the sculpture. This information is stored in computers as 3-D coordinates

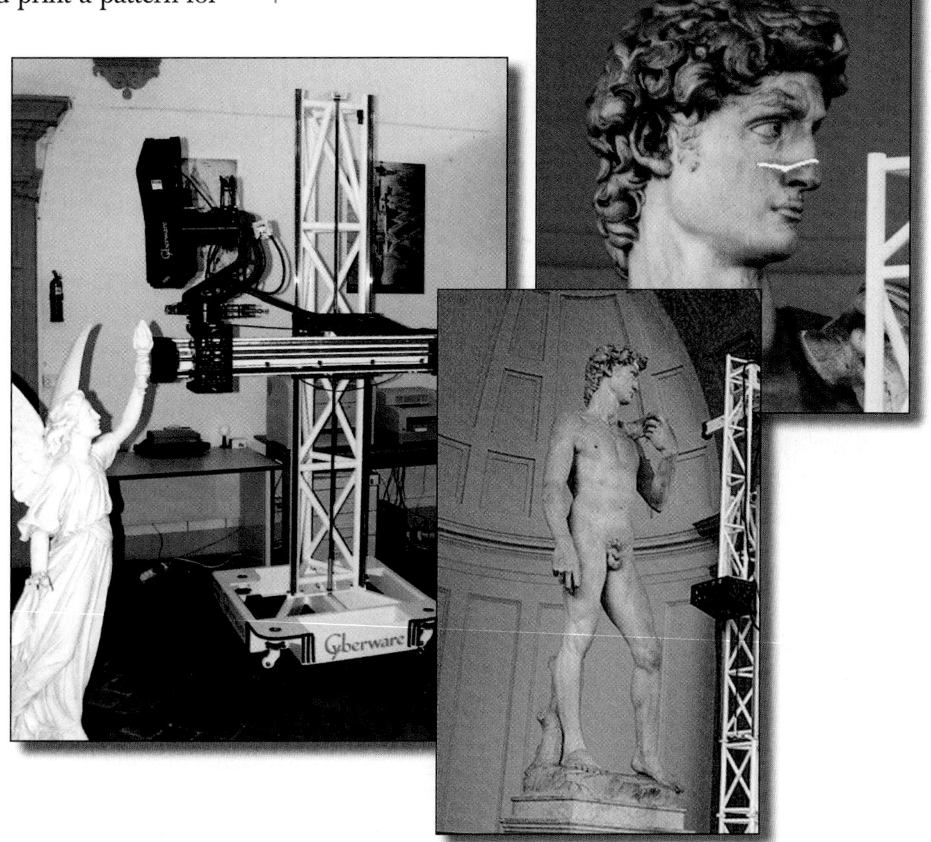

Figure 4-12 In order to create 3-D scans of larger statues, the 3-D scanning system includes a vertical truss, a horizontal arm for vertical movement, a pan-tilt head for horizontal movement, and the scanner head – all on a rolling base.

for later processing into a surface model of the sculpture. For larger sculptures, such as Michelangelo's *David*, the scanner head must be placed on a rolling assembly that allows the scanner to move around the object so each side of the object can be scanned.

Once you have created the model for your sculpture, you can use a CNC milling machine to shape your desired medium. The manufacturing industry uses CNC milling machines for complex manufacturing of items such as jet engines and car parts. In sculpture, CNC milling machines use CAD models or 3-D models as the input to the CNC milling machine. The software reads the models and determines the geometry of the object. After you enter some milling parameters (type of cutting tool, required accuracy, and so on), the CNC system software automatically calculates the milling paths and then guides the tools on the milling machine to sculpt the object, as defined by the model. CNC milling machines can range in size from desktop versions that can mill smaller objects such as bottles and jewelry to large machines used to mill larger objects. The Chicago Field Museum, for example, relied on a large CNC milling machine to create sculpted bones to replace foot bones that were missing from the original fossil set of the *Tyrannosaurus rex* (Figure 4-13).

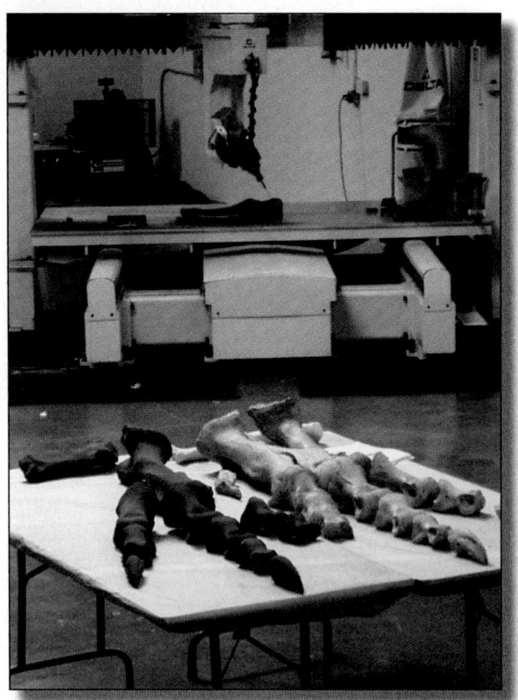

Figure 4-13 CNC milling machines can range in size from desktop versions that can mill smaller objects to large machines used to mill larger objects, such as the foot bones of a Tyrannosaurus Rex.

Finally, you can use a computer to create sculpture that can be shared electronically, such as over the Web. Telesculpture involves creating a sculpture – either virtual models fashioned using CAD and 3-D modeling tools or physical models sculpted and then scanned or photographed – and then sharing that artwork over the Web with other artists. Sharing the telesculpture allows other artists to collaborate in the artistic process, use those models to create physical sculptures, or simply appreciate the form and structure of the 3-D models. Those involved in telesculpture note that the electronic sculptures are more permanent than physical material, such as stone or clay, and that telesculpture allows art to be shared with a global audience, either via Web sites or in virtual reality worlds where the sculptures are included as part of the virtual landscape.

Graphic Arts

Today, almost every computer can be used to create some graphics (and, in fact, most of us have become accustomed to a graphical user interface to interact with our computer). Although computer graphics encompasses a wide range of artistic expression, it essentially involves drawing pictures on computers, also called **rendering**. The graphics created on a computer can be illustrations, cartoons, simulations, designs for new products, logos, backgrounds for a music video, or stylized art. Using computers, graphic artists can create pictures of realistic objects or items that do not yet (and may never) exist.

Some suggest that creating art on a computer means the computer does the work. In reality, the artistic process is executed on a computer, but only at the direction of the artist. When creating graphics using a computer, the artistic process is similar to creating art using pen and paper or paintbrush, oil, and canvas – the artist envisions the image, plans the approach to create the image, and then uses software (instead of pen or paintbrush) to create the graphic. **Illustration software**, such as Adobe Illustrator, allows you to illustrate and render digital art, just as you would use a pencil, brush, or pastels to create traditional art. Instead of using a pencil or a brush, however, you now use the mouse or a graphics tablet as your input device. The software has the computer equivalents of all the tools that an artist would use manually: brushes, pencils, spraying tools, erasers, different types of paper, and so on. Using the software, you also can add effects with special filters or edit and retouch a graphic, picture element, or "pixel," by pixel.

Other unique types of graphics software include software for creating fractal art. A **fractal** is a geometric pattern that is repeated at ever smaller (or larger) scales to produce irregular shapes and surfaces that cannot be represented by classical geometry. A fractal has symmetry of scale, which means you can zoom in on part of a fractal shape an infinite number of times and it still looks the same.

In terms of art, a **computer-generated fractal** is a unique art form that uses mathematical formulas to create art with a vast range of structure, detail, color and light (Figure 4-14). The fractal essentially is a graphical image that represents the behavior of a mathematical equation repeated over and over. The formula used determines how each of the millions of pixels in the image is formed and colored. Artists then can modify the formulas and change color algorithms to create unique images of abstract shapes or representations of waves, plants, landscapes, and planets.

Software used to create fractal art provides tools that allow artists to define what mathematical formulas to use to create the art, set color schemes, and define geometrical patterns to use (Figure 4-14). Some fractal creation software even allows you to distribute the resource-intensive process of performing the calculations to multiple computers on a network (using the same distributed computing principles of SETI@home, as discussed in Chapter 3).

Photography

A **digital camera** allows users to take pictures and store the electronic images digitally on a storage medium, instead of on traditional film. Digital cameras appeal to a wide range of users, including professional photographers. For example, real estate agents use digital cameras so they can easily post images to a Web site for review by

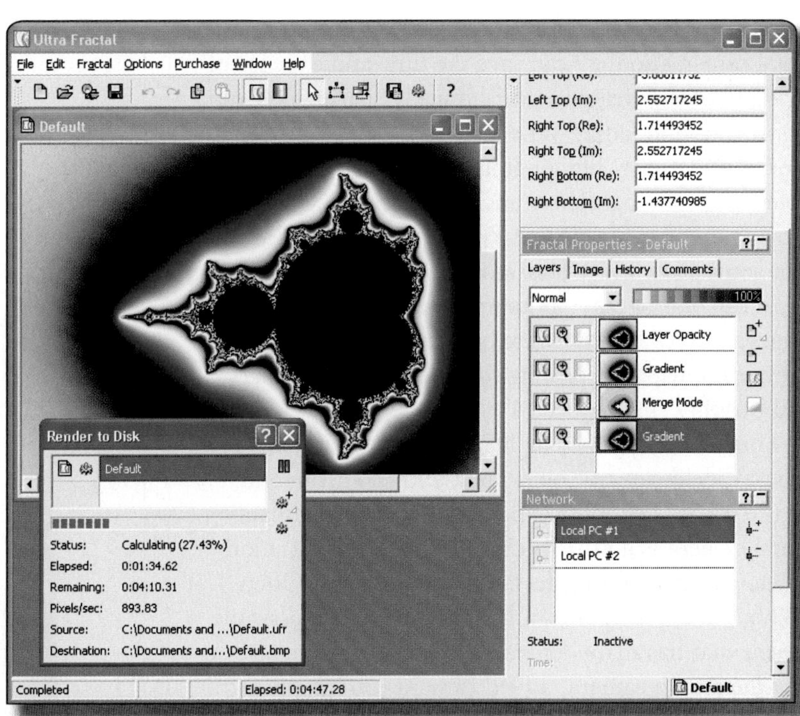

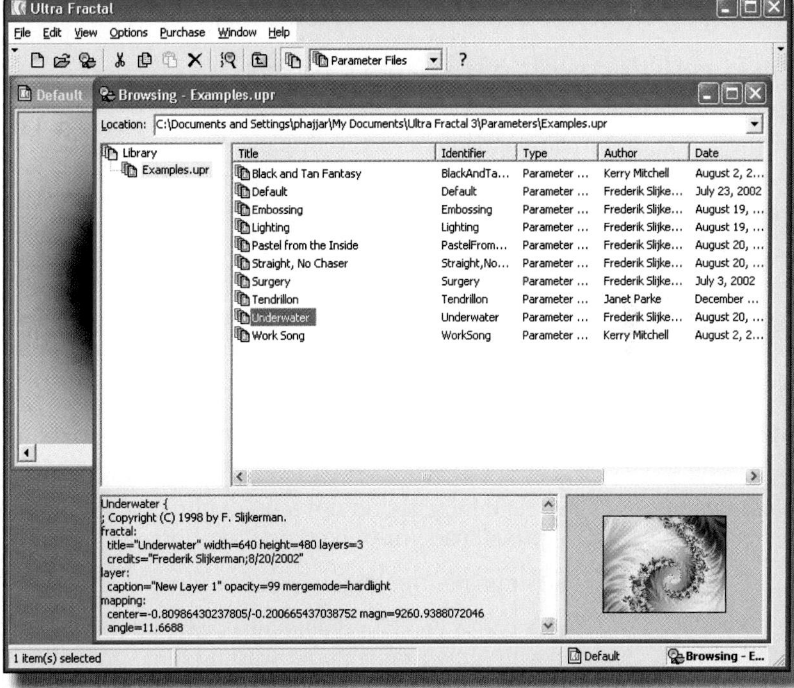

Figure 4-14 Software used to create fractal art provides tools to allow artists to define what mathematical formulas to use to create the art, set color schemes, define geometrical patterns – and even distribute calculations over a group of networked computers.

clients and customers. Home and business users use digital cameras so they can save the time and expense of having photos developed, while quickly sharing images with friends and family via e-mail and Web sites. While some consider only film photography true art, professional photographers and artists are using and enjoying the benefits of digital photography (Table 4-1). Photojournalists and professional photographers use digital cameras to take photographs and then refine the images using editing software before creating prints on high-quality paper or posting them to an online gallery on the Web.

Three basic types of digital cameras are studio cameras, field cameras, and point-and-shoot cameras (Figure 4-15). The most expensive and highest-quality digital camera is a **studio camera**, which is a stationary camera used for professional studio work. Often used by photojournalists, a **field camera** is a portable camera that has many lenses and other attachments. Like the studio camera, a field camera can be quite expensive. A **point-and-shoot camera** is much more affordable and lightweight and provides acceptable quality photographic images for the home or business user.

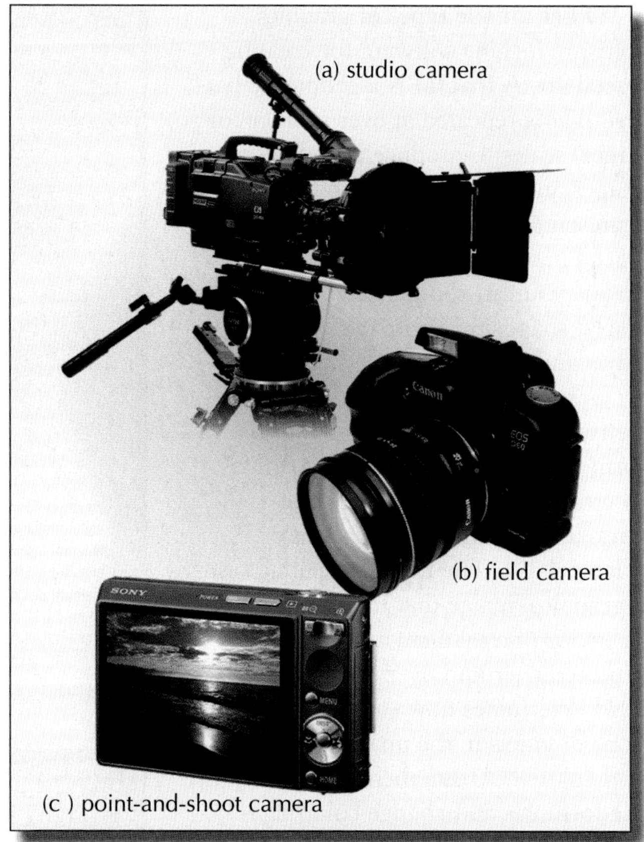

Figure 4-15 Several types of digital cameras are available on the market, with features designed for specific types of users.

BEHIND THE SCENES: DIGITAL PHOTO CAPTURE

Figure 4-16 illustrates how one type of digital camera transforms the captured image into a screen display. As you point the camera lens towards the image you want to photograph and click the button to take the picture,

Table 4-1 Digital Photography Benefits

BENEFIT	DESCRIPTION
Speed	▪ Digital images allow for instant previews right after the photo is taken so you know if you have captured the shot you want
Cost savings	▪ Digital images do not require film processing time or cost (although you will pay to have prints made or printed on your home printer). ▪ Eliminates the ongoing cost of film ▪ Because you can delete a bad photo, you can take many more experimental photos without worrying about wasting film
Environmental benefits	▪ Without traditional developing, the use and disposal of photographic chemicals is reduced substantially.
Flexibility	▪ Like any electronic images, digital photos can be e-mailed, posted to Web sites, included in documents, and more. ▪ Can be posted to photo printing services to get hard copy prints ▪ Can be organized into albums on the Web or on your computer
Editing	▪ Digital photos can be retouched and manipulated on a computer, without losing quality

Digital photography offers many benefits over traditional film photography.

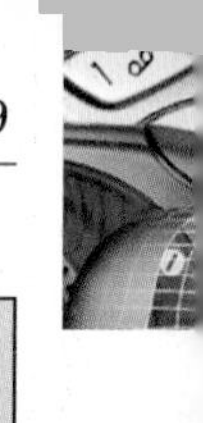

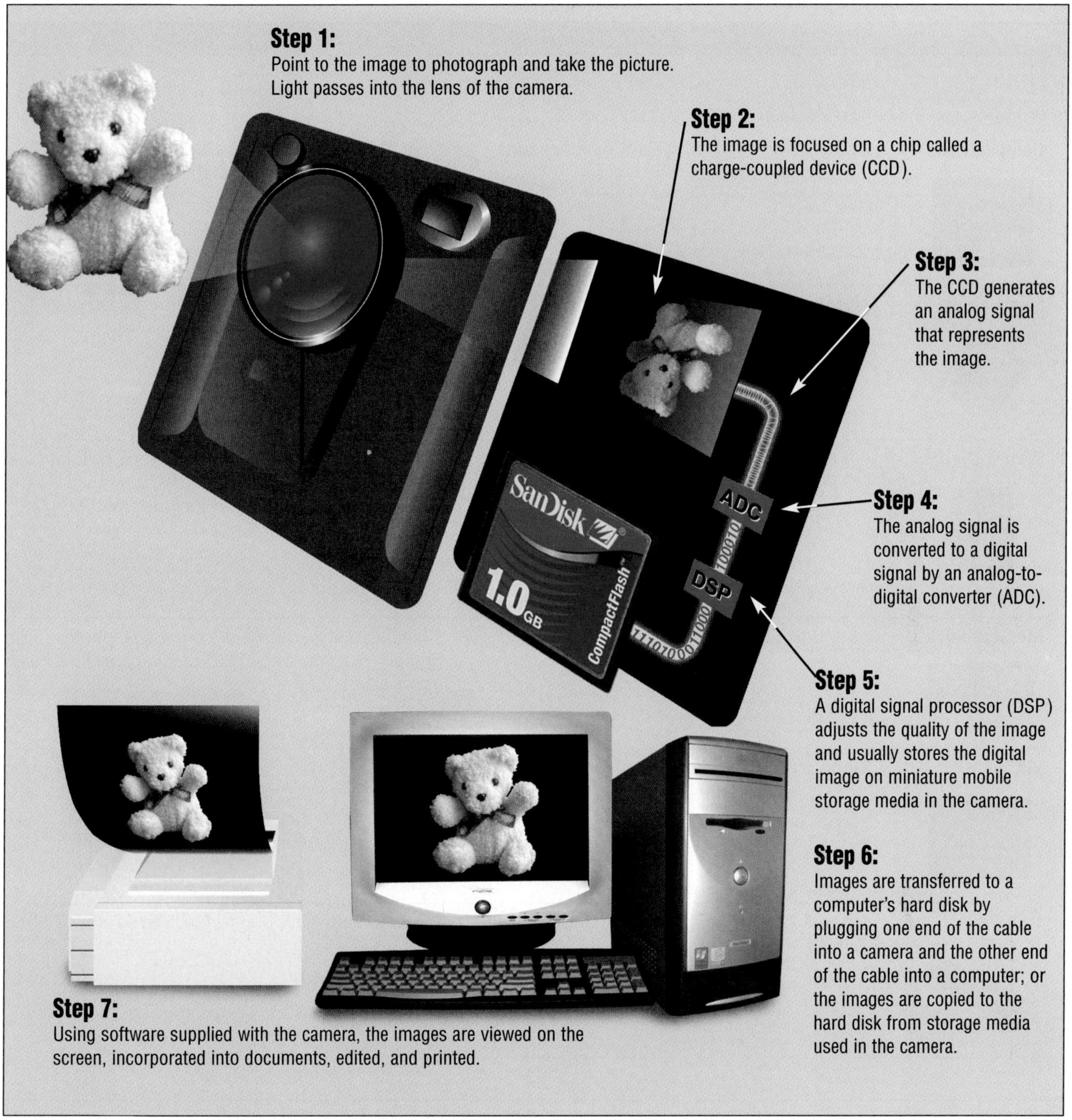

Step 1:
Point to the image to photograph and take the picture. Light passes into the lens of the camera.

Step 2:
The image is focused on a chip called a charge-coupled device (CCD).

Step 3:
The CCD generates an analog signal that represents the image.

Step 4:
The analog signal is converted to a digital signal by an analog-to-digital converter (ADC).

Step 5:
A digital signal processor (DSP) adjusts the quality of the image and usually stores the digital image on miniature mobile storage media in the camera.

Step 6:
Images are transferred to a computer's hard disk by plugging one end of the cable into a camera and the other end of the cable into a computer; or the images are copied to the hard disk from storage media used in the camera.

Step 7:
Using software supplied with the camera, the images are viewed on the screen, incorporated into documents, edited, and printed.

ADC
DSP
SanDisk
1.0GB
CompactFlash

Figure 4-16 How a digital camera works.

light passes into the lens of the camera. The image is focused on a chip called a **charge-coupled device (CCD)**. The CCD generates an analog signal that represents the image; that analog signal then is converted to a digital signal by an analog-to-digital converter (ADC). A digital signal processor (DSP) adjusts the quality of the image and stores the digital image on the storage media in the camera.

Digital cameras use a variety of storage media to store images. These media include familiar storage media, such as CDs, as well as miniature storage media such as a flash memory card, a memory stick, or a USB drive (Figure 4-17). Once captured, the images are transferred from the camera to a computer's hard disk either by connecting the camera to a computer using a cable or copying the images from the miniature storage media to the hard disk.

Table 4-2 Miniature Mobile Storage Media

DEVICE NAME	STORAGE CAPACITY	TYPE	USE
CompactFlash	Up to 4 GB	Flash memory card	Digital cameras, PDAs, notebook computers, printers, music players, cellular telephones
Smart Media	16 MB to 128 MB	Flash memory card	Digital cameras, PDAs, photo printers, cellular telephones
Secure Digital	Up to 2 GB	Flash memory card	Digital cameras, PDAs, music players, cellular telephones, digital video cameras, car navigation systems, e-books. Also includes mini-SD and micro-SD cards
Memory Stick	16 MB to 128 MB	Flash memory card	Digital cameras, notebook computers, photo printers. Memory Stick PRO media capacities go up to 4 GB
xD	Up to 2 GB	Flash memory card	Digital cameras
USBDrive	Up to 8 GB	Flash memory card	Plugs into any USB port to function as a mini hard disk

A variety of miniature mobile storage media.

DIGITAL PHOTO EDITING Using software, the images captured on a digital camera can be viewed, edited, incorporated into documents, and printed. Some digital cameras allow users to review and edit images while they still are stored on media in the camera. Most users, including professional photographers and photojournalists, prefer to download, or transfer a copy of, the images from the digital camera to a computer's hard disk. With some digital cameras, you can download images using a cable that connects between the digital camera and the USB port or FireWire port on the system unit. If the camera stores photos on storage media, such as an SD card, you can insert the media into a reading device that connects wirelessly or attaches to a USB port in the system unit (Figure 4-17). Many newer computers also come with built-in card readers to make it easier to transfer and store images.

Once the photos are stored on a computer's hard disk, a photographer can edit the images using photo-editing software or image-editing software. **Photo-editing software** or **image-editing software** allows you to edit digital photographs to adjust the contrast and brightness and correct lighting problems

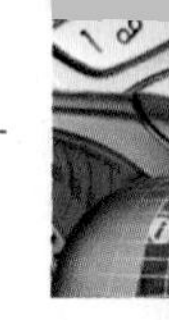

Figure 4-17 To download digital photos, you can insert the media, such as an SD card, into a reading device that connects wirelessly or attaches to a USB port in the system unit. You even can get a mouse with a built-in card reader.

(Figure 4-18a), to remove red-eye, to crop an image and remove unnecessary or unwanted elements (such as your thumb or the random stranger in the background), and to add elements. You also can use photo-editing software to add color to black-and-white photos and even remove blemishes and wrinkles (Figure 4-18b). Professional artists use photo-editing software to create stunning images by adding special effects or to transform a single photo into a digital image that looks like an oil painting or an entirely new artwork (Figure 4-18c).

You also can use photo-editing software to print photographs or create electronic photo albums. Home photographers often post their digital photographs to online photo processing and printing sites, such as Snapfish, where they can share photo albums with friends or order prints of specific photos. Photographers and photojournalists often post their photos to online galleries that showcase their work, as well as to their own Web sites.

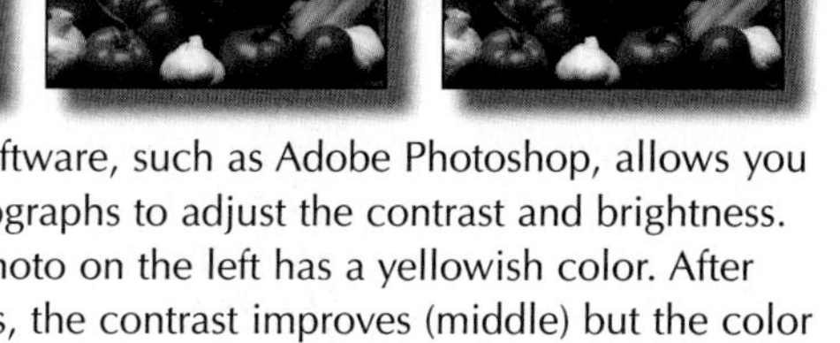

(a) Photo-editing software, such as Adobe Photoshop, allows you to edit digital photographs to adjust the contrast and brightness. For example, the photo on the left has a yellowish color. After balancing the levels, the contrast improves (middle) but the color cast is still visible. Finally, after balancing the color, the yellowish cast is removed and the true bright colors of the peppers come through.

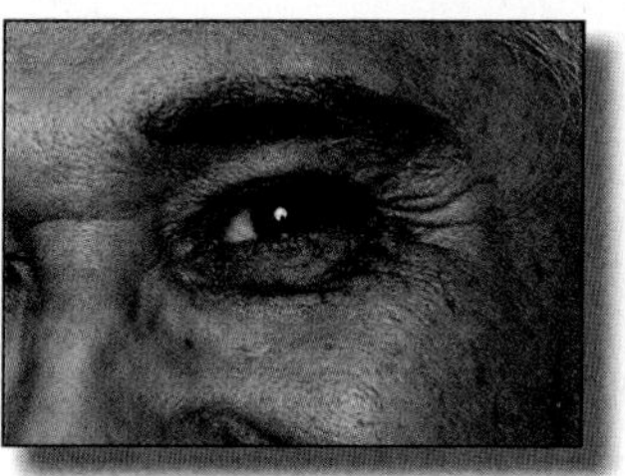

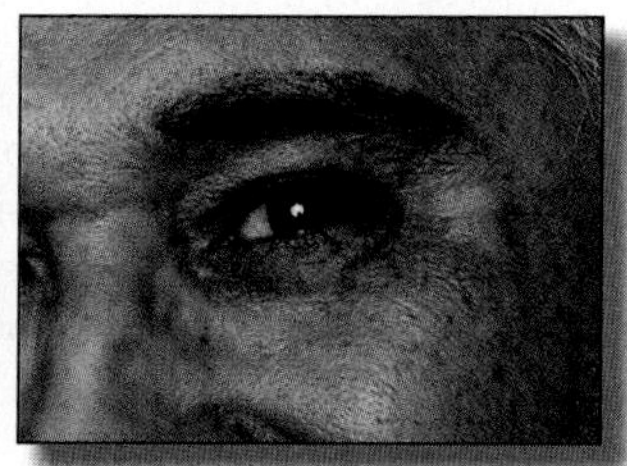

(b) Photo-editing software allows you to remove blemishes and wrinkles from a photograph. Here, for example, the wrinkles below the eye are removed digitally.

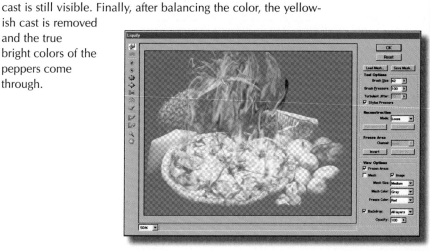

(c) Professional artists can create stunning images by adding special effects, such as the steam rising from the pizza in the first image. Photo-editing tools also allow you to take a digital photo of a tomato and create new versions that look like an oil painting or an entirely new artwork.

Figure 4-18

@ISSUE: Picture Imperfect

Today, many commercial artists, photojournalists, and creators of billboards, book covers, and print ads use photo-editing or image-editing software to create their work. Using this software, they can alter digital photographs and import graphics to add clouds to a blue sky, edit a picture so that it looks as if a group of people are standing in front of the Colosseum in Rome, add people to a photo, or remove a person from a picture altogether. For example, with photo-editing software you could recreate a photo where you are shaking hands with Elvis Presley in a Las Vegas lounge.

Some individuals and organizations have raised concerns about the use of computers to alter output, primarily graphical output such as retouched photographs and video feeds. Many believe that digital photograph retouching is acceptable, as long as the editing does not significantly change the content or the meaning of the photographs. One group that completely opposes any manipulation of an image, however, is the National Press Photographers Association (NPPA). The association believes that allowing even the slightest alteration eventually could lead to photographs being deliberately altered to misrepresent the truth. To underscore this, the NPAA's code of ethics states: "As journalists, we believe that credibility is our greatest asset. In documentary photojournalism, it is wrong to alter the content of a photograph in any way (electronically or in the darkroom) that deceives the public. We believe the guidelines for fair and accurate reporting should be the criteria for judging what may be done electronically to a photograph."

One Los Angeles Times staff photographer discovered the hard way how seriously the NPPA and his employer take the intentional manipulation of an image. He was fired for editing together two photos to make one dramatic photo of a British soldier and a crowd of people outside the Iraqi city of Basra. In a front-page editor's note, the L.A. Times acknowledged the issue and ran the original photos on their Web site (Figure 4-19).

The editor's note admitted that the photographer used photo-editing software to combine elements of two different images to produce the front-page photo. As shown in Figure 4-20, the final, front-page photograph shows a civilian carrying a child toward a soldier, who has a hand outstretched as if he were signaling the civilian to halt. When several readers noticed that some civilians appeared twice in the final photograph, the L.A. Times contacted the photographer, who admitted to altering the image to improve the composition. Because L.A. Times' policy forbids altering the content of news photographs, the photographer was fired.

In fast-moving situations, the job of a photographer — to get the perfect shot — can be challenging. With powerful photo- and image-editing tools, it is all too simple and tempting to take an almost perfect shot and alter it ever so slightly to make it the perfect shot.

Digital retouching is an area in which few legal precedents have been established, so it is an ethical question for professional photographers, photojournalists, and others whose jobs are based on sharing accurate images with the public. Beyond the ethical concerns, some worry about the erosion of accuracy and authenticity, combined with the so-called "CNN effect." The CNN effect is a term used to describe the ability of mass media to influence political and military decision makers. Insiders say that the CNN effect is real, as all offices in the Pentagon, White House, and other key government agencies are tuned to CNN, all of the time. Given that, a terrorist group could set world political events in motion by distributing one well-altered photo or video. By the time the alteration was discovered (if ever), the situation might have escalated beyond the government's ability to pull back.

Most agree that journalists must maintain high standards of accuracy and truth in their reporting and photography, as evidenced by the reaction of the L.A. Times and the public. Every picture tells a story, but the picture should tell the story of what actually happened and not what the photographer thinks should have happened. Few, however, would react negatively to having their picture altered slightly to remove a few wrinkles or eliminate a few pounds before it runs on the cover of Time Magazine. Is that also unethical — or is that type of alteration acceptable? As a photographer, where would you draw the line between creating the picture perfect cover and creating an imperfect representation of reality?

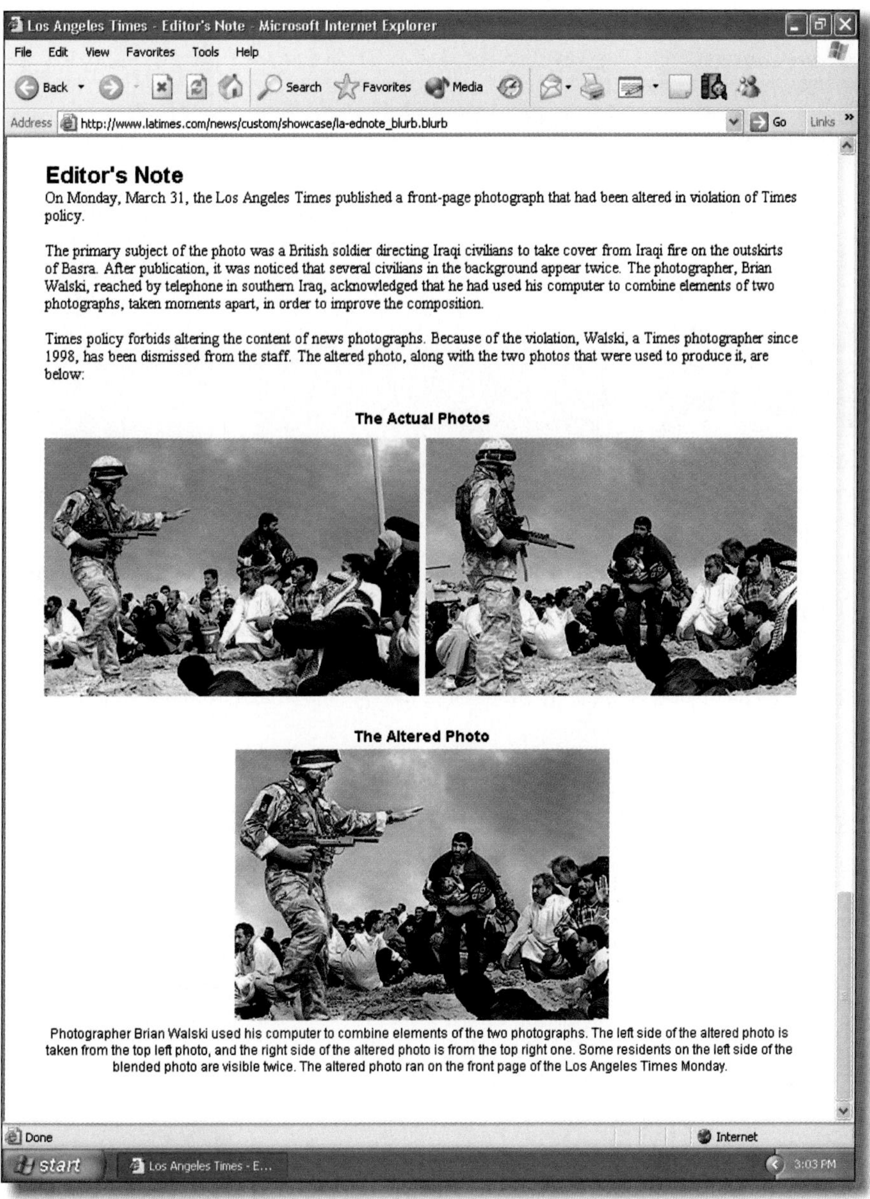

Editor's Note

On Monday, March 31, the Los Angeles Times published a front-page photograph that had been altered in violation of Times policy.

The primary subject of the photo was a British soldier directing Iraqi civilians to take cover from Iraqi fire on the outskirts of Basra. After publication, it was noticed that several civilians in the background appear twice. The photographer, Brian Walski, reached by telephone in southern Iraq, acknowledged that he had used his computer to combine elements of two photographs, taken moments apart, in order to improve the composition.

Times policy forbids altering the content of news photographs. Because of the violation, Walski, a Times photographer since 1998, has been dismissed from the staff. The altered photo, along with the two photos that were used to produce it, are below:

The Actual Photos

The Altered Photo

Photographer Brian Walski used his computer to combine elements of the two photographs. The left side of the altered photo is taken from the top left photo, and the right side of the altered photo is from the top right one. Some residents on the left side of the blended photo are visible twice. The altered photo ran on the front page of the Los Angeles Times Monday.

Figure 4-19 When the Los Angeles Times discovered that this front-page photo had been altered, the photographer was dismissed. At the top are the two original photographs, which, to a photographer's trained eye, are less compelling than the final altered photograph. In the photograph on the left, the soldier has his hand outstretched in an effort to halt or calm the civilians, but the civilian with the child is not making eye contact. In the photograph at the right, the civilian has moved forward and has made eye contact with the soldier, but the soldier is in an easy stance with his weapon under his arm. The final altered photo creates a dramatic scene and uses a trick of perspective to make it appear as if the weapon is pointed at the child.

Copyright Concerns

Because digital photos and computer graphics are easily shared and transferred over the Internet, they raise unique copyright concerns. One way to ensure that copyrighted photos, graphics, and animations are used only by those who have permission is to add a digital watermark to the files before posting them to the Internet.

Digital watermarking allows you to embed a digital code in audio, images, video, and documents. The code is imperceptible during normal use, but readable by computers and software provided by companies such as Digimarc. To create a digital watermark, you use Digimarc's software to make subtle changes to the data that is part of the original digital content. The changes made by the software are so small that the human eye cannot see Digimarc digital watermarks (Figure 4-20). Yet, the digital watermark can be recognized by simple reading devices or applications enabled with the appropriate Digimarc software.

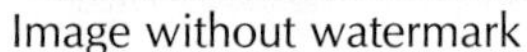

Image without watermark | Image with watermark | View of imperceptible watermark

Figure 4-20 Digimarc's software embeds a digital watermark by making imperceptible changes to the data of the original digital content. The first photo shows the original image; the second the image with the watermark, which cannot be seen by the human eye. The third image shows the changes made to the image to embed the watermark, which includes information on the copyright owner, contact information, and more. This calculation is made by subtracting the original image from the watermarked image.

To determine if any digitally watermarked images are posted on Web sites or are on your hard drive, you can use software that detects and allows you to view the information stored in a digital watermark. For example, Digimarc's ImageBridge reader software can be configured to work with your browser or Windows Explorer (Figure 4-21). The software detects images digitally watermarked using Digimarc software and displays a special icon next to the image. You can right-click the image to review the copyright information embedded in the digital watermark.

Figure 4-21 ImageBridge reader software detects images digitally watermarked using Digimarc software and allows you to review the information embedded in the digital watermark.

COMPUTERS IN ENTERTAINMENT

Computers have changed the world of entertainment in ways unimaginable just a few years ago. For example, movies and television shows once were shot on rolls and rolls of film that had to be developed at the end of each day of shooting. In 2002, *Star Wars Episode II: Attack of the Clones* was the first major motion picture shot, distributed, and shown in purely digital format. The entire movie was shot using only digital video and was distributed to many movie theaters via a satellite system. Now, movie distributors and theaters are starting to upgrade to digital projection. Instead of delivering the latest movie release on film, distributors deliver the 150 GB to 200 GB movie on a hard drive. The drive is used to store the movie on a server which then sends it to the projector in the theater. There currently are about 1,200 such digital projection theatres in the United States. As cinemas are upgraded to handle digital projection, the projection systems in the theaters can display almost any digital content – from digital satellite signals to DVDs to digital cable. Cinemas thus could broadcast other types of events – big sporting events, concerts, or Broadway productions – and pull in an entirely new type of audience.

In the area of television and movies, computers have allowed for advances in video editing, colorization, animation, and motion capture. Computers also have changed sports, from the CAD-created equipment to the simulators used to train athletes.

Television and Movies

As noted, technology developments in film and television have shifted the industry from a film-based world to one based on digital video. On the sets of television shows and movies, camerapersons use digital video cameras to capture raw footage. Instead of literally cutting unwanted scenes from film and splicing it back at the correct point, video editors complete postproduction editing of raw footage digitally and add titles, soundtracks, and special effects to produce even higher-quality results.

BEHIND THE SCENES: DIGITAL VIDEO CAPTURE

The newest generation of video cameras, called **digital video (DV) cameras**, record video as digital signals instead of analog signals. In addition to capturing live full-motion video, many digital video cameras also can capture still frames.

Capturing digital video works much in the same way as capturing digital photos. As you point the camera lens towards the scene and press a button to record the video, light passes into the lens of the camera. The image is focused on a chip called a charge-coupled device (CCD). For the best picture quality, professional digital video cameras have three CCDs to capture three different light spectrums (red, green, and blue). The CCDs generate an analog signal that represents the image. The analog signal then is converted to a digital signal by an analog-to-digital converter (ADC). A digital signal processor (DSP) adjusts the quality of the image and stores the digital image on the storage media in the camera.

There are hundreds of digital video cameras on the market today (Figure 4-22). The most expensive, highest-quality camera is a **studio DV camera**, which is a stationary camera used for professional studio work, such as filming on a movie set. A **field DV camera** is a portable camera that has many lenses and other attachments; sports camerapersons, who need the ability to get close to the action with a camera, often use field cameras. A **point-and-shoot DV camera** is much more affordable and lightweight and provides acceptable quality photographic images for the home or business user.

Figure 4-22 Digital video cameras have a range of features to provide the highest-quality video possible for each type of user.

DV cameras record and store data on one of several different types of media. For point-and-shoot DV cameras the most popular media is a MiniDV tape. For professional work using field and studio DV cameras, a higher-quality Digital Betacam and DVCAM tapes are the most widely used media. As you record digital video, the digital data is stored on the MiniDV or DVCAM tape. To transfer the images from the tape to a computer hard drive, you connect the DV camera to a USB or FireWire port on the system unit and start the software used to support the video transfer.

DIGITAL VIDEO EDITING Once the video is stored on hard disk, it can be viewed and edited using video-editing software. **Video editing software**, such as Apple Final Cut Pro and Adobe Premiere, allows you to edit digital video to split the video into scenes, cut out unwanted parts, add special effects, and more. The raw video shot during a television or movie shoot is called the dailies. Traditionally, after a day of shooting, directors, producers, and camerapersons gather in a screening room to take a look at the dailies. The production team views the dailies from the DVCAM tape to determine where to make cuts in the footage. Editors then move the digital video from the tapes to the postproduction editing machines.

If you were editing the dailies from a movie or television show, the first step in the editing process is **splitting**, which involves segmenting the video into smaller pieces, or scenes, that you can manage more easily. Most video-editing software automatically splits the video into scenes. After splitting, you would cut out unwanted scenes or portions of scenes (and save the bloopers for the extras on the DVD version of the movie). This process is called **pruning**.

When you have all of the scenes you want to use in the final production, you would then edit each individual scene. You can crop, or change the size of scenes to cut out irrelevant footage, and correct any lighting issues. If video has been recorded over a long period – and some movies can take years to make – using different cameras under different lighting conditions may result in digital video with varied lighting. Using color correction tools help you analyze the video and match brightness, colors, and other attributes of video clips to create a smoother look to the video.

After editing all of the scenes, you can add logos or titles to scenes. For a foreign film, for example, you could add subtitles to translate the film into English. You also can add opening and closing credits, as a simple credit roll or a highly animated sequence. Video editing software provides templates for titles and credits, so that you can select a template as a baseline and then customize the font, color, shadows, and more. Some video-editing software even allows you to import text files listing credits to save production time and avoid misspellings.

You may want to add special effects, such as warping, zoom motion, or morphing. **Morphing** is a special effect in which one video image is transformed into another image over the course of several frames of video, creating the illusion of metamorphosis (Figure 4-23). Movies such

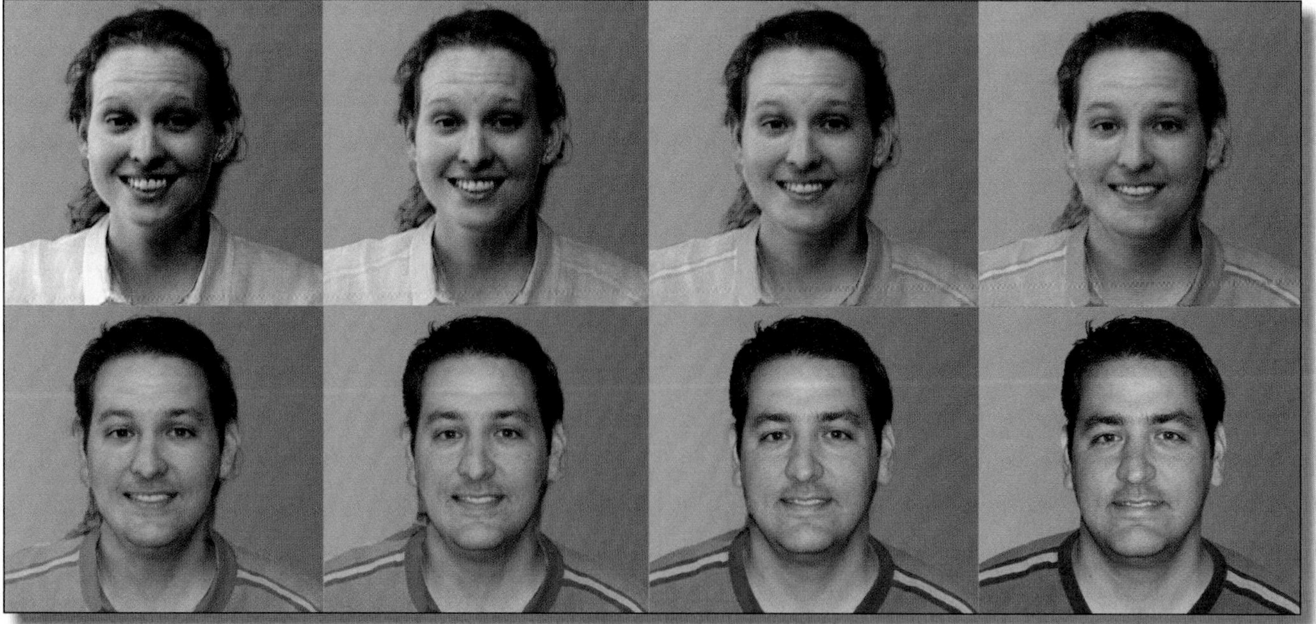

Figure 4-23 Morphing creates the illusion of metamorphosis over time, to allow for unique special effects in film and music videos.

as *Terminator II* and *The Mask* used morphing techniques to show humans changing into altered creatures and then back. You also can add animations to video to put new, entirely digital characters into a movie or television show. You will learn more about animation later in this chapter.

Video composition – the process of integrating two or more elements into one complete scene – allows you to frame a particular scene to make it more interesting. Video composition software, such as Apple Shake, provides tools that allow you to include visual effects such as sunlight, rain, characters, and more. Another step in the video composition process is combining (compositing) cartoon or other animated figures with realistic settings. In creating the *Lord of the Rings: The Two Towers,* editors used video composition software to integrate numerous visual effects, including live action from the set; computer graphics elements such as water, smoke, pine needles; digital lighting; and even the computer-created character Gollum. Some shots featured as many as 400 separate elements, which were integrated using video composition.

Video composition also is used to integrate special effects created using a blue screen or green screen, also called a chroma-key screen. The **blue screen** or **green screen technique** films the motion of the main subject against a blue or green background. The actual background scene later is filled in digitally. This technique allows actors and scale models to find themselves in totally imaginary situations – hurtling through the atmosphere in space ships, flying through the air, or scaling walls (like Superman and Spiderman) – and have it look completely real on television or in the theater. The same technique also is used to project a weather map full of computer graphics behind the meteorologist and to make news reporters look as if they are on location, when they never left town (Figure 4-24).

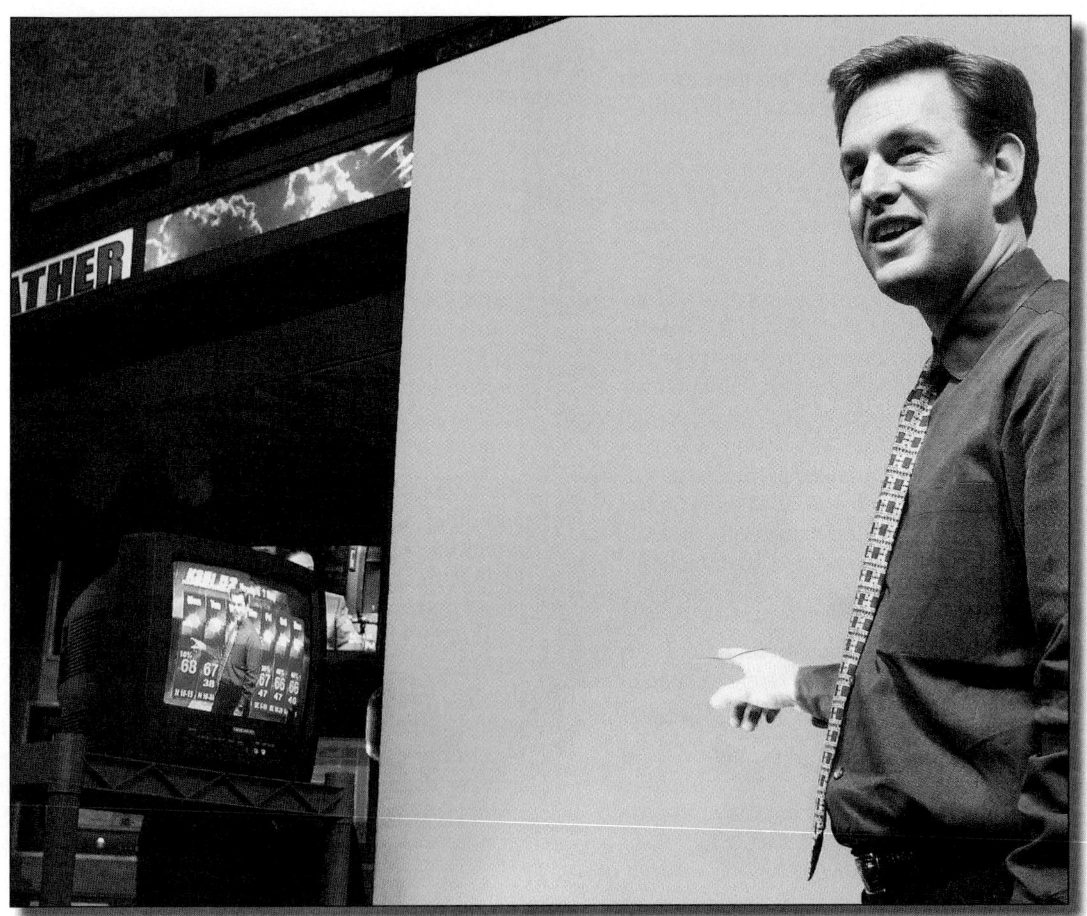

Figure 4-24 Meteorologists typically stand in front of a blue or green screen, not a weather map, which is added in the background using computer graphics.The digital weather map flow, with data and animation, is created before the meteorologists go on the air. Once they are in front of the camera, they click through a pre-programmed weather segment and narrate it. The weather segment, as well as the whole news program, is managed by the news director in the control room.

The next step in editing a video is to add audio effects, including voice-over narration and background music. Many video editing programs allow you to add additional tracks, or layers, of sound to a video, in addition to the sound that was recorded on the video camera. You also can add special audio effects. The final step in editing a video is to combine the scenes into a complete video. This process involves placing the scenes in order and adding transitional effects between scenes. Video-editing software allows you to combine scenes and separate each scene with a transition, such as fading, wiping, and more, to create the quick cuts between images and scenes that are the hallmark of today's commercial and music videos.

@ISSUE: Digital Video Editing: What You See Is...

In today's news and sporting events, computer graphics are a huge part of the experience. Thanks to advances made in computer technology, broadcasters easily can generate computer graphics within minutes to enhance a news story or to show key statistics from a football game. These computer graphics sometimes even become the news. For example, to accompany a story about tornadoes ripping through the Midwest a graphics editor quickly can create a computer-generated map showing the destructive paths of the tornadoes and the estimated damage. Or, instead of using video footage to report on a plane crash, an animation of how the crash occurred can be produced. In these situations, the use of computer graphics and digital video editing add to the viewing experience. Another type of graphics being added to broadcasts, however, is causing some concern.

To date, some of the best-known examples of video editing in realtime (that is, as the video is fed live to your television) can be found in professional sports broadcasts. During the Super Bowl, for example, viewers around the world saw a first-down line stretched across the gridiron. The line, however, was not anywhere near the field. Instead, it was a computer graphic created and inserted into the live feed of the broadcast. To help determine where to insert the orange pixels, several game cameras were fitted with sensors that tracked the cameras' positions and zoom levels. Adding to the illusion of reality is the ability of the computer system to account for people live on the field so that the line was occluded, or blocked, as a player or referee walked over it (not literally, of course).

Sports is using the same technology — referred to as a Live Video Insertion System (L-VIS) — to add still or video images to live broadcasts so that they look as if they are part of the original scene. What is the most common use? To place more advertisements in front of the viewer. Thanks to the L-VIS system, the Coca-Cola logo on the soccer field in a televised game may or may not be real. Using this same system, advertisers can target different portions of the audience with different types of ads — even on the same patch of grass. During the Super Bowl, Canadian viewers saw ads that featured the Global TV blimp — except Global TV does not own a blimp.

Virtual signage, as it officially is called, is increasingly noticeable. To create a virtual sign using the L-VIS system, a computer scans a wall or surface before a game. Another computer uses this scan to create a digital canvas where the graphics can be placed. At any point in the game, the computer can use its powerful video-processing engine to insert an electronic image in real time into any video stream, which causes about a 3 frame or .2 second delay (less than the delay introduced by a satellite uplink). When an object passes in front of the virtual ad, the computer compensates by occluding that spot on the ad, and the illusion is complete. Because it is just a part of the game, more people see the ad — including those who normally channel surf or head to the kitchen during commercials.

The alteration of reality is not just happening in sports and other entertainment programming, it also is part of the broadcast news. One of the first instances of altering graphics in the news occurred in 1994 when an ABC News correspondent supposedly was reporting from Capitol Hill after the President's State of the Union address. In reality, she was standing in her overcoat in the ABC news studio in front of a blue screen. Graphics editors added a backdrop of Capitol Hill behind the reporter to complete the effect. Although ABC contended that the deception was not intended to mislead and did not change the content of her report, it leads one to wonder why the alteration was even necessary. Would

(continued)

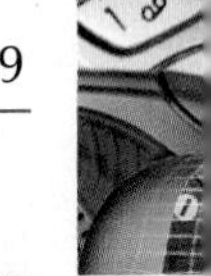

@ISSUE: Digital Video Editing: What You See Is... *(continued)*

fewer viewers have believed her story if they knew she was not standing in front of Capitol Hill?

A more recent incident occurred during the news broadcast of the 2000 New Year's celebrations in Times Square — when a virtual CBS logo triggered a debate about the ethics behind virtual signage. If you were in Times Square, you saw a Jumbotron screen with an NBC logo; however, if you watched the broadcast on CBS, they creatively had covered up the NBC-sponsored sign with a digital CBS logo in the background.

For many, while virtual ads in sporting events are annoying, the altering of the live video by a news organization is too much. Television news outlets, many contend, must present only true and accurate reporting in all instances, and viewers should be able to rely on the fact that the video footage they see behind a news reporter is real. Because the digitally inserted images seem incredibly real, viewers can have a hard time separating reality from virtual signage. Further, in another example of the CNN effect, most viewers do not doubt the validity or the reality of a news broadcast, especially when the footage they are watching is live.

While viewers are growing more savvy about what is real and what is a virtual first-down line, sign, or blimp, many note that no one has yet answered the question of when this digital technology interferes with the core ideals of television broadcasting. At what point does the use of digital graphic technology become a violation of journalism ethics? Critics note that news outlets have one core purpose — to inform viewers of the truth, not to market to them and or entertain them. As digital graphics technology continues to provide new tools to alter the images we see on television, broadcasters will find new applications to entertain, inform, and educate the public. The question, of course: how is the viewing public to know what is intended to supplement reality, and what is meant to replace reality? In a world where you used to be sure that what you saw was the real thing, now you may have to think twice. Is what you see actual reality — or a uniquely computer-generated fiction?

COLORIZATION Computers also have been used to **colorize** – that is, to add color to – black-and-white movies so that they appeal to modern audiences used to seeing color in movies. To add color to a movie, an editor must add color frame by frame, adding the colors one at a time to each part of the individual frame. Using computers helps to speed the process. First, the old film is scanned into the computer to create a digital version. An artist then can view the movie frame by frame on the computer. Using video-editing software, the artist draws the outline for each color area, and the computer fills it in.

To further speed the process, an artist may add color only to every tenth frame or just to key frames. Typically, in a movie or television show, the positions of actors and background objects vary little from frame to frame. Given that, the artist might manually color every tenth frame and let the computer fill in the frames in between in a process called interpolation. **Interpolation** involves having the computer software use algorithms to determine which colors to include between the manually colored frames and then automatically fill in the correct colors. As you will learn, computer animators rely on a similar technique – called tweening – to create realistic animations.

Just the opposite of colorization is **digital grading**. Using special software, an original film image can be color-corrected to enhance a scene that was too dark when filmed, or change the color of an object. For example, digital grading helped film makers change Captain Picard's face to blue as he was assimilated by the Borg in *Star Trek: First Contact.* It also was used in *The Lord of the Rings: The Fellowship of the Ring* to drain color from Boromir's face as he died.

Computer-Generated Imagery and Animation

The art of giving motion to objects is referred to as animation, or **computer-generated imagery (CGI)**. **Computer animation** involves using a computer to animate an object, either as a two-dimensional (2-D) or three-dimensional (3-D) object. New computer hardware and software has given computer graphic artists and animators many new tools to create more vivid, lifelike, and fantastic animations than ever.

As a 2-D animation artist, you draw an object or scene much as you would with illustration software. To create a 3-D animation, every object in the scene has to be sculpted in 3-D to form what is called a wire frame model. A **wireframe model** actually is made up of a mesh-like set of lines that follow the contours of the object. The object can be drawn or scanned using a 3-D scanner. The wireframe forms the basis for generating an artificial character. Skin, hair, scales, or other textures can be mapped on to the wireframe to complete the

digitally created character. The software then generates the actual still image of the object and adds the appropriate effects, such as shadows and reflections (Figure 4-25). The act of applying the final effects and textures is called rendering; depending on the complexity of the image, the rendering process can take a few minutes or more. Once rendering is complete, the final image is displayed on your computer screen.

Once you have the 2-D images or 3-D model, you must animate the sequence. A popular method called key frame animation is employed by most animation software, be it 2-D or 3-D. **Key frame animation** focuses on the key points, or frames, in an animation sequence (usually where the action starts or stops or changes course). For example, to animate a car driving off a cliff and crashing in the road below, the key points are the top of the cliff and the road. The animation software program can compute the positions between the top and bottom of the animation sequence in a process called **tweening**. The animator provides information on the key frames and the software tweens for all the frames in between.

Alternatively, you can use movements acquired using motion capture to provide lifelike moves for a 3-D animated character. Just as motion capture is used to create new dance movements, that lifelike monster in your favorite movie or computer game most likely got his moves thanks to motion capture. As moviegoers and

Figure 4-25 In 3-D animation, the wireframe forms the basis for generating an artificial character or object. Skin, hair, human or reptile skin, or other textures can be mapped on to the wireframe to complete the digitally created character or object. After specifying texture, lighting, and other effects, you render the image to create the final 3-D object.

computer gamers demand increasingly realistic action and animation in games, motion capture technology is allowing programmers to develop television shows, movies, and games populated by animated characters with natural, highly realistic human movements. In the 2004 movie, *The Polar Express*, Tom Hanks and other actors were filmed on a large motion-capture stage with nearly 200 cameras as they moved through their performances. The data collected was then used by animators to create the realistic images seen in the movie.

With animation software, the motion captured using a motion capture system can also be mapped onto a model to create highly realistic scenes such as sports games or battles with multiple animated characters. That realistic motion makes characters more believable and keeps moviegoers intrigued. Motion capture also gives video games star quality. By using motion capture to capture the movements and expressions of leading athletes, a game programmer can portray both the athletic and personal qualities of these stars and give the game player a chance to coach these stars.

The entertainment industry rapidly has embraced the dynamic technologies of CGI, 3-D animation, and motion capture. CGI is used in numerous movies today. In *Pirates of the Caribbean: Dead Man's Chest* and *Pirates of the Caribbean: At World's End,* the crew members of Davy Jones' *Flying Dutchman* are all made possible with CGI (Figure 4-26). The computer-generated crew members were blended with live footage, using CGI software and video-editing software to integrate the live footage with the computer-animated creatures. Computer-generated characters not only are modeled on real actors or animals; animators can create entirely new characters. For example, 3-D animation and motion capture was used to give the Pillsbury Doughboy lifelike movement and to add life to characters in Keebler and Monopoly commercials. Game programmers such as Sony, SEGA, and Microsoft are using motion capture to give fictional characters like Lara Croft hundreds of body motions.

Sports

Over the last two decades, computers have become as much a part of sports as the arenas and equipment used by athletes. CAD software is used to design all types of sports equipment, from sneakers to baseball gloves to

Figure 4-26 In *Pirates of the Caribbean: Dead Man's Chest,* CGI crew members were blended with live footage to make it appear as if the Flying Dutchman's captain and crew were interacting with the humans.

Formula One race cars. Computers also are used as virtual coaches and nutritionists. For example, using a specialized software program you can input details about your diet, exercise, and training plan, and the computer will output expert information on diet, fitness, and training schedules to help you improve your performance. Even the machines at the gym use computers to calculate the workout time, the calories burned, the effort expended, and so on.

Coaches and athletes use video cameras and motion capture to analyze and improve performance. With baseball, for example, pitchers or hitters can record their performances on digital video and play the video in slow motion to look for the smallest movement that might be affecting performance (Figure 4-27). The attention to movement detail is even more intense for gymnasts, in a sport where the slightest shift in technique can be the deciding factor between a gold or silver medal. Using motion capture, a coach can track the exact movements of an athlete's body during an activity – such as throwing a curve ball, jumping a hurdle, or completing a back handspring – and then compare the athlete's actual movements with the optimum movements needed for the perfect throw, jump, or flip. Their training movements then can be analyzed over and over again until the athlete has the technique exactly right.

Computers also are found on the field and around a course. For example, to ensure that every clock on the Olympic courses are in sync, many Olympic venues rely on clocks

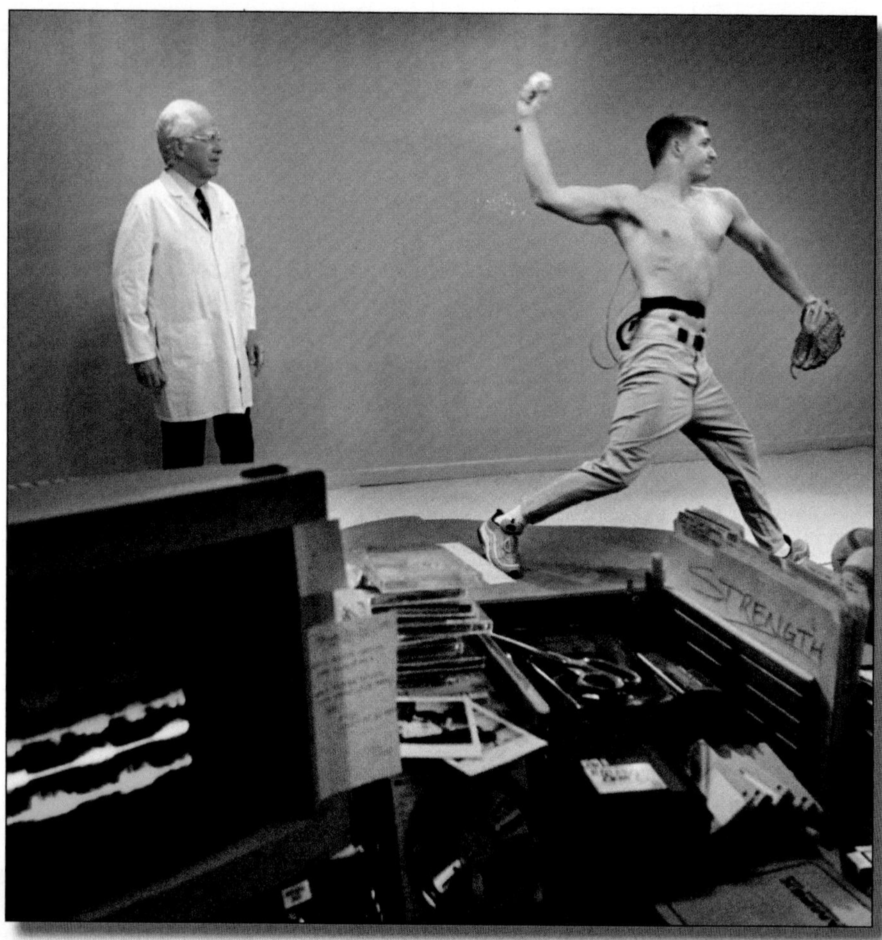

Figure 4-27 Using motion capture, a pitcher can track and analyze his exact movement during a pitch. The sensors are placed at key points to track movement which is then transmitted to and charted by a computer for analysis.

Figure 4-28 Marathoners and bikers rely on transponders strapped to their ankles or bikes to mark the time they officially pass the finish line.

coordinated by a GPS-based system that keeps every course on exactly the same time (except for the less than one second it loses every 20,000 years). Cross-country skiers, biathletes, and bikers have transponders strapped to their ankles or bikes to mark the time the athlete officially passes the finish line (Figure 4-28). The transmitters are synched with the GPS-based clock system to calculate an athlete's final time precisely; the same transponders are used to measure the split times along the course, which can be miles long and far from any television camera.

The advent and rapid improvement of virtual reality technologies even are becoming part of athletic and gymnastic training. The U.S. Olympic bobsled team already uses a virtual reality simulator so that they can practice their sport when no snow is on the ground. Virtual reality body suits also can allow you to learn new movements, such as a ski jump. The computer lets you rehearse a move by shifting your head to the left a fraction or tucking your elbows in just a bit. The virtual reality system adjusts to your actions and tells you when your moves would result in a crash or a perfect landing.

Some sports, such as ski racing, are using computer technology to create "skiing ghosts" that race alongside the real skiers on the race course. In this case, footage from the fastest skier in a race is superimposed on the course alongside the skier actually racing to give a head-to-head view of how the leader and the current challenger stack up on the turns. For obvious safety reasons, this could never be done in real life.

Even umpires can be aided by computer technology. A system called QuesTec Umpire Information System helps evaluate the accuracy of umpires calling strikes at home plate. The system uses cameras that record each pitch digitally from multiple angles and can isolate a pitch to within two-fifths of an inch. All of this data is recorded for each pitch during a game. Umpires can view pitch data, digital video clips, and batter snapshots on their laptops after a game to help them determine how accurately they called strikes and balls. The three-dimensional perspective allows the umpires to get a good sense of the true movement and location of the baseball (Figure 4-29). The system also can play back pitches in an animated 3-D environment, which includes a digitally created field and background designed to look and feel like an actual stadium. Many umpires are less than enthusiastic about the new system, but developers of the technology and baseball officials say the objective feedback will help make calls more consistent.

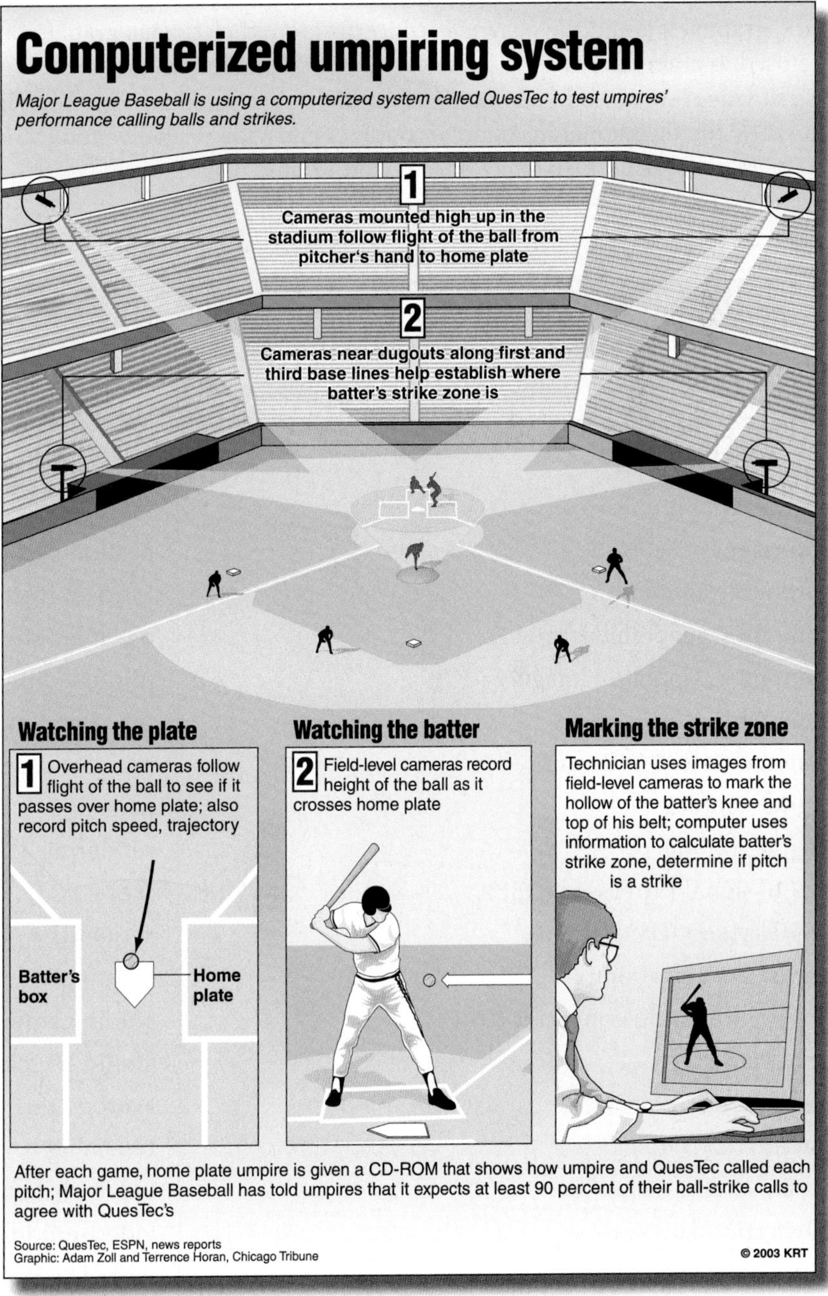

Figure 4-29 A system called QuesTec Umpire Information System records each pitch digitally to allow umpires to determine their accuracy in calling strikes and balls.

CONCLUSION

In this chapter, you learned how computers are used in the arena of arts and entertainment. After learning how computers convert analog data, such as music, to digital data, you learned how computers are changing every aspect of the music industry, from the way artists write and record songs to how they perform and distribute their music. The chapter also reviewed the use of computers in dance, and you learned how dance notation software, motion capture, and other computer technologies help dancers choreograph, record, and enhance their performances. You also discovered how computers are used in theater to help with set, costume, and lighting design, as well as ticket sales; and in sculpture to create 3-D models, control milling machines, and share telesculpture electronically. You learned how computers are used in the graphic arts to create a wide range of images, including computer-generated fractals. You also learned about digital photography, including how images are captured and edited to create unique photographic art, and the copyright concerns around electronic graphics and photos. You found out how computers are used in entertainment, with a focus on how television and movie creators use computers to capture and edit digital video, create computer animations, and colorize old movies. You also learned about the ethical questions raised by the digital manipulation of graphics and video. Finally, you learned about the use of computers in sports, to create equipment, help athletes train, and to time results.

Key Terms

analog-to-digital converter (ADC)
audio-editing software
blue screen
charge-coupled device (CCD)
colorize
computer animation
computer-generated fractal
computer-generated imagery (CGI)
copyright
dance notation software
digital camera
digital grading
digital signal processor (DSP)
digital video (DV) cameras
digital watermarking
digital-to-analog converter (DAC)
field camera
field DV camera
fractal
green screen technique
illustration software
image-editing software
interpolation
key frame animation
MIDI port
MIDI protocol
morphing
motion capture
Musical Instrument Digital Interface (MIDI)
music notation software
photo-editing software
point-and-shoot camera
point-and-shoot DV camera
pruning
rendering
score
sequencer
splitting
studio camera
studio DV camera
synthesizer
tweening
video composition
video-editing software
virtual signage
wireframe model

Chapter Review

Multiple Choice

Select the best answer.

1. A(n) _____ compresses digital data to save space.
(a) digital signal processor (DSP)
(b) analog-to-digital converter (ADC)
(c) musical digital interface (MDI)
(d) digital-to-analog converter (DAC)

2. Typically, music notation software allows notes to be entered by _____.
(a) typing notes on a computer keyboard or playing a tune on a MIDI keyboard
(b) clicking note buttons and then clicking them on to a staff in the score
(c) importing existing MIDI files or scanning printed sheet music
(d) all of the above

3. A _____ is a special type of serial port that connects the computer to an electronic musical instrument or other input device, such as an electronic piano keyboard.
(a) USB port
(b) MIDI port
(c) DAC port
(d) SCSI port

4. A sequencer is a software program or dedicated device that _____.
(a) generates an analog signal to represent the image
(b) uses mathematical formulas to create art with a vast range of structure, detail, color and light
(c) records, processes, edits, and plays back MIDI data through an instrument or computer speaker
(d) transforms one image into another image over the course of several frames of video

5. _____ captures movement as a series of symbols so that it can be shared with others.
(a) Dance notation software
(b) Audio-editing software
(c) Illustration software
(d) Image-editing software

6. Computer graphics essentially involves drawing pictures on computers, also called _____.
(a) tweening
(b) morphing
(c) pruning
(d) rendering

7. The most expensive and highest-quality digital camera is a _____, which is a stationary camera used for professional work.
(a) field camera
(b) point-and-shoot camera
(c) studio camera
(d) Web camera

8. The first step in the video-editing process is _____, which involves segmenting the video into smaller pieces that can be managed more easily.
(a) pruning
(b) splitting
(c) rendering
(d) morphing

9. _____ is a process used in colorizing films that involves having computer software determine which colors to include between manually colored frames and then automatically fill in the correct colors.
(a) Blue screen
(b) Video composition
(c) Interpolation
(d) Metamorphosis

10. To create a 3-D animation, every object in a scene is sculpted in 3-D to form a _____, which is made up of a mesh-like set of lines that follow the contours of the object.
(a) MIDI protocol
(b) wireframe model
(c) digital watermark
(d) computer-generated fractal

Chapter Review

Short Answer

Write a brief answer to each of the following questions.

1. How is an analog-to-digital converter (ADC) different from a digital-to-analog converter (DAC), and why are they necessary?
2. How is computer-aided design software used in the theater?
3. What is a fractal and how is a computer-generated fractal produced?
4. What is photo-editing software and how is it used?
5. How do coaches, athletes, and officials use computers to improve their performance?

Web Research

Use a search engine such as Google (google.com) to research the following questions. Then, write a one-page, double-spaced report or create a presentation, unless otherwise directed.

1. A 2006 survey of college students found that more than half downloaded music and movies illegally, accounting for more than 1.3 billion illegal downloads that year. After the recent Supreme Court ruling against Grokster, the RIAA stepped up its campaign to stop illegal music file downloading by students on college campuses. Use the Web to research the latest actions by the RIAA and some of the legal cases affecting the state of music copyright violation today. Given the aggressive stance of the RIAA and the success of online music stores such as Apple's iTunes, do you think illegal downloads will decline in the future? Why or why not? Knowing that downloading copyrighted material is illegal, why do you think people still engage in this activity?
2. A watermark is a barely visible image impressed on stationery that identifies the manufacturer of the stationery. A **digital watermark** is an invisible code inserted into a graphic, audio, or video file that identifies the file's copyright information. Use the Web to learn more about digital watermarks and how they are used to protect intellectual property rights on the Internet. What does the future look like for this technology?

Group Exercises

Working with a group of your classmates, complete the following team questions.

1. Digital cameras capture images as digital bitmapped files. Conventional film cameras capture images as transparencies on film. Although digital cameras make it easy to store, enhance, and share pictures, many photographers feel that, dollar for dollar, conventional film cameras take better pictures. Some estimate that it takes a 10 megapixel digital camera to produce the quality of prints available from a film camera. Have each member of your team visit a camera shop and compare a digital camera with a comparably priced conventional film camera. Consider the features of both cameras. If possible, compare photographs taken with each type of camera. Then, meet with your team, share your findings, and prepare a PowerPoint presentation showing the advantages, and disadvantages, of digital cameras versus conventional film cameras.
2. Computer-generated imagery (CGI) has been featured in many films. In some movies, the animation has had a leading role, as in the 2-D animation in *Beauty and the Beast* or the 3-D animation in the series of *Toy Story* and *Shrek* films. In other films, the animation has played a supporting role, as in *Jurassic Park*, *Titanic*, the *Harry Potter* series, and all three *Pirates of the Caribbean* movies. Have each member of your team screen a movie in which CGI is used. Consider the type of animation, how it is used, and how well it is done. Reflect on how CGI contributes to the film's story line. Could the movie have been as good, or better, without computer animation? Research the history of computer animation and CGI to gain an appreciation for what it takes to create such images. Then, meet with your team, share your impressions, and prepare a PowerPoint presentation that summarizes CGI and animation history, and shows how computer animation adds to, or detracts from, popular movies.

Computers in the Transportation Industry 5

Design and Manufacturing
- Design
- Testing
  - *Aerodynamics Testing*
  - *Crash Testing*
- Manufacturing
- Inventory Control

Automobiles and Trucking
- Inside an Automobile
  - *Fuel Injection and Other Functions*
  - *Antilock Braking System (ABS)*
- Collision Warning Systems
- Night Vision
- Smart Tires
- Entertainment Systems
- Smart Cars

On the Road
- Computerized Mapping
- Onboard Global Positioning Systems
- Telematics
- Route Optimization
- Electronic Toll Collection
- Intelligent Highways

Trains and Buses

Airlines
- Air Traffic Control
- Reservations and Ticketing
- Self-Service Check In
- Fuel Calculation
- Training Using Flight Simulators

Conclusion

Every day, millions of people — including you — travel from home to work, school, the shopping mall, or across the country as part of their daily routine. No matter what transportation mode you choose — whether a car, train, bus, or airplane — computers are behind the scenes helping to control the basic functions of the vehicle, controlling traffic lights, or providing communication to air traffic control to land the plane safely on the runway. The transportation industry also relies on computers to help design, test, and manufacture the wide range of vehicles that travel along the roadways, tracks, and skies. In the near future, computers also will be at the heart of highways that can track traffic and help reroute cars to reduce congestion.

In this chapter, you will learn more about the use of computers in the transportation industry. First, you will learn about how computers are used to help design, test, and manufacture vehicles. Next, you will learn about the use of computers inside cars and trucks to help control basic systems, provide early warnings about possible collisions, provide safety features, and new entertainment options. You also will learn about the future of computerized cars, called smart cars, and review the potential downsides of relying on computer automation to guide a vehicle safely. After learning about how computerized mapping, onboard GPS systems, and telematics help you navigate safely to your destination, you will learn more about how computers help with route optimization for truck fleets, electronic toll collection, and intelligent highways. Next, you will learn about how computers are used in public transportation such as trains and buses. Finally, you will learn about the use of computers in the airline industry, to handle air traffic control, reservations and check-in, fuel calculation, and training, along with the privacy questions raised by computerized passenger-screening systems.

DESIGN AND MANUFACTURING

Computers are used in all aspects of the design and manufacturing of automobiles, trains, planes, and other vehicles. Using computer technology helps companies design, test, and produce a vast number of new vehicles each year, each with new features. By relying on computers and other technologies to help support the production process, manufacturers can shorten development and manufacturing cycles, while lowering production costs and creating vehicles with better gas mileage and improved safety features.

Design

As you learned in Chapter 1, computer-aided design (CAD) is the use of a computer and special software to assist in product design. Many vehicle manufacturers use CAD to create graphics and models of a new vehicle on screen, so that they can modify a design, dynamically change product features, and perform calculations to optimize the design for production.

Using computer-aided design allows automobile manufacturers to take a more efficient and flexible approach to product design. For example, instead of creating paper or clay models of a concept car, designers can use CAD software to create many different, highly detailed three-dimensional models, showing options with different headlights, hood shapes, tail lamps, or other features. These highly detailed models even can show how the sunlight reflects off the vehicle's sheet-metal panels. After getting feedback from customers and executives, designers quickly can add, subtract, or combine features of several car models and then again review it with key stakeholders in the design process. The ability to make design changes quickly not only reduces cycle time (the time from idea to shipping product), it significantly reduces costs involved in reworking physical models.

In the airline industry, the use of CAD reached a milestone in 1995, when the Boeing 777 became the first airplane to be completely digitally designed from preassembled parts. The 238 design teams working on the airplane were linked from their computers to a large mainframe and, using CAD software, could review three-dimensional images of parts created by other teams. The teams also could simulate the assembly of those parts on the screen, easily correcting errors when two parts were misaligned.

Testing

One of the major benefits of using computers in the vehicle design process is the ability to test the design of a car, plane, train, or other vehicle before it is built. Sophisticated CAE (computer-aided engineering) programs simulate the effects of wind, temperatures, weight, and stress on various car components, to help engineers understand how the car will handle certain driving conditions. CAE software gives designers and engineers the ability to analyze designs in the early stages of the product development process, rather than after products are manufactured when changes are costly, time consuming, and even dangerous. For example, as discussed in Chapter 1, BMW engineers use CAE tools to analyze how components, such as axle links or wheels, will react under stress, before taking the time to build models of each component.

AERODYNAMICS TESTING Designers also use CAE to evaluate a vehicle as a total aerodynamic system. DaimlerChrysler, for example, has used computerized tools to help understand and redesign cars to reduce vibration noise caused by air being taken into and flowing around and through the car. To test aerodynamics of a car, plane, train, or other vehicle, designers use several tools, including wind tunnel testing and Computational Fluid Dynamics (CFD). **Computational Fluid Dynamics (CFD)** involves programming specific equations into computers, running simulations, and allowing the computer to analyze how the air (or any other fluid) flows over a shape. Using such models can help manufacturers create less wind resistant and more fuel efficient, quieter, safer vehicles.

A **wind tunnel** is a tubelike structure where wind is produced (usually by a large fan) to flow over the test object, such as a model of a car. The object is connected to instruments that measure and record the aerodynamic forces that act upon it. To use such a wind tunnel, designers quickly can create a small-scale prototype by using the CAD model as the input to a CNC milling machine. As you learned in Chapter 4, the software reads the models, automatically calculates the milling paths, and then guides the tools on the milling machine to cut the object, as defined by the model.

Another type of wind tunnel is a computer-generated wind tunnel, or virtual wind tunnel. A **virtual wind tunnel** is a software program that allows you to import a 3-D model of an object and then simulate the effects of wind as they would be in a physical wind tunnel (Figure 5-1). A virtual wind tunnel relies on CFD to predict how air will flow around a plane, car, or other vehicle.

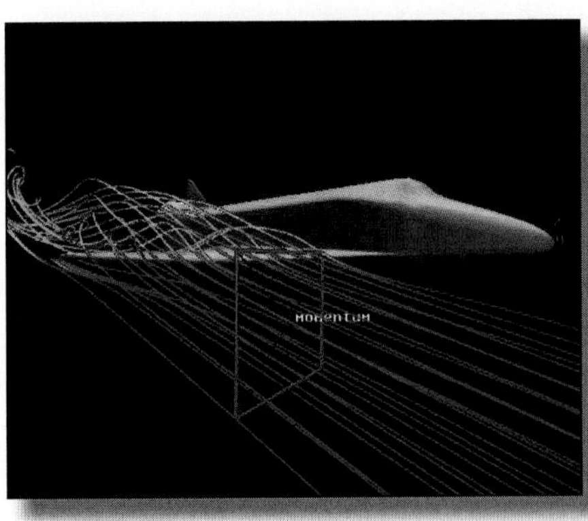

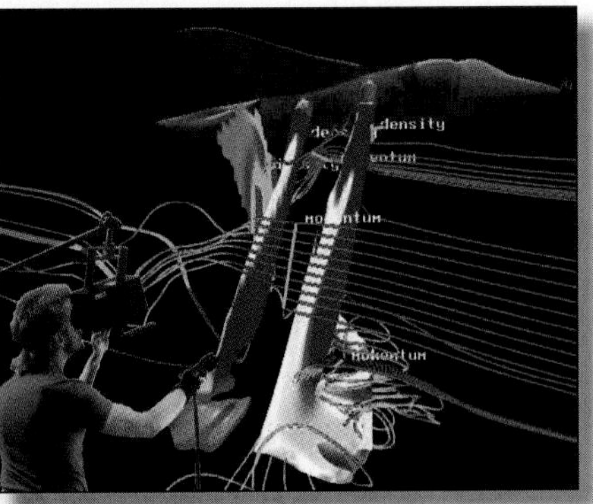

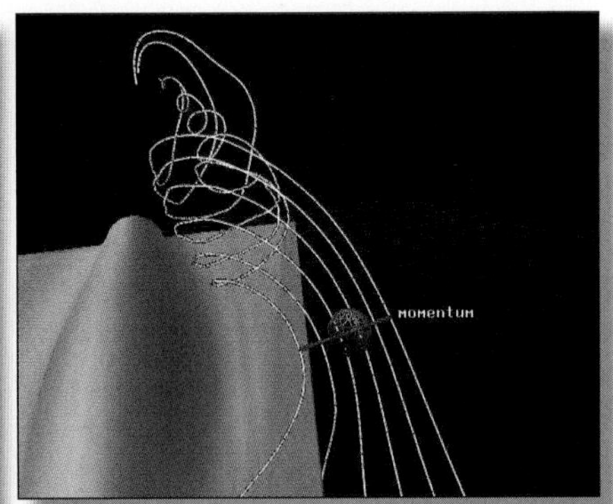

Figure 5-1 A virtual wind tunnel is a software program that allows you to import a 3-D model of an object and then simulate the effects of wind as they would be in a physical wind tunnel.

For pilots or race car drivers, being able to predict the performance of any vehicle under stress is critically important. Because actual testing in live situations can be very dangerous, pilots and drivers use CAE and simulations to test components and instruments. The simulation software even allows them to examine how individual flying or driving styles or a specific environment will affect performance. The drivers and pilots also use virtual wind tunnels and other training devices to ensure optimal performance.

CRASH TESTING Computers also are used to help test the damage a collision might cause to a car and, more importantly, its passengers. To conduct computerized crash analyses, engineers disassemble a car and weigh and measure each piece. That information is input into a software program that is used to create a computerized model of the vehicle. Engineers then can use the software to simulate the car crashing into another object, such as a tree, fence, or another car (Figure 5-2).

Running a car crash simulation, however, requires an enormous amount of processing power to take into account all of the possible inputs: acceleration, speed, road surfaces, car materials, number of passengers, types of restraints, air bag deployment, and so on. Most labs rely on supercomputers or **parallel processing**, in which the computing process is shared by two or more computers, in order to handle the processing load. A typical crash test might solve anywhere from five to thirty million equations simultaneously, so the parallel processing capability is essential. Additionally, some vehicle manufacturers will run close to 10,000 crash simulations a month, with most vehicle designs getting as many as 175 simulations. Even with the cost of the computing power, using computerized crash analysis

Results of a car crashing into a rigid barrier, such as a wall or post.

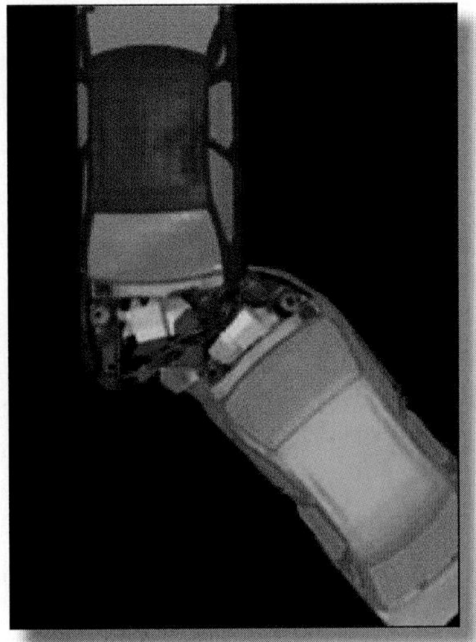

Results of a head-on collision between two cars.

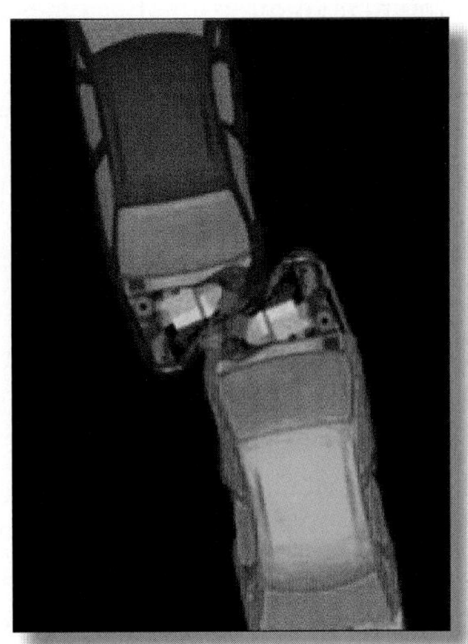

Results of a collision between two cars in which the front of one comes in at an angle to the front of the other.

Figure 5-2 Computerized crash analysis helps to test the damage a collision might cause to a car and its passengers.

costs around $3,000 to $4,000 per crash – a significant savings over the cost of crashing actual cars (around $75,000 per crash). Using computerized crash testing also provides a much more controlled environment, so researchers can isolate specific variables.

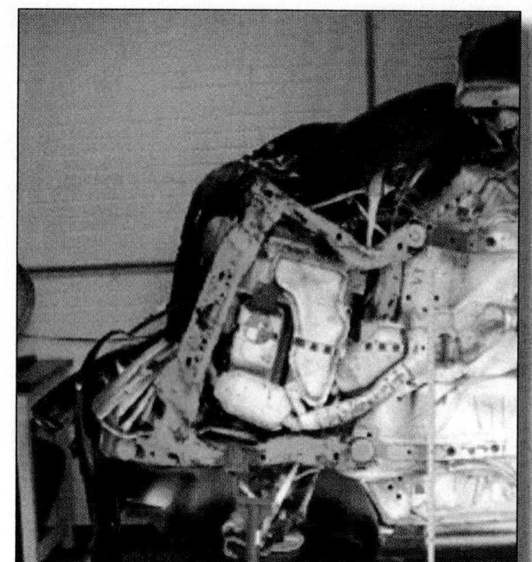

View of underside of test vehicle after two-vehicle crash. The tire at top is the driver-side tire.

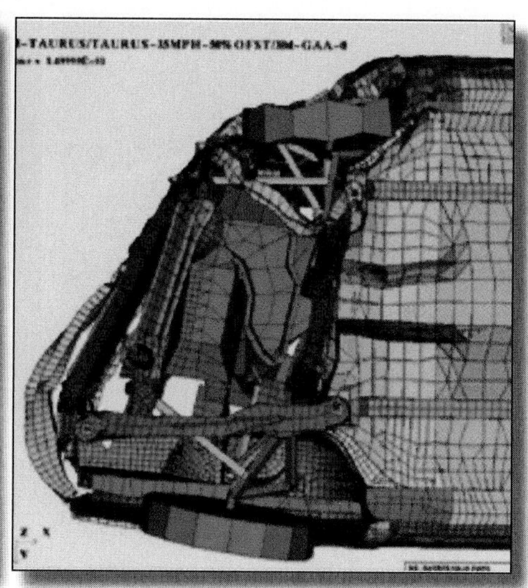

Simulated result of the test vehicle after a two vehicle crash is almost identical to the real crash.

Figure 5-3 If the computer crash models are sound, the results of a simulated crash very closely match real-world results.

The government recently has used car crash simulations, for example, to study the effects of collisions between sport utility vehicles and smaller cars and to determine the strength of guardrails. Similar crash analyses are used to better understand how lighter materials aimed at providing greater fuel efficiency can withstand crashes. If the models used in the simulations are sound, the computerized crash test results very closely match what will happen in the real world (Figure 5-3).

Manufacturing

Once a vehicle design is complete, fully tested, and approved for production, computer-aided manufacturing helps speed the process of creating the actual vehicle. As you have learned, the manufacturing process also relies on computers to direct the machines that produce and assemble a product – an approach to manufacturing called computer-aided manufacturing (CAM).

During the design process, digital assembly software shows the number of welds and the number of robots needed to assemble a vehicle, along with other tooling and fixtures. This allows the production lines to prepare adequately for the production of any vehicle. Further, the CAD design specifications can serve as inputs to CAM production equipment such as CNC milling machines, robots, software-controlled drills, welding, and tooling machines.

The assembly line in a manufacturing plant fundamentally is changed by the use of computers. Robots, for example, are used to help build various parts and assemble the finished vehicles (Figure 5-4). Robots are much more durable, faster, and efficient than humans and can complete tasks, such as welding or heavy lifting, that would be dangerous to humans. Although such robots are costly, the manufacturer benefits from the speed and reliability of the machines.

Inventory Control

As discussed in Chapter 1, a key challenge for a factory and its warehouse is to manage its inventory,

Figure 5-4 The assembly line in a manufacturing plant uses robots to safely complete a wide range of tasks.

so enough parts are available to continue production, but the warehouse is not left with overstocked parts that may become obsolete. Vehicle manufacturers rely on inventory control systems to track the current supplies of inventory and match this against anticipated future orders to ensure that enough components, such as rotors and engines, will be available to manufacture the shipment of new buses scheduled for delivery.

Vehicle parts suppliers and service technicians – including your local car repair shop – also rely on computerized inventory control systems to help them track thousands of parts for numerous makes and models (Figure 5-5). An automotive part inventory control system, for example, typically uses a database management system customized to keep track of each part, part number, stock on hand, inventory location, part manufacturer, unit cost, the selling price to the customer, and more. The inventory software generally also can store information on a specific collection of parts called a kit, which are needed to complete a job such as fixing worn out brake pads. By setting up a kit code, the repair shop can set up special prices for the kit, while being able to track the individual components in each kit separately.

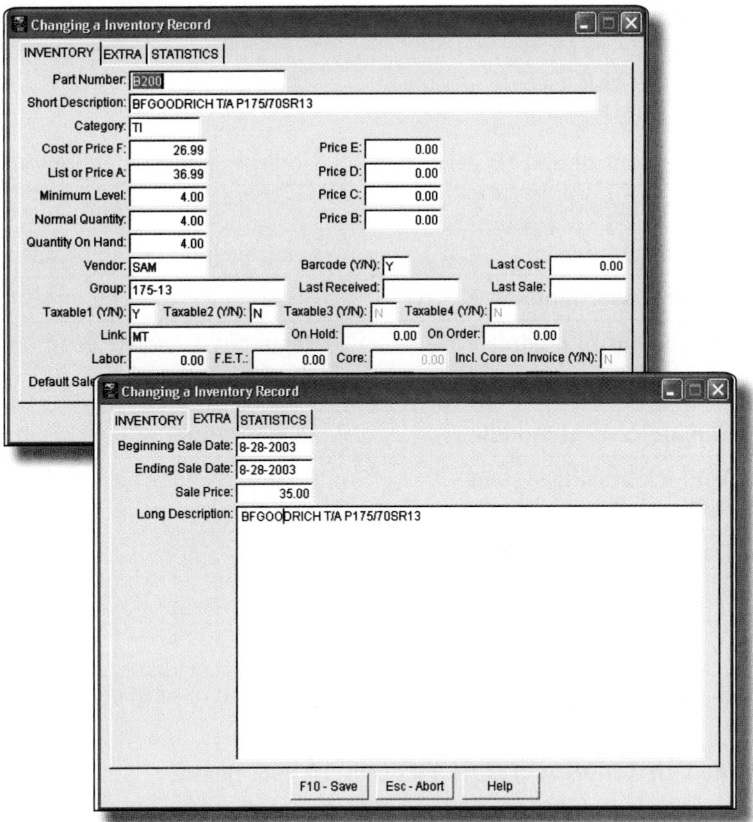

Figure 5-5 Automotive parts suppliers also rely on inventory control software, such as Auto Repair Boss, to help them track thousands of parts for numerous makes and models of cars.

AUTOMOBILES AND TRUCKING

Computers are not just used to design, test, and manufacture automobiles. They also are used to control numerous aspects of the car's basic functions. Computer-controlled devices in your car perform tasks such as ensuring the fuel is mixed in the correct amounts or displaying warning messages if you are about to back up into an object, such as a bicycle, parking meter, or another car. Other computer-controlled devices monitor your car's tire pressure to ensure they are inflated correctly. Someday soon computers may even help to drive the car, helping you to avoid collisions and maintain a safe driving speed and distance.

Inside an Automobile

The next time you get into your car, pay close attention to the sounds, lights, and other messages your car outputs to you. Computer chips are used to generate the chimes you hear when you open doors and press buttons. In fact, although you might think of your car as a largely mechanical machine, cars today actually are highly sophisticated machines with more than one hundred microprocessors used to control various functions and subsystems in the car. Figure 5-6 shows several of the key computerized modules used in today's automobiles; Table 5-1 lists each component, along with the functions it performs.

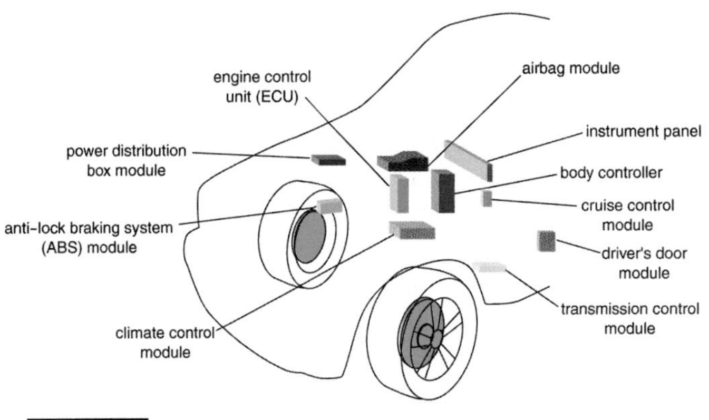

Figure 5-6 Today's cars use more than one hundred microprocessors to control various functions and subsystems.

Table 5-1 Computerized Vehicle Components and Modules	
COMPUTER COMPONENT OR MODULE	*CONTROLS*
Engine control unit (ECU)	Controls engine functions such as fuel-to-air ratio, spark timing, and so on
Airbag module	Controls airbag deployment
Body controller	Controls interior lights, door locks, power windows, power seats, and so on
Driver's door module	Communicates commands from switches on door to body controller
Cruise control module	Regulates speed while in cruise control
Instrument panel	Controls gauges and indicator lights using data from the communications bus
Climate control module	Monitors interior temperature and controls heating and cooling systems
Antilock braking system (ABS) module	Controls antilock brakes and may handle traction control and stability control systems
Transmission controller	Controls automatic transmission
Power distribution box module	Controls relays in the power distribution box

In today's vehicles, microprocessors are at the heart of subsystems that provide safe, comfortable, and efficient driving.

FUEL INJECTION AND OTHER FUNCTIONS Before emissions laws were enacted, manufacturers could build a car engine without microprocessors. As emissions laws became increasingly strict, cars needed more advanced control schemes to regulate the air and fuel mixture in the car and remove pollution from the exhaust. A microprocessor called an electronic control unit (ECU) provided this control. Today, the **engine control unit (ECU)** is the most powerful computer in most cars. It communicates with a wide range of vehicle components, ranging from the engine management systems and suspension control, to power window regulators and lighting systems.

The most processor-intense job performed by the ECU is controlling the engine. To do this, the ECU monitors the outputs of the car and then adjusts the inputs to the car accordingly. As you drive down the highway, the ECU gathers data from dozens of different sensors – monitoring outputs such as the temperature of the coolant or the amount of oxygen in the exhaust. These outputs serve as inputs to the ECU, which processes the data, checks against the ideal values in data tables, and then determines when to fire spark plugs, closes and opens the fuel injectors, and turns the cooling system on and off. These functions performed by the ECU are aimed at providing you with the best gas mileage, while reducing the amount of pollution in your car emissions.

The ECU is actually a small circuit board, much like the motherboard in your personal computer. It includes a processor and other components, such as analog-to-digital converters that allow the digital ECU to interpret outputs from analog sensors such as the oxygen sensors. The ECU also includes several communications chips and a **communications bus** to allow the various modules in the car to send data to and from the ECU. This communications bus works just like the communications bus in your personal computer, passing data to and from the central processing unit.

As the car runs, various modules in the car collect data: the ECU knows the coolant temperature and engine speed; the transmission controller knows the vehicle speed; the airbag module knows if there is a problem with the airbags. All of these modules send this data onto the communications bus to the ECU. Several times each second, the ECU sends a packet that contains this data (for example, speed, temperature, airflow) over the communications bus to the instrument panel. The instrument panel is programmed to look for certain packets. Whenever it sees a specific packet, it updates the appropriate gauge or indicator. A packet with the car's speed, for example, changes the reading on the speedometer, while a packet indicating low fuel will cause the low fuel light to come on. Other packets tell the car to generate a computerized voice telling you that your door is ajar or the headlights are on.

Another benefit of having a communications bus is that each module in the car can communicate errors or faults to the ECU, which stores the faults. A mechanic later can read the fault data using a special tool that connects to the diagnostic port in the car (Figure 5-7). This can make it easier for technicians to diagnose

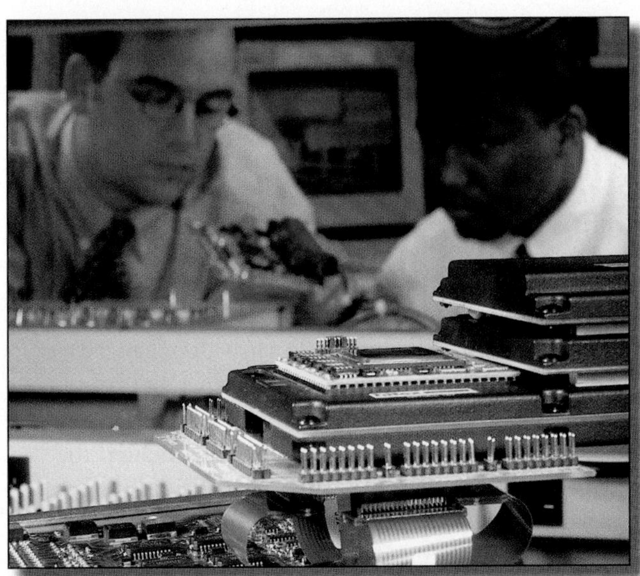

Figure 5-7 Each module in the car can communicate errors or faults to the ECU, which stores the faults. A mechanic later can read the fault data using a special tool that connects to the diagnostic port in the car and sends the data to a computer.

problems with the car, especially intermittent problems, which often are hard to describe and seem to vanish just as you take the car to the mechanic for repairs.

ANTILOCK BRAKING SYSTEM (ABS) Computer technology also is used to control the antilock braking system in your car. An **antilock braking system (ABS)** is designed to keep your wheels from locking up or skidding as you brake to slow down, so that you have more traction and control to steer the car out of harm's way. A simple ABS system relies on a microprocessor that serves as the ABS controller (Figure 5-8). The ABS controller continually watches the speed sensors, looking for rapid or unusual decelerations that indicate a car wheel is about to lock up and cause loss of traction. To help control the braking on any of the car wheels, the ABS controller sends messages to the brake valves to ensure the tire slows at the same rate as the car, which gives the car maximum braking power. With older cars, drivers were taught to pump the brakes to prevent the wheels from locking up. In a car with an ABS system, if you press your brakes hard in an emergency situation, you will feel a pulsing in the brake pedal as the ABS system rapidly opens and closes the brake valves, relieving the driver of the need to pump the brakes manually.

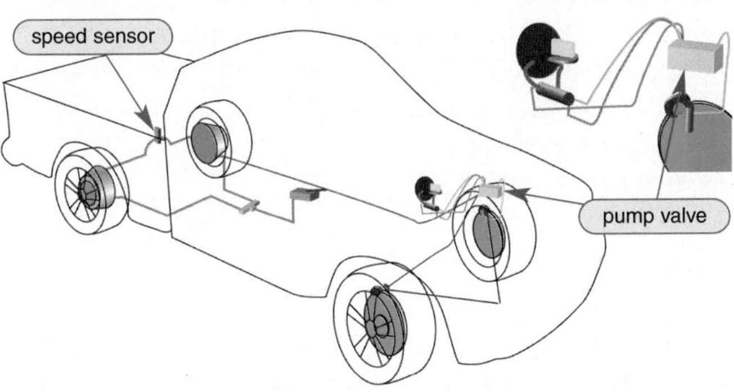

Figure 5-8 A simple ABS system relies on a microprocessor that receives input from the speed sensors and then triggers the appropriate action by the brake pumps and valves.

Collision Warning Systems

Although standard in many trucks, more and more cars are outfitted with **collision warning systems (CWS)** that alert the driver when the vehicle ahead is dangerously close or if the car is about to hit an object behind the car.

Cars and trucks equipped with a collision warning system have a central processor that sits above the engine block, as well as sensors on the bumper and below each door (Figure 5-9). The system uses radar

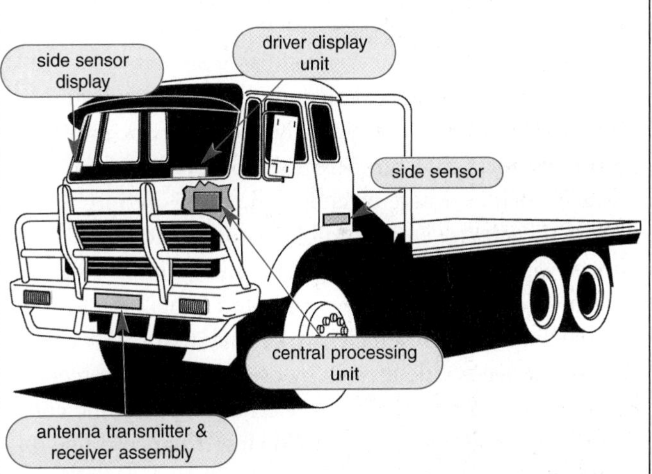

Figure 5-9 Collision warning systems (CWS), such as the Eaton Vorad Collision Warning System, can help warn cars and trucks about potential obstacles. The components include:

- Driver Display Unit: Installed in the dash or integrated into instrument cluster. Displays warnings and emits audible tones giving the driver additional time to take action.
- Antenna Transmitter and Receiver Assembly: Has a range of 350 feet to transmit information from sensors.
- Side Sensor Display: Displays lights on a pillar inside the cab and warns when a vehicle is alongside, out of the driver's view.
- Side Sensor: Detects vehicles alongside, out of the driver's view.
- Central Processing Unit: Determines if it should set off driver alerts at speeds from .25 to 100 MPH.

to detect objects up to 350 feet ahead, while other radars on both sides of the truck's cab pick up objects in the blind spots alongside the vehicle. When the radar detects a potential hazard, the sensor sends the data to the central processor, which in turn sends signals to the small display unit inside the truck cab. The driver display unit outputs a warning in the form of lights and audible tones at quick intervals to warn the driver to maneuver the car to avoid an accident (Figure 5-10).

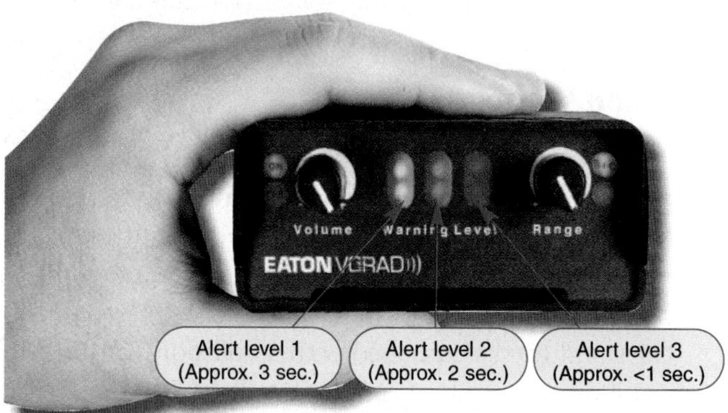

Figure 5-10 The driver display unit outputs a warning in the form of lights and audible tones at quick intervals to warn the driver to maneuver the vehicle to avoid an accident.

Also called collision avoidance systems, a collision warning system in a car typically uses a sensor mounted on the bumpers that can detect the proximity of an obstacle such as a bike or child. Like the CWS in trucks, the system emits audible beeps as the rear bumper approaches the obstacle. Some systems also flash a warning using ceiling mounted lights.

Truck and other vehicle owners say that CWS can help to reduce accident rates by as much as 70 percent. Further, drivers report that over time, they become conditioned to maintain greater following distances. The units, which cost around $2,500, quickly pay for themselves in the form of lower insurance premiums, fewer accidents and repairs, and lower fuel costs due to changes in the drivers' braking patterns.

Other work vehicles, such as snowplows, also will benefit from collision warning systems. In the midst of severe storms, drivers must navigate roads in low-visibility conditions that make road markings, guardrails, and even oncoming or stalled cars, almost impossible to see. Having CWS technology included in the snowplows helps warn drivers about potential hazards and helps to keep them safely driving down snow-covered roads.

New car manufacturers also are starting to offer collision avoidance technologies in their vehicles. In 2007, Lexus introduced an option in its LS460 model that actually lets the car *park itself*. By using bumper-mounted sensors that work in conjunction with its rearview mirror camera, the vehicle can parallel park without clipping the cars in front or behind, all the while displaying its progress on a touch screen in the car's dashboard.

Night Vision

Even more advanced computer systems soon may be standard equipment in snowplows and other vehicles, with the goal of providing the driver with enhanced visibility. Some cars have night vision systems that help provide a view of obstacles that otherwise would be unseen in the dark. The system, which is installed behind the car's grill, comes on at dusk automatically and uses an infrared camera to detect people or animals in the darkness or past the glare of an oncoming car's headlights. The system then generates a black and white image of the road on a small LCD display, which is projected onto the lower part of the windshield so that the driver can see it in their peripheral vision (Figure 5-11).

In commercial vehicles, such as snowplows, even more sophisticated systems incorporate global positioning systems (GPS), radar, onboard databases, and display units to provide a virtual image of the road, including unseen obstacles. The GPS allows the system to locate the snowplow within 25 meters, while radar tuned to a system mounted on a nearby transmission tower, helps pinpoint the plow's position that is accurate to within a few centimeters. Using the location information, the system accesses the onboard unit to provide images of road features, such as turns, intersections, and medians. Inside the snowplow, these images appear on a display unit in clear view of the driver, who can use the virtual image of the road to help navigate the snowy road surfaces in the midst of a storm.

Figure 5-11 A night vision system, which generates a black-and-white image on a small LCD display, shows any obstacles that might be in the dark ahead.

Smart Tires

Computers even monitor your tires as you drive. The SmarTire pressure-monitoring system utilizes a special wireless radio transmitter that is mounted to the tire rim (Figure 5-12). As you start to drive, an internal switch activated by the tire rotation turns on the battery-operated transmitters, which then transmit tire pressure and temperature to a receiver mounted in the car every few minutes. The receiver plugs into the cigarette lighter or other power socket.

When the pressure and temperture data sent from the sensors deviates from programmed levels, the receiver outputs a message to the display module to alert you to the problem. The message indicates the issue and which tire tripped the warning. The early warning gives you time to safely pull over and address the problem, whether it is a slow leak that will eventually wear down the tire tread, or under-inflation that could cause a blowout.

In the future, systems may be able to adjust tire pressure dynamically, depending on where you are driving. For example, logging trucks might have onboard computers that communicate via satellite to geographic information systems and weather databases. Depending on the terrain and weather conditions where the truck is driving, the system will be able to adjust the pressure in the truck's tires. By having tire pressure right for the road conditions, trucks can go faster and tires last longer (which means the system pays for itself in a few months).

Figure 5-12 The SmarTire tire pressure monitoring system utilizes a special wireless radio transmitter (a) which is mounted to the tire rim (b) and transmits tire pressure and temperature to a receiver mounted in the car. The receiver communicates with a display module (c), that displays information about problems.

Entertainment Systems

Advances in computers are not just focused on providing new safety features. They also are focused on keeping you and your passengers entertained as you drive. Most new family cars that come out on the market allow you to choose from a range of entertainment system options, including LCD monitors to play movies from a DVD player, video game units, and stereos that play MP3 music. If you want to watch a movie, you can pop a DVD in the DVD player, which is wired through the car's standard speaker system and to one or more small LCD monitors mounted in the ceiling or on the backs of the front seats (Figure 5-13). Passengers can listen to the audio using wireless headphones and even control the volume using their own volume controls. The in-car video game units, such as the Sony PlayStation, also are wired to the same LCD monitors and in-car sound system.

Car stereos that support MP3s allow you to record your MP3 files onto a CD-R or CD-RW disc and then play it in the CD player. Other options include using a

Figure 5-13 The COBY DVD entertainment system has a wireless remote control, an LCD display, and wireless headphones so passengers can watch movies while the driver listens to the radio.

cassette tape adapter, which looks like a normal cassette but has a connector to your portable MP3 player, such as an Apple iPod or Microsoft Zune. You put the cassette tape adapter in your tape deck, connect your MP3 player, and turn it on. The sound plays through your car's stereo system. Some newer in-car systems have replaced a CD changer with a 20 GB hard disk-based MP3 player, which requires you to download tunes from your computer to the MP3 player using a docking station. The newest crop of upscale vehicles comes with integrated iPod adapters, USB connectors, in-dash displays and databases to organize and manage playlists, and much more.

If these choices for entertainment are not enough, there is always satellite radio. **Satellite radio**, also called digital radio, works in a manner similar to regular car radio, but instead of signals that travel only 30–40 miles from their source, satellite radio signals are broadcast using satellites that are, for most services, more than 22,000 miles above earth. Because the signals are broadcast nationally, listeners can tune in to their favorite satellite radio station using a special receiver (Figure 5-14) without worrying the signal will fade on long road trips. Back in the late 1990s, the Federal Communications Commission (FCC) allocated a spectrum in the 2.3 GHz range for nationwide broadcasting of digital audio radio services. Today, three companies – Sirius, XM, and Worldspace – broadcast hundreds of different programming formats and choices to listeners around the globe.

Smart Cars

Today's cars have more and more sophisticated features to add to safety, comfort, and enjoyment. Many newer high-end cars have voice-activated control that uses speech recognition technology to allow you to complete tasks that otherwise might require you to turn your eyes away from the road – tasks like turning on the radio, adjusting the temperature, or dialing your cellular phone.

Cars of the future may have even more computerized functions to help enhance the driving experience. Cars with these new features – often referred to as **smart cars** – will rely on computers to make your car aware of your needs and preferences, road and weather conditions, and other external information, and then automatically modify its own behavior accordingly.

One relatively new smart feature available for cars and trucks is called adaptive cruise control. **Adaptive cruise control (ACC)** is a system that maintains a safe driving interval between your car and other vehicles by changing gears or by applying the brakes. Current systems use sensors much like those used in collision warning systems to determine the relationship between your car and other vehicles (Figure 5-15). The sensors use either radar or lidar. **Lidar**, which is short for "light detecting and ranging," is a technology used to determine location, position, and speed, much like radar. They key difference is that lidar uses lasers, not radio waves, to determine the range to an object (Table 5-2).

Figure 5-14 Satellite radio services provide vehicle owners a choice of dozens of radio station formats — from talk radio to classic rock — without the worry of static or fading signals during long road trips.

Figure 5-15 To help maintain a safe distance between vehicles, adaptive cruise control uses forward looking radar or lidar and then electronically adjusts vehicle speed. When traffic clears, the vehicle returns to the set speed.

Table 5-2 Radar Versus Lidar

RADAR	*LIDAR*
Acronym for RAdio Detection And Ranging	Acronym for LIght Detection And Ranging
Radar transmits radio waves into the atmosphere at a target, which scatters some of the power back to the radar's receiver.	Lidar transmits laser light at a target. Lidars operate at a higher frequency than radar, in the ultraviolet, visible, and infrared region of the electromagnetic spectrum.
Radar antenna sends out a short, high-power pulse of radio waves at a known frequency. The same antenna is used to receive the much-weaker signals that return.	The lidar's transmitter is a laser, while its receiver is an optical telescope.

Whether using radar or lidar, when the sensors in the adaptive cruise control system sense an object is too close, it will send a message to the transmission or braking systems to change gears or apply the brakes. Although many high-end luxury cars already have adaptive cruise control systems, the technology is not foolproof. Radar is more expensive to install than lidar, but the laser-based system often mistakenly interprets rain and snow as oncoming vehicles. Someday soon, however, adaptive cruise control and collision warning systems may use a range of sensors, digital video cameras and electronic control units inside your car to track other vehicles, adjust driving speeds accordingly, and keep you and your car out of harm's way. Similar technologies may actually steer the cars in safely spaced lines of cars on major freeways.

There are other projects under way in the smart car arena aimed at changing the way you interact with your car. One such project involves using cameras to allow you to simply point or wave to control your car. The system also has microphones attached to the driver's seat belt so that the vehicle's speech recognition system can accept verbal commands from the driver and an LCD monitor featuring navigation tips, your daily schedule, and even your e-mail. Other smart car features being developed include headlights that use sensors attached to the steering wheel and back axle to see around corners; improved night vision; and wireless communication with motorcycle riders through their safety helmets.

Finally, tomorrow's smart car will be able to use wireless communications to pass information between vehicles. For example, the car in the right lane next to you could send a wireless signal to your car to indicate that the driver intends to make a left turn, which would cut you off in the intersection. Knowing this, you can respond by slowing down and allowing him to complete the turn before you move through the intersection.

ON THE ROAD

Computers and other technological improvements have made everyone's driving experiences on the road a bit safer, less stressful, and more efficient – helping to ensure you actually can enjoy the ride. For example, a number of Web sites, such as Traffic.com, SmarTraveler.com, and local or state Web sites, provide updated traffic reports that highlight routes with congestion, construction, or accidents that might cause delays (Figure 5-16). Using computers allows you to generate printed maps customized to your specific route, rely on

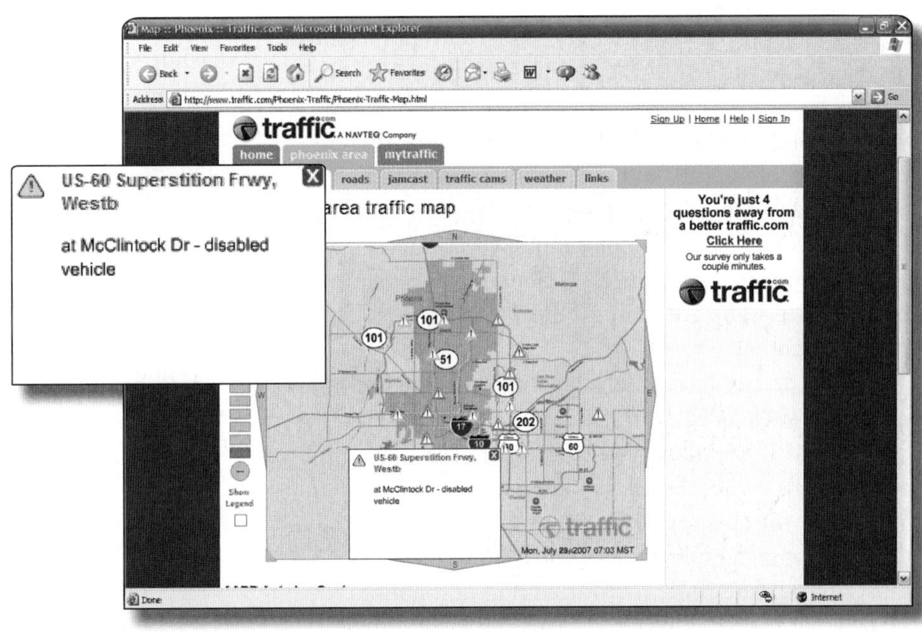

Figure 5-16 Web sites, such as Traffic.com, SmarTraveler.com, and local or state Web sites, provide updated traffic reports 24 hours a day.

real-time directions communicated from your GPS system, or even contact a call center for directions to the nearest gas station; truck drivers even use computers to determine the most efficient route to their drop off location.

Other computer systems, such as electronic toll booths and intelligent highways help you to move quickly – and safely – to your destination. These applications, and some of those discussed below, are simply a small part of a movement toward **Intelligent Transportation Systems (ITS)**, which is the application of computer, communications, and electronic technologies to help improve transportation by making it safer and more efficient.

Computerized Mapping

Planning an automobile trip used to require that you pore over printed maps and manually calculate the distance between your starting location and your destination. Determining the actual mileage or driving time was difficult. You would have to reference a different resource to find overnight accommodations along the route. Now, you quickly can get directions from your starting point to your destination location using trip planner and map Web sites such as FreeTrip.com, Google maps, MapQuest, or MapBlast.com (Figure 5-17). When you use one of these Web sites, you simply input a starting location and ending destination and then indicate your preference for either a scenic route or the shortest distance route. These Web sites use your input to query a vast database of geographical information and search for the most appropriate route to your ending destination. The resulting map then is displayed on the Web site for you to save, print, or even download to your PDA. Some automobile clubs, such as the American Automobile Association (AAA), have Web site features that allow you to generate printed maps that show scenic drives, restaurants, shopping, and motel, hotel, and bed-and-breakfast accommodations along the desired route. Whether for a long trip – or simply to get directions to your friend's new apartment – online map sites have taken much of the guesswork out of driving from one place to another.

If you do not have Internet access, mapping software programs such as Microsoft Streets & Tips or DeLorme Street Atlas USA, allow you to generate the same types of maps or driving directions (Figure 5-18). Like map Web sites, the software uses your input to query a vast database of geographical information and search for the most appropriate route to your ending destination. Depending on the number of maps available for the program, the maps might be stored on your hard drive or on a CD-ROM or DVD-ROM.

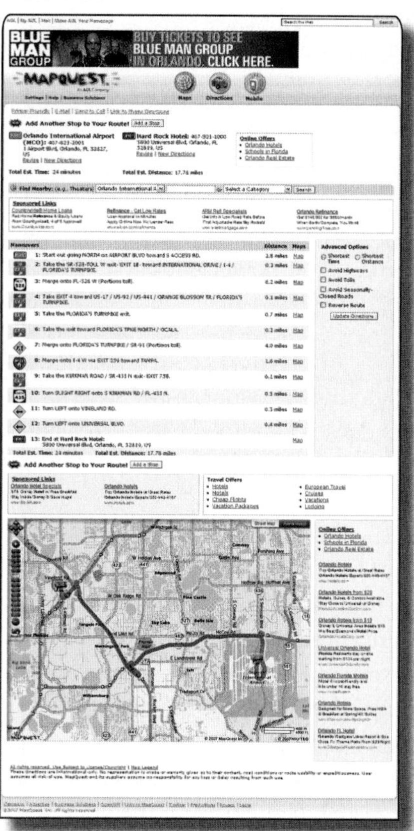

Figure 5-17 Map Web sites such as MapQuest allow the user to get driving directions between two locations — including tourist attractions, hotels, airports, and more.

An exciting new use of maps on the Internet is the creation of "mashups." A **mashup** is a map overlayed with information about anything that might be located within that map's region. The items located on the mashup map appear as little bulbs pointing to spots on the map, and the information about each spot can be retrieved by clicking the little bulb. Mashups exist for mapping restaurants, crimes in a neighborhood, parking spots in a city, the whereabouts of singles in an urban area, traffic conditions, and lots more.

Onboard Global Positioning Systems

Some people like to have a real-time navigation aid, such as a global positioning system (GPS) device, instead of a printed map. For example, if you are the only person in the car, it is difficult, not to mention dangerous, to read a printed map while driving. Further, if your travel plans change, the map instantly becomes obsolete. With a GPS device, also referred to as an onboard satellite navigation system, your car's current location can be tracked at any point, based on the signals sent to and received from the GPS satellites around the globe. The GPS device, like other GPS receivers,

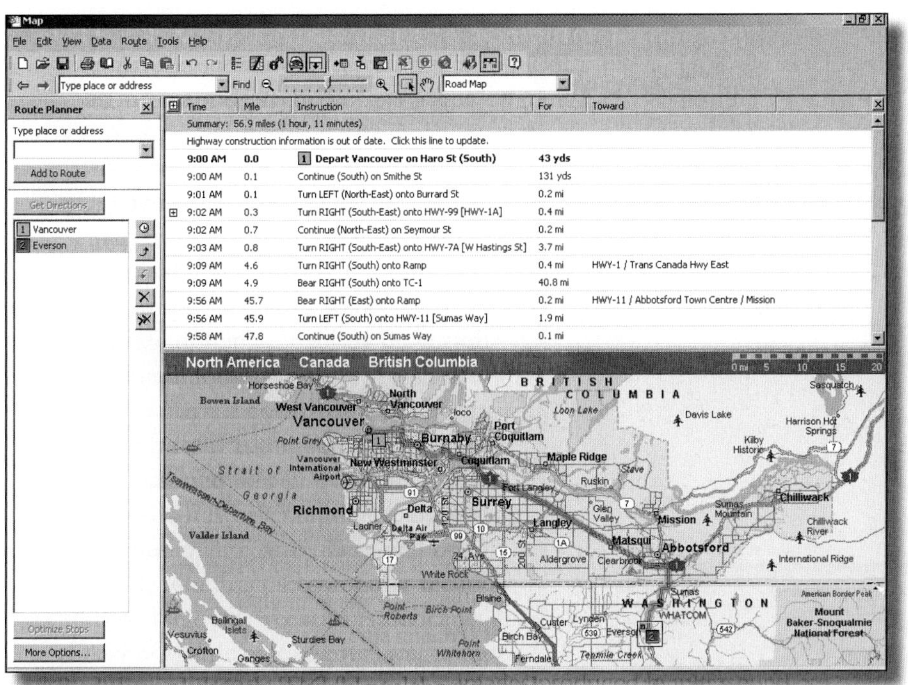

Figure 5-18 Mapping software programs such as Microsoft Streets & Trips allow the user to generate computerized maps or driving directions. Some packages even connect to the Internet to update construction information that might affect your route.

includes a display unit to output key information about your location; many onboard navigation systems also use voice output so you can keep your eyes on the road (Figure 5-19). Currently, about 1.5% of new car buyers opt for this upgraded feature.

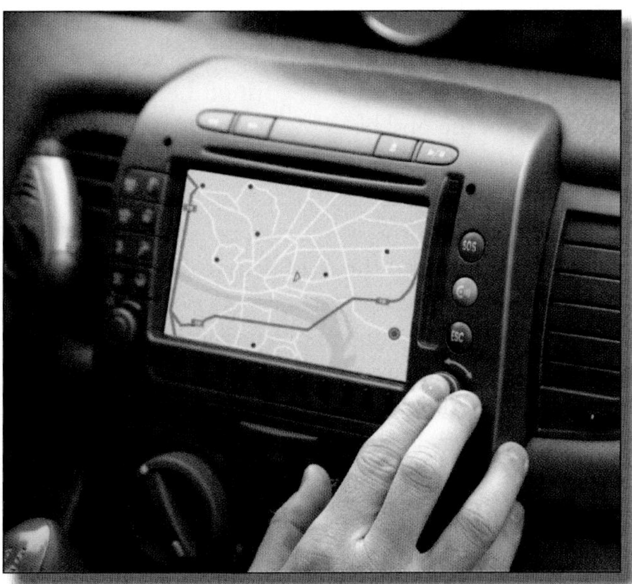

Figure 5-19 A GPS system in your car includes a display unit to output key information about your location, as well as voice output, so you can keep your eyes on the road.

To get started, you can input a destination location to a specific address, an airport, or other attraction. The navigation system determines your current location and then automatically creates a route to your destination location. As you drive, the navigation system uses GPS signals to monitor your location along the route. As you come within a certain distance of a turn or highway exit, it will indicate this to you on the display and via voice output – for example, telling you that you should make a right turn in 1.2 miles. If you drive off the calculated route, the navigation system will determine your location and recalculate the route needed to get you back on track. Having real-time, turn-by-turn directions voiced to you as you drive makes it easier than ever to navigate in unfamiliar areas with confusing roads.

Onboard navigation systems were first introduced as an optional feature in luxury vehicles and rental cars. Today, navigation systems cost less and are more widely available, which means they soon may be standard equipment in more cars. Some navigation systems are built right into the control panel, while others are stand-alone units installed after the car is manufactured. Alternatively, you can install special GPS software on your handheld or laptop computer to give it the features of a built-in GPS system that provides directions to any destination's location you need.

GPS devices also are used to track fleets of commercial trucks as they haul goods to their destination. A simple GPS tracking device is placed in the cab or trailer. The corporate office can track the location of any truck using a Web-based interface (Figure 5-20). The system also allows them to determine if the truck currently is moving or stopped.

Telematics

Telematics is an emerging technology field that combines computers, location-sensing technology, such as GPS, and wireless data in a car. One specific type of telematics, referred to as **call center telematics**, also rely on a cellular connection to a call center staffed with a limited number of people. The OnStar system, which uses a cellular phone-based system to connect

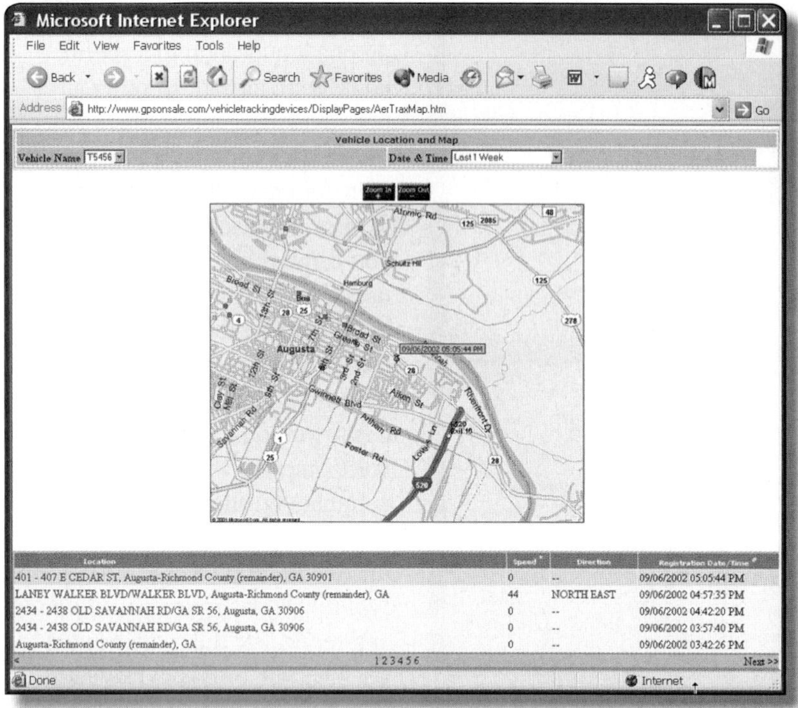

Figure 5-20 GPS devices also are used to track fleets of commercial trucks as they haul goods to their destinations. A simple GPS tracking device is placed in the cab or trailer. The office can track the location of any truck using a Web-based interface.

you with a live operator, is perhaps the best-known example of call center telematics. With the OnStar system, for example, you press a button in your car (often on or near the rearview mirror) to request a connection with an OnStar advisor in a remote call center (Figure 5-21). The advisor, who immediately can locate your car based on the GPS coordinates, can help by giving you directions to a nearby gas station, dispatch emergency vehicles if you have an accident, or even call ahead to make reservations at restaurants. The telematics system even can read any system data stored in the engine control unit to determine why your car broke down or if the air bags deployed during an accident. The OnStar advisor then can contact and route roadside assistance to your location. In the event of an accident, they determine if airbags have deployed and will dispatch emergency assistance if necessary. In the case of a breakdown, they can also guide a roadside assistance response vehicle to the car's location. If you are locked out of your car, you even can place a call to OnStar to have them unlock your car remotely.

While OnStar is a GM-branded call center telematics system, other car manufacturers provide similar systems under different brand names (BMW's service, for example, is called BMW Assist). These services do charge a fee. Subscriptions start at about $17 per month for basic service.

voice connection
air bag deployment
crash severity info
data transmission

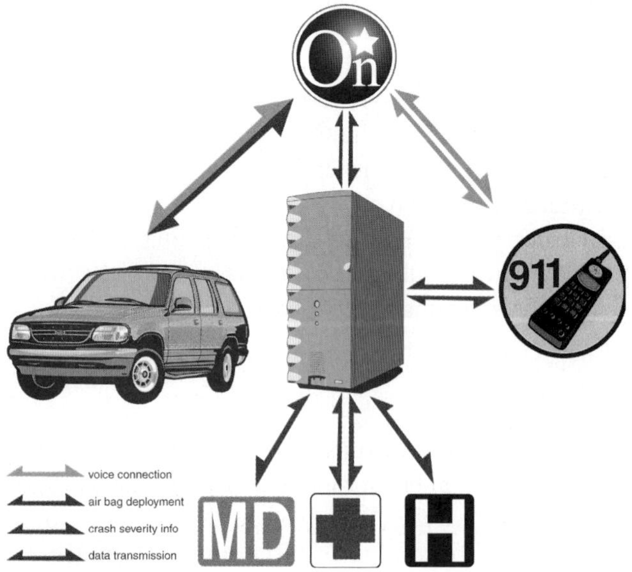

Figure 5-21 With the OnStar system, you press a button in your car to connect to an OnStar advisor over a cellular radio-based system.

Someday soon, even more advanced automotive telematics systems might be able to communicate directly with your service center and send fault data stored in the engine control unit to the service center computers. Based on this information, the automotive technician can greet you at the service desk with a printout of the data from your car, along with a list of the parts required to fix the problem.

Route Optimization

As you drive down the road next to a truck, consider the job at hand: getting the load of goods to the right location in as timely a manner as possible, while minimizing the total distance traveled by company vehicles. Even a veteran truck driver cannot possibly know the best route to every delivery location. Trucking companies thus use computers and route optimization software to ensure that their truck drivers are taking the best route to their locations and hitting locations in the appropriate sequence (Figure 5-22). In the past, most truck drivers and companies relied on a manual system for planning delivery routes – using paper maps and estimated travel times to determine the best delivery routes. A computerized route-optimization program,

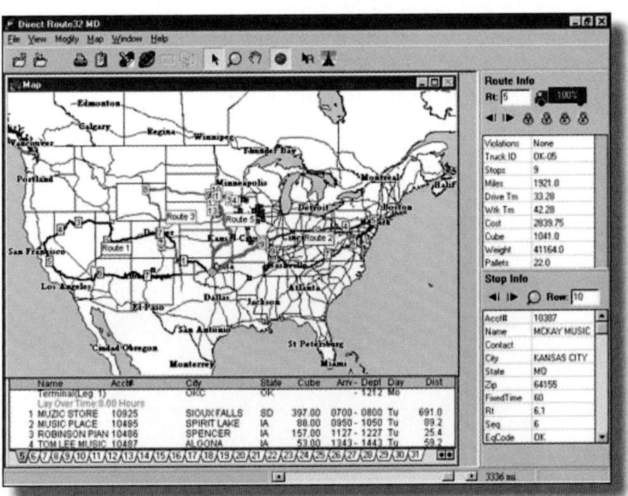

Figure 5-22 Trucking companies use computers and route optimization software such as Direct Route to ensure that their truck drivers are taking the best route to their locations and hitting locations in the appropriate sequence.

however, can schedule drivers and optimize routes based on customer locations and types, road network distances, vehicle costs and capacities, and time windows for delivery and more. The map databases utilized by the software systems also include information about which roads are restricted to certain types of vehicles, to ensure truck drivers do not try to drive on a road with low underpasses or bridges. These software packages often also calculate fuel consumption based on the suggested route, along with other costs, such as tolls.

Some of these state-of-the-art truck systems also include a satellite communications link with the company headquarters. Information on troubleshooting mechanical problems, directions, weather reports, and other important communications can be delivered to the truck from anywhere in the country in a matter of seconds. This keeps the trucker in communication with the dispatcher to discuss delivery schedules and courses of action should there be bad weather or mechanical problems. It also allows the dispatcher to track the location of the truck and monitor fuel consumption and engine performance.

Electronic Toll Collection

Every day, on highways around the world, millions of car and truck drivers pass through toll booths on their way to and from their destination. Some systems have workers who take the tolls by hand; other toll booths use automated baskets that tabulate the coins you toss in a basket and then open a gate to let you pass through. While the latter is faster than the former, both require you to find toll money, come to a stop, pay the toll, and then pass through the toll booth.

To help speed up this process, many of today's toll roads use an electronic toll-collection system that detects and processes tolls electronically (Figure 5-23). An **electronic toll-collection system** uses a vehicle-mounted transponder that stores your account information. The **transponder** is a small battery-operated, radio frequency identification (RFID) unit that you attach to your car windshield. The transponder, which you may have to purchase, stores basic account information, such as an identification number.

Antennas are positioned above each toll lane to emit radio frequencies that communicate with the transponder. As you pass through the toll lane, an antenna activates the transponder, identifies the transponder, and reads your account information. To ensure that all cars are counted and billed accurately, some electronic toll-collection systems also use a light curtain and treadles. A light curtain is a beam of light directed across a lane. When that beam of light is broken, the system knows a car has entered. Treadles, which are sensor strips embedded in the road, detect the number of axles on a vehicle so the vehicle is charged the correct toll. After

Figure 5-23 Many of today's toll roads use an electronic toll-collection system that detects and processes tolls electronically (a). To use the system, you need a transponder (b) that stores basic account information, such as an identification number.

deducting the toll amount from your prepaid account or credit/debit card, a lighted display or a gate opens, indicating that the toll has been paid.

All of the lanes in the electronic toll-collection system are networked together. Each lane has a **lane controller**, which is a computer that controls the lane equipment and tracks vehicles passing through. All of the lane controllers at a toll plaza are connected on a local area network (LAN). The toll plaza LANs are connected to a central database via a wide area network (WAN). The database stores the identification number and other information about each transponder along with key customer information and the desired payment method.

Different states use various types of electronic toll-collection systems, including E-ZPass, Fastrak, Sun Pass, and TxTag, but all work in largely the same way. Using these systems can help speed traffic through otherwise congested toll plazas. Even though drivers have to slow down to use the toll booths (optimal tag reading speeds range from a few miles an hour to up to 55 MPH on highways serviced by E-ZPass that have special express lanes without toll booths), you do not have to stop to deposit the payment, nor do you have to worry about finding change. At this point, however, the various systems used by the states are not compatible, so you may find yourself back in the cash only lane once you cross state borders.

Intelligent Highways

As you drive to class or work, especially if you are on a major highway, look at the various technologies in place to help track and control traffic. For example, the sensor loops used to trigger a red-light system at an intersection also are placed in roads throughout the country to help determine traffic speed. Recall that the sensor loops are a length of electrical wire buried just under the asphalt. The wire is charged with an electrical current to generate a magnetic field. When a car passes over the sensor loop, it changes the magnetic field. By monitoring these changes and determining how quickly cars pass between sensor loops, transportation officials can determine traffic speed. This data on the number of cars and traffic speed is transmitted to a central computer, which is monitored by local transportation departments. If the data suggests that traffic volume is very high or cars are slowing significantly, the transportation department can watch live footage from video cameras along the road to understand exactly what the source of the problem is (Figure 5-24). Local television stations also can broadcast live feeds from the cameras. Officials then can provide up-to-the minute messages on dynamic message signs (the same ones used to display AMBER alert messages) to alert drivers to congestion ahead and suggest alternate routes (Figure 5-25).

As new technology becomes available, transportation officials are looking for new, less expensive ways to

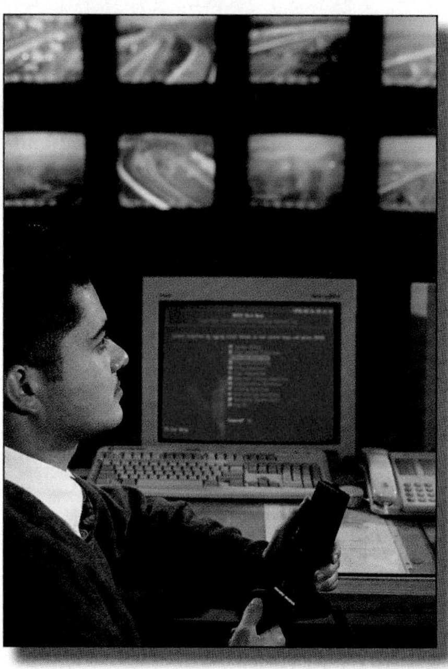

Figure 5-24 From this room, the transportation department can watch live footage from video cameras along interstates for incidents that could create traffic problems. This immediate view helps provide better information on the source of the problem, which means better information can be communicated to travelers.

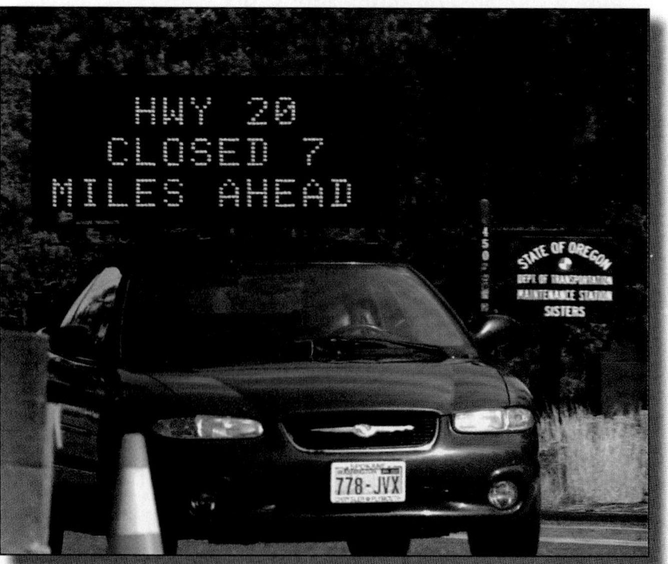

Figure 5-25 With intelligent highways, transportation officials will be able to provide up-to-the minute messages on dynamic message signs to alert drivers to congestion ahead and suggest alternate routes.

track traffic flow and communicate potential trouble spots to drivers. One possibility is to use the radio frequencies emitted by cell phones to track where drivers are on a highway and determine traffic patterns using that data. Other systems would track the radio signals from small RFID devices, such as the transponders used in electronic toll-collection systems. For example, in a system called Cellocate, a small battery-powered RFID device would be placed in your car. Receivers called listening posts are placed on towers or high buildings. As you drive past a listening post, it collects data from your RFID device and sends it to a central server. The server calculates your location and then sends this information back to the user, who can access your vehicle location via a Web site or a software program interface. Both systems, however, have created privacy concerns, because they make it possible for a company or agency to track you wherever you drive.

As information is collected from these systems, the data would be stored in a large database that would be accessible over the Web. You could query the Web site database for information on a specific route to get map-based information about where the roads are congested. Cell-phone service providers also could call you with a customized traffic report, based on the road and direction in which you are traveling.

@ISSUE: How Smart, How Safe?

Without question, computers and technology have helped to provide numerous safety and control features to almost every type of transportation, from cars to trains to planes. Collision warning systems in cars and trucks help reduce accidents, while trains rely on computerized systems to keep them on the correct routes. Modern airplanes rely on **fly by wire** technology, which means that computers on the plane transmit the pilot inputs into electrical signals that are sent through wires to control landing gear, spoilers, and other components of the planes. The computers make the job of the pilot easier, for example, by automatically trimming the plane even when it is being flown by the pilot.

And yet, despite the numerous safety benefits computers can bring to transportation, some people have reservations about using technology to replace human intellectual abilities. Others have concerns that, with the computers in command, humans might lose control and have no way to override the computer in the event of computer malfunction or another emergency. Still others question how to protect these systems and their infrastructure from hackers or others who might intentionally introduce bugs into the system in order to cause others harm.

In some cases, computer system issues are merely frustrating, as in the case of the collapse of the air traffic control service in Britain in April 2002. After a computer handling the flight data failed, air traffic controllers had to keep track of aircraft using paper and pen, thus leaving many planes temporarily grounded. In another example, a 24-inch snowfall caused one street traffic light to stay red continually, because the sensor loops buried under the snow could not sense cars and thus never sent data to tell the computer to change the light to green. Frustrated motorists simply ran the red light, thus adding one more driving hazard on a snowy street.

In other cases, computer system issues can prove more serious — and even fatal. For example, in December of 1995, an American Airlines Boeing 757 hit mountainous terrain while attempting to perform an escape maneuver. The crew had accepted a straight-in arrival approach to Cali Runway 19, but the crew was not familiar with the arrival they were given. Confused over the clearance, the crew spent valuable time trying to program the flight management computer to fly the clearance they thought they had been given, which caused the aircraft to turn left away from the arrival path. When the crew noticed it 90 seconds later, they tried to recover, but a continued descent caused them to crash into a mountain. In this case, a confusing human-computer interface proved deadly. More than 160 lives were lost.

In some cases, man's distrust of the machines is actually the source of the issue, as evidenced in the crash of a British Midlands flight in January 1989. The plane suffered a failure of a fan blade in the left engine. Although the cockpit instruments correctly indicated that the severe vibration was coming from the left engine, the pilots' distrust of the instruments led them to disbelieve instrument readings and incorrectly diagnose that the problem was with the right engine. The crew shut down the wrong engine and then attempted an emergency landing. The plane, relying solely on the single engine with the fan blade failure, landed short of the runway in a crash in which 47 of the 126 people on board died.

Even if the systems are working correctly, hackers can cause issues. The so-called Roanoke Phantom, for example, tapped into air traffic control radio systems for nearly six weeks in the early 1990s and transmitted false air traffic control instructions to pilots around Roanoke Regional Airport in Virginia. The phony controller, Rodney Eugene Bocook, instructed pilots to change altitudes and direction and even to abort landings. The FAA tracked down Bocock before any serious incidents occurred and he was convicted in federal court of endangering the safety of an aircraft in flight, issuing misinformation to pilots, sending out false distress calls, and using indecent and profane language on the aviation frequencies.

Given the potential for computer failure, hacking, and programmer error, many people are less than comfortable

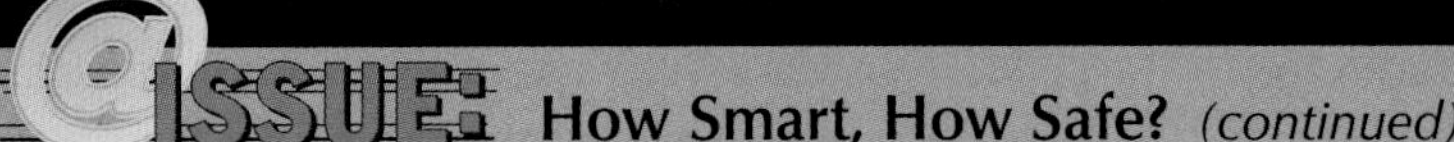

How Smart, How Safe? *(continued)*

introducing more and more automation and computer control into the vehicles that carry us to and from home, work, the library, the grocery store, and the baseball field every day. For example, a driver of a fully automated car might be less alert than a driver in full control of his or her car — which only contributes to more serious issues in the rare event when the computer fails and the driver needs to be attentive enough to notice and resolve the problem.

How do you feel about computer systems controlling your vehicle? Would you trust a smart car to drive you to and from work every day? These are just a few of the questions being asked, even as more "intelligent" and "smart" vehicles are hitting the roads, railways, and skies each day. In the end, however, it is only human for drivers and passengers to wonder just how smart — and how safe — these systems are.

TRAINS AND BUSES

Computers not only are used to help with control and safety features of individual vehicles; they also play a key role in passenger vehicles, such as trains and buses, and their use for private and public transportation.

As with cars, for decades, computers have been used inside buses and each train car to control various systems, such as fuel injection, instrument panels, and so on. Today, computers also are used in a networked system that allows one car of a train to communicate with the others. For example, each car in a train has a computer system to control the brakes. Instead of having each system function as a stand-alone unit, many trains now use computerized braking systems in which all of the car computers are networked and take commands on when and how to brake from the locomotive. The engineer in the locomotive uses controls on the instrument panel in the locomotive to send these commands to the other cars.

Engineers and dispatchers also use computers to determine the routes a train should take. When a dispatcher authorizes you to take the train over a specific route, a computer program assures that operations are safe and then transmits the route information to each active train via a radio frequency network. An onboard computer in each locomotive then displays the correct route to the locomotive engineer. GPS systems are used to track and locate the train at any point in its travels and the onboard computer accesses a database to compare the actual location and speed of the train with the information radioed by authorities. If the engineer attempts to steer the train along a route different than the one set by the dispatcher, the computer system will alert the engineer and, if necessary, stop the train.

The routes and stops of trains in an airport are almost entirely controlled by computers. If you board one of these airport trains, often called trams, you will notice that the trains have no human driver. Instead, the train movements are controlled by a computerized train control system, which instructs the trains to move along a preprogrammed path according to a set schedule and route. The trains are supervised automatically from a main control center, where humans can intervene and override the computer system, if something goes wrong. Such train systems typically use voice output to inform passengers that doors are about to close, or open at the next stop. The train systems also are linked to the passenger information displays over the train doors, which indicate the train's route.

Buses – and especially bus drivers – also are being affected by advances in computer technology. Already in use in France and Las Vegas, new, highly computerized buses are steered not by people, but by an optical guidance system that includes networked cameras, computers, and motors (Figure 5-26). The buses still have human drivers who control the bus' speed by braking and accelerating. The drivers do not, however, steer the buses: steering is handled by a computer and a dashboard-mounted camera focused on high-contrast markings painted on a road. The image-processing software in the computer continuously compares the bus' trajectory with the stripes painted on the road. If the software notes even a tiny deviation from those markings, a motor mounted on the steering column gently steers the bus back on course. For some, the idea of riding

Figure 5-26 An optically guided Civis bus, like this one in France, uses a dashboard camera to watch the road markings to keep the bus on course.

a bus on autopilot is a little unnerving; thus far, however, the optically guided steering has proven to be more accurate than human steering. Of course, in the event of emergency, a human driver can take over, thus automatically overriding the optical guidance system.

To ensure that riders always know when the next bus is coming, each bus is equipped with global positioning satellite devices to track their location. This information is transmitted wirelessly to displays at bus stops, so riders have an exact time when the next bus will arrive.

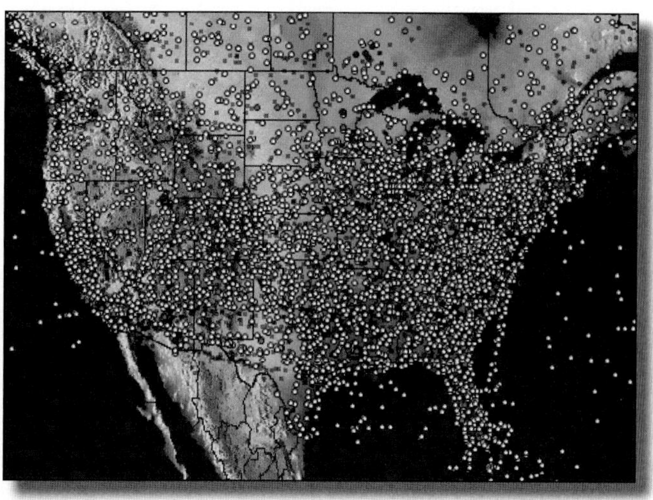

Figure 5-27 On a typical day, air traffic controllers monitor 87,000 flights over the United States. In this snapshot, each white dot represents a flight in the air.

AIRLINES

The modern airline industry depends on computers for almost every aspect of the business. Airplanes, like automobiles, are designed by using computers and computer-aided design and engineering. As with automobiles, simulations are completed in wind tunnel tests prior to manufacturing to ensure the plane designs are safe and efficient. The airplanes themselves rely on computers for system control, communication back to air traffic control towers, and to provide customers with in-flight entertainment over small LCD screens. Numerous airport services are automated by computers, including the display screens that display flight, gate, and status information, the electronic announcements made over the intercom, and even car rental services. Pilots also are carrying laptop computers with electronic versions of the dozen or so airplane manuals required on the flight deck.

In this section you will learn more about the use of computers to help train pilots on flight simulators, to manage ticketing and reservations processes, to support air traffic control, and to calculate the fuel required in each plane, based on its route and load.

Figure 5-28 Air traffic controllers rely heavily on computers to help track the flight patterns of thousands of aircraft to guide them to landing safely, while minimizing airport delays.

Air Traffic Control

According to the National Air Traffic Controllers Association, roughly 5,000 planes are in the sky above the United States at any given moment, which translates to more than 87,000 flights per day carrying close to two million passengers. As shown in Figure 5-27, having that many aircraft in the air at one time does not leave much room for error. The job of managing the take-off, flight, and landing of all of these commercial and private aircraft lies squarely in the hands of air traffic controllers across the United States. These air traffic controllers rely heavily on computers to help track the flight patterns of thousands of aircraft, ensure they are traveling at safe distances, and help reroute them around bad weather, while minimizing airport delays (Figure 5-28).

At the core of the air traffic control system is the Air Traffic Control System Command Center. The **Air Traffic Control System Command Center (ATSCC)** oversees all air traffic control in the United States, including helping to manage centers where problems such as bad weather, or traffic overload, exist. The United States airspace is divided into 21 centers, as shown in Figure 5-29 on the next page, each of which is subdivided into smaller airspaces. As your plane flies out of one airspace into another, the air traffic controllers from the new airspace take over monitoring the plane and giving instructions to the pilot.

Before any flight can take off, the pilot completes a pre-flight routine that includes transmitting a flight plan to the air traffic control tower. The flight plan includes

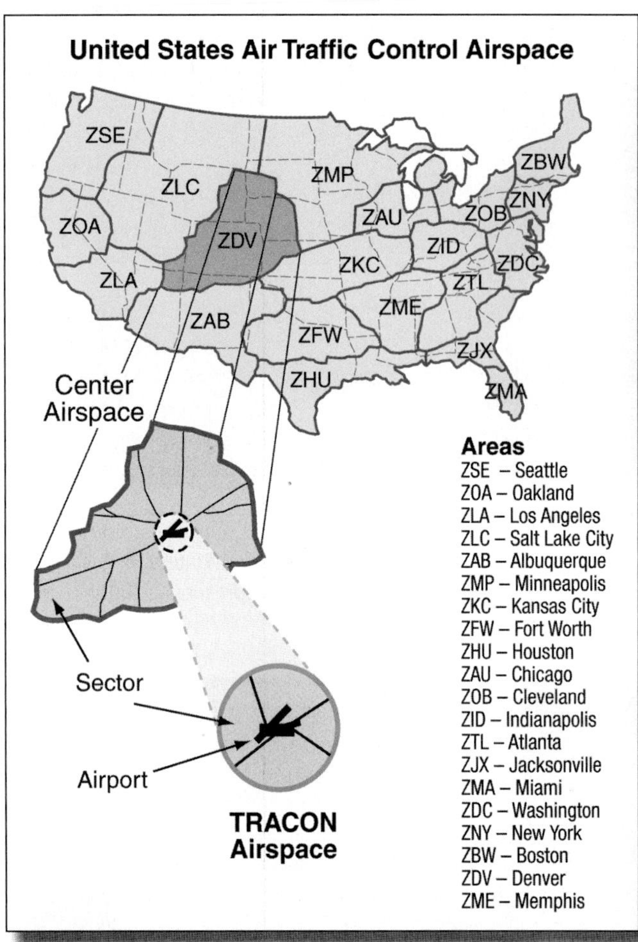

Figure 5-29 The United States airspace is divided into 21 centers, each of which is subdivided into smaller airspaces.

the airline name, flight number, intended airspeed and cruising altitude, the flight route, and the unique beacon code assigned to that aircraft. In the air traffic control tower, a flight data person reviews the weather and enters the flight plan into the FAA host computer. The computer generates an electronic **flight progress strip**, which contains all of the necessary data for tracking that plane during its flight and will be constantly updated. Once the flight plan has been approved, the flight data person gives clearance to the pilot and passes the strip to the ground controller in the tower, who guides the flight through take-off. As the plane moves from one airspace center to the next, the flight progress strip is passed from controller to controller, each of whom monitors the plane until it moves into the next airspace.

When the plane reaches the airspace for the destination airport, air traffic controllers will direct the plane to line up with other planes heading into the airport for a runway approach. Up until the point when the plane is 10 miles from the runway, all of the air traffic control has been based on information sent over radar and computers to air traffic control centers. Within 10 miles of the runways however, a local controller in the airport tower also will check the runways and the skies above the runways with binoculars and surface radar. When the local controller determines that it is safe, he or she gives the pilot clearance to land. Once the plane lands, a ground controller takes over, using ground radar information to direct the plane to the terminal gate.

As technology improves, the FAA continually has updated the technology used by air traffic controllers. Since the 1960s, the FAA has been a leader in using computers to help air traffic controllers direct aircraft. As new technologies became available, the FAA added new computers to those in use, retiring the older equipment. For example, the FAA currently is running a program called Standard Terminal Automation Replacement System (STARS) to help replace the older computers and displays being used by air traffic controllers. Also being installed are the Airport Movement Area Safety System and the Airport Surface Detection Equipment Model-X, which are designed to reduce runway accidents, or "incursions."

Inside the airplane, computers help to give pilots another set of eyes. Systems such as the Automatic Dependent Surveillance-Broadcast (ADS-B) system and the Traffic Alert and Collision Avoidance System, or TCAS, use a special display screen to show the pilot the relative positions and speed of aircraft up to 40 miles away, thus allowing pilots to identify aircraft on conflicting flight paths. The system also sounds an audible alarm when it determines that another aircraft will pass too closely to another plane. TCAS provides a backup to the air traffic controllers systems used to separate planes in normal flight patterns. In addition to enhancing collision avoidance capabilities, the ADS-B and the TCAS allow pilots and controllers to work together to reduce delays.

Reservations and Ticketing

When you call a travel agent or an airline, or visit a travel Web site to purchase an airline ticket, the agent uses a computer to access a computerized reservation system or global distribution system to check what seats are available on your flight, confirm the reservation, take your payment information, and then book the ticket for you. A **computerized reservation system (CRS)**, now more often referred to as a **global distribution system (GDS),** is an electronic system that allows travel providers to display information about available flights and seats and to manage the inventory. The use of global distribution systems is not just limited to airline reservationists; agents at travel agencies, tour operators, hotels, and car rental firms use GDS to check on available inventory, whether it's a seat on a plane, a hotel room, or a mid-size car.

The first and most widely known global distribution system was SABRE (Semi-Automated Business Research Environment), first conceived when American Airlines President C.R Smith and R. Blair Smith, a senior sales representative for IBM, met on an airplane in 1953. During the conversation, they speculated on the best way to build a data-processing system that would create a complete airline seat reservation system and make all the data instantly available to any travel agent. Seven years later, in 1960, the SABRE system was installed at its first travel agency. The revolutionary system was the first real-time business application of computer technology – and is actually the first example of electronic commerce.

The SABRE system gave American Airlines a unique competitive advantage: as travel agents used the Sabre system to gain rapid access to flight information, American flights were listed at the top whenever possible, so that agents were more likely to book customers on American flights. Since then, other airlines and technology companies have created their own GDS, including Galileo/Apollo, Amadeus, and Worldspan.

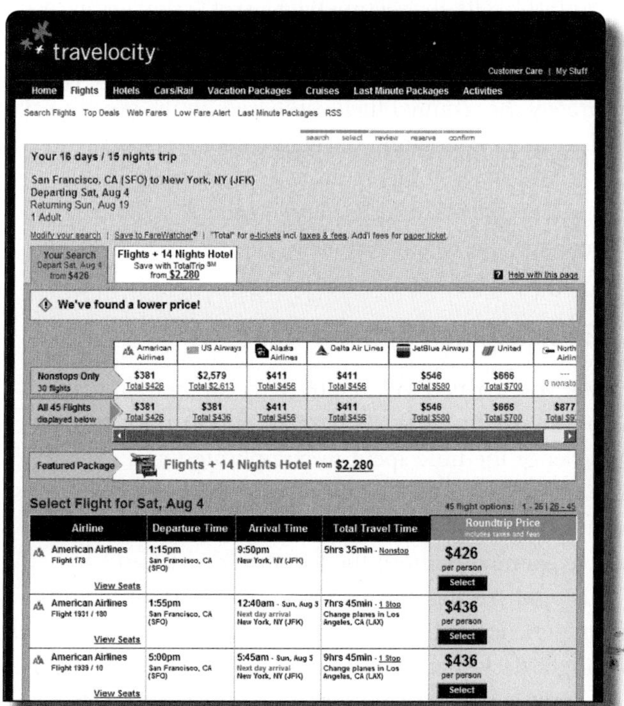

Figure 5-30 Online travel Web sites rely on GDS systems to provide behind-the-scenes logic needed to determine what flights and seats are available. Travelocity, for example, uses the SABRE system to allow customers to design and book airline trips.

The GDS systems are examples of a massive client-server system, in which hundreds of terminals from reservationists around the globe connect to the system over networks, in order to access the data in the GDS database. You can even access the GDS databases over the Internet, by visiting a travel Web site, such as Travelocity (owned by privately held Sabre Holdings, the company formed when American Airlines spun off the SABRE system in 2000) or Expedia (originally formed within Microsoft in 1995, but now operates independently and offers additional travel Web sites such as hotels.com and hotwire.com among others).

Many of the online travel Web sites rely on the GDS systems to provide behind-the-scenes logic needed to determine what flights and seats are available. Travelocity, for example, uses the Sabre system to allow customers to design and book trips themselves by tapping into reservations and information for hundreds of airlines, hotels, car rental companies, and many cruise and vacation packages (Figure 5-30). The Expedia Web site uses the Worldspan travel system to locate the best prices for your desired flight times.

When you access the Travelocity Web site, you can enter your desired flight dates and times. When you submit the request, the programming behind the Web pages queries the GDS database and sorts through an entire range of flights between cities to try to find the lowest fare available. The Web site also offers travelers the option of receiving RSS (real simple syndication) feeds of last-minute travel deals, cell phone flight delay alerts, and a downloadable Windows Vista dashboard "FareWatcher" gadget that alerts you when travel to your three favorite destinations drops in price.

Some GDS systems, such as Sabre Airline Solutions, also provide additional software tools that airlines use to maintain and store airline schedules, fares, and inventory, as well as a number of airport and customer relationship management functions, such as managing frequent flyer programs.

Self-Service Check In

After you have booked your flight and arrive at the airport the day of your flight, you need to check in and receive your boarding pass. In the past, checking in required you to wait in line and work with an agent, who confirmed your reservation and printed out your boarding pass. Today, however, you are just as likely to check in at a computerized kiosk or terminal with a touch screen and print out your own boarding pass (Figure 5-31).

To use a self-service kiosk, you typically must enter your frequent flier number or swipe a credit card to

Figure 5-31 For faster service at the airport, you can check in at a computerized kiosk and print your own boarding pass.

allow the machine to retrieve your reservation data. The machine reads your information from the magnetic stripe on the card and then queries the reservation database for your travel information.

Once the reservation is found, you can use the touch screen as an input device to confirm the information is correct. Next, the system may display a diagram of the plane, showing your seat and other seats on the plane that are taken or available; you can change your seat reservation by touching the seat you would like. Next, you can indicate whether you are checking any luggage and, if you want, request or buy an upgrade or add your frequent flier number to the reservation. The terminal then prints out your boarding pass with your desired seats, including boarding passes for any connecting flights on that airline.

Most airlines now allow you to check in over the Web, up to 24 hours before your flight. After logging into the Web site, you enter relevant flight information and then print your boarding pass from your home or office on the next page. Armed with your boarding pass, you can head straight to security, avoiding any long lines at the check-in counter, assuming, of course, you are not checking any bags. Most major hotel chains also offer computer kiosks linked to the airline Web sites so guests may check in and print boarding passes before leaving the hotel.

Fuel Calculation

The price of jet fuel is the largest variable cost for any airline, other than labor. Airlines thus work to ensure that planes carry just enough fuel to fly safely to their destination – as well as extra fuel to handle other factors, such as circling the airport due to air traffic or extra weight caused by ice on the wings.

Fuel calculations are part of the daily routine of hundreds of pilots, flight engineers, and dispatchers. During flight planning, crews must balance fuel requirements required to get to their destination with the weight of passengers and cargo. Fuel quantity is usually measured by checking on the gallons added, looking at cockpit gauges, or physically testing the fuel tank volume using dipsticks. In the past, the fuel requirements for a particular flight were calculated manually using a variety of complex formulas, which took into account the weight of the payload and weather conditions.

This manual approach, however, was open to error. A pilot in command might mistakenly miscalculate or transpose numbers, changing the number of gallons required from 91 to 19. Today, computer programs running on laptop or handheld computers can be used to aid in fuel calculations. Pilots at the former Britannia Airways (now called Thomsonfly), for example, are given laptop computers with software that allows pilots to generate flight calculations, including calculating fuel requirements for a specific flight. Using the software, pilots are able to determine accurately the required fuel load based on the specific payload, weather conditions, passenger count, and more. Being able to assess fuel requirements correctly helps reduce the cost to the airline and ensures that the aircraft has enough fuel to land correctly.

Training Using Flight Simulators

As you learned in Chapter 2, computer simulations often are used to give soldiers an opportunity to experience the time spent in complicated and expensive military vehicles. Similar types of computer simulations are used to train airline pilots, to give them the benefits of live training without the associated risks and cost.

Typically, a flight simulation involves modeling the experience of being inside the cockpit of a plane, with the flight deck that includes navigation, communications, and flight control instruments. A **flight simulator**, or **airplane simulator**, is a device that duplicates a specific airplane's cockpit and is capable of closely representing the actual aircraft through various ground and flight routines (Figure 5-32). Some flight simulators use a generic

Figure 5-32 A flight simulation involves modeling the experience of being inside the cockpit of a plane, with the flight deck that includes navigation, communications, and flight control instruments.

flight deck, with displays that can be reprogrammed to simulate aircraft displays from different types of planes.

In addition to creating realistic modeling of an airplane's instruments, controls, and view, high-tech flight simulators also must be able to simulate the rumble of an uneven runway when the airplane lands or the thrust effect that occurs when brakes are used. During the training session, an instructor station system – typically a standard personal computer – monitors the pilot's flight and can instruct the simulator to replicate an instrument failure or turbulence; send commands from a simulated air traffic controller; or change the airport at which the pilot will land.

Using computers for training simulations has several benefits. First, new pilots can practice scenarios repeatedly and learn from mistakes without additional cost or danger. Pilots also have a chance to become familiar with the instrumentation of a new type of plane, before actually getting in the cockpit. Further, because the flight simulator records every event in sequence, a flight training instructor can review and replay portions of the simulation to offer feedback and analysis. The end result is better-trained, more confident pilots, who can bring you safely to your destination.

@ISSUE: TSA's Secure Flight: Sacrificing Privacy for Safety?

Since September 11, 2001, when commercial airliners were hijacked by terrorists and used to kill thousands in the air and on the ground, most airline passengers have been willing to endure a little inconvenience in the name of safety and air travel security. Stringent baggage screenings, liquids limited to 3.4 ounce containers in clear one-quart zip-top bags, shoe removal, and electronic equipment scrutiny are now standard at all U.S. airports. Given the recent attempts of passengers trying to smuggle liquids and shoe-based explosives, many believe the restrictions to be reasonable, if inconvenient. With each new attempted security breach and subsequent new checkpoint restriction, however, comes the inevitable question: just how much privacy are we willing to sacrifice for safety?

For some time, airlines have run a basic screening program that has the ability to screen passengers based on payment method and reservation dates. As soon as a ticket is purchased, a **Passenger Name Record (PNR)** is created that contains all the profile information for that passenger's flight. When activities such as purchasing a one-way ticket with cash occur, for example, it triggers a flag, suggesting a possible security issue with that passenger. The system, however, did not flag the September 11th terrorists. In November of 2001, President Bush signed into law the **Aviation and Transportation Security Act**, which created the **Transportation Security Agency (TSA)** in an attempt to revamp, standardize, and strengthen security screening at the nation's airports. In 2004, the **Intelligence Reform and Terrorism Prevention Act (IRTPA)** was signed into law, officially transferring from the airlines to the TSA the responsibility of comparing PNR data to information contained in the federal terrorist watch lists, among other things, with the goal of tightening the passenger prescreening process.

Shortly after the TSA was created, the agency got to work on creating an ambitious, new computerized system, called **Computer Assisted Passenger Pre-Screening II (CAPPS II)**, which was intended to strengthen the existing screening system used by the airlines – the original CAPPS. The system was meant to search government watch lists, financial records and credit histories, private sector employment screening databases, and other sources in an attempt to identify suspicious activity. Public outcry over the potential for privacy violations and abuse forced the government to scrap the program in 2004 and develop another method for accomplishing its security mission.

The result has been a program called **Secure Flight**. The Secure Flight program is intended to "enhance the security of domestic commercial air travel within the United States through the use of improved watch list matching," according to the TSA. As designed, the program's goals are to identify known and suspected terrorists, prevent those on the government's No Fly list from boarding a plane, perform a secondary screen of passengers identified through the pre-screening process, assist with passenger air travel, and protect the privacy of individuals in the system. Still in its infancy, the program hopes to balance the need for air travel security with passenger privacy rights and civil liberties. As you can imagine, privacy watchdogs and consumer rights agencies are keeping a close eye on this one.

@ISSUE: TSA's Secure Flight: Sacrificing Privacy for Safety? *(continued)*

In conjunction with Secure Flight, the federal government has granted private sector enterprises the opportunity to participate in its "Registered Traveler" program. This program is viewed as a means for accelerating the security screening process by pre-profiling and maintaining a database of individuals who are willing to give up some privacy and submit to background checks and biometric data collection in exchange for speedier passage through airport security checkpoints. One such company is Clear (www.flyclear.com). To get a Clear smart card (Figure 5-33), the applicant must first submit basic biographic data, such as full legal name, address, and height, online to the company. Then, the applicant must appear in person at a Clear enrollment station for government-issued identification verification, iris and fingerprint capture, and a photo. An annual fee of $99.95 is required before the Clear card is issued. At airports with Clear card security stations, card holders bypass the long security lines and speed through a separate Clear security station by presenting their smart cards to gain access to the terminal. The Clear system currently is in place at the airports in Orlando, Cincinnati, Indianapolis, New York's JFK, and San Jose, California.

Figure 5-33 Smart cards, such as this one issued by Clear, allow pre-screened passengers to speed their way through airport security at selected airports.

Another technology in the early stages of testing is an X-ray screening device that uses a technique called "backscatter." The machine is designed to take an X-ray of a passenger's body in an attempt to detect concealed weapons and explosives.

In test at Phoenix's Sky Harbor International Airport, the device is meant to be used as a secondary screening method for passengers that do not pass the primary security screening. For those concerned about X-ray exposure, the TSA offers a physical pat-down search as an alternative to the scan. Privacy advocates worry that the X-ray images are too invasive, since they clearly depict the outline of the passenger's body plus anything attached to it, such as jewelry. TSA officials state the X-ray images will not be viewable by other passengers moving through the security checkpoint since the machines are to be used in a remote screening location. Once a passenger clears the backscatter station, the image taken is deleted from the system, so nothing is stored for later access. The backscatter devices have already been tested at London's Heathrow airport, and are in use in some prisons.

Have all these new approaches ended the discussion about air travel security and passenger data privacy? Not by a long shot. With most of the systems still in test and preliminary roll-out stages, many people are waiting to see just how effective they are in securing our nation's airports and air travel systems. Some see the systems as a necessary component in the government's responsibility for maintaining homeland security. Others, however, see a slippery slope ahead that could lead to the government intruding even further into the private lives of its citizens, all in the name of national security and terror prevention. As you book your next flight to visit family, take a vacation, or head to a business meeting, consider what data you had to provide the agency — and the government — in order to make your reservation and clear security. How much more privacy are you willing to sacrifice should it be required for your safety in the future?

CONCLUSION

In this chapter, you learned about the use of computers in the transportation industry. First, you learned about the use of computers to help design, test, and manufacture vehicles, as well as the use of computers to control basic systems inside cars and trucks. You also learned how computers are used for ABS brakes, collision warning systems, night vision, and other safety features, as well as for new entertainment options. After a review of how smart cars could change your driving experience, you also learned about the potential downsides of relying on computer automation to guide a vehicle safely. After learning about how computerized mapping, onboard GPS systems, and telematics help you navigate safely to your destination, you also learned about using computers for route optimization for truck fleets, electronic toll collection, and intelligent highways. You also learned about how computers are used in trains and buses that are guided by computer systems. Finally, you learned about the use of computers in the airline industry, including air traffic control, reservations and check-in, fuel calculation, and training, along with the privacy questions raised by the new Secure Flight system, and other airport security systems.

Key Terms

adaptive cruise control (ACC)
Air Traffic Control System Command Center (ATSCC)
airplane simulator
antilock braking system (ABS)
Aviation and Transportation Security Act of 2001
call center telematics
collision warning systems (CWS)
communications bus
Computational Fluid Dynamics (CFD)
Computer Assisted Passenger Pre-Screening II (CAPPS II)
computerized reservation system (CRS)
electronic toll collection system
engine control unit (ECU)
flight progress strip
flight simulator
fly by wire
global distribution system (GDS)
Intelligence Reform and Terrorism Prevention Act (IRTPA) of 2004
Intelligent Transportation Systems (ITS)
lane controller
lidar
mashup
parallel processing
Passenger Name Record (PNR)
satellite radio
Secure Flight
smart cars
telematics
transponder
Transportation Security Agency (TSA)
virtual wind tunnel
wind tunnel

Chapter Review

Multiple Choice

Select the best answer.

1. The _____, which is the most powerful computer in most cars, communicates with a wide range of vehicle components.
   (a) adaptive cruise control (ACC)
   (b) computational fluid dynamic (CFD)
   (c) flight progress strip (FPS)
   (d) engine control unit (ECU)

2. A(n) _____ is designed to keep a car's wheels from seizing up or skidding as a driver slows down, so more traction is available to steer out of harm's way.
   (a) collision warning system (CWS)
   (b) intelligent transportation system (ITS)
   (c) antilock braking system (ABS)
   (d) computerized reservation system (CRS)

3. The key difference between lidar and radar in adaptive cruise control systems is that lidar _____.
   (a) is a technology used to determine location, position, and speed
   (b) uses lasers, not radio waves, to determine the range to an object
   (c) is more expensive to install than radar
   (d) all of the above

4. With a _____ device, also referred to as an onboard satellite navigation system, a car's current location can be tracked at any point, based on signals sent to and received from satellites around the globe.
   (a) CWS
   (b) GPS
   (c) ITS
   (d) ABS

5. _____ is an emerging technology field that combines computers, location-sensing technology such as GPS, and wireless data in a car.
   (a) transponder
   (b) communications bus
   (c) telematics
   (d) lane controller

6. The _____ system, which uses a cellular radio-based system to connect drivers with a live operator, is a GM-branded call center telematics system.
   (a) FreeTrip
   (b) SmarTire
   (c) OnStar
   (d) MapQuest

7. A _____ is a small battery-operated, radio frequency identification (RFID) unit that you attach to your car windshield to use an electronic toll-collection system.
   (a) transponder
   (b) communications bus
   (c) telematics
   (d) lane controller

8. A global distribution system (GDS) is an electronic system that allows _____.
   (a) travel providers to display information about available flights and to manage inventory
   (b) airplane pilots to calculate fuel requirements based on weather conditions
   (c) drivers to recognize when a vehicle is dangerously close to an object
   (d) dispatchers to determine the routes a train should take

9. Today, many airline travelers check in at a computerized kiosk or terminal with a _____ and print out their own boarding passes.
   (a) touch screen
   (b) keyboard
   (c) joystick
   (d) pointing stick

10. A benefit of using computers for flight training simulations is that _____.
   (a) new pilots can practice scenarios repeatedly and learn from mistakes
   (b) pilots can become familiar with the instrumentation in a new type of plane
   (c) flight trainers can review and replay portions of a simulation to offer feedback
   (d) all of the above

Chapter Review

Short Answer

Write a brief answer to each of the following questions.

1. How do manufacturers use computer-aided design (CAD) and computer-aided engineering (CAE) to design and test vehicles?
2. How is a wind tunnel different from a virtual wind tunnel?
3. Why do many labs rely on parallel processing when running a crash simulation?
4. What is call center telematics and how is it used?
5. How are flight simulators used to train pilots?

Web Research

Use a search engine such as Google (google.com) to research the following questions. Then, write a one-page, double-spaced report or create a presentation, unless otherwise directed.

1. At one time, planning a road trip involved the frustrating scrutiny of one or more maps (and the even more frustrating task of trying to refold them). Today, a number of Web sites offer **maps**, driving directions, and travel guides that can help even the most reluctant traveler. Use the Web to compare at least two Web sites that can be used to plan a road trip, weighing the strengths, and weaknesses, of each site.
2. According to a report in MarketResearch.com, **electronic toll-collection** systems reduce operating costs, improve traffic flow, and are convenient and efficient. Use the Web to learn more about specific electronic toll-collection systems used in one or more states. Investigate the advantages, and disadvantages, of the system for both the state and for drivers.

Group Exercises

Working with a group of your classmates, complete the following team questions.

1. One exciting new Internet development is the creation of mashups. Considered one of the hottest new growth areas for second generation applications, experts predict Web users can now find upwards of ten or more new mashups a day. For some, combining maps with other location-based sets of data seems a natural means of conveying information. For others, mashups may present new privacy concerns as the locations of individuals (singles, criminals) can now be plotted for the world to see. With your group, do some research on mashups – what are they, how do they work, what are some examples of current mashups? What types of mashups would your group like to see? What types of mashups might be better left undeveloped? Create a PowerPoint presentation to inform your classmates about mashups, give examples, and present both the pros and cons of making mashups available.
2. At the 2000 Paris Motor Show, Citröen unveiled the first automobile with an onboard computer. The AutoPC let drivers access e-mail, receive weather and traffic data, and obtain navigation information, and allowed passengers to watch movies on DVD. Today, a number of automakers offer optional onboard computer systems, with a range of capabilities. But, are they worth the cost? Have each member of your team visit a local auto dealer and find a car that is offered with, and without, an onboard computer. Note the capabilities of the computer and compare the cost of the two cars. Then, meet with your team, share your findings, and prepare a PowerPoint presentation showing the features, and cost, of an onboard computer system and determine if the option is worth the investment.

Computers in Education 6

Changing Times, Changing Schools
- The Factory Model
- A New Model for a New Century

Importance of Computer Fluency

Computers as Learning Tools
- Computer-Aided Instruction
- Web-Based Training
- Internet Resources
- Programming Tools
- Educational Games and Simulations
- Software Tools

Computers as Teaching Tools
- Presentation Tools
- Communications Tools
  - *E-Mail*
  - *Mailing Lists*
  - *Newsgroups and Message Boards*
  - *Video Conferencing and Chat*
  - *Podcasting*
- Learning Management Systems

Distance Learning

Technology in the Classroom: Benefits and Opportunities
- Benefits of Technology in the Classroom
- Opportunities for Improvement

Defining an Information Age Education

Conclusion

In today's classroom, computers and other technologies are as ubiquitous as desks, textbooks, and pencils. Teachers use PowerPoint slides to support their lectures, while students complete their English reports on computers in the lab. Looking up a book in the library requires a computerized card catalog, although many students rely on the Internet to find research to support a thesis. Even students in kindergarten are using computer-based tutorials to learn basic reading and math skills in a fun and interactive way, while employees at companies worldwide are taking online training classes to keep their accounting certifications current. After class, teachers are logging on to e-mail to share curriculum ideas and lesson plans with other teachers, whether in the same district or across the globe.

In fact, the uses of the computer in education are almost limitless — and this chapter presents only a few of the ways computer and educational technologies are changing today's classrooms. In this chapter, you will learn how the teaching and learning models used in schools have changed over the years and about the importance of computer fluency in the Information Age. You will discover how computers are used as learning tools to help students practice skills, gather information, and think creatively, and as teaching tools to support presentations, communication, and class administration. After discussing distance learning, the chapter reviews the benefits of using technology in the classroom, as well as areas where there still are opportunities for improvement. Finally, you will consider what skills and knowledge are key to preparing students to be successful in the 21st century.

CHANGING TIMES, CHANGING SCHOOLS

As a general rule, the educational model used in America's schools has been a reflection of the time and the culture (Figure 6-1). Before the end of the Civil War, society was agrarian, with most people living on farms. During that time, students learned in one-room schools, with one teacher. The curriculum was focused on basic subjects – reading, writing, and elementary mathematics – as well as the skills needed to live and work on a farm. School days were short, to allow students time for morning and evening chores, and let out completely for the summer so children could help on the farm.

The Factory Model

Towards the end of the 19th century, as the industrial revolution continued, more of the country's population moved into cities and worked in factories. Schools were built around an educational model called the factory model, which learned its lessons from the automation and routine of the factory. A factory model school, typically a large building with numerous classrooms, was designed to be an efficient learning institution with a standard curriculum for all students. The curriculum focused on providing students with the basic skills needed to perform in a factory job – a job they were likely to keep for life. In the classroom, students sat in orderly rows with the teacher at the front, quietly listening to the teacher share facts they were expected to learn by rote.

Today, many schools still are organized around the factory model. Most of the school day is spent listening to lectures in various classes. Students move, as if on a conveyor belt, from one class to the next, each with a new lesson on a new subject. Different learning styles generally are not taken into account by the teaching approach, which involves presenting facts, assigning hands-on individual work, and administering standardized tests.

A New Model for a New Century

Many teachers and instructors have recognized that the factory model no longer may be the most appropriate way to educate students. Students in large classrooms, bored by listening to lectures (and used to watching fast-moving music videos and action movies), are not learning as effectively as they could. Many of today's jobs require teamwork not fostered by the factory model's focus on individual work. Instead of having just one job, you and other high school and college graduates may have six to eight jobs during your career – many of which will involve information work. As information workers, you will be asked to analyze, retrieve, process, and store information – quite a difference from the factory model classroom where you simply take in facts for later output on a test.

Realizing the need for change, in 2002, President Bush signed into law the **No Child Left Behind Act** (known as NCLB), which aims to improve student academic assessment achievement programs and boost education system quality, among other initiatives. In response to both changing times and NCLB, K-12 schools, as well as postsecondary schools, are moving away from

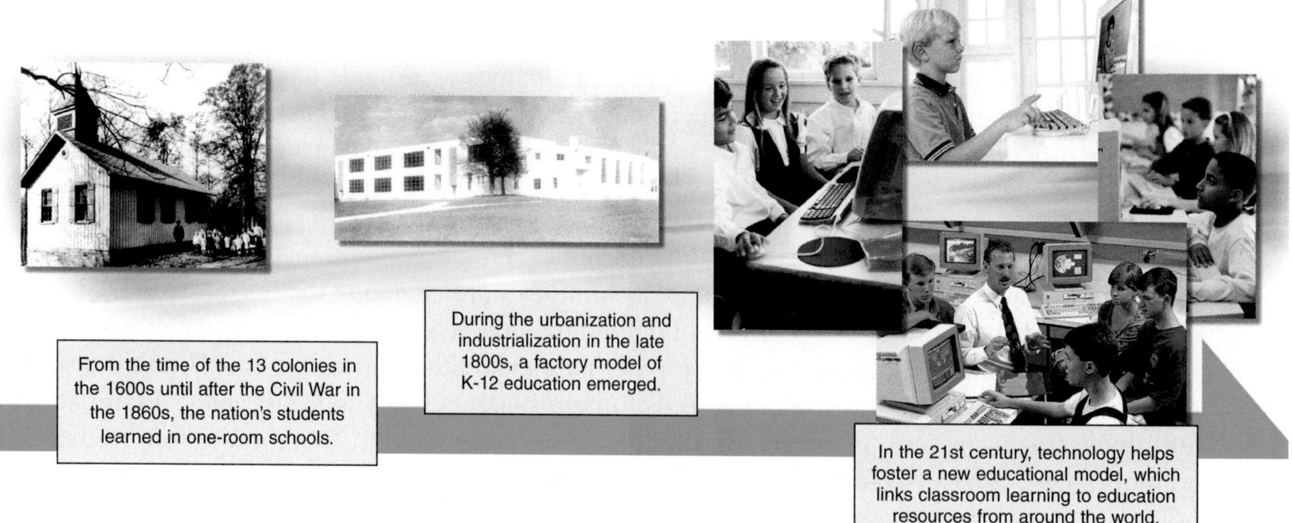

From the time of the 13 colonies in the 1600s until after the Civil War in the 1860s, the nation's students learned in one-room schools.
During the urbanization and industrialization in the late 1800s, a factory model of K-12 education emerged.
In the 21st century, technology helps foster a new educational model, which links classroom learning to education resources from around the world.

Figure 6-1 The educational model used in America's schools has changed over time to reflect the culture and the technologies available to teachers and students.

traditional learning environments to newer ones, focused on student-centered learning. In some cases, computer technology is helping educators make the change. Table 6-1 lists the characteristics representing traditional learning environments, as compared to newer learning strategies and the technologies and tools used to support learning in this new environment.

A key to the success of this new learning environment is an emphasis on the use of technology as a teaching and learning tool. You and many of your friends likely grew up with computers in your home, so having computers in the classroom seems a natural extension. Computers in school open the classroom's four walls up to the world and allow students to gather information from around the globe – whether an economics lesson from a local bank president, environmental information from state agencies, or history shared by a companion school in Melbourne, Australia.

Table 6-1 Traditional Versus Newer Learning Environments

TRADITIONAL LEARNING ENVIRONMENTS	*NEW LEARNING ENVIRONMENTS*
Teacher-centered instruction	Student-centered learning
Single-sense stimulation	Multisensory stimulation
Single-path progression	Multipath progression
Single media	Multimedia
Isolated work	Collaborative work
Information delivery	Information exchange
Passive learning	Active, exploratory, inquiry-based learning
Factual, knowledge-based learning	Critical thinking and informed decision making
Reactive response	Proactive, planned action
Isolated, artificial context	Authentic, real-world context

This chart shows characteristics that represent traditional approaches to learning for K-12 students and the corresponding characteristics often associated with new learning environments. You will learn more about the technologies used to support new learning environments in this chapter.

IMPORTANCE OF COMPUTER FLUENCY

As you learned in a previous chapter, computer technology is an integral part of many aspects of our lives. The ability to use computer technology and to evaluate electronic information has become a basic skill for students and employees at all levels and in many industries. Because of this, many believe that computer fluency is vital to success. **Computer fluency** entails having knowledge and understanding of computers and their uses, as well as how computers affect your life and world. Computer fluency also involves the ability to use computers and other technologies; to organize, and interpret the information that technology makes available; and, perhaps most important, to be a lifelong learner of new and emerging technologies. The exact concepts and skills that define computer fluency can differ, depending on a school's or company's specific definition of what it means to be computer fluent. In general, however, computer fluency involves understanding computers and the ability to learn and use new technologies as they evolve.

Computer fluency differs from **computer literacy**, which traditionally has been more focused on an understanding of application software functions, such as copying and pasting, or even specialization in a computer area, such as Web development. Instead, computer fluency is a foundation that not only supports an understanding of today's computer technologies, it also includes the ability to independently learn and use new technologies and recognize their societal impact. While it is important to have specific computer skills, such as creating a document with a word processor, being a lifelong learner of new and emerging technologies will allow you to adapt and apply your knowledge to new uses of computers on the job, at school, and at home.

Being fluent with computers also improves your employability. Almost every job today involves using computers, whether ringing up sales on a computerized cash register, controlling a nuclear power plant, or accessing a reporting Web site to view latest sales trends (Figure 6-2). Having computer fluency shows potential employers that you are comfortable with computers in the workplace, which will make you more productive on the job. Further, by learning to use a computer to find information and complete tasks – for example, by using the Internet to do research on a topic or negotiate the purchase of a new car – you will develop a set of personally and professionally valuable skills, which, in turn, give you a sense of satisfaction. It will also improve your confidence at school, on the job, and in the rest of your life. Table 6-2 outlines key benefits of computer fluency for you and for your employer.

Figure 6-2 In today's job market, computer fluency is an important skill – and its importance will increase as more and more computers are used in the workplace.

Table 6-2 Benefits of Computer Fluency

INDIVIDUAL	*CORPORATION*
Enhances your employability	Provides a standard for employee recruitment
Increases your productivity, effectiveness and efficiency by helping you to complete tasks more quickly (e.g., online banking, updating address information via the Internet)	Enhances employee's ability to be productive, effective, and efficient on the job
Helps you to find, retrieve, store, and analyze information used at work, school, and at home	Reduces support costs and calls to organizations' Help desks
Improves your confidence when dealing with computers in everyday life	Increases employee satisfaction, by improving confidence when using computers in the workplace
May generate an interest in further study of computers and related fields	Makes newer technologies easier to grasp

Computer fluency has many benefits both for individuals and corporations.

@ISSUE: Narrowing the Digital Divide

Educated people. Higher-income families. Urbanites. Industrially developed nations. Upper-class neighborhoods. Individuals without disabilities. Statistics show that people in these groups have more access to technology than uneducated people, lower-income families, those living in rural areas, less industrially developed nations, lower-class neighborhoods, and individuals with disabilities. The concept that people can be split into two groups — those who have access to computer technology and those who do not — sometimes is called the digital divide. One study claims that those with less access to technology are at least a generation behind with respect to education. Another study alleges that those with less access to technology are less successful.

The good news is that the digital divide might be getting smaller. A 2003 study by the Corporation for Public Broadcasting shows that youngsters of all income levels and ethnic groups increasingly use the Internet (in fact, the study showed that children under 17 now spend nearly as much time in front of a computer as they do watching television). In another 2003 study, a Baltimore market-research firm surveyed 500 college-bound high-school students of different races and found increasingly smaller differences in computer use in school between white and black students. For example, 81 percent of white students had access to computers at school, compared with 71 percent of black students. And today's students have grown up "wired," using e-mail, instant messaging, and text messaging as often as they use the phone.

The news, however, is not all positive. Critics of the Baltimore study note that the digital divide still exists among students who are not planning to go to four-year colleges. Even schools — which play a key role in helping to bridge the digital divide by making computers a core part of the curriculum — are not working on a level playing field. While most low-income and minority kids have Internet access through their schools, they may have to compete with 500 other students for time on one of five computers. In rural America, schools are slower to get Internet access because of the high cost of putting in telecommunications networks. K-12 schools across the United States still are struggling to connect classrooms to the Internet. Despite the enormous success of initiatives such as the federal E-Rate program (designed to help eligible schools and libraries get affordable access to modern telecommunications and information systems), schools still must contend with old computers, aging buildings with faulty wiring, and limited hardware funds. Recent budget cuts have exacerbated the problem.

Still, policymakers and educators are working to ensure that all children have access to computers in the school, even if they do not have them at home. Private corporations such as Cisco, Dell, Microsoft, and 3Com also are pitching in, donating hardware, software, and network connections to help schools out.

So, while signs of increased Internet use are encouraging, the persistent gaps between ethnic and income groups remain a cause for concern. As computer fluency becomes a key part of being successful in today's society, some public-policy experts worry that less-affluent sectors could become more isolated as they do not develop the skills needed to succeed in the digital era. Skeptics, however, note that the research focuses on statistics only and does not isolate other cultural factors, such as parental support and student interest. Other questions that are as yet unanswered include: does access to technology such as a computer and the Internet makes you more successful? Are students who do not have computers at home facing an academic disadvantage in competing for good grades? Are job seekers who have a computer more likely to find a job than those without a computer?

Educators understand that technology is not a magic potion that ensures educational and life success. While most research shows that students using technology are more motivated and get better grades, simply having computers in a school does not mean that every student will actively use them. The key is to narrow the gap to ensure that, at the very least, every student has the same opportunities, regardless of gender, race, income, or location. For now, it seems, the digital divide in the United States might actually be starting to narrow.

COMPUTERS AS LEARNING TOOLS

Computers today are used to help teach a wide range of subjects – not just computer concepts or application software skills. Students complete history, science, and language assignments and do research on computers in lab rooms and at home (Figure 6-3). They carry out group assignments by doing research on the Internet and having videoconferences with students from other schools. Vocabulary lessons are reinforced using computer-based tutorials instead of flash cards.

All of these are examples of using computers and other technologies to facilitate learning, a practice referred to by a wide range of names and acronyms, including **Technology-Based Training (TBT)**, **Computer-Based Education (CBE)**, and **Computer-Based Instruction (CBI)**. Technology-based training can include learning from a CD-ROM, via the Internet, or using chat or e-mail to communicate

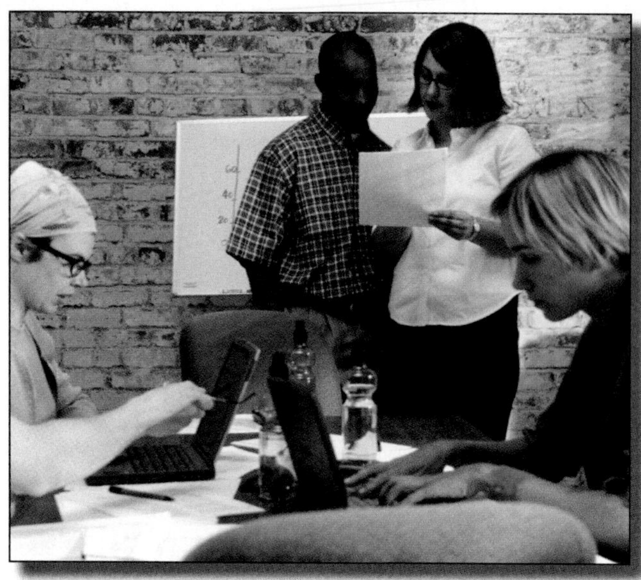

Figure 6-3 Computers are used to help teach a wide range of subjects. In a lab setting, for example, students can work together to research information and data to be used for science experiments or other group projects.

with other students. Technology-based training and education can be delivered in the classroom on stand-alone computers, on computers connected by a local area network, or via the Internet – or a combination of these approaches. Regardless of the specific hardware, software, and network setup, TBT is centered on one idea: that the computer and other technologies can be used as effective tools to help students learn and to support teachers in the instructional process.

In the following section, you will learn more about some of the computer technologies used to support the learning process, including computer-aided instruction, tutorials, programming tools, simulations and games, and productivity tools.

Computer-Aided Instruction

One of the ways computers are used in the classroom is through computer-aided instruction. **Computer-aided instruction (CAI)**, also referred to as **computer-based training (CBT)**, is a type of education in which students learn by using instructional software to complete exercises. CAI typically consists of self-directed, self-paced tutorials on a specific topic, such as learning subjunctive verbs in Spanish, understanding geometry, learning basic reading and language skills (Figure 6-4), or preparing for the SAT or GRE exams. CAI is delivered to students on a CD-ROM or DVD-ROM or via the local area network.

Computer-aided instruction was introduced in the 1980s, with programs that were almost entirely text-based and linear so that a student simply clicked a button in the software program to move from screen to screen. Despite the software's limitations, research showed that CAI could be a successful learning tool, resulting in learning of equal or higher quality than traditional instruction. Newer CAI software programs incorporate multimedia – graphics, sound, animation, and video – to provide a more engaging learning experience.

CAI generally is used to support skill-driven learning, which involves gaining an understanding of specific information and skills, while receiving regular feedback and support. CAI software often uses tutorials focused on a specific topic, such as using a mouse, mastering the multiplication tables, or learning how to balance your checkbook. Computer-based tutorials are programmed to respond in a certain way, based on your input. This is one of the unique benefits of CAI: you are required to actively participate in the program and engage in the learning process, rather than passively receive information. The tutorials also are programmed to provide

Figure 6-4 In the classroom, teachers rely on computer-assisted instruction to teach young learners basic reading skills and language skills.

almost immediate output or some confirmation of your input. If you click the next button, for example, the program will display the next screen. Answering a quiz question will cause the program to display information to let you know if your answer is correct or incorrect (Figure 6-5).

Some tutorials are linear in nature, while others offer branching based on student input. A linear tutorial moves in a specific sequence, presenting information in a predefined order. After you respond to a question, the tutorial likely will provide **feedback** – that is, information about the correctness of your response – and then move to the next screen. A tutorial that uses **branching**, by contrast, might do more than confirm if a response is correct or incorrect. If your answer is correct, it might confirm that you are correct and then move on to the next question. If your answer is incorrect, the tutorial instead might branch off to a section that provides more information on that topic. This approach is called **remediation**, which involves providing direction to review specific content that will help you better understand the topic. After reviewing the information, the program might allow you to return to the question to try again. Other tutorials may use branching in a more optional way, providing links that you can click to access more information on particular topics.

Tutorials also can be programmed to perform a **needs assessment**, which is a formal process of identifying discrepancies between your current understanding of a topic and an understanding defined as mastery of the topic. The needs assessment typically takes the form of a **pre-test**, which is a test you take prior to the training experience to determine whether or not you need to take the training and, if so, what areas you should focus on. A math tutorial, for example, begins with diagnostic testing to evaluate your strengths and weaknesses and then creates a personalized study plan targeted to your needs (Figure 6-6). Many tutorials also have a corresponding **post-tests**, which is a test you take after training to measure how much you have learned. Schools and companies often directly compare pretest and posttest scores to determine how much students have benefited overall from the training experience.

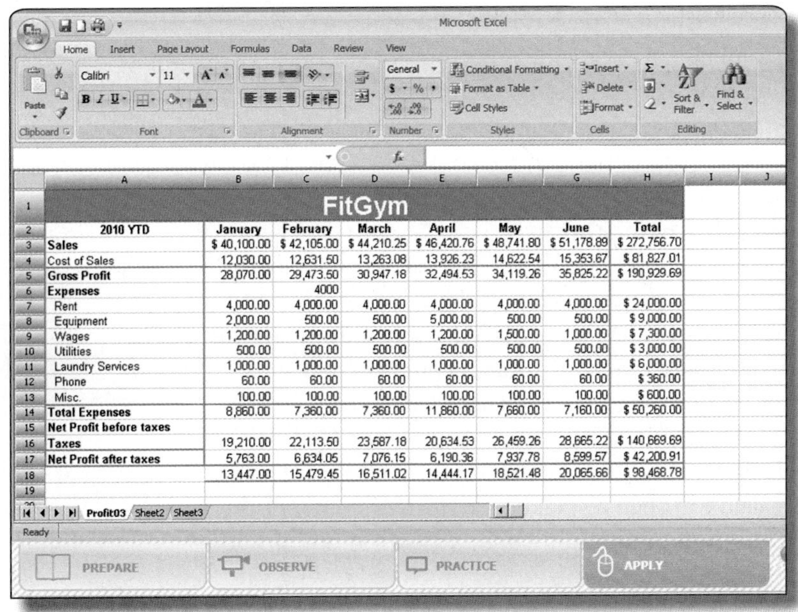

FitGym							
2010 YTD	January	February	March	April	May	June	Total
Sales	$ 40,100.00	$ 42,105.00	$ 44,210.25	$ 46,420.76	$ 48,741.80	$ 51,178.89	$ 272,756.70
Cost of Sales	12,030.00	12,631.50	13,263.08	13,926.23	14,622.54	15,353.67	$ 81,827.01
Gross Profit	28,070.00	29,473.50	30,947.18	32,494.53	34,119.26	35,825.22	$ 190,929.69
Expenses		4000					
Rent	4,000.00	4,000.00	4,000.00	4,000.00	4,000.00	4,000.00	$ 24,000.00
Equipment	2,000.00	500.00	500.00	5,000.00	500.00	500.00	$ 9,000.00
Wages	1,200.00	1,200.00	1,200.00	1,200.00	1,500.00	1,000.00	$ 7,300.00
Utilities	500.00	500.00	500.00	500.00	500.00	500.00	$ 3,000.00
Laundry Services	1,000.00	1,000.00	1,000.00	1,000.00	1,000.00	1,000.00	$ 6,000.00
Phone	60.00	60.00	60.00	60.00	60.00	60.00	$ 360.00
Misc.	100.00	100.00	100.00	100.00	100.00	100.00	$ 600.00
Total Expenses	8,860.00	7,360.00	7,360.00	11,860.00	7,660.00	7,160.00	$ 50,260.00
Net Profit before taxes							
Taxes	19,210.00	22,113.50	23,587.18	20,634.53	26,459.26	28,665.22	$ 140,669.69
Net Profit after taxes	5,763.00	6,634.05	7,076.15	6,190.36	7,937.78	8,599.57	$ 42,200.91
	13,447.00	15,479.45	16,511.02	14,444.17	18,521.48	20,065.66	$ 98,468.78

Figure 6-5 Most tutorials provide almost immediate output or feedback. Answering a quiz question, for example, causes the program to display feedback to let you know if you are correct or incorrect.

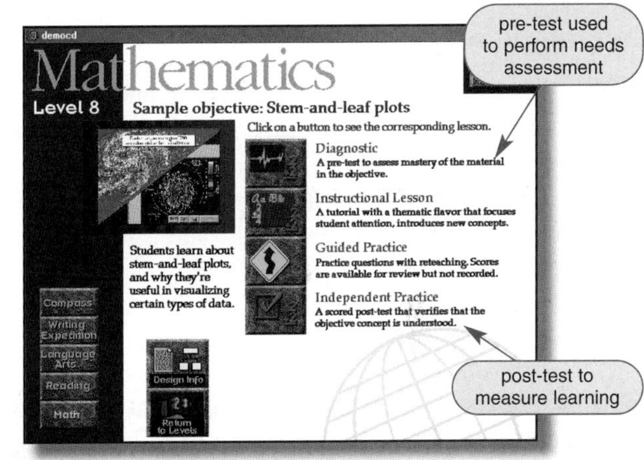

Figure 6-6 An interactive math program allows students to pretest their knowledge or take a scored posttest to measure learning.

Web-Based Training

Web-based training (WBT) is a type of computer-based training that involves delivery of education content via the Internet, a private intranet, or an extranet. Similar to CBT, Web-based training typically consists of self-directed, self-paced instruction on a topic. WBT is popular in business, industry, and schools for teaching new skills or enhancing the existing skills of employees, teachers, or students. As with CBT, students actively become involved in the learning process when using WBT, instead of passively receiving information.

Many Web sites offer WBT to the general public. Such training covers a wide range of topics, from learning how to change a flat tire to mastering better time-management skills to creating documents in Word (Figure 6-7). Some of the WBT courses at these Web sites are free, while others require registration and payment to take the course.

A good example of WBT is the use of online courses to study for major college entrance exams, such as the ACT, SAT, GRE, and MCAT. Study aids are developed and made available through companies such as Sylvan, Kaplan, Princeton Review, and others. Professional certification exams, such as the Certified Public Accountant (CPA), also have WBT study materials available. When test-takers are ready to attempt the exams, in most cases they can be scheduled online and taken on the computer at a local proctored testing site.

WBT often is combined with other materials – links to references, bulletin boards, discussion groups, and more – for distance learning courses. Distance learning will be covered later in this chapter.

Internet Resources

The Internet provides a vast resource of information on almost any topic. The Internet is a particularly valuable source of reference materials, such as encyclopedias, dictionaries, and other collections of facts (Figure 6-8). With Internet access you now have a quick and easy way to research topics, using online encyclopedias such as Encyclopedia.com, the Encyclopedia Britannica, and the Encarta Encyclopedia Center. Online dictionaries and thesauruses in numerous languages also make it easier than ever for you to check the spelling and meaning of

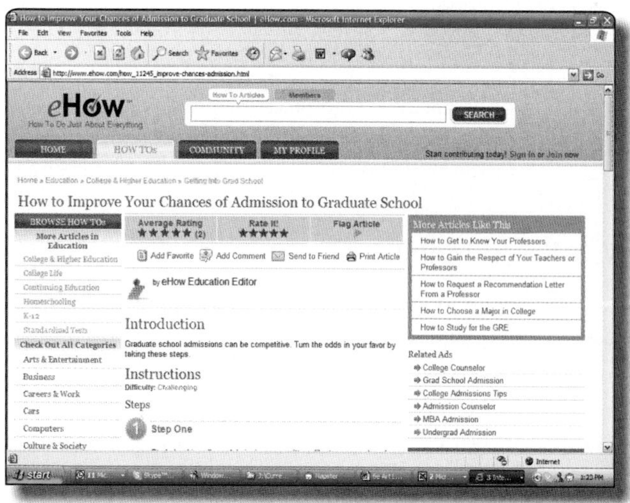

Figure 6-7 Web-based training is available on a wide range of topics, including mastering better time-management skills. Some courses are free, while other require registration fees.

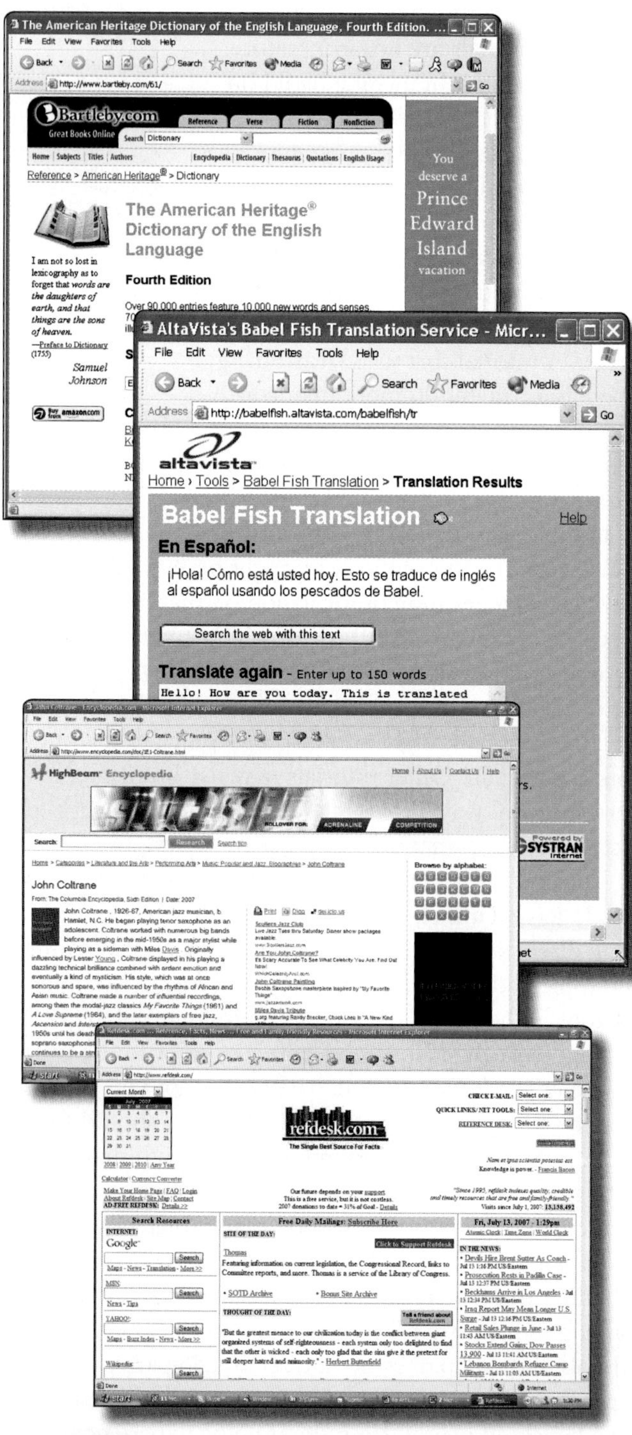

Figure 6-8 The Internet is a particularly valuable source of reference materials, such as encyclopedias, dictionaries, and other collections of facts.

words or to find synonyms. Other sites, such as Refdesk.com, provide links to reference tools on almost any topic or content, including map resources, language translators, measurement converters, currency and time zone converters, and postal zip codes.

Students also access news Web sites to better understand current events and international affairs. Some news sources even provide special student-friendly versions of their news sites (Figure 6-9). CNN, for example, has a CNN Student News site that provides top news stories written by CNN journalists and teachers. The stories are written at a level appropriate for students in middle and high school and are accompanied by a lesson plan or discussion activity. USA Today hosts the USA Today Education Web site, which provides student-friendly news stories and accompanying daily lesson plans.

One unique and fun way that teachers can incorporate the Internet into the classroom is to use WebQuests. A **WebQuest** is a project that has students use Internet resources to answer open-ended questions presented around a particular topic. In every WebQuest, you are asked to use Internet-based research to help understand or problem-solve a real-world issue. A WebQuest called A Forest Forever, for example, asks you to decide the fate of a forest just designated as a National Forest by understanding issues affecting America's forests and then working with other students to create a PowerPoint presentation with recommendations (Figure 6-10). Students not only are challenged to find Internet resources, they also have an opportunity to organize the information and interpret the information in their own way.

Students also are learning to use a variety of search tools, including directories, search engines, and metasearch engines, to help them gather information on the Web. In addition to learning how to write search queries, students also are learning how to evaluate the credibility of the Web sites and pages listed in the search results using the steps outlined in Chapter 3 (see Table 3-3).

Programming Tools

A unique way that computers are used in the classroom is to teach students basic programming skills. Even if you have no plans to be a programmer in your future career, many educators believe that learning

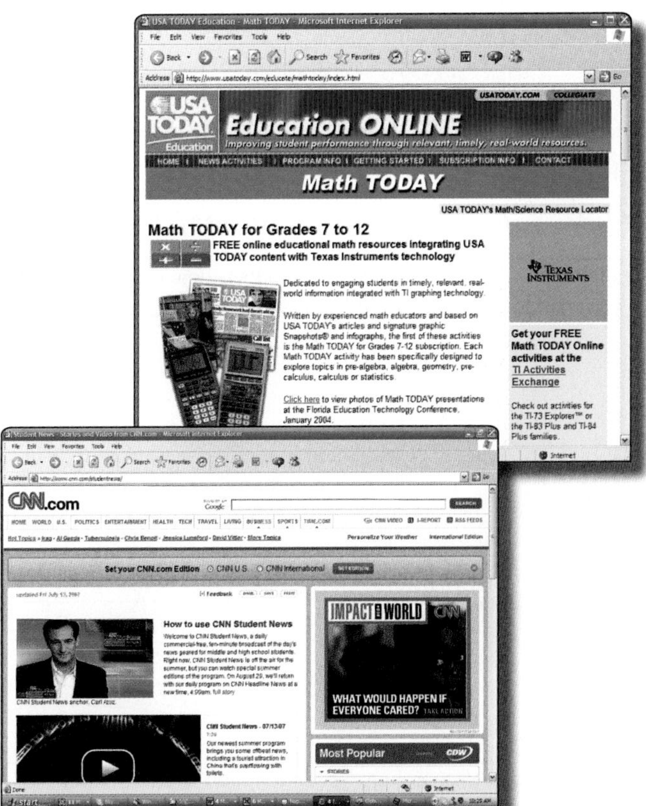

Figure 6-9 Many news sources, such as CNN and USA Today, provide special student-friendly versions of their news sites.

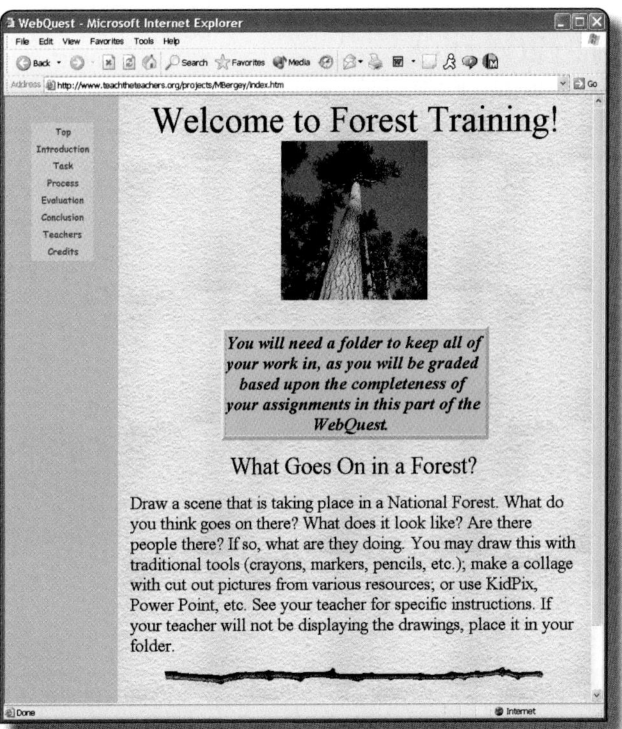

Figure 6-10 WebQuests ask students to use Internet-based research to develop a creative response to an issue or topic.

programming basics teaches you to think in an organized, systematic way about a problem you are attempting to solve (Figure 6-11). You then can apply that same logical thinking approach to a nonprogramming situation, such as figuring out the best way to organize a series of tasks in a construction or engineering project.

A popular way to teach students basic programming is by allowing them to build simple programs in LOGO. **LOGO** is a simplified programming language invented at the Massachusetts Institute of Technology by Seymour Papert. Papert created LOGO with the goal of helping new programmers to learn basic skills in the construction of scenes, called **microworlds**. At the core of LOGO is a set of geometric commands that are sent to a turtle-like object on the computer screen (Figure 6-12). The syntax of the language is simplified enough to allow learners to explore and experiment with creating their own microworlds.

One interesting approach to using LOGO is to write simple instructions to program LEGO robots created using LEGO Mindstorms bricks (Figure 6-13). The LEGO Mindstorms system consists of several key pieces, including the RCX, which is a programmable LEGO brick. You can build a model of a car, machine, animal, or a never-before-seen object around the RCX. You then can program the RCX to perform certain actions using the software provided with the LEGO Mindstorms system (called ROBOLAB) or with LOGO. The program can be downloaded to the RCX using an infrared transmitter that is connected to your computer. Infrared sensors allow the robot to accept the download and store the data. A remote control enables you to activate the RCX brick

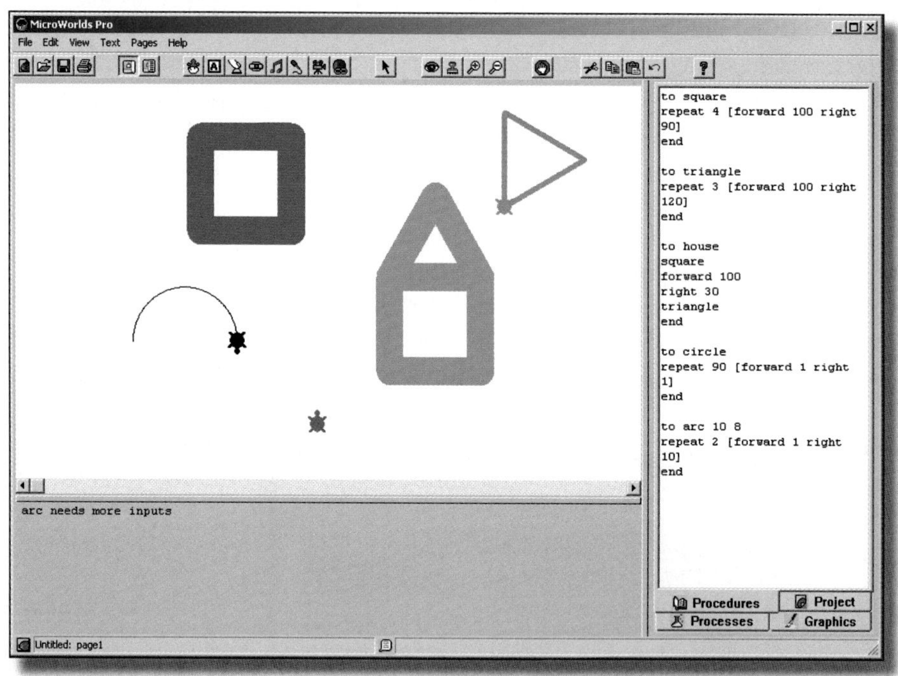

Figure 6-12 LOGO is a simplified programming language that allows new programmers to use geometric commands to move a turtle-like object on the computer screen.

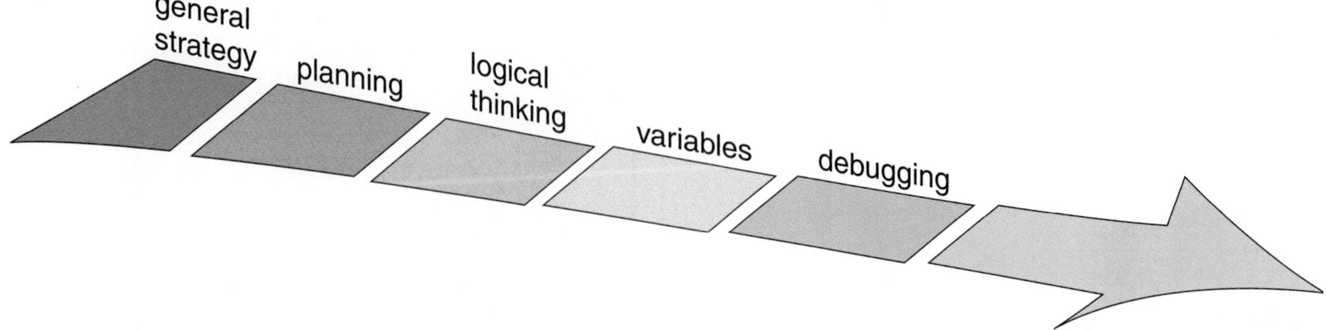

Figure 6-11 Programming is a complex task, requiring a problem-solving mindset. Researchers have identified five key skills required in the programming process: general strategy, planning, logical thinking, variables, and debugging.

from a distance. It communicates with the RCX brick using infrared light, just like a television remote control.

The LEGO Mindstorms system is built around a constructivist learning philosophy that suggests students learn best when they build knowledge for themselves, instead of simply memorizing information. Constructivism also notes that students learn best when they are excited about a topic and thus want to learn. The LEGO Mindstorms system follows these principles, giving students a fun, hands-on experience building their own invention – something they can care about. The process is open-ended; students can be encouraged to experiment and create entirely new machines each time.

Figure 6-13 The LEGO Mindstorms system allows students to build a model around programmable RCX bricks.

Educational Games and Simulations

Computer-based games and simulations are an effective way to teach new concepts and skills, by allowing students to invent new things or explore new environments. **Educational games** are designed to help students learn concepts while playing a game with specific rules. These games can be an effective way to teach information through repetition and practice. They also can promote a spirit of competition, by allowing students to compete against other students or the game itself.

Many educational games create environments that require students to use problem-solving skills to find solutions. For example, with the Carmen Sandiego series, as students follow clues to try to find the criminal mastermind, Carmen Sandiego, they learn about geography, culture, music, and history (Figure 6-14). Another popular educational game is the CD-ROM based Oregon Trail. As the leader of a wagon party, you must make key decisions, such as what supplies to pack or which route to travel to get your group of pioneers safely to the Oregon Territory. Not only does the software present history in a highly engaging way, it also helps you learn basic organizational, resource management, decision-making, and problem solving skills. The game also helps you understand the consequences of your actions (for example, not packing enough ammunition or food for your trip).

As you have learned, computer simulations use computers and software to create a realistic experience to show how events might occur under certain conditions. In the classroom, simulations allow students to study topics that would be too expensive, dangerous, or impractical to practice in real life. For example, asking students to manage the power output from a nuclear power plant clearly is both dangerous and impractical. Using a Web-based simulation, such as the Nuclear Power Plant Simulator, allows you to experience the process of manipulating the control rods and coolant at the plant, in an effort to generate maximum power without having a meltdown (Figure 6-15a). Alternatively, students can run a lemonade stand to learn basic economic principles and the ups and downs of managing a business (Figure 6-15b).

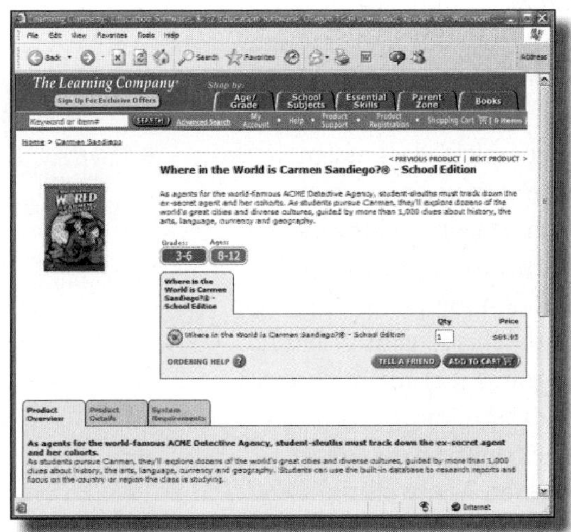

Figure 6-14 For more than a decade, students of all ages have been chasing the elusive Carmen Sandiego and her counterparts, while learning about geography, culture, music, and history.

Table 6-3 lists several examples of topics where using a simulation provides a fun, interactive, and effective way to teach a topic that you otherwise only might read about in a textbook or on a static Web page.

In addition to bringing complex topics to life, computer-based simulations and educational games give students a chance to engage actively in real-world situations – or in whole new worlds that they could not possibly experience in real life.

Software Tools

In the classroom, computers are used not only to convey information, but also as tools that help you create a professional-looking English paper, build a presentation for your speech on comparative politics, or construct a Web page to show the findings of your team's biology project. Teaching students how to use application software is critically important in preparing students for work in the information economy. Many companies will not even consider a candidate without some basic application software skills, such as using a word processor, presentation software, or e-mail.

For this reason, students at all levels – from kindergarten into graduate school – are learning to use application software, also called productivity software, to complete class assignments. Learning to use application software, such as word processing, spreadsheet, database, presentation graphics, and desktop publishing software, gives students a comfort level with the programs that might encourage them to explore more advanced features, either on their own or in additional classes. Many classes also teach students to use Web browsers to navigate the many learning resources available on the Internet, as well as to use HTML editors and other Web publishing tools to create personal Web pages.

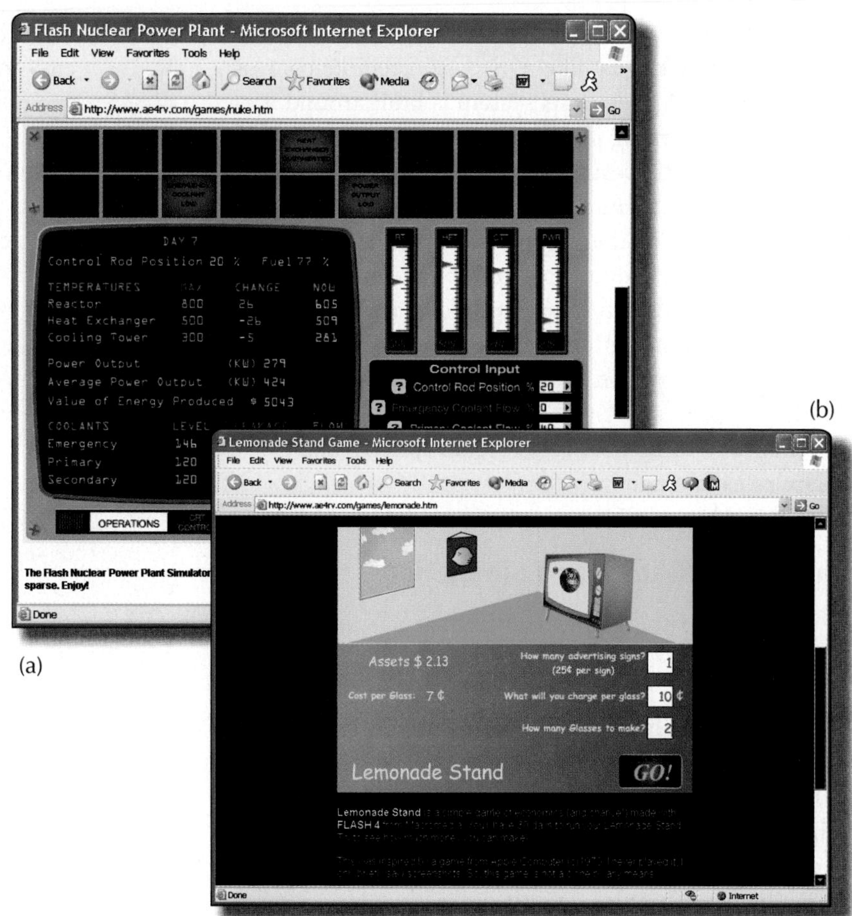

Figure 6-15 Using simulations allows you to study topics that are too expensive, dangerous, or impractical to practice in real life. The Web-based Nuclear Power Plant Simulator allows you to experience the process of manipulating the control rods and coolant in an effort to generate maximum power without having a meltdown (Figure 6-15a). Alternatively, running a lemonade stand lets you learn basic economic principles and the ups and downs of running a business (Figure 6-15b).

Table 6-3 Simulation Characteristics

CHARACTERISTIC	*EXAMPLES OF SIMULATIONS*
Expensive to practice	■ Running a business ■ Launching a rocket
Dangerous to practice	■ Flying a jet ■ Managing a nuclear power plant
Too slow to see the processes involved	■ Motion of glaciers ■ Ozone pollution ■ Creation of diamonds
Too fast to see the processes involved	■ Motion of sound waves ■ Speed of light
Too large to see the processes involved	■ Motion of the planets ■ Plate tectonics ■ Formation of a black hole
Too small to see the processes involved	■ Bonding of atoms in molecules ■ Cell mitosis

In addition to teaching students to use basic application software, some teachers also encourage them to use special-purpose software to learn more about a specific subject. As you learned in previous chapters, students in a music class might use notation software to record the melody of a new song, while art students might create computer-generated fractal art. Students in a creative writing class might use collaborative writing groupware to work collectively on creative writing and editing projects. Students in a science lab might record rainfall amounts in a geographic information system (GIS) to help analyze patterns of precipitation.

Students also are learning to use multimedia-authoring software to create presentations to share with the class or to turn in, much as they would a written report. Multimedia-authoring software allows users to combine text, graphics, audio, video, and animation into an interactive application. For example, thousands of schools around the world use HyperStudio as a multimedia-authoring software tool. HyperStudio makes it easy to create presentations using a series of slides and placing text, sounds, and video clips on them (Figure 6-16). The program also lets you create a hyperlink from a button or word in your project directly to a Web page. When saved, the presentation is called a **stack**. The stack can be presented to the class, handed in on a floppy disk, e-mailed to the teacher, or even posted to the Web.

Students also use presentation graphics software, such as Microsoft PowerPoint or Apple Keynote, to create multimedia presentations. **Presentation graphics software** is application software that allows you to create visual aids for presentations to communicate ideas, messages, and other information to a group (Figure 6-17). The presentation can be viewed as slides, sometimes called a **slide show**, which can be displayed on a large monitor or projection screen. PowerPoint and Keynote both provide templates to help students design slides, as well as graphics, audio, and video clips to enhance a presentation. Students can use these slide shows as support for a class presentation on a specific topic.

(a) Card 1 — Title Card

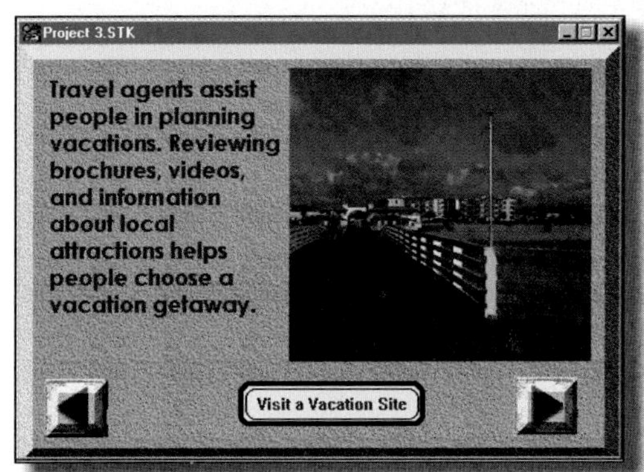

(b) Card 2

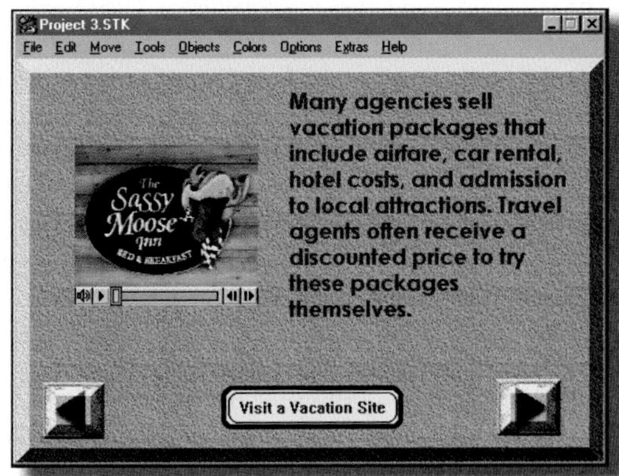

(c) Card 3

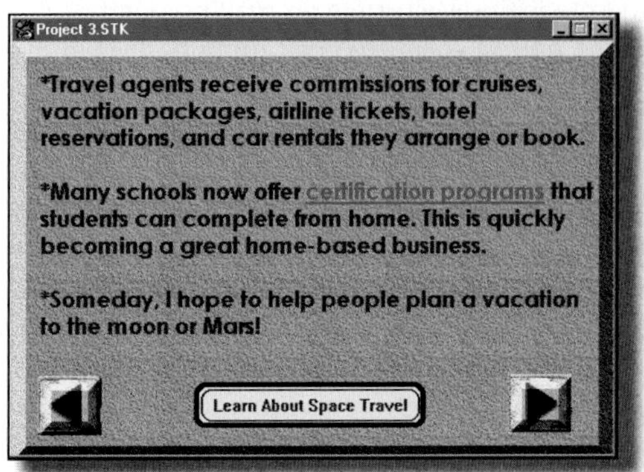

(d) Card 4

Figure 6-16 Multimedia-authoring software such as HyperStudio makes it easy for students to create presentations called stacks, which include text, sounds, graphics, and more. Students can hand in the stacks on disk, via e-mail, or even post their stacks to the Web.

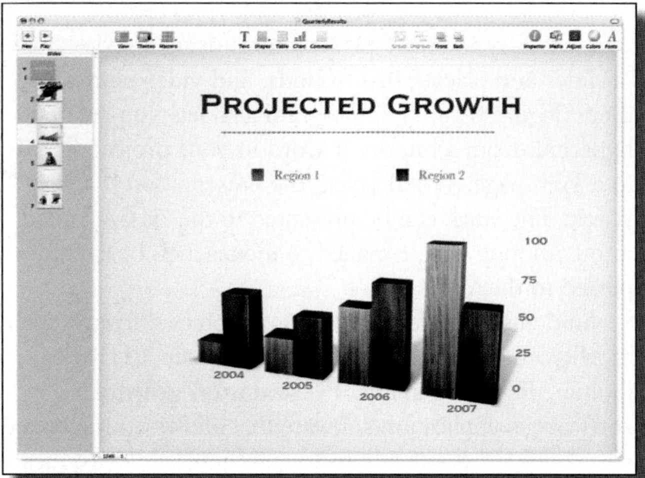

(a) Keynote

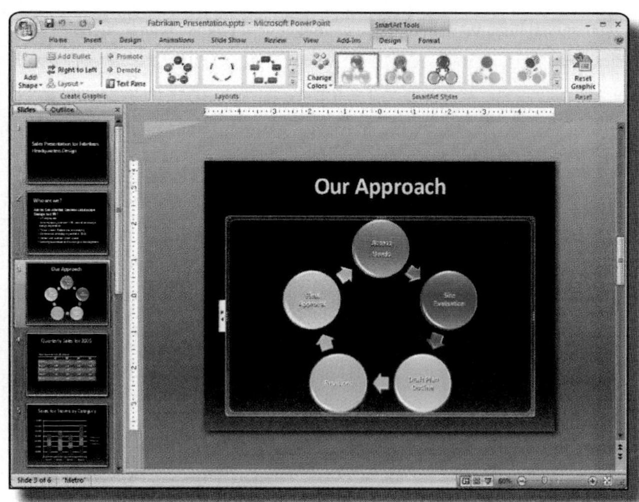

(b) PowerPoint

Figure 6-17 Presentation graphics software, such a Apple Keynote and Microsoft PowerPoint, allows students to create visual aids for presentations to share with the class.

@ISSUE: Privacy Protection for Pupils

Computers in the classroom bring with them numerous benefits, as well as potential privacy concerns. For the most part, schools take great care to ensure that your safety, health, and privacy are protected while you are on school grounds. Your right to privacy has limits at your school, however, just as it does in the workplace. For example, if you send an e-mail from a school computer, the school has a legal right to review its contents. Messages sent within the school, as well as those sent outside of the school, also can be subject to monitoring by the school. A school can review cookie files on a computer, which can reveal every Web site visited from that computer. If someone logs on to a lab computer with your username and password, you might be falsely accused of visiting Web sites on making bombs — and be the first person suspected of calling in the bomb threat to the school last week.

The concern is not just how you use school computers; it also is about what they are storing about you on the computers. Schools possess and store a significant amount of data about you, including your personal information, address, all of your grades, health issues, disciplinary actions, and more. Schools thus must take steps to ensure that only appropriate personnel see this information. Hackers present a daunting challenge because they might be able to access the school database and post your most sensitive information on the Internet.

Even the simplest and most innocent act can cause issues. For example, suppose a school creates a track team Web page, listing names, contact information, and a small paragraph about each athlete's hobbies and interests outside of school. A student from another school, upset about losing the state tournament to you, accesses the Web site, notices that your hobbies include playing with your dog, and starts placing phone calls to you at home, threatening to poison your puppy.

Schools now recognize the importance in explicitly defining privacy policies and guidelines on the disclosure of student or faculty information. Most schools thus include specific information in the school's acceptable use policy (AUP) to inform staff and students about their privacy rights related to the use of the school's computer network. Most policies are simple, but the general policy is that any e-mail messages, cookies, documents, or other electronic files stored on the school's computer or network are subject to search. Like your locker, the school can examine the contents of computers at any time to ensure that students are using the system responsibly. While most schools only will do so if needed — for example, if there is reason to suspect an activity or material that violates the school's code of conduct or the law — it is important to remember the school's policy as you are using school computers.

(continued)

@ISSUE: Privacy Protection for Pupils *(continued)*

Further, even as schools are working to protect themselves by clearly spelling out acceptable use policies, some schools are providing companies with students' personal information. In an effort to get new computers, software, and networking equipment for your school, the administration may agree to provide access to your personal information or allow companies to display ads on computers in the lab. Critics are quick to suggest that if the cost of a commercial deal is subjecting students to online advertising or allowing corporate marketers to mine students' private personal information, then the price is too high.

Student profiling also is not uncommon. A company called American Student List sells databases of children's names in grades K-12, overlaid with data on sex, age, race, and more. They gather the information from surveys given to students in school — surveys students might believe are for college admissions and other education-related purposes. In fact, that data sometimes is used for the secondary purpose of marketing credit cards, magazines, student recognition products (such as the "Who's Who Among American High School Students" list), and job recruitment opportunities. In fact, a complaint was lodged in 2003 against American Student List and another company, The National Research Center for College and University Admissions, Inc. for misleading both high school educators and students about the use of the data collected. Two other student data collection companies — Education Research Center of America, Inc. and Student Marketing Group, Inc. — settled FTC charges in 2003 regarding their deceptive data collection methods for non-education-related uses.

Privacy advocates also express concerns about the use of fingerprint recognition in school libraries. In 2002, thousands of pupils in schools across the United Kingdom had their fingerprints taken so they could be recognized by the fingerprint recognition system installed in school libraries. For libraries, a fingerprint recognition system cuts costs and prevents children from having to carry library cards around. The system involves scanning each child's thumbprint, which is stored in a computer and used to prove the child's identity every time he or she borrows a book.

Groups like EPIC are vocal about the fact that students should not shed all of their rights at the front door to the school, including the right to privacy. In fact, several laws are aimed at protecting student privacy, most notably the Family Educational Rights and Privacy Act (FERPA) — also called the Buckley Amendment.

The FERPA protects the confidentiality of student education records at any school that receives federal funds (which includes almost every school in the United States, including private schools). FERPA gives students the right to review their own education records and request corrections, as well as to disallow a school from releasing their personally identifiable information. The act also prohibits educational institutions from disclosing personally identifiable information in education records without the written consent of the student, or if the student is a minor, the student's parents.

FERPA is not foolproof, however, and includes many exceptions that allow student records to be released without consent. Most involve sharing the information with other schools or financial aid organizations, but schools also will supply the information to comply with a judicial order or lawfully issued subpoena. The act includes the nebulous phrase that schools can release records to "organizations conducting certain studies for or on behalf of a school" without student consent. For many, that phrase leaves a huge loophole in the law, allowing companies like American Student List to gain data from students.

To understand your school's stance on student privacy and just how it might be using your data, take the time to visit your school's Web site or read the student handbook. Most likely, they are protecting your privacy as closely as you would yourself. There is no harm in asking — but there just might be in not taking the time to ask.

COMPUTERS AS TEACHING TOOLS

At school, teachers use computers to assist with classroom instruction. Presentation tools, for example, help teachers support lectures with engaging multimedia explanations of concepts. Technologies such as e-mail, chat, and discussion groups help teachers stay in touch with other instructors and students, both in and out of the classroom. Teachers also use computer-based systems to support the administrative aspects of the classroom – test administration, grading, scheduling, and more – so that they can focus on the teaching process. This section reviews several ways that teachers use computers as teaching tools in today's classrooms, including the use of presentation tools, communications tools, and learning management systems.

Presentation Tools

Teachers use multimedia-authoring and presentation graphics software to create presentations to deliver in the classroom. Software packages such as PowerPoint and Keynote offer tools to support lectures and create class handouts. Presentation graphics software allows you to view a finished presentation in a variety of formats. An outline includes only the text from each slide, such as the slide title and key points (Figure 6-18a). Audience handouts, which include images of two of more slides on a page, can be used as class handouts on which students can take notes (Figure 6-18b). Teachers also can print notes to help themselves deliver the presentation. A notes page shows an image of the slide along with any additional notes the teacher wants to see while discussing a topic or slide (Figure 6-18c).

Multimedia-authoring software allows instructors to create interactive presentations for student use. Once created, the multimedia presentations often are used as computer-based or Web-based training tools, with tutorials on special topics. Teachers also can use multimedia-authoring software to create simulations that bring topics to life. For example, using multimedia-authoring software tools a teacher can create a simulation of how the planets orbit the sun so that students more easily can envision the motion of the planets by seeing it on a computer screen.

Teachers also are replacing the traditional blackboard with an **interactive whiteboard**, also called an **electronic whiteboard**, which turns a computer and a data projector into a powerful tool for teaching and learning (Figure 6-19). Many electronic whiteboards allow you to write notes, draw diagrams, or highlight key information on the whiteboard using your finger,

Figure 6-19 Sophisticated electronic whiteboards, such as the SMART Board, produced by SMART Technologies, allow you to press on its large touch-sensitive surface to access and control any computer application. In addition, you can write notes, draw diagrams, and highlight information using a pen from the SMART Pen Tray or just your finger.

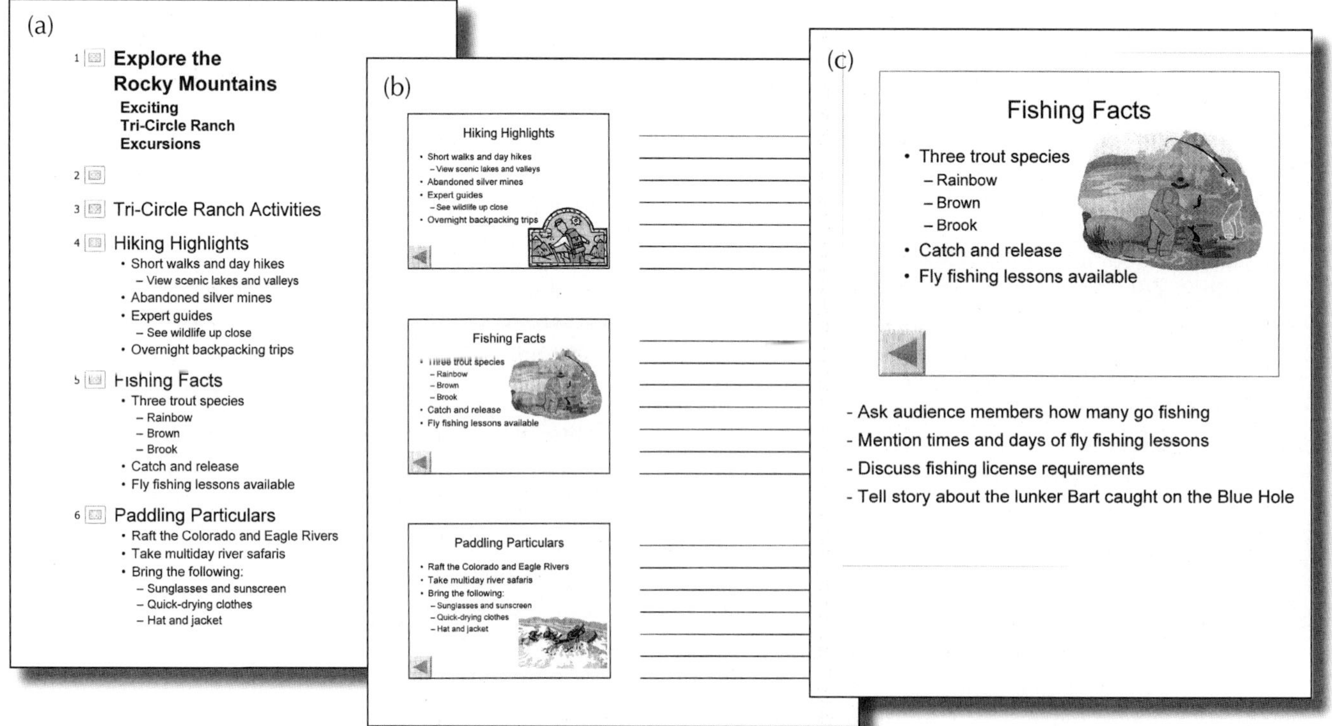

Figure 6-18 In addition to viewing the presentation as slides, presentation graphics software allows users to print the presentation as an outline, as audience handouts, or as notes pages for the speaker.

regular whiteboard pens, or special pens included with the whiteboard. The teacher then can save the notes electronically, print them, and then hand the notes out to students as follow-up to a lecture.

Another new technology that instructors are starting to use is the classroom response system, or "clickers." Also know as *audience response systems* or *student response systems*, a **classroom response system (CRS)** uses RF or infrared signals to transmit student-generated responses to the instructor's computer from handheld keypads. The system typically consists of individual student handheld response units similar to TV remote controls, add-in software for presentation software such as PowerPoint, and an RF or infrared receiving unit attached to the instructor's computer. The instructor can use the system during class to survey or quiz students, but instead of asking for a show of hands or paper responses, students can register their choices by simply clicking the appropriate button on their keypad to send a signal to the teacher. If presentation software is being used, the tabulated results of all student responses is automatically tallied and can be shown immediately to the class for timely feedback and correction if needed. Figure 6-20 shows one such example of the keypad devices and their use in class.

Communications Tools

Even if most of the communication between teachers and students occurs in the classroom, today's teachers can utilize new communications tools to further promote interaction. Some of these tools allow a class to communicate with other classes or teachers from around the world, while others allow teachers to communicate to parents and students outside of the classroom.

Figure 6-20 Classroom response systems (CRS) can be used to take attendance, increase participation, and provide immediate feedback to students as they are quizzed during class time.

E-MAIL E-mail, which is the most widely used Internet application for all users, provides an excellent communications tool for teachers. Using e-mail, teachers can send information to parents on upcoming student projects or field trips, communicate with fellow teachers to share curriculum ideas, or remind students to bring pictures from home for a community art project.

MAILING LISTS Teachers also benefit from **mailing lists**, or **listservs**, in which e-mails on certain topics are sent to members who have subscribed to the list. A mailing list allows teachers to receive e-mails from and send e-mails to a group of teachers to exchange information, thoughts, and ideas about particular subjects, such as technology in the classroom or new ways to teach earth science. Hundreds of education-related mailing lists are available for teachers to gather and share information. A computer called a **list server** handles the job of directing the e-mail to all members of the list. To run, a mailing list requires a machine that will act as the list server for the list; special software, typically listserv or majordomo, to facilitate the exchange of e-mail among members; and a **moderator** or **list owner** who does various administrative tasks to keep the list running. To receive e-mail from a mailing list, you must first join, or **subscribe** to the list. To stop receiving e-mails, you can **unsubscribe** from the mailing list.

NEWSGROUPS AND MESSAGE BOARDS Newsgroups are another resource for teachers to gather information. Most schools have bulletin boards in central locations, such as the school lobby, student union building, and faculty offices. The bulletin boards provide a way to post information about events, new policies, and schedules; teachers can stop by and read the information others have posted. **Usenet newsgroups**, often simply called **newsgroups**, essentially are an electronic version of the old bulletin board, in which users can post messages and browse through, read, and respond to postings.

The entire collection of newsgroups available on the Internet is called Usenet, which contains thousands of newsgroups on a number of topics. Usenet newsgroups were developed in the late 1970s to provide students at several universities with the ability to communicate with large numbers of people in close-to-real time. To read and post articles in a newsgroup, you need special software known as an **NNTP client** or **newsreader**.

A popular Web-based type of discussion forum that does not require a newsreader is a **message board**. Many Web sites have message boards, instead of newsgroups, because they are easier to use. Also called **discussion groups**, these Web-based discussion areas supply teachers with a common community to share ideas. There are hundreds of discussion group focused on education available on the Web, with many aimed at specific topics such as distance education, technology in the classroom, teaching English, music in K-12 classes, and more (Figure 6-21).

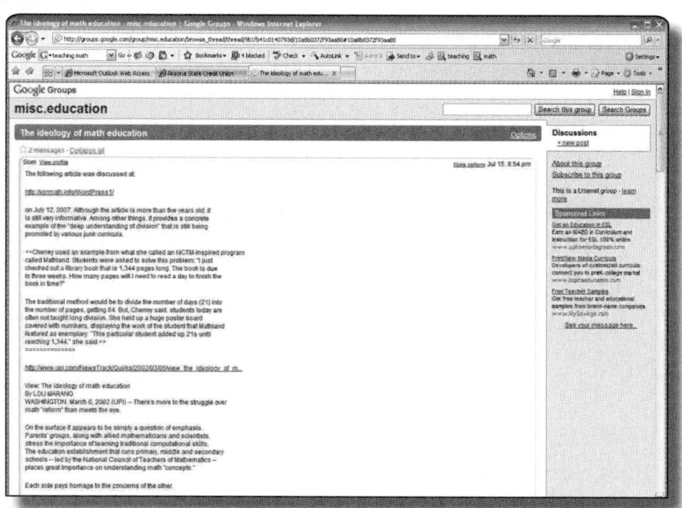

Figure 6-21 Teachers can use a Web site, such as Google Groups, to find discussion groups focused on specific topics such as distance education, technology in the classroom, teaching English, music in K-12 classes, and more.

VIDEO CONFERENCING AND CHAT Teachers are using computers to help introduce new communication tools into the learning process. Using video conferencing, teachers can connect students who may be in separate classrooms in different countries. A **video conference** is a meeting between two or more geographically separated people who use a network or the Internet to transmit audio and video data. To participate in a video conference, you need video conferencing software, such as NetMeeting, along with a microphone, speakers, and a video camera attached to a computer. With video conferencing, a teacher can link her classroom to a classroom in London to talk about how the United Kingdom's parliamentary government system is similar to and different from the United States government (Figure 6-22). The video conferencing software also can include tools to allow students to share electronic files or write notes on a whiteboard, a Paint-like program in which you can diagram or sketch ideas.

Similar tools, such as chat, allow for real-time communication. **Real time** means that the people who are communicating are online at the same time. A chat is a real-time typed conversation that takes place on a computer. A chat room is a location on an Internet server that permits users to chat with each other. Anyone in the chat room can participate in the conversation, which usually is specific to a particulate topic. Some chat rooms support voice chats and video chats, in which you can hear or see fellow students as they chat.

PODCASTING The most recent new use of technology for communication with students involves podcasting. **Podcasting** is a technique for publishing both audio and video programs on the Internet. The name comes from Apple's popular MP3 player, the iPod, and "broadcasting." Podcasts are fairly common on commercial news Web sites and iTunes, but are just starting to find a home in education. For example, some educators are experimenting with podcasting class lectures, exams reviews, and chapter summaries, while textbook publishers are making available podcasts of current events that educators can use to supplement their daily lesson plans. Apple even has a Web page dedicated to podcasting in education!

Learning Management Systems

Teachers also use computer-based systems to support the administrative aspects of the classroom. A

Figure 6-22 The Global Schoolhouse Project uses videoconferencing, e-mail, and other tools to link classrooms around the world, so they can collaborate on shared projects and learn together.

learning management system (LMS) is a computer-based management administration system that tracks students' progress and performance in the classroom. The specific terms used to describe a learning management system have changed over time: the original term, **computer-managed instruction**, or **CMI**, changed to **integrated learning systems (ILS)** and now to learning management system or LMS. All of these terms refer to the set of software tools used to support classroom administration, including conducting registration, managing schedules and course catalogs, testing and placement, analyzing student performance, and other management functions. LMS can be used in a traditional classroom setting that uses CBT to provide content or as part of a course that uses Web-based training.

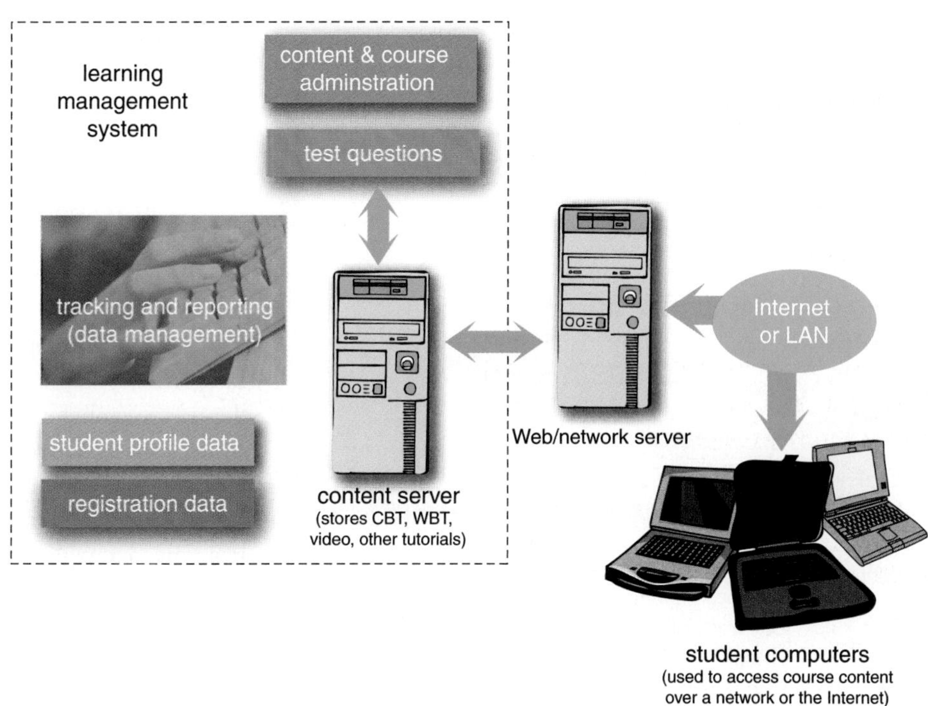

Figure 6-23 A learning management system delivers course content and testing and provides tools for student registration, grading, and reporting.

A learning management system can include a wide range of functions (Figure 6-23). In general, most systems include:

- Tools to create and share course pages, such as syllabi, homework assignments, and class updates
- Roster operations tools to allow students to register for courses and maintain their personal student profiles
- A test engine to create, deliver, and score tests with a range of questions: true/false, multiple choice, matching, fill in the blank, and even essays
- A database or other repository of electronic course content, called **courseware**, which can include text, graphics, videos, CBT, WBT, and more
- Grade book, tracking, and reporting tools to allow instructors and students to track student progress and test scores (the system even may e-mail grades to students)
- Communications tools, such as chat, discussion groups, or e-mail, to allow students to communicate with other students and to allow instructors to e-mail updates and grades to students

As shown in Figure 6-23, an LMS allows students to take courses over a network in a school classroom or via the Internet from home, a hotel room, or anywhere in the world. Students and instructors must log into the system with a username and password. Once they are logged in, the system usually displays personalized content showing a list of courses in which that student currently is enrolled, upcoming homework assignments, messages posted by the teacher, and so on.

DISTANCE LEARNING

Distance learning (DL) is the delivery of education at one location, while the learning takes place at another location. Also called **e-learning**, distance learning courses use computers and other technologies to extend education from the classroom to anywhere students can access an Internet-connected computer (Figure 6-24).

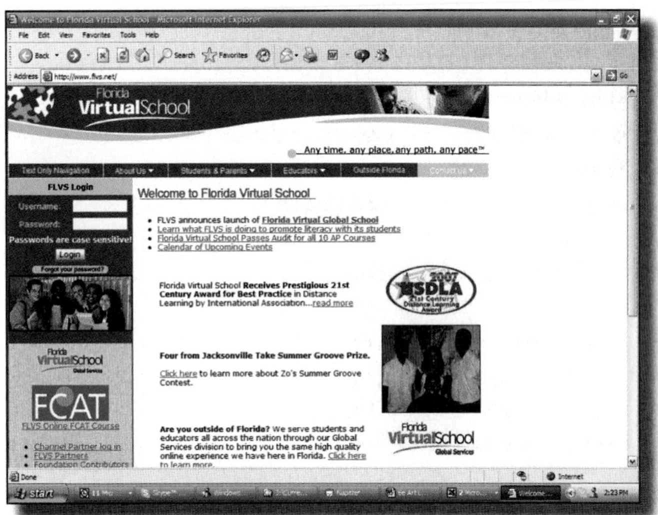

Figure 6-24 Distance learning (DL) courses use computers and other technologies to extend education beyond the four walls of the school. For example, the Florida Virtual School is an Internet-based, public high school with over 31,000 students, many of whom use the distance learning program to take courses not available in their school, such as Advanced Placement (AP) courses or electives such as Latin.

Web-based training companies often specialize in providing teachers and instructors with the tools needed for the preparation, management, and distribution of distance learning courses. Some learning management systems, for example, supply teachers with tools to create rich, educational, Web-based training sites and allow students to access the Web-based learning environment over the Web. Tools at the site also let students check their progress, take practice tests, search for topics, send e-mail, and participate in discussions or chats.

Depending on the type of course, a distance learning class may or may not have a teacher or facilitator who provides course guidelines, manages discussion boards, delivers lectures, and so forth. A distance learning course with a teacher presenting content and guiding the class typically is referred to as instructor-led training (ILT). That term is used to differentiate those courses from self-paced training courses that do not have an instructor, such as Web-based software skills tutorials available over the Internet.

Distance learning courses also fall into two other categories, synchronous or asynchronous, based on how the course timing is structured. When distance learning courses are **synchronous**, the class is structured more like a normal classroom, which means students and instructors attend class at a specific time and information is shared in real time. Technologies used to support a synchronous e-learning class include real-time chat, video conferencing, and instant messaging. When distance learning courses are **asynchronous**, learning does not take place at a specific time. Instead, students access course resources at whatever time is convenient, work through the assignments at their own pace, and communicate with the instructor or other students through e-mail, mailing lists, newsgroups, or message boards. Many courses use a combination of approaches, with students attending class sessions conducted synchronously, while asynchronously accessing additional resources such as PowerPoint slide shows, news articles, or Web-based simulations. Both approaches have advantages and disadvantages, as shown in Table 6-4.

Distance learning courses are ideal for students who live far from a school or college campus or work full- or part-time. By eliminating the barriers of distance, distance learning allows students to attend class from anywhere in the world and at times that fit their schedules. Distance

Table 6-4 Synchronous Versus Asynchronous Course Delivery Models

ASYNCHRONOUS	*SYNCHRONOUS*
Advantages	**Advantages**
■ Convenient and accessible: students can access training at any time, 24 hours a day, seven days a week. ■ Self-paced content allows students to work on their own timeline. ■ Course content is entirely consistent.	■ Instant feedback on a student's performance. ■ Allows the training to be adjusted immediately if needed. ■ Gives students the same sense of community as a live classroom.
Disadvantages	**Disadvantages**
■ Student may feel isolated or be less motivated without any real-time human interaction. ■ Does not provide immediate feedback on a student's performance, leaving adjustments to training until after an evaluation is completed	■ Training is not self-paced, which means students must work at the timeline of the rest of the class. ■ Can be difficult to schedule courses in different time zones. ■ Students' availability needs to be managed.

learning also benefits those who live in rural locations; if their smaller schools do not offer more specialized courses, students can attend those courses at a major university as a distance learning course. DL also is ideal for physically challenged students who are capable of learning, but are unable to travel to school on an everyday basis. According to the American Federation of Teachers, U.S. high school students in all 50 states may take online courses in public schools. Many of these students use e-learning to complete freshmen college courses while still in high school or to explore possible careers by taking courses in special areas such as engineering or computer technology.

Many companies and organizations, such as Motorola, Circuit City, Merck, McDonald's, General Motors, and the U.S. Army, have historically offered e-learning opportunities to employees, to help workers stay up to date on skills or help them move into new jobs. Companies often choose DL instead of face-to-face training sessions because DL reduces travel costs and cuts back on the need for trainers and centralized training facilities. For organizations like the U.S. Armed Forces, distance learning is a perfect way to train enlisted men and officers around the world. The U.S. Army, for instance, sponsors an eArmyU distance learning program, which gives enlistees the chance to enroll in thousands of online courses and 145 degree and online certification programs from colleges and universities around the country.

@ISSUE: Ready to Go the Distance (Learning)?

Upon first consideration, distance learning courses seem to have everything going for them: you can attend class in your pajamas, order a pizza as sustenance during the lecture, and — if the classes are taught asynchronously — take a break from class mid-day to go to the gym. Plus, with the teacher miles away, he or she is unlikely to call on you while you are mid-daydream. How could you turn down a learning experience like that?

You may want to reconsider. The reality is that that the dropout rate for higher-education distance learning courses typically is 20 percent higher than it is for traditional classroom-based courses. At community colleges, the dropout rate for distance learning courses often reaches 50 percent or more. The reason for such high dropout rates? Students enroll in distance learning courses without adequately considering whether or not they are good e-learning candidates — and then, too late, find out they are not.

Many schools provide online surveys with questions you should consider before enrolling in a distance learning course, some of which are listed in Table 6-5. Most of these surveys focus on four key areas:

- *Motivation*: Be sure you understand your main motivation for taking a distance learning course — whether to enhance skills and knowledge for your job, to help you change careers, to complete a degree started years ago, or to learn a new skill. Understanding your own motivation will help you when you are feeling overwhelmed by coursework or have writer's block while composing your final paper.
- *Discipline and time management*: Distance learning requires more self-discipline than traditional classroom-based learning and demands excellent time management skills. Generally, students drawn to distance learning courses are trying to juggle numerous responsibilities: full-time work, taking care of children, managing a household, and other everyday tasks. Life does not stop just because you are in a distance learning course. To be successful in a distance learning class, you will need to manage your commitments outside of class, as well as in class. Be sure to ask yourself: am I disciplined enough to set a schedule and meet the dates? Can I avoid procrastination? Can I work with family or friends to help take on some of my commitments so I have time for class and homework?
- *Solid study skills*: Students with good study skills are more likely to perform well in a distance learning course. Instead of listening to lectures in a classroom, much of the distance learning course will involve reading content online or in a book, typing e-mail or instant messages, and completing exams. Having solid reading, writing, and test-taking skills thus are critical to your e-learning success. You also need to be able read and follow detailed instructions on your own, because the instructor may not be immediately available to answer questions. If your study skills are better than average, you likely will do better than average in a distance learning course. If you need help honing your study skills, many Web sites and books are available to provide help.
- *Computer skills and Internet access*: Most distance learning courses are Web-based, which means you need to be comfortable using a computer and the Internet. To make the learning experience more convenient, it also is best if you have a computer with Internet access someplace easily accessible — at home, at work, or wherever you primarily want to access the course content. Before signing up for an e-learning course, ask yourself: am I already comfortable with using the Internet as a means of communication and research? Do I own or have access to a computer with Internet access and e-mail? If the answers are yes, then you are one step closer to being ready for a distance learning course.

@ISSUE: Ready to Go the Distance (Learning)? *(continued)*

Without question, distance learning courses provide significant advantages for students who are working full- or part-time or are not geographically close to a college that offers a particular course. Before entering any online class, however, be sure to ask the questions outlined here to help determine if you are ready for e-learning. Just like a classroom-based course, distance learning classes will present challenges: assignments with short deadlines, concepts that are difficult to grasp, and papers that require significant research. However, distance learning allows you to take courses when it is convenient for you, to study at home or at the office, or to access learning resources online any time you need them. And the rewards for completing the distance learning course are the same as with any class: new skills, new knowledge, and a new point to add to your transcript and resume. Plus, with a distance learning course, you can celebrate your final class by finishing the last slice of pizza as you e-mail your final exam to your instructor (just be sure to keep the tomato sauce off the keyboard!).

Table 6-5 Distance Learning Success Indicators

- Am I self-directed and highly motivated?
- Am I self-disciplined and do I work well independently?
- Are my writing and communication skills better than average?
- Do I try to solve problems and work through difficulties independently?
- Can I read and follow detailed instructions on my own?
- Do I manage my time well?
- Can I establish a regular weekly schedule and complete assigned work by the required dates?
- Am I already comfortable with using the Internet as a means of communication and research?
- Do I own or have access to a computer with access to e-mail and the Internet?
- Do I have enough time to take a distance learning courses? (Distance learning courses require as much or more time per week as classroom-based courses.)

Questions to ask yourself before enrolling in a distance learning course. If you answer Yes to most of these questions, then you may be ready for a distance learning course.

TECHNOLOGY IN THE CLASSROOM: BENEFITS AND OPPORTUNITIES

With computers as common in the classroom as the blackboard and notebooks, educators and parents are eager to assess what the impact of technology in the classroom has been – and where there is room for improvement.

Benefits of Technology in the Classroom

Researchers and educators have worked hard to assess the value that technology brings to the learning process and educational experience. One of the challenges of assessing technology's impact is that it is difficult to separate the use of technology from the key role of teachers in the learning process (Figure 6-25). Most evaluations, however, show that if teachers are trained to integrate technology into the classroom effectively, computers and technology tools can be a valuable addition to the learning environment. Some of the positive effects that technology has in the classroom include:

- Bringing interesting and engaging courses into the classroom, with studies that are based on real-world problems and encourage active participation. For example, students can use simulations such as Oregon Trail or hands-on projects such as LEGO Mindstorms to define a problem, test ideas, and receive feedback.

Figure 6-25 Teachers make a difference in the quality of their students' education when they integrate technology effectively.

- Giving students a sense of purpose. Research has demonstrated that completing realistic tasks, such as creating a project Web site, results in increased learning, stronger writing, and longer retention. Even more important, students engaged in building their own products develop a sense of purpose and value – and an understanding of how to contribute to their community.
- Allowing students to work in teams with other students or practitioners beyond the school classroom. Students learn collaboration and research skills, which are critically important for future success.
- Providing learning experiences that support thinking and problem solving. For example, when students use the Internet to find resources, they are constructing (not receiving) knowledge and building valuable research skills.
- Helping create virtual communities of teachers, administrators, parents, students, practicing scientists, and other interested community people, to explore new ways to improve learning.
- Expanding learning opportunities to all students, who can participate in courses using distance learning tools.

Overall, most educators and researchers agree that under the right conditions, technology advances children's academic achievement. In many cases, technology is a positive addition to, rather than a replacement for, traditional classroom activities. For example, as part of the Hands-On Universe program, high school astronomy and physics classes are reviewing computer images captured by automated telescopes at the University of California, Berkeley, Lawrence Berkeley Lab (Figure 6-26). The program is a huge success; two groups of students even discovered previously unknown supernovas. Conventional testing, however, does not have an accurate way to assess learning captured during these kinds of complex learning experiences, nor the student's ability to apply these concepts to new situations. It thus can be difficult to accurately assess technology's true impact on learning in and out of the classroom.

Opportunities for Improvement

Technology, by its very nature, is simply a set of tools. Providing computers, software, and Internet connections is just the first step in ensuring all students have access to technology. The successful use and integration of those tools in the classroom depends on a number of factors, including having well-trained teachers, adequate hardware, and the support of the school and community. All too often,

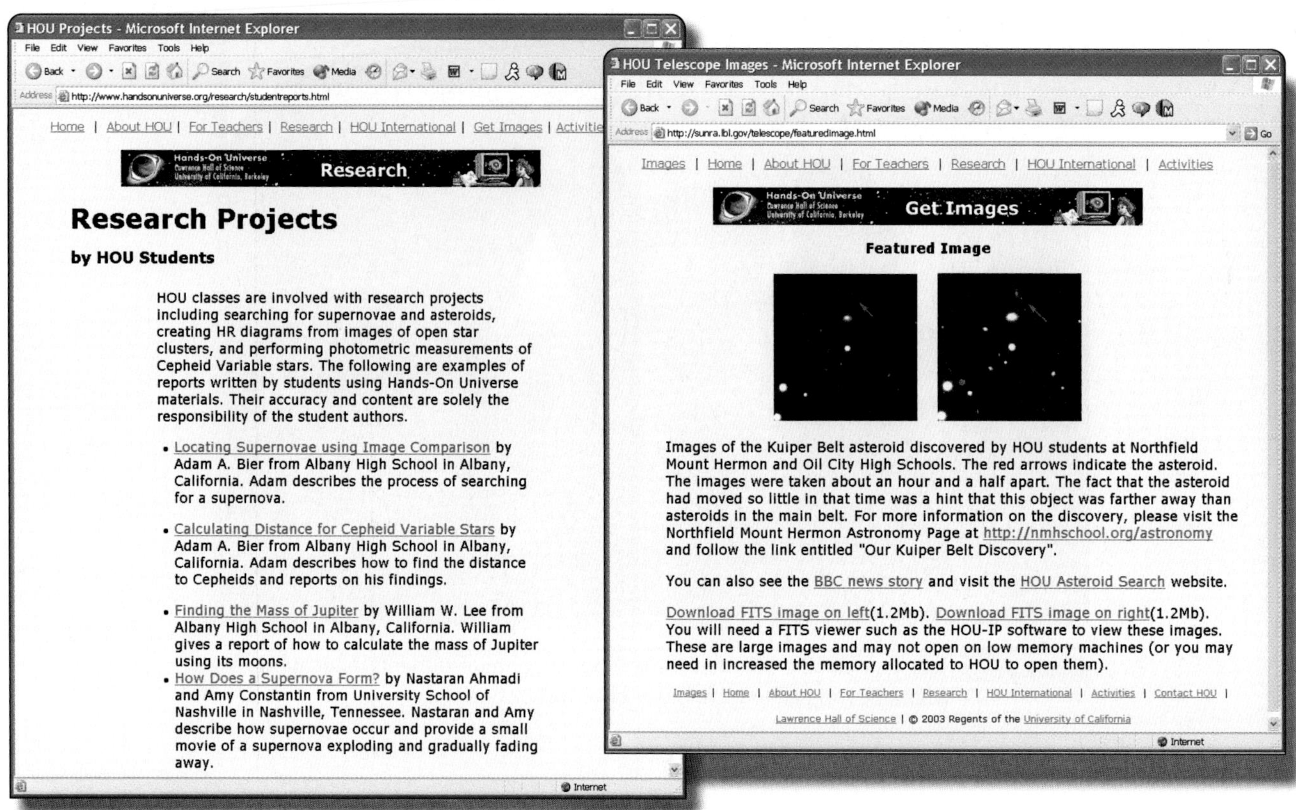

Figure 6-26 The Hands-On Universe program allows students to review images captured by automated telescopes and posted to the Internet – and then share their findings with other students and researchers.

teachers are not well-trained on how to integrate technology into their current curriculum. Even if software, hardware, and Internet connections are available, teachers may not use them if they lack the skill or understanding of how to integrate them into their daily classroom activities.

Training and mentorship programs allow teachers to learn computer and integration concepts from experienced teachers (Figure 6-27). In understaffed schools, teachers are so strapped for time they do not have the chance to recreate classroom lessons; design worksheets, handouts, and instructions for computer activities; or attend training sessions on how to better incorporate technology tools.

While some schools have modern computing facilities, older schools with less funding may lack the wiring and power to support Internet access or a computer lab. Even those with computers may be using outdated hardware and software, which limits the ability of students to learn skills relevant to today's workplace. Other factors limiting the effective use of computers in the classroom include school cultures that are resistant to change and a lack of strong leadership to help with funding and training initiatives.

For computers to have a positive impact in the classroom, it is important to have the support of school leadership to provide financial and cultural assistance. If school leadership supports technology in the classrooms, it helps ensure that the school will have a plan for ongoing funding and equipment and training updates, as well as a focus on encouraging the community to support the school's efforts. School leaders must recognize the need for ongoing professional development among all staff. Further, they must be committed to providing ongoing funds to update hardware and software every few years. Installing and managing a computer lab is not a one-time funding need: computer equipment and software demand replacement or upgrades every few years – and finding the funding often is difficult.

Finally, a key to success for schools in the information age is a cultural shift away from the factory model that has been used since the Industrial Revolution. For teachers, students, and the community to benefit fully

Figure 6-27 Training and mentorship programs allow teachers to learn computer and integration concepts from experienced teachers.

from using technology for teaching and learning, the current learning model must change to allow for a more student-centered model. As educational technology increasingly becomes a part of every school, tomorrow's classroom will have a curriculum focused on skills required for success in the 21st century, teachers well-trained in how to integrate technology in the classroom, standard modern computing facilities, and leaders who recognize the critical role technology plays in defining an excellent education in the Information Age.

DEFINING AN INFORMATION AGE EDUCATION

As noted earlier in the chapter, computers and technology not only have changed how students learn, they also have changed what skills and concepts students need to learn. While computer fluency is a key part of an Information Age education, computer fluency is not the only skill students need to be successful.

Researchers and educators have spent significant time in determining the skills and knowledge students need to live, learn, and work successfully in the digital age, where computers are a key part of everyday life. The essential skills required of students have not changed: students must have basic math, reading, and writing skills. Further, students should have familiarity with liberal arts and social studies to foster an understanding of people, societies, and how cultures turn information into knowledge.

As previously noted, students also should have computer fluency so they not only can use computers and other technologies, but also so they have a comfort level that allows them to learn to use new technologies quickly. Students should be effective users of basic productivity tools to make them attractive to employees. Finally, students need to learn how to use information. For example, with all of the information available on the Internet students will need to be able to find appropriate information, evaluate that information, organize the information, and then process the information effectively.

CONCLUSION

In this chapter, you learned how the teaching and learning models used in schools have changed over the years, from the factory model to a newer student-centered model. You also learned how computers are changing the classroom and about the importance of computer fluency in the Information Age. You discovered how computers are used as learning tools in the form of computer-based training and Web-based training. After reviewing how Internet resources are used in the classroom, you found out how programming tools, simulations and games, and software tools give students an opportunity for hands-on learning. After seeing how computers are used as teaching tools to support presentations, communication, and class administration, you learned how distance learning has made classrooms open to anyone, at any time. You reviewed the benefits of using technology in the classroom, as well the areas where there are opportunities for improvement. Finally, you learned what skills and knowledge are key to preparing you and other students to be successful in the 21st century.

Key Terms

asynchronous
branching
classroom response system (CRS)
Computer-Based Education (CBE)
Computer-Based Instruction (CBI)
computer fluency
computer literacy
computer managed instruction (CMI)
computer-aided instruction (CAI)
computer-based training (CBT)
courseware
discussion groups
distance learning (DL)
educational games
e-learning
electronic whiteboard
feedback
integrated learning systems (ILS)
interactive whiteboard
learning management system (LMS)
list owner
list server
listservs
LOGO
mailing lists
message board
microworlds
moderator
needs assessment
newsgroups
newsreader
NNTP client
No Child Left Behind Act (NCLB)
podcast
posttests
presentation graphics software
pretest
real time
remediation
slide show
stack
subscribe
synchronous
Technology-Based Training (TBT)
unsubscribe
Usenet newsgroups
video conference
Web-based training (WBT)
WebQuest

Chapter Review

Multiple Choice

Select the best answer.

1. Computer-based tutorials can be programmed to perform a needs assessment, which identifies _____.
   (a) the type of hardware required to run the tutorial successfully
   (b) discrepancies between current understanding of a topic and an understanding defined as mastery
   (c) directions for reviewing specific content to help better understand a topic
   (d) all of the above

2. _____ is a type of computer-based training that involves delivery of education content via the Internet, a private intranet, or an extranet.
   (a) Web-based training (WBT)
   (b) Computer-aided instruction (CAI)
   (c) Technology-based training (TBT)
   (d) Computer managed instruction (CMI)

3. A _____ is a project that has students use Internet resources to answer open-ended questions presented around a particular topic.
   (a) mailing list
   (b) pretest
   (c) WebQuest
   (d) list server

4. _____ is a simplified programming language that helps new programmers learn basic skills in the construction of scenes, called microworlds.
   (a) LOGO
   (b) FORTRAN
   (c) COBOL
   (d) BASIC

5. Using simulations to study a topic is especially effective when the concept being studied is particularly complex or is too _____ to practice in real life.
   (a) expensive
   (b) dangerous
   (c) impractical
   (d) all of the above

6. HyperStudio makes it easy to create a multimedia presentation called a _____, which can be presented to a class, handed in on a floppy disk, or even posted to the Web.
   (a) feedback
   (b) stack
   (c) listserv
   (d) slide

7. Students can use _____, such as Microsoft PowerPoint or Apple Keynote, to create visual aids that communicate ideas, messages, and other information to a group.
   (a) word-processing software
   (b) presentation graphics software
   (c) database software
   (d) desktop publishing software

8. A _____, also called a discussion group, is a Web-based discussion forum that does not require a newsreader and provides teachers with a common community to share ideas.
   (a) newsgroup
   (b) mailing list
   (c) message board
   (d) video conference

9. When distance learning courses are asynchronous, _____.
   (a) learning does not take place at a specific time
   (b) information is shared in realtime
   (c) the courses must be supported by video conferencing or instant messaging
   (d) all of the above

10. All of the following terms refer to a set of software tools used to support classroom administration *except* _____.
    (a) learning management system (LMS)
    (b) computer-managed instruction (CMI)
    (c) integrated learning systems (ILS)
    (d) computer-based training (CBT)

Chapter Review

Short Answer

Write a brief answer to each of the following questions.

1. What is computer fluency and why is it important?
2. In computer-aided instruction, how is a linear tutorial different from a branching tutorial?
3. What communications tools do teachers use to promote interaction outside of the classroom?
4. What is a learning management system?
5. What are some positive effects that technology has had in the classroom?

Web Research

Use a search engine such as Google (google.com) to research the following questions. Then, write a one-page, double-spaced report or create a presentation, unless otherwise directed.

1. The explosive growth of content on the Web in recent years has dramatically altered the way students conduct research for school projects. Instead of spending hours poring over school library card catalogs and pulling reference books from the library shelves and stacks, students now scan dozens of online hits from Google searches, and pull their references from their computer screens at home. Educators are starting to notice, however, that students are challenged to pick the best quality sources from among the vast array presented. And educators now are debating whether certain sites, such as Wikipedia, should be banned entirely because of their collaborative or subjective content development natures. The debate has even triggered the introduction of a bill to the U.S. Senate that would require federally funded schools or libraries to block access to "interactive sites" that may include blogs, encyclopedias like Wikipedia, and social networks. Check with your school library – how has the Internet affected the services reference librarians offer students doing research? Have they seen a reduction in the number of students coming through the doors to do research, or changes in the way students do that research? Locate the current news regarding the banning of Wikipedia and the status of the Senate bill. Where do you stand with regard to the debate – should interactive encyclopedic resources be banned?

2. Podcasting has started to work its way into the heart of education. Some educators are starting to augment their traditional and distance learning courses with podcasts of lesson summaries, daily news reports, and other materials in their attempt to use the technology to engage students in the learning process. Use the Web to find out how popular podcasting is in education. What topics areas are offered? What form do the podcasts take – audio only, or is video available? As a student, what types of podcasts would you be interested in using? What length seems appropriate, given your topical choices – 10 minutes, half an hour? Provide your instructor with your recommendations regarding the use of podcasts in this course.

Group Exercises

Working with a group of your classmates, complete the following team questions.

1. Almost all public schools provide computers in the classroom, and most offer Internet access. The extent to which computers contribute to learning, however, varies greatly from school to school. The principal of one school that effectively integrated computers into its curriculum claims that, in order to use computer technology successfully, the technology must be transparent, teachers must be committed to using the technology, and the community must be involved in the technology program. Have each member of your team visit a local school and interview a teacher and/or administrator about how computers are used. Consider how, and why, computers contribute or do not contribute to the learning process. What technologies are not present, but should be? What would it take to implement them? Then, meet with your team and compare how computers are used in each school. Prepare a PowerPoint presentation showing the factors that are most important to the successful use of computers in the classroom.

Chapter Review

2. Educational software is available on a wide variety of skills and subjects. The software lets students learn at their own pace, shows infinite patience, and usually offers an entertaining approach. Unlike human instructors, however, educational software often does not recognize unique problems, fails to address individual goals, and provides limited feedback. Have each member of your team research a software vendor and find an educational software package. Note the subject or skill being taught, the audience at which the software is directed, the approach used, and any special features. If possible, view a demonstration of the software. Then, meet with your team, share your findings, and prepare a PowerPoint presentation explaining the ages and topics for which you feel educational software is most, and least, suited.

Computer Viruses and Computer Crime 7

Computer Viruses, Worms, and Trojan Horses
- **Computer Viruses**
- **Types of Viruses**
- **How Viruses Work: Infection and Delivery**
  - *Infection*
  - *Delivery*
- **Trojan Horses and Worms**
- **Botnets and Zombies**
- **Hoaxes**
- **Protecting Your Computer**
  - *Using Antivirus Software*
  - *Handling E-Mail*
  - *Disabling Macros*

Computer Crime

Types of Computer Crime
- *Unauthorized Access and Use*
- *Hardware Theft*
- *Information Theft*
- *Intellectual Property and Software Theft*

Methods of Committing Computer Crimes
- *Obtaining Passwords*
- *Salami Shaving*
- *Data Diddling*
- *Denial-of-Service Attacks*

Identifying and Prosecuting Computer Criminals
- *Who Is a Computer Criminal?*
- *Prosecuting Computer Criminals*

Conclusion

As you have learned in previous chapters, people today rely on computers to create, manage, store, and communicate critical information at work, at home, and in school. They use computers to support elections, design cars, guide missiles, predict hurricanes, and steer trains, buses, and planes. Because of the critically important role computers play in our lives, it is important that they, and the data they store, are not corrupted by a nasty computer virus or do not fall prey to a computer criminal who steals information or changes lines of code. Consider the consequences, for example, if a computer criminal accessed a police database to obtain the addresses of the officers who arrested him — and then paid them a less-than-friendly personal visit? Or if a cyberterrorist deliberately altered the software used to control a guided missile?

In this chapter, you will learn about a number of computer security risks, including computer viruses and computer crime. A **computer security risk** is any event or action that could cause a loss of, or damage to, computer hardware, software, data, information, and processing capability. Some breaches of computer security are accidental; others are planned. This chapter addresses some of the more common computer security risks, including computer viruses, worms, and Trojan horses, and how you can protect yourself from these electronic villains. The chapter also looks at the wide range of acts considered to be computer crime, as well as the challenge posed in identifying and prosecuting computer criminals. Chapter 9 will address ways you can protect yourself from computer crime using security tools and procedures.

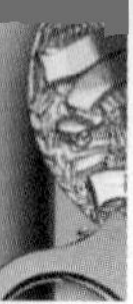

COMPUTER VIRUSES, WORMS, AND TROJAN HORSES

MyDoom. W32/Nimda. Netsky. Code Red. Slammer. All of these are types of malicious logic programs created with the intention of changing the way your computer works. A **malicious logic program**, also called a **malicious software program** or **malware**, is any program that acts without a user's knowledge and deliberately changes the computer's operations. Malicious logic programs include computer viruses, worms, and Trojan horses. Recent studies reveal that half the current threats globally are from Trojan horses, 40% from worms, and 10% from viruses. The United States has the highest level of malicious activity in the world, although the country only has about 19% of the world's Internet users. No matter where you live, however, you are not immune from the annoyance and potential damage of malware.

Computer Viruses

Like the common cold, thousands of variations of computer viruses exist. A **computer virus** is a potentially damaging computer program designed to infect a computer, replicate itself, and negatively affect the way a computer works – without your knowledge or permission. Some viruses are malicious and are intended to destroy disk sectors or alter data on your computer, possibly deleting the executable file for your browser or corrupting the Word document that contains your final English composition paper. One of the most destructive malware programs launched this decade was the ILOVEYOU virus (Figure 7-1). Spread via e-mail in 2000, the program racked up millions in both software damage and lost productivity worldwide. The program combined features of both a traditional virus and a worm, and spread when users opened the message attachment containing the malware program, described in the following section.

Despite the many variations of viruses that exist, all viruses have three characteristics:

- A virus can search for new programs, software, documents, or other files to infect.
- A virus can reproduce by adding itself to other files or creating copies of itself and distributing the copies.
- A virus can perform an unwanted function on a computer, such as destroying files, corrupting part of the hard disk, or simply displaying an annoying message.

After a computer virus has infected a single computer it can use that computer as a host to replicate and spread throughout the computer – or any networks to which it is attached – and can damage files and system software, including the operating system. Figure 7-2 shows how a virus can spread from one system to

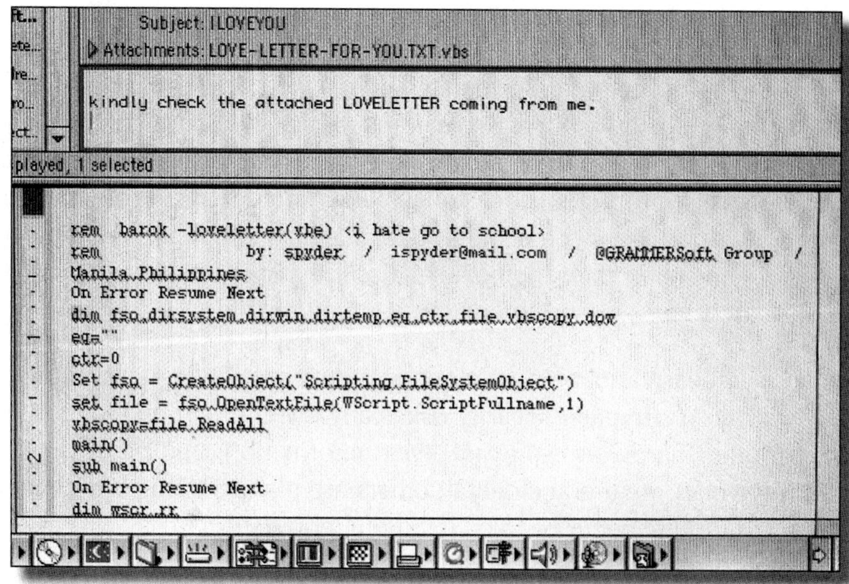

Figure 7-1 Many worms and viruses, such as the ILOVEYOU virus, rely on the distribution ease of e-mail to spread and infect many computers at once. Messages contain an image similar to the one pictured here. When the attachment is opened, the virus spreads by sending itself to all addresses in the recipient's e-mail address book.

another. Once running, the virus then can infect other programs or documents. Computer viruses also pass from computer to computer, just as a biological virus passes from person to person.

Even smart phones are not immune. A smart phone infected with the Cabir virus will not be able to make calls until the user responds to a message prompt on the phone (Figure 7-3). Once the user agrees to the prompt, the virus uses the phone's Bluetooth capability to send itself to every other Bluetooth-enabled device in range. When the users of those phones respond to the message prompt, their phones then send the message out. In order for a virus to spread, it needs a common platform. In the case of the Cabir smart phone virus, the dominant Symbian 8 operating system appears to be that platform. So far, 30 countries have been infected.

Types of Viruses

Although there are numerous variations of viruses, five main types of viruses exist: file viruses, macro viruses, boot sector viruses, master boot record viruses, and multipartite viruses.

A **file virus** inserts virus code into program files, as opposed to document or data files. A file virus often infects an executable file, a file used to start a program, which usually is run by clicking an icon or shortcut on the desktop or by entering the name of the program at a com-

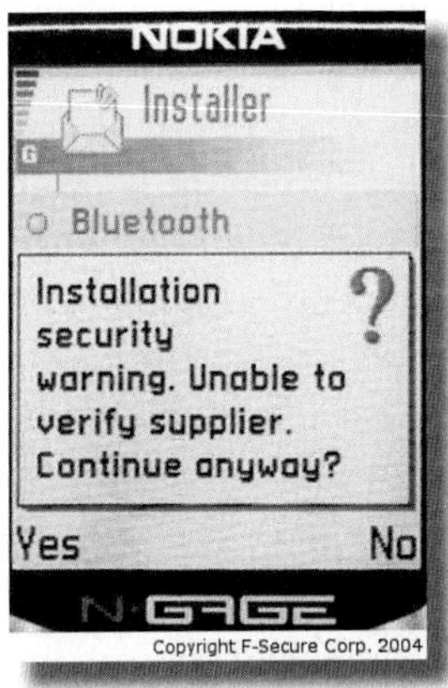

Figure 7-3 A smart phone infected with the Cabir virus will not permit the user to make phone calls until the user approves its installation. Once installed, the virus uses Bluetooth to send itself to other smart phones.

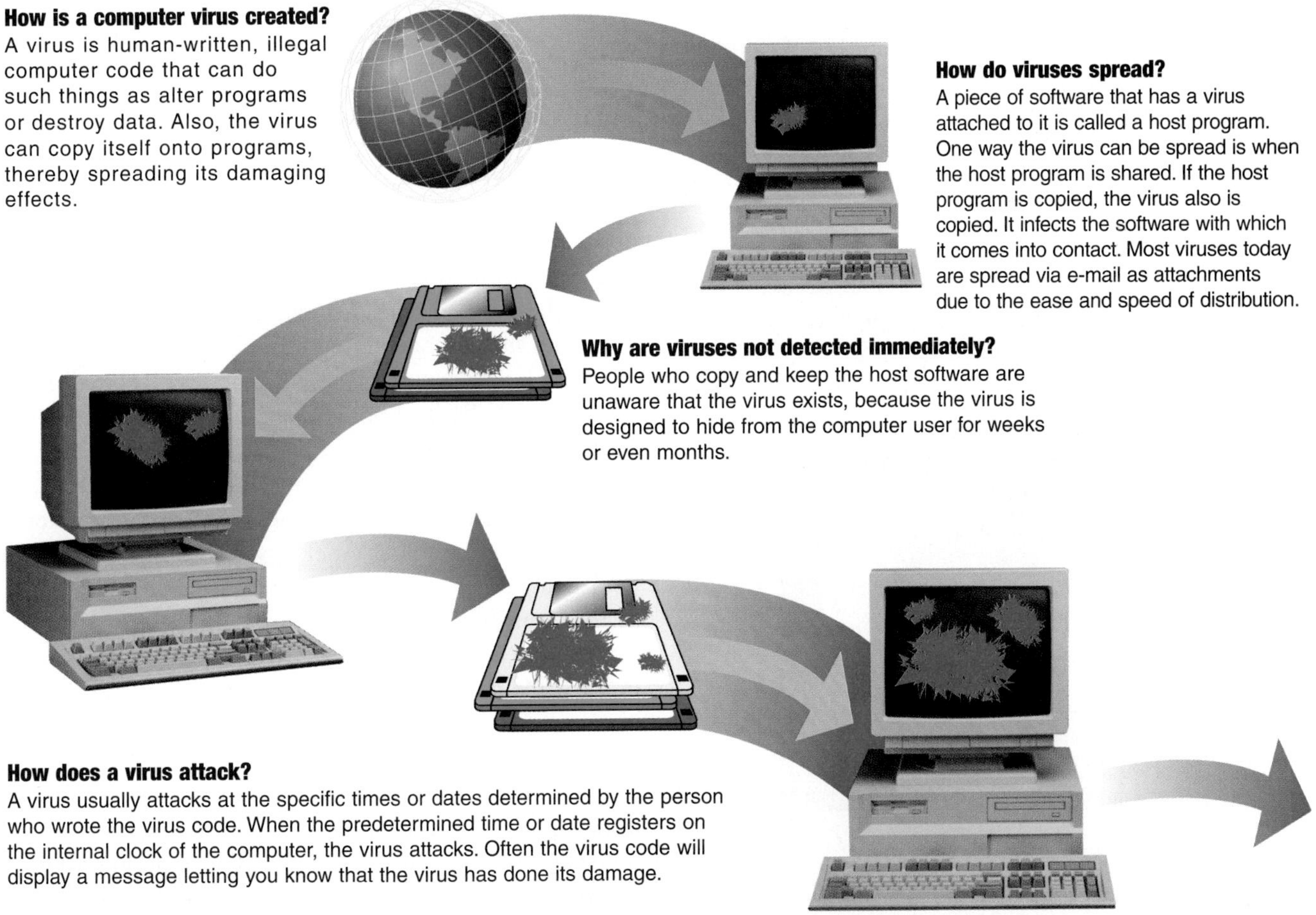

How is a computer virus created?
A virus is human-written, illegal computer code that can do such things as alter programs or destroy data. Also, the virus can copy itself onto programs, thereby spreading its damaging effects.

How do viruses spread?
A piece of software that has a virus attached to it is called a host program. One way the virus can be spread is when the host program is shared. If the host program is copied, the virus also is copied. It infects the software with which it comes into contact. Most viruses today are spread via e-mail as attachments due to the ease and speed of distribution.

Why are viruses not detected immediately?
People who copy and keep the host software are unaware that the virus exists, because the virus is designed to hide from the computer user for weeks or even months.

How does a virus attack?
A virus usually attacks at the specific times or dates determined by the person who wrote the virus code. When the predetermined time or date registers on the internal clock of the computer, the virus attacks. Often the virus code will display a message letting you know that the virus has done its damage.

Figure 7-2 Like biological viruses, a computer virus can infect a single computer and then spread to infect many others.

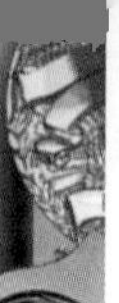

mand prompt. Once the executable file or other infected file is run, the virus spreads to any program that accesses the infected program. For example, the Silly Willy virus searched for and infected executable files on a computer with new code. When you ran an infected executable file, the system display cleared and a message displayed on your computer screen (Figure 7-4). The virus then accessed your hard drive. Although it did not reformat the disk, after some time a new message was displayed and the virus then attempted to format the floppy disk.

A **macro virus** uses the macro language of an application, such as a word-processing program, to hide virus code. Macro viruses infect Microsoft Word, Excel, PowerPoint, and Access files, although newer strains now are turning up in other programs as well. When a document with an infected macro is opened, the macro virus is loaded into memory. Certain actions, such as opening or saving the document, activate the virus so that the virus runs, does its damage, and copies itself into other documents. Macro viruses often are made part of templates so that any document created using the template is infected. The macro virus Wallpaper (also called Pirate) is activated when an infected document is opened. At that point, the virus infects Word templates and other macros, so that it infects other documents each time you open, print, or create a document from a template. Some versions of Wallpaper activate on the thirty-first day of each month, at which point the virus attempts to replace the Windows Desktop wallpaper with a picture of a skull (Figure 7-5).

A **boot sector virus** replaces the boot program used to start the computer system with a modified, infected version of the boot program. The virus is named for the **boot sector**, which is the first sector of a floppy disk or hard disk and is used to store the boot program. The **boot program**, which contains information about the contents and characteristics of the disk, includes information needed to start the computer. When the infected boot program is run, it loads the virus into the computer's memory. Once the virus is in memory, it also spreads to any floppy disk inserted into the computer. Parity Boot is a boot sector virus that displays the message PARITY CHECK and freezes the operating system when you boot the computer. Because the message is an actual error message that a computer displays to indicate faulty memory, you might think your computer has a memory fault rather than a boot sector virus infection.

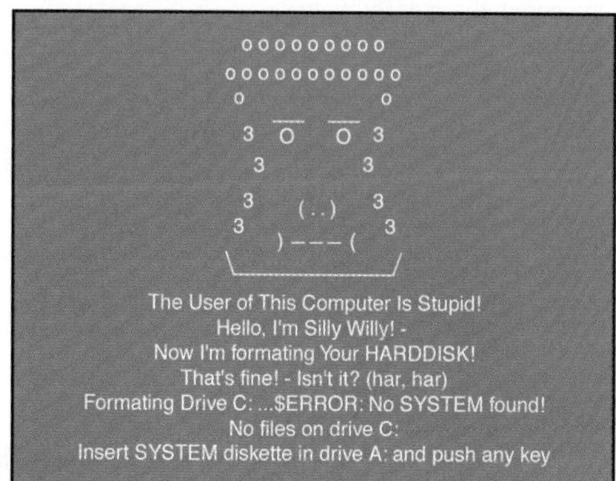

Figure 7-4 As seen here, when a user ran an executable file infected by the Silly Willy virus, the system display cleared and an animated face appeared in the upper-left hand corner of the screen.

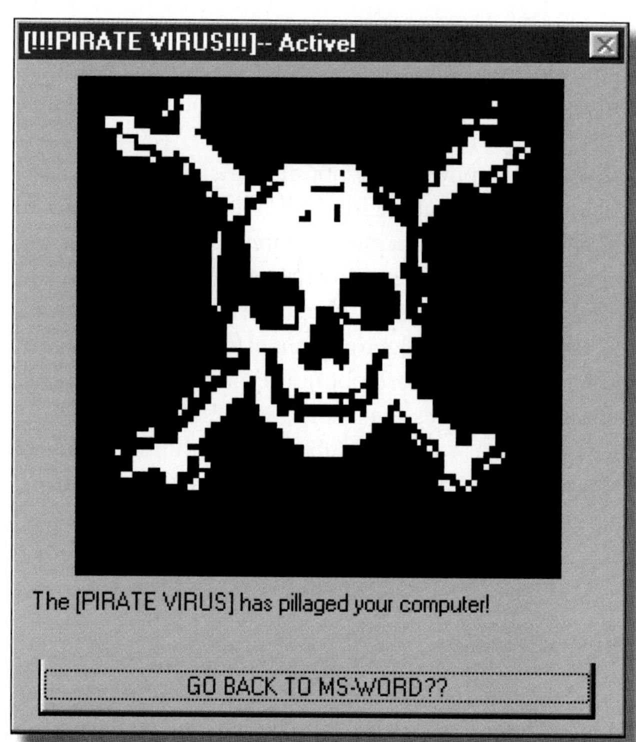

Figure 7-5 The macro virus Wallpaper is activated when an infected document is opened. Some versions of Wallpaper activate on the 31st day of each month, at which point the virus attempts to replace the Windows Desktop wallpaper with a picture of a skull and then shows a message box with the same skull image.

Master boot record (MBR) viruses attack disks in the same manner as boot sector viruses; the difference is that a master boot record virus normally saves a legitimate copy of the master boot record in a different location on the hard disk. Because the operating system cannot access the boot information, the computer will not start from the hard disk. Examples of master boot record viruses are NYB, AntiExe, and Unashamed.

A **multipartite virus**, also called a **polypartite virus**, has characteristics of a boot sector virus and a file

virus in that it infects both boot records and program files. Many of these viruses are very destructive, deleting and corrupting files, erasing computer memory, overwriting the master boot record, and deleting floppy disk drivers so you cannot reboot your machine from a floppy disk. Multipartite viruses, such as One_Half, Emperor, Anthrax and Tequila, also are difficult to repair. If the boot area is cleaned but the files are not, the boot area will be reinfected. Conversely, if the virus is not removed from the boot area, any files that you have cleaned will be reinfected.

How Viruses Work: Infection and Delivery

Unlike the biological viruses that cause the common cold, people create computer viruses. To create a virus, a programmer must write the virus code and then test the code to ensure the virus can replicate itself, conceal itself, monitor for certain events, and then deliver its **payload** – the destructive event or prank the virus was created to deliver. Most viruses have two phases to their execution: infection and delivery.

INFECTION To start the infection phase, a virus must be activated. Today, the most common way viruses spread is by people running infected programs disguised as e-mail attachments. During the infection phase, viruses typically perform three actions.

First, the virus *replicates* by attaching itself to program files. As you have learned, a macro virus hides in the macro language of an application, such as Microsoft Word. Boot sector viruses target the boot program and execute when the computer boots up. A file virus attaches itself to program files. The file virus, Win32.Hatred, replicates by first infecting Windows executable files for the Calculator, Notepad, Help, and other applications on the hard disk. The virus then scans the computer to locate .EXE files on other drives and stores this information in the system registry. The next time an infected file is run, the virus reads the registry and continues infecting the next drive.

Second, viruses *conceal* themselves to avoid detection. A **stealth virus** disguises itself by hiding in fake code sections, which it inserts within working code in a file. **Polymorphic** viruses actually change their code as they infect computers. Win32.Hatred uses both concealment techniques. The virus writes itself to the last file section, while modifying the file header to hide the increased file size. It also uses a polymorphic engine to scramble and encrypt the virus code as it infects files.

Finally, viruses *watch* for a certain condition or event and *release* their payload when that condition or event occurs. The event might be booting up the computer or reaching a date on the system clock. Win32.Hatred, for instance, delivers its payload when the computer clock hits the seventh day of any month. If the triggering condition does not exist, the virus simply replicates.

DELIVERY During the delivery phase, the virus unleashes its payload. The payload might be a harmless prank that displays a silly message, or it might be destructive – corrupting or deleting data and files. When Win32.Hatred delivers its payload on the seventh of any month, it displays the author's message (Figure 7-6) and then covers the screen with black dots. The virus also deletes several antivirus files as it infects the system. The most dangerous viruses do not have an obvious payload, but instead quietly modify files. A virus, for example, could randomly change numbers in an inventory program or introduce delays to slow a computer. Table 7-1 outlines some common symptoms of virus infections, so you can better detect if a virus that delivered its payload has infected your computer.

Some viruses are considered to be logic bombs or time bombs. A **logic bomb** is a program that is activated when a certain condition is detected. A disgruntled worker, for example, could infect a network server with a logic bomb that starts destroying files if his name is added to a list of terminated employees. A **time bomb** is a type of logic bomb that is activated on a particular date. Win32.Hatred, which delivers its payload on the seventh of any month, is an example of a time bomb. A well-known time bomb is the Michelangelo virus, which destroys data on your hard disk on March 6, which is Michelangelo's birthday.

Trojan Horses and Worms

Other kinds of electronic bugaboos exist, in addition to viruses. While often called viruses, Trojan horse

Win32.Hatred by Lord Julus (c) 1999
Today is the 7th !! Today is the day of hate !!
With Heart feel Hatred ! Black blood runs thru my veins !
Hatred !! Hatred !!
(escape is your escape)

Figure 7-6 When Win32.Hatred delivers its payload on the seventh of any month, it displays the author's message and then covers the screen with black dots. The virus also deletes several antivirus files as it infects the system.

Table 7-1

SIGNS OF A VIRUS INFECTION

- An unusual message with a graphic image displays on the computer monitor.
- An unusual sound or music plays randomly.
- The available memory on your computer is less than what should be available.
- A program or file is suddenly missing.
- An unknown program or file suddenly appears.
- The size of a file changes without explanation.
- A file becomes corrupted.
- A program or file does not work properly.

applications and worms actually are part of the broader category of malicious logic programs (Figure 7-7).

A **Trojan horse** is a destructive program disguised as a real application, such as a screen saver. A Trojan horse is named for Greek myth in which the Greeks give a giant wooden horse to their foes, the Trojans, as

IT'S NOT A VIRUS. IT'S A WORM.
©JOHN S. PRITCHETT

Figure 7-7 While often called viruses, worms and Trojan horse applications actually are part of a broader category called malicious logic programs.

a peace gesture. After it was taken inside the walled city of Troy, however, the horse proved to contain Greek soldiers. Unlike viruses, Trojan horses do not replicate. To spread, they rely on you and other computer users to believe they are legitimate programs, thus infecting your computer when you open an e-mail attachment or download and run a file from the Internet.

Once on your computer, a certain condition or action usually triggers the Trojan horse to release its payload. When it runs, a Trojan horse can capture information, such as user names and passwords, from your system or open up a backdoor that allows a hacker to control your computer remotely. For example, the Trojan horse PWSteal, places itself in the \Windows\System folder as the Molecule.exe and Molecule.dll files and then runs when you start your computer. Once activated, the Trojan horse attempts to steal login names and passwords, which then are sent to the Trojan horse author's anonymous e-mail address. The Trojan horse Infostealer affects gamers who play the popular online World of Warcraft game. The program steals the player's user ID, password, operating system information, and local IP address, and delivers it to another Web site for collection.

A **worm**, such as the CodeRed or Sircam worm, is a malicious logic program that replicates by creating copies of itself, either on one computer or any number of computers on a network. Unlike viruses, which replicate by attaching themselves to program files, worms do not infect other program files. Instead, a worm copies itself from one computer's disk drive to another (often using e-mail as a way to spread the program). As a worm copies itself repeatedly in memory or on a disk drive, eventually no memory or disk space remains. By using up the system resources, the worm can cause a computer or entire network to shut down.

Worms can perform a variety of tasks, although many are mass-mailing e-mail worms that read e-mail addresses from your address book and then continue spreading the worm by sending e-mail messages to those addresses. The Code Red worm (Figure 7-8) spread through a vulnerability in the Microsoft Internet Information Server. After infection of a user's computer, the worm attacked other systems and used the infected computers as part of a denial of service attack on the White House's Web site (www.whitehouse.gov). The Sircam worm is a mass mailing e-mail worm that uses your Windows Address book to collect e-mail addresses. The worm then attaches itself to a random document from your infected computer and sends the now-infected file via e-mail to a list of people in your address book. When the recipient opens the file – which they likely will do because it appears to have been sent by a coworker or friend – his or her computer also is

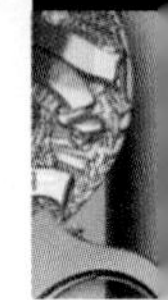

Figure 7-8 The Code Red worm, seen here, not only delivered a message to the user's screen, but also caused the infected computer to participate in a denial of service attack on the White House's Web site (www.whitehouse.gov).

infected and the worm repeats the e-mailing process on that computer, thus continuing to spread.

One of the biggest problems with the Sircam worm is that, in the process of e-mailing random files to anyone in your address book, it could attach personal letters, poetry, forms having Social Security numbers, tax returns, and documents listing usernames and passwords. Sircam infected computers at homes, businesses, universities, and even the Federal Bureau of Investigation's cyberprotection unit, resulting in at least eight documents sent to citizens outside of the FBI. Luckily, none of the documents were particularly sensitive or classified. The incident, however, pointed to the serious damage a worm such as Sircam could cause, perhaps sending out important personal information, medical records, or national security secrets to your next-door neighbor, your boss, or a coworker in a foreign country.

Botnets and Zombies

A growing form of malware is "bot" programs. **Bots**, or **botnets**, are programs that are installed on a user's machine without their knowledge or consent. They allow an external user to remotely control the computer as part of a larger coordinated attack, such as a denial of service attack. A **zombie** is the name given to the compromised computer. In addition to playing a role in denial of service attacks, bot programs can distribute spam, spread spyware and adware, log keystrokes, and harvest confidential information from zombie computer systems, leading to potential identity theft. Symantec, one of the leaders in Internet security services, recently reported an average of nearly 64,000 computers daily infected with a bot program. China has the most bot-infected computers, at 26% of that country's total. The United States has the highest number of bot "command and control" computers, at 40% of the global total. In a recent high-profile case, Jeanson Ancheta pled guilty to running a botnet system consisting of hundreds of thousands of networked zombies that he leased to advertising companies for the distribution of spam. In 2007, two Dutch hackers were sentenced to prison for launching the Toxbot Trojan horse program that allowed them to commandeer millions of computers worldwide to collect credit card numbers, eBay and PayPal account information, and purchase iPods, PlayStation consoles and other electronic equipment. With the growth of botnets in recent years, the FBI decided to launch "Operation Bot Roast," which recently busted Robert Alan Soloway of Seattle for using a botnet to send millions of junk e-mails since 2003.

Hoaxes

At some point, you may have received an e-mail that described some new, extremely destructive type of virus, telling you to delete a file from your hard drive. It is likely, however, that the virus described in the e-mail does not exist, and the warning is untrue. A **virus hoax** is an e-mail message that spreads a false virus warning, usually in chain letter fashion, from person to person (Figure 7-9). An e-mail describing a hoax generally has no file attachment or any references to a third party who can validate the claim. The message in the e-mail itself also can tip you off that the virus described is a hoax. Some of the common phrases found in these e-mails include:

- If you receive an e-mail titled [*virus hoax e-mail name here*], do not open it!
- Delete it immediately!
- It contains the [*virus hoax name here*] virus.
- It will delete everything on your hard drive and [*other unlikely destructive events here*].
- Delete the file, [*file name here*], to remove the virus from your hard drive.
- Forward this warning to everyone you know!

Most virus hoax warnings use similar language, making them relatively easy to identify. Before ignoring the e-mail or following its instructions and deleting files you might need, you should check with reputable

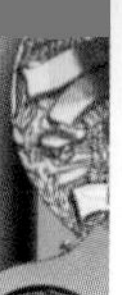

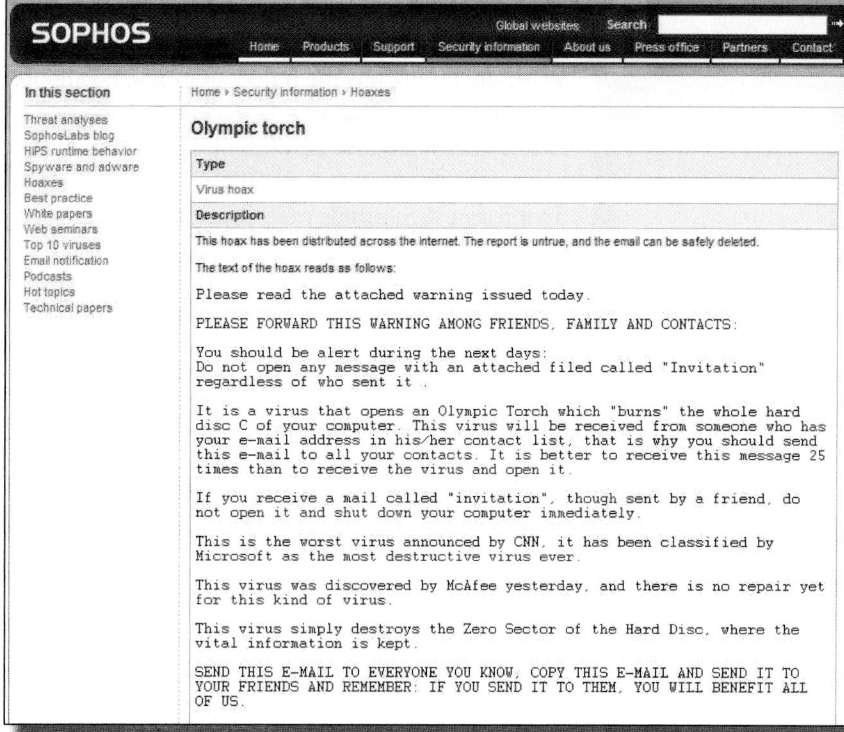

Figure 7-9 Characteristics of a hoax e-mail include a lack of credible third-party references to verify the message's contents, no attachments, stating that a well-known company or agency has already verified the nature of the "threat," and instructions to send the message to all your friends.

references to determine if a virus warning is legitimate or a hoax. The Web sites of many antivirus software makers, such as Symantec, McAfee, and F-Secure post lists of hoaxes (Figure 7-10).

Protecting Your Computer

Just as everyone is susceptible to the common cold, every computer is susceptible to a computer virus. In 1995, the chance that a virus would infect your computer was 1 in 1000; by 2002, the odds were only 1 in 9, and getting worse. By one expert's account, an unprotected computer on a network can be compromised in an average of 12 minutes. Even with better antivirus software, viruses are tough to avoid as creative programmers craft new electronic ways to contaminate your computer.

The cost of being struck by a virus can be staggering. A single Fortune 500 company hit by the Melissa virus, for example, calculated that it lost $10 million from the infection – the costs of lost productivity and lost network operation time. A virus that hits your personal computer has the same effects, reducing your productivity and causing enormous frustration by corrupting key documents or deleting your digital camera photos from your last vacation. It also can result in monetary loss, including charges for technical troubleshooting service to get your computer diagnosed, disinfected, and ready for use.

It is impossible to guarantee that a computer or network is safe from a computer virus, worm, or Trojan horse. A good start, however, is to stay informed about new virus alerts and virus hoaxes. You can take several other precautions to protect your home and work computers from malicious logic programs, as listed in Table 7-2. The following section explores some of these precautionary measures.

USING ANTIVIRUS SOFTWARE

First and foremost, install an antivirus program on your computer and update it frequently. An **antivirus program** protects a computer against viruses by identifying and removing any computer viruses found in memory, on storage media, or on incoming files. Most antivirus programs also protect against worms and Trojan horses. Table 7-3 lists several popular antivirus programs.

When you purchase a new computer it often includes antivirus software, although you later may have to pay to update your subscription. Many schools also provide site licenses for antivirus software (Figure 7-11), which give faculty, staff, and students the license to install antivirus software packages on their campus or home computers. After logging in with a username and password, users can download the software from the school Web site. Most schools now use the same Web sites to post virus news, with information on how to identify and avoid new viruses.

An antivirus program scans for programs that attempt to modify the boot program, the operating system, and other programs that normally are read but not modified. Many antivirus programs also automatically scan files downloaded from the Web, e-mail attachments, opened files, and all removable media inserted into the computer.

One technique that antivirus programs use to identify a virus is to look for virus signatures. A **virus signature**, also called a **virus definition**, is a known pattern of virus code. Computer users should update their antivirus program's signature files regularly.

Updating signature files brings in any new virus definitions that have been added since the last update (Figure 7-12). This extremely important activity allows the antivirus software to protect against viruses written since the antivirus program was released. Most antivirus programs contain an auto-update feature that regularly prompts users to download the new virus signatures. The vendor usually provides this service to registered users at no cost for a specified time.

Another technique that antivirus programs use to detect viruses is to inoculate existing program files. To **inoculate** a program file, the antivirus program records information such as the file size and file creation date in a separate inoculation file. The antivirus program then uses this information to detect if a virus tampers with the data describing the inoculated program file.

If an antivirus program identifies an infected file, it attempts to remove the virus, worm, or Trojan horse. If the antivirus program cannot remove the infection, it often quarantines the infected file. A **quarantine** is a separate area of a hard disk that holds the infected file until the infection can be removed. This step ensures other files will not become infected. Users also can quarantine suspicious files themselves.

In addition to detecting, inoculating, and removing viruses, worms and Trojan horses, most antivirus programs have utilities that create a recovery disk. The **recovery disk**, also called a **rescue disk**, is a removable disk that contains an uninfected copy of key operating system commands and start-up information that enables the computer to restart correctly. Once you have restarted the computer using the recovery disk, the antivirus program can attempt to repair damaged files. If it cannot repair the damaged files, you may have to restore them with uninfected backup copies of the files.

In extreme cases, you may need to reformat the hard disk to remove a virus. Having uninfected, or clean, backups of all files is important. Chapter 9 addresses backup and restore procedures you can use to ensure you always have a clean set of backup files.

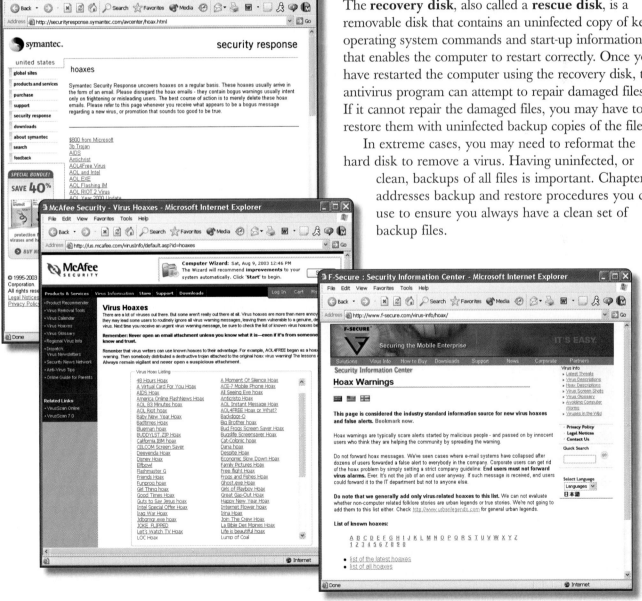

Figure 7-10 The Web sites of Symantec, McAfee, and F-Secure post lists of hoaxes so you can determine if a virus warning is legitimate or a hoax.

Table 7-2

TIPS FOR PREVENTING VIRUS, WORM, AND TROJAN HORSE INFECTIONS	
1.	Install an antivirus program on all of your computers. Obtain updates to the antivirus signature files on a regular basis.
2.	Never open an e-mail attachment unless you are expecting it, and it is from a trusted source. ■ Never open e-mail attachments with the file extensions VBS, SHS or PIF or double file extensions such as NAME.BMP.EXE or NAME.TXT.VBS. These extensions are almost never used in normal attachments, but they are frequently used by viruses and worms. ■ If you feel that an e-mail you get from a friend is somehow strange - if it is in a foreign language or if it just says odd things, double-check with the friend before opening any attachments. ■ Do not trust the icons of an attachment file. Worms often send executable files which have an icon resembling icons of picture, text, or archive files to fool the user.
3.	Scan for viruses in all e-mail attachments you intend to open. Turn off message preview.
4.	If the antivirus program flags an e-mail attachment as infected, delete the attachment immediately.
5.	Check all downloaded programs for viruses, worms, or Trojan horses. These malicious logic programs often are placed in seemingly innocent programs, so they will affect a large number of users.
6.	Set the macro security in programs so you can enable or disable macros. Only enable macros if the document is from a trusted source and you are expecting it.
7.	Before using any removable media, use the antivirus scan program to check the media for infection. Incorporate this procedure even for shrink-wrapped software from major developers. Some commercial software has been infected and distributed to unsuspecting users this way.
8.	Install a personal firewall software program.
9.	Write-protect your recovery disk by sliding the write-protect tab into the write-protect position.
10.	Back up your files regularly. Scan the backup program before backing up disks and files to ensure the backup program is virus free.

Computer users can use a number of safe computing tips to minimize the risk of virus, worm, and Trojan horse infections.

Table 7-3

ANTIVIRUS PROGRAMS
Command BitDefender AntiVirus
eTrust InoculateIT
F-Secure Anti-Virus
McAfee VirusScan
McAfee Virex
Norton AntiVirus
Webroot Spy Sweeper with Antivirus
ZoneAlarm Internet Security Suite

Popular antivirus programs can help protect your computer against viruses, worms, and Trojan horses.

HANDLING E-MAIL Viruses commonly infect computers through e-mail attachments. Figure 7-13 shows how a virus can spread from one computer to another via an infected e-mail attachment. To help ensure that you are not the recipient of a virus sent via e-mail, follow these guidelines:

- Many e-mail programs allow users to preview an e-mail message without opening it. Some viruses and worms can deliver their payload when a user simply previews the message. Thus, you should turn off message preview in e-mail programs.
- Never open an e-mail attachment unless you are expecting the attachment and it is from a trusted source. A **trusted source** is a company or person you believe will not knowingly send a virus-infected file. If the e-mail is from an unknown source or an untrusted source, do not open or execute any attachments. If the message seems particularly odd, you may want to delete the e-mail message immediately.

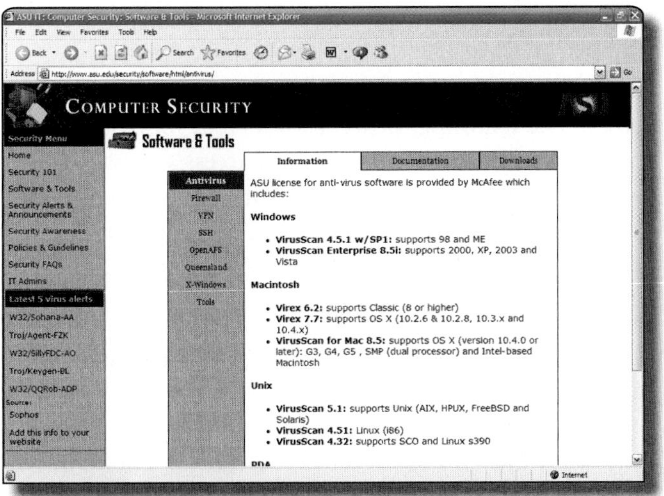

Figure 7-11 Many schools provide site licenses for antivirus software, which gives faculty, staff, and student the license to install antivirus software packages on their campus or home computers.

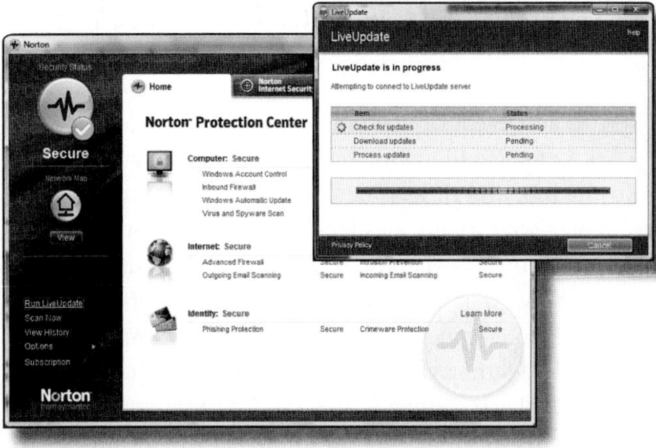

Figure 7-12 Many vendors of antivirus programs allow registered users to update signature files automatically from the Web at no cost, while they have a valid subscription.

DISABLING MACROS As you have learned, some viruses are hidden in macros, which are instructions saved in an application such as a word processing or spreadsheet program. In applications that allow users to write macros, set the macro security level to medium. With a medium security level, the application software warns users that a document they are attempting to open contains a macro. From this warning, a user can choose to disable or enable the macro. If the document is from a trusted source, the user can enable the macro. Otherwise, it should be disabled.

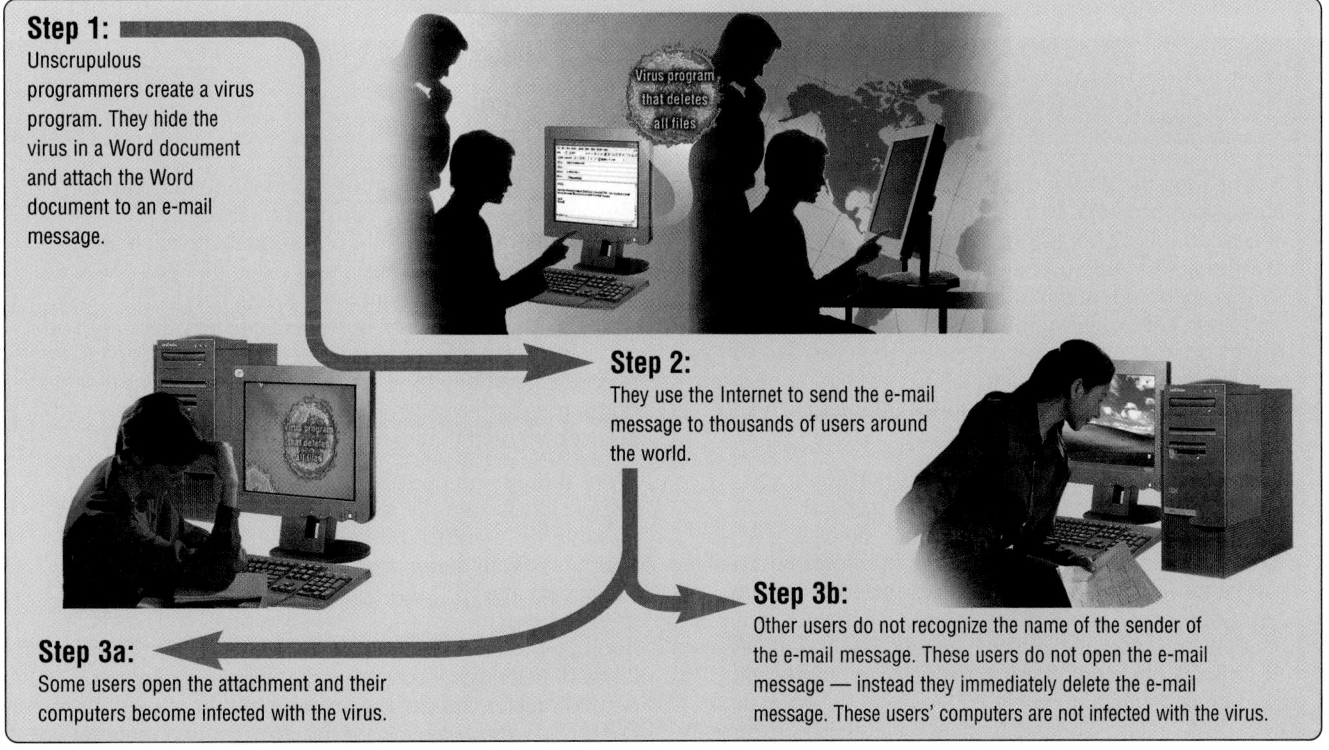

Step 1:
Unscrupulous programmers create a virus program. They hide the virus in a Word document and attach the Word document to an e-mail message.
Virus program that deletes all files
Step 2:
They use the Internet to send the e-mail message to thousands of users around the world.
Step 3a:
Some users open the attachment and their computers become infected with the virus.
Step 3b:
Other users do not recognize the name of the sender of the e-mail message. These users do not open the e-mail message — instead they immediately delete the e-mail message. These users' computers are not infected with the virus.

Figure 7-13 Viruses commonly are spread from one computer to another via an infected e-mail attachment.

COMPUTER CRIME

As you have learned, a computer security risk is any event or action that could cause a loss of, or damage to, computer hardware, software, data, information, and processing capability. Some breaches of computer security are accidental; others are planned. An intentional breach of computer security often involves a deliberate act that is against the law. Any illegal act involving a computer generally is referred to as a **computer crime**. The term **cybercrime** refers to online or Internet-based illegal acts. Today, cybercrime is number 3 on the FBI's top ten priorities list.

Computer crime is a serious problem for today's corporations. A recent IBM survey found that nearly 60% of U.S. businesses believe cybercrime is more costly to them than physical crime. In the United Kingdom, high-tech crime costs firms with more than 1,000 employees over $4.6 billion annually. Even organizations using a range of security tools and technologies are not protected entirely. And, because only 30 percent of incidents are reported to law enforcement agencies, computer criminals can gamble on the notion they never will be caught or prosecuted for their crimes.

Types of Computer Crime

Although many different types of computer crimes are committed, most either are crimes against a computer that damages the system or data, or crimes that use a computer as a tool, such as in the theft of funds or unauthorized access to confidential information in databases. The following section reviews four major types of computer crime – unauthorized access and use, hardware theft, intellectual property theft and software piracy, and information theft – and their impact. Chapter 9 will present a detailed look at safeguards you can put in place to help prevent these crimes.

UNAUTHORIZED ACCESS AND USE **Unauthorized access** is the use of a computer or network without permission. An individual who tries to access a computer or network illegally is called a **cracker**. The term, **hacker**, although originally a complimentary word for a computer enthusiast, now has a derogatory connotation with essentially the same definition as cracker. These computer criminals typically break into a system by connecting to it and then logging in as a legitimate user. Some intruders do no damage; others leave some evidence of their presence either by leaving a message or deliberately altering data. Examples of unauthorized access include gaining access to a bank's computer system to complete unauthorized transfers of funds from customers' bank accounts or to an online bookstore's database to steal credit card numbers.

Unauthorized use is the use of a computer or its data for unapproved or potentially illegal activities. Unauthorized use includes a variety of activities, from

@ISSUE: Cyberslacking

It is nearing the end of the workday and you are thinking about your brother's birthday next week, so you quickly access an online bookstore and order a book by his favorite author. Or you need a mid-morning work break, so you spend a few minutes on eBay, YouTube, or Facebook checking out the latest posts. Or you only have slow dial-up Internet access at home, so as soon as you get to work you log onto a P2P file-sharing network and use your company's high-speed Internet access to download music or movie files.

Most workers assume that no one gets hurt when you spend time on the Internet for personal reasons. The statistics, however, show that is far from the case. One survey found that U.S. employees spend five hours per week surfing the Web for personal reasons, including reading news, shopping, gambling, and even viewing pornography. Sending and receiving personal e-mail and instant messaging at work also contributes to the problem. In the U.K., one survey found that nearly 25% of workers spend more than 30% of their workday "wilfing," aimlessly searching the Web in a "what was I looking for" (wilf) mode. Shopping, news, and travel sites are the biggest culprits.

Cyberslacking, or using the Internet and the Web for personal reasons at work, costs companies around the world billions of dollars in lost productivity each year. Further, downloading music and video files eats away at a company's expensive Internet access bandwidth, slowing down legitimate business activities. Sending and receiving personal e-mail and downloading files can expose a company to viruses and other security breaches, not to mention lawsuits if the downloaded contents contain copyrighted material.

What should you do to access the Internet at work responsibly? Carefully read and understand your company's Internet access policies and follow them. When in doubt, ask your supervisor for clarification on policies. Resist the urge to shop, chat, play online games, send personal e-mail, or send instant messages to friends during work hours, unless your company permits these kinds of activities. Remember that downloading copyrighted music, videos, and software either at work or at home — without paying for the downloaded material is piracy and you are breaking the law.

the seemingly harmless to the very destructive. It is not unlikely that, at some point, you may have used a computer for some unauthorized activity. Examples of unauthorized use can be as innocent as using your company's computer to send personal e-mail or using your company's spreadsheet software to track your softball league scores, or as criminal as accessing a bank computer to steal money from someone else's bank account.

Unauthorized access and use often are the first step in committing other crimes. In the examples of a criminal illegally accessing a bank computer, the unauthorized access to the bank's computer simply is the first step towards completing the theft of funds – thus making this a three-fold crime of unauthorized access, unauthorized use, and financial theft.

Once a criminal has gained access to a system, he or she can use the computer resources and data to commit crimes. For example, in 1994, a Russian in St. Petersburg dialed into Citibank's cash management system and used valid user identification numbers and passwords of two other banks (one in Argentina and one in Indonesia) to transfer money to his own account. The theft totaled an estimated $10 million.

HARDWARE THEFT **Hardware theft** is the act of stealing, defacing, or destroying computer equipment. Hardware theft also includes vandalism, which can range from someone cutting a computer cable to individuals breaking into a university computer lab and smashing computers.

Hardware theft and vandalism are not major threats to you as a home computer user, unless a thief breaks into your home. Companies, schools, government agencies, and other organizations, however, are at risk for hardware theft and vandalism. For example, in 2007 alone, thousands of employees at Alcatel-Lucent were placed at risk when a contractor lost a hard drive containing personal employment data when it shipped the drive via UPS. The Transportation Security Agency (TSA) also lost a computer hard drive containing Social Security numbers, bank data, and payroll information for about 100,000 employees. CDs with information on 2.9 million Georgia Medicaid and children's health program recipients were stolen. And in April, the IRS admitted that nearly 500 laptops and computer devices, some with sensitive taxpayer data, could not be located. In order to inform the public that their personal data may have been compromised, California passed SB 1386, the Security Breach Information Act, effective July 2003, that obligates companies storing unencrypted personal data to notify individuals when such data is either lost or stolen. Most states have since followed suit.

Users of smaller computers – laptops, notebook computers, or PDAs – are the most susceptible to hardware theft. It is estimated that more than 750,000 notebook computers are stolen each year, because the size and weight of these computers makes them an easy target. Crowded airport security screening areas are helpful for thieves, who can pick up a computer and walk away unnoticed while the owner waits to complete his or her security screening. Internet cafes with wireless hot spots also are target-rich environments for thieves.

Once a thief has the computer, he or she can access whatever information is on the machine. Some thieves, for example, focus on stealing computers from company executives so they can use the stolen computer to access confidential information illegally. Others target government agencies, such as the Department of Veterans Affairs, which had a laptop containing sensitive information on 26 million U.S. military veterans stolen in 2006. This particular laptop was eventually recovered, but the FBI reports that 97 percent of stolen PCs are never recovered.

INFORMATION THEFT As discussed in Chapter 1, information is a valuable asset to companies working in the Information Age. Instead of only producing tangible goods, businesses and industries are using information to provide core services or as their main product. **Information theft** occurs when someone steals personal or confidential information. An unethical company executive may steal or buy stolen information to learn more about a competitor. A corrupt individual may steal credit card numbers to make fraudulent purchases.
Information theft often involves other types of computer crime. For example, an individual might gain unauthorized access to a computer and then steal credit card numbers. This is exactly what happened at Tucson-based CardSystems Solutions in 2005. More than 40 million credit card numbers were stolen by someone using malware over an undetermined amount of time. Most of the stolen card numbers were for VISA and MasterCard accounts. In 2007, Scott Levine of Florida was convicted of stealing information from data-management company Acxiom Corp. in the largest database theft to date. Levine's company, Snipermail.com, stole 1.6 billion customer records containing names, e-mail addresses, and mailing addresses.

Both business and home users can fall victim to information theft. When information is stolen, it can cause as much damage as other kinds of computer crime, if not more. Underground Web sites offering stolen credit cards and verification numbers only charge between one to six dollars per data set (upwards of $18 for more detailed identity information), yet the losses to business and

individuals can run into the billions, as evidenced by the theft of 45.7 million credit card records experienced by retailer TJ Maxx in 2006. The company stated losses of approximately $1.6 billion, and took a $12 million charge against revenue in the first quarter of 2007 alone.

One serious type of information theft targeted at individuals is identity theft. **Identity theft** occurs when someone appropriates your personal information without your knowledge to commit fraud or theft. After stealing your name, Social Security number, credit card number, or some other piece of your personal information, an identity thief can rent an apartment, get a job, start cellular phone service, or open a credit card account in your name and then never pay off the debts, thus ruining your credit history.

How do identity thieves get your information? It can be stolen, as noted above, although that is hard for an individual to control. Any time that you give someone personal information, whether verbally or in writing, a potential thief can use the information for his or her own gain. You may unwittingly give information when completing surveys or questionnaires or when talking to telemarketers who ask for information in exchange for goods or services. Papers in your trash can provide valuable information for thieves. More computer-savvy thieves can hack into your computer or company databases to get your personal information, while customer service reps can use their position to steal your information. Identity thieves also can scour the Internet for any personal information you have shared. In many cases, you do have control over the sharing of this information.

Congress passed the **Identity Theft and Assumption Deterrence Act of 1998 (Identity Theft Act)** to address the problem of identity theft. Specifically, the act made it a federal crime to use another person's identification knowingly to conduct any unlawful activity. Identity theft continues to be a major problem that demands the attention of law enforcement agencies such as the U.S. Secret Service and the FBI. In 2003, President Bush signed the **Fair and Accurate Credit Transactions Act (FACT Act)** which, among other things, requires merchants to delete all but the last five digits in a credit card number from a receipt. In 2004, the President signed the **Identity Theft Penalty Enforcement Act**, giving law enforcement new tools to prosecute those who violate the financial privacy of U.S. citizens.

@ISSUE: Identity Theft: Turning Your Good Name Bad

Someone's identity is stolen every day. Waiters in restaurants steal credit card information. Landlords glean Social Security numbers from credit reports. These individual instances of identity theft, however, pale in comparison to the largest identity fraud case in U.S. history in which a group of three men downloaded 30,000 credit reports without authorization and sold them to accomplices for up to $60 a piece. At the heart of the crime was Philip Cummings, a Help desk employee of Teledata Communications (TCI), a company that lets banks and other lenders access credit histories compiled by the three-biggest credit rating firms, Equifax, Experian, and TransUnion.

Beginning in 1999, Cummings had access to the passwords and codes used by TCI's customers to download consumer credit reports for business purposes. With these codes, he was able to retrieve credit reports for himself. He also gave the passwords and codes to co-conspirators and received $30 for each credit report obtained using the stolen codes. The credit reports then were passed on to at least 20 other people. The group operated over a period of three years, using the credit information found in the reports to steal funds from bank accounts and make fraudulent purchases. Somewhat unbelievably, the group still was able to access the information even after Cummings left TCI in March 2000, since he gave a co-conspirator a preprogrammed laptop computer and taught him how to access the credit bureaus and download the reports.

Consumers whose credit reports were stolen in this scheme had reported many forms of identity fraud. Bank accounts holding tens of thousands of dollars in savings were depleted, thousands of dollars in credit card bills were racked up, address changes were made at financial institutions so that checks, debit cards, ATM cards, and credit cards could be sent to unauthorized locations. In 2005, the Federal Trade Commission (FTC) received over 685,000 consumer fraud and identity theft complaints, with consumers reporting losses of more than $680 million.

While most cases of identity theft do not occur on such a massive scale, identity theft is the number one non-violent crime in the United States. The Federal Trade Commission reports that identity theft incidents are on the rise. As shown in Table 7-4, identity thieves get your personal information in any number of ways. In addition to simple techniques such as rummaging through the trash, a practice referred to as dumpster diving, thieves can gain access to your personal information through the Internet. So much of your personal information can be found on Web sites that, with some basic software packages, a thief can build a profile of you based on personal information that you have entered

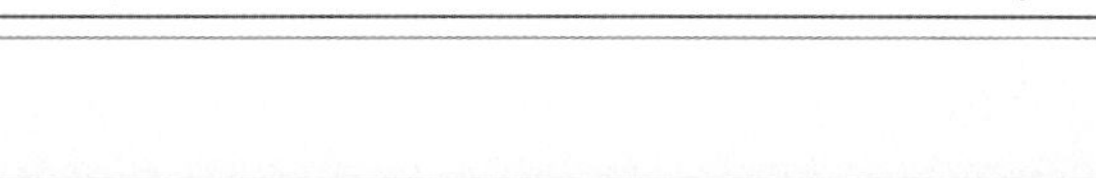

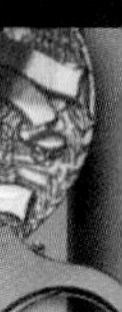

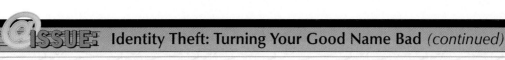

ISSUE: Identity Theft: Turning Your Good Name Bad *(continued)*

willingly in e-mails, discussion groups, Web sites, chat rooms, and more. The Internet not only gives thieves access to our personal information, it helps them use that information. On the Web, a thief does not have to be there, in person, to make a fraudulent credit card purchase or to apply for credit in your name. Identity thieves also can use public computers to hide their whereabouts further.

With your name, Social Security number, credit card number, or some other piece of your personal information in hand, identity thieves quickly can turn your good name bad. A thief can open a new credit card account, using your name, date of birth, and Social Security number. The thief can call your credit card issuer and, pretending to be you, change the mailing address on your credit card account. Then, your imposter runs up charges on your account. Because your bills are being sent to the new address, you may not immediately realize there's a problem. When they use the credit card and don't pay the bills, the delinquent account is reported on your credit report. In the end, your credit rating is destroyed — and you might not even know it until you are denied a loan or mortgage or, worse, are contacted by the police for the felony crime of writing bad checks over $300.

The costs of identify theft can be high. Lenders suffer losses of more than $1 billion annually due to identity theft. Individuals pay as well, with their time, money, and sense of security. Consider the following:

- You will spend an average of $1,200 on out-of-pocket expenses to cover monies spent by an identify thief.
- You will spend an average of 30 hours straightening out the mess. Because many companies are not open at night or on weekends, you may have to take time off from work or school to visit government offices that are open only during business hours.
- If you are sued or arrested for crimes someone committed in your name, you may need to hire a lawyer — at a cost of thousands of dollars.
- If you are denied credit because of the theft, you may lose a chance to buy a home, get a school loan, or purchase a new car. You also may have to pay costs to reapply for a loan.

No single age group is immune from identity theft. Most at risk, however, are people age 18-29 (29% of the total); individuals age 30-39 are next (24%). Your hometown may play a role in your risk, however. Topping the list of cities with the most identity theft cases is the Phoenix metropolitan area, followed by Las Vegas, Riverside-San Bernardino-Ontario, CA, and the Dallas-Fort Worth metro area.

How can you avoid identify theft? Table 7-5 lists several best practices to follow to help avoid identify theft — or at least quickly right the wrong if your identity is stolen. At the end of the day, using common sense when giving out information, paying attention to your bills, and obtaining regular credit reports are the simplest ways to be sure your good name stays just that — yours.

Table 7-4

HOW IDENTITY THIEVES GET YOUR PERSONAL INFORMATION:	HOW IDENTITY THIEVES USE YOUR PERSONAL INFORMATION:
▪ They steal wallets and purses containing your identification and credit and bank cards. ▪ They steal your mail, including your bank and credit card statements, preapproved credit offers, telephone calling cards and tax information. ▪ They complete a change of address form to divert your mail to another location. ▪ They rummage through your trash, or the trash of businesses, for personal data in a practice known as dumpster diving. ▪ They fraudulently obtain your credit report by posing as a landlord, employer, or someone else who may have a legitimate need for — and a legal right to — the information. ▪ They get your business or personnel records at work. ▪ They find personal information in your home. ▪ They use personal information you share on the Internet. ▪ They buy your personal information from inside sources. For example, an identity thief may pay a store employee for information about you that appears on an application for goods, services, or credit.	▪ They call your credit card issuer and, pretending to be you, ask to change the mailing address on your credit card account. The imposter then runs up charges on your account. Because your bills are being sent to the new address, it may take some time before you realize there's a problem. ▪ They open a new credit card account, using your name, date of birth and SSN. When they use the credit card and don't pay the bills, the delinquent account is reported on your credit report. ▪ They establish phone or wireless service in your name. ▪ They open a bank account in your name and write bad checks on that account. ▪ They file for bankruptcy under your name to avoid paying debts they've incurred under your name, or to avoid eviction. ▪ They counterfeit checks or debit cards, and drain your bank account. ▪ They buy cars by taking out auto loans in your name.

How identify thieves ruin your good name.

INTELLECTUAL PROPERTY AND SOFTWARE THEFT

Intellectual property refers to unique and original works such as ideas, inventions, writings, art, processes, company and product names, and logos. As discussed in Chapters 4 and 8, **intellectual property rights** are the rights to which creators are entitled for their work. **Intellectual property theft** occurs when someone steals someone else's intellectual property. Intellectual property theft typically involves ex-employees taking critical company information when they leave a job, whether to help out in a new job or for more disreputable purposes, like blackmail. The information might be the company's price lists or product catalog or more highly confidential information such as a cutting-edge sports car design, the secret barbecue sauce recipe that made the company famous, or a blockbuster film pre-release. Because much of this information is stored digitally on computers, stealing it is as simple as copying the data to removable media or e-mailing the information to a personal e-mail address, so it can be downloaded and reviewed on a home computer. For example, in June 2003, two and a half weeks before the nationwide theatrical release of the *The Hulk*, Universal Studios sent digital copies of the movie to ad agencies. After making an unauthorized copy, an employee defeated the movie's security tag and posted the copy to a Web site where movie enthusiasts routinely gather to post and trade copies of bootleg movies. The employee eventually pled guilty to copyright infringement and faces a maximum sentence of three years in prison and a fine of $250,000, or twice the gross gain or gross loss from the offense.

Copyright infringement is one of the most common types of intellectual property theft. As you have learned, a copyright protects any tangible form of expression, including music, movies, and software. The music and movie industries have been hit hard by copyright infringement over the last few years, as the Internet and P2P file-sharing networks like LimeWire and KaZaA made it easy for users to share music, video, and other works protected by U.S. copyright law. As you learned in Chapter 4, the Recording Industry Association of America (RIAA) and the Motion Picture Association of American (MPAA) are working aggressively to stop the piracy of copyrighted material by suing the P2P file-sharing networks and individuals. As evidenced by these suits, the price of piracy can be very high: in the

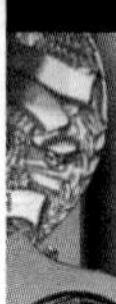

Table 7-5

TIPS TO AVOID IDENTITY THEFT

- Before revealing personal identifying information, find out how it will be used and if it will be shared with others. Ask if you have a choice about the use of your information: can you choose to have it kept confidential?
- Give your Social Security number only when absolutely necessary. Do not carry your card in your wallet. Ask to use other types of identifiers when possible.
- Use only one credit card to shop online and keep the credit limit low. Shop at familiar, reputable Web sites.
- Enroll in a program like Verified by Visa or MasterCard's SecureCode, which enables card owners to add a password to their existing credit card. To ensure that only the card owner can use their credit card online, cardholders are prompted to enter the password during the e-commerce transaction.
- Pay attention to your billing cycles. Follow up with creditors if bills do not arrive on time.
- Minimize the identification information and the number of cards you carry to what you actually need. If your driver's license or credit cards are lost or stolen, notify the creditors by phone immediately, and call the credit bureaus to ask that a "fraud alert" be placed in your file.
- Order a copy of your credit report from the three credit reporting agencies every year at www.annualcreditreport.com. Make sure it's accurate and includes only those activities you've authorized.
- Keep items with personal information in a safe place; shred them when you don't need them anymore. Make sure charge receipts, copies of credit applications, insurance forms, bank checks and statements, expired charge cards, and credit offers you get in the mail are disposed of appropriately.
- Never give away any personal information about yourself in chat rooms.
- Don't include your telephone number or home address as part of your signature on e-mails.
- Remove your name from the marketing lists of the three credit reporting bureaus by calling 1-888-5OPTOUT or visiting www.optoutprescreen.com. This limits the number of pre-approved credit offers you receive.
- Never respond to "phishing" e-mail messages. Your bank, eBay, or other entities will never ask for your personal information and passwords in this manner. Just delete these messages.

Although not foolproof, several simple precautions can help you avoid being the victim of an identity thief.

spring of 2007, the RIAA sent pre-lawsuit letters to students at more than 60 college campuses around the country indicating they would be sued if they did not settle with the RIAA for their illegal music downloading activity. The RIAA has settled with over 500 students nationwide, some for $3,000. Those students who do not settle face minimum damages of $750 per copyright violation. In 2005, the MPAA sued a 67-year-old man whose 12-year old grandson had illegally downloaded four movies to the computer in his home. The lawsuit sought damages of $600,000, but the man settled for $4,000. The music and movie trade groups are continuing the crackdown by alerting ISPs, colleges and universities, and large corporations to potential copyright abuse on their networks and asking for their help in identifying those responsible.

Another widespread form of intellectual property theft is software theft. **Software theft** occurs when someone steals software media, intentionally erases software programs, or illegally copies a software program. Like hardware theft, software theft can take many forms. One type of software theft involves someone physically stealing the media that contains the software. For example, a dishonest student at the school library might steal the Microsoft Encarta CD-ROM from the reference desk. Another type of software theft can occur when a programmer is terminated from, or stops working for, a company. Although the programs are company property, some programmers intentionally remove programs they have written from company computers.

Software also can be stolen from software manufacturers. This type of theft, called **software piracy**, is the unauthorized and illegal duplication of copyrighted software. Software piracy is by far the most common from of software theft. Even after you have purchased a software package, you do not have the right to copy, loan, rent, or in any way distribute the software. Doing so not only is a violation of copyright law, it also is a federal crime. Despite this, recent statistics show that 35 percent of the world's software is pirated.

Software piracy continues for several reasons. In some countries, legal protection for software does not exist. In other countries, like the United States, the laws are difficult to enforce. Many buyers believe they have a right to make copies of software for which they paid hundreds – even thousands – of dollars. Finally, software piracy is a

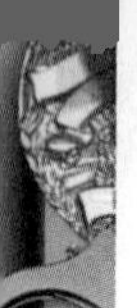

relatively simple crime to commit. In minutes, you can copy a software CD-ROM to a CD-RW to share with a friend; alternatively, you can post the software to a P2P file-sharing network and make it available to thousands of users around the world.

Software piracy, however, is a serious crime. Not only does it increase the chance of spreading viruses and drive up the cost of software, software companies take it very seriously. If you or your company is caught copying software, you can be held liable under both civil and criminal law. In a civil action, a copyright owner can stop you from using its software immediately and request monetary damages up to $150,000 for each program copied. In addition, the government can criminally prosecute you and fine you up to $250,000, sentence you to five years in jail, or both. Organizations like the Business Software Alliance (BSA) – created by a number of worldwide software companies – work to promote a better understanding of the impacts of software piracy and, as needed, to take legal action against software pirates (Figure 7-14).

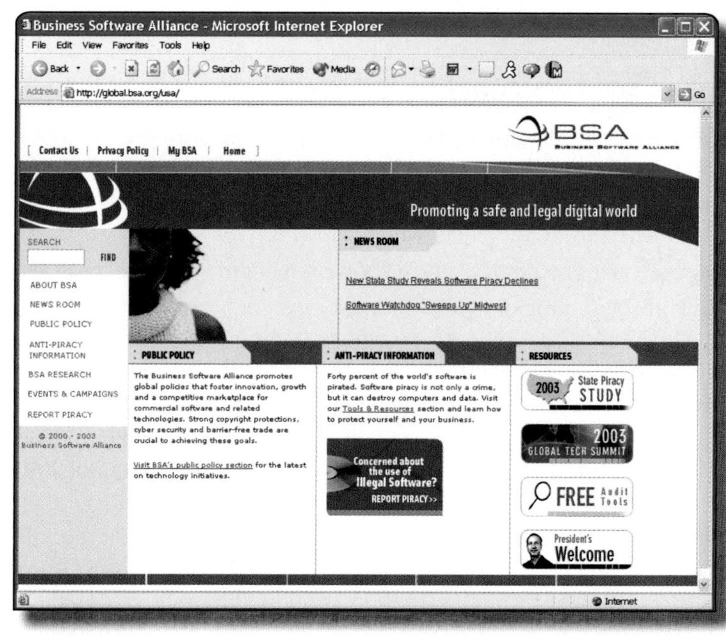

Figure 7-14 The Business Software Alliance (BSA) works to promote a better understanding of the impacts of software piracy and, as needed, take legal action against software pirates.

Methods of Committing Computer Crimes

As evidenced by the examples above, computer criminals can use a variety of methods to commit computer crime. Sometimes, finding the information needed to commit a crime is as simple as dumpster diving to find passwords or computer manuals listing access codes. For employees, their position in a company may give them access to the computers and data they need to commit crimes unnoticed. In other cases, the crime is blatant, such as when three men broke into a Sun Microsystems data center and stole 15 servers. The Internet brings with it numerous security risks, including attacks by malicious logic programs such as worms, as well are more targeted attacks using denial-of-service attacks.

OBTAINING PASSWORDS One of the most basic ways to gain unauthorized access to a computer or network is to obtain passwords. Sometimes, users choose passwords that are easy for someone else to guess: their birthday; the name of their daughter, wife, or pet; or simply the word, "password," which is the most common choice. As noted above, dumpster diving also can help computer criminals find passwords written on sticky notes or notepads and then simply discarded.

One simple but amazingly effective strategy for gaining unauthorized access to a computer or network is called social engineering. **Social engineering** involves tricking a user into revealing his or her password. Sometimes social engineering is as simple as asking someone if you can use their system account to log on, since your password has expired. A growing social engineering trick is to use pre-texting to gain confidential information. With pre-texting, the criminal creates a fictitious scenario for gathering this information. Usually perpetrated over the phone, the scenarios can involve problems with customer or technical support at a bank or credit card issuer. The ruse claims a need for the confidential information in order to fix some problem with the account. Pre-texting is common in e-mail phishing attempts as well. With **phishing**, an e-mail is sent from what appears to be a legitimate company – often a financial institution – asking for verification of account information and PINs, and contains a link to the phisher's Web site to provide this information. When surrendered, the information can be used to drain the accounts, leaving the victim penniless. Phish attempts do not always pretend to be from financial institutions, however. One recent phish attempt preyed on the frenzy surrounding the release of the Apple iPhone by informing targets they had won the coveted device, which would be theirs upon surrender of personal information. Another phish attempt sought account information from MySpace users. And a phish e-mail claiming to come from the Department of Justice and the IRS attempted to defraud citizens in 2007. Industry groups state that close to 1,000 unique phish mailings are circulated each day, with an average lifespan of just one hour. Individuals who clicked the e-mail link and provided account information lost $2.8 billion in 2006, with amounts averaging $1,244 per victim. An example of a typical phish e-mail message is shown in Figure 7-15. Another social engineering trick is for a hacker to send an e-mail, posing as a system administrator, claiming to need your password for some system administration work or telling everyone on the network to change their password to a generic password (Figure 7-16). The hacker then can use the password to access the system.

Another way that a different user can obtain your password is a technique called shoulder surfing. **Shoulder surfing** involves observing someone, perhaps by looking over his or her shoulder, to get information. Shoulder surfing is a surprisingly effective way to get information. In the office or the school lab, for example, you probably trust the coworker or student chatting with you as you log on to your PC – and thus do not think twice about hiding your password entry from view. Shoulder surfing also works well in crowded places, where a cracker can stand next to you and watch as you enter your PIN at an ATM (Figure 7-17) or fill out a form to update your car registration. Someone also can shoulder surf at a distance with the aid of binoculars. To prevent shoulder surfing, experts recommend that you shield paperwork, a keypad, or your keyboard by using your back, elbow, or hand to block the view of prying eyes.

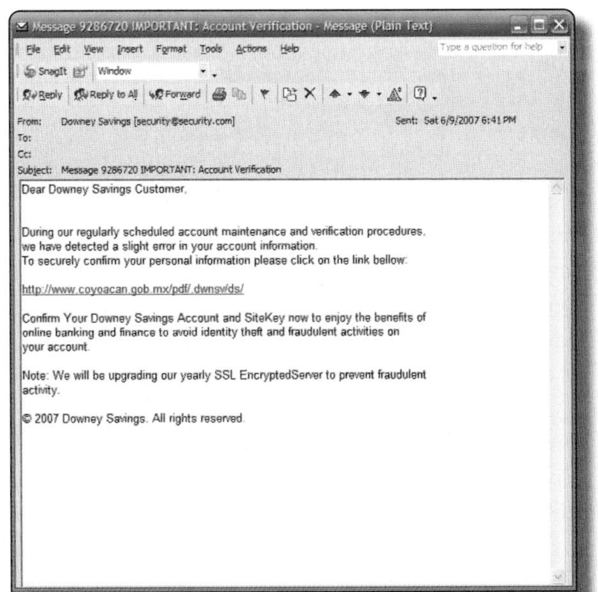

Figure 7-15 Most phish e-mails claim to come from a financial institution that needs to verify your account information, such as account number and password or PIN. If you receive such a message, do not click the embedded link! Just delete the message.

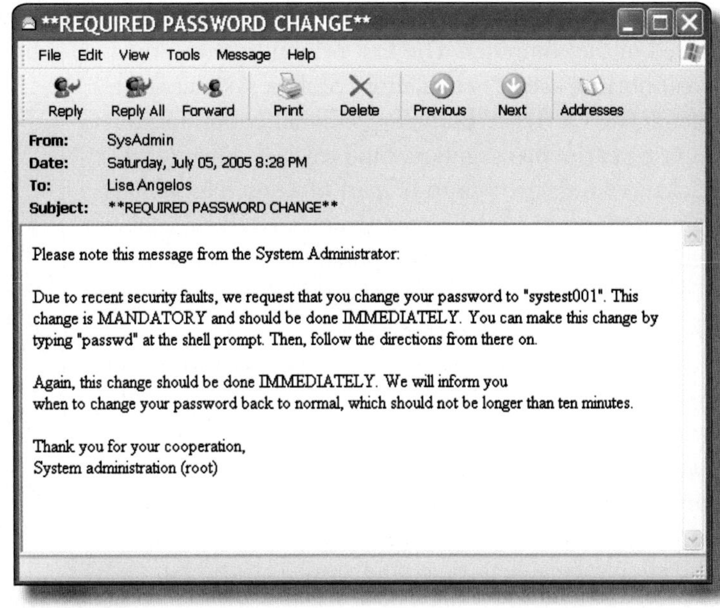

Figure 7-16 A social engineering trick is for a hacker to send an e-mail, posing as a system administrator, telling everyone on the network to change their password to a generic password.

A more sophisticated method used to obtain passwords involves using packet sniffers. A **packet sniffer** is a program or device that monitors data traveling over a network in packets. While network administrators use sniffers for legitimate network management functions, hackers also use them. A hacker uses the packet sniffer to scan all messages traveling on a network to look for passwords, credit card numbers, and other sensitive data. If you log into a computer across a network – perhaps accessing your school e-mail account over the Internet from home – you may end up giving your password to hackers. An unauthorized sniffer is difficult to detect on a network, and hackers who have placed packet sniffers on heavily used networks have collected thousands of passwords.

One other way to access passwords and other data on a computer or network is to have superuser status. On a computer or network, a **superuser** or **system administrator** is a privileged user who has unrestricted access to the whole system, including being able to override file security. In a well-publicized incident in 1988, a West German citizen exploited security loopholes in the UNIX operating system to give himself superuser status. For almost two years, he was able to gain access to more than 30 computers belonging to the United States military. Having superuser status on one machine allowed him to read and alter material stored in the computer. The first person to notice the unauthorized access was Clifford Stoll, a systems manager at the Lawrence Berkeley National Laboratory. After a year of investigation, Stoll tracked down the hacker, who turned out to be part of a spy ring selling computer secrets to the Soviet Union's KGB for money and drugs. The details of this pursuit are revealed in Stoll's 1989 book, *The Cuckoo's Egg: Tracking a Spy through the Maze of Computer Espionage.*

Given all the possible ways another user can obtain your password, you should select a password carefully and try to create one that no one can guess. Longer passwords provide greater security than shorter ones; the password should include letters and numbers and, if possible, be at least eight characters long. Ideally, you also should be able to type your password without looking at the keyboard. Table 7-6 offers some tips on how to choose a good password.

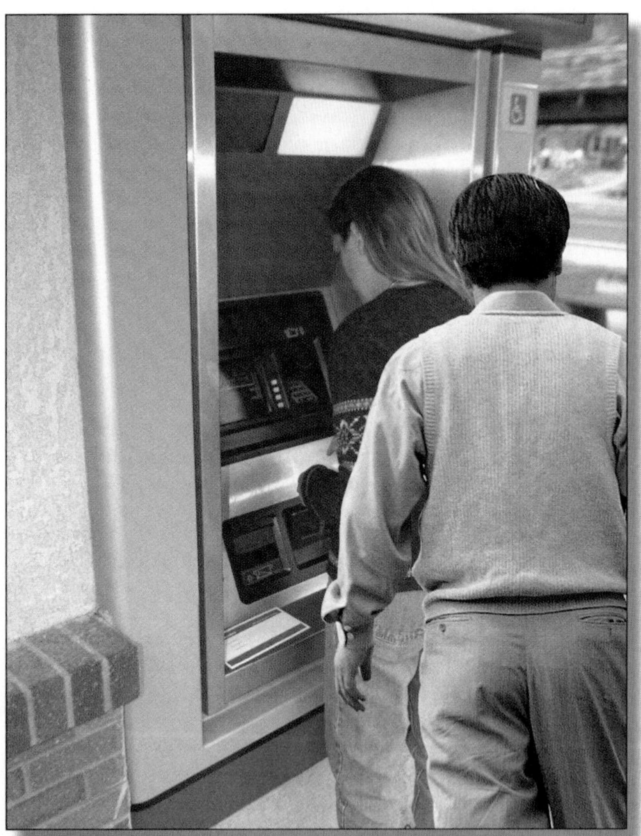

Figure 7-17 Using shoulder surfing, someone can watch as you enter your PIN number at an ATM machine keypad. To prevent shoulder surfing, experts recommend that you shield paperwork, a keypad, or your keyboard by using your back, elbow, or hand to block the view of prying eyes.

SALAMI SHAVING One unique method computer criminals use to steal or embezzle funds is a technique called salami shaving. Using **salami shaving**, a programmer alters a program so that a very small amount of money is taken, or "shaved," from a large number of transactions. For example, each time your bank computes monthly interest, the value is rounded (say, from \$0.8428329 to \$0.84). A programmer could alter the bank system so that the fractional cents were placed into his or her account. With thousands of accounts, the round off amount can be huge, but individuals are unlikely to notice. A variation on the approach was taken by a Taco Bell employee who reprogrammed his drive-up-window cash register to ring up a \$2.99 item as a \$.01 item, so that he could pocket \$2.98 each time the item was ordered (he collected \$3,600 before he was caught).

DATA DIDDLING Another approach to computer crime is **data diddling**, which is illegal or unauthorized data alteration. Data diddling does not require sophisticated knowledge of computers; it can be as simple as a change to a number in a spreadsheet showing financial projections, a false order entry in a database to indicate an item has been sold, or an alteration to the account numbers for direct deposit paychecks. Some creative uses of data diddling involved a case in which clerks in an upscale department store changed the accounts of customers so they were listed as bankrupt. The store wrote off the losses, while the customers paid the clerks 10 percent of the \$33 million they saved by not having to pay their bills. In another case in 2003, a Los Angeles man participated in a scheme with hackers from Romania who gained unauthorized access to the online ordering system of Ingram Micro, Hewlett-Packard, and Office Depot and then placed hundreds of thousands of dollars of fraudulent orders for computer equipment. The equipment was sent to locations in the Los Angeles area and then repackaged and sent to Eastern Europe, where the hackers resold it for a profit.

In another case, computer criminals accessed and modified data in Penn Central Railroad's freight flow system, so that boxcars would be routed to a small railroad company outside Chicago. The data then was modified so that Penn Central would not realize the boxcars were missing. Some estimates indicated that

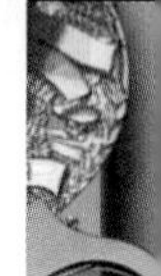

Table 7-6 Password Dos and Don'ts

DO	DON'T
■ Make the password at least eight characters long, if supported by the software. ■ Use uppercase and lowercase letters throughout the password. ■ Use numbers and punctuation in the password. ■ Choose a password you can type quickly, without looking at the keyboard (this helps prevent shoulder surfing). ■ Change your password often. ■ Keep your password private; do not share it with anyone. ■ Memorize your password so that you do not have to write it down.	■ Use any word in the dictionary. ■ Use two short words together (fluffycat) or separated by a symbol or numbers (surf_wave). ■ Use any proper name, such as the name of a geographical location or famous person. ■ Use a sequence of letters or numbers from the keyboard (for example, CVBNM or 56789). ■ Use personal information in your password, such as your last name, pet's name, birthday, or words related to hobbies you enjoy. ■ Post your password near your computer.

Choosing a good password is your first line of defense against password guessing and other hacking tools. Some tips on choosing a password are listed above.

data diddling resulted in almost 400 boxcars being stolen; further investigation showed that the boxcars had been repainted and used by other railroad companies. Wanting to minimize attention to the crime, Penn Central chose not to prosecute.

DENIAL OF SERVICE ATTACKS A **denial-of-service** attack, or **DoS attack**, is an assault on a single computer, usually a network server, with the intention of disrupting service on the targeted system. Malicious hackers carry out a DoS attack in a variety of ways. For example, they may access a single computer to send an influx of confusing data messages or useless traffic to a computer network. The target system eventually is overloaded by the messages and forced to shut down, thus blocking legitimate users from using the network.

A more devastating type of DoS attack is a **distributed denial of service**, or **DDoS**, attack, in which multiple computers are accessed and used to attack multiple computer networks. Typically, a hacker will exploit a security hole in one computer system, making it the DDoS master. The hacker then uses the master system to identify other systems that can be accessed. Next, the hacker installs a denial of service software tool on the accessed systems (sometimes thousands of computer). Once the DoS tools are installed on numerous computers, the hacker uses the master computers to execute commands that instruct the controlled computers to launch a flood of traffic against a specified target. As seen earlier in this chapter, botnets and zombies often play roles in DDoS attacks.

DDoS attacks have been able to stop operations temporarily at several major Web sites and the domain name servers that route data over the Internet. One of the more well-known distributed denial-of-service attacks occurred in 2000, when a 15-year old calling himself MafiaBoy launched attacks on several major Web sites, including CNN.com, Yahoo.com, and Amazon.com. (MafiaBoy later was caught after bragging about his exploits in a chat room). In October 2002, a DDoS attack flooded all thirteen of the root servers of the Internet Domain Name System, which are used to translate domain names – such as course.com – to the IP address computers understand. Without the DNS, users were not able to access most Web sites. During the attack, eight or nine of the DNS servers were disabled temporarily or severely hampered in serving legitimate user requests; thankfully, four or five of the 13 servers remained online throughout the attack and the majority of Internet users did not experience any interruption in service. The popular Internet auction site, eBay, was hit in late 2005.

The government and other law enforcement agencies are acutely aware of the serious nature of denial-of-service attacks. Industry experts believe there are close to 35,000 DOS attacks launched daily around the globe. In 2007, a rash of DOS attacks took place in Russia, shutting down media and political Web sites in an attempt to disrupt public information delivery prior to major elections. Companies or individuals requiring assistance or information about DDoS attacks and other Internet security breaches can contact or visit the Web

site of the Computer Emergency Response Team Coordination Center (CERT/CC), which is a federally funded research and development center (Figure 7-18).

Identifying and Prosecuting Computer Criminals

Identifying and prosecuting computer criminals remains a major challenge for law enforcement officials. Cybercriminals are not an easily categorized group: they can be malicious hackers, virus programmers, unhappy employees, software pirates, spies, terrorists, or just a kid enjoying the thrill of illegally accessing the school library computer. Cybercriminals also can be tough to locate. With the Internet connecting computers around the world, a cybercriminal can commit crimes on computers in Indiana while sitting in Budapest. The laws surrounding cybercrime also are just starting to be tightened, providing for stronger punishments in the hope of deterring future crime.

WHO IS A COMPUTER CRIMINAL? Most computer criminals are ordinary people, not computer wizards or criminal masterminds. When thinking about computer crime, most people think of hackers, who access computers or networks from outside of the corporate network to enter systems, steal data and information, and interrupt service. Although it is difficult to develop a profile of a typical hacker, many are males aged 19 to 35 who are relatively sophisticated computer users. The same profile fits programmers who create malicious logic programs intended to damage the computers of unsuspecting users.

Another set of computer criminals is authorized users who commit unauthorized acts. Angry, disgruntled, or dishonest employees often have direct access to systems, know core processes (for example, how funds are processed or paychecks are deposited), and even may be aware of security holes. This type of computer criminal may appear highly improbable, as they often are middle class, white-collar employees who otherwise seem to be solid employees. Because they seem unlikely to be criminals, such individuals are particularly well equipped to use their knowledge to commit computer crimes.

Depending on the criminal, the motives behind the crimes can vary widely, although most stories about computer crime have common themes: they are white-collar crimes, in which no one gets physically hurt. The goal of the crime is to beat the system, in some way, whether that means stealing money from an already wealthy organization or outsmarting the computer security at a firm.

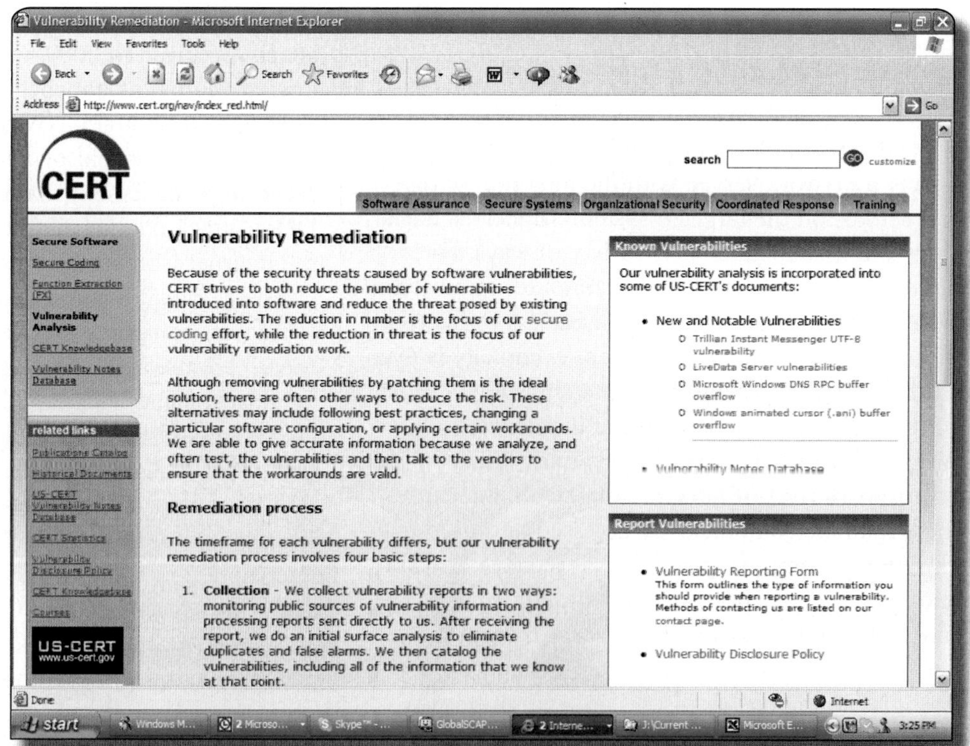

Figure 7-18 Companies or individuals requiring assistance or information about DDoS attacks and other Internet security breaches can contact or visit the Web site of the Computer Emergency Response Team Coordination Center (CERT/CC), which is a federally funded research and development center.

For some hackers, breaking into a system is an exciting adventure, which shows their level of computing skill to others in the hacker community. As an example, in July 2003, computer experts were tipped off to a loosely organized competition that dared hackers to break into and deface Web sites. Hackers took on the challenge, hitting small business, personal, and church Web sites. No major Web sites were hit, thanks to improved security. Hacking Web sites also gives hackers a public forum in which to express their point of view, as when Falun Gong practitioners claimed their Web sites were attacked and hacked into by the Chinese government, when pro-Napster hackers defaced Web sites to show support for the file-sharing service, when anti-Bush hackers replaced the photo on George W. Bush's campaign Web site with a hammer and sickle or when pro-American hackers hacked the Web site of the Al-Jazeera news network (Figure 7-19).

Other criminals have much more malicious intentions. Terrorists, cyberstalkers, and sexual predators all can use computers as tools to help them commit crimes or share their ideological viewpoints. Spies and others can hack into computers to steal security and military secrets or commit industrial espionage.

The motive behind some computer crimes is purely financial, in which an individual identifies and takes advantage of an opportunity to make money. An entirely different motive drives angry exemployees or existing employees who want to exact revenge on their companies. For example, one fired engineer, who also worked as the company's network administrator, launched a logic bomb. Three weeks after he was fired, employees came to work and could not start their computers. A check of the network and its computers showed that the logic bomb had destroyed all of the firm's software and erased all network files, causing $10 million in damages.

Figure 7-19 During Operation Iraqi Freedom, hackers defaced numerous Web sites as a protest against the United States, Iraq, or the war in general. For example, the Al-Jazeera news network was the target of many pro-American defacement attacks, such as the one above, as well as denial-of-service attacks.

PROSECUTING COMPUTER CRIMINALS In many ways, computer crimes simply are newer versions of long-established crimes – theft, fraud, vandalism, trespassing, harassment, child pornography, and copyright infringement – made new again with the addition of computers. And yet, prosecuting computer criminals can be difficult.

Cybercriminals are not confined by geography, like traditional criminals. Any individual, armed with nothing more than a computer, can commit crimes that impact individuals, businesses, and governments – all without leaving the sofa. Truly savvy computer criminals also become adept at covering their tracks, routing communications through other networks around the globe to hide the source of the crime. Because these crimes can take place in many countries in the space of minutes, international law enforcement officials also must cooperate with each other to find and take legal action against cybercriminals (Figure 7-20).

Making the prospect of identifying and prosecuting computer criminals even more difficult is that many computer crimes go unreported. While computer crime is a big headline-maker, the crimes reported on the evening news are a small part of the actual crimes

Figure 7-20 Swedish computer experts Frederik Bjoerck, left, and Johan Ekstrom, right, at the Stokholm University helped the FBI track down the author of the Melissa virus and the "I LOVE YOU" bug.

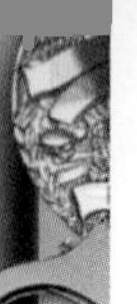

committed. In fact, although over 80 percent of firms report suffering from insider abuse of network access, only 30 per cent of companies reported computer crimes to law enforcement officials.

Companies often hesitate to pursue civil or criminal recourse, worried that the bad publicity might cause more damage than the crime itself. Companies also know that the legal process required to prosecute a criminal is long and costly. Even if found guilty, a computer criminal – who may have caused millions of dollars in losses in a crime involving bits of data – is likely to get a much lighter sentence than a criminal who committed a physical act, such as theft or assault.

Things are changing, however, and computer criminals are starting to get more than just a slap on the wrist. Judges and juries are beginning to understand exactly how much damage a computer criminal can cause, as they increasingly recognize the value of information and data. The public also is becoming aware that computer crimes are a loss for everyone, forcing credit-card companies to raise rates to cover losses due to identify theft and causing downtime when a denial-of-service attack brings your ISP to a halt.

Law enforcement agencies are becoming trained in the processes necessary to investigate computer crimes. The U.S Department of Justice, for example, has a Computer Crime and Intellectual Property Section (CCIPS) focused solely on prosecuting computer crimes and cybercrimes (Figure 7-21). Further, laws are being written to address computer crime directly, as shown in Table 7-7, and the sentences are getting tougher. The first person convicted under the Computer Fraud and Abuse Act was Robert T. Morris, Jr., a Cornell graduate student who introduced a worm into the Internet and brought down around 6,000 computers. Morris was sentenced to three years probation, ordered to pay a $10,000 fine, required to serve 40 hours community service, and forced to pay $91 per month to cover his probation supervision. In 2003, a leader of a huge counterfeit video piracy ring received a 46-month prison term, while just four months later, a computer hacker was sentenced to one year and one day and ordered to pay over $88,000 restitution for a series of computer intrusions and credit-card fraud totaling approximately $7,000.

Companies are realizing that the publicity that results from prosecuting a computer crime actually can be good. If handled correctly, the legal action sends strong, positive messages. It shows customers that the company takes the protection of their customers seriously; that it is improving its security (which its competitors may not be doing) and that it wants to save customers money by reducing losses due to crime.

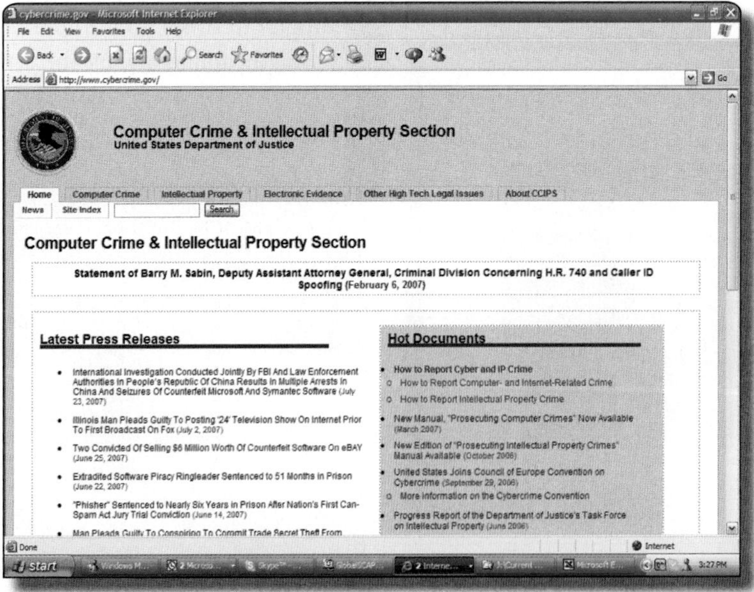

Figure 7-21 Law enforcement agencies are becoming trained in the processes necessary to investigate computer crimes. The U.S Department of Justice, for example, has a Computer Crime and Intellectual Property Section (CCIPS) focused solely on prosecuting computer and cybercrimes.

Table 7-7 Recent Cybercrime Legislation

2004	**Identity Theft Penalty Enhancement Act**	Established in federal criminal court the offense of aggravated identity theft (the use of a stolen identity to commit criminal acts); also made it possible to add an additional penalty just for identity theft on top of the penalty for the actual theft committed.
2003	**Fair and Accurate Credit Transactions Act (FACT Act)**	Requires merchants to delete all but the last five digits from retail receipts; permits every citizen the right to a free credit report annually from the major credit reporting bureaus; strengthens and simplifies fraud monitoring and reporting processes; requires lenders and credit agencies to take action against fraud as soon as it is detected, even if unreported by victims.
2002	**Cyber Security Enhancement Act**	Addresses weaknesses in current law by directing the U.S. Sentencing Commission to review and amend federal computer crime sentencing guidelines; empowers judges to issue appropriately tough sentences for computer crime by allowing them to consider intent, violations of privacy rights and the sophistication of the offense in addition to actual loss.
2001	**USA PATRIOT Act**	Expands the government's surveillance rights; extends the types of information that law enforcement authorities may obtain with a subpoena to include e-mail, voice mail, or even the remote IP address from which a computer connects to a provider Also allows for "roving wiretaps," so that law enforcement officials can get court orders to wiretap a cellular or disposable phone a suspected terrorist would use. Obtaining such records will make the process of identifying computer criminals and tracing their Internet communications faster and easier.
1998	**Identity Theft and Assumption Deterrence Act**	Makes it a crime to knowingly transfer or use, without permission, a name, birth certificate, or Social Security number as a means of identification. Also covers credit card numbers, cellular phone serial numbers, or any other information that can uniquely identify an individual.
1997	**No Electronic Theft (NET) Act**	Permits federal prosecution of large-scale, willful copyright infringement even where the infringer does not act for a commercial purpose or for private financial gain, thus closing the loophole in criminal enforcement of copyright infringement.
1994	**Computer Abuse Amendments Act (also called 18 U.S.C.§ 1030)**	Focused on further defining fraud and related activity in connection with computers.
1986	**Electronic Communications Privacy Act**	Limited unlawful access to stored electronic communications (although the term "e-mail" is absent from the ECPA, legislative history indicates that e-mail falls within the coverage of the statute).
1984	**Computer Fraud and Abuse Act**	Made fraud and related activity (unauthorized access, sharing damaging programs such as viruses) in connection with computers illegal.

Over the last few decades, many laws have been written to address computer crime directly; several of these laws are shown here.

CONCLUSION

In this chapter, you learned about a number of computer security risks. You learned about the many types of viruses that are likely to infect your computer, as well as how they work using a two-stage infection and delivery process. You also found out how Trojan horses and worms work and how to avoid falling for a virus hoax. Finally, you learned how to protect your computer from malicious logic programs to ensure the safety of your data and programs. You also learned about computer crime, including the many types of computer crime ranging from unauthorized use to intellectual property and software theft. After discovering several ways that computer criminals commit their offenses, you found out more about the two-fold challenge of identifying and then prosecuting computer criminals. In Chapter 9, you will learn about various safeguards, security tools, and procedures you can use to protect yourself from computer crime.

Key Terms

antivirus program
boot program
boot sector
boot sector virus
bot or botnet
computer crime
computer security risk
computer virus
cracker
cybercrime
cyberslacking
data diddling
denial-of-service attack (DoS)
distributed denial-of-service attack (DDoS)
Fair and Accurate Credit Transactions (FACT) Act
file virus
hacker
hardware theft
identity theft
Identity Theft and Assumption Deterrence Act of 1998
Identity Theft Penalty Enhancement Act
information theft
inoculate
intellectual property (IP)
intellectual property rights
intellectual property theft
logic bomb
macro virus
malicious logic program
malicious software program
malware
master boot record (MBR) viruses
multipartite virus
packet sniffer
payload
phishing
polymorphic
polypartite virus
quarantine
recovery disk
rescue disk
salami method
salami shaving
shoulder surfing
social engineering
software piracy
software theft
stealth virus
superuser
system administrator
time bomb
Trojan horse
trusted source
unauthorized access
unauthorized use
virus definition
virus hoax
virus signature
worm
zombie

Chapter Review

Multiple Choice

Select the best answer.

1. A boot sector virus _____.

a. inserts virus code into program files, as opposed to document or data files

b. uses the macro language of an application to hide virus code

c. replaces the program used to start the computer system with a modified, infected version

d. infects both the macro language or an application and program files

2. A virus's _____ is the destructive event or prank the virus was created to deliver, such as deleting data or files or displaying a silly message.

a. cracker

b. trusted source

c. payload

d. signature

3. A(n) _____ is a malicious logic program disguised as a real application, such as a screen saver.

a. antivirus program

b. Trojan horse

c. worm

d. virus hoax

4. Most antivirus programs have utilities that create a _____, which contains an uninfected copy of key operating system commands and start-up information that enables the computer to restart correctly.

a. time bomb

b. recovery disk

c. boot program

d. packet sniffer

5. The term cybercrime refers to _____.

a. the act of stealing, defacing, or destroying computer equipment

b. using the Internet and the Web for personal reasons at work

c. online or Internet-based illegal acts

d. stealing software media or illegally copying a software program

6. Although _____ once was a complimentary word for a computer enthusiast, the term now has a negative connotation and means anyone who tries to access a computer or network illegally.

a. hacker

b. superuser

c. payload

d. zombie

7. A serious type of information theft is _____, which occurs when someone appropriates personal information to commit fraud or theft

a. identity theft

b. hardware theft

c. intellectual property theft

d. software theft

8. Salami shaving is a method computer criminals use to steal or embezzle funds by _____.

a. observing someone, perhaps by looking over his or her shoulder, to get information

b. tricking a user into revealing his or her password

c. turning off or disabling message preview in e-mail programs

d. altering a program so that a very small amount is taken from a large number of transactions

9. A _____ is an assault on a single computer, usually a network server, with the intention of disrupting service on the targeted system.

a. master boot record (MBR)

b. virus definition (VD)

c. social engineer (SE)

d. denial-of-service attack (DoS)

10. Prosecuting computer criminals can be difficult because _____.

a. cybercriminals are not confined by geography, like traditional criminals

b. many computer crimes go unreported

c. companies often hesitate to pursue civil or criminal recourse, worried about the bad publicity

d. all of the above

Chapter Review

Short Answer

Write a brief answer to each of the following questions.

1. What three actions typically are performed during a computer virus's infection phase?
2. How is a time bomb different from a logic bomb?
3. How does an antivirus program inoculate a file and quarantine an infected file?
4. What is software piracy and why does it continue?
5. How can an unauthorized user obtain a password?

Web Research

Use a search engine such as Google (google.com) to research the following questions. Then, write a one-page, double-spaced report or create a presentation, unless otherwise directed.

1. An old saying claims that, "An ounce of prevention is worth a pound of cure." An **antivirus program** is an ounce of prevention that can protect computer users from the pound of cost associated with a computer virus infection. Use the Web to locate one or more manufacturers of antivirus programs and find out how you can protect your computer from computer viruses.

2. As you learned in this chapter, botnets and their zombie computers are starting to reach beyond the annoyance of denial of service attacks. Use the Web to learn more about uses of botnets, what law enforcement is doing to combat their use, and what measures individuals can take to prevent their own computer systems from becoming zombies.

Group Exercises

Working with a group of your classmates, complete the following team questions.

1. With the growing number of notebook computer users has come increasing concern about the vulnerability of portable computers. In one year, an insurer of personal computers reported claims for almost $1 billion worth of equipment. Among incidents reported were accidental damage (238,000 cases), theft (208,000 cases), power surges (38,000 cases), and loss during transit (19,000 cases). To protect notebook computers and the information they hold, manufacturers have developed a range of products. Have each member of your team visit a computer vendor and make a list of products available to help safeguard portable computers. What is the purpose of each product? How much does it cost? How is it used? Which products do salespeople recommend? Why? Then, meet with your team and compare your findings. Prepare a PowerPoint presentation on the safeguards available to protect portable computers.

2. A relatively new career option is computer security officer or consultant. These individuals are responsible for protecting the privacy of an organization's records and helping to prosecute people who illegally access an organization's computers. Computer security officers can have a number of backgrounds — programmers, police officers, even hackers. Many schools offer courses in computer security, but the lack of standardized qualifications leads to a wide range of compensation. Some security consultants, however, make more than $400 per hour. Have each member or your team interview a computer security consultant or a security officer at your school or local organization. What are the gravest security threats? How should these threats be handled? What should be done with violators? Then, meet with your team, share your findings, and prepare a PowerPoint presentation explaining the responsibilities of a computer security officer.

Computers, Law, and Ethics 8

Law Versus Ethics
Computers and the Law
- **E-Commerce Laws**
  - *Digital Signatures*
  - *Online Advertising*
- **Intellectual Property**
  - *Copyright Infringement*
  - *Software Piracy*
- **Objectionable Content**
- **Online Gambling**
- **Cyberlibel**
- **Cyberstalking**

Computers and Ethics
- **Ethical Decision Making: A Framework**
- **Ethics for Computer Professionals**
  - *Codes of Ethics and Professional Conduct*
  - *Professionalism and Responsibility*
- **Ethics in Business**
  - *Advertising and Marketing*
  - *Digital Manipulation*
  - *Protecting Customer Data*
- **Ethical Use of Intellectual Property**
  - *Music, Movie, and Software Piracy*
  - *Plagiarism*

Conclusion

Each day, new computer technologies are put to use in ways previously not considered: to monitor the heartbeat of a newborn, to profile the credit and spending habits of a household, to create a stunning new piece of art, or to steer a car from a skid to a safe stop. Without question, our world increasingly is dependent on and dominated by computers and other technologies. In most instances, computer technology has had a positive effect on the world, making our lives easier, more productive, safer, and more entertaining. At the same time, the use of computers raises a number of important issues, including how to create laws to address computer crimes and how computers and technologies should be used ethically. As a computer user, you will have the opportunity to make choices about how you use that technology; ethics can help guide your decisions.

In this chapter, you will learn the differences between law and ethics, as well as their relationship. Next, you will learn about laws focused on the use of computers, including e-commerce and intellectual property laws, as well as legal guidance set forth around objectionable content, online gambling, cyberlibel, and cyberstalking. You then will consider the relationship between computers and ethics, reviewing an ethical decision-making framework that can help you determine what you consider an ethical approach to your schoolwork, your profession, your personal life, and your use of computers. After reviewing ethical issues faced by computer professionals and in business, you also will examine the ethical issues surrounding the use of intellectual property.

LAW VERSUS ETHICS

Before reviewing various legal and ethical aspects of computing, it is important to understand the relationship between the law and ethics. The **law** is a consistent set of rules that are widely published, generally accepted, and usually enforced. Laws exist to govern conduct between individuals in a society; they are requirements to act in a given way, not just expectations or suggestions to act in that way. Because laws strictly define what actions are acceptable or unacceptable, they can help simplify choices of behavior.

Ethics, by contrast, often require complex decision making. **Ethics** are the standards that help guide your behavior, actions, and choices. Ethics are grounded in a notion of responsibility and accountability. The word "ethics" is derived from the Greek word *ethos*, meaning character, and from the Latin word meaning mores (customs). Together, these words define how individuals choose to interact with one another (as opposed to how the law dictates they must interact). In philosophy, the study of ethics defines what is good for an individual and for society and then establishes good behaviors and duties that people owe themselves and one another. Table 8-1 outlines the key characteristics of the law and ethics, to show some of the differences.

Despite their differences, ethical values and legal principles usually are closely related (Figure 8-1). The law often incorporates ethical standards to which most citizens subscribe (for example, laws prohibiting murder, vandalism, and identity theft serve to enforce conduct that most would agree is ethical). Ethical obligations, however, often involve issues that are outside of or go beyond the law. For example, if you were an employee in your school's registrar's office, you could access student grades from the registrar's database. Look up grades for your friends, so they do not have to wait for delivery of the grades in the mail. Is it illegal? No. Is it ethical? That is a more personal decision, grounded in your sense of responsibility and accountability, your personal values, your religious beliefs, and so on.

While law and ethics often are intertwined, and law often embodies ethical principles, the two are not interchangeable. The law does not ban some acts that would be widely condemned as unethical, but the law does prohibit certain acts that some might not perceive as unethical. For example, lying to a friend is not illegal, but most people would consider it unethical. On the other hand, sharing copyrighted songs via a P2P (peer-to-peer) file-sharing network is illegal, but many people do not have an ethical conflict with downloading copyrighted MP3s for free.

Table 8-1 Law Versus Ethics

CHARACTERISTICS OF LAW	CHARACTERISTICS OF ETHICS
Law must be consistent – that is, two laws cannot contradict each other, because people cannot obey both.	Ethics involves learning what is right and wrong, making personal judgments about what is right and wrong, and then doing the right thing.
Laws are universal and apply to everyone in a society (for example, a country, state, or town).	Most ethical decisions have multiple alternatives and may have mixed outcomes.
Laws are published, in written form, so they are available to everyone within the society.	Ethics often are not documented; they are personal value judgments about right and wrong.
Laws include requirements that have to be generally obeyed.	Most ethical decisions have personal implications.
Laws must be enforced, so that individuals are compelled to obey the law if they do not choose to do so voluntarily.	Most ethical decisions have extended and uncertain consequences; making ethical decisions requires consideration of potential consequences for all involved.

Law and ethics have unique and different characteristics.

Figure 8-1 Ethical values and legal principles are closely related, because many laws mandate ethical conduct.

COMPUTERS AND THE LAW

As you learned in Chapter 7, numerous types of computer crimes are committed each day, causing losses to individuals and corporations. You also learned that, while identifying and prosecuting computer criminals remains a major challenge for law enforcement officials, the laws surrounding cybercrime also are being strengthened, providing for stronger punishments in the hope of deterring future crime.

A new area of law, called **cyberlaw**, seeks to address legal and regulatory issues relating to the Internet and the World Wide Web. Because of the effect of computers on our lives, cyberlaw is a rapidly growing field. In some cases, cyberlaw deals with computer crimes that simply are newer versions of long-established crimes – theft, fraud, vandalism, trespassing, harassment, child pornography, and copyright infringement. In other cases, computers and technology are enabling entirely new types of crime that previously were not possible, such as cyberstalking and sharing copyrighted music files over file-sharing networks.

Lawmakers are working to craft laws to ensure that rules and regulations are clearly established to address these new iterations of old crimes, as well as entirely new crimes. Several key laws have been passed in the area of cyberlaw in an effort to ensure that cyberspace is appropriately regulated, just like physical space. The following sections review several areas where lawmakers have focused their legislative powers to define new laws. It also reviews the legal challenges of enforcing cyberlaw when the scene of the crime – the Internet – has a vast global reach and thus often defies the jurisdiction of any one law enforcement agency.

E-Commerce Laws

The incredible growth of e-commerce has created an entirely new set of legal challenges. Each day, traditional and online retailers, banks, and many other businesses conduct transactions with consumers and other businesses. These transactions may take place within a single state, within a country, or across national borders using the Internet. The challenge for lawmakers is how to regulate e-commerce transactions as they do transactions at the local Old Navy retailer, without infringing on privacy or making the process so complicated that you would rather just head to the local store.

DIGITAL SIGNATURES In 2000, the **Electronic Signatures in Global and National Commerce Act (E-SIGN)** was signed into law. E-SIGN, also referred to as the Millennium Digital Commerce Act, specifies that in the United States a digital signature has the same legal weight as a traditional signature written on paper. Prior to the passage of the law, contracts in the United States were not valid unless they were signed, by hand, with pen and ink. Using digital signatures, two company CEOs can complete a business transaction and sign the contract, without having to fly thousands of miles for a meeting or send the hard copy back and forth using costly overnight mail services. The law is designed to make you feel more secure about sealing big-ticket deals online, such as buying a car, by making an electronic signature just as binding as one in ink.

Just as your handwritten signature identifies you as you, a digital signature can provide that same identification, only electronically. A **digital signature** is an encoded, or encrypted, code that a person, Web site, or company attaches to an electronic message, document, or file to verify the identity of the sender (Figure 8-2).

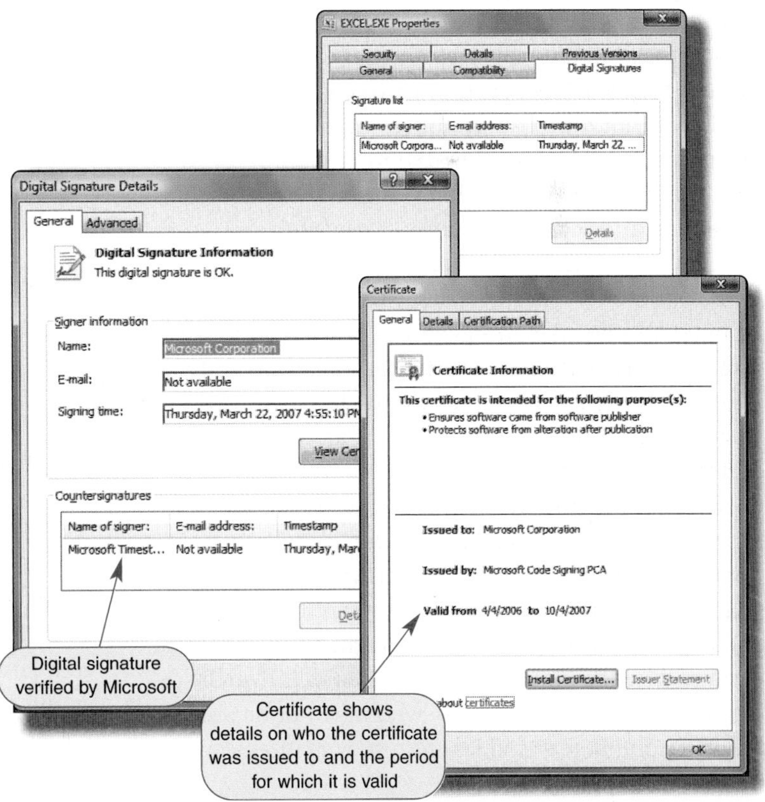

Figure 8-2 Many companies digitally sign installation files, so that you can ensure they are legitimate, unaltered files before you install the program. To view a program's digital signature using Windows Vista, right-click the file, click Properties, then click the Digital Signatures tab. Click the Detail button to view more information about the digital signature. Not all files will have a digital signature.

The code usually consists of the user's name and a hash of all or a part of the message. A **hash**, also called the **message digest**, is a mathematical formula that generates a code from the contents of the message. Thus, the hash differs for each message. Receivers of the message decode, or decrypt, the digital signature. The recipient then generates a new hash of the received message and compares it with the one in the digital signature to ensure that they match. Chapter 9 will discuss the encryption technology used in digital signatures in more detail.

Digital signatures, also called electronic signatures or e-signatures, can be used to ensure that an impostor is not participating in an Internet transaction. That is, digital signatures help to prevent online forgery. A digital signature also can verify that the content of an electronic message or document, which easily can be changed, has not been modified.

On the day of the signing, President Clinton used a magnetic card containing his digital signature to sign the bill into law electronically, although he later used pen and ink to sign a paper copy to make the document official. The law also says certain urgent notices – such as cancellation of utilities, eviction notices, cancellation of health or life insurance, and product recalls – must be sent on paper in order to ensure that consumers do not miss critical notices simply because their computers were down. The need to rely on paper to back up digital signatures points to some of the technical, social, and security questions about the law.

One concern is the lack of technical standards. E-SIGN does not specify a single technology that must be used to create digital signatures. Many companies now are working to develop the hardware and software individuals will use to sign messages and documents electronically, but it is not yet clear if all of these systems will work together correctly.

Critics claim that the use of digital signatures will increase the digital divide by favoring middle- and upper-class families owning computers. While the bill guarantees consumers a choice between digital and pen-and-paper contracts, a car dealer might charge you an extra service fee for using a paper contract. If such scenarios arise, poorer families – who may not be able to afford a computer – and less tech-savvy citizens are at a distinct disadvantage.

Finally, an unfortunate by-product of new laws and new technologies is new criminals. Thieves could forge your digital signature, just as they can steal a credit-card number, and then sign for a new car loan. With a credit card, you only are liable for the first $50. E-SIGN, however, does not specify a dollar limit on purchases made using stolen digital signatures, meaning losses suffered by consumers could be financially devastating. Table 8-2 lists some basic guidelines on how to use digital signatures safely when signing electronic contracts.

Table 8-2

TIPS FOR CONSUMERS USING ELECTRONIC SIGNATURES TO SIGN ONLINE CONTRACTS

- Do not consent to an electronic contract or to receive electronic notices if you are uncomfortable using a computer or do not understand how to use e-mail.
- Do not consent to an electronic contract or to receive electronic documents until you are certain that your computer's software and hardware are compatible with the business' computer system.
- Remember that you can opt to receive documents on paper instead of electronically if you prefer.
- As with any contract, read the fine print. Don't agree to a contract that you do not understand.
- Keep backup paper copies of the electronic documents you receive, and keep a list of the businesses with which you agree to receive electronic documents.
- Notify the businesses of any changes that may affect your ability to receive e-mail, such as changing your e-mail address, your hardware, or your software.
- Close any unused e-mail accounts.
- Don't give out your e-mail address to any business if you don't want to receive e-mail notices from that business.
- Be sure to notify the business if you have any problems receiving its e-mails or opening its documents.

The Consumers Union, publisher of Consumer Reports magazine, provides several tips for consumers using electronic signatures to sign online contracts.

ONLINE ADVERTISING Consider the thousands of advertisements you have seen while browsing on the Web – whether simple banner ads or pop-up ads that appear annoyingly in front of the Web page you want to view. Without question, the Internet has opened up an entirely new field for advertising, connecting advertisers and customers with text, interactive graphics, video and audio promising weight loss, offering better Internet service, or encouraging you to see the latest Disney movie or refinance your mortgage.

In the United States, the same laws that apply to other forms of advertising govern advertising on the Internet. These laws, embodied in the **Federal Trade Commission Act**, state that advertising in any medium – print, television, radio, or Internet ads – must be truthful and must not mislead consumers. An advertisement can be misleading if relevant information is left out or if the claim implies something that is not true. For example, a banner ad promoting a buy one, get one free sale is misleading if it does not also note other conditions, such as that you have to make a minimum $500.00 purchase and sign up for a credit card. Any claims in an ad also must be substantiated, especially when the product is health, safety, or performance related. For example, if a product promises you can learn to speed read in ten minutes, the company must have data to support that claim.

Interestingly, it is not only the company running the ad that is responsible to evaluate ads for truthfulness. The Federal Trade Commission (FTC) also holds Web site designers and advertising agencies responsible for reviewing advertisements to ensure that claims in the ad are substantiated. If an online ad is found to be in violation of the Federal Trade Commission Act or any other law, you can be hit with fines up to $11,000 per violation and, in the case of civil lawsuits, responsible for refunds to customers for actual damages. Of course, these laws only apply to the United States, so ads being run on Web sites outside of the United States are not subject to the same punishments. As with all content on the Internet, be sure to evaluate the claims made in any ad carefully to ensure the claims in the ad are credible.

@ISSUE: Hacktivism: Heroes or Criminals?

Although sometimes merely a harmless prank, hacking is a crime — and one with serious consequences. Hackers can be prosecuted under the Computer Fraud and Abuse Act of 1986 and several state laws, which make it a crime to access or use a computer without authorization, to alter data in a computer without authorization, or to commit other acts with the intent of causing damage to the computer or data. The threat of punishment, however, rarely is a deterrent for many in the hacking community, because their motives for hacking matter more than the risk of being caught.

What drives hackers? For some, hacking is strictly about the challenge and excitement of breaking into a computer or network. For these hackers, a successful hack is a badge of honor in the hacking community. For others, hacking is a way to express a political view, protest a government's censorship of free speech, or bring examples of human rights violations into public view. The new agenda for these hackers is a kind of electronic civil disobedience that allows them to challenge authority using their computer skills. This type of electronic protest, dubbed **hacktivism**, has started to change the rules of protest and civil disobedience. Instead of sit-ins, hacktivists use computer break-ins; their protest signs are the Web pages they post on hacked Web sites. The approach is effective and its use is on the rise, and becoming increasingly organized.

For example, to protest corruption and censorship of the Mexican government, a hacker group called X-pilot rewrote the home page of a Mexican government site. Nike.com was hacked to protest its labor policies, and visitors were redirected to an Australian labor rights site. In 2000, a hacker group calling itself the Federation of Random Action protested Occidental Petroleum's plans to explore for oil on U'wa Indian ancestral land by launching a distributed denial-of-service (DDoS) attacks on two Occidental Petroleum sites and a third site run by Fidelity Investments, an Occidental shareholder.

Another group, Hacktivismo, is a semiorganized group of programmers from around the world who disapprove of destructive techniques like defacing Web sites or launching DDoS attacks (Figure 8-3). Instead, as the Hacktivismo Declaration notes, "the international hacking community has a moral imperative to act" to use their technological skills to advance human rights. Their focus is protecting the free speech and universal access that are cornerstones of the Internet.

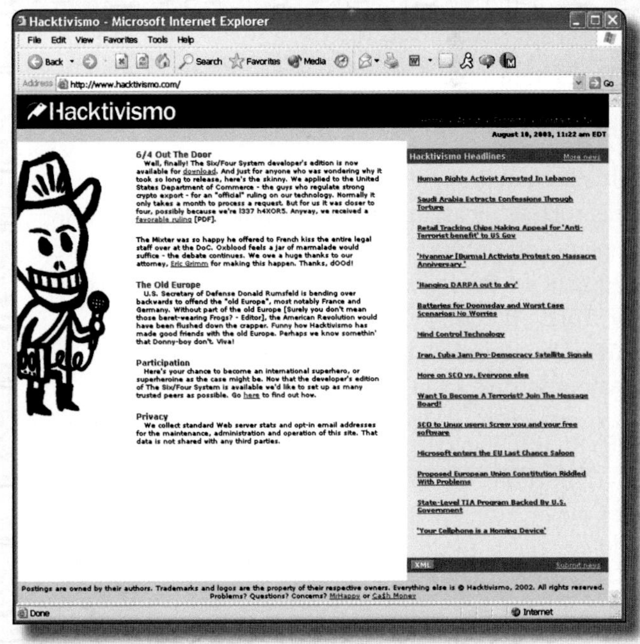

Figure 8-3 The hacktivist group Hacktivismo focuses on protecting the free speech and universal access that are cornerstones of the Internet.

(continued)

ISSUE: Hacktivism: Heroes or Criminals? *(continued)*

Core targets for Hacktivismo are countries such as Saudi Arabia, Iran, China, Myanmar, Singapore, and at least 20 others that use firewalls to restrict citizens' access to the Internet. In these countries, firewalls are used to limit the Web pages available to citizens; any content that contains news stories or religious or political views contrary to the government's views can be blocked, as well as information on health, education, or entertainment. Firewalls also may be configured to log the IP addresses of users who have requested access to banned sites and to snoop on e-mail communications. Using these firewalls, a government effectively can limit its citizens' access to what otherwise is the most vast information resource available. In these countries, the consequences of trying to access a site blocked by a firewall can be severe, including jail.

To combat these countries, Hacktivismo focuses on writing and distributing software that interferes with governments' efforts to censor the Internet. Hacktivismo distributed their first program, Camera/Shy, as an Internet Explorer-based browser. The browser received banned content as encrypted content within ordinary .gif images, which passed by the filters of most censors.

Hacktivismo has released a software tool, called Six/Four, in commemoration of the Tiananmen Square massacre which occurred on June 4, 1989. Six/Four is based around a concept of trusted network access, allowing users from countries with limited access to receive permission to connect and have their Internet requests and responses handled through this secure network — instead of a government-monitored Internet service provider. In an interesting twist, even Six/Four's software license is focused on supporting human rights. The license forbids users from using the software in a malicious manner or to introduce harmful changes to the software's source code.

Hacktivism raises some interesting ethical questions. Consider your position on hacktivists from several points of view: a citizen of a country where many Web sites are banned; a corporate executive of a hacked site; a customer of a Web site brought down by hacktivists; and a supporter of free speech. From the point of view of each of those groups, should hacking a Web site — which is illegal under United States law — be a crime if it is done with a greater purpose, such as sharing a political concern? Are some techniques used by hacktivists more ethical than others, or are all of the techniques simply criminal acts that should be punished as such? Can hacktivism really have an impact?

In some cases, the companies targeted probably would argue that, regardless of some higher moral purpose, hacking remains a crime. Others believe that hacktivists merely are practicing civil disobedience — the equivalent of a 60s-style sit-in — using new technologies. Hacktivism is a new and interesting frontier, and the way in which companies, governments, and individuals will respond to hacktivists remains yet to be seen.

Intellectual Property

Intellectual property refers to unique and original works such as ideas, inventions, writings, art, processes, company and product names, and logos. Intellectual property rights are the rights to which creators are entitled for their work. Although intellectual property theft takes many different forms, the following section addresses copyright infringement, along with software piracy.

COPYRIGHT INFRINGEMENT As you have learned, a copyright protects any tangible form of expression and gives the creator, whether a company or individual, exclusive rights to duplicate, publish, and sell its materials. The wide availability of digital content – from art to books to software – makes it easier than ever for you and others to make copies of the content. In some cases, copying the content might not be a copyright infringement, while in other cases, it is. In fact, many areas of copyright law are not clear, because copyright law gives the public fair use of copyrighted material.

Fair use essentially is a limitation on the exclusive rights of copyright holders. The **Copyright Act** gives copyright holders the exclusive right to reproduce their works for a limited time period, because that work is their intellectual property. But, fair use allows some use of copyrighted material, such as for educational and critical purposes. Section 107 of the copyright law includes four factors that should be used to define whether a use of copyrighted material in a particular case is fair use (Table 8-3). For some, however, the vague definition is subject to wide interpretation and raises many questions:

- Should individuals be able to download the contents of your Web site, modify it, and then put it back up on the Web as their own?
- Should a faculty member have the right to print material from the Web and distribute it to members of the class for teaching purposes only?
- Should someone be able to scan photographs or pages from a book, publish them to the Web, and allow others to download them?

- Should you be able to record a season's worth of Grey's Anatomy and then hold a private showing for your friends?
- Should you be able to print the lyrics to your favorite Greenday song on the your MySpace page?
- Should students be able to post their term papers on the Web, making them available for other students to download and use as their own work?

Table 8-3

FOUR FACTORS USED TO DETERMINE FAIR USE
1. The purpose and character of the use, including whether such use is of a commercial nature or is for nonprofit educational purposes
2. The nature of the copyrighted work
3. The amount and substantiality of the portion used in relation to the copyrighted work as a whole
4. The effect of the use upon the potential market for, or value of, the copyrighted work. The fact that a work is unpublished shall not itself bar a finding of fair use if such finding is made upon consideration of all the above factors.

Section 107 of copyright law includes four factors that should be used to determine whether using copyrighted material in a particular case is fair use.

To date, U.S. courts have recognized that use of copyrighted material for criticism, comment, news reporting, teaching, scholarship, or research falls into the category of fair use. In 1984, the Supreme Court also found that "time-shifting" – such as private, non-commercial home recording of television programs to permit later viewing – is fair use. The law still is not entirely settled, however, on several other issues. For example, is it fair use for you to make a backup copy of an audio CD you own for personal use only? Another question revolves around "space-shifting" or "format-shifting," which involves taking content you own in one format and putting it into another format for personal, non-commercial use. Ripping an audio CD into an MP3 format, for example, is one way users are space-shifting copyrighted content.

In 1998, the U.S. Congress passed the **Digital Millennium Copyright Act (DMCA)**, the most comprehensive reform of United States copyright law in years, with changes focused on responding to new questions raised by digital content. The core focus of the law is to protect copyright owners. Some of the key tenets of the law include:

- Making it a crime to circumvent antipiracy measures built into most commercial software.
- Outlawing the manufacture, sale, or distribution of code-cracking devices used to copy software illegally.
- Providing exemptions from anticircumvention provisions for nonprofit libraries, archives, and educational institutions under certain circumstances.
- Limiting Internet service providers from copyright infringement liability for simply transmitting information over the Internet. Service providers, however, are expected to remove material from users' Web sites that appears to constitute copyright infringement.
- Limiting liability of nonprofit institutions of higher education for copyright infringement by faculty members or graduate students.

Before and after passage of the bill, the Digital Millennium Copyright Act had much opposition, fostering concern among some groups and creating vocal critics in others. In particular, many have opposed the anti-circumvention provisions claiming that, instead of stopping copyright infringement, they stifle free speech, curb scientific research, and violate fair use.

For example, companies creating copy-protected DVDs and CDs limit consumers' ability to make legitimate, personal copies of content they have purchased. One case widely cited as an example of how DMCA can stifle free speech is when the Motion Picture Association of America (MPAA) sued hacker magazine *2600: The Hacker Quarterly* for publishing, in print and on its Web site, links to a DVD descrambling source code called DeCSS (De Contents Scramble System). DeCSS, written by a Norwegian programmer Jon Johansen, allowed computer users to scramble the signal on DVDs, thus allowing them to be watched on any computer, rather than only an MPAA-approved DVD player. The major movie studios represented by the MPAA claimed that the distribution of DeCSS threatened their copyright protection and was illegal under the DMCA.

2600: The Hacker Quarterly claimed that publishing the code, which originally was written to allow DVDs to be used on Linux-based systems, was not illegal given that fair-use doctrines state the public can use copyrighted material for noncommercial purposes. Further, despite the claims of the MPAA, DeCSS does nothing to allow users to make unauthorized copies of DVDs – it only allows them to play a DVD on a computer or DVD player. Finally, the use of a hyperlink in print and on the Web is a free speech issue. The court ruled in favor of the MPAA, prohibiting publishing or linking to the DeCSS. They noted that a hyperlink violates the law if it points to illegal material with the purpose of disseminating that illegal material – that is, the link is illegal because of its function, even if it also is speech. Supporters agreed with the ruling's support of guidelines outlined in DMCA; critics found the ruling a threat to free speech and fair use. Later, in July 2003, anti-DMCA groups were pleased when a court ruled that Johansen did nothing wrong in using his DeCSS program to unscramble DVD scrambling codes that stopped him from using his Linux PC to play back DVDs he had bought.

Another unique aspect of the Digital Millennium Copyright Act is the policing role it gives to online service providers, such as Web hosting firms, search tools, and Internet service providers. As outlined in Section 512 of the law, such firms are given **safe harbor** – that is, they are not subject to copyright infringement laws – if they notify users of their policies regarding copyright infringement and the consequences of repeated infringing activity. They also must set up a way to deal with copyright complaints and quickly remove or disable access to material identified in a copyright holder's complaint. Service providers, such as Google.com, Earthlink, and Yahoo!, since have posted explicit notices of how they handle potential copyright infringements under the Digital Millennium Copyright Act (Figure 8-4).

Copyright law also has been affected by two other pieces of legislation – the Copyright Term Extension Act and the TEACH Act – which are described in Table 8-4.

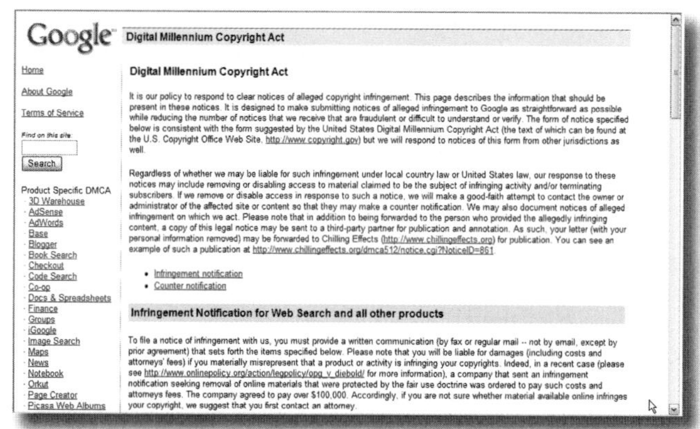

Figure 8-4 Service providers, such as Google.com, Earthlink, and Yahoo!, have posted explicit notices of how they handle potential copyright infringements under the Digital Millennium Copyright Act.

Table 8-4

COPYRIGHT PROTECTION LAWS

Law	Description
Technology, Education, and Copyright Harmonization (TEACH) Act (2002)	Redefines the terms and conditions on which educational institutions throughout the country may use copyright protected materials in distance education — including on Web sites and by other digital means — without permission from the copyright owner and without payment of royalties.
Digital Millennium Copyright Act (1998)	Makes it illegal to circumvent antipiracy measures built into commercial software, as well as outlawing the manufacturing or sale or devices to illegally copy software to other copy-protected resources.
Copyright Term Extension Act (1998)	Retroactively extended the duration of copyright ▪ in the case of individual works, from the life of author plus 50 years to the life of the author plus 70 years ▪ in the case of works of corporate authorship and works first published before January 1, 1978, from 75 years to 95 years These rules provide for the same term of protection as exists in Europe.
No Electronic Theft (NET) Act (1997)	Expands piracy laws to include distribution of copyrighted material over the Internet and set penalties for willfully infringing a copyright for purpose of commercial advantage or private financial gain

Some newer copyright and piracy laws.

SOFTWARE PIRACY As discussed in Chapter 7, software piracy is the unauthorized and illegal duplication of copyrighted software. Even after you purchase a software package, you do not have the right to copy, loan, rent, or in any way distribute the software. Doing so not only is a violation of copyright law, it also is a federal crime.

Software manufacturers issue license agreements to protect themselves from software piracy. A **license agreement** gives you the right to use the software – but you do not own the software. The license agreement provides specific conditions for the use of the software, which must be accepted before using the software (Figure 8-5). The terms usually are displayed when you install the software. In the case of software on the Web, the terms are displayed on a page at the manufacturer's Web site. Use of the software constitutes the acceptance of the terms on the user's part.

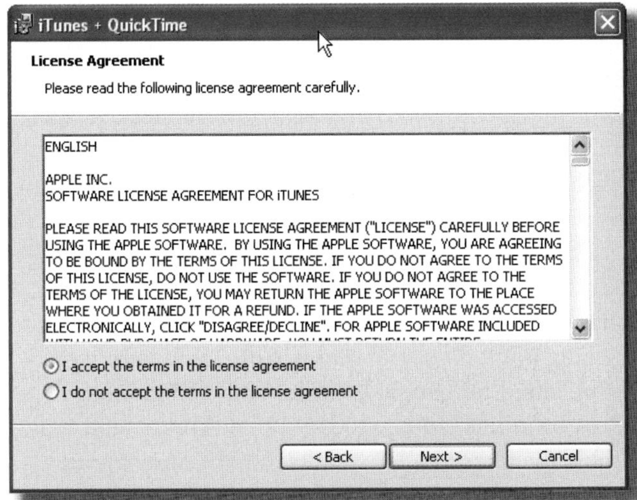

Figure 8-5 A user must accept the terms of the end-user license agreement before using the software.

The most common type of license included with software purchases by individual users is a single-user license agreement, also called an end-user license agreement. An **end-user license agreement (EULA)** typically includes many of the following conditions that specify a user's responsibility upon acceptance of the agreement. Under most end-user license agreements, users are permitted to:

- Install the software only on one computer (some agreements allow users to install the software on one desktop computer and one notebook computer).
- Make a copy of the software as a backup.
- Give or sell the software to another individual, but only if the software is removed from the user's computer first.

Users are not permitted to:

- Install the software on a network, such as a school computer lab.
- Give copies to friends or colleagues while continuing to use the software.
- Export, rent, or lease the software.

Unless otherwise specified by a license agreement, you do not have the right to copy or in any way distribute software. Software is protected by federal copyright law. The violation of this law can take place in a number of ways, from an individual making a copy of a program to give to a friend to a software piracy ring duplicating and selling thousands of copies of software CDs. In 1997, the U.S. government signed the **No Electronic Theft (NET) Act** to strengthen the copyright and trademark laws, in an effort to extend copyright protection in the digital age. The NET Act closed a copyright law loophole that allowed an MIT student, David LaMacchia, to avoid prosecution for distributing free copyrighted software on the Web. To address the loophole, the NET Act punishes all software pirates who willfully copy, distribute, and traffic in protected software on the Web, whether or not they enjoy a financial gain. The law amended existing copyright law to:

- Allow for the prosecution of individuals in cases involving large-scale illegal reproduction or distribution of copyrighted works, even if the infringers do not have a profit motive.
- Clarify that reproduction and distribution can be electronic (for example, over the Internet) or physical (on a CD, DVD, or in print).
- Increase the penalties for copyright infringement and allow for increased penalties for second or subsequent felony copyright offenses.

In 2002, a Massachusetts man was sentenced to 18 months in federal prison for his role as leader of an international computer software piracy ring that copied and sold stolen copies of thousands of software programs, including programs not yet commercially available, that were worth more than $1 million. Five of the members of the ring were employees of the computer chip maker, Intel, who supplied computer hardware to the group in exchange for access to the group's pirated software. The case was one of the most significant investigations of copyright infringement on the Internet ever conducted by the FBI, and one of the first to be prosecuted under the No Electronic Theft (NET) Act.

Critics of the new law claim that the sentences made acceptable by the NET Act might unfairly punish unwitting violators, particularly those without profit motives. The example cited by one opponent was that, under the law, if a father gave his old computer to his college-bound daughter and then reloaded the software on his computer, he could be prosecuted criminally under the NET Act.

Objectionable Content

One of the most hotly contested aspects of the Internet involves objectionable materials, including obscene or indecent content, racist literature, or other materials containing violence, objectionable language, nudity, and so on. Some believe that such material should be banned, while others feel that such content should be restricted and made unavailable to minors. Opponents of restriction argue that banning any materials violates constitutional guarantees of free speech.

Several attempts have been made to legislate in this area. Responding to pressure for restrictions, President Clinton signed the **Communications Decency Act (CDA)**, which made it a criminal offense to distribute indecent or patently offensive material online. The law was appealed immediately and, in June 1996, was declared unconstitutional by the U.S. Supreme Court, which held that the government has no right to limit free speech if less restrictive means – such as content filtering – are available. The court's ruling accorded speech on the Internet the same First Amendment free speech rights given to the printed word, TV interviews, signs held by protesters, and other forms of communication.

Two years later, a more narrowly focused law, **Child Online Protection Act** (not to be confused with Children's Online Privacy Protection Act or COPPA which requires Web sites to protect the personal information of persons under 13 years of age) was intended to focus on commercial distributors of material harmful to children. The American Civil Liberties Union (ACLU) and a group of other plaintiffs immediately subjected COPA to a First Amendment challenge; the courts overturned COPA, again noting that the government has no right to restrict free speech if less restrictive means are available. Another problem with the law was the question of what constitutes material harmful to children.

In December of 2000, Congress passed the **Children's Internet Protection Act** and the **Neighborhood Children's Internet Protection Act** as part of a larger federal appropriations measure. The laws required that any school or library receiving federal funding for Internet access must have filtering software on all computers with Internet access. The filters must protect against access to certain visual depictions that are obscene, including child pornography, or that might be harmful to minors. After several court challenges in which the filtering mandate was declared unconstitutional on First Amendment grounds, the Supreme Court ruled in June 2003 that the filtering requirement is constitutional for public libraries.

Those opposed to the Children's Internet Protection Act note that Internet filtering software suffers from underblocking in some instances and overblocking in others. On the day of the Supreme Court ruling, the Electronic Frontier Foundation released a study showing that, in some cases, filtering software failed to block Web sites with pornography, while blocking out sites addressing state-mandated curriculum topics. Although newer filtering software can use algorithms to analyze words in context, some filtering software blocked out punctuation primers and a page on Heroines of the Revolutionary War, while allowing certain pornography and sex Web sites through.

This technology raises First Amendment concerns because of its potential to be overinclusive in blocking content. Concerns are increased because the extent of blocking often is unclear and not disclosed, and may not be based on parental choice. To avoid limiting access by adults, authorized school or library staff may disable the filter to allow adults to have unrestricted Internet access for any lawful purpose.

Online Gambling

The Internet used to be flooded with ads promoting offshore casinos and online sports betting sites, but it is now illegal for Americans to bet through these Web sites. In 1998, the **Internet Gambling Prohibition Act** made it illegal to bet via the Internet or any other interactive computer service in the United States. In making online gambling illegal, the law attempts to reduce the potential problems caused by the ease and anonymity of online gambling, including access to underage gamblers, unfair payouts, and addiction. In 2006, the **Unlawful Gambling Enforcement Act** made it illegal for U.S. financial institutions to process payments of any kind for Internet gambling that is illegal under U.S. federal or state law.

The legislation has had a dramatic impact on the international online gambling industry, which derived close to 60% of its $12 billion annual revenues from U.S. citizens. Yet those offshore sites that remained in business in countries such as Curacao, Antigua, Barbuda, and the United Kingdom (Figure 8-6) have reported revenue growth despite the U.S. ban.

The tide may soon turn, however. In 2007, the World Trade Organization filed suit against the United States, claiming the ban is a blatant move to protect domestic, land-based gambling revenue. And the same year, Rep. Barney Frank introduced a bill called The Internet Gambling Regulation and Enforcement Act which aims to allow the U.S. Treasury Department to add regulation and licensing for online entities to its existing responsibilities for domestic gaming operations.

Although online gambling comprises about 5% of the overall $258 billion gambling market – which includes casinos, card rooms and government-sponsored lotteries – both opponents and proponents of current legislation agree the fight isn't yet over.

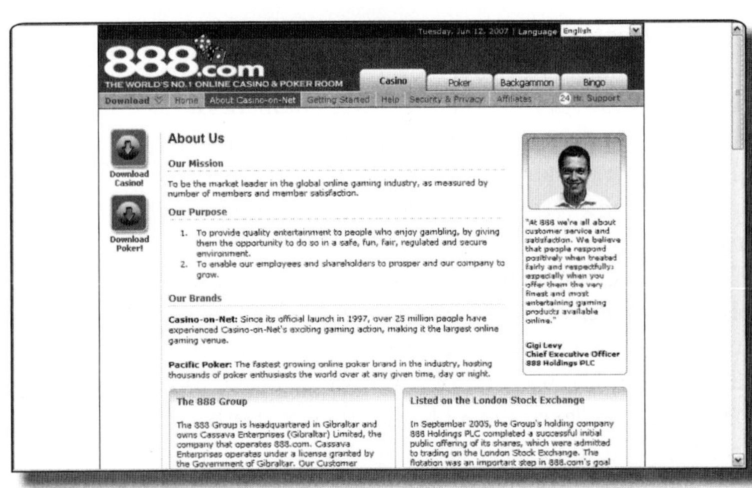

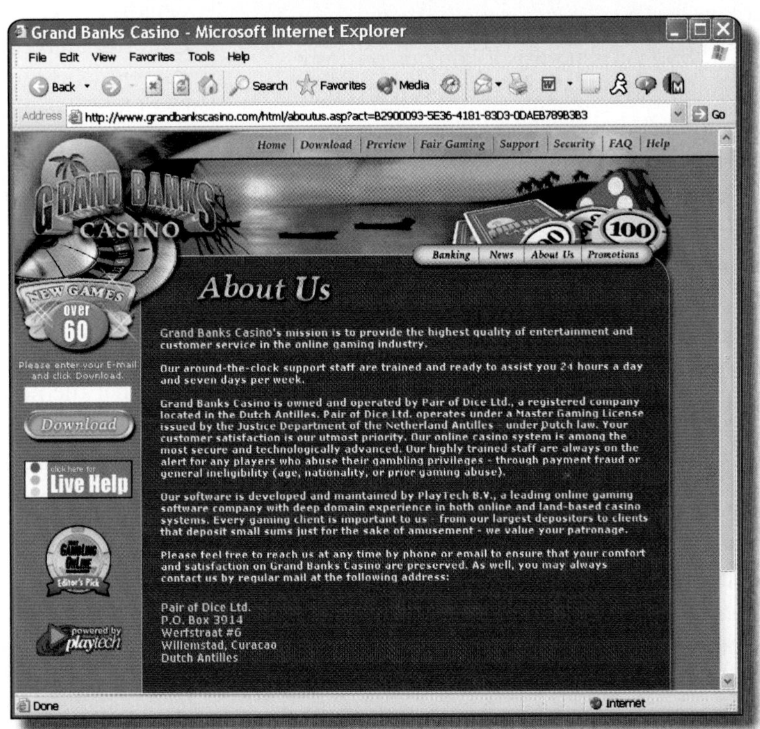

Figure 8-6 Many online gambling sites are managed from locations outside of the United States. Many of these sites have an About Us section that lists the country from which the site is run.

Cyberlibel

Although free speech rights are a key part of the U.S Constitution, courts have to balance the reputation of one person with the free speech rights of the other. **Defamation** involves making a false statement that harms the reputation of someone else and causes damage. In most cases, the falsehood must be intentional for it to be considered defamation. The damage may be tangible losses, such as the loss of a job, or the damage may be intangible, such as the loss of reputation and respect in a community.

Defamation can include **libel**, the publishing of a falsehood that harms someone, or **slander**, the same doctrine applied to the spoken word. With the explosive growth of the Internet, individuals can share information instantly and inexpensively via e-mail, Web pages, blogs, discussion groups, and more. Committing an act of libel thus can take place in seconds, and the effect can be global. The anonymity allowed by the Internet also makes users less inhibited about the content of their messages and postings. Perhaps the most unique feature of the Internet, however, is that it allows anyone with access to be a publisher – and to be sued as a publisher.

Cyberlibel – the act of committing libel using Internet technology – is still a relatively new aspect of cyberlaw. Legal scholars point to three landmark cases that reveal the climate of the courts. In the first major published Internet libel case, Cubby, Inc. vs. CompuServe Inc. (1991), the plaintiff sued CompuServe for a defamatory remark posted on one of the company's forums. CompuServe argued that the company was not the publisher of content, and did not retain editorial control over such postings. Instead, CompuServe claimed its service was that of a distributor of published works, which relieved them of liability. The courts agreed, and ruled in favor of CompuServe.

A similar case was brought against network service provider Prodigy and its online forums by Stratton Oakmont in 1995. At issue was a libelous post on Prodigy's popular "Money Talk" forum that stated, among other things, that Stratton Oakmont was a "cult of brokers who either lie for a living or get fired." The president of the company filed suit against Prodigy. In this instance, Prodigy was found to be a publisher, not a distributor, of content since the company maintained a clear policy of retaining the right to edit, remove, and filter messages in its system in order to ensure a "family" atmosphere. In this case, the courts ruled in favor of the plaintiff.

And finally, in Zeran vs. America Online (1996), the service provider was sued by a user who had his personal information posted in connection with advertisements for souvenirs glorifying the Oklahoma City bombing. An unknown AOL user had obtained Kenneth Zeran's information and posted the ads on AOL, resulting in numerous disturbing threats and harassment. Zeran sued AOL claiming negligence in allowing such postings to occur, even though he had complained to AOL upon learning of the hoax. AOL used the Communications Decency Act of 1996 as its defense, claiming the immunity the law provides to Internet service providers. In this case, the courts ruled in favor of AOL and upheld the fact that Internet service providers cannot be held liable for the posting of defamatory remarks by third parties. As Internet communication continues to grow, cyberlibel will become an issue of increasing importance, and lawmakers may need to define a version of libel laws that addresses the unique nature of the Internet. Until then, anyone is potentially answerable for libel on the Internet, whether an Internet service provider, newsgroup moderator, or e-mail provider.

Cyberstalking

Although there is no universally accepted definition of **cyberstalking**, the term generally refers to the use of the Internet, e-mail, or other electronic communications devices to stalk another person. **Stalking** usually involves harassment or other threatening behavior in which an individual engages repeatedly, such as following you, appearing at your home or place of business, making harassing phone calls, leaving written messages or objects, or vandalizing your property.

The incidents of cyberstalking are growing each year. Women remain the most likely targets of cyberstalkers, but men increasingly are being targeted. Children even are cyberstalking other children. Unfortunately, cyberstalking moves from cyberspace to the real world with tragic consequences. For example, in California, a 50-year-old former security guard pleaded guilty on April 28, 1999, to stalking, computer fraud, and sexual assault after using the Internet to solicit and eventually rape a woman who rejected his romantic advances. In New Hampshire, a 21-year old man murdered a 20-year old woman and then killed himself. For days, the police did not know the motive behind the crime, until they confiscated his computer and discovered that the murderer had created two Web sites on which he expressed his loneliness and alternating love and hatred for the woman, who was a former classmate. In addition to describing his favorite weapon – an AR-15 assault rifle – his online journals tell how the man paid Internet search agencies to find the woman's Social Security number and place of employment.

While stalking and cyberstalking share many characteristics, the Internet and other communications technologies provide new avenues that stalkers can use to find and pursue their victims. Cyberstalkers locate their victims in chat rooms, bulletin boards, social networks, online auction sites, or newsgroups. Once they have selected a victim, cyberstalkers can send threatening e-mails with a mouse click. Other cyberstalkers even set up timed messages to be sent while they are away from the computer. California ranks first for both victims and harassers, with harassment via e-mail occurring in 31% of cases. In one case, California law enforcement authorities say they have encountered situations where victims repeatedly received the message "187" on their pagers – the section of the California Penal Code for murder. Cyberstalkers also can get other Internet users to harass a victim by posting a controversial message on a message board, using the name, phone number, or e-mail address of the victim. Identifying a cyberstalker often is difficult, as a

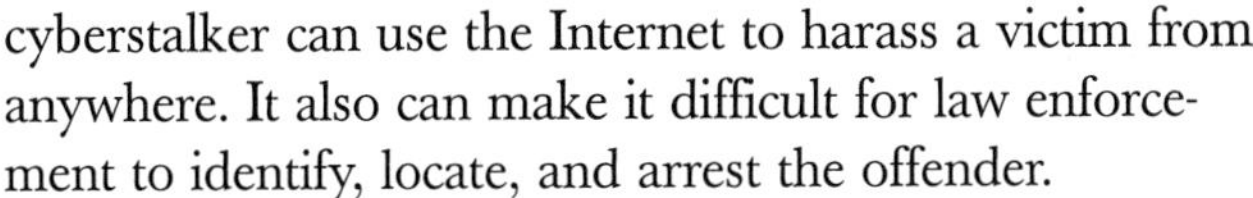

cyberstalker can use the Internet to harass a victim from anywhere. It also can make it difficult for law enforcement to identify, locate, and arrest the offender.

Federal antistalking laws provide some protection against cyberstalkers, making it a federal crime to transmit any communication containing a threat to injure the person of another, including communications via the telephone, e-mail, pagers, or the Internet. All 50 states and the District of Columbia have enacted stalking laws, and most states have laws that explicitly cover cyberstalking. Table 8-5 lists some tips on how to avoid cyberstalking and what to do if you are being cyberstalked.

Table 8-5

PREVENTION TIPS

- Do not share personal information in public spaces anywhere online, nor give it to strangers, including in e-mail or chat rooms. Do not use your real name or nickname as your screen name or user ID. Pick a name that is gender- and age-neutral. And do not post personal information as part of any user profiles.
- Be extremely cautious about meeting online acquaintances in person. If you choose to meet, do so in a public place and take along a friend.
- Make sure that your ISP and Internet Relay Chat (IRC) network have an acceptable use policy that prohibits cyberstalking. And if your network fails to respond to your complaints, consider switching to a provider that is more responsive to user complaints.
- If a situation online becomes hostile, log off or surf elsewhere. If a situation frightens you, contact a local law enforcement agency.

WHAT TO DO IF YOU ARE BEING CYBERSTALKED

- If you are receiving unwanted contact, make clear to that person that you would like him or her not to contact you again.
- Save all communications for evidence. Do not edit or alter them in any way. Also, keep a record of your contacts with Internet system administrators or law enforcement officials.
- You may want to consider blocking or filtering messages from the harasser. Many e-mail programs such as Microsoft Outlook have a filter feature, and software can be easily obtained that will automatically delete e-mails from a particular e-mail address or those that contain offensive words. Chat room contact can be blocked as well. Although formats differ, a common chat room command to block someone would be to type: /ignore <person's screen name> (without the brackets). However, in some circumstances (such as

Table 8-5 *(continued)*

threats of violence), it may be more appropriate to save the information and contact law enforcement authorities.

- If harassment continues after you have asked the person to stop, contact the harasser's Internet service provider (ISP). Most ISP's have clear policies prohibiting the use of their services to abuse another person. Often, an ISP can try to stop the conduct by direct contact with the stalker or by closing their account. If you receive abusive e-mails, identify the domain (after the "@" sign) and contact that ISP. Most ISP's have an e-mail address such as abuse@(domain name) or postmaster@(domain name) that can be used for complaints. If the ISP has a Web site, visit it for information on how to file a complaint.
- Contact your local police department and inform them of the situation in as much detail as possible. In appropriate cases, they may refer the matter to state or federal authorities.

Some tips on how to avoid cyberstalking and what to do if you are being cyberstalked from divorcesource.com.

COMPUTERS AND ETHICS

As discussed in the previous section, many new laws are being passed and existing laws are being amended to address issues surrounding the use of computer technology to commit wrongdoing. Often, however, rapid changes in technology leave gray areas in which behavior is not defined by law. Lacking legal direction, individuals must rely on ethics to guide decisions.

Depending on the particular moment in your life, you may be led by a different set of ethics. In your personal life, you are guided by your personal ethics, which may be influenced by your upbringing, religion, culture, core values, and so on – whatever aspects of your life have helped to define your sense of right and wrong. On the job, your actions are guided by professional ethics. Ethics that define how you choose to use computers are considered **computer ethics**.

This section introduces you to a framework for ethical decision making and reviews specific ethical issues related to the work of computer professionals and businesses, and the use of intellectual property. The list of ethical concerns included here is by no means comprehensive. In fact, whether at school, at work, at home, or with a group of friends, you will encounter ethical issues every day, perhaps different each time – that require a different response each time. The examples here merely are topics to highlight some key issues and

stimulate your thinking about computer ethics in a structured way, so that you are better prepared to handle ethical dilemmas when they arise.

Ethical Decision Making: A Framework

Ethical decision making is not always simple. Most likely, you already have been confronted with situations in which you had to choose between several competing interests or decide between two conflicting ethical demands. To help you deal with such situations in the future, consider the principles promoted by several ethical viewpoints:

- *The golden rule:* Quite simply, this viewpoint states that you should treat others as you would have them treat you. Think about the effects of your actions from the viewpoint of someone who will be affected by those actions. What action would they have you choose? How would you feel if someone else made this decision and it affected you?
- *Universal law:* This viewpoint is based on Kant's categorical imperative, which states that, if an action is not right for everyone to take, then it is not right for anyone to take. What would happen if everyone chose to take the action you are considering?
- *The greatest good/least harm:* This utilitarian view suggests that, when choosing between two actions, you should select the one that achieves the greatest good for the greatest number and causes the least harm. Of any two actions, the most ethical one will produce the greatest balance of benefits over harms.
- *The slippery slope rule:* This view suggests an action that brings about a small but acceptable change might, if taken repeatedly, lead to an unacceptable change. The first action thus should not be taken because, once you start down this slippery slope, repeating such actions could end in unacceptable or unexpected results.
- *What is not yours is not yours:* This viewpoint asks that you assume tangible and intangible objects belong to someone unless specifically stated otherwise. If something created by or owned by someone else is useful to you, the creator or owner deserves to be compensated.

As a guide in deciding on a course of action, follow these steps and ask yourself these questions:

1. Get the facts. Are you being asked to do something that you think might be wrong? Are you aware of potentially illegal or unethical conduct on the part of others? Are you trying to make a decision while unsure about the ethical course of action?
2. Think before you act. Clearly define the conflict you are facing. Try to understand why you are concerned about making a decision: is it an ethical issue or a legal one? What values and principles are at stake?
3. Consider who might be affected. Identify those whom your actions might impact or who have an interest in your actions. Those impacted might include coworkers, student colleagues, customers, suppliers, stockholders, the government, or even the community as a whole.
4. Consider your options and their consequences. By considering how different courses of action might affect the different groups listed above, you may be able to reach a decision that is acceptable to most (although it may not satisfy everyone).
5. Test your decision. Review the questions to support ethical decision making in Table 8-6 to help determine the best course of action. If possible, consult others for their opinions and viewpoints. If you cannot directly ask others, consider what they would recommend or expect you to do. Would you feel at ease with your action or decision if your parents, teachers, friends, spouse, or employer became aware of it?

Once you have made a choice, communicate your decision and rationale to those it might affect. Later, it might be important to reflect on your decision and consider how your choice or actions turned out for all concerned. Another key question to ask: if you had to do it over again, what, if anything, would you do differently? Later in the chapter the @Issue section, Doing the Right Thing, will give you a chance to apply this framework when evaluating and resolving ethical dilemmas.

Ethics for Computer Professionals

Recognizing that individuals and organizations need specific standards for the ethical use of computer

Table 8-6

QUESTIONS TO SUPPORT ETHICAL DECISION MAKING

- Is it legal?
- Is it against school or employer codes of conduct or professional standards?
- Does it feel right?
- Will it reflect negatively on you or your organization?
- Who else could be affected by this (coworkers, friends, customers, you, etc.)?
- If you were in the other person's situation, what decision would you choose?
- Would you be embarrassed if others knew you took this course of action?
- Is there an alternative action that does not pose an ethical conflict?
- Which decision would you be proud to share with someone whom you truly respect?
- Which decision would you want to read about yourself on the front page of your local paper?
- Will you be able to sleep at night after you make the decision?

If you are not sure what decision to make, try asking yourself the simple questions listed here.

technology, a number of computer-related organizations have established codes of conduct.

CODES OF ETHICS AND PROFESSIONAL CONDUCT A **code of conduct** or **code of ethics** is a set of written guidelines that outlines the obligations and responsibilities individuals have to their employers, schools, public, or society as a whole. Computer professionals, in particular, have a unique set of ethical guidelines to follow. Codes of conduct are good standards to help determine whether a specific action taken while using a computer is ethical or unethical.

Many of the major professional organizations in the computer and information technology field, such as the Association for Computing Machinery (ACM) and the Data Processing Management Association, have codes of professional conduct that outline the obligations of members as computing professionals (Figure 8-7).

Many businesses have adopted similar codes of conduct and made them known to their employees. Others require employees to read and sign off on The Ten Commandments of Computer Ethics promoted by the Computer Ethics Institute (Figure 8-8). One of the issues with ethical decision making in business is that some people believe ethical decisions are the responsibility of management, not the employees. This often is true in service departments, such as accounting or information technology, in which employees' jobs are structured to provide whatever services management wants. For example, suppose a company president tells a junior accountant to alter the quarterly reports to show higher than average sales, in the hopes of causing a rise in stock price. Rather than questioning the ethics (and legality) of altering data, the junior accountant may simply do what he or she was asked – hiding behind the notion that ethics are the responsibility of management. In fact, establishing codes of conduct that apply to an entire organization can help all employees, from the part-time staff member to the chairman of the board, make ethical discussions, by providing a standard against which they can measure their actions.

PROFESSIONALISM AND RESPONSIBILITY Computer professionals have a unique responsibility towards society, as the software and technology products they build control cars and airplanes, help with medical diagnoses, predict hurricanes, and more.

The Therac-25 is just one startling example of what can happen when computing professionals do not act ethically and professionally. The Therac-25 was a computerized radiation therapy machine. Not only did the software ease the laborious set-up process, but it also monitored the safety of the machine. Due to serious errors in the software, the Therac-25 massively overdosed patients at least six times between June 1985 and January 1987. Each radiation overdose was several times the normal therapeutic dose and resulted in a patient's severe injury or even death. Any number of individuals and groups were responsible for the problem not being found before so many deaths: the programmer, who had a responsibility to make his superiors aware of the dangers inherent in doing safety monitoring only in the software; the manufacturer, Canadian Medical Corporation, which did not conduct appropriate and systematic safety analysis; the FDA for not pulling the Therac-25 after the first accident, and so on. The scenario highlights the critical importance of highly ethical and professional behavior on the part of software engineers, companies, the government, and professional organizations.

Ethics in Business

Each day, individuals all over the world make business decisions that affect customers, employees, partners, suppliers, and others with whom the business has a relationship. Many different factors can drive the decisions made by businesses: making the most profit, cutting costs, getting good publicity, finding the fastest way to complete a job, creating an entirely new product, or, more simply, the desire to make an ethical decision.

Business ethics are the standards that drive a company's decisions, policies, and actions. In the wake of corporate scandals such as Enron, Tyco, and WorldCom, many companies are making it a point to promote their focus on ethics and its positive impact on the workplace. This section reviews ethical questions facing businesses, including advertising and marketing practices, the use of customer data, and digital manipulation of pictures and other data.

PREAMBLE

...The Code and its supplemented Guidelines are intended to serve as a basis for ethical decision making in the conduct of professional work. Secondarily, they may serve as a basis for judging the merit of a formal complaint pertaining to violation of professional ethical standards...

IMPERATIVES

- Contribute to society and human well-being.
- Avoid harm to others.
- Be honest and trustworthy.
- Be fair and take action not to discriminate.
- Honor property rights including copyrights and patent.
- Give proper credit for intellectual property.
- Respect the privacy of others.
- Honor confidentiality.
- Strive to achieve the highest quality, effectiveness, and dignity in both the process and products of professional work.
- Acquire and maintain professional competence.
- Know and respect existing laws pertaining to professional work
- Accept and provide appropriate professional review.
- Give comprehensive and thorough evaluations of computer systems and their impacts, including analysis of possible risks.
- Honor contracts, agreements, and assigned responsibilities.
- Improve public understanding of computing and its consequences.
- Access computing and communication resources only when authorized to do so.

Figure 8-7 The above excerpts are from the Association for Computing Machinery (ACM) Code of Ethics and Professional Conduct. A copy of the complete ACM Code of Ethics and Professional Conduct is available on their Web site at www.acm.org.

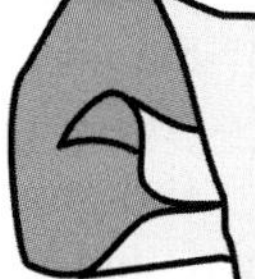

The Ten Commandments of Computer Ethics

1. Thou shalt not use a computer to harm other people.
2. Thou shalt not interfere with other people's computer work.
3. Thou shalt not snoop around in other people's files.
4. Thou shalt not use a computer to steal.
5. Thou shalt not use a computer to bear false witness.
6. Thou shalt not use or copy software for which you have not paid.
7. Thou shalt not use other people's computer resources without authorization.
8. Thou shalt not appropriate other people's intellectual output.
9. Thou shalt think about the social consequences of the program you write.
10. Thou shalt use a computer in ways that show consideration and respect.

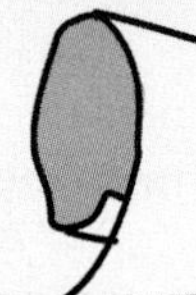

Figure 8-8 Some companies and schools require employees and students to read and sign off on The Ten Commandments of Computer Ethics as promoted by the Computer Ethics Institute.

ADVERTISING AND MARKETING As previously noted, the Federal Trade Commission Act requires that advertising in any medium must be truthful and must not mislead consumers. Yet, what is legal in advertising may not always be ethical. For example, a credit-card company Web site might, in accordance with the letter of the law, include all of the terms and conditions of which you need to be aware before applying for the credit card. Is it ethical, however, for that company to include information about monthly and annual service fees on a separate Web page, in very small print? And to make the link to that page hard to find on the page with the online credit-card application?

The profusion of ads on the Internet raises questions about a Web site's responsibility to mark links or graphics as advertisements, as opposed to editorial content. In 2002, CNN.com began running simple text-based ads as links, next to the news headlines. The links connected readers to marketing Web pages, not news stories, which raised concern among some journalism ethics experts. In their view, the ethical approach would have been to label the links clearly as being sponsored or paid for by advertisers. In a new twist, news Web sites such as CNN.com receive sponsored search listings from Yahoo! Search Marketing, and will return advertising links, along with news stories, when you conduct a search from their site (Figure 8-9). In 2007, Microsoft bought Aquantive, a similar Internet search marketing company, for $6 billion in order to stake their claim to a portion of the growing online advertising business, estimated at $55 billion in 2007. Ethics experts warn that mixing ads in with search results on news and information sites will further blur the lines between editorial content and advertising. Customers searching the site expect to find news – and may, in fact, think that the advertising link is a story or an endorsement of a product by the paper. The news firms counter that the results page clearly distinguishes the sponsored listings (provided by Yahoo! Search Marketing) from the other search results listings (provided by Google, which recently bought DoubleClick for $3.1 billion).

Another advertising practice that raises some ethical questions is the practice of adding advertising images to live broadcasts. As you learned in Chapter 4, advertisers are using the Live Video Insertion System (L-VIS) to add still or video images to live broadcasts, most often to place more advertisements in front of the viewer. Using the system, advertisers can add a Coca-Cola logo to the middle of a soccer field, or place ads for a local bank on the walls behind the batter in a baseball stadium. Many question the ethics behind altering reality and then presenting it to viewers as reality. Although

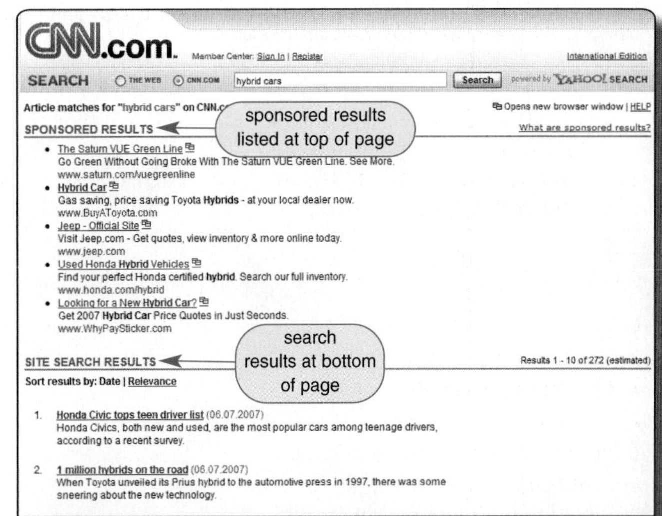

Figure 8-9 When you conduct a search on the CNN.com site, sponsered advertising links, along with news stories, related to the search topic are displayed. Ethics experts worry about mixing ads with news content; the news firms counter that the results page clearly distinguishes the sponsored listings from the other search results listings.

no intentionally misleading information is being communicated to viewers, the entire context of the advertisement is a falsehood. In a world where you used to be sure that what you saw was reality, the use of the L-VIS and other systems may make you question that reality.

DIGITAL MANIPULATION Computers and editing software make it increasingly easy to modify images and photographs to create more compelling or controversial images. For example, as you learned in Chapter 4, adding graphics to television broadcasts is not just part of sports and other entertainment programming – it also is part of the broadcast news. Using computers, news stations can film reporters in front of a blue screen and then add a backdrop digitally to make it appear as if the reporter is on location. Figure 8-10 illustrates how a sign has been digitally placed on the grass of the racetrack to add excitement to the photograph.

Newspaper correspondents also have been found editing photos to create a more unique photo, such as

Figure 8-10 With the help of digital technology, it is easy for images to be manipulated so that viewers at home see an image greatly enhanced from what is seen live.

the Los Angeles Times photographer who was fired for editing together two photos to make one dramatic photo of a British soldier and a crowd of people outside the Iraqi city of Basra. The code of ethics of the National Press Photographers Association (NPPA) strongly denounces any alteration of photographs, noting that even the slightest modification eventually could lead to photographs deliberately altered to misrepresent the truth. The code of ethics also notes: "As journalists, we believe that credibility is our greatest asset. In documentary photojournalism, it is wrong to alter the content of a photograph in any way (electronically or in the darkroom) that deceives the public."

The case of the Los Angeles Times photographer, however, certainly is not the first time computers were used to manipulate photos for print. One of the most controversial incidents occurred in 1994 when Newsweek and TIME magazine both ran photos of O.J. Simpson on their covers, shortly after he was arrested for murder. Newsweek ran an untouched mug shot of Simpson; TIME ran a digitally edited version of the photo that used effects intended to create a more sinister shot (Figure 8-11). The effect was that Simpson's skin tone looked darker on the cover of TIME, drawing hard criticism from Simpson supporters who felt the cover was racially insensitive. TIME defended the move, saying the image was not a news photograph, but a photo illustration.

Three years later, Newsweek and TIME again ran similar covers, this time featuring the parents of the McCaughey septuplets. TIME ran an unaltered photograph of the couple, while Newsweek ran a digitally edited photo in which the mother's teeth had been touched up. This time, critics questioned if Newsweek felt a more attractive version of the new mother would sell more magazines. Newsweek later apologized for the manipulation.

In fact, it is impossible to know how many of the images you see on television, in print, or on the news have been digitally edited. In most cases – on billboards, book covers, and print ads – digital editing is the norm, used to create interesting visual effects that catch a viewer's eye. In the case of the news, however, editing photographs raises ethical questions.

Digital retouching is an area in which few legal precedents have been established, so it seems to pose an ethical question for professional photographers, photojournalists, and others whose professions are based on sharing accurate images with the public. Others argue that digital photograph retouching is acceptable, as long as the editing does not significantly change the content or the meaning of the photographs.

Most agree that journalists must maintain high standards of accuracy and truth in their reporting and photography, as evidenced by reaction of the LA Times

Figure 8-11 One of the most controversial incidents of digital photo editing occurred in 1994 when Newsweek and TIME magazine both ran photos of O.J. Simpson on their covers, shortly after he was arrested for murder. Before publishing the photograph, Time's editors chose to artificially darken Simpson's skin tone using digital editing.

and the public. Every picture tells a story, but the picture should tell the story of what actually happened, and not what the photographer thinks happened. Few, however, would react negatively to having their picture altered slightly to remove a few wrinkles or pounds before it runs on the cover of TIME Magazine. Is that also unethical – or is that type of alteration acceptable? As a photographer, where would you draw the line between creating the picture perfect cover – and creating an imperfect representation of reality?

PROTECTING CUSTOMER DATA Businesses are the caretakers of millions of data records about customers and employees. Each time you complete a purchase in a store or online using a credit or debit card, information about your purchase is stored in a large marketing database. Banks, mail-order catalogs, your Internet service provider, e-commerce Web sites – in fact, any Web site where you have registered – all store data about you.

For businesses, this data is a huge asset. Firms can analyze sales and customer data to better target marketing campaigns, product development, or sales efforts. Companies also can sell this customer data to a third party, who may be eager to pay for a list of customer information to use for an e-mail advertising or a telemarketing campaign. Some companies are prevented legally from selling customer information, whether due to contracts or their own privacy policies. In other cases, no such legal restrictions apply, which leaves the company with an ethical decision as to whether or not the short-term financial gain of selling customer data is worth the potential long-term loss of customer loyalty. Just because a company can sell customer data, should it do so?

Another question is raised when a company changes its privacy policy or the manner in which it allows you to opt-out from receiving offers – after you already have disclosed your personal information. In 2001, for example, eBay was criticized widely when, after discovering a bug in its registration system, it changed the personalized settings for roughly 6 million customers. The registration form was supposed to have "yes" as the default answer to such questions as, "Do you want to receive calls from telemarketers?" The bug had changed the default answers to "no," so any customers registering between April and November of 2000 did not have to click to change the answers to "no." Instead of leaving the responses as they were, eBay changed the "no" responses for 6 million customers to "yes"; customers were notified of the change and were given 14 days to change the settings before they took effect. Many of the eBay customers found this just one more reason to question the ethical stances of eBay, which had already changed its policy to allow for the sending of marketing materials and giving telemarketers phone numbers.

The issue led some privacy groups to question the business practice of automatically registering consumers for services and then requiring them to opt out. For example, on numerous Web sites, you automatically are opted in to receiving e-mails, offers from third parties, and so on. You then must go to another page, after the registration, to change your preferences to opt out (Figure 8-12). Some charge that the more ethical approach would be to assume customers prefer to opt out, by default, instead of taking advantage of customers who might not notice the check box on the page or forget to update their profile later.

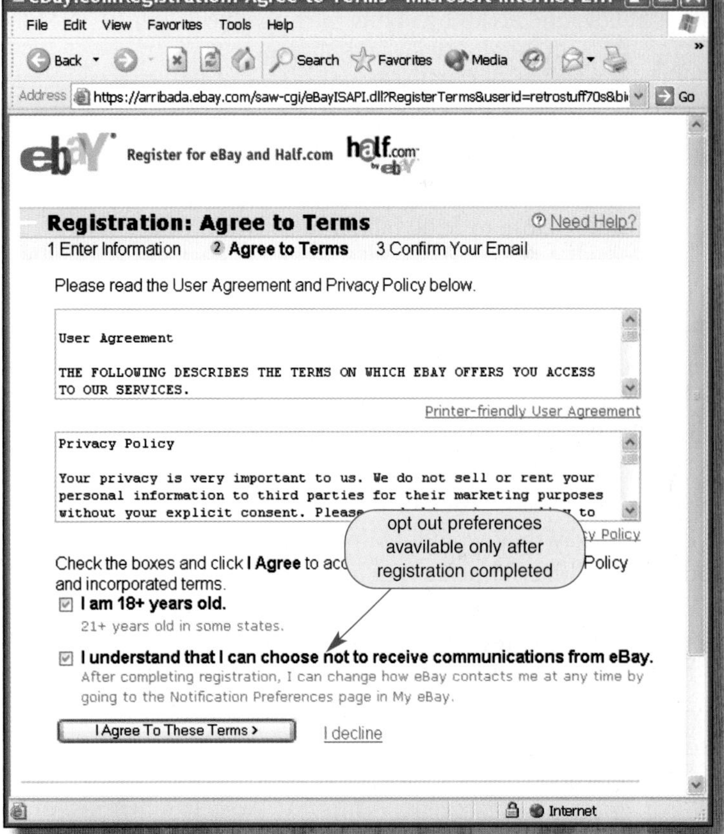

Figure 8-12 Many question the ethics of automatically registering consumers for services and then requiring them to opt out. For example, on numerous Web sites, you automatically are opted in to receiving e-mails, offers from third parties, and so on. You then must go to another page, after the registration, to change your preferences to opt out.

Ethical Use of Intellectual Property

Business and individuals need to consider the law and ethics when using intellectual property such as reports, books, Web page content, software, music, movies, and more. Much of this material is protected by copyright law, which limits use of the content, except as allowed for by fair-use doctrine. Despite the clear legal implications, many persist in copying software, music, movies, and other content for uses that go beyond those considered legal or ethical.

MUSIC, MOVIE, AND SOFTWARE PIRACY Piracy of music, movies, and software creates interesting – and often contradictory – viewpoints when considered in the context of ethical conduct. As you have learned, the laws protecting software, movies, music, and other copyrighted content from being copied and distributed are quite clear: under most circumstances, copying copyrighted content is illegal and can result in both civil and criminal prosecution. Despite this, software piracy and the downloading of countless numbers of songs and movies persist and many, who are well aware of the law, do not believe the act to be in any way unethical.

A 2005 study by the Business Software Alliance (BSA) and IDC reported that for every two dollars spent on legal software purchases, one dollar's worth was obtained illegally. The PC software market is expected to grow by $300 billion over the next few years, meaning close to $200 billion in software will likely be pirated. The country with the highest piracy rate is Vietnam (90%), with Zimbabwe (90%), Indonesia (87%), and China (86%) following closely behind. The United States ranks lowest at 21%.

In an earlier BSA study, the organization found that many of these users appear to make decisions based on saving money: when asked if they would consider downloading an unlicensed or pirated version, almost half of them say they would. Despite this, the same study showed that 85 percent of Internet users feel that strong intellectual property protection is important to protect companies, researchers, and authors.

The reasons for the contradiction could be based on any number of factors. For one, the growing number of Internet users and the increased availability of high-speed connections make it easier to download large music, software, or movie files. Many buyers rationalize their piracy, believing they have a right to make copies of DVDs and software for which they paid tens, hundreds, even thousands of dollars. Others argue that CDs cost too much, with prices close to $20 for discs that contain only a few memorable songs. Piracy also is quite convenient (offering an almost endless supply of songs from a huge range of artists) and a relatively simple crime to commit. In minutes, you can copy a software CD-ROM or music CD to a CD-RW to share with a friend; download an artist's latest tracks from a P2P file-sharing network; or get a sneak preview of a movie before it hits the theater. Most users also feel that software or other content piracy is a victimless crime, using the faulty logic that the software company, music label, or movie studio already makes millions, so they can afford to have a few of their programs, songs, and movies downloaded for free. A study from the U.K. found that attitudes also play a role, especially among "Generation Y" – those born between 1979 and 1994. The study reports that when there is a "lack of fear" of consequences as is found with illegal music downloads, inappropriate behaviors emerge.

The reality is that these acts are not victimless crimes, nor are they ethical. In 2005, software piracy cost the worldwide software industry $34.3 billion in lost revenue. In the United States alone, software piracy cost the industry more than one hundred thousand jobs – any one of which could be the job of a friend or family member. One of every three CDs sold today is pirated equating to nearly $5 billion in lost revenues globally; the music industry blames a recent sales slump on the vast number of songs being downloaded for free. As losses hit particular labels, the impact is felt throughout the industry (Figure 8-13). In this case, victims include the artists whose work gets no reward, record producers who have to cut their artists because it is impossible to compete against theft, and consumers who get less diversity and less choice. In all cases, local, state, and federal governments also lose tax revenues, which may mean cuts of local services, such as firefighters. Another reason to think twice before buying a pirated software, movie, or music CD is that piracy nurtures organized crime. The money you paid for a pirated CD may be channeled into the drug trade, money laundering, or other forms of serious organized criminal activity. The Recording Industry Association of America (RIAA) has recently begun to send students at many U.S. colleges and universities "pre-lawsuit" letters in an attempt to deter illegal file traffiking. In 2006, more than 60% of teens surveyed admitted to downloading music and movies illegally, so RIAA is hoping their action will both educate and curb this activity. Preliminary data may provide some hope. Investment bank Piper Jaffray found that 36% of U.S. teens bought their music from online services such as iTunes in 2006, up from 28% the year before. In the same period, file sharing via P2P networks dropped eight percent.

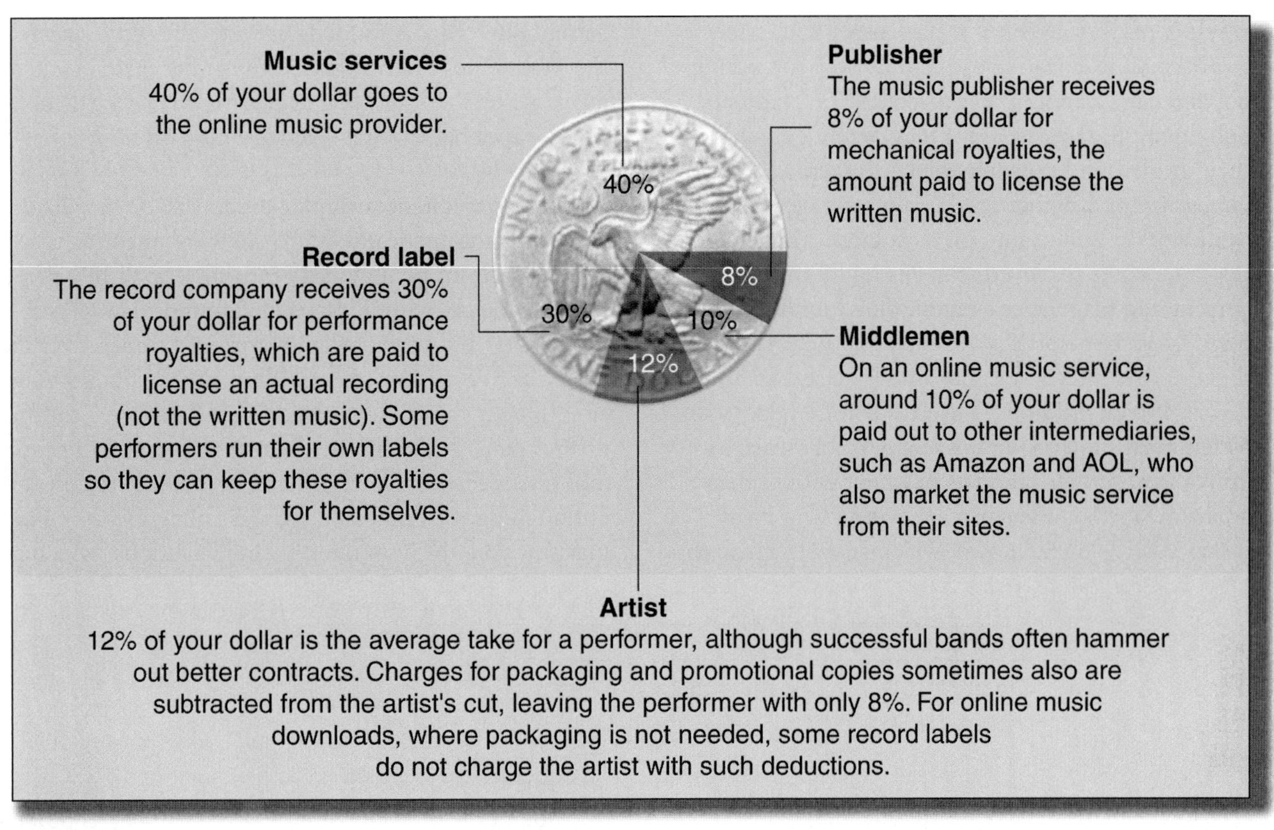

Music services
40% of your dollar goes to the online music provider.
Publisher
The music publisher receives 8% of your dollar for mechanical royalties, the amount paid to license the written music.
40%
8%
30%
10%
12%
Record label
The record company receives 30% of your dollar for performance royalties, which are paid to license an actual recording (not the written music). Some performers run their own labels so they can keep these royalties for themselves.
Middlemen
On an online music service, around 10% of your dollar is paid out to other intermediaries, such as Amazon and AOL, who also market the music service from their sites.
Artist
12% of your dollar is the average take for a performer, although successful bands often hammer out better contracts. Charges for packaging and promotional copies sometimes also are subtracted from the artist's cut, leaving the performer with only 8%. For online music downloads, where packaging is not needed, some record labels do not charge the artist with such deductions.

Figure 8-13 Many online music services like Apple's iTunes Music Store and MusicNet charge about $1 per song. Many argue that stealing a few songs does not hurt anyone, especially multi-million dollar artists and record labels. The graph above shows the breakdown of where your money goes for each digital file you download for free, assuming about $1 per song. In February 2006, iTunes downloaded its one billionth song.

Some argue that piracy and illegal copying, especially in the case of music and movies, causes fans to buy more copies of releases by the same artists and actors. They also note that making music, movies, and software available freely on the Internet increases the exposure for new artists and actors, as well as programmers hoping to get a new product on the market quickly. What do you think?

One unique type of software – **shareware** – relies solely on ethical behavior of users to earn profits. Shareware is copyrighted software that is distributed free for a trial period. To use a shareware program beyond that period, you send a payment to the person or company who developed the program. Developers of shareware rely on the honor system, trusting users to send payment if software use extends beyond the stated trial period. In some cases, shareware is a scaled-down or limited version of the full software and payment entitles the user to a fully functional product.

Businesses, public or private schools, and universities are not exempt from copyright laws. In fact, because of their unique position of influence, businesses and schools must be committed to upholding copyright laws by adhering to license agreements, communicating polices around using corporate servers for music and movie sharing, and not making copies of software beyond license agreements. Businesses and schools should make every effort to uphold the law, because it is by their example that employees and students will learn to have respect for intellectual property.

PLAGIARISM The act of using the ideas or writings of another individual without clearly acknowledging the source of that information, and representing those ideas as your own is known as plagiarism. Because so many works are available on the Internet – books, online dictionaries and encyclopedias, research articles, and magazines – it is easier than ever to plagiarize content, either mistakenly or intentionally. Students also can buy entire term papers online at numerous term paper Web sites, such as PaperDue, Genius Papers, and even Cheaters.com. These sites entice stressed students by touting the hundreds of terms papers they have available on almost any subject for free, for a small fee, or in return for another paper.

Plagiarism is a violation of copyright law and most school honor codes, and is – to most people – unethical.

Many students, however, view plagiarism and other types of academic cheating as the only way to excel in school and earn a spot in a good college or graduate school. Some students feel as if they are judged entirely on their grades, and thus are willing to sacrifice ethics and integrity for a higher grade point average. For others, ethics never comes into play: Rutgers' Management Education Center surveyed students and found that over 41 percent had plagiarized content they found on the Internet. Over two-thirds of the students surveyed did not believe that Internet plagiarism was a serious infraction, even if they did not themselves commit plagiarism.

What most students do not realize is that teachers typically can tell when students have not written their own papers. Further, they also are getting help from Web sites such as turnitin.com, which allow teachers to submit questionable student papers. The service searches the Web for any phrases or sections that match content available on the Internet and returns color-coded copies of the paper back to the teacher within 48 hours (Figure 8-14).

The consequences of plagiarism can be serious, including automatically failing an assignment or a course, or even being expelled from school. In a recent high-profile case, a judicial board found that 34 Duke University first-year graduate business students cheated on a take-home final exam. Nine students faced expulsion, fifteen students were suspended for one year and given failing grades in the course, nine failed the course, and one received a failing grade on just the exam, although appeals may change this ruling. To avoid plagiarism, you always should include citations, which are

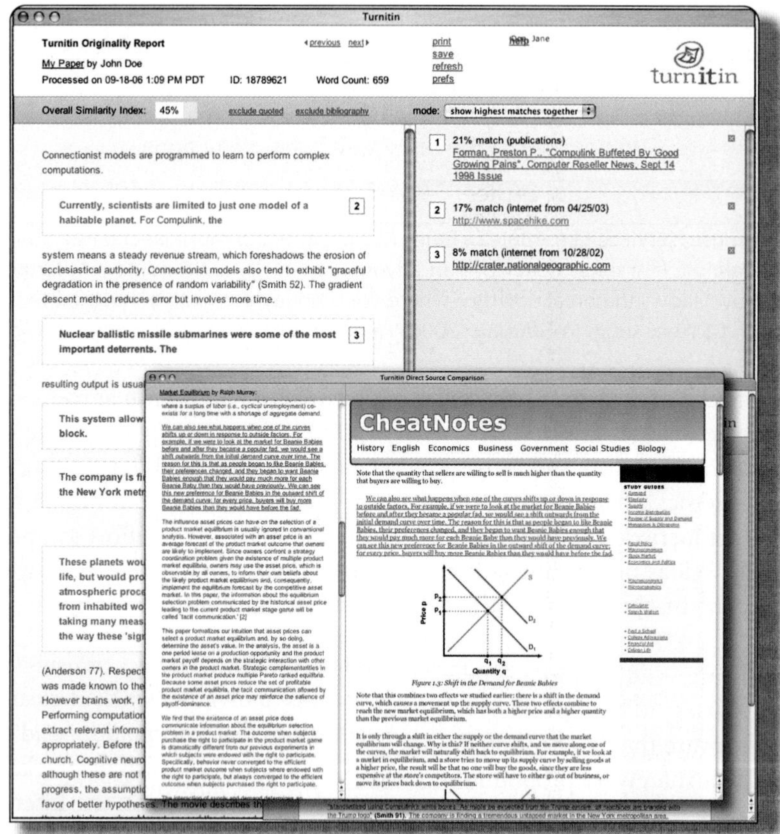

Figure 8-14 Turnitin.com allows instructors to see quickly how original the content in a student's report is. In this case, the red text is identified as being plagiarized directly from a Web site.

references used to identify content from another source. Citations for print material should include information about the work's author, title, publishing company, publishing date, and page numbers. Citations for Web sites should include the author, the document title, the date of publication, the date you accessed the page, and the URL. Table 8-7 provides some information on how to cite sources. For more information on citing sources, you should consult your instructor, who can guide you to any number of valuable print and online resources. If you use Word 2007, be sure to use the software's new References tab to properly cite and format sources and Web sites.

Table 8-7

EXAMPLES OF HOW TO CITE SOURCE MATERIAL

Source	Example
Book	Smith, John, and Keith Allan. Writing Your First Novel. Boston: Bookworks Publishing, 2004
Magazine or newspaper article	Weiss, Paul. "Ripken Reaches 3000 Hits, Millions of Fans." Baltimore Sun 12Jan. 2003, late ed.: A11.
Web site	Narahari, Vasu. Programming in Visual Basic. 17 Dec. 2003. College of William and Mary. 15 Nov. 2002 http://www.wm.edu/progvb/intro.asp>.
Article on Web site	Lanes, Scott. "Quick Guide to Barbecue." New York Times on the Web 5 May 2002. 5 June 2002 <http://search.nytimes.com/search/daily/bin/fastweb?getdoc+site+site+87604+0+wAAA+%22a%7#@#Ebody%7Eon%7Emt.%7grill%22>.
Online book	Kelly, Brent and Shuen Sheh. Introduction. Buying a New Car Online. New York: Edmunds Press, 2000. 15 Jan. 2001. <http://www.buynewcaronline.com/online/start.htm>.
Article in a reference database on CD-ROM	"World War I." Encarta. CD-ROM. Microsoft, 2002.
E-mail message	Portal, Danilo. "How to Format a Resume." E-mail to Mason Jesus. 10 Jan. 2002.
Web discussion group posting	Marcy, Meehan. "Government Reviewing New Privacy Law" Online posting. 30 Apr. 2003 Online Privacy Forum. 28 May 2003 <http://privacy.govwatch.com/2003/forum>.

One of the most widely used types of citation is the MLA style, examples of which are shown here, with a specific focus on how to cite electronic resources. More information on citing sources is available in style manuals such as The *MLA Handbook for Writers of Research Papers*, published by the Modern Language Association; *The Chicago Manual of Style*, published by the University of Chicago; and *A Manual for Writers of Term Papers, Theses and Dissertations*, by Kate L. Turabian.

Ethics: What Is the Right Thing?

As you have seen in this chapter, computers, technology, and the Internet create numerous new ethical dilemmas that challenge every user, almost every day. This @Issue box presents several scenarios where ethical issues potentially are involved. As you read each of the following scenarios, use the framework for ethical decision making described earlier in this chapter and try to identity the competing interests, decide what you think about the actions of the various characters, and then determine how you would have handled the situation. No answer is right or wrong; ethics, as you have learned, are not about hard and fast rules; instead, they are viewpoints of the right way to handle a situation in a manner each individual personally deems ethical.

1. Maria worked for years at a well-known marketing firm, Shuman Advertising, helping to build their now-sizable database of customers by placing cold calls to customers and gathering customer information for direct mail and e-mail lists. Recently, Maria took a new job as marketing manager at an e-mail marketing firm, Celerity Communications. Her bonus is based on how quickly she can expand their current e-mail lists to include 100,000 new customers. Maria still has copies of many of the lists she compiled on her home computer while working late nights for Shuman Advertising. She decides to start adding to the Celerity e-mail lists using these customers, and copies the information into the database the next day.

2. Your friend Ben downloads and installs a trial version of a new computer game. The game is pretty simple, but for Ben it is the perfect way to clear his mind when he needs a study break. The trial period for the game is long over, but Ben does not plan to pay for the software, as he only uses it once or twice a week and, in his words, "It's an easy program to write anyway — I could do it in a few hours."

3. A tax software company is running behind in getting their product to market before the tax season — and the program still has a few key bugs. The company decides to release the product with the bugs, so that they will have time to duplicate the CDs, print manuals, package the software, and ship it to stores. While the manufacturing group is handling that, they will clean up those last few bugs and release a patch for the software to fix the few bugs. The patch will be available free on the Internet or, if a customer requests a CD with the patch, for $5.00 to cover shipping and handling.

4. Minh is a programmer for a Web site development company and finds that, as the company is getting more last-minute requests for Web page updates, he often works late nights.To spend more time at home, Minh asks his manager if he can set up his home computer so that he can finish these jobs at home each night. His manager approves. Excited about the prospect of getting home at a decent hour for a change, Minh quickly makes copies of all the software and data he will need to complete the job at home and rushes home to have dinner with his family before heading back to work on his home computer.

5. You finally are publishing your first novel and your publisher wants to include your photo inside the book jacket. After the photo shoot, the graphics editor decides that giving you slightly lighter hair will give you a younger, fresher look — exactly the look your readers will love. She calls you and asks your permission to make the change, and then asks if there are other changes you would like while she is working on the photo. You mention that yes, you would love it if she could remove the wrinkles at the corner of your eyes and add color to make your eyes seem a more intense brown.

6. In the last few weeks, a multinational company, Petraxol, has been in the news, getting serious criticism for their poor environmental record. Just last week, one of the firm's oil tankers spilled gallons of oil off Buzzards Bay near your home and seriously impacted the fishing industry. Two days after the spill, hackers accessed the company's Web site and altered the company's home page by posting graphic images of dead fish, birds, and other wildlife that died from being covered in oil. The images actually were from an oil spill almost fifteen years ago, when an Axton oil tanker wrecked off the Alaskan coast — but they made the point. The hacker group later posted messages to discussion groups, taking full responsibility for the hack and encouraging others to hack other oil company sites to send a message that these firms must be held responsible for the negative impact they have on the environment.

CONCLUSION

In this chapter, you learned about the differences between law and ethics, as well as their relationship. You learned more about laws focused on the use of computers, including e-commerce laws pertaining to digital signatures and online advertising. You also learned about how intellectual property laws have been structured to protect an author's copyright, and how the copying of music and movies and software piracy persists, despite those laws. Next, the chapter reviewed laws concerning Internet content and online gambling, as well as newer legal areas such as cyberlibel, cyberstalking, and hacktivisim.

You learned about ethics and were introduced to an ethical decision-making framework to help you determine what is ethical and unethical. You then learned about ethics for computer professionals and ethical questions that face businesses in the areas of advertising, presenting true unedited images of the world, and serving as caretaker of customer data. Finally, you were asked to consider the ethical use of intellectual property and issues related to music, movie, and software piracy, as well as plagiarism. As noted in the chapter, the list of ethical concerns included here is by no means comprehensive; instead, it presents several topics to highlight a few key issues and further your thinking about computer ethics in a structured way, so that you are better prepared to handle ethical dilemmas when they arise.

Key Terms

business ethics
Child Online Protection Act
Children Internet Protection Act
code of conduct
code of ethics
Communications Decency Act (CDA)
computer ethics
Copyright Act
cyberlaw
cyberlibel
cyberstalking
defamation
Digital Millennium Copyright Act (DMCA)
digital signature
Electronic Signatures in Global and National Commerce Act (E-SIGN)
end-user license agreement (EULA)
ethics
fair use
Federal Trade Commission Act
hacktivism
hash
Internet Gambling Prohibition Act
law
libel
license agreement
message digest
Neighborhood Children's Internet Protection Act
No Electronic Theft (NET) Act
plagiarism
safe harbor
shareware
slander
stalking
Unlawful Gambling Enforcement Act (2006)

Chapter Review

Multiple Choice

Select the best answer.

1. A new area of law, called cyberlaw, seeks to address legal and regulatory issues relating to the _____.

(a) theft of computer hardware and software
(b) use of computers for unauthorized activities
(c) unrestricted access to company intranets
(d) Internet and the World Wide Web

2. A _____ is an encoded, or encrypted, code that a person, Web site, or company attaches to an electronic message or document to verify the identity of the sender.

(a) safe harbor
(b) license agreement
(c) digital signature
(d) code of ethics

3. Upon acceptance of an end-user license agreement, software users typically are permitted to _____.

(a) make a copy of the software as backup
(b) install the software on a network
(c) export, rent, or lease the software
(d) all of the above

4. The _____, which made it a criminal offense to distribute patently offensive material online, was declared unconstitutional by the U.S. Supreme Court in 1996.

(a) Communications Decency Act (CDA)
(b) No Electronic Theft (NET) Act
(c) Children's Internet Protection Act (CIPA)
(d) Internet Gambling Prohibition Act (IGPA)

5. _____ involves making a false statement that harms the reputation of someone else and causes damage.

(a) Stalking
(b) Piracy
(c) Defamation
(d) Plagiarism

6. Universal law is an ethical viewpoint based on Kant's categorical imperative, which states that _____.

(a) you should treat others as you would have them treat you
(b) tangible and intangible objects belong to someone unless specifically stated otherwise
(c) an action that brings about an acceptable change might lead to an unacceptable change
(d) if an action is not right for everyone to take, then it is not right for anyone to take

7. As a guide in deciding on a course of action, follow all of these steps except _____.

(a) get the facts
(b) act before you think
(c) consider who might be affected
(d) test your decision

8. The code of ethics of the National Press Photographers Association (NPPA) _____.

(a) endorses any alteration of photographs
(b) accepts alteration of photographs only if it enhances the image
(c) accepts alteration of photographs only to make a point
(d) strongly denounces any alteration of photographs

9. _____ is copyrighted software that is distributed free for a trial period, after which a payment should be sent to the person or company who developed the program.

(a) Groupware
(b) Shareware
(c) Public-domain software
(d) Custom software

10. _____, which is the act of taking the ideas or writings of another and representing them as your own, has been made easier by the Internet.

(a) Plagiarism
(b) Slander
(c) Hacktivism
(d) Candor

Chapter Review

Short Answer

Write a brief answer to each of the following questions.

1. How is law different from ethics?
2. How does fair use limit the rights of copyright holders?
3. What are key tenets of the Digital Millennium Copyright Act?
4. How did the No Electronic Theft (NET) Act amend existing copyright law?
5. Despite what some people believe, why is software piracy not a victimless crime?

Web Research

Use a search engine such as Google (google.com) to research the following questions. Then, write a one-page double-spaced report or create a presentation, unless otherwise directed.

1. Recently, a Kansas teacher failed almost half of her class for plagiarizing material from the Internet, although the decision later was amended. The Internet has made **plagiarism** easier for students to commit, and harder for teachers to detect. Use the Web to learn more about Internet plagiarism, how it impacts students and schools, and what can be done to combat it.

2. To avoid libel, newspapers and magazines employ fact checkers to verify stories and editors to screen letters from readers. The Internet, however, offers no such safeguards, and **cyberlibel** can touch both public and private figures. Use the Web to find out more about cyberlibel and what steps lawmakers and the courts are taking to protect people from unproved allegations.

Group Exercises

Working with a group of your classmates, complete the following team questions.

1. The Children's Internet Protection Act mandates that, to receive federal funding, libraries must install filtering software on computers to prevent patrons from accessing obscene or harmful material on the Internet. Many librarians have seen objectionable material on library computer screens, but most oppose filtering software, contending that it limits free speech and blocks some Web sites containing legitimate educational information. Have each member of your team visit a local school or public library and interview a librarian about filtering software. Is the software necessary? Why? Can the library modify, or work around, the filtering software so it does not block sites of educational value? What other measures could be taken to protect children? Then, meet with your team, share your findings, and prepare a PowerPoint presentation on controlling Internet access on library computers.

2. A doctor who worked long hours for a health care company was furious when, after purchasing a gift for her children online, she received a memo from headquarters warning that she could be fired for personal use of company computers. According to one survey, 90 percent of workers admit to using office computers for reasons not related to business. Concerns about wasted time and resources, together with worries about possible liability for employee actions, have led many companies to issue codes of conduct governing computer use at work. Have each member of your team visit a company that has a code of conduct. Interview someone familiar with the code. What is permitted? What is prohibited? What are the consequences if the code is violated? Then, meet with your team, share your findings, and prepare a PowerPoint presentation comparing various codes of conduct.

Computers, Privacy, and Security

Security Concerns
- System Failure
- Secure Internet Transactions and E-Mail

Privacy Concerns
- Collecting Customer Data
  - *Electronic Profiling; Opt Out and Opt In*
- Spam
- Online Activity Tracking
  - *Cookies; Spyware; Web Bugs*

Protecting Security and Privacy
- Privacy Laws
- Protecting Against System Failure
- Backing up Data
- Defining a Disaster Recovery Plan
- Protecting Against Unauthorized Access and Use
  - *Firewalls; Intrusion Detection Software; Usernames and Passwords; Possessed Objects; Biometric Devices; Callback System; Audit Trails*
- Protecting Against Hardware Theft
- Protecting Online Security and Privacy
  - *Using Data Encryption; Securing Internet Transactions; Securing E-mail Messages; Reducing Spam; Limiting Personal Information Sharing; Managing Cookies, Spyware, and Web Bugs*

Security and Privacy in the Workplace
- Employee Monitoring and Surveillance
- Legal Rights of Employers and Employees

Computers, Security, and Privacy: A Balancing Act

Conclusion

For years, businesses have used computers and databases to collect and store information. Much of that information was stored on a corporate network and thus was not accessible to you or others outside of the company. With the rise of the Internet, data once stored offline was made available online, giving the public a view into the data for the first time. Although this provides many benefits, it also causes security and privacy concerns. As an example, in 1993, MacWorld magazine reported that, by spending just $112 and about 75 minutes online they found stacks of information on such public figures as George Lucas, Janet Reno, Joe Montana, and Clint Eastwood, including home addresses and phone numbers, Social Security numbers, birth dates, campaign contributions, marriage records, and more. Many local, state, and federal government agencies make a wide range of records available online, including voter registration data, real estate owner information, and more (Figure 9-1).

Although this is just one example, scenarios like these cause concern for many. As such personal information becomes more accessible, each of us — companies, associations, government agencies, and consumers — must take precautions to protect our security and privacy. Some security issues were discussed in Chapter 7. In this chapter, you will learn about additional security concerns, such as system failure and securing online transactions and e-mail. You also will learn about privacy concerns related to the collection of customer data, spam, and technologies used to track your activity online. Next, you will discover ways to protect your security and privacy, including privacy laws and safeguards against system failure, unauthorized access and use, and hardware theft. You then will review how to protect your security and privacy online. Finally, the chapter considers the issue of security and privacy in the workplace.

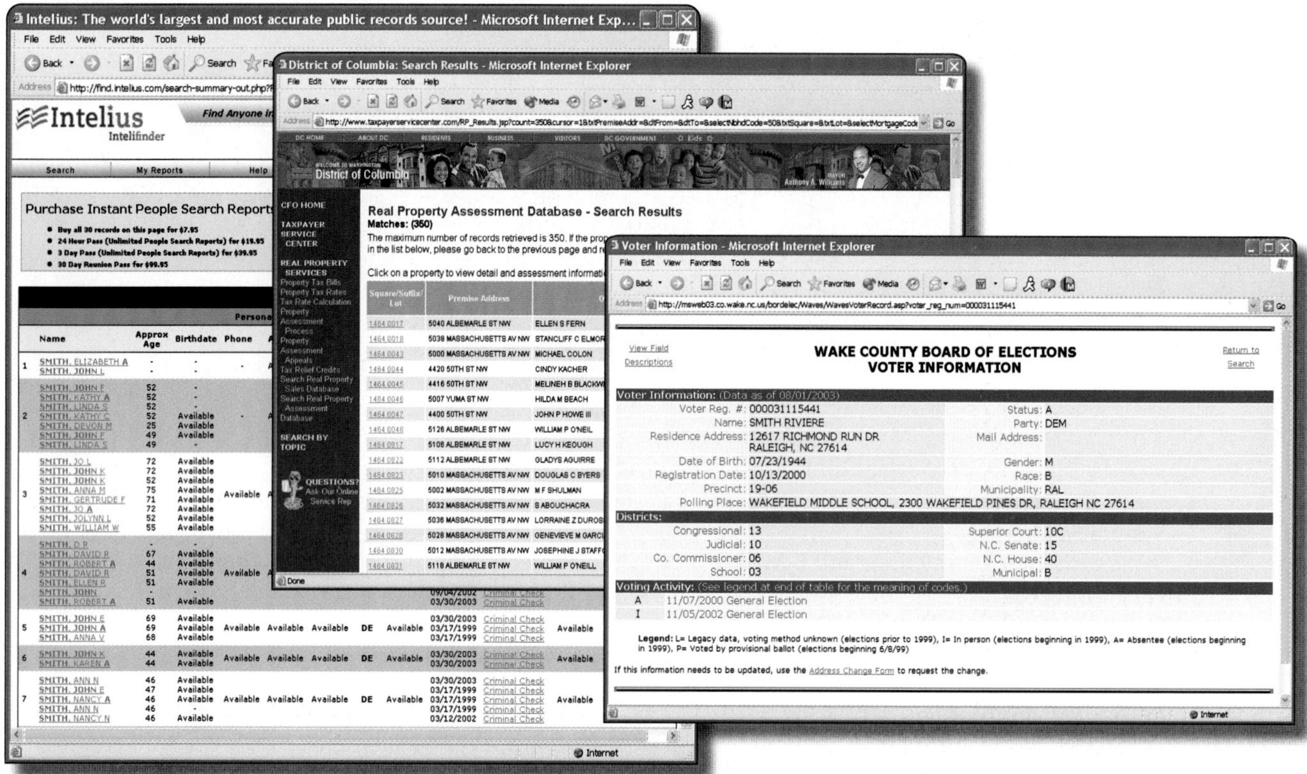

Figure 9-1 With just a few clicks, anyone can learn your home address, phone number, directions to your house, if you are a registered voter and which elections you voted in, as well as the value of any property you own. For a hundred dollars, even more of your personal information can be obtained, including criminal background, credit history, relatives, roommates and neighbors, bankruptcies, civil judgments against you, and more.

SECURITY CONCERNS

As you learned, a computer security risk is any event or action that could cause a loss of or damage to computer hardware, software, data, information, and processing ability. Chapter 7 introduced you to several major computer security risks, including malicious logic software and various types of computer crime. Chapter 8 covered personal security risks that can result from computer use, including cyberstalking and identify theft. This section covers two additional security concerns: system failure and unsecured Internet transactions and e-mail messages.

System Failure

A **system failure** is the prolonged malfunction of a computer. System failure can cause loss of hardware, software, data, or information. A variety of causes can lead to system failure, including natural disasters such as fires, floods, or storms; random events such as electrical power problems; and even errors in computer programs.

Older or malfunctioning hardware also can produce system failure, as can objects as small as dirt, hair, smoke, or other particles that can cause your hard disk to have a head crash. A **head crash** occurs when the read/write head of a hard disk drive touches the platter that stores the data, usually resulting in a loss of data or sometimes the loss of the entire drive. Although internal hard disks are built to withstand the shock of a fall and are sealed to keep out contaminants, head crashes do occur occasionally.

One of the more common causes of system failure is an electrical power variation, such as an undervoltage or overvoltage. An **undervoltage** occurs when the electrical supply drops. In North America, a wall plug typically supplies electricity at 120 volts. Any significant drop below 120 volts is considered an undervoltage. A *brownout* is a prolonged undervoltage. A *blackout* is a complete power failure. Usually, an undervoltage causes data loss – such as when your computer shuts off due to lack of power and you lose the report on which you were working. Undervoltages generally do not cause damage to hardware.

An **overvoltage**, or power surge, occurs when the incoming electrical power increases significantly above the normal 120 volts. A momentary overvoltage, called a **spike**, occurs when the increase in power lasts for more than one millisecond. Uncontrollable disturbances such as lightning can trigger spikes in power. Overvoltages

can cause immediate and permanent damage to hardware, possibly causing you to lose all of the data on your computer. If your computer is networked, an overvoltage also can damage other computers on the network. At home, the risk of damage from overvoltage can be minimized by using surge protectors or by unplugging the computer during lightning storms.

Secure Internet Transactions and E-Mail

Information transmitted over networks has a higher degree of security risk than information kept on a company's premises. In a business, network administrators usually take measures to protect the network from security risks. On the Internet, where no central administrator is present, the security risks are greater.

When you send an e-mail or submit data over the Internet, the data is routed through dozens of networks, any of which can be monitored to view the data in your message or submission. On an e-commerce site, intercepted data might include your home address, phone number, and credit card number. Sending an unprotected e-mail message is similar to sending a postcard through the United States mail: anyone along the route can read it. You never can be sure who might intercept it, who might read it, or to whom it might be forwarded. Earlier versions of Microsoft Outlook and Netscape Navigator, for example, had a security hole so that, if a sender embedded a few lines of JavaScript code in the message, the e-mail program secretly would return all forwarded e-mail to the original sender. How many times have you forwarded an e-mail to someone else with a comment you definitely would not want the sender to see? As evidenced by this simple example, if a message contains personal or confidential information, users should protect the message. Today, companies regularly make available software patches to fix security holes in their products; typically you can download a patch from their Web site for free.

PRIVACY CONCERNS

As you have learned, information privacy refers to the right of individuals and companies to deny or restrict the collection and use of information about them. When you use your computer to send e-mail, register to receive daily sports scores, or purchase a CD over the Internet, your privacy potentially can be compromised and some of your personal information, along with your online activity, may be shared in ways of which you are unaware. Software such as spyware and keystroke loggers allows companies to monitor your online activity, from what sites you visit to how long you linger on a shopping, dating, or social network site.

In the past, your personal information was stored in paper records kept in separate locations, not in large databases. Today, your personal information is stored in numerous databases on computers and servers in any number of locations. Your doctor and your health insurance company store your medical history, while your supermarket has all of your purchases recorded so they can better market to you. Credit card companies use databases to profile your purchasing behavior in order to determine the appropriate level of customer service and the types of promotional materials to send you. The government has countless databases recording where you live and if you own your home, how much money you make, and what investments you have. Do you own a gun? Are you married? Do you have a criminal record? They have that stored too.

The fact that your personal information is tracked by numerous organizations, in and of itself, may not be an issue. Some of your personal information may not be information you consider private. For example, you might not mind if the grocery store tracks your purchases or if a company knows you are a registered nurse. Another set of your personal information, however, may be information that you want to keep private. This set of information – your private information – might include your medical history or Web surfing activity.

Computer technology has made private information increasingly difficult to protect. The following sections review technologies and practices that raise privacy concerns, including how companies collect and use customer data, spam, and online activity tracking.

Collecting Customer Data

When you fill out a form such as a product warranty registration, a magazine subscription, or a contest entry form, the merchant that receives the form probably enters it in a database. Likewise, every time you click an advertisement on a Web site or register a software program online, your information, purchase history, and preferences are entered into a database.

ELECTRONIC PROFILING Once a company has your personal information in a database, the merchant can sell your data to national marketing firms and Internet advertising firms. By combining this data with information from public sources such as driver's licenses and

vehicle registrations, these firms can create electronic profiles of you and other individuals.

These marketing and advertising firms focus on being able to collect accurate, in-depth information about individuals and creating a customer profile or electronic profile for each person. The electronic profile may contain such personal details as your name, age, address, telephone number, buying habits, marital status, number of dependents, pets, or the type of car you own. Also called database marketing, the companies typically collect data about your demographics and buying activity in order to identify their best customers – customers that generate the most sales or profit – and to understand how to market to those customers. Even your cell phone can provide marketers valuable information for customizing their sales pitches. When you respond to an ad to send a text message to a particular number, the recipient not only gets your cell phone number, but can determine where you live based on that phone number, and where you were when you sent the message. This information can then be used to blast messages back to your phone about special offers or upcoming events in the area.

Companies also can sell your electronic profile to other companies. A car dealership, for example, may want to send a print flyer or e-mail message to all sports car owners in the vicinity. Thus, the dealership may contact a marketing firm to purchase a list that includes the name, address, and e-mail address of all sports car owners living in the Pacific Northwest.

Direct marketers and their supporters say that using information in this way lowers overall selling costs, which lowers product prices. Customers who receive personalized messages of interest may concede that electronic profiling allows companies to pinpoint what types of offers are appropriate for them, so a new homeowner gets information on cleaning services instead of renter's insurance. Critics contend that the information in an electronic profile reveals more about an individual than anyone has a right to know. They claim that companies not only should inform individuals if they plan to provide personal information to other firms, they also should explain exactly how they will use your personal information. Further, the companies need to make it simple for consumers to limit the way their information is used.

OPT OUT AND OPT IN As you have learned, some organizations offer you choices about how your personal information is used. For example, many marketers let you opt in to receiving marketing messages, which means you will not receive e-mails and other types of marketing messages unless you sign up and specifically request they be sent to you (many companies allow you to opt in via their Web site). You also can opt in to allow companies to share your personal information.

Other firms allow you to opt out – that is, to instruct them not to have your information shared with others or used for promotional purposes. Marketing e-mails often include an opt-out link at the bottom that you can click to be removed from the mailing list; businesses also make opt-out services available to customers online or over the phone.

A company's privacy policy should explain opt-out and opt-in rules and provide a statement of what will and will not be done with any sensitive data you disclose. Many online and offline companies have privacy policies, which are made available to customers on their Web sites and in print materials. A credit card company, for example, probably has a privacy policy that it occasionally will mail with your statement. This began with passage of the Gramm-Leach-Bliley Act (GLBA) or Financial Modernization Act of 1999. Many companies also have links to privacy policies on their Web sites.

Privacy advocates note that consumers hardly ever read such privacy policies. Those who do read the policies often find them confusing because they are filled with technical legal language. Privacy policies also change, sometimes without customers being aware of those changes. If one company is bought by or merged with another, ownership of customer data may be transferred. For example, in 2002, the bankrupt Web site DrKoop.com attempted to sell its assets to the online consumer health site, Vitacost.com – assets that included personal medical histories entered by almost one million visitors when the Web site was thriving. Users sued DrKoop.com and successfully prevented the sale of all of their sensitive information, with the exception of their e-mail addresses.

Spam

With your e-mail address in hand, companies, marketers, and government agencies may use your information simply to process your order, or they may use it to market products, services, or promotions to you. A company quickly can use your information to make you a target for spam, either from them or from other firms. **Spam** is any unsolicited junk e-mail message or newsgroup posting sent to many recipients or newsgroups at once, invading your privacy by sending a flood of e-mails you have not requested and do not want to receive. The content of spam ranges from selling a product or service to promoting a business opportunity to advertising offensive material. Spam also can include

viruses or spyware, which pose security risks to your computer and your privacy. A newer, growing form of spam is "image-based," requiring dramatic increases in both network bandwidth and storage. According to one study, volumes spiked 300 percent in 2006 due to this type of spam.

In January 2004, Congress passed the **CAN-SPAM** Act of 2003 (Controlling the Assault of Non-Solicited Pornography and Marketing Act) in an attempt to control the types of unsolicited advertising and promotional messages sent. The law bans false or misleading header information, deceptive subject lines, and requires a mechanism for opting-out of future mailings. It also requires that commercial mailings be identified as such, complete with a physical address for the sender. Violations start at $11,000.

Has this legislation stopped spammers? No, although it has led to some high-profile legal action, most notably the recent indictment and arrest of Robert Alan Soloway of Seattle. He was charged with the sending of tens of millions of e-mails using forged e-mail addresses and domains on "zombie" computers – those of unsuspecting owners who have no idea their computers are part of the scheme – and faces fines upwards of $772,000.

Like most individuals with an e-mail address, you probably are familiar with (and tired of) receiving spam. One study indicates the average user receives more than 1,000 spam e-mail messages each year, with the most popular types of spam promoting pharmaceutical products and stocks. The flood of unsolicited e-mail is growing so fast that spam accounts for almost half of all U.S. e-mail traffic. Spam has become one of the most annoying aspects of using a computer, as well an expense for individuals and companies who must pay for the connections and disk space necessary to handle all of the junk mail. However, studies are showing that we are getting used to spam as a part of Internet life. Over 70% of e-mail users have some form of spam-blocker installed. And some experts predict that as more people migrate away from e-mail to text messaging, it may become even less of a concern.

Online Activity Tracking

Several different technologies allow companies, advertisers, and others to track your activity while you are on the Internet. These technologies – including cookies, spyware, and Web bugs –- are discussed in this section.

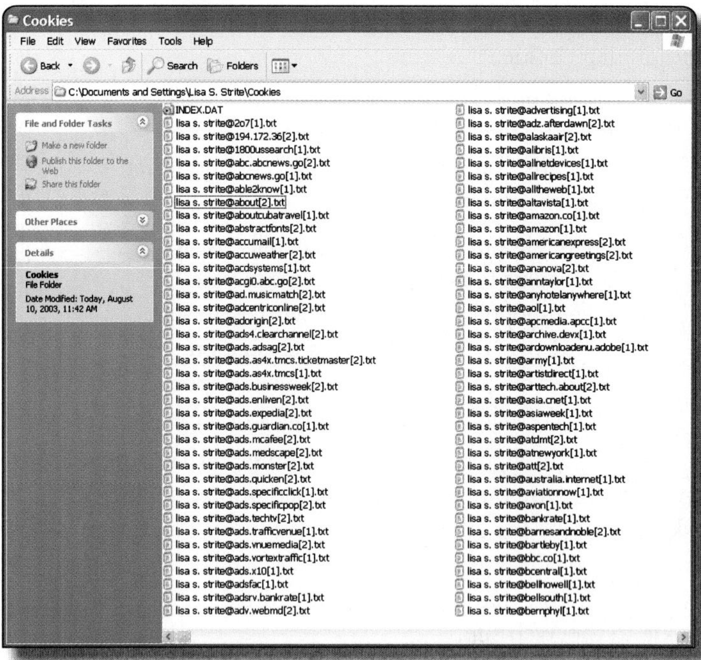

Figure 9-2 A cookie is a small text file that a Web server stores on your computer. Cookie files typically contain data about you, such as your user name or viewing preferences. The name of the file often provides some information as to which Web site placed the cookie on your computer.

COOKIES E-commerce and other Web applications often rely on cookies to identify users and display customized content. A **cookie** is a small text file that a Web server stores on your computer (Figure 9-2). The name comes from Unix programming objects, or tokens, called "magic cookies." They are attached to a user or a program and can change, depending on what is accessed by the user or program. Cookie files typically contain data about you, such as your user name or viewing preferences.

Web sites use cookies for a variety of purposes:

- Most Web sites that allow for personalization use cookies to store user preferences on your hard disk. On such sites, you may be asked to fill in a form requesting personal information, such as your name, zip code, or site preferences. Yahoo, for example, uses a cookie to store information about your customized My Yahoo page, including the background colors, the selected content, the weather reports or sports scores to display, and more (Figure 9-3).
- Some Web sites use cookies to store your username and password, so that you do not have to log in each time you visit the Web site. For additional security, some Web sites

store your username, but not your password, in a cookie.

- Companies also use cookies to track which pages on the Web site you visited most often, what ads you have seen or clicked, and other Web site statistics.
- Online shopping Web sites generally use a session cookie to keep track of items in your online shopping cart. This allows you to start an order on one day and then finish it on another day. Session cookies usually expire after a certain time, such as a week or a month.

As shown in Figure 9-4, many commercial Web sites send a cookie to your browser; your computer's hard disk then stores the cookie in a cookies file. The next time you visit the Web site, your browser retrieves the cookie from your hard disk and sends the data in the cookie to the Web site.

Cookies come in several varieties: temporary or persistent, and first party or third party. Table 9-1 describes the different types of cookies placed on your computer. The name of a cookie file often provides some information on whether a cookie is a first-party or third-party cookie and which Web site placed the cookie on your computer. For example, the cookie file named dsimpson@foxnews[1].txt most likely is a first-party cookie placed on your computer by the Fox News Web site. A cookie file named dsimpson@ads.specificclick[1].txt most likely is a third-party cookie placed on your computer from an ad delivered by the SpecificCLICK ad network. The ad might have been displayed on any one of the Web sites you visited.

Some Web sites sell or trade information stored in your cookies to advertisers, a practice many believe to be unethical. Web sites also can use third-party cookies to record **click stream data**, which is data about the Web pages you visit and the links you click on a Web site, even after you leave the Web site and navigate to other Web sites. As previously discussed, a Web site can read data only from its own cookie file. If you visit a Web page with ads from a third-party advertiser, however, both the Web site and the third-party advertiser can place cookies on your hard disk. When you visit another Web page with ads from the same third-party advertiser, that Web page can send a request to the third-party advertiser to ask for information about you, some of which might have been collected at the previous Web site and stored in the third-party cookie.

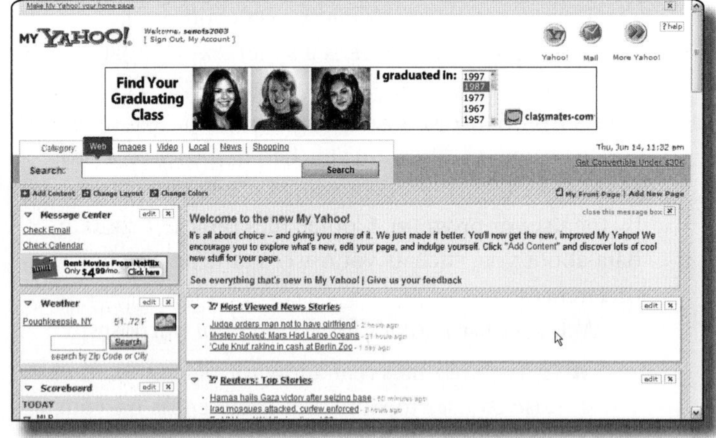

Figure 9-3 Yahoo uses a cookie to store information about your customized My Yahoo page, including the background colors; selected content; which weather reports, horoscopes, or sports scores to display; and more. The cookie even stores information about how you would like the information laid out on the Web page.

Figure 9-4 How cookies work.

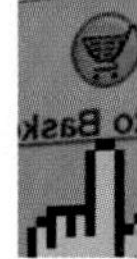

Table 9-1 Types of Cookies and Their Uses

COOKIE	DESCRIPTION
Temporary cookie or session cookie	Used to store information during a session or visit to a Web site. A session cookie typically stores data such as the list of items in your shopping cart or graphic elements that repeat from page to page. Session cookies usually expire after a certain time, such as a week or a month. Temporary or session cookies pose little privacy risk and help make your browsing experience more efficient.
Persistent cookie	Stored on the hard disk of your computer even after you close the browser. The next time you visit the Web site, it can access the cookie from your hard disk to customize your Web page or automatically log you in. Although hundreds of persistent cookies can be stored on your computer, a Web site can read data only from its own cookie file. It cannot access or view any other data on your hard disk, including another cookie.
First-party cookie	Persistent cookie placed on your hard disk by the Web site you currently are viewing. First-party cookies allow the Web site to customize your browsing experience to fit your preferences. These cookies also can record any personal information that you provide on a Web site. For example, if you create a profile for yourself with an ID and password, your e-mail address, or your name and address, that information can be stored in a cookie or in the Web site database.
Third-party cookie	A temporary or persistent cookie that originates on a Web site different from the one you are viewing currently. For example, if you view a Web site that includes advertisements from a third-party firm, a third-party cookie might be placed on your computer. Many online advertising firms, such as DoubleClick, SpecificCLICK, 24/7 Real Media, and Advertising.com, use third-party cookies to track your Web page use so they can target their advertisements.

Cookies come in several varieties: temporary or persistent and first party or third party, each of which is used for different purposes.

SPYWARE **Spyware** is a program placed on a computer without the user's knowledge that secretly collects information about the user. Spyware can enter a computer as a virus or can be included in another program, such as a game or utility. While you are online, the spyware program runs on your computer or a network server to communicate information it collects to some outside source or allow intruders to breach network security.

Some employers use spyware to collect information about an employee's program usage or Web surfing activity. Internet advertising firms often use spyware, which they refer to as **adware**, to collect information about your Web browsing habits.

WEB BUGS Another type of spyware is called a Web bug. A **Web bug** or **Web beacon** is a graphic embedded in Web pages used to collect information about visitors to the site. Online advertising networks refer to Web bugs as **invisible GIFs** or **clear GIFs** (Figure 9-5).

Web bugs gather information such as a computer's IP address, the type of browser used to retrieve the bug, the Web address of the page from which the user came, the time the page was viewed, and a previously set cookie value.

Web bugs are used to:

- Add information to an ad network cookie on your hard drive. The information in the cookie is used to access your profile in the ad network database, which determines what banner ad displays on a Web page.
- Provide an independent accounting of how many people have visited a Web site.
- Gather statistics about Web browser usage at different places on the Internet.
- Determine how many recipients of HTML e-mails read a marketing e-mail message and when they read it.

Web sites commonly use Web bugs to customize a user's experience or to gather statistics on the site, but the invisible, and sometimes undisclosed, nature of Web bugs fuels privacy debates.

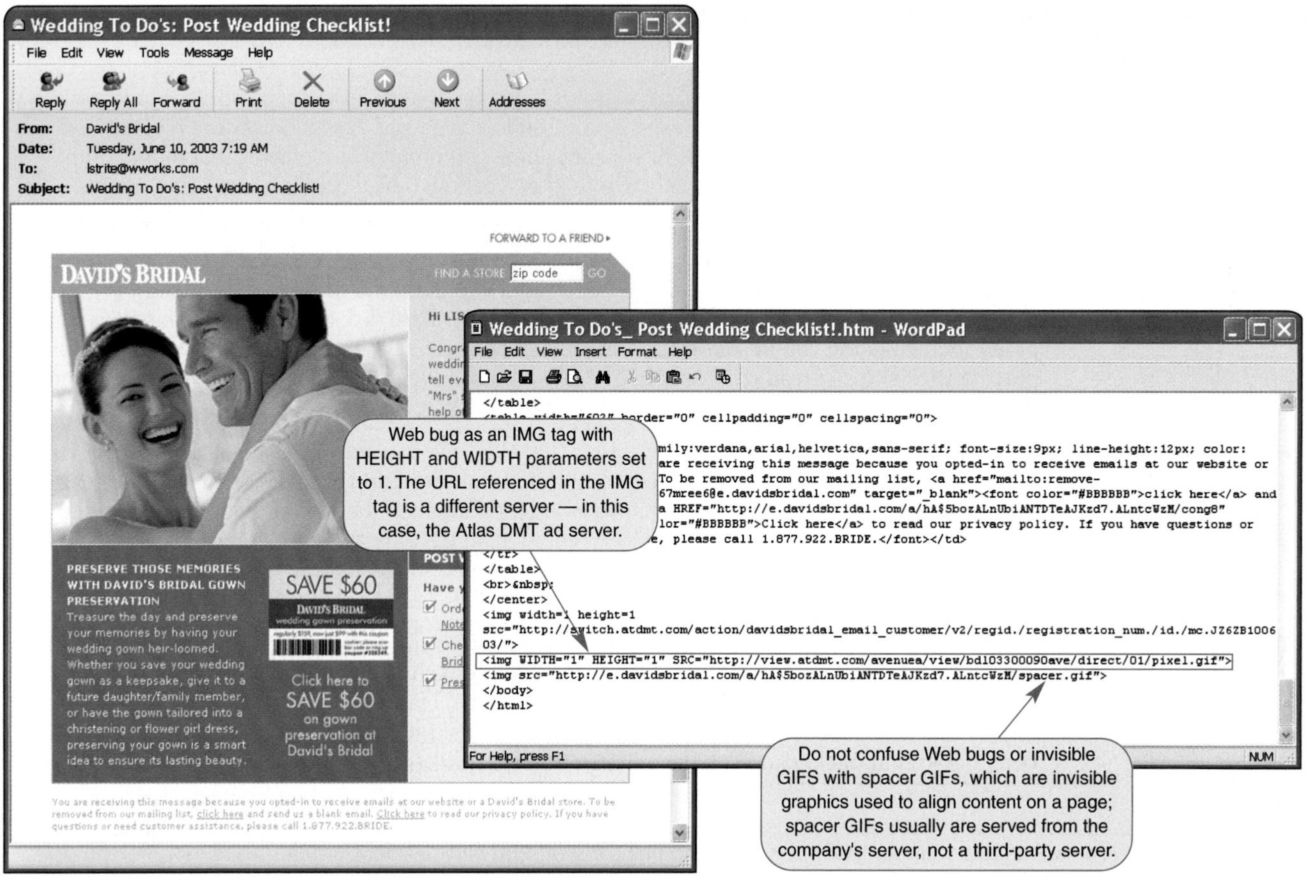

Web bug as an IMG tag with HEIGHT and WIDTH parameters set to 1. The URL referenced in the IMG tag is a different server — in this case, the Atlas DMT ad server.

Do not confuse Web bugs or invisible GIFS with spacer GIFs, which are invisible graphics used to align content on a page; spacer GIFs usually are served from the company's server, not a third-party server.

Figure 9-5 You can determine if a Web page or e-mail message uses Web bugs by viewing the HTML source code and searching for IMG (image) tags. A Web bug typically is an IMG tag with HEIGHT and WIDTH parameters set to 1. The URL referenced in the IMG tag is a different server than the rest of the Web page.

@ISSUE: Carnivore: Sniffing out Bad Guys and Good?

For years, people have talked about Carnivore, a program the FBI uses to keep an eye on the e-mail and Web activity of potential criminals. The original idea behind the Carnivore system was that law enforcement could monitor e-mail traffic sent from a criminal suspect to gather evidence. Today, Carnivore also is used to monitor Web pages viewed and files downloaded. Although Carnivore recently was renamed DCS1000, in an effort to sound less intimidating, the program remains a real threat to privacy in the eyes of many.

How does Carnivore work? Carnivore is a packet sniffer, which looks at every packet in a data transmission to determine if any of the packets include data for which the Feds might be looking. To set up Carnivore to monitor the Internet activity of a suspected criminal or terrorist, the FBI first must obtain a court order. Then, the FBI and an Internet service provider define an access point on the network where they can monitor data from the suspect (preferably an access point that does not contain other traffic from regular, unsuspecting citizens like you). The FBI connects a tapping device at the access point — the purpose of which is to create a copy of any data that flows through the access point. This collected data is passed into a collection system where it is filtered to remove any data traffic not eligible for view under court orders. The other data — information sent to and from the suspect's computer — is stored for review by the FBI (Figure 9-6).

Despite complaints from privacy advocates, the FBI stands by their use of Carnivore, noting that the Internet increasingly is a communications tool for some of the most serious criminals: terrorists, spies, organized crime rings, and drug traffickers. Carnivore was used extensively in the days and weeks after 9/11, as law enforcement scrambled to identify who was responsible for the terrorist act and if other such attacks were in the works. Being able to use a tool like Carnivore gives them an opportunity to gather hard, firsthand evidence of some of these activities. The FBI further notes that Carnivore is used for gathering evidence against known criminals, not

(continued)

@ISSUE: Carnivore: Sniffing out Bad Guys and Good? *(continued)*

for monitoring the Internet for potentially illegal acts of regular computer users. They also cite the tight court restrictions, which limit a court order allowing the use of Carnivore to 30 days and require reports back to the judge every 7 to 10 days.

In 2000, when it first was revealed that the FBI was using Carnivore, privacy advocates, citizens, and even members of Congress loudly voiced their concerns about the privacy implications. Many expressed worry that the FBI will not reveal precisely how Carnivore works; some questioned if the software allows the FBI to review data not covered under the court order, either intentionally or due to flaws in the program. A related concern is that Carnivore could be abused by law enforcement as a monitoring tool, instead of an evidence-gathering tool. Although the FBI claims to have never used Carnivore in this way, the system is capable of broadly capturing and reviewing Internet traffic, as opposed to the precisely targeted reviews currently being used.

The Electronic Privacy Information Center recently reported that technical flaws in Carnivore actually might have hindered an FBI antiterrorism investigation, possibly involving Osama bin Laden. The report, based on released FBI documents, notes that Carnivore had captured e-mails from individuals not covered under court order, a violation of federal wiretap law. The Bureau document states that the "FBI technical person was apparently so upset that he destroyed all the e-mail take, including the take on [the authorized target]." Two other documents written one week later mention that Carnivore sometimes causes "the improper capture of data," and that "[s]uch unauthorized interceptions not only can violate a citizen's privacy but also can seriously 'contaminate' ongoing investigations".

Carnivore thus remains a controversial system that is hotly debated for its potential privacy risks, while being a somewhat inelegant tool that does not allow for highly sophisticated Internet traffic analysis (which may, in the end, make it more dangerous than a very powerful, highly targeted packet-sniffing program). A Justice Department review panel was in the process of evaluating the use of Carnivore shortly before the September 11th terrorist attacks. Since then, interest in limiting Carnivore seems to have waned (see @Issue: How PATRIOTic Are You?). The FBI continues to defend Carnivore, noting that electronic surveillance has helped secure convictions for over 25,600 dangerous felons over the past 13 years, and Carnivore is just the latest in a string of successful surveillance tools. In today's world, where organized crime rings meet in chat rooms to discuss plans and drug runners send cryptic e-mails with instructions on the next drop, some are willing to pay for the price of safety with the potential loss of some privacy.

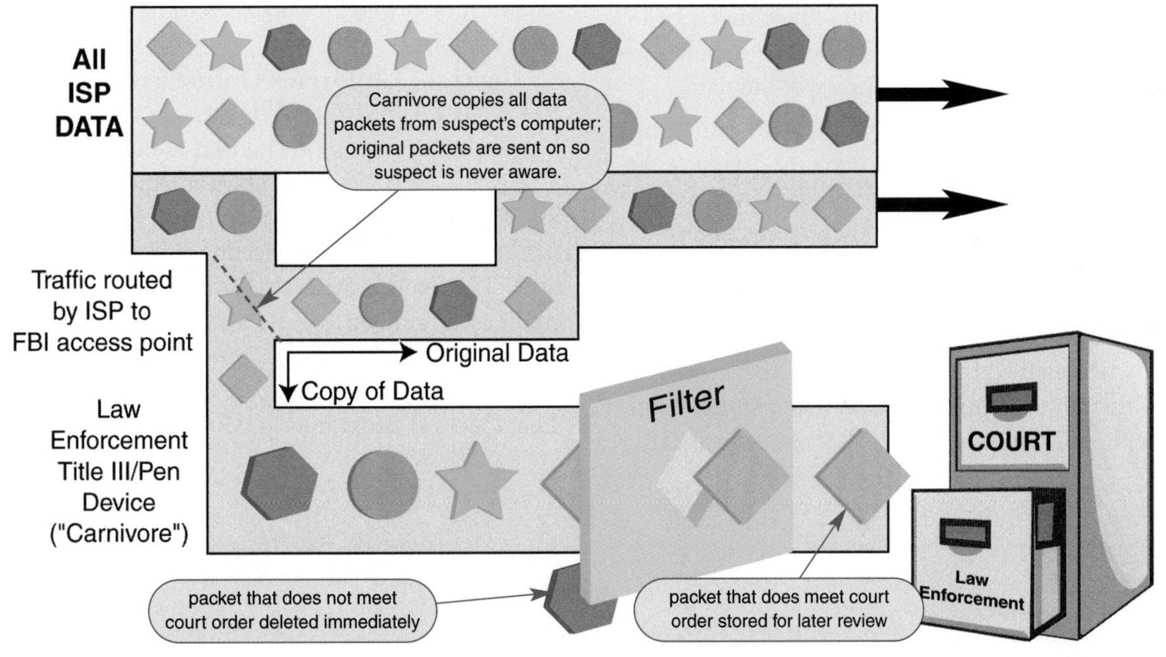

Figure 9-6 Carnivore is a packet-sniffing program used to review all data sent to and from a suspected criminal's computer.

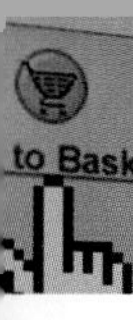

PROTECTING SECURITY AND PRIVACY

As indicated by the security and privacy risks reviewed thus far, protecting your security and privacy can be a challenge in today's highly connected and technology-rich world. By remaining aware of potential risks, employing common sense, using sound precautions, and implementing safeguards, you can maintain your security and privacy. The following section reviews several practices, laws, and tools that can help.

Privacy Laws

The concern about privacy has led to the enactment of federal and state laws regarding the storage and disclosure of personal data (Table 9-2). Common points in some of these laws include the following:

1. Information collected and stored about individuals should be limited to what is necessary to carry out the function of the business or government agency collecting the data.
2. Once collected, provisions should be made to restrict access to the data to those employees within the organization who need access to it to perform their job duties.
3. Personal information should be released outside the organization collecting the data only when the person has agreed to its disclosure.
4. When information is collected about an individual, the individual should know that the data is being collected and have the opportunity to determine the accuracy of the data.

Several federal laws deal specifically with computers. The 1986 **Electronic Communications Privacy Act** (ECPA) provides the same protection that covers mail and telephone communications to new forms of electronic communications. The law, which grew out of the Watergate scandal of the 1970s, prohibits access to stored communication or transmitted messages such as e-mail or voice mail without consent or a court order, and only then in the course of a criminal investigation. One exception under this law is a business, which can monitor its employees, as you learned in Chapter 1. Under the guidelines stated in the ECPA, the FBI can use its Carnivore packet-sniffing program to monitor e-mail and online activity of suspected criminals and terrorists. If you are not a suspected criminal or terrorist, however, the FBI cannot legally monitor your online activity. With regard to commercial Web sites, the ECPA requires that companies adhere to their stated privacy policies. The 1984 and 1994 **Computer Fraud and Abuse Acts** outlawed unauthorized access to federal government computers and the transmission of harmful computer code such as viruses.

One law with an apparent legal loophole is the 1970 **Fair Credit Reporting Act.** The act limits the people who legally can view a credit report to only those with a legitimate business need. The problem is that it does not define a legitimate business need. The result is that just about anyone can say they have a legitimate business need and gain access to your credit report. Ever wonder why you get so many credit card offers in the mail? Credit card issuers regularly scan consumer credit histories to determine which offers to send. Some would say this is a legitimate business need.

Credit reports contain much more than just balance and payment information on mortgages and credit cards. The largest credit bureaus maintain information on family income, number of dependents, employment history, bank balances, driving records, lawsuits, and Social Security numbers. In total, credit bureaus have more than 400 million records on more than 160 million people. Some credit bureaus sell combinations of the data they have in their databases to direct marketing organizations.

Under the **Children's Online Privacy Protection Act (COPPA)** of 1998, Web sites are required to protect personal information on children under the age of 13. The Act, which went into effect in April 2000, requires that Web sites get explicit permission from parents before marketing to or collecting personal data from children. The explicit permission often is in the form of a credit card number.

Many Web sites demonstrate their commitment to privacy by applying to be part of the TRUSTe program. The TRUSTe program is a voluntary program in which

Table 9-2 U.S. Privacy Laws

DATE	LAW	PURPOSE
2003	**Controlling the Assault of Non-Solicited Pornography and Marketing (CAN-SPAM) Act**	Establishes requirements for those who send commercial e-mail and defines penalties for violating the law.
2001	**Provide Appropriate Tools Required to Intercept and Obstruct Terrorism (PATRIOT) Act (renewed 2006)**	Gives law enforcement the right to monitor people's activities, including Web and e-mail habits.
1999	**Gramm-Leach-Bliley Act (GLBA) or Financial Modernization Act**	Protects consumers from unauthorized disclosures of financial information and requires entities to periodically report information disclosure policies to consumers.
1998	**Children's Online Privacy Protection Act (COPPA)**	Requires Web sites to get explicit permission from parents before marketing to, or collecting personal information from, children under age 13. Also requires protection of the personal information collected.
1998	**Digital Millennium Copyright Act (DMCA)**	Makes it illegal to circumvent antipiracy schemes in commercial software; outlaws sale of devices that copy software illegally.
1997	**No Electronic Theft (NET) Act**	Closes a narrow loophole in the law that allowed people to give away copyrighted material (such as software) on the Internet without legal repercussions.
1996	**National Information Infrastructure Protection Act**	Penalizes theft of information across state lines, threats against networks, and computer system trespassing.
1994	**Computer Abuse Amendments Act**	Amends 1984 act to outlaw transmission of harmful computer code such as viruses.
1992	**Cable Act**	Extends the privacy of the Cable Communications Policy Act of 1984 to include cellular and other wireless services.
1991	**Telephone Consumer Protection Act**	Restricts activities of telemarketers.
1988	**Computer Matching and Privacy Protection Act**	Regulates the use of government data to determine the eligibility of individuals for federal benefits.
1988	**Video Privacy Protection Act**	Forbids retailers from releasing or selling video-rental records without customer consent or a court order.
1986	**Electronic Communications Privacy Act (ECPA)**	Provides the same right of privacy protection for the postal delivery service and telephone companies to the new forms of electronic communications, such as voice mail, e-mail, and cellular telephones.
1984	**Cable Communications Policy Act**	Regulates disclosure of cable television subscriber records.
1984	**Computer Fraud and Abuse Act**	Outlaws unauthorized access of federal government computers.
1978	**Right to Financial Privacy Act**	Strictly outlines procedures federal agencies must follow when looking at customer records in banks.
1974	**Privacy Act**	Forbids federal agencies from allowing information to be used for a Treason other than that for which it was collected.
1974	**Family Educational Rights and Privacy Act**	Gives students and parents access to school records and limits disclosure of records to unauthorized parties.
1970	**Fair Credit Reporting Act**	Prohibits credit reporting agencies from releasing credit information to unauthorized people and allows consumers to review their own credit records.

Summary of the major U.S. laws concerning privacy.

a company's Web site and business practices are reviewed by TRUSTe to ensure that the Web site adheres to established privacy principles and complies with ongoing TRUSTe review and consumer resolution procedures. Once approved, the Web site can display the TRUSTe trustmark, which is a seal displayed by member Web sites, as shown in Figure 9-7.

Even if a Web site displays a TRUSTe trustmark, you should review its privacy policy. In general, to be an informed consumer and Web user you should make a practice of viewing the privacy statement for Web sites you frequent to see exactly what information the Web site collects and how it uses the information. Be sure the privacy policy states how it handles your personally identifiable information (PII), such as your e-mail address, your name and address, or even more sensitive personal information, such as financial data, political party affiliation, or religious beliefs.

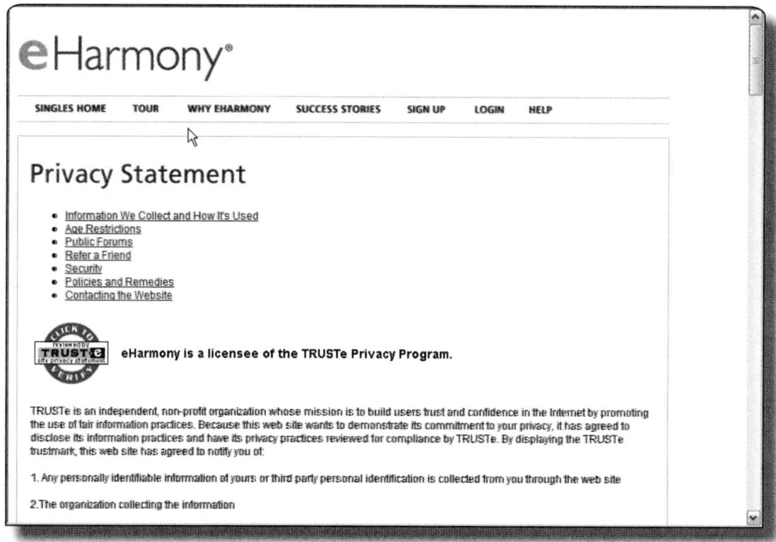

Figure 9-7 TRUSTe reviews Web site's practices to ensure that the Web site adheres to established privacy principles. Once approved, the Web site can display the TRUSTe trustmark.

@ISSUE: How PATRIOTic Are You?

September 11, 2001 was a day that changed much of life in America. The belief that Americans were safe and secure in their own country was shaken to the core. Further adding to the shock was learning that, not only had many of the men guilty of the terrorist attack lived in the United States, they even trained at U.S. flight schools. In the stunned pain following that day, intelligence and law enforcement officials rushed to demand laws to give them more authority to identify, ferret out, and convict anyone with terrorist intentions. Congress quickly complied, passing the USA PATRIOT Act on October 26th, only a month and a half after the September 11th attacks.

The USA PATRIOT Act, which is an acronym for Uniting and Strengthening America by Providing Appropriate Tools Required to Intercept and Obstruct Terrorism Act, includes provisions that:

- Relax restrictions on information sharing between law enforcement and intelligence agencies
- Authorize roving wiretaps to allow law enforcement to intercept any communications made to or by a suspect, without specifying the exact telephone line or computer to be monitored
- Allow detention of noncitizens for up to seven days without charges
- Expand police access to e-mail records and voice mail records
- Increase government monitoring of financial transactions
- Permit law enforcement to access a wide range of tangible records, including library and bookstore records
- Allow for "sneak and peek" searches of homes and offices, in which search warrants are presented after the search

The law also has many other changes that allow the FBI to search chat rooms, bulletin boards, and Web sites and to monitor individuals at public places and events, even if there is no credible evidence of wrongdoing. Despite the name of the law, such powers are not limited to investigating terrorist acts: law enforcement can apply these powers for any violation of federal law, including drug crimes, white-collar crime, and copyright violations.

(continued)

ISSUE: How PATRIOTic Are You? *(continued)*

Concerned critics worry that the USA PATRIOT Act may compromise our civil liberties in ways never before imagined. The law, for example, allows the FBI to access business records, medical records, educational records, and library records without showing any credible knowledge that these documents include evidence to help solve a crime — or that a crime even was committed. Instead, government agencies only need to cite an ongoing investigation related to terrorism or intelligence activities and the records are theirs for the reading. Authorities note that, when you consider some of the 9/11 hijackers had used library computers to communicate with one another and research the attacks, the law seems less outrageous.

The American Civil Liberties Union (ACLU) and others, however, remain critical of the government for passing the law, stating that the USA PATRIOT Act does little to protect citizens, while seriously infringing on civil liberties in America. Yet a 2006 Harris poll found that when law enforcement agencies are investigating terrorism, 70% of U.S. adults favor expanded camera surveillance on streets and in public places, 61% favor closer monitoring of banking and credit card transactions, 62% favor monitoring Internet chat rooms and other forums, and 52% favor monitoring cell phones and e-mail.

Despite varying opinion on the matter, on March 9, 2006, President George W. Bush signed the USA PATRIOT Improvement and Reauthorization Act of 2005, extending the original sixteen components of the legislation passed in 2001. The law also added 30 new civil liberties safeguards to provide both protection for citizens and tools for law enforcement, even though no verified civil liberties abuses have been documented to date.

The attempt to secure the United States while at the same time ensure American civil liberties is a balancing act. The government is working to provide tools to make the country safer which, by necessity, requires some limits on civil liberties, including increased airport security, new rules on registration for foreign students, and the possibility of a national ID card. President Bush noted in his address to the nation in November 2001, "After September the 11th, our government assumed new responsibilities to strengthen security at home and track down our enemies abroad. And the American people are accepting new responsibilities, as well." Following the signing of the reauthorization on March 9, 2006, President Bush stated the legislation "strengthens the Justice Department so it can better detect and disrupt terrorist threats. And the bill gives law enforcement new tools to combat threats to our citizens from international terrorists to local drug dealers."

After September 11th, Americans, in a surge of patriotism, offered public services and charitable donations in record numbers. With the PATRIOT Act, the government was given stronger monitoring and surveillance powers than ever before. But, when the two collide — your desire to keep your country and family safe and the government's new rights to monitor your communications and behavior — which wins out? In the light of further eroding civil liberties, just how PATRIOTic will you be?

Protecting Against System Failure

In the event of a system failure, having backups of your data and files is critically important. To protect against electrical power variations, you should use a surge protector. A **surge protector**, also called a surge suppressor, has special electrical components to smooth out overvoltages, provide a stable current flow, and keep an overvoltage from reaching the computer and other electronic equipment (Figure 9-8). Sometimes resembling a power strip, a surge protector plugs into the power outlet. The computer, phone lines, and other devices, such as a printer, are plugged into the surge protector. The surge protector absorbs small overvoltages, generally without damage to the computer and

Figure 9-8 Circuits inside a surge protector safeguard against overvoltages and undervoltages. To ensure you get a quality surge protector, you should purchase a surge protector that meets Underwriters Laboratories (UL) 1149 standard, which allows no more than 500 maximum volts to pass through the line.

equipment. If a huge power surge occurs, such as that from a lightning strike, some surge protectors shut off all power to a computer to avoid damage.

For additional electrical protection, some systems connect to an uninterruptible power supply. An **uninterruptible power supply (UPS)** is a device that contains surge protection circuits and one or more batteries that can provide power during a temporary or permanent loss of power (Figure 9-9). A UPS connects between your computer and a power source. UPS software can shut down a computer cleanly if power is out for a certain number of minutes.

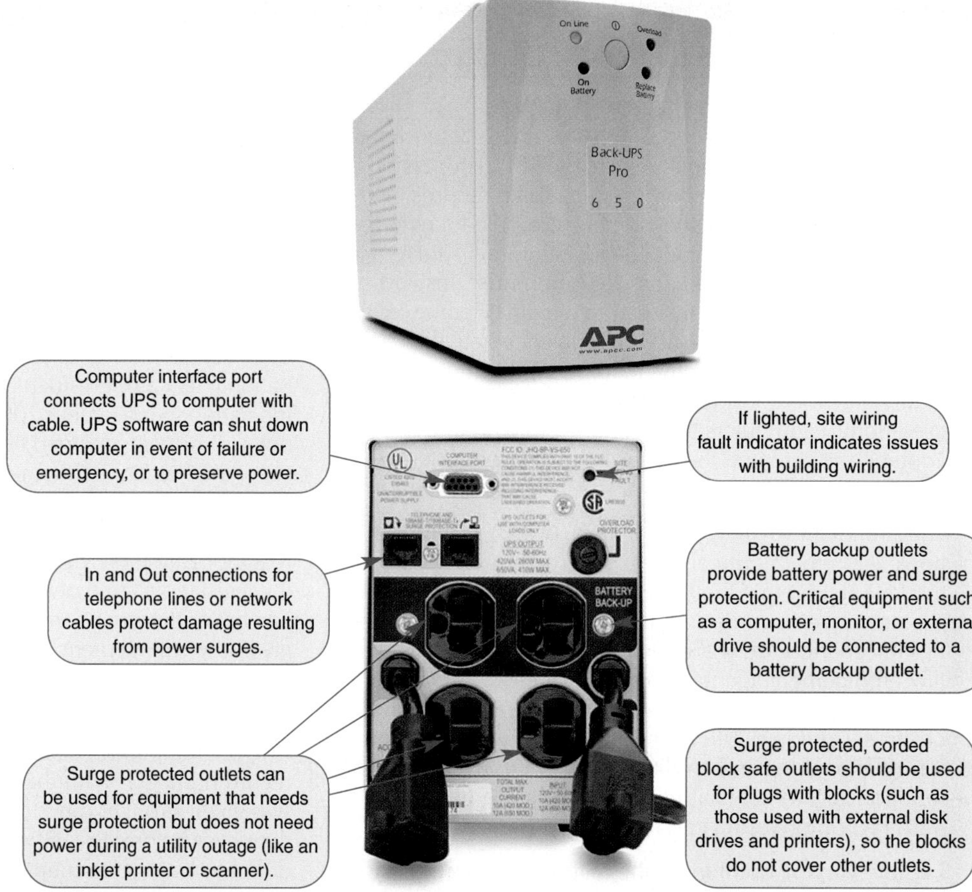

Figure 9-9 If power fails, an uninterruptible power supply (UPS) uses batteries to provide electricity for a limited amount of time. A UPS should provide several types of outlets for your computer and other equipment, as well as network connections or phone lines.

Backing Up Data

Performing a regular backup of critical files on your computer is one of the most important aspects of being a responsible computer user. A **backup** is a duplicate of a file, program, or disk that can be used if the original is lost, damaged, or destroyed. To **back up** a file means to make a copy of it. In the case of a system failure or the discovery of corrupted files, you can restore the files by copying the backed up files to their original location on the computer. Creating backups allows you to recover months or years of work that can be lost in an instant if your hard disk crashes or your computer is stolen. You always should back up critical files including documents that you create, such as your Quicken or Microsoft Money data and your contact database, as well your e-mail program.

Backup files can be stored on any storage media, including external hard drives, CD-RWs, DVD+RWs, Zip disks, and others. Backup copies should be kept in a safe place, such as a fireproof and heatproof safe or **off site** – that is, in a location away from the computer site. Keeping backup files off site ensures that a single disaster, such as a fire, does not destroy both the computer and the backup copies of the data. You can store the backup at a friend or family member's home, a bank safe deposit box, or on an Internet hard drive. Your school may provide a limited amount of storage space on its network for student use as well. An **Internet hard drive**, also called **online storage**, is a service that provides storage for computer users, usually for a minimal monthly fee. Xdrive and IBackup are examples of companies that provide online storage solutions you can use to back up files. If you do not have a high-speed Internet connection, however, it might be impractical, because the time required to download and upload files can be daunting.

Several approaches can be used to back up files. The most basic approach is simply to make a copy of important files on a USB drive, CD-RW, or other media on a regular basis. Alternatively, you can use a backup utility that allows you to select which drives or folders to copy, where to store the backup files, and when to perform the backup. These programs usually give you a choice between several different types of backup, as described

Table 9-3 Backup Utilities

TYPE OF BACKUP	DESCRIPTION	ADVANTAGES	DISADVANTAGES
Full backup	Copies all of the files in a computer	Fastest recovery method, because all files are backed up	Longest backup time
Differential backup	Copies only files that have changed since the last full backup	Fast backup method; Requires minimal storage space to back up	Recovery is time consuming because the last full backup plus the differential backup are needed to recreate a file
Incremental backup	Copies only files that have changed since the last full or incremental backup	Fastest backup method, because only most recent changes are backed up; Requires minimal storage space to back up	Recovery is most time consuming because the last full backup and all incremental backups are needed to recreate a file
Selective backup	Allows users to back up specific files	Fast backup method; Provides great flexibility	Difficult to manage individual backups; Least manageable of the backup methods

Businesses and home computer users can perform four different types of backup, as outlined above.

in Table 9-3. Windows includes a backup utility with many of these features; for a program with more features, you can buy a backup software package that automates the backup process, in case you forget to back files up regularly.

Backup procedures specify a regular plan of copying and storing important data and program files. Generally, you should perform a full backup at regular intervals, such as at the end of each week and at the end of the month. Between full backups, you can perform differential or incremental backups. Figure 9-10 illustrates a sample approach a company might follow for backing up its computers for one month. Whatever backup procedures a company adopts, they should be stated clearly, documented in writing, and followed consistently.

April 2008

MONDAY	TUESDAY	WEDNESDAY	THURSDAY	FRIDAY	SAT/SUN
29 DAILY INCREMENTAL	30 DAILY INCREMENTAL	31 END OF MONTH FULL BACKUP	1 DAILY INCREMENTAL	2 WEEKLY FULL BACKUP	3/4
5 DAILY INCREMENTAL	6 DAILY INCREMENTAL	7 DAILY INCREMENTAL	8 DAILY INCREMENTAL	9 WEEKLY FULL BACKUP	10/11
12 DAILY INCREMENTAL	13 DAILY INCREMENTAL	14 DAILY INCREMENTAL	15 DAILY INCREMENTAL	16 WEEKLY FULL BACKUP	17/18
19 DAILY INCREMENTAL	20 DAILY INCREMENTAL	21 DAILY INCREMENTAL	22 DAILY INCREMENTAL	23 WEEKLY FULL BACKUP	24/25
26 DAILY INCREMENTAL	27 DAILY INCREMENTAL	28 DAILY INCREMENTAL	29 DAILY INCREMENTAL	30/1 END OF MONTH FULL BACKUP	2/3

Figure 9-10 This calendar illustrates a monthly backup procedure that uses different backup methods. This combination of full and incremental backups provides an efficient way to protect data.

Defining a Disaster Recovery Plan

A **disaster recovery plan** is a written plan describing the steps a company would take to restore computer operations in the event of a disaster. Although a disaster may seem an unlikely occurrence, the aftermath of the terrorist attacks that destroyed the World Trade Center in New York and significantly damaged the Pentagon in Washington, D.C., left dozens of businesses and schools seriously considering their disaster recovery plans. Many of the larger companies within the World Trade Center, including Morgan Stanley and Smith Barney, had disaster recovery plans in place with their data being backed up and held at off-site locations, as well an alternate network. Businesses without a solid disaster recovery plan, however, may not be so lucky. According to Gartner Group, two out of five enterprises that experience a disaster, such as a hurricane, fire, earthquake, or terrorist attack, go out of business within five years.

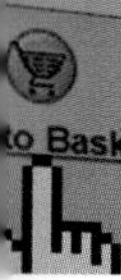

A disaster recovery plan contains four components (Table 9-4):

- The *emergency plan* specifies the steps to be taken immediately after a disaster strikes.
- The *backup plan* stipulates how a company uses backup files and equipment to resume information processing.
- The *recovery plan* identifies the actions to be taken to restore full information-processing operations.
- The *test plan* contains information for simulating disasters and recording an organization's ability to recover.

Companies may maintain a *hot site*, which is a separate facility that mirrors the systems and operations of the main site, or a *cold site*, a site that mirrors the main site, but does not become operational until the main site is unavailable. Typically, a business has a contract with a disaster recovery service company that offers hot and cold site services with a monthly service charge; these companies also may offer backup services. In another approach, one company has a cold site which actually is a converted barn on the property of the president; the barn is set up with computers and networking so that the technology team and other essential workers can move there in any emergency. When using a cold site, some time elapses between the disaster and when the cold site becomes functional.

Table 9-4 Disaster Recovery Plan

COMPONENT	DESCRIPTION
Emergency plan	Specifies the steps to be taken immediately after a disaster strikes. Should contain the following information: ■ Names and telephone numbers of people and organizations to notify (e.g., management, fire department, police department) ■ Procedures to follow with the computer equipment, including shutdown, power shut-off, file removal ■ Employee evacuation procedures ■ Return procedures — that is, who can reenter the facility and what actions they are to perform
Backup plan	Specifies how the company will use backup files and equipment to start information processing. Also identifies: ■ Location of backup data, supplies, and equipment ■ Location of an alternate computer facility in the event a company's normal location is destroyed or unusable ■ Personnel responsible for gathering backup resources and transporting them to the alternate computer facility ■ A schedule indicating the order in which and approximate time by which each application should be up and running
Recovery plan	Identifies the actions to be taken to restore full information-processing operations. May involve creating separate committees to handle different areas of recovery (e.g., hardware, software, facilities).
Test plan	Contains information for simulating disasters and recording an organization's ability to recover. After running a simulated disaster, the test plan should be updated to include information not specified in the plan.

A disaster recovery plan contains four key components, as described above.

Protecting Against Unauthorized Access and Use

For some businesses, information is their most valuable asset. Safeguarding that information from unauthorized access is one of their greatest concerns. Companies and individuals can take several measures to protect against unauthorized access and use. Many systems implement access controls using a two-phase process called identification and authentication. **Identification** verifies that an individual is a valid user. **Authentication** verifies that the individual is the person he or she claims to be. Other types of controls include firewalls, intrusion detection software, usernames and passwords, possessed objects, biometric devices, callback systems, and audit trails, which are reviewed in the following section.

FIREWALLS A **firewall** is a security system consisting of hardware and/or software that prevents unauthorized access to data, information, and storage media on a network (Figure 9-11). Companies use firewalls to deny network access to outsiders and to restrict employee access to sensitive data, such as payroll or personnel records.

Large companies often route all of their communications through a proxy server. A **proxy server** is a server outside of the company's network that controls which communications pass into the company's network. That is, the proxy server carefully screens all incoming and outgoing messages. Proxy servers use a variety of screening techniques. Some check the domain name IP address of a message for legitimacy. Others require that messages have digital signatures.

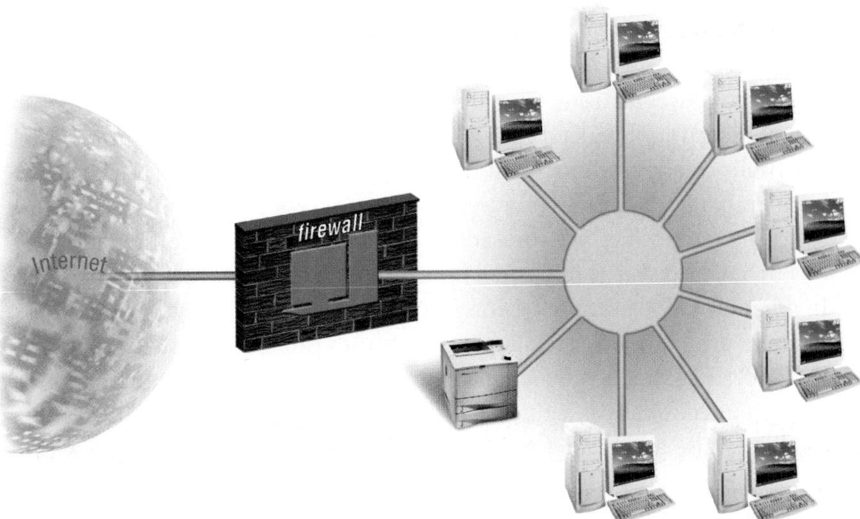

Figure 9-11 A firewall helps to prevent unauthorized access to data, information, and storage media on a network.

A **personal firewall** is a utility program that detects and protects a personal computer and its data from unauthorized intrusions. Personal firewalls constantly monitor all transmissions to and from the computer and inform you of any attempted intrusion. Some operating systems, such as Windows XP and Vista, include personal firewalls. For added protection, you can purchase standalone personal firewall software. Table 9-5 lists several popular personal firewall software programs.

Table 9-5

- BlackICE PC Protection
- McAfee Firewall
- Norton Personal Firewall
- Sygate Personal Firewall
- Tiny Personal Firewall
- ZoneAlarm

Popular personal firewall products.

If your personal computer is connected to the Internet for long periods of time, especially if you have a high-speed connection such as a cable or DSL connection, you should consider a personal firewall. You also might want to consider a personal firewall if you connect to the Internet via a public wireless network, such as Wi-Fi hotspots found in airports and even parks (Figure 9-12). Although some do, many of these public wireless networks do not provide firewalls or other security measures to ensure your data transmissions are safe. Because wireless networks use over-the-air communications that may be intercepted by packet sniffers and other devices, you should use a personal firewall while connecting to the Internet over a public wireless network.

Figure 9-12 Some cities have installed wireless access points in parks to allow users to connect to the Internet using their laptops. If you connect to the Internet via a public wireless network, such as Wi-Fi hotspots, you should consider using a personal firewall.

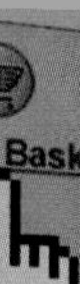

INTRUSION DETECTION SOFTWARE To provide even more protection against potential hackers, larger companies sometimes use intrusion detection software to identify possible security breaks. Intrusion detection software automatically analyzes all network traffic, assesses system vulnerabilities, identifies any unauthorized access (intrusions), and notifies network administrators of suspicious behavior patterns or system breaches.

In addition to intrusion detection software, some companies have programs called honeypots. A **honeypot** is a computer system, or software simulating a computer system, which intentionally is set up with security holes designed to entice an intruder to hack a computer (the term was coined by Clifford Stoll in *Cuckoo's Egg*, his story of hacker tracking). Honeypots divert a hacker from real systems, while allowing a company to learn more about how hackers are exploiting the network. They also enable the company to catch hackers who have been doing damage elsewhere on the network.

Although the use of honeypots is accepted widely, the legality of using a honeypot and monitoring every keystroke has not yet been explored fully. Monitoring – federal criminal law calls it interception of communications – carries up to five years in prison under the Federal Wiretap Act. In most cases, honeypots fall into the exemptions outlined by the law, but some remain potentially illegal.

USERNAMES AND PASSWORDS As you learned in Chapter 7, one of the most basic ways to gain unauthorized access to a computer, network, or user account is to obtain authorized usernames and passwords. Some systems assign a username or user ID to each user. For example, a school may have you use your student identification number as your user ID. With other systems, such as most commercial Web sites, you can select your own user name. Many users select a combination of their first and last names. For example, a user named Cleo Bonner might choose CBonner as her user name. Most systems require that users select their own passwords. In some cases, users choose passwords that are easy for someone else to guess: their birthday; the name of their daughter, wife, or pet; or simply the word, password.

Chapter 7 reviewed the numerous methods that exist for someone to obtain your username, password, or both, including shoulder surfing, dumpster diving, social engineering, and the use of packet sniffers. Given all the possible ways another user can obtain your password, you should select a password carefully and try to create one that no one can guess. Longer passwords provide greater security than shorter ones. As shown in Figure 9-13, each character added to a password significantly increases the number of possible combinations and the length of time it might take for a human or a computer to guess the password. The password should include letters and numbers and, if possible, be at least eight characters long. Some organizations now require users to set "strong passwords" in order to gain access to secure areas. A **strong password** consists of letters, numbers and special characters, and is at least eight characters long. Some systems even allow the use of a space, so you can set a "pass phrase" with two or more words to add some complexity. Ideally, you also should be able to type your password without looking at the keyboard. For more tips on choosing a good password, refer to Table 7-6 in Chapter 7.

PASSWORD PROTECTION

		AVERAGE TIME TO DISCOVER	
Number of Characters	**Possible Combinations**	**Human**	**Computer**
1	36	3 minutes	.000018 second
2	1,300	2 hours	.00065 second
3	47,000	3 days	.02 second
4	1,700,000	3 months	1 second
5	60,000,000	10 years	30 seconds
10	3,700,000,000,000,000	580 million years	59 years

- *Possible characters include the letters A–Z and numbers 0–9*
- *Human discovery assumes 1 try every 10 seconds*
- *Computer discovery assumes one million tries per second*
- *Average time assumes the password would be discovered in approximately half the time it would take to try all possible combinations*

Figure 9-13 This table shows the effect of increasing the length of a password that consists of letters and numbers. The longer the password, the more effort required to discover it. Long passwords, however, are more difficult for users to remember.

POSSESSED OBJECTS A **possessed object** is any item that you must carry to gain access to a facility or computer. Your ATM card, for example, is a possessed object that allows you to access your bank account via an automated teller machine. Hotels often use card keys to allow guests to access their rooms. Many companies and even schools also use

possessed objects, such as badges or cards, to allow access to a building or specific areas within a building. Possessed objects, like your ATM card, often are used in conjunction with a password or PIN to provide an additional level of security.

BIOMETRIC DEVICES A **biometric device** authenticates a person's identity by translating a personal characteristic, such as facial features, the pattern of the iris in your eye, fingerprints, your signature, or the sound of your voice, into a digital code (Figure 9-14). When you attempt to access an area, a biometric device reads your personal characteristic and then compares it with the digital code stored in the computer. If the digital code in the computer does not match the personal characteristic code, the computer denies access to the individual.

Biometric devices are gaining popularity as a security precaution because they are virtually foolproof methods of identification and authentication. Users can forget their usernames and passwords. Possessed objects can be lost, copied, duplicated, or stolen. Personal characteristics, by contrast, are unique and cannot be forgotten and misplaced.

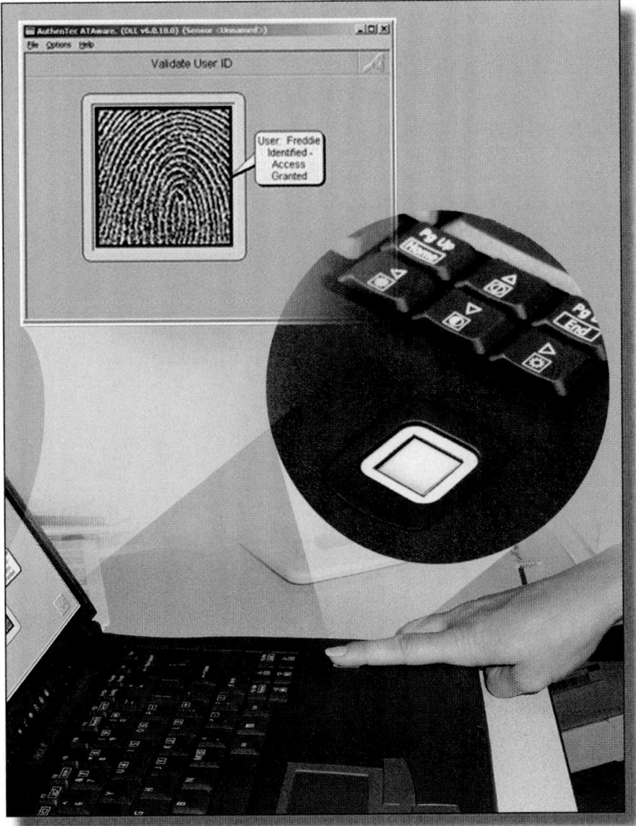

Figure 9-14 Some personal computers use fingerprint scanners to authenticate that the correct user is trying to access the computer.

Biometric devices do have some disadvantages. For example, if you cut your finger, a fingerprint scanner might reject you as a legitimate user. Biometric devices also can be expensive, although digital fingerprint readers for use with a personal computer can cost less than $100. Biometric devices also raise some concerns that having biometric information stored in a database could lead to abuses in personal freedom and privacy.

CALLBACK SYSTEM With a **callback system**, you connect to a computer only after the computer calls you back at a previously established phone number. Some networks use callback systems as an access control or as a way to authenticate mobile users. To initiate a call from a callback system, you call a computer and enter a username and password. If these entries are valid, the computer instructs you to hang up and then calls you back at the authorized number. A callback system provides an added layer of security. Even if a person steals or guesses a username or password, that person also must be at the authorized telephone number to access the computer system.

Callback systems work best for users who regularly work at the same remote location, such as at home or at a branch office. Users who need to access a computer from different locations and telephone numbers can use a callback system, but they must go through security procedures to change the callback number stored by the callback system each time they move to a new location.

AUDIT TRAILS A computer should maintain an **audit trail** or **log** that records in a file both successful and unsuccessful attempts to access the system. An unsuccessful access attempt could result from something as simple as mistyping your password, or it could stem from a hacker trying thousands of passwords.

Companies typically investigate unsuccessful access attempts immediately to ensure they are not intentional breaches of security. They also should review successful access for irregularities, such as the use of the computer after normal hours or from remote locations.

Protecting Against Hardware Theft

To reduce the chance of theft, companies and schools use a variety of security measures. Physical access controls, such as locked doors and windows, usually are adequate to protect computer equipment. Many businesses and schools, and some homeowners, install alarm systems for additional security. School computer labs and other areas with large numbers of semifrequent computer users often attach physical security devices such as cables that lock the equipment to a desk or a

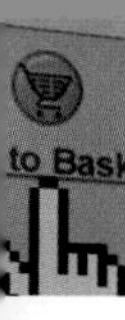

cabinet. Small locking devices also can secure access to a hard disk, CD or DVD drive.

As previously noted, users of smaller computers – laptops, notebook computers, or PDAs – are the most susceptible to hardware theft. It is estimated that more than 500,000 notebook computers are stolen each year, because the size and weight of these computers makes them easy targets. Mobile users must take special care to protect their equipment. Common sense is a start: you never should leave a notebook computer or PDA unattended in a public place such as an airport or restaurant, or out in the open, such as on the seat of a car.

Some users attach a physical device, such as a cable, to lock a mobile computer temporarily to a stationary object. For example, at a hotel, you can lock your notebook computer to a desk or table when you leave the room. Other mobile users install a mini-security system in the notebook computer that shuts down the computer or sounds an alarm if the computer moves outside a specified distance.

Protecting Online Security and Privacy

Safeguarding your security and privacy online involves using tools and technologies, such as encryption

Table 9-6

TIPS FOR PROTECTING ONLINE PRIVACY

Only give out information that is essential.	Do not provide your name, mailing address, e-mail address, or telephone number unless it is necessary. Examples include commercial sites that ask you to fill out surveys when you make your first purchase, or sites offering free services such as Web-based e-mail that may also request information about your income and lifestyle. If you are unsure about the credibility of a Web site, especially a Web site of an online-only firm, then do not provide any information about yourself or complete any financial transactions with that site.
Do not reveal personal information inadvertently.	Your browser can reveal your personal details, without you knowing, unless you change your browser settings. In your browser's Setup, Options, or Preferences menus, you can see that your browser includes information such as your name and e-mail address, which Web sites can read when you visit (Figure 9-15). If you do not use the e-mail component of your browser, remove your name and e-mail address from the Account Settings for e-mail.
Mind your cookies.	Change your browser's privacy settings to alert you to or to block all cookies. Consider using a cookie manager software program that selectively blocks cookies.
Limit the personal information you post on the Web or share with others online.	Avoid having your home address, telephone number, or personal e-mail address posted on the Web, either in a chat room, Web page, database, or Web site that can be accessed by the general public. If you must post this information, use a made-up address or PO box, instead of your home address. Instead of a personal e-mail address, you can use the address from a free Web-based e-mail account.
Be aware of Web security issues.	Never submit a credit card number or other financial data over a connection that is not secure. Use encryption if you are sharing sensitive information with others via e-mail. Run a program to find spyware and identify Web bugs on your computer or on Web sites.
Keep your primary e-mail address clean.	Instead of using your main personal e-mail account to post to newsgroups, mailing lists, or chat rooms or when ordering products over the Web, use a "disposable" e-mail account, such as a free Web-based e-mail account. If these sites start to send volumes of spam, your primary e-mail account should remain largely unaffected — and you can discontinue using the disposable e-mail account and find another one.
Do not reply to spammers.	If you are spammed, do not waste time replying with whatever unsubscribe instructions are listed in the e-mail. Doing so only tells spammers that the e-mail address is valid and active — and you likely will find your e-mail address on the lists of countless others spammers in short order.
Read privacy polices and review security seals.	Review the privacy policy of Web sites that you visit frequently, especially ones where you are providing your personal information to determine how that information might be used. Check to see if the Web site backs up their privacy policy with a seal program such as TRUSTe or BBBonline, which provide a baseline of privacy standards.

Following these tips from the Electronic Frontier Foundation (EFF) and airsafe.com can help you maintain your privacy online, by limiting the amount of personal information you share and limiting other's access to your private data.

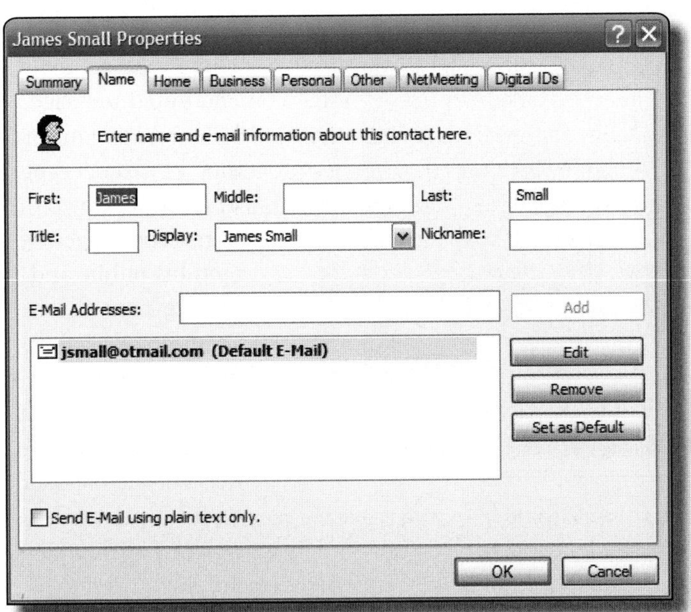

Figure 9-15 Your browser can reveal your personal details, such as your name and e-mail address, which Web sites can read when you visit. If you do not use the e-mail component of your browser, remove your name and e-mail address from the Account Settings for e-mail.

and digital certificates and cookie managers, as well as smart computing practices, such as limiting the personal information you share on Web sites. Table 9-6 lists several important tips on how to maintain security and privacy while online; this section reviews several of these tips in more detail.

USING DATA ENCRYPTION As you have learned, information theft occurs when someone steals personal or confidential information. The use of access controls, such as usernames/passwords or biometric devices, can help protect information stored on computers located on a company's premises. Information transmitted over networks, however, has a higher degree of risk, because unscrupulous users can intercept it during transmission.

To keep users from reading intercepted data, many companies and individuals rely on encryption. Encryption is the process of converting readable data into unreadable characters to prevent unauthorized access. To read encrypted data, the recipient must **decrypt**, or decipher, the data into a readable form. In the encryption process, the unencrypted, readable data is called **plaintext**, while the encrypted data is called **ciphertext**.

Many methods of data encryption exist. Table 9-7 shows some examples of simple encryption methods. Figure 9-16 on the next page shows the contents of a sample encrypted file. An encryption key often uses more than one of these methods, such as a combination or transposition and substitution along with a complex formula to rearrange the characters.

The two basic types of encryption keys are private key and public key. With **private key encryption**, also called **symmetric key encryption**, both the originator and recipient use the same secret key to encrypt and decrypt the data. **Public key encryption**, also called **asymmetric key encryption**, uses two encryption keys: a public key and a private key. Public key encryption software generates both your private key and public key. A message encrypted with your public key only can be decrypted with your private key, and vice versa. The public key is made known to those with whom you communicate.

Table 9-7 Methods of Encryption

NAME	*METHOD*	*PLAINTEXT*	*CIPHERTEXT*	*EXPLANATION*
Transposition	Switch the order of characters	PASSWORD	APSSOWDR	Adjacent characters swapped
Substitution	Replace characters with other characters	ACCESS	DRROYY	Each letter replaced with another
Expansion	Insert characters between existing characters	VIRUS	XVXIXRXUXS	Letter X inserted before each character
Compaction	Remove characters and store elsewhere	IDENTIFICATION	IDNTFIATON	Every third letter removed (E, I, C, I)

This table shows four simple methods of encryption, which is the process of translating plaintext into ciphertext. Most encryption programs use a combination of these four methods, along with other formulas.

Figure 9-16 A sample encrypted file, referred to as ciphertext.

For example, public keys are posted on a Web page or e-mailed. A central administrator can publish a list of public keys on a public-key server. The private key, by contrast, is to be kept confidential.

To send an encrypted e-mail message with public key encryption, the sender uses the receiver's public key to encrypt the message. Then, the receiver uses his or her private key to decrypt the message (Figure 9-17). For example, if Sylvia wants to send Doug an encrypted message, she would use Doug's public key to encrypt the message. When Doug receives the encrypted message, he would use his private key to decrypt it. Doug's encryption software generated his public and private keys. Sylvia used Doug's public key to encrypt the message. Thus, only Doug will be able to decrypt the message with his private key.

RSA encryption is a powerful public key encryption technology used to encrypt data transmitted over the Internet. Many software and public encryption programs, such as Pretty Good Privacy (PGP) and newer versions of Netscape Navigator and Microsoft Internet Explorer, use RSA technology,

SECURING INTERNET TRANSACTIONS To provide secure data transmission, many Web browsers use encryption. Some browsers offer a protection level

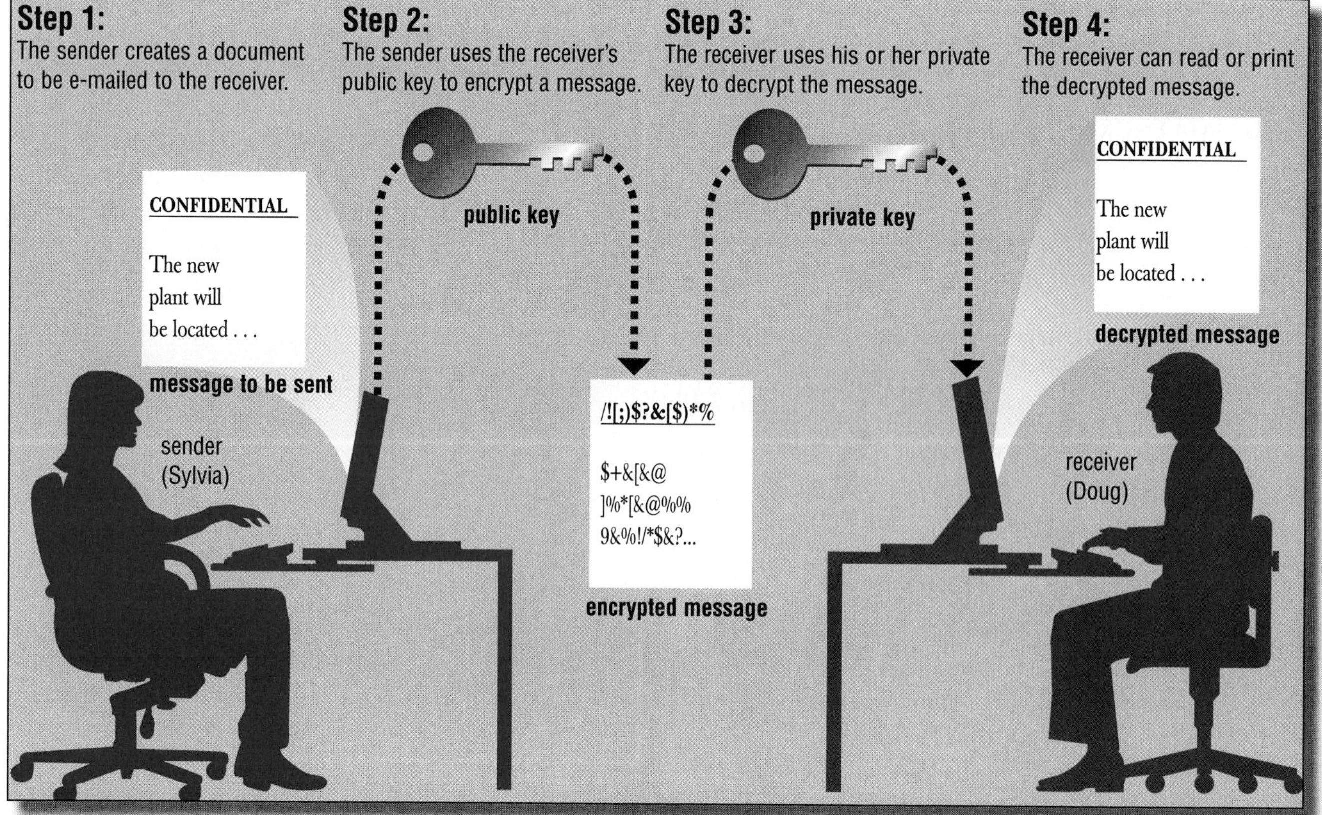

Figure 9-17 How public key encryption works.

known as 40-bit encryption. Many also offer 128-bit encryption, which is an even higher level of protection because it has a longer encryption key. Applications requiring more security, such as banks, brokerage firms, or online retailers that use credit card or other financial information, require 128-bit encryption.

A Web site that uses encryption techniques to secure its data is known as a **secure site.** Secure sites use digital certificates along with a security protocol. Two popular security protocols are Secure Sockets Layer and Secure HTTP. Credit card transactions sometimes use the Secure Electronics Transactions Specification.

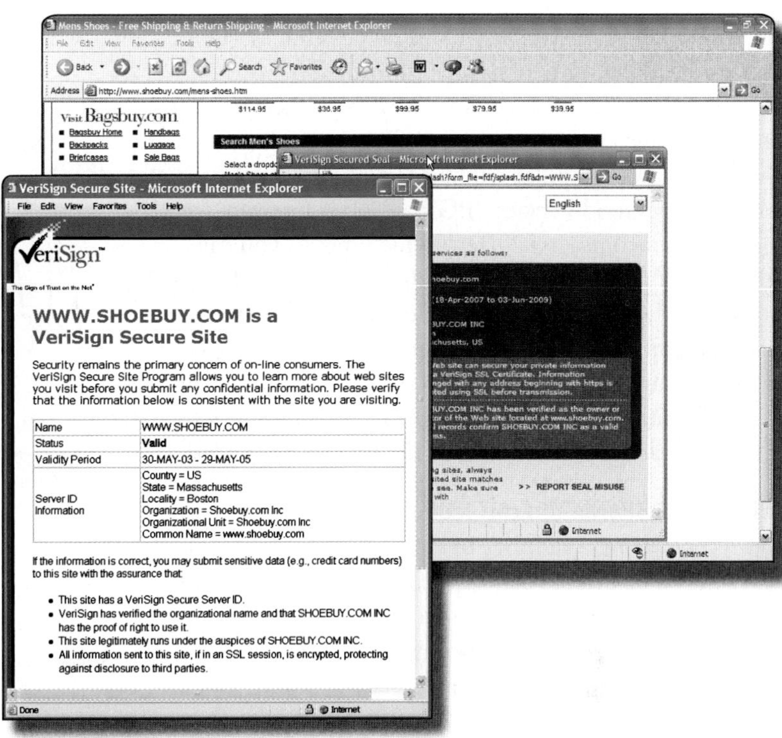

Figure 9-18 Verisign is a certificate authority that issues and verifies digital certificates.

A **digital certificate** is a notice that guarantees a user or a Web site is legitimate. E-commerce applications commonly use digital certificates. A **certificate authority (CA)** is an authorized person or company that issues and verifies digital certificates. Users apply for a digital certificate from a CA. A digital certificate typically contains information such as the user's name, the issuing CA's name and signature, and the serial number of the certificate. The information in a digital certificate is encrypted.

Secure Sockets Layer (**SSL***)* provides encryption of all data that passes between a client and an Internet server. SSL requires that the server have a digital certificate (Figure 9-18). Once the server has a digital certificate, the Web browser communicates securely with the client. Web addresses of pages that use SSL typically begin with https, instead of http (Figure 9-19). SSL is available in both 40-bit and 128-bit encryption.

Secure HTTP (S-HTTP) allows users to choose an encryption scheme for data that passes between a client and a server. With S-HTTP, the client and server both must have digital certificates. S-HTTP is more difficult to use than SSL, but it is more secure. Applications that must verify the authenticity of a client, such as online banking, use S-HTTP.

The **Secure Electronics Transactions (SET) Specification** uses encryption to secure financial transactions on the Internet, such as payment by credit card. To make purchases through a Web site that uses SET, users typically download a *wallet program,* which stores their credit card information on their computer, and then select the wallet as the method of payment. The SET Specification is quite complex, making it slow on some computers.

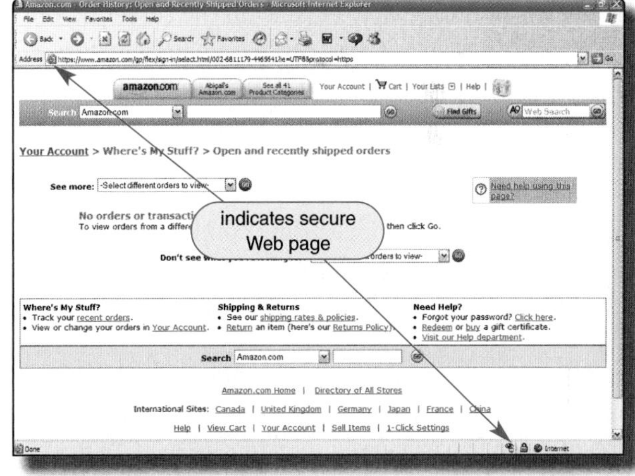

Figure 9-19 Web addresses of secure Web pages often begin with https instead of http and show a secure padlock icon at the bottom of the page. Double-clicking the padlock icon will display information about the digital certificate for the Web site.

SECURING E-MAIL MESSAGES If an e-mail message contains personal or confidential information, you should protect the message. Two ways to protect an e-mail message are to encrypt it and to sign it digitally. One of the more popular e-mail encryption programs is called Pretty Good Privacy (PGP). PGP is freeware for personal, noncommercial users, which means you can download it at no cost (Figure 9-20).

A digital signature is an encoded, or encrypted, code that a person, Web site, or company attaches to an electronic message or document to verify the identity of the sender. Digital signatures help prevent e-mail forgery by verifying that the content of an e-mail has not changed.

Figure 9-20 An encrypted e-mail message is scrambled and unreadable until it is decrypted.

REDUCING SPAM You can reduce the amount of spam you receive using a number of techniques. Some e-mail programs have built-in settings that allow you to specify junk e-mail address or block e-mail addresses from spammers, and then automatically delete the spam. You also can sign up for e-mail filtering services from your ISP. **E-mail filtering** is a service that blocks e-mail messages from designated sources, so they never get to your Inbox. These services typically collect the spam in a central location that users can view at any time. An alternative to e-mail filters is to purchase an **anti-spam program**, such as MailWasher or McAfee SpamKiller, that allows you to review e-mails on the server before you download them so you can delete spam before spending time downloading it. Unfortunately, the programs sometimes delete real e-mail messages as well.

Even with these programs it can be hard to identify all spam because, using special software, spammers can generate millions of e-mails using combinations of letters and numbers, such as tsa79, placed in front of the domain name portion (such as @aol.com) of an e-mail address.

Also, the use of image-based spam, which contains unwanted content inside graphics, is on the rise. This type of spam is particularly difficult for spam filters to detect because the message is embedded in graphic elements that are programmed to randomize as e-mail messages are sent by the millions from the spammer. As a result, the message looks unique to the spam filter each time it's delivered.

LIMITING PERSONAL INFORMATION SHARING Maintaining privacy is an important issue for most Web users. Organizations such as the Electronic Privacy Information Center (EPIC) and the Center for Democracy and Technology (CDT) have Web sites dedicated to informing consumers about privacy issues. As a result of the influence of EPIC and CDT, the U.S. Senate is considering a new law, called the Online Personal Privacy Act. The law would focus on four main principles:

- *Notice*: Web sites must give clear notice as to what information they collect, how that data will be used, and whether it will be released to third parties.
- *Consent*: Web sites must get consumers to specifically opt in, or give consent to, having their personally identifiable information collected.
- *Opt out and Opt in*: Companies must offer a way for consumers to opt out, or refuse consent, before any personally identifiable information is collected. Consumers would be given opt-in protection for sensitive personal information (such as financial and health information, ethnicity, religious preferences) and opt-out protection for nonsensitive personal information (such as your name and address and marketplace purchases).
- *Permanence*: If a new company takes control of a Web site as a result of merger or acquisition, the consumer's original opt-in or opt-out preference remains in effect.

While Web site owners have a responsibility to post and adhere to privacy policies, consumers should make efforts to protect their own privacy. Many Web users take little time to consider who is collecting data about their online behavior, for what purpose they are using the data, if they sell the data to other companies, and if they can match it to personally identifiable information.

Of particular concern is the growing use of social networks such as MySpace and Facebook, where millions of registered users document their lives for others to see. Employers also use these types of sites to perform background checks on potential new hires in addition to the more traditional means of learning about job candidates' pasts.

When you register for a Web site, review their privacy policy and opt-out and opt-in polices. As you enter information into the form, read the language carefully to ensure you fully understand whether you must opt out or opt in to ensure your data is not shared. Also, do not share your personal information too quickly: if a form only has two required fields, do not complete the other fields on the form. If a Web site asks you to participate in a survey, decline the offer.

If you are purchasing a product, you will have to give accurate billing information. On a free site, however, if you are not comfortable providing the data requested, you probably can find a site that offers similar services and information, but does not require so much information. Some suggest that, instead of entering your personal data, you enter a fake name or address (unless the site terms specifically state you must provide correct information). Others argue that this practice is unethical and in some places illegal. If you do enter a fake address, however, use an obviously fake address and do not use someone else's real address.

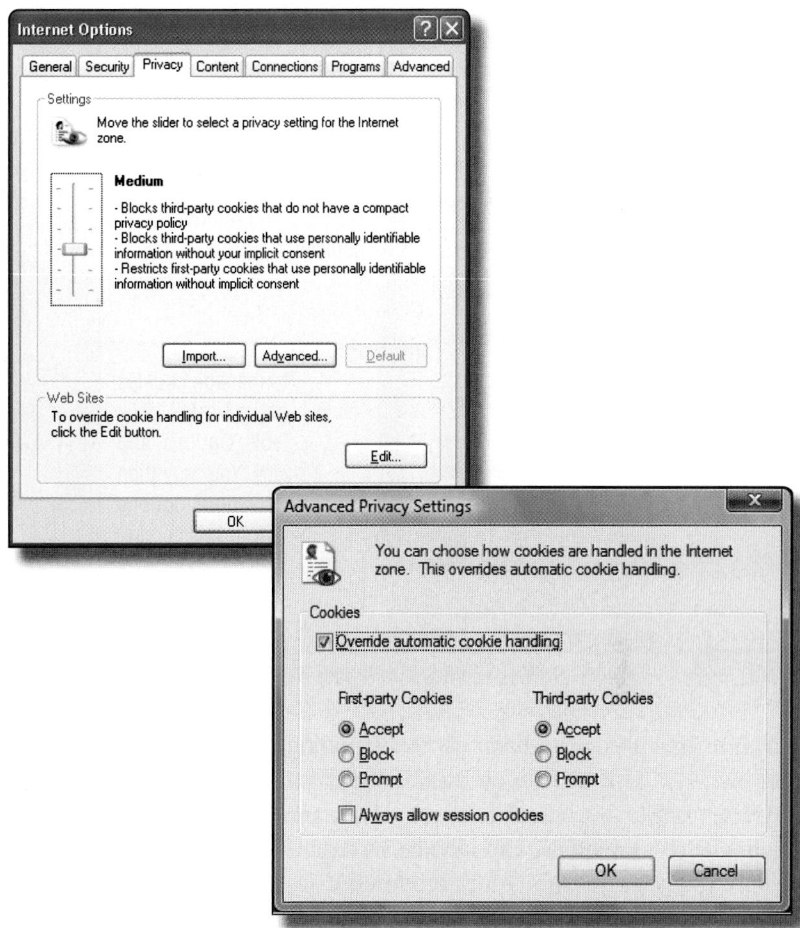

Figure 9-21 You can change your browser's privacy settings to specify whether you accept all cookies automatically, accept third-party or first-party cookies only, or refuse all cookies.

MANAGING COOKIES, SPYWARE, AND WEB BUGS

To reduce any privacy risk posted by cookies, you can change your browser's privacy settings to specify whether you accept all cookies automatically, accept temporary or first-party cookies only, or refuse all cookies (Figure 9-21). You also can delete all cookies from your hard drive, using features in your Web browser (Figure 9-22).

Keep in mind that, when changing browser privacy settings, you might not want to refuse all cookies. Some Web sites require the use of cookies; if you do not accept cookies, you will not be able to purchase merchandise, tickets, or services or benefit from customized content. If you delete all cookies from your computer, you may find that your automatic log in and personal preference data are not available when you visit a Web site.

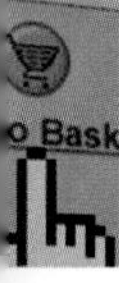

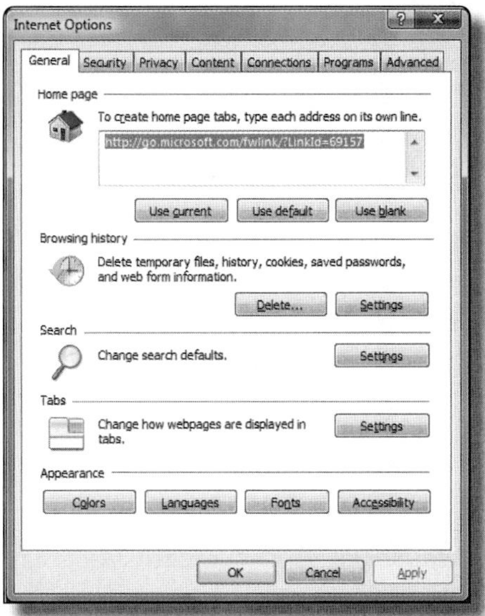

To delete cookies using Internet Explorer 7, click Tools, Internet Options, then Delete under Browsing history. The Delete Cookies button then lets you remove all cookies.

To manage cookies using Firefox, click Tools, Options, and Privacy. You may then choose various options from this screen.

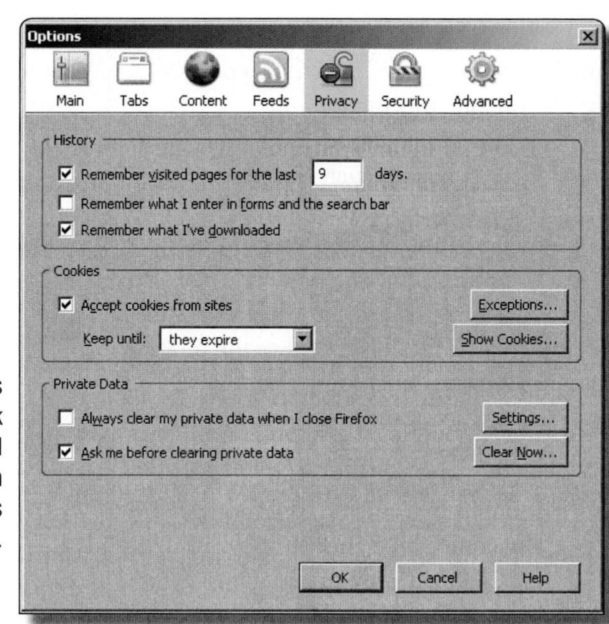

Figure 9-22 Deleting cookies from a computer hard drive requires only a few simple steps.

To ensure you do not have spyware running on your computer, check your computer for spyware using a software program such as Ad-Aware. Ad-Aware, which is a free download, can identify and remove spyware and adware from your computer. It scans all of the drives on your computer for adware and other types of spyware and then safely removes the software. The programming languages, Java, JavaScript, and ActiveX, also can be used for spyware. You can change your browser's settings to turn off support for these languages; if a Web site you trust and want to use requires the languages, you can turn them back on. Ad-aware also provides protection from Web bugs, as do software programs such as Bugnosis. Your best best may be to install a program that combines multiple security features to manage your privacy risk. Table 9-8 lists some of the more popular programs on the market today.

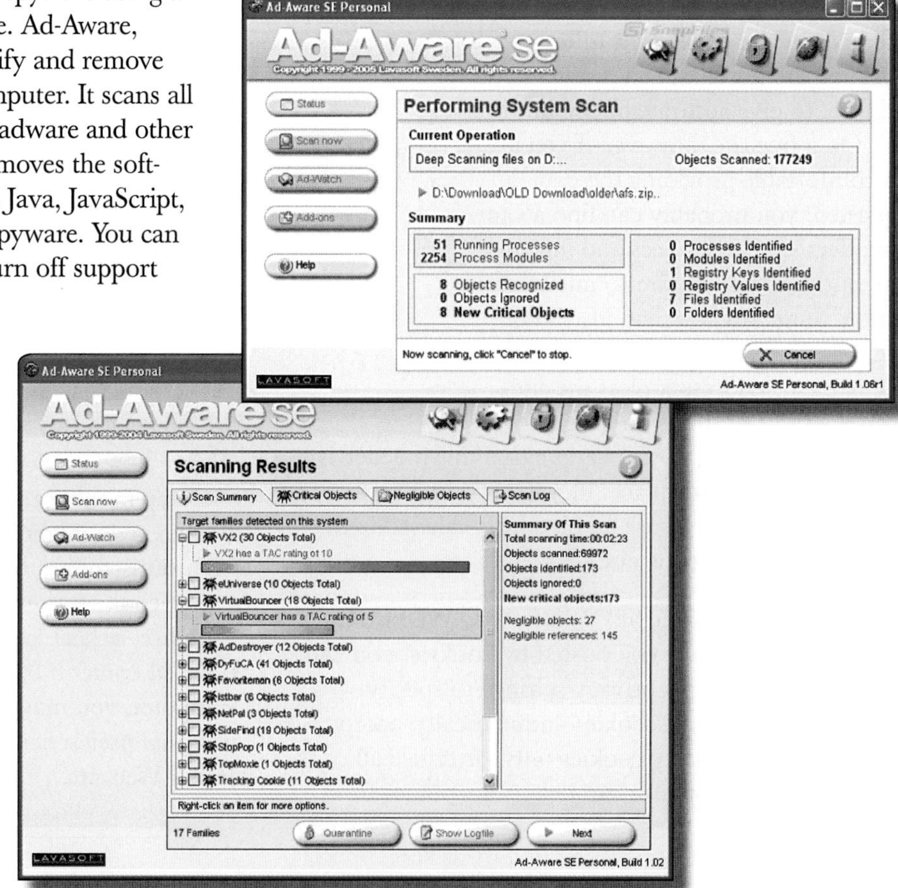

Figure 9-23 Ad-Aware, which is a free download, can identify and remove spyware and adware from your computer. After scanning all of your system drives to identify tracking cookies and spyware, Ad-Aware displays a list of files and allows you to delete all of the files from your system.

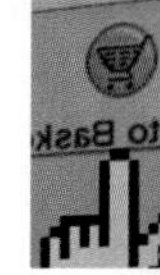

Table 9-8

PROGRAM NAME
ZoneAlarm Anti-Spyware
Norton AntiVirus
Trend Micro AntiVirus plus AntiSpyware
Windows Defender
McAfee VirusScan Plus
Webroot Spy Sweeper with Anti-Virus
Spyware Doctor
Spybot – Search & Destroy

Several full-featured system security programs are available today for managing privacy risks.

SECURITY AND PRIVACY IN THE WORKPLACE

Just about anywhere you go today in public, a surveillance camera may be watching you. Surveillance cameras are used to monitor highway traffic, airports, banks, retail stores, and even many workplaces. As you learned in Chapter 1, employee monitoring involves the use of computers to observe, record, and review an employee's use of a computer. Employee monitoring and surveillance also involves the use of video cameras and other technologies to keep close watch over employees on the job. The use of both types of supervision has increased in the last few years, as the costs of the technology come down and the number of employees with Internet access continues to rise. This section reviews the use of employee monitoring and surveillance tools, as well as the legal rights of employers and employees.

Employee Monitoring and Surveillance

According to a 2005 study by the American Management Association (AMA), 76 percent of major U.S. firms monitor workers' Web site connections. Thirty-six percent of employers track content, keystrokes, and time spent at the keyboard, while another 50% store and review employees' computer files. E-mail is also stored and reviewed by 55% of firms surveyed. Twenty-five percent of companies said they had fired employees for misuse of telecommunication equipment and 26% have fired employees for misusing the Internet.

With more than 65% of the U.S. adult population online each day, employers are concerned about and challenged by issues such as slowdowns in employee productivity, and even legal liability when an employee uses corporate networks to pirate software or send harassing e-mails.

Companies can take several measures to prevent unauthorized use of corporate computing resources. At a minimum, they should have an acceptable use policy (AUP) that outlines the activities for which computers may and may not be used. A company's AUP also should specify the acceptable use of computers by employees for personal reasons. Some companies prohibit such use entirely. Others allow personal use on an employee's own time, such as a lunch hour. Whatever the policy, a company should document it and explain it to employees. The AMA survey revealed that 84% of employers now have established policies regarding e-mail use and 81% have policies covering Internet activity. With the growth of instant messaging and blogs, 42% of companies have policies regarding IM, and 20% document acceptable use of personal blogs on company time.

To ensure that employees are abiding by the acceptable use policy, companies may use employee monitoring and surveillance. Employee monitoring can track communications such as e-mail messages, the Web sites an employee visits, and the amount of time an employee spends away from the computer. Keystroke monitoring also can be used to measure an employee's productivity by counting the employee's keystrokes per hour.

Many software programs, called **employee Internet management (EIM) software**, exist to help employers monitor their employees' Internet use, block Web sites, and report on possible infractions. EIM products like Websense Enterprise allow companies to

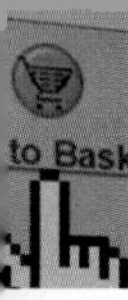

limit which sites employees can access; others capture employee Web activity and generate reports to show where that activity violates a company's acceptable use policy. E-mail monitoring software, such as MIMESweeper, filters through e-mail, searching for keywords or phrases that are unacceptable or might be grounds for legal action.

During the time when employees are away from their desks, video cameras and computers are used to keep track of their actions, whether in the stock room or in the lunch room. The increasingly small size of digital video cameras allows them to be installed almost anywhere, including in smoke detectors. The recorded video can be stored on a regular VCR or a digital video recorder (DVR) for easy review by managers. The video also can be streamed over the Internet for real-time monitoring (Figure 9-24).

Legal Rights of Employers and Employees

While employees often are upset to find their workday is monitored at and away from their desks, employers are focused on using employee monitoring and surveillance tools to ensure network security; manage productivity; make certain employees are safe; and guarantee that employees are not using computers in a way that might damage the company's reputation.

As you learned in Chapter 1, the law establishes that it is legal for your employer to monitor your use of their computer equipment and your time at the workplace. Video surveillance also is legal, in most cases. Some states do have laws to recognize a general right to privacy and certain states have passed laws limiting an employer's rights to videotape in places where employees should reasonably be able to expect privacy, such as the bathroom. Privacy and workers' rights advocates say the prevalence of cameras is a complaint of many workers. Employers, however, typically win out in the courts when they claim the use of cameras strictly is to limit criminal activity – not to monitor an employee's productivity to determine if he or she is worthy of a pay raise.

In the end, under current law, your right to privacy at work has definite limits. If you send an e-mail from a work computer, your employer has a legal right to review its contents. The Web sites you visit are open to review as well, as are any documents you create or files you download. Table 9-9 on the next page lists several important tips on using computers at work, smartly, ethically, and safely.

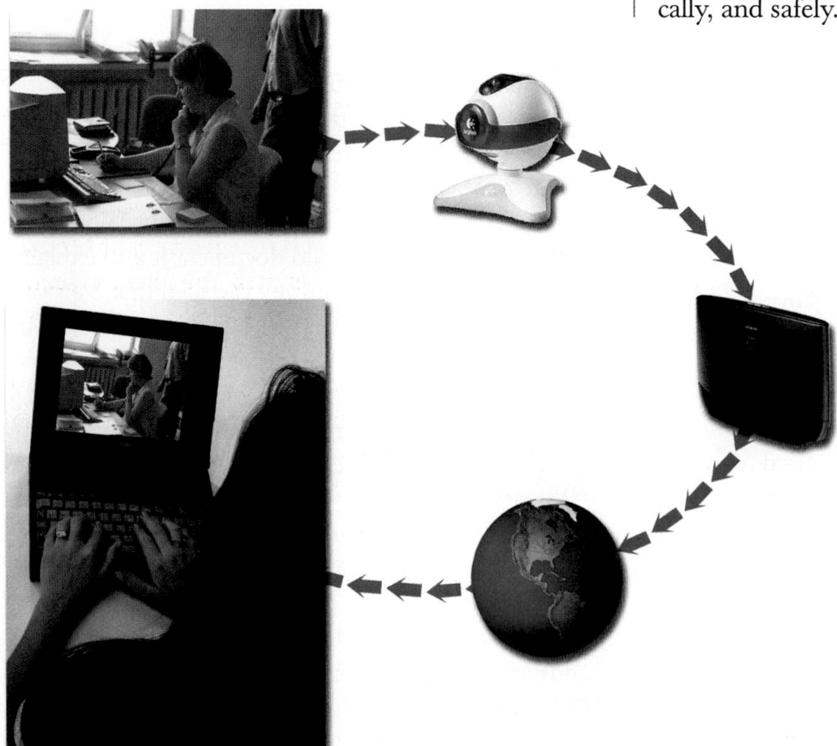

Figure 9-24 A surveillance video camera can be installed anywhere in the workplace — over a cash register, in the mail room, or over employee's desks — to capture their actions. These video cameras can send images to a video server, which streams it to the Internet. A supervisor then can log into a secure Web site from anywhere and check in on employees.

Table 9-9

TIPS FOR USING COMPUTERS AT WORK

- Know your organization's rules for using computers. Read and be sure you understand the organization's acceptable use policy (AUP). If your organization does not have an AUP, ask your manager or instructor for explicit instructions and then document it in written form.
- Limit use of your computer for personal reasons. Sending instant messages to friends or doing your banking online from work likely are not the best use of your company's time or computing resources. Most acceptable use policies limit how workers can use the Web while at work, so refer to the AUP for guidance.
- Avoid visiting Web sites that contain material that is inappropriate for the workplace. If you accidentally stumble on an inappropriate Web site, report it to the appropriate part of the organization, so that your motives are not questioned. Keep the report brief, however; the network administrator otherwise will be overwhelmed with such notices.
- Remember that your Web use can be monitored and reviewed.
- Remember that e-mails are the property of your organization; anything you type can be reviewed for content or intent.
- Document and report illegal, suspicious, or unusual activity you notice on the organization's networks to the appropriate part of the organization. For example, if you notice a huge stash of pirated MP3s on the shared server, be sure to let the network administrator know.
- Exercise common sense whenever you use the Web. Your organization's AUP might not address all of the situations that can arise. Using common sense and the ethical decision making framework outlined in Chapter 8 can help you decide on the best course of action.

Following these tips (adapted from airspace.com) can help you avoid potential problems caused by your computer use at work or school.

COMPUTERS, SECURITY, AND PRIVACY: A BALANCING ACT

As you have learned throughout this book, computers provide innumerable benefits to you and the rest of society. Computers allow your doctor to send your medical records to a specialist across the country in seconds for a second opinion. Computers let the police spread Amber alerts almost immediately, so that kidnapped children quickly can be found. New computerized devices in your car help keep you safe, provide maps to ensure you do not get lost, and allow 911 to locate you in an instant. With computers turning the Internet into an art gallery, concert hall, and classroom, artists, musicians, and educators are able to share ideas, research, and creations with others around the world.

Computers do so much, so well, that many are willing to accept the possible security and privacy risks opened up by computers and technology. Employers, for example, worry about legal action that might result from an employee's misuse of e-mail, but are unwilling to limit e-mail access at the cost of the productivity gains. You eagerly buy CDs, clothes, and gifts from your favorite e-commerce sites, accepting the possibility that your credit card somehow might be obtained by a hacker. You continue to update your car registration and handle your banking online, fully aware of the risks, because the alternative – standing in line at the Registry of Motor Vehicles or at the bank – is entirely too inconvenient.

In the end, maintaining security and privacy in the Information Age proves to be a balancing act. Users must weigh the desire to enjoy the conveniences, services, content, and entertainment made available by computers against the need to take realistic and practical steps to ensure their security and privacy. Likewise, governments, companies, and other organizations need to ensure that the information they collect and store is used ethically and responsibly, and that users always have the opportunity to request that their information be treated with the utmost privacy. As technology changes, security and privacy challenges will continue to change. Staying aware of and understanding these issues is the first step to ensuring your security and privacy, even as you enjoy the benefits of computers in the world all around you.

CONCLUSION

In this chapter, you learned about security concerns in addition to those discussed in Chapter 7, including system failure and securing online transactions and e-mail. You learned about privacy concerns related to the collection of customer data for electronic profiling and the need to allow customers to opt out or opt in. The chapter also reviewed privacy concerns around spam, cookies, spyware, and Web bugs used to track your activity online. You discovered ways to protect your security and privacy, including piracy laws, system backups, and safeguards against system failure. The chapter looked at several key ways to protect against hardware theft and to limit unauthorized access and use, including firewalls, intrusion detection software, and access controls. You considered ways to protect your security and privacy online, as well as the question of how much privacy employees have in the workplace. Finally, issues such as the government's use of Carnivore and the questions raised by the USA PATRIOT Act suggest that managing the value of computers and technology and the risks they pose to our security and privacy is – and will remain – a balancing act.

Key Terms

adware
antispam program
asymmetric key encryption
audit trail
authentication
back up
backup
biometric device
callback system
CAN-SPAM Act
certificate authority (CA)
Children's Online Privacy Protection Act (COPPA)
ciphertext
clear GIFs
click stream data
Computer Fraud and Abuse Acts
cookie
decrypt
differential backup
digital certificate
disaster recovery plan
Electronic Communications Privacy Act (ECPA)
e-mail filtering
employee Internet management (EIM) software
Fair Credit Reporting Act
firewall
first-party cookie
full backup
Gramm-Leach-Bliley Act (GLBA)
head crash
honeypot
identification
incremental backup
Internet hard drive
invisible GIFs
log
off site
online storage
overvoltage
persistent cookie
personal firewall
plaintext
possessed object
private key encryption
proxy server
public key encryption
Secure Electronic Transactions (SET) Specification
secure HTTP (S-HTTP)
secure site
secure sockets layer (SSL)
selective backup
session cookie
spam
spike
spyware
strong password
surge protector
symmetric key encryption
system failure
temporary cookie
third-party cookie
undervoltage
uninterruptible power supply (UPS)
Web beacon
Web bug

Chapter Review

Multiple Choice

Select the best answer.

1. A momentary overvoltage, called a _____, occurs when the increase in power lasts for more than one millisecond.
   (a) spike
   (b) head crash
   (c) spam
   (d) firewall

2. A _____ is a small text file that a Web server stores on your computer.
   (a) cookie
   (b) honeypot
   (c) backup
   (d) plaintext

3. A _____ is stored on the hard disk of your computer even after you close the browser.
   (a) temporary cookie
   (b) session cookie
   (c) persistent cookie
   (d) all of the above

4. Web sites can use third-party cookies to record click stream data, which is data about the _____.
   (a) source of the content and information displayed on a Web page
   (b) author and software used to create the Web site
   (c) number and characteristics of visitors to a Web site
   (d) Web pages you visit and the links you click on a Web site

5. _____ is a program placed on a computer without the user's knowledge that secretly collects information about the user.
   (a) Spyware
   (b) A digital certificate
   (c) Ciphertext
   (d) A Web beacon

6. The 1984 and 1994 Computer Fraud and Abuse Acts _____.
   (a) provide the same protection that covers mail and telephone communications to new forms of electronic communications
   (b) outlaw unauthorized access to federal government computers and the transmission of harmful computer code such as viruses
   (c) limit the people who legally can view a credit report to only those with a legitimate business need
   (d) require that Web sites get explicit permission from parents before marketing to or collecting personal data from children

7. A(n) _____ authenticates a person's identity by translating a personal characteristic, such a facial features or fingerprints, into a digital code.
   (a) possessed object
   (b) audit trail
   (c) biometric device
   (d) callback system

8. To send an encrypted e-mail message with public key encryption, the sender uses _____ to encrypt the message.
   (a) his or her private key
   (b) his or her public key
   (c) the receiver's private key
   (d) the receiver's public key

9. A Web site that uses encryption techniques to secure its data is known as a _____.
   (a) secure site
   (b) certificate authority
   (c) proxy server
   (d) selective backup

10. The law establishes that it is _____ at the workplace.
    (a) illegal for your employer to monitor your use of his or her computer equipment or your time
    (b) legal for your employer to monitor your use of his or her computer equipment, but not your time
    (c) legal for your employer to monitor your time, but not your use of computer equipment
    (d) legal for your employer to monitor your use of his or her computer equipment and your time

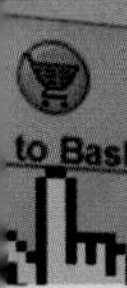

Chapter Review

Short Answer

Write a brief answer to each of the following questions.

1. How is an undervoltage different from an overvoltage?
2. Why do Web sites use cookies?
3. What is a backup and why should backups be kept off site?
4. How is private key encryption different from public key encryption?
5. How is e-mail filtering different from an antispam program?

Web Research

Use a search engine such as Google (google.com) to research the following questions. Then, write a one-page, double-spaced report or create a presentation, unless otherwise directed.

1. In one survey, almost one-third of business respondents ranked spam as their most effective marketing tool, and almost half had considered spam as a marketing option. Marketing budgets for **spam** are estimated at more than $1.3 billion. Use the Web to find out more about how companies use spam and its effectiveness as an advertising option. How does the CAN-SPAM Act affect the use of spam as a marketing tool? Locate news stories for several recent arrests of alleged spammers. What did they do, and why is it illegal?

2. Slowly but surely, Web bugs are infesting the Internet. Five years ago, less than 1 percent of personal Web pages housed the cyber-insects; today, **Web bugs** swarm on more than 15 percent of corporate home pages, and almost 20 percent of personal Web pages. Use the Web to learn more about these ubiquitous creepy-crawlies and the concerns they pose for some privacy advocates.

Group Exercises

Working with a group of your classmates, complete the following team questions.

1. Computer security experts believe there are thousands of hackers. Some are sophisticated programmers, but many are so-called "script kiddies" who use tools written by expert programmers to gain unauthorized access to computer systems. Although hackers may be most worrisome to large corporate networks, no computer connected to the Internet is immune to their incursions. Home computers with always-on, high-speed connections may be the most vulnerable to script-kiddy assaults. A personal firewall can help ward off these invasions. Have each member of your team visit a software vendor and find a personal firewall package. What is the name of the software package? Who is the manufacturer? What are the system requirements? What does the software do? How is the software installed? How much does it cost? Then, meet with your team, share your findings, and prepare a PowerPoint presentation comparing personal firewalls.

2. Information can be a company's most valuable asset. Yet, information also can be the most difficult asset to protect. In a test of the vulnerability of various computer systems, a Web security firm was able to sign up at a bank for credit cards at 129 percent interest, make unauthorized trades at a mutual fund, access employee schedules at an airline, and change information in patient files at a health care center. Have each member of your team visit an information-intensive organization and interview someone on how the information is protected. What security measures are used? Why? What, if any, problems have been experienced? What additional security measures are anticipated, or being considered, for the future? Then, meet with your team, share your findings, and prepare a PowerPoint presentation showing how different organizations protect their information.

3-D (three-dimensional)
  animation, 99–101
  modeling software, 85–86

A
ABS (antilock braking system) module, **112**, 113
ACC (adaptive cruise control), **116–117**
Access (Microsoft), 168
accounting systems, 8
ACH (automated clearing house), **12–13**
acquirers, 6
Acrobat Reader (Adobe), 15
ActiveX (Microsoft), 246
ADC (analog-to-digital converter), **76**, 78, 89, 95
Adobe Acrobat Reader, 15
Adobe Illustrator, 86
Adobe Photoshop, 91
Adobe Premiere, 96
ADS-B (Automatic Dependent Surveillance-Broadcast) system, 126
advertising, 196–197, 209, 216. *See also* adware; marketing
adware, 227, 246. *See also* advertising; marketing
aerodynamic testing, 108–109
AFIS (Automated Fingerprint Identification System), 37–38
Agricultural Revolution, 2, 23
airbag module, **112**
airplane(s), 108, 123, 128–129. *See also* airline industry
  air traffic control systems, 125–130
  simulators, **128–129**
airline industry, 123, 125–130. *See also* airplanes
algorithms, 47
ALI (automatic location identifier), 41
Amazon, 8–9, 213
AMBER (America's Missing: Broadcast Emergency Response), 40–41, 122, 249
American Airlines, 127
ANI (automatic number identifier), 41
animation
  3-D (three-dimensional), 99–101
  described, **99–101**, 103
  key frame, **100**
anti-spam programs, **244**. *See also* spam
antivirus programs, **172–175**, 247. *See also* viruses
AOL (America Online), 41, 204, 213
Apple Final Cut Pro, 96
Apple Keynote, 147, 150
Apple Shake, 97
Applied Digital Solutions, 42
Arizona State University, 80
arts, 75–82
asymmetric encryption, **241**
asynchronous courses, **154**
ATMs (automatic teller machines), 10–12, 14, 238–239
  computer crime and, 183, 184
  described, **11**
ATSCC (Air Traffic Control System Command Center), **125**
audio. *See also* music
  converters, **76**, 78, 89, 95
  -editing software, **79–80**
audit trails, 239
AUP (acceptable use policy), 148, 247, 249
authentication, **236**
AutoCAD (AutoDesk), 82
automobiles, 108–117. *See also* transportation
Aviation and Transportation Security Act, **129**

B
backups, 173, **234–235**, 236
banking, 10–15, 184
  bar code(s)
  described, **6**
scanners, **6**
BCIS (Bureau of Citizenship and Immigration Services), 44
bill
  payment services, 14–15
  presentment, **15**
biometric devices, **239**
blackouts, **222**
blue screen technique, **97**
body controller, **112**
boot programs, **168**
boot sector
  described, **168**
  viruses, **168**
border patrols, 44
botnets, **171**, 185
bots, **171**
braking systems, 124–125
branching, **141**
Braverman, Harry, 20
browsers, 243–246
Buckley Amendment. *See* FERPA (Family Educational Rights and Privacy Act)
Bureau of Customs and Border Protection, 44
bus transportation, 124–125
Bush, George W., 233
business uses, of computers, 1–26

C
Cable Act, 231
Cable Communications Policy Act, 231
CAD (computer-aided design), **4–5**, 84–86, 101–103, 108, 110
CAD (computer-assisted diagnosis), **55–56**
Cadbury, 4
CADE (Customer Account Data Engine), 37
CAE (computer-aided engineering), **4–5**
CAI (computer-aided instruction), **140–141**
call center telematics, **119–120**
callback systems, **239**
CAM (computer-aided manufacturing), **4–5**, 110
CAN-SPAM Act, 225, 231
CAPPS II (Computer Assisted Passenger Pre-Screening II), **129**
card readers, **11**
Carnivore, 228–229
cars. *See* automobiles; transportation
CAs (certificate authorities), 243
CAS (computer-aided surgery), **58**, 59
cash dispensers, 11
CASPIAN (Consumers Against Supermarket Privacy Invasion and Numbering), 10
CAT (computerized axial tomography) scan, **55**, 58, 59
CBE (Computer-Based Education), **139**
CBI (Computer-Based Instruction), **139**
CBT (computer-based training), **140–141**, 153
CCD (charge-coupled device), 89, 95
CDA (Communications Decency Act), **202**
CDs (compact discs). *See also* music
  players for, in automobiles, 115–116
  piracy and, 212–215
cell phones, 15, 21, 224
Cellocate, 123
censorship, 198
Census Bureau, 34
CERT/CC (Computer Emergency Response Team Coordination Center), 186
CFD (Computation Fluid Dynamics), **108**
CGI (computer-generated imagery), **99–101**
chat, 29–30, **152**, 181
Child Online Protection Act, **202**
children
  finding missing, 40–41, 122, 249
  legislation protecting, 202, 230–231
  microchips and, 42
Children's Internet Protection Act, **202**
China, 212
choreography, 82–83
CIM (computer-integrated manufacturing), **4**
ciphertext, **241**
citations, 215
citizens, tracking, 43
civil disobedience, 197
Civil War, 136
clear GIFs, **227–228**
click stream data, **226**
climate control module, **112**
clinical data capture imaging, 54–58
club cards, 10
C-MAN (Costal-Marine Automated Network), 64–65
CMI (computer-managed instruction), **153**
CNN (Cable News Network), 92, 143, 185, 209
code of conduct, 207, 208
CODIS (Combined DNA Index System), 37
colorization, **99**
communications bus, **112**
Communications Decency Act, 204
CompactFlash cards, **90**
computer(s)
  fluency, **137–138**
  -generated fractals, **87**
  literacy, **137–138**
  models, **67–70**
  programming, 143–145
  simulations, **47**, 60–61, 67–70, 145–146
computer crime
  described, **176–189**
  types of, 176–182
Computer Abuse Amendments Act, 189, 231
Computer Fraud and Abuse Act, 188, 189, 230–231
Computer Matching and Privacy Protection Act, 231
consumer preferences, 8–9
contracts, 196
cookies, 225–227, 240, 245–246
COPPA (Children's Online Privacy Protection Act), **230–231**
copyright(s). *See also* intellectual property
  computer crime and, 180–182
  described, **80**
  graphics and, 93–94
  laws, 198–200
  music and, 80–82, 180–181, 212–216
  overview, 198–200
Copyright Act, **198–199**
Copyright Term Extension Act, 200
Corporation for Public Broadcasting, 139
courseware, **153**
CPR (computer-based patient record), 52
crackers, **176**
crash testing, 109–110
credit
  -authorization systems, **6**
  cards, 177–178
crime. *See* computer crime
criminal records, 38–39
crisis management, 44
CRS (computerized reservation system), **126**
CRS (classroom response system), **151**
cruise control module, **112**
C-Span, 30
customer data. *See also* data
  collecting, 223–229
  protection of, 211
customer service, 21
CVS (computer vision syndrome), **19**
CWS (collision warning systems), 113–114
Cyber Security Enhancement Act, 189
cybercrime, **176**. *See also* computer crime
cyberlaw, **195**. *See also* laws
cyberlibel, **203–204**
cyberslacking, **176**
cyberstalking, **204–205**

D
DAC (digital-to-analog converter), **76**
Daley, Richard M., 33
dance notation software, 82–84
data. *See also* databases
  capture imaging, 54–58
  click stream, **226**
  collecting, 223–229
  diddling, **184–185**
  modeling, 67–70
  protection of, 211
database(s). *See also* data
  education and, 149
  law enforcement, 38, 40
  marketing/sales, **8–9**
DDoS (distributed denial-of-service) attack, **185–186**, 197
decryption, **241**
defamation, **203**
Dell Computer, 5
deposit slots, 11
de-skilling, use of the term, **20–22**
diagnostic systems, 54–58
Digimarc, 93–94
digital
  cameras, **87–93**, 95–99
  certificates, **243**
  divide, **23**, 139
  grading, **99**
  signatures, **195–216**
  watermarks, 93–94
  x rays, **54–55**, 59
Digital Angel, 42
Digital Michelangelo project, 85–86
direct deposit, **12**
disaster recovery plans, 235–236
discussion groups, **151–152**
display screens, on ATMs, 11
distance learning (DL), **153–156**
distributed computing, **66**
DMCA (Digital Millennium Copyright Act), **199**, 200, 231
DNA, 37, 65, 67
Dole, Bob, 29–30
domain names, 185–186
DOS (denial-of-service) attacks, 185–186
DoubleClick, 209, 227
DRE (direct recording electronic) machines, 31–32, 32
driver's door module, **112**
DSP (digital signal processor), **76**, 89, 95
Duke University, 215
DV (digital video) cameras, **95–99**
DVD (digital video disc) players, 115–116, 199–200

E
EAS (Emergency Alert System), 40–41
e-bills, **15**
EBT (electron beam tomography), 55
ECGs (electrocardiograms), **54–55**
e-commerce, 195–197. *See also* transactions
ECPA (Electronic Communications Privacy Act), **189**, 230, 231
ECU (engine control unit), **112**
education. *See also* training
  communication tools, 151–152
  computers as teaching tools, 149–152
  games and, 145–146
  Internet resources, 142–143
  learning management systems, 152–153
  overview, 135–163
  plagiarism and, 213–214
  programming tools and, 143–145
  software tools and, 146–148
educational games, **145–146**
EEG (electroencephalography), **55**
e-File, 35–36
EFT (electronic funds transfer), 10–15
EIM (employee Internet management) software, 247–248
e-learning. *See* distance learning (DL)
elections, 28–33
Electronic Communications Privacy Act. *See* ECPA (Electronic Communications Privacy Act)
electronic profiling, 223–224
electronic toll-collection system, **121–122**
electronic whiteboard. See interactive whiteboard
e-mail
  citations in, 215
  education and, 151
  encryption and, 244
  filtering, **244**
  monitoring, 247–249
  security and, 174, 223, 244
  viruses and, 174
employees
  legal rights of, 248–249
  monitoring, 19–22, 247–249
EMR (electronic medical record), **52**, 53
encryption, 11, 196, 240–241
Enhanced 911 (E-911), **41–42**
entertainment, 75, 94–103
  copyrights and, 199–200, 212–216
  systems, in automobiles, 115–116
environmental impact modeling, 68
epidemiology, **60**
ergonomics, **17–19**
E-SIGN (Electronic Signatures in Global and National Commerce Act), 195–196, 196

ethics
business, **207–209**
characteristics of, 194
code of, **207**, 208
computer, **205–216**
decision making and, 206
described, **194**
law versus, 194
overview, 193–220
EULA (end-user license agreement), **201**
evidence, tracking, 37–43
Excel (Microsoft), 168

F
FAA (Federal Aviation Administration), 123, 126
FACT (Fair and Accurate Credit Transactions Act), **178**, 189
factory model school, 136
Fair Credit Reporting Act, **230**, 231
fair use, **198–199**
Family Educational Rights and Privacy Act, 231
FBI (Federal Bureau of Investigation), 37, 38–39, 230
Carnivore system and, 228–229
computer crime and, 176
viruses and, 171
FCC (Federal Communications Commission), 116
FDA (Food and Drug Administration), 55
Federal Trade Commission Act, **196–197**
feedback, **141**
FERPA (Family Educational Rights and Privacy Act), 149
field
cameras, **88**
DV cameras, **95–96**
file viruses, **167–168**
Final Cut Pro (Apple), 96
Financial Modernization Act, 224
firewalls, 174, **237**
FireWire ports, 90
first-party cookies, **227**. *See also* cookies
flash memory cards, 89–90
flight
progress trip, **126**
simulators, **128–129**
fly by wire technology, **123**
font size, 18
Ford Motors, 8
fractals, **87**
FTC (Federal Trade Commission), 178, 196–197
fuel
calculation, 128
injection, 112–113

G
gambling, 202–203
games, 145–146
GDS (global distribution system), **126–127**
genes, **65**
genomes, **65**
GFDL (Geophysical Fluid Dynamics Laboratory), 68
GIFs (Graphics Interchange Format). *See* clear GIFs
GIS (geographic information system), **68–70**, 147
GLBA (Gramm-Leach-Bliley Act), 231, 224
GlucoWatch, 58–59
government, use of computer by, 27–37. *See also* legislation; *specific agencies*
GPS (global positioning system), 41, 42, 45–47
sports and, 103
transportation industry and, 114, 118–120, 124
graphics. *See also* images; photographs
arts, 86–87
clear GIFs, **227–228**
digital manipulation of, ethics and, 209–211
green screen technique, **97**

H
hackers, 148, **176**, 186–187
hacktivism, **197**, 198
haptic feedback, **60**
hardware theft, **177**, 239–240
Harley-Davidson, 21
hash, **196**
head crashes, **222**
help desks, 21
Hershey's, 4
HIPAA (Health Information Portability and Accountability Act), **53**
homeland security, 43–44
honeypots, **238**
HTML (HyperText Transfer Protocol)
editors, 146
music and, 78
security and, 227, 228
HTTP (HyperText Transfer Protocol), 243
Human Genome Project, 65, 67
hurricanes, 63. *See also* weather data

I
IBM (International Business Machines), 127
identification, **236**
identity theft, **178**, 179–181, 189
Identity Theft Act, **178**
Identity Theft Penalty Enforcement Act, **178**, 189
illustration software, **86–87**
ILS (integrated learning systems), **153**
image(s). *See also* graphics; photographs
-editing software, **90–92**
-guided surgery, **58–59**
Industrial Revolution, 2, 23
industry, use of computers by, 1–26
Information Age
described, **2**
moving into, 2–3, 159
information theft, **177–180**
inoculation, of program files, **173**
instrument panel, **112**
intellectual property. *See also* copyrights
described, **180**
ethical use of, 212–216
overview, 198–202
rights, **180**
theft, **180–182**
intelligent highways, 122–123
interactive whiteboard, **150**
Internet
-based voting, **31–32**
hard drive, **234**
Internet Gambling Prohibition Act, **202**
interpolation, **99**
intrusion detection software, 238
Intuit Turbo Tax, 35
inventory control systems, **5**, 7–8, 110–111
invisible GIFs, **227–228**
iPhone, **182**
IRS (Internal Revenue Service), 34–37, 177, 182
IRTPA (Intelligence Reform and Terrorism Prevention Act), **129**
ISBN (International Standard Book Numbering), 6
ISPs (Internet Service Providers), 41, 204–205, 213, 244
ITS (Intelligent Transportation Systems), **118**
iTunes, 80

J
Jaffray, Piper, 212
Japan, 56
Java, 246
JavaScript, 246
job-scheduling systems, **5**
just-in-time manufacturing, **5**
Justice Department (United States), 32, 182, 188

K
Kanka, Megan, 38
Kennedy, John F., 28, 33
key frame animation, **100**. *See also* animation
keyboards
ergonomics, 17–18
MIDI, 77, 80
Keynote (Apple), 147, 150
keypads, 11
kiosks, 127–128L

L
Labor Department (United States), 22–23
LaMacchia, David, 201
LANs (local area networks), 122
law(s). *See also* legislation
computer crime, 188, 189
e-commerce, 195–197
employee monitoring and, 19–22
enforcement, 27, 37–43, 188–189
overview, 193–220
privacy, 19–22, 240–247
use of the term, **194**
LCDs (liquid crystal displays), 114, 115, 117, 125
legislation. *See also* laws
Aviation and Transportation Security Act, **129**
Cable Act, 231
Cable Communications Policy Act, 231
CAN-SPAM Act, 225, 231
Child Online Protection Act, **202**
Children's Internet Protection Act, **202**
Communications Decency Act, 204
Computer Abuse Amendments Act, 189, 231
Computer Fraud and Abuse Act, 188, 189, 230–231
Computer Matching and Privacy Protection Act, 231
Copyright Act, 198–199
Copyright Term Extension Act, 200
Cyber Security Enhancement Act, 189
Fair Credit Reporting Act, 230, 231
Family Educational Rights and Privacy Act, 231
Federal Trade Commission Act, **196–197**
Financial Modernization Act, 224
Identity Theft Act, 178
Identity Theft Penalty Enforcement Act, **178**, 189
Internet Gambling Prohibition Act, 202
National Information Infrastructure Protection Act, 231
Neighborhood Children's Internet Protection Act, **202**
NET (No Electronic Theft) Act, 189, **200**, 201, 202, 231
Online Personal Privacy Act, 244
PATRIOT Act, 231
Privacy Act, 231
Right To Financial Privacy Act, 231
TEACH (Technology, Education, and Copyright Harmonization) Act, 200
Telephone Consumer Protection Act, 231
Unlawful Gambling Enforcement Act, **202**
USA PATRIOT Act, 189, 232–233
Video Privacy Protection Act, 231
LEGO, 144–145, 156
libel, 203–204
Library of Congress, 28
license agreements, **201**
list
owners, **151**
servers, **151**
listservs, **151**
LMS (learning management systems), **152–153**
logic bombs, **169**
LOGO, 144
logs. *See* audit trails
LoJack device, 40
Los Angeles Times, 92–93, 210
Luddites, **3**, 23
L-VIS (Live Video Insertion System), 98–99, 209

M
macro(s)
disabling, 175
viruses, **168**
mailing lists, **151**
malicious logic program, **166**
malicious software program, **166**
manufacturing, 3–5, 108–111
maps, 118
marketing, 6–10, 209, 223–224, 230–232. *See also* advertising
mashups, **118**
MBR (master boot record) viruses, **168**
medical
imaging, 54–58
informatics, **52**
information, credibility of, 61–62
records, 52–53, 56–57
research, 60–61
training, 60–61
uses of computers, 51–62
MEDLINEplus Web site, 56–57
Megan's Law, 38
memory sticks, 89–90
message
boards, **151–152**
digest, **196**
Mexico, 197
microchips, 42, 43
Microsoft Access, 168
Microsoft ActiveX, 246
Microsoft Excel, 168
Microsoft NetMeeting, 152
Microsoft PowerPoint, 147, 150–151, 154, 168
Microsoft Word, 168
Microsoft Zune, 116
microworlds, **144**
MIDI (Musical Instrument Digital Interface), 77, 80. *See also* music
described, **78**
ports, 78, 79
protocol, **79**
military, 27, 45–47
computer crime and, 177, 183–184
education and, 155
Millennium Digital Commerce Act. *See* E-SIGN (Electronic Signatures in Global and National Commerce Act)
moderators, **151**
monitoring
employees, 19–22, 247–249
patients, 58
morphing, **96–97**
Morris, Robert T., 188
motion capture, **83–84**
mouse, 18
movies, 95–99. *See also* entertainment; video
MRI (magnetic resonance imaging), **55**, 56, 58
MRP (manufacturing resource planning), **4–5**
multipartite viruses, 168–169
music. *See also* audio; MIDI (Musical Instrument Digital Interface)
composing, 76–78
copyrights and, 80–82, 180–181, 212–216
distributing, 80–81
editing, 79
notation software, **77–78**
overview, 76–82
performing, 80
playing, 78–80, 115–116
recording, 78–80

N
National Aeronautics and Space Administration (NASA), 44
National Cancer Institute, 60, 61
National Information Infrastructure Protection Act, 231
NCIC (National Crime Information Center), 38, 40
NCLB (No Child Left Behind Act), 136–137
NCMEC (National Center for Missing and Exploited Children), 41
needs assessment, 141
Neighborhood Children's Internet Protection Act, **202**
NET (No Electronic Theft) Act, 189, **200**, 201, 202, 231
NetBank, 14
NetMeeting (Microsoft), 152
new economy, **2**
newsgroups, **151–152**
newsreaders, **151–152**
NICS (National Instance Criminal Background Check System), 38
night vision, 114
911 system, 41–42, 249

NNTP client, **151–152**
NOAA (National Oceanic and Atmospheric Administration), 64

O
objectionable content, **202**
OCR (optical character recognition), **34–35**
off site, 234
office. *See also* workplace
  environment, technology improvements to, 15–17
  ergonomics, 17–18
  human factors and, 17–19
  "paperless," 15–17
Olympics, 102–103
OncoLink, 56–57
online
  activity tracking, 225–226
  storage, **234**
Online Personal Privacy Act, 244
OnStar system, 120
opt in, **224**, 244–245
opt out, **9**, 224, 244–245
optical mark recognition systems, **31**
Osaka University, 56
overvoltage, **222**
Owens Corning, 15–16

P
P2P file-sharing networks, 81, 182, 212
PackBots, 45–46
packet sniffers, **183**, 228–229
pagers, usage frequency of, 21
"paperless" offices, 15–17
parallel processing, **109–110**
passwords, 148, 181–185, 238
patient histories, 52
PATRIOT Act, 231
payload, **169**
PDAs (personal digital assistants), 15, 21
  law enforcement and, 37
  maps and, 118
  medical care and, 57
  theft of, 177, 240
PDF (Portable Document Format), 15, 37
PDR (*Physician's Desk Reference*), 56–57
persistent cookies, 227. *See also* cookies
personal firewalls, 237
PGP (Pretty Good Privacy), 242, 244
pharmaceutical records, 56–58
PHI (personal health information), **52**
phishing, **182**
photographs. *See also* graphics
  digital manipulation of, ethics and, 209–211
  editing software for, **90–92**
  taking digital, 87–93
Photoshop (Adobe), 91
PINs (personal identification numbers), 11, 32–33, 238–239
  described, 6
  computer crime and, 182, 183, 184
pixels, 86
plagiarism, 213–214
plaintext, 241
PNR (Passenger Name Record), **129**
podcasts, 152
point-and-shoot
  cameras, **88**
  DV camera, **95**
political polling, **28–29**
polymorphic viruses, **169**
polypartite viruses, **168–169**
POS (point-of-sale) systems, **6–7**, 8, 10
possessed objects, **238–239**
POSTNET bar codes, 6, 33–34
power distribution box module, **112**
PowerPoint (Microsoft), 147, 150–151, 154, 168
presentation
  graphics software, **147–148**
  tools, 150–151
privacy. *See also* security
  education and, 148–149
  employee monitoring and, 19–22
  ethics and, 211
  laws, 19–22, 240–247
  overview, 221–252
  protecting, 230–247
  in the workplace, 247–249
Privacy Act, 231
private key encryption, **241**
production-scheduling systems, **5**
programming, 143–145
proxy servers, **237**
pruning, **96**
public key encryption, 241
punch card system, **30**, 31

Q
quarantines, **173**
QueTec Umpire Information System, 103

R
radio, satellite, **116**
radiosondes, **63**
railways, 124–125
real time, use of the term, **152**
recovery disks, **173**
remediation, **141**
remote sensing, **64**
rescue disks, **173**
reservation systems, 126–127
retail sales, 6–10, 13
RFIDs (Radio Frequency ID Tags), 121–123
Right To Financial Privacy Act, 231
robotics, 6, 45–47, 110, 144–145
route optimization, **120–121**
RSI (repetitive stress injuries), **18**

S
SABRE (Semi-Automated Business Research Environment), 127
safe harbor, **200**
salami shaving, **184**
sales databases, 8–9
SARS (Sudden Acute Respiratory Syndrome), 60
satellite radio, **116**
satellites, 63–64, 116
science, 51, 62–70
  data classification/analysis, 64–67
  data collection, 63–67
scientific method, **62**
sculpture, 85–86
SD (Secure Digital) cards, **90–91**
Secure Flight, **129–130**
Secure HTTP (S-HTTP), **243**
secure sites, **243**
security. *See also* privacy; viruses
  authentication, **236**
  education and, 148–149
  e-mail and, 174, 223, 244
  encryption, 11, 196, 240–241
  firewalls, 174, **237**
  overview, 164–192, 221–252
  passwords, 148, 181–185, 238
  risks, **165**
  Web bugs and, **227–228**, 245–246
self-service check in, 127–128
sequencers, **79**
server(s)
  computer crime and, 185–186
  encryption and, 243
  proxy, **237**
session cookies, **227**. *See also* cookies
SET (Secure Electronics Transactions Specification), **243**
SETI@Home, 66
shareware, **213**
shoulder surfing, **183**
signatures, **195–216**
simulations, **47**, 60–61, 67–70, 145–146
skilling, use of the term, **20–22**
slander, **203–204**
slide shows, **147**
SMART Board, 150
smart bombs, 46
smart cards, **13–14**, 33, 130
smart cars, 116–117
smart tires, 115
Smith, C. R., 127
Smith, R. Blair, 127
social engineering, **182**, 183
Social Security, 12, 36, 179, 180, 181
software
  piracy, 181–182, 201–202, 212–216
  theft, **181**
sound. *See* audio
Soviet Union, 184
Space Shuttle, 44
spam, **9**, 224–225, 240, 244
spikes, **222**
sports, 98, 101–103
spyware, 245–246
SSL (Secure Sockets Layer), **243**
stacks, **147**
stalking, **204–205**
State Department (United States), 43
stealth viruses, 169
Stoll, Clifford, 184
studio
  cameras, **88**
  DV cameras, **95–96**
subscribing, to mailing lists, **151**
superusers, **183**
surge protectors, **233**
surveillance, 44, 248
symmetric key encryption, 241
synchronous courses, **154**
synthesizers, **78**
sypware, **227**
system
  administrators, **183**
  failures, **222**, 233–234

T
TAB (tablature), 77
tax preparation software, **35–36**
TaxCut (H&R Block), 35
TBT (Technology-Based Training), **139**, 140
TCAS (Traffic Alert and Collision Avoidance System), 126
TEACH (Technology, Education, and Copyright Harmonization) Act, 200
techno-stress, 20
telecommuting, **16–17**
telematics, **119–120**
telemedicine, **59–60**
Telephone Consumer Protection Act, 231
telepresence surgery, **59–60**
television, 95–99. *See also* entertainment
temporary cookies, **227**. *See also* cookies
terrorism, 43, 187, 228–229, 232–233
testing
  aerodynamic, 108–109
  crash, 109–110
theater, 84–85
third-party cookies, **227**. See also cookies
three-dimensional (3-D)
  animation, 99–101
  modeling software, 85–86
ticketing systems, 126–127
time bombs, **169**
traffic
  laws, 39–40
  reports, 117–118
training, 128–129, 140–141, 153. *See also* education
trains, 124–125
transactions, 223, 242–243. *See also* e-commerce
transmission controller, **112**
transponders, **121–122**
transportation industry, 107–134
Travelocity, 127
Treasury Department (United States), 203
Trojan horses, **169–171**
troop movements, 46–47
trucking, 111–117
TRUSTe program, 230–232
trusted source, **174**
TSA (Transportation Security Agency), **129**, 177

U
UAVs (unmanned aerial vehicles), **45**
ultrasound, **55**
unauthorized
  access, **176–177**, 236–239
  use, **176–177**, 236–239
undervoltage, **222**
unemployment, 22–23
University of California, 66, 157
UNIX, 183
Unlawful Gambling Enforcement Act, **202**
unsubscribing, to mailing lists, **151**
UPC (Universal Product Code), **6**
UPS (uninterruptible power supply), **234**
USA PATRIOT Act, 189, 232–233
USB (Universal Serial Bus)
  drives, 89–90, 234
  ports, in automobiles, 116
Usenet newsgroups, **151–152**
user IDs, 238
usernames, 148, 238
USPS (United States Postal Service), 33–37
U.S. Bureau of Customs and Border Protection, 44
U.S. Census Bureau, 34
U.S. State Department (United States), 43
U.S. Treasury Department (United States), 203
U.S. VISIT system (Visitor and Immigrant Status Indication Technology), 43–44

V
vehicles, stolen, 40. *See also* automobiles
VeriChip, 42, 43
Veterans benefits, 12
video
  composition, **97**
  conferencing, **152**
  editing software, 96–99
  surveillance, 248
Video Privacy Protection Act, 231
virtual
  signage, **98**
  wind tunnels, **108–109**
voting systems, 30–33
virus(s), 166–175, 187
  described, **166**
  hoaxes, **171–172**
  signatures (definitions), **172–173**
  types of, 167–169

W
WANs (wide area networks), 122
watermarks, 93–94
WBT (Web-based training), **141–142**, 153
weather data, 63, 64, 68
Web beacons. *See* Web bugs
Web browsers, 243–246
Web bugs, **227–228**, 245–246
WebQuest, **143**
Wi-Fi, 237
wind tunnels, 108
wireframe models, **99–101**
wireless 911, 41–42
wiretapping, 232–233
WMS (warehouse management systems), **5**
Word (Microsoft), 168
workers, autonomy of, **21**
workplace. *See also* office environment
  balancing home life with the demands of, 22
  employee monitoring and, 19–22
  quality of life in the, 19–22
  security and privacy in the, 247–249
World War II, 45
worms, **169–171**
WTO (World Trade Organization), 203

X
x rays, digital, **54–55**, 59

Y
Yahoo!, 14, 57, 61, 185, 200, 209

Z
zombies, **171**, 186
Zune (Microsoft), 116